Dedication

"Is it finished yet?", Marni, Adam, and my wife Ricki, 1978.

My family displayed remarkable patience and were a source of encouragement throughout the preparation of this book.

Paul Halpern

Preface

In preparing this textbook, there were a number of goals that I set for myself. First, I found the Fourth Edition of *Essentials of Managerial Finance,* by J. Fred Weston and Eugene F. Brigham, the U.S. textbook on which this book is based, to be clearly written, well organized, and, in general, comprehensive in its coverage of the major topics in financial management. Therefore, I attempted to be consistent with the style of the original text and I did not tamper significantly with the format of the original text. The only major change was the insertion of a chapter on International Financial Management (Chapter 22) and the deletion of a descriptive chapter on the Timing of Financial Policy. Second, my intention was to present any new material at the same level as the original text. Third, and most important, I did not want the Canadian edition of the basic text to be a cosmetic Canadianization.

Of course, all the expected changes needed to include Canadian material have been made. This required either a complete or a major rewrite of a number of chapter, e.g., Tax Environment (Chapter 2), Capital Budgeting (Chapter 11), and The Market for Long-Term Securities (Chapter 13), among others. A number of the remaining chapters required the insertion of new materials to describe the Canadian environment. However, I tried to minimize change for the sake of change.

There are some chapters in which I have rewritten the discussions of financial theory, e.g., cost of capital, mergers, and term loans and leases. In addition, some differences of opinion on the interpretation and application of the theory between the U.S. authors and myself required some rewriting of the material in the U.S. text.

Although I tried to maintain the same theoretical level as the original text, in some instances the discussions are slightly more rigorous. However, based on my experience in teaching the introductory course in finance, I believe that students will be able to handle the greater rigor.

In order to maintain the overall theoretical level of the original text, one area of financial theory has not been considered at all. This area, called capital asset pricing, is an important theoretical tool, but a complete presentation requires some statistical sophistication. In addition, the application of capital asset pricing to traditional, multi-period capital budgeting is not as straight-forward as some introductory textbooks would lead us to believe. Finally, while our discussions of capital structure, dividend policy, and cost of capital have presented all the relevant issues, analysis has been simplified.

In a number of ways, preparing a good Canadian version of a U.S. text-book is more difficult than writing a new textbook. I hope that both students and instructors find that *Essentials of Canadian Managerial Finance* is complete in its discussion of the Canadian material and the changes in some of the other material improves upon the presentation of the original text.

In this text, I have not sought to avoid the many unresolved areas of business financial theory and practice. Although the text could have been simplified in many places by avoiding the difficult issues, I preferred to provide a basic framework based on the "received doctrine"; then to go on to present materials on a number of important but controversial issues.

The level and difficulty of the material is somewhat uneven. Certain sections are simply descriptions of the institutional features of the financial environment and, as such, are not difficult to understand. Other parts — notably the material on capital budgeting, uncertainty, and the cost of capital — are by nature rather abstract, and as such, are difficult for those not used to thinking in abstract terms.

Ancillary Materials

The *Study Guide* highlights the key points in the text and presents a comprehensive set of problems similar to those at the end of each chapter. Each problem is solved in detail, so a student who has difficulty working the end-of-chapter problems can be aided by reviewing the *Study Guide*.

An *Instructor's Manual* is also available which includes answers to the questions and problems in the text.

Acknowledgements: Canadian Edition

There are a number of individuals who have assisted me in obtaining Canadian material for the text and in reviewing drafts of particular chapters. In addition, I have benefited from discussions with a number of my colleagues who have made valuable suggestions on the presentation of the theoretical material. These individuals have provided valuable assistance and have improved the quality of the book. I am indebted to the following cast of individuals and companies for their assistance: L. Bernardi, W.B. Coutts, J. Dermer, Esbe Scientific, K. Garfinkel, Genstar, M.J. Gordon, W. Johnson, W. Leaney, J. McCallum, J. McFadyen, C. Nichol, R. Prichard, M. Trebilcock, and S. Turnbull.

I owe special thanks to Larry Gould for reviewing, in great detail, a number of important chapters. Also, David Johnston has been of great assistance in finding material for the text and reviewing the chapters of the text. His assistance in the preparation of Chapters 3 and 22 was extremely valuable.

Finally, I would like to thank the staff of Holt, Rinehart and Winston of Canada, Limited — especially J. Dill, K. Leland and J. McKeon. Faced with the approaching deadlines for the publication of the book, they displayed remarkable understanding as my progress on the book frequently stalled.

Toronto, Ontario   Paul Halpern
January, 1979

Acknowledgments: U.S. Edition

In its several revisions, the book has been worked on and critically reviewed by numerous individuals, and we have received many detailed comments and suggestions from instructors (and students) using the book in our own schools and elsewhere. All this help has improved the quality of the book, and we are deeply indebted to the following individuals, and others, for their help: M. Adler, E. Altman, J. Andrews, R. Aubey, P. Bacon, W. Beranek, V. Brewer, W. Brueggeman, R. Carleson, S. Choudhury, P. Cooley, C. Cox, D. Fischer, R. Gray, J. Griggs, R. Haugen, S. Hawk, R. Hehre, J. Henry, A. Herrmann, G. Hettenhouse, R. Himes, C. Johnson, R. Jones, D. Kaplan, M. Kaufman, D. Knight, H. Krogh, R. LeClair, W. Lee, D. Longmore, J. Longstreet, H. Magee, P. Malone, R. Moore, T. Morton, T. Nantell, R. Nelson, R. Norgaard, J. Pappas, R. Pettit, R. Pettway, J. Pinkerton, G. Pogue, W. Regan, F. Reilly, R. Rentz, R. Richards, C. Rini, R. Roenfeldt, W. Sharpe, K. Smith, P. Smith, D. Sorenson, M. Tysseland, P. Vanderheiden, D. Woods, J. Yeakel, and D. Ziegenbein for their careful reviews of this and previous editions.

We owe special thanks to Roger Bey, Keith Johnson, and Ramon Johnson for providing us with a set of problems they had developed for their classes, and also for providing us with detailed reviews of the manuscript of this book.

The Universities of California and Florida, and our colleagues on these campuses, provided us with intellectual support in bringing the book to completion. Finally, we are indebted to the Dryden Press staff—principally Mary Ellen Stocker and Martha Cobb—for their special efforts in getting the manuscript into production and for following through to the bound book.

The field of finance will continue to experience significant changes. It is stimulating to participate in these exciting developments, and we sincerely hope that *Essentials* will contribute to a better understanding of the theory and practice of finance.

Los Angeles, California   J. Fred Weston
Gainesville, Florida   Eugene F. Brigham
September 1976

Contents

Part Six
Integrated Topics in Financial
Management 571

Overview of Finance: Analysis, Planning, and Control

Part One

Part One consists of six chapters. The first describes the scope and nature of managerial finance and serves as an introduction to the book. Next, in Chapter 2, we examine the tax system; since a high percentage of business income is paid to the government, taxes are an important consideration in finance. In addition specific provisions in the tax system induce particular behavior by firms and individuals. In Chapter 3 we examine the construction and use of the basic ratios of financial analysis; through ratio analysis, the firm's strengths and weaknesses can be pinpointed. The impact of inflation on financial ratios and proposals to adjust for this impact are discussed in the appendix to this chapter. Chapter 4 explains two key tools used in financial planning: break-even analysis, and the sources and uses of funds statement. In Chapter 5 we take up financial forecasting in both the long and the short run: given a projected increase in sales, how much money must the financial manager raise from external sources to support this level of sales? Finally, in Chapter 6, we consider the budget system through which management controls and coordinates the firm.

Finance deals, in the main, with very specific questions: Should we lease or buy the new machine? Should we expand capacity at a particular plant? Should we raise capital this year by long-term or short-term debt or by selling stock? Should we go along with the marketing department, which wants to expand inventories, or with the production department, which wants to reduce them? Specific questions such as these, which are typical of the types of decisions facing the financial manager, are considered in the remainder of the book. But here in Part One we take an *overview* of the firm. Because all specific decisions are made within the context of the firm's overall position, this overview is critical to an understanding of any specific proposal.

Scope and Nature of Managerial Finance

What is managerial finance? What is finance's function in the firm? What specific tasks are assigned to the financial manager? What tools and techniques are available, and how does one go about measuring the manager's performance? On a broader scale, what is the role of finance in the Canadian economy, and how can managerial finance be used to further national goals? Providing at least tentative answers to these questions is the principal purpose of this book.

CHANGING ROLE OF FINANCIAL MANAGEMENT

As with many things in the contemporary world, financial management has undergone significant changes over the years. When finance first emerged as a separate field of study in the early 1900s, the emphasis was on legalistic matters such as mergers, consolidations, the formation of new firms, and the various types of securities issued by corporations. Industrialization was spreading rapidly and firms were faced with the critical problem of obtaining capital for expansion. Compared to today, the capital markets were primitive and the transfer of funds from savers to investors was relatively difficult. Imperfections in the capital markets and in the information provided did not generate confidence in investors to purchase bonds or stocks. In this environment, when capital markets were just beginning to become important in the industrialization process, it is easy to see why finance concentrated so heavily on legal issues relating to the issuance of securities.

The emphasis remained on securities through the 1920s; however, the events in the depression of the 1930s resulted in interest in bankruptcy and

3

reorganization. Finance, however, remained a descriptive, legalistic subject.

This type of analysis continued in the 1940s and the 1950s, and finance was viewed from the outside rather than from within the firm's management. However, some time was devoted to budgeting and other internal control procedures, and, stimulated by the work of Joel Dean, capital budgeting was beginning to receive attention.[1]

The evolutionary pace quickened during the late 1950s. Whereas the right-hand side of the balance sheet (liabilities and capital) had received more attention in the earlier era, increasing emphasis was being placed on asset analysis during the last half of that decade. Mathematical models were developed and applied to inventories, cash, accounts receivable, and fixed assets. Increasingly, the focus of finance shifted from the outsider's to the insider's point of view, as financial decisions within the firm were recognized to be the critical issues in corporate finance. Descriptive, institutional materials on capital markets and financing instruments were still studied, but these topics were considered within the context of corporate financial decisions.

The emphasis on decision-making has continued in recent years, with the increasing belief that sound capital budgeting procedures required accurate measurements of the cost of capital. In addition, great strides in the theory of finance have permitted an improved understanding of the basic concept of finance — the trade-off of risk and return. There has been a renewed interest in a number of topics that were important in the days of institutional finance. These include mergers and consolidations due to the increased merger activity in the late 1960s and early 1970s; bankruptcy and reorganization due to the important theoretical discussions of the impact of bankruptcy cost on financial decisions; and finally, analysis of the types of securities issued by firms. Although the topics appear to be the same, the analysis is based on models of economic and financial activity and is not solely descriptive.

Meanwhile, a number of new topics have become important. First, accelerated progress in transportation and communications has brought the countries of the world closer together; this, in turn, has stimulated interest in international finance. Second, high rates of inflation, along with uncertainty as to the actual inflation rate that will exist in the future, have become important problems for financial managers in their planning function. Finally, public awareness of air and water pollution has had a direct impact on firms through the planning and investment decision processes. Financial managers must now be aware of the costs of ecological damage and the benefits of attempting to reduce this damage.

Therefore, the current responsibilities of financial managers are a result of the evolution of financial management. While the specifics vary among organizations, some finance tasks are basic. Funds are raised from external sources and allocated to different uses within the organization. The flow of

[1] Joel Dean, *Capital Budgeting* (New York: Columbia University Press, 1951).

funds involved in the operations of an enterprise is managed. Benefits to the financing sources take the form of returns, repayments, products, and services. These key financial functions must be performed in all organizations, be they business firms, governmental units or agencies, or nonprofit organizations such as museums or the Red Cross.

The main functions of financial managers are planning for, acquiring, and utilizing funds in ways that maximize the efficiency of the organization's operation. This requires knowledge of the financial markets from which funds are drawn; knowledge of how sound investment decisions are made; and knowledge of how efficient operations are stimulated. Managers must consider a large number of alternative sources and uses of funds in making financial decisions. They must choose, for example, internal or external funds, long-term or short-term projects, long-term or short-term fund sources, and higher or lower rates of growth.

Up to this point, the discussion of the finance function has applied to all types of organizations. What is unique about business organizations is that they are directly and measurably subject to the discipline of the financial markets. These markets are continually determining the valuations of business firms' securities, thereby providing measures of the firms' performances. A consequence of this reassessment of managerial performance by the capital markets is the change in relative valuation levels of business firms. That is, changes in valuation signal changes in performance. Therefore, valuations stimulate businesses' efficiency and provide incentives to business managers to improve their performance. It is difficult to test the efficiency and performance of organizations other than business firms because of the absence of institutions such as financial markets which continually place valuations on them and assess their performance.

The Impact of Inflation on Financial Management

During the 1960s prices rose at an average rate of about 2½ to 3 percent per year with higher than average rates occurring in the latter part of the decade. However, in the 1970s, the average rate, up to the end of 1977, was 7.5 percent with rates as high as 11 percent per year. In addition, there appears to have been substantial variation in the observed inflation rates. This "double digit" inflation, along with the uncertainty of inflation, has had an important impact on business firms and especially on their financial operations. As a result, many functions undertaken by the financial manager are becoming more difficult and established financial policies and practices are undergoing changes. Some of these are outlined below.

1. *Interest rates.* The rate of interest on Government of Canada securities (called the default-free rate) consists of a "real rate of interest" of about 3 percent plus an "inflation premium" that reflects the capital market's

expectations of the long-run rate of inflation. Therefore, an increase in the expected rate of inflation is quickly translated into higher default-free interest rates. Since the cost of money to firms is equal to the default-free rate plus a risk premium, increases in the default-free rate induced by higher expected rates of inflation are quickly passed on to business borrowers.

The higher interest rates *per se* are not a major problem if the earnings of the firm increase with the inflation rate. In fact, conventional wisdom was that the assets of a corporation would generate cash flows that would increase by the same amount as the inflation rate. However, earnings in all firms have not kept pace with inflation, and thus the true cost of borrowing has increased.

2. *Planning difficulties.* Businesses operate on the basis of long-run plans. For example, a firm builds a plant only after making a thorough analysis of expected costs and revenues over the life of the plant. If the inflation rate is stable, even though it might be high, and if the financial manager is aware of the response of the firm's earnings to inflation, then the planning function is not more complicated. But if the inflation rate is variable, planning becomes very difficult. In this case, the cost of materials and labor change dramatically in unexpected directions. In addition, various suppliers of inputs, for example, labor, are unwilling to enter into long-term contracts. Therefore, accurate forecasts of revenues and costs are especially important, yet exceedingly hard to make. Efforts are, of course, being made to improve forecasting techniques, and financial planning must include more flexibility to reflect the increased level of uncertainty in the economy. Incidentally, the increased uncertainty in many industries tends to raise the risk premiums for firms in those industries, driving their costs of capital still higher.

3. *Bond price declines.* The price of a long-term bond is based on the market's expectations of the long-run inflation rate. To the extent that there are unanticipated changes in inflation rates, bond prices will become more variable. Lenders, in an effort to protect themselves against these risks of unanticipated bond price movements, are beginning (a) to put more funds into short-term than into long-term debt, and (b) to insist upon bonds whose interest rates vary with "the general level of interest rates" as measured by an index of interest rates. Brazil, Israel and other inflation-plagued countries have used such index bonds for years. In fact, there are now in existence in Canada floating rate, preferred shares which have a dividend payment linked to an index of interest rates. Unless inflation in Canada is controlled, a more extensive use of these "linked" bonds will occur.

4. *Accounting problems.* With high rates of inflation, reported profits are distorted. The sale of low-cost inventories results in higher reported profits, but cash flows are held down as firms restock with higher-cost inventories. Similarly, depreciation charges are inadequate, as they do not reflect the new costs of replacing plant and equipment. If a firm is unaware of the

"shakiness" of profits that reflect inventory valuation and inadequate depreciation charges, and if it plans dividends and capital expenditures on the basis of such figures, then it could develop serious financial problems.

The existence of double digit and uncertain inflation is a disturbing and challenging new experience for financial managers around the world. Although no one knows what the full impact of continued inflation will be, one thing is clear — if the current inflationary conditions continue, a number of financial policies and practices will have to be modified to meet this situation.

Organization of a Firm's Finance Department

In the typical firm, the chief financial officer, who has the title of vice-president -finance, reports to the chief executive officer and has accountable to him two key officers, the treasurer and the comptroller. The treasurer and his staff are responsible for raising capital and dealing with suppliers of capital, as well as for the firm's credit policy. The comptroller and his staff are responsible for the accounting and budgeting systems, including capital budgeting. In a sense, the treasurer handles the outside finance functions and the comptroller the inside functions, while the vice-president-finance has the overall responsibility for both.

GOALS OF THE FIRM

Throughout the book we operate on the assumption that management's primary goal is to make all financial and investment decisions so as to maximize the wealth of its existing shareholders. Wealth is defined as the sum of the dividends paid to the existing shareholders plus the market value of their shares. Clearly, if an investment or financial decision results in an increased dividend with the same share price, or an increased share price with the same dividend, then shareholders are better off. Just how good is this assumption — does management really try to maximize shareholder wealth, or is it equally interested in profits, in sales, in survival, in the personal satisfaction of the managers themselves, in employees' welfare, or in the good of the community and society at large? Further, does management really try to *maximize*, or does it "satisfice"? That is, does it seek satisfactory rather than optimal results?

Profits versus Wealth

Let us consider the question of profits versus wealth. Suppose management is interested primarily in shareholders, making its decisions so as to maximize their welfare. Will profit maximization be best for shareholders? In answering this question, we must decide whether the profit figure in question is total corporate profits or earnings per share. As we noted before, in making any financial or investment decision, management must be interested in the welfare of the existing shareholders and their claim on total corporate profits. Thus, if the firm undertakes an investment decision, total corporate profits may increase; but if new equity has been issued to finance the project, the number of shares will increase and the earnings per share may fall. Each shareholder before the investment decision was made had a claim on the earnings per share. If earnings per share fall, then the price per share may fall, and hence the existing shareholder's wealth is reduced. Thus, to the extent that profits are important, management should concentrate on earnings per share rather than on total corporate profits.

Earnings per Share   Will maximization of earnings per share maximize shareholder welfare, or should other factors be considered? Consider the timing of the earnings. Suppose one project will cause earnings per share to rise by $.20 per year for five years, or $1.00 in total, while another project has no effect on earnings for four years but increases earnings by $1.25 in the fifth year. Both projects are riskless. Which project is better? The answer depends upon which project adds the most to the value of the stock, and this in turn depends upon the time value of money to investors. In any event, timing is an important reason to concentrate upon wealth as measured by the price of the stock rather than upon earnings alone.

Risk   Still another issue relates to risk. Suppose one project is expected to increase earnings per share by $1.00, while another is expected to raise earnings by $1.20 per share. The first project is not very risky; if it is undertaken, earnings will almost certainly rise by about $1.00 per share. The other project is quite risky, so while our best guess is that earnings will rise by $1.20 per share, we must recognize the possibility that there may be no increase whatever. The final decision will depend upon the aversion to risk displayed by investors in the market place. If, based on this market risk aversion, one of these projects is accepted and the other is rejected, the market value of the shares will increase.

Recognizing all these factors, managers interested in shareholder welfare should seek to maximize shareholder wealth. In most instances this is equivalent to the maximization of the firm's stock price.[2] The price of the stock

[2]This rule may lead to unusual behavior when a firm is close to bankruptcy. At this point, the equity holders realize that there is little or no chance that they will receive anything if the firm becomes bankrupt since the bondholders have a prior claim. The equity holders are willing to undertake very risky projects which have a high probability of losing the money invested and a very low probability of a high payoff. This type of project will increase the risk of bondholders. A good example of this type of investment would be a lottery ticket. The shareholders need not worry if the investment does not pay off since they are protected by limited liability. If the investment pays off, they can pay the bondholders and have something left over for themselves. This type of investment decision can maximize the wealth of equity holders at the expense of the wealth of the bondholders. It is no wonder that bondholders attempt to protect themselves from this type of investment decision by requiring restrictions on management's investment activities.

reflects the market's evaluation of the firm's prospective earnings stream over time, the riskiness of this stream, and a host of other factors which include financial policies such as the dividend and debt-equity decisions. The higher the price of the stock, the better is management's performance from the standpoint of the shareholders; thus, market price provides a performance index by which management can be judged.[3]

Maximizing Shareholder Wealth versus Other Goals

In theory, shareholders own the firm and elect the management team; management, in turn, is supposed to operate in the best interests of the shareholders. We know, however, that the stock of most large firms is widely held, so the managers of such firms have a great deal of autonomy. This being the case, might not managements pursue goals other than maximizing shareholder wealth? Some alternative goals are examined in this section.

Maximizing versus "Satisficing"   First, consider the question of *maximizing,* which involves seeking the best possible outcome, versus "satisficing," which involves a willingness to settle for something less. Some argue that the management of a large, well-entrenched corporation could work to keep shareholder returns at a fair or "reasonable" level and then devote part of its efforts and resources to public service activities, to employee benefits, to higher management salaries, or to golf.

Similarly, an entrenched management could avoid risky ventures, even when the possible gains to shareholders are high enough to warrant taking the gamble. The theory behind this argument is that shareholders are generally well-diversified, holding portfolios of many different stocks, so if one company takes a chance and loses, the shareholders lose only a small part of their wealth. Managers, on the other hand, are not diversified, so setbacks affect them more seriously. Accordingly, some argue that the managers of widely held firms tend to play it safe rather than aggressively seek to maximize the prices of their firm's shares. In addition, this inadequate management diversification argument has been used to explain why companies undertake mergers with firms in totally unrelated fields. These conglomerate mergers provide the managers with the diversification that they desire.

It is extremely difficult to determine whether a particular management team is trying to maximize shareholder wealth or is merely attempting to satisfice on this factor while pursuing other goals. For example, how can we tell whether or not voluntary employee or community benefit programs are in the long-run best interests of the shareholders? Are relatively high management

[3] A firm's stock price might, of course, decline because of factors beyond management's control. Accordingly, it is useful to look at comparative statistics; even though a firm's stock declines by 10 percent, management will have performed well if the economy or other firms in the industry decline by 20 percent.

salaries really necessary to attract and retain excellent managers who, in turn, will keep the firm ahead of its competition? When a risky venture is turned down, does this reflect management conservatism or a correct judgment that the risks of the venture outweigh the potential rewards?

It is impossible to give definitive answers to these questions. Several empirical studies have been undertaken but the evidence remains cloudy. It is true that more and more firms are tying management's compensation to the company's performance, and research suggests that this motivates management to operate in a manner consistent with stock price maximization. Additionally, in recent years take-over bids and proxy fights have removed a number of supposedly entrenched managements; the recognition that such actions can take place has doubtless stimulated many other firms to attempt to maximize share prices.[4] A firm operating in a competitive market, or almost any firm during an economic downturn, will be forced to undertake actions that are reasonably consistent with shareholder wealth maximization. Finally, managements are interested in maintaining a high level of personal marketability; if they are eagerly sought after by other firms, they will be able to obtain higher current compensation. In order to maintain this marketability, their company must be perceived as being successful and the obvious measure of success is the firm's stock price. Thus, while managers may have other goals in addition to shareholder wealth maximization, there are reasons to view this as a dominant goal for most firms. And even though a management group may pursue other goals, shareholder wealth is bound to be of considerable importance. Often the same types of actions that could maximize wealth are also necessary to keep it at a satisfactory level; it may therefore be difficult, in practice, to determine which goal is dominant.

Social Responsibility One final point that deserves consideration is *social responsibility:* Should businesses operate strictly in the shareholders' best interests, or are they also partly responsible for the welfare of society at large? In tackling this question, consider first the firms whose rates of return on investment are close to normal, that is, close to the average for all firms. If such companies attempt to be socially responsible, thereby increasing their costs over what they otherwise would have been, and if the other businesses in the industry do not follow suit, then the socially oriented firms will probably be forced to abandon their efforts. Thus, any socially responsible acts that raise costs will be difficult, if not impossible, in industries subject to keen competition.

What about firms with profits above normal levels — can they not devote resources to social projects? Undoubtedly they can; many large, successful

---

[4]A take-over bid is an offer by one company to buy the stock of another; while a proxy fight involves an attempt to gain control by getting shareholders to vote a new management group into office. Both actions are facilitated by low stock prices, so self-preservation can lead management to try to keep the stock value as high as possible.

firms do engage in community projects, employee benefit programs, and the like to a greater degree than would appear to be called for by pure profit or wealth maximization.[5] Still, publicly owned firms are constrained in such actions by capital market factors. Suppose a saver who has funds to invest is considering two alternative firms. One firm devotes a substantial part of its resources to social actions, while the other concentrates on profits and stock prices. Most investors are likely to shun the socially oriented firm, which will put it at a disadvantage in the capital market. After all, why should the shareholders of one corporation subsidize society to a greater extent than the shareholders of other businesses? Perhaps it is up to the individual shareholder to decide how much, and to whom, funds for social action should be distributed. Thus, even highly profitable firms (unless they are closely held as opposed to publicly owned) are generally constrained against taking unilateral cost-increasing social actions. This conclusion holds not only for donations of funds for social action, but also for expenditures to protect the environment.

Does all this mean that firms should not exercise social responsibility? Not at all — it simply means that most cost-increasing actions may have to be put on a mandatory rather than voluntary basis, at least initially, to insure that the burden of such action falls uniformly across all businesses.[6] Thus, fair hiring practices, minority training programs, product safety, pollution abatement, anti-combines activities, and the like are more likely to be effective if realistic rules are established initially and enforced by government agencies. It is critical that industry and government cooperate in establishing the rules of corporate behavior and that firms follow the spirit as well as the letter of the law in their actions. Thus, the rules of the game become constraints, and firms should strive to maximize shareholder wealth subject to these constraints. Throughout the book, we shall assume that managements operate in this manner.

FINANCIAL DECISIONS: RISK-RETURN TRADE-OFF

Financial decisions affect the value of a firm's stock by influencing both the size of the earnings stream, or profitability, and the riskiness of the firm. These relationships are diagrammed in Figure 1-1. Policy decisions, which are made subject to government constraints, affect both profitability and risk; these two factors jointly determine the value of the firm.

---

[5]Even firms such as these often find it necessary to justify such programs at shareholder meetings by appeals to long-run wealth maximization.

[6]If the costs of degrading the environment fall on a particular group, this group can pay the offending company to reduce its output, and hence its polluting activities. Thus, no governmental action is required. If, however, the costs of the pollution are borne by a large group which cannot come together to pay the offending company, then the government may have to step in.

FIGURE 1-1   Valuation As the Central Focus of the Finance Function

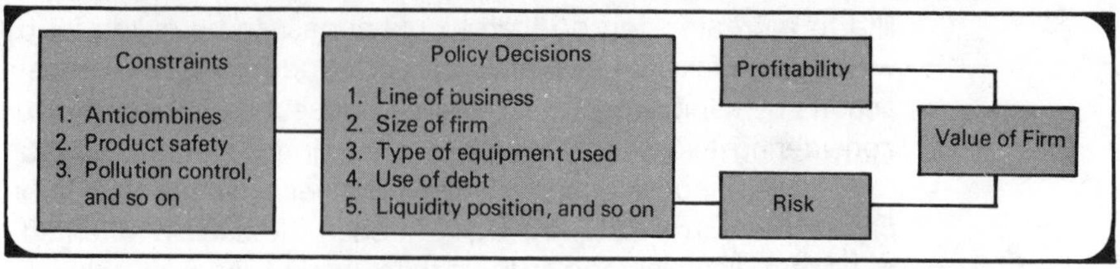

The primary policy decision is that of choosing the industry in which to operate — the product-market mix of the firm. When this choice has been made, both profitability and risk are determined by decisions relating to the size of the firm, the types of equipment used, the extent to which debt is employed, the firm's liquidity position, and so on. Such decisions generally affect both risk and profitability. An increase in the cash position, for instance, reduces risk; however, since cash is not an earning asset, converting other assets to cash also reduces profitability. Similarly, the use of additional debt raises the rate of return, or the profitability, on the shareholders' net worth; at the same time, more debt means more risk. The financial manager seeks to strike the particular balance between risk and profitability that will maximize the wealth of the firm's shareholders. That is called a *risk-return tradeoff,* and most financial decisions involve such tradeoffs between risk and return.

ORGANIZATION AND STRUCTURE OF THIS BOOK

The optimal structure for a finance text, if one exists, is most illusive. On the one hand, it is desirable to set out a theoretical structure first, then use the theory in later sections to explain behavior and to attack real-world decision problems. On the other hand, it is easier to understand the theoretical concepts of finance if one has a working knowledge of certain institutional details. Given this conflict, what should come first, theory or institutional background? We have wrestled with this problem, experimenting with both approaches in our own classes, and the following outline of the six parts of the book reflects our own experience and that of others who shared their ideas and preferences with us.

Part One: Overview of finance: taxes, financial analysis, planning, and control
Part Two: Working capital management
Part Three: Decisions involving long-term assets
Part Four: Sources and forms of long-term financing
Part Five: Financial structure, the cost of capital, and dividend policy
Part Six: Integrated topics in financial management

The contents of each part are next discussed briefly to provide an overview of both the book and the field of managerial finance.

Part One: Overview of Finance: Financial Analysis, Planning, and Control

Part One, which consists of Chapters 1–6, develops certain key concepts and commonly used tools of financial analysis. Included are such topics as ratio analysis, operating leverage, sources and uses of funds analysis, financial forecasting, and financial control techniques. The material provides a useful overview of finance, and the ideas and terminology developed facilitate an understanding of all the other parts of the book.

Part Two: Working Capital Management

Financial management involves the acquisition and use of assets, and to a large extent these actions are reflected in the firm's balance sheet. Accordingly, to a degree, the book is organized in a balance sheet sequence, with Part Two focusing on the top part of the balance sheet, or the "working capital" section. Working capital refers to the firm's short-term, or current, assets and liabilities, and the emphasis is placed on determining optimal levels for these items. Chapter 7 is on the theory of working capital, Chapter 8 concerns current assets, and Chapter 9 discusses current liabilities. The theory chapter sets forth a rational framework within which to consider decisions affecting the specific balance sheet items that make up working capital. Firms make two kinds of working capital decisions: (1) *strategic* decisions relating to target working capital levels, and (2) *tactical* decisions that relate to day-to-day operations. The strategic decisions are fundamentally related to the tradeoff between risk and return we discussed earlier, to alternative sources of capital, to management's view of the term structure of interest rates, to the effectiveness of internal control procedures (that is, inventory control), to credit policy decisions, and so forth. The tactical operating decisions involve short-run adjustments in current assets and current liabilities to meet temporary conditions. The most obvious short-run adjustment relates to changing sales levels—fixed assets and long-term liabilities are inflexible in the short run, so changes in market demand must be met by working capital adjustments. Working capital is also adjusted from the target levels to reflect changes in long- and short-run interest rates and other changes in the availability of, and the need for, funds.

In Chapter 8 we discuss some factors bearing on (1) target levels of each kind of current asset and (2) methods for economizing on the investment in each kind of current asset. For example, the target inventory level is determined jointly by costs of stock-outs, costs of carrying and ordering inventories, order lead times and usage rates, and the probability distributions of each of those factors. With this in mind, we base our discussion of inventories on the standard EOQ-plus-safety-stock inventory model. Then, in Chapter 9, we examine the sources and forms of short-term credit.

Part Three: Decisions Involving Long-Term Assets

In Part Three we move into the lower part of the balance sheet, examining the decisions involved in fixed-asset acquisitions. After a discussion of compound interest in Chapter 10, we take up capital budgeting techniques, explaining in some detail the mechanics of capital budgeting in Chapter 11. Next, in Chapter 12, we expand the discussion to include uncertainty, covering the basic concepts of probability distributions, the tradeoff between risk and rate of return, decision trees, and simulation.

Part Four: Sources and Forms of Long-Term Financing

In Part Four we move to the lower right-hand side of the balance sheet, examining the various kinds of long-term capital available to finance long-term investments. Chapter 13 presents an overview of the capital markets, explaining briefly certain institutional material without which no basic finance course is complete. Chapter 14 analyzes the financial characteristics of common shares. Chapter 15 examines bonds and preferred shares, Chapter 16 analyzes term loans and leases, and Chapter 17 discusses the nature and use of warrants and convertibles.

Part Five: Financial Structure, the Cost of Capital, and Dividend Policy

In Part Five we pull together the threads developed in earlier chapters. We show how (1) financial structure affects both risk and expected returns; (2) risk and return interact to determine the optimal capital structure; (3) the cost of capital, which is required when making fixed-asset decisions, is calculated; and (4) investment opportunities and cost of capital considerations interact to determine the way the firm should distribute its profits between dividends and retained earnings.

Part Six: Integrated Topics in Financial Management

In the final four chapters we take up important but somewhat specialized topics that draw upon the concepts developed in the earlier sections. In Chapter 23 the external growth of firms through mergers and holding companies, as well as the factors affecting this development, is introduced. Throughout most of the text we deal with growing and successful firms; however, many firms face financial difficulties, so the causes and possible remedies to these difficulties are discussed in Chapter 24. In Chapter 22 multinational finance is discussed. The analysis draws on a number of concepts from planning and capital budgeting as well as some new ones such as risk in foreign exchange markets. Finally, in Chapter 25, we discuss the financial situation facing the small business firm and show how the tools of financial analysis may be applied to such a company. Chapter 25 also serves as a summary of the book.

QUESTIONS

1-1. The field of finance may be thought of as having gone through five developmental periods: (1) the time up through 1929; (2) the 1930s and early 1940s; (3) the late 1940s and early 1950s; (4) the middle and late 1950s; and (5) the 1960s and 1970s. What was the major emphasis in each period, and what economic circumstances led to this emphasis?

1-2. Why is shareholder wealth maximization thought to be a better operating goal than profit maximization?

1-3. The steel industry is dominated by the three large domestic firms, plus European, U.S., and Japanese firms. How effective would a voluntary pollution control effort be in such an industry? How might the steel firms participate in setting mandatory pollution control standards? How might Canadian standards affect our balance of payments?

1-4. The Carr Carriage Company has 1000 shares of common stock outstanding with a current price of $100 per share. The current earnings per share are $10. The company decides to retain the $10 per share and invest the funds to earn a 5 percent rate of return in every future year. The earnings per share increase to $10.50 and the stock price rises to $105. However, the firm could have paid out the earnings as dividends and the shareholders could have invested the funds in a project of equivalent risk to earn 10 percent. If the dividend were paid, the stock price per share would remain at $100.

Since the earnings per share and the stock price of the company have increased, the investment decision maximized the wealth of shareholders. Do you agree that this decision maximizes shareholders' wealth?

The Tax Environment

2

There are a number of techniques available to governments to generate tax revenues. These include sales, property and excise taxes, and customs duties. In this chapter, we are interested in the taxation of income of incorporated businesses (both private and public)[1], unincorporated businesses and individuals. This chapter will deal with the basic elements in corporate and individual taxation as they affect the financing and investment decisions of corporations. Since we do not intend to present a comprehensive introduction to taxation, many of the intricacies of tax law are not covered.

Specific provisions in the Income Tax Act will play an important role in the investment and financing decisions of taxpayers. For example, the debt-equity choice of a corporation is influenced by the fact that interest payments, and not dividends, are a tax-deductible expense; the dividends paid by firms may be affected by the dividend tax credit given to shareholders. In addition, the tax environment will have an impact on leasing decisions, on investment decisions such as the purchase of machinery, and on financing decisions such as refunding an outstanding bond or preferred share issue.

The capacity to influence these decisions through provisions in the tax structure is one important ingredient in governmental fiscal policy. Fiscal policy is that set of governmental decisions which attempts to influence the level of economic activity by altering the receipts and expenditures of the federal and provincial governments.

---

[1] A corporation that is resident in Canada is considered a public corporation when at least one class of its shares are listed on a Canadian stock exchange or if it meets certain requirements and elects to be a public corporation. A private corporation is defined as a corporation that is not public and not controlled, directly or indirectly, by a public corporation.

16

Through the taxation system, the government can influence real corporate investment. First, the tax rates applied to taxable income can be lowered. This increases the after-tax profitability of investment projects and increases the probability of their acceptance by firms. Second, the depreciation charge allowed for tax purposes — called the *capital cost allowance* — can be changed. For example, the government may permit a higher capital cost allowance deduction through the use of an accelerated write off. This will result in a lower tax liability in the early years of a project and enhance the after-tax profitability of investment projects. Third, the government can permit an investment tax credit for the purchase of new depreciable assets. This credit allows a given proportion of the cost of an asset to be deducted from federal taxes payable in the year of acquisition. The investment tax credit alters the after-tax profitability of the investment. Finally, the government can exempt certain income from taxation. This will certainly result in a stimulus to generate income in this form. A good example of this type of provision is the interest, dividend and capital gains exemption for individuals and the exclusion of one half of capital gains from income. Therefore, the government can, by altering certain tax regulations, have an important impact on the real investment activity of corporations and the personal investment choices of individuals.

In this chapter, we will discuss the ingredients in the determination of the taxes payable by any taxpayer, corporate or individual. Although these two groups of taxpayers will be considered separately, there is an important similarity that must be noted in the calculation of taxes payable. For any taxpayer, the derivation of taxes payable requires the determination of (a) the base on which the tax is to be calculated, (b) the tax rates to be used, and (c) any credits that provide a direct offset to taxes payable. In Figure 2-1, a schematic approach is given for the calculation of taxes payable. This figure outlines the components in the calculation of final taxes payable and gives examples for both individuals and corporations. The base on which taxes are calculated is called *taxable income* and is shown in Line 5. This is calculated as net income (Line 3), less permissible deductions (Line 4). The *taxes payable* (Line 6) are calculated by applying the appropriate tax rate to taxable income. The final component is the *tax credit* (Line 7) which is applied directly to taxes payable to obtain the final value of taxes payable.[2]

In the discussion to follow in this chapter, we will briefly investigate each of the components highlighted in Figure 2-1; first for corporations and then for individuals. Our major interest is in corporate taxation, but the area of individual

---

[2] In Figure 2-1, the taxpayer appears to calculate net income as the difference between the sum of income from all sources (Line 1), less the sum of all expenses (Line 2). This is not strictly correct, since the Income Tax Act requires the taxpayer to calculate the difference between income and expenses for each source of income. Net income is then calculated as the sum of these differences over all sources. The two approaches are different if, for example, there is a loss on one source of income which cannot be applied to positive net income from another source. We feel that the categories presented in Line 1 and 2 are useful from a descriptive and logical point of view, but this caveat should be kept in mind.

FIGURE 2-1   Schematic Representation of Calculation of Taxes Payable

	Components in calculating taxes payable	Examples of entries for each component	
		Corporate	Individual
Line 1	Income accruing to taxpayer	— sum of all sources of income	— sum of all sources of income
Line 2	Less: deductions of acceptable expenses	— expenses generally deducted in calculating net income on an accounting statement	— scheduled in Income Tax Act
Line 3	Net income		
Line 4	Less: permissible deductions	— examples: charitable donations, deduction for taxable dividends received, capital and non-capital losses of previous years	examples: personal exemptions, charitable donations, deduction for investment income, capital losses of previous years
Line 5	Taxable income		
Line 6	Taxes payable before any credits		
Line 7	Less: tax credits	— investment tax credit	— investment tax credit, dividend tax credit
Line 8	Final taxes payable		

taxation will be investigated, especially where it has an impact on financial variables, and thus on corporate decision making.

In the following, corporate and personal taxation will be considered separately. This distinction is somewhat arbitrary since there are some tax provisions which are similar for both categories. The purpose of the division is to present a self-contained discussion of each type of taxation, corporate and personal.

CORPORATE TAXATION: COMPONENTS OF INCOME

The first component included in income is active business income. Here, the use of the word "active" is designed to distinguish between income derived from the activities of a corporation and income derived from its property, such as rent, or interest paid to it on loans. The tax department does not consider a corporation to be carrying on an *active* business if virtually all of its income is from royalties, dividends or interest (unless the company is a money lending institution). Another component included in corporate income is the full value of intercorporate dividends, whether or not the dividend paying corporation is resident in Canada. A third component of income is net capital gains. The sale of any financial asset at a price that differs from the purchase price of the asset will result in a capital gain or a capital loss. In calculating the tax liability for a capital gain or loss, the sale price of the asset is compared to the adjusted cost base of that asset. This base reflects either the actual price paid for the asset (if purchased after 1972) or an imputed value of the asset on valuation day, December 31, 1971, (if the asset was purchased prior to 1972). In calculating the capital gain or loss, the expenses incurred in the disposition of the asset are deducted from the proceeds of sale.

If there is a capital gain on the sale of the asset, the *taxable capital gain,* which is equal to one half of the full capital gain, is included as regular income and taxed at regular rates. Therefore, capital gains are taxed at an effective rate equal to one half the ordinary rate. When there is a capital loss, these losses are netted against the capital gains. If gains exceed losses, one half of the net gain is included in income as a taxable capital gain. If capital losses exceed capital gains, one half of the net losses (called allowable capital losses) can be applied to taxable capital gains one year back, and as many years in the future as necessary to absorb the remainder.

DEDUCTIONS FROM INCOME

Expenses can be deduced in calculating taxable income as long as they meet the criterion that they were incurred to earn income. Several important categories of expense will be discussed at this point and others will be considered in later chapters — for example, bond discount and underwriting expenses are dealt with in Chapter 15; lease payments in Chapter 16, and so forth. The deductions that will be investigated here are:

  (i) interest expenses,
  (ii) dividend deductions,
  (iii) application of losses — capital and non-capital, and
  (iv) capital cost allowances.

Interest Expenses

Interest charges on debt issued for business purposes are a tax-deductible expense. On the other hand, common and preferred dividends and interest charges on income bonds are not tax-deductible. Thus, interest charges generate a tax benefit which is not available from other conventional financing methods. For example, to pay $1 in interest requires that the corporation earn

$1 before taxes; however, to pay $1 in taxable dividends, the corporation with a 48 percent tax rate must earn $1.92 before taxes.

Dividend Deductions

In calculating net income, dividends received from other corporations are included. If the dividends are from taxable Canadian corporations, the full amount of the dividend may be deducted in the calculation of taxable income. Thus, certain intercorporate dividends are tax free.

Application of Losses

Non-capital (operating) losses   Non-capital losses can be applied to reduce taxable income from the previous year. In addition, these losses can be carried forward for five years. Any tax loss not completely used up within those five years cannot be applied in the sixth or subsequent years. In using the non-capital losses in any year, the losses can be deducted from the taxable income in a year which includes both a capital gain component *and* non-capital income.

Capital losses   If the allowable capital losses exceed the taxable capital gains in any particular year, then the difference, called the *net allowable capital losses,* can be applied only against the taxable capital gains included in taxable income and not against non-capital income. These losses can be carried back one year and forward indefinitely.

Capital Cost Allowance (CCA)

In the preparation of accounting statements, the cost of an asset is allocated over its useful life by means of an annual depreciation expense. In computing taxable income, the analogous expense is the *capital cost allowance* (CCA). Unlike the depreciation charge, the CCA deduction is not based on an estimate of the useful life of an asset. The capital cost allowance is calculated by applying a fixed capital cost rate to a declining capital cost balance. Thus, if the original capital cost of the asset is $1,000 and the capital cost rate is 10 percent, then CCA will be $100 in the first year. In the second year, the 10 percent rate is applied to the *undepreciated capital cost* (UCC) of $900 and this gives a CCA of $90. It is obvious that any particular piece of depreciable property will never be fully depreciated when this declining-balance method is used.

Each depreciable asset fits into one of many asset classes available. The maximum CCA rate applicable to a particular class is specified in the Income Tax Regulations. The taxpayer may use a rate lower than that specified — in fact, no CCA need be claimed in any particular year.

When a taxpayer has a number of assets in a particular class, these assets are grouped into one unit (called a *pool*) for CCA calculations. Even if assets are scrapped (but not sold) or are obsolete, they still remain in the pool for CCA calculations. When assets of a particular class are purchased or sold, the value of the undepreciated capital cost of the pool is affected. In general, the costs of assets acquired are added to the undepreciated capital cost of a pool. The UCC in a pool will be reduced by the application of CCA deductions and by the proceeds of disposal of assets in the pool. The CCA expense for a particular year is based on the value of UCC of the pool at the end of the year.[3]

Examples of the assets that belong in the various pools and the maximum CCA rate applicable to these classes are noted below.

Class	Asset	Maximum CCA rate
3	Buildings and other structures (e.g. windmills)	5%
6	Frame buildings, fences	10%
8	Machinery, equipment, furniture, miscellaneous assets	20%
10	Automotive equipment, trailers	30%

As an example of the calculation of UCC and CCA charges, consider an asset with an original capital cost of $1,000 and a capital cost rate of 20 percent.

TABLE 2–1 Calculation of CCA and UCC for an asset with original cost $1,000 and capital cost rate of 20%

Year	(1) UCC at year end used for CCA expense	(2) CCA charge (0.2 × UCC)	(3) UCC balance after deduction of current CCA charge
1	$1,000	$200	$800
2	800	160	640
3	640	128	512
4	512	102	410
5	410	82	328

In the first year, the UCC at the year end that is used for the CCA charge is equal to the original cost of $1,000. The CCA charge for the year is the capital cost rate of 20 percent times the UCC balance. The third column is the UCC balance after the current CCA charge is subtracted (i.e. Column (3) equals Column (1) minus Column (2) for a given year). The value in Column (3) in a

---

[3] Since the capital cost allowance is calculated on the UCC balance *after* acquisitions and sales, the CCA charge claimed on an asset acquired anytime during the year will equal the CCA charge as if the asset were owned for the full year.

particular year becomes the UCC base for CCA charges in the following year.[4]

Notice that we have stopped the calculations at year five. However, if the asset is not sold, the UCC balance never reaches zero, and thus, there is always a CCA deduction — although its value becomes very small.

The declining-balance fixed rate CCA technique is amenable to mathematical modelling. Without presenting their derivation, formulas for the undepreciated capital cost and the capital cost allowance for any year are presented below.

$$UCC_j = C_0(1 - d)^{j-1} \qquad\qquad 2-1$$

$$CCA_j = dC_0(1 - d)^{j-1} \ = dUCC_j \qquad\qquad 2-2$$

where UCC_j is the undepreciated capital cost at the end of year j

CCA_j is the capital cost allowance expense for year j

C_0 is the original cost of the asset

d is the capital cost rate of the class

j is the year in question.

Equation 2–1 is used to calculate the undepreciated capital cost in year j and this is the base on which the capital cost allowance for year j is calculated.

To demonstrate how these formulas can be used, consider the example presented in Table 2–1. For the third year, we calculate CAA_3 and UCC_3 using Equations 2–1 and 2–2. $C_0 = \$1,000$ and $d = 0.2$:

$$\begin{aligned} UCC &= C_0(1 - d)^2 \\ &= 1,000(1 - 0.2)^2 \\ &= \$640 \end{aligned}$$

$$\begin{aligned} CCA_3 &= dC_0(1 - d)^2 \\ &= (0.2)\$1,000(1 - 0.2)^2 \\ &= \$128 \end{aligned}$$

If we wanted to know the CCA charge for the fifteenth year, we would use:

$$\begin{aligned} CCA_{15} &= dC_0(1 - d)^{14} \\ &= \$8.80 \end{aligned}$$

Sale of Assets

If there are any dispositions of assets in a pool, the impact on the undepreciated capital cost is determined first; and then the capital cost allowance is calculated by applying the capital cost rate to the undepreciated capital cost adjusted for dispositions.

---

[4] If this example reflected the UCC in a pool, the value for Column (1) for any year would equal the value in Column (3) for the previous year, adjusted for additions and sales.

When a taxpayer has a number of assets in the same class, the assets are grouped together in a pool and the pool is treated as a unit for the purposes of CCA calculations. When assets are sold from a pool, the *proceeds of sale* (if not in excess of the original cost) are subtracted from the pool as a whole to obtain the UCC value. As long as the resulting UCC of the pool is positive, there are no important tax problems to be considered. However, there may be instances in which the subtraction of the proceeds of sale will result in a negative balance of UCC. This negative balance is referred to as *recaptured depreciation* and it is considered as income and taxed at regular corporate income rates. Therefore, any recapture will occur only if the proceeds of sale are in excess of the undepreciated capital cost of the *pool* and not of the asset sold. In Table 2–2, there are four examples of the calculation of the UCC of the pool after the sale of an asset. In the first example, the proceeds of sale are less than the UCC value of the pool before the sale. Therefore, the resulting UCC balance is $5,000. In the second example, the proceeds of sale are less than the original cost of the asset, but exceed the UCC before the sale. The subtraction of the proceeds from the before-sale UCC value would give a balance after the sale of – $5,000. This $5,000 is recaptured depreciation and is included in regular income. The UCC of the pool after the sale is zero.

TABLE 2–2   Calculation of UCC Balance after the Sale of an Asset

	I	II	III	IV
UCC balance before sale	20,000	20,000	20,000	50,000
Assets sold:				
Original cost	$ 30,000	$ 30,000	$ 30,000	$ 10,000
Proceeds of sale	15,000	25,000	35,000	25,000
Recapture	—	5,000	10,000	—
Capital gain	—	—	5,000	15,000
UCC of pool after sale	5,000	—	—	40,000

A further complication enters this analysis if the proceeds from the sale of an asset exceed the original cost of the asset. This excess is treated as a capital gain in computing the tax liability. In examples III and IV, the capital gain impact is shown. In example III, the proceeds of sale (35,000) exceed the original cost of the asset and the UCC of the pool. The capital gain is equal to $5,000 (i.e. proceeds less original cost). Subtracting the proceeds of sale less the capital gain (i.e. the original cost of $30,000) from the pre-sale UCC results in a – $10,000 value. Therefore, the UCC balance after the sale is zero and there is a $10,000 recapture. Finally, example IV presents a capital gain of $15,000. To calculate the UCC balance after the sale, the proceeds less the capital gain (i.e. $25,000 – $15,000 = $10,000) is subtracted from the pre-sale UCC value (i.e. $50,000 – $10,000 = $40,000). The resulting value of $40,000 is equal to the UCC of the pool after the sale.

To summarize the discussion, the capital cost of the purchased assets is added to the undepreciated capital cost of the class. The sale proceeds are subtracted from the pool up to the original cost of the asset. At the end of the year, after all the purchases and sales, if the UCC of the pool is positive and there are still assets in the pool, then the capital cost rate is applied to the UCC. If the UCC of the pool is negative, take recapture. If the proceeds of sale exceed the original capital cost of the asset, then the taxpayer must take one-half of the capital gain into net income.[5]

Capital Cost Allowance: Accelerated Write-offs

For certain types of depreciable assets, the capital cost allowance is computed on a straight-line basis over a prescribed number of years. The assets may be written off over two years with the maximum claim in the first year equal to 50 percent of the capital cost. In the second year, the maximum claim is the remaining UCC, even if nothing was claimed in the first year. (In this case, the claim would be 100 percent.) This accelerated write-off has an impact on tax liability and will be of concern in discussing the decision to invest in assets. The assets recognized for this accelerated write-off are certain manufacturing and processing machinery and equipment acquired after May 8, 1972 (Class 29), energy conservation equipment acquired after May 25, 1976 and before 1980 (Class 34), and air pollution equipment acquired before 1980 (Class 27).

COMPUTATION OF TAX

Up to this point we have described the major components in the calculation of taxable income. Now we will consider the basic tax rates applied to the taxable income base. In the following section, any adjustments to taxes payable through tax credits will be investigated.

The basic federal tax rate for Canadian corporations is 46 percent. However, through a special incentive provision relating to manufacturing and processing profits, the basic federal rate is, in effect, reduced to 40 percent on these profits.[6]

For all provinces except Ontario and Quebec, the federal government collects both federal and provincial taxes and rebates the provincial shares. Of

[5] If there is only one asset in the class, or if there are no assets in the class after more than one asset is sold, then there is a small modification to the above discussion. If the proceeds of sale are less than the UCC balance before the sale, the difference is called a terminal loss and is written off against income. This is the only major difference. Both recapture and capital gains are handled in the same way as in Table 2. As an example of a terminal loss, consider an asset with an original cost of $20,000 and a UCC value of $10,240 that is sold for $8,000. Since the sale price is less than the UCC value, there is a terminal loss of $2,240.

[6] The impact is to reduce the tax rate by 6% for profits subject to tax at the basic federal rate. However, the provision is in reality a tax credit which is applied to taxes payable derived from using the basic federal rate.

the basic 46 percent rate, a corporation may deduct a tax abatement equal to 10 percent of its income earned in a province. However, provinces can levy taxes in excess of this 10 percent abatement. For example, the 1977 provincial rates were 12 percent for Ontario[7] and Quebec, 11 percent for Alberta and 15 percent for British Columbia. Thus, the effective total tax will reflect the basic 46 percent and the excess of the provincial corporate tax over 10 percent. For example, the effective 1978 tax rates for a corporation earning all of its profits in Ontario (at 13 percent in 1978) are presented below:

TABLE 2-3   Calculation of Effective Tax Rates for 1978

	Basic Corporate Tax		Corporate Tax on Manufacturing and Processing Profits	
Basic federal tax rate		46%		46%
Less: abatement for provincial tax	10%		10%	
Manufacturing and processing deduction	—	10	6%	16
Net federal tax rate		36%		30%
Provincial tax (Ontario)		13		13
Effective tax rate		49%		43%

To encourage the formation of business, there is a federal small business tax deduction[8]. The effect of this provision is to reduce the federal tax rate on income eligible for the small business deduction to 25 percent (i.e. the basic federal rate is reduced by the small business deduction of 21 percent).

A further small business deduction is applied against provincial tax in five provinces (Ontario, Manitoba, Saskatchewan, British Columbia and New Brunswick). The lower rate in these provinces is applicable to income which is eligible for the federal small business deduction. The reduced federal rate is applicable to the first $150,000 of active business income. Income in any year over this value is taxed at the normal tax rates.

There is also a deduction on profits from manufacturing and processing. On profits eligible for the small business deduction, the manufacturing and processing deduction is 5 percent. The net effect of the combined deductions is to reduce the federal tax rate to 20 percent on the first $150,000 of manufacturing and processing profits earned by Canadian-controlled private corporations.

This small business reduced rate may not continue indefinitely. The taxable income of the corporation is accumulated beginning after 1971, and the small business rate is applied as long as the cumulative total (which may be

[7] As of April, 1978, the province of Ontario increased the provincial rate to 13 percent.

[8] This deduction is applicable only to Canadian-controlled private corporations as defined in the Income Tax Act.

reduced by the dividends paid) is less than $750,000. The effective tax rates for corporations with less than $150,000 of business income are presented below in Table 2–4. Again, the example will be for a corporation with all of its profits in Ontario, and the Ontario tax provisions concerning small business income will be used.

TABLE 2–4 Calculation of Effective Tax Rates for 1978, Small Business Deduction

	Basic Corporate Tax		Corporate Tax on Manufacturing and Processing Profit	
Basic federal tax rate		46%		46%
Less: abatement for provincial tax	10%		10%	
Manufacturing and processing deduction	–		5	
Small business deduction	21	31	21	36
Net federal tax		15%		10%
Provincial tax (Ontario)	13%		13%	
Less: provincial small business deduction	3	10	3	10
Total effective tax rate		25%		20%

Tax Credits

The final component in determining the actual taxes payable is the tax credit. The application of the tax rate to the taxable income provides the federal taxes payable. However, there are certain provisions which permit a credit against income taxes payable and this reduces the actual amount of federal taxes payable. These provisions include tax credits for political donations and the investment tax credit, but we will consider only the investment tax credit which can be used by individuals as well as corporate tax payers.

For prescribed buildings, machinery and equipment, there is an investment tax credit of 5 percent of the capital cost of the assets. In certain designated regions, the tax credit is 7.5 percent and it reaches 10 percent in the Gaspé and the Atlantic Provinces. The tax credit may be applied to federal tax payable in the year of acquisition, and when applied, it results in an abatement of federal taxes. There are limitations on the amount of the tax credit that can be used in the year of acquisition.

When the investment tax credit is utilized, the undepreciated capital cost of the asset must be reduced by the value of the investment tax credit used in each year. As of January, 1978, the investment tax credit will be applicable to assets acquired after June 23, 1975 and before July 1, 1980, at which time it will no longer be applicable for assets acquired after this date.

Payment of Taxes

The actual payment pattern for taxes will have an impact on cash flows for investment decisions. Incorporated businesses must make installment payments over a fourteen or fifteen month period. An installment payment is due on the last day of each month of the corporation's tax year and the balance of the tax payable, if any, is due two months after the end of the taxation year. If the company has claimed the small business deduction in the preceeding year, the final installment payment is due at the end of the third month after the end of the taxation year. Finally, an unincorporated business is required to make installment payments of its tax liability at the end of each calendar quarter. Any balance remaining is due by April 30 of the following year.

PERSONAL TAXATION

As described in Figure 2–1, the computation of both corporate and individual taxes payable follows the same basic steps. Since this text is not intended to cover personal finance, our coverage of the tax environment for individuals will be limited. We are interested in those income tax provisions which have an indirect impact on a corporation's actions. These include the taxation of capital gains and dividends.

Calculation of Taxable Income

In addition to employment income, income from property is included in taxable income. This latter category includes dividends, interest, and capital gains. We will defer the discussion of dividends to a subsequent section.

The full amount of interest income is included in the net income calculation, but this is not true for capital gains. Just as in the calculation of capital gains in corporate taxable income, capital gains for individuals can be netted against capital losses. When the resulting value is positive (i.e. when there is a net capital gain), one half of this capital gain is included in regular income. Thus, capital gains are taxed at an effective rate of one half the ordinary tax rate for individuals. When the net figure is negative, one half of this capital loss (i.e. the allowable capital loss) can be deducted from other sources of income in the same year. The maximum deduction is $2,000.

A number of exemptions and deductions are made from net income to obtain taxable income. These deductions include personal deductions, and gifts among others. To offset the impact of inflation, some of these exemptions and deductions have been indexed through a linkage to increases in the consumer price index (CPI); however, the indexing is lagged by approximately one year. For example, for the taxation year 1977, the CPI for the year ending September 30, 1976, was the basis for the indexing.

Of the possible deductions that could be considered, we will investigate two: (a) the interest, dividend and capital gains deductions, and (b) the application of unused allowable capital losses. The first deduction permits the taxpayer to deduct up to $1,000 from the aggregate amount of Canadian sources of interest received, the taxable portion of capital gains on Canadian securities and adjusted dividends.[9] The second deduction permits unused allowable capital losses to be carried over from previous years. The unused allowable capital losses can be deducted from the taxable capital gains in the preceding year and from a maximum of $2,000 of other income in that year as long as there was non-capital income remaining after the deduction of non-capital losses. If the taxpayer was particularly unlucky, any remaining allowable capital losses can be applied forward until the remainder is absorbed. However, the maximum deduction permitted against non-capital income in any *future* year is $2,000.

Tax Rates: Individuals

As in corporate taxation, both the federal and provincial governments levy personal income taxes. Each province imposes a tax on income earned in the province at whatever level it chooses. For all provinces except Quebec, this tax is expressed as a percentage (or surtax) of the basic federal income tax payable. The percentage rates vary among provinces. In 1978, Alberta had the lowest rate with 38.5 percent while Newfoundland had the highest at 57.5 percent. Quebec was the only province that had a progressive tax scheme. For all provinces except Quebec, the provincial tax is collected by the federal government and transferred to the province.

The tax rates applicable to individuals on their employment income are also used for unincorporated businesses such as sole proprietorships and partnerships.

In addition to indexing exemptions and deductions, the tax brackets for taxable income are also indexed. Table 2–5 shows the tax rates for 1978.

The tax rate structure is graduated so that the higher the income, the higher the tax liability. For example, consider the taxable income level $13,689 in Table 2–5. At this income level, the federal tax payable is $2,618 plus 25 percent on the next $3,042 of taxable income. The 25 percent value reflects the marginal federal tax rate—the tax rate applicable for every dollar of taxable income above $13,689, assuming the investor remains in the same tax bracket. Notice that the marginal federal tax rates increase from 6 to 43 percent as taxable income increases. In addition, the average federal tax rates increase from 11 to 33.1 percent (see Column 3). Columns (4) and (5) are calculated based on the Province of Ontario surtax of 44 percent of the basic federal tax payable.

[9] The dividends received are adjusted by adding 50% of the value of the dividend received. This final figure is called grossed-up dividends and is described in more detail in a subsequent section.

TABLE 2-5 Rates of Federal Income Tax, 1978[a]

Taxable income (1)	Tax (2)		Average tax rate at upper level of interval (3) Federal	(4) Total[b]	Total marginal tax rate[b] (5)
760 or less	6%				
761	$ 46 + 16% on next	$ 760	11.1%	15.9%	23.0%
1,521	168 + 17% on next	1,521	14.0	20.2	24.5
3,042	427 + 18% on next	1,521	15.4	22.1	25.9
4,563	701 + 19% on next	3,042	16.8	24.2	27.4
7,605	1,279 + 21% on next	3,042	18.0	25.9	30.2
10,647	1,918 + 23% on next	3,042	19.1	27.5	33.1
13,689	2,618 + 25% on next	3,042	20.2	29.1	36.0
16,731	3,379 + 28% on next	4,563	21.9	31.5	40.3
21,294	4,657 + 32% on next	15,210	26.1	37.6	46.1
36,504	9,524 + 36% on next	22,815	29.9	43.1	51.8
59,319	17,737 + 39% on next	31,941	33.1	47.7	56.2
91,260	30,194 + 43% on remainder				61.9

[a] The total tax payable is subject to a federal credit of 9 percent of the basic federal tax (minimum of $300, maximum of $500).

[b] Includes Province of Ontario surtax at 44 percent of federal tax payable. In Column (4), the average total tax rate is calulated as the average federal tax rate plus the provincial surcharge of 44 percent. In Column (5), the total marginal tax rate is equal to the federal marginal tax rate plus the provincial surcharge.

The average rates of taxation can be used to compare the tax burdens of different forms of business structure. For example, the tax burden of a sole proprietorship (which uses the tax table presented in Table 2–5 to calculate its tax liability) versus an incorporated business can be compared using the average tax rates.

Dividend Taxation

An example of a provision that has an impact on both taxable income and tax credits is the taxation of dividends from a company resident in Canada. Shareholders are subject to taxation on these dividends; however, there is an adjustment to both preferred and common share dividends received from Canadian sources which reduces the effective taxation at the personal level. The adjustment is a dividend tax credit which reduces the amount of federal, and hence provincial, tax payable.

The amount of gross federal tax payable, before the tax credit is applied, is found by applying the appropriate marginal federal tax rate to adjusted dividends received. To obtain the adjusted dividends, a gross-up is added to the actual dividends received. The gross-up is 50 percent of the dividends received. The tax credit, which is equal to 75 percent of the gross-up, is then deducted from federal tax payable to obtain the net federal tax payable. The provincial tax is found by applying the provincial surcharge to net federal tax payable.

As an example, consider a shareholder who receives $1,000 in cash dividends. To calculate the after-tax dividend received and the effective tax rate, two examples are presented based on the 1978 income tax regulations. Assume there are two investors in Ontario (which has a 44 percent surtax on federal tax payable) with 28 and 39 percent marginal federal tax rates and that the $1,000 exemption on interest, dividends, and capital gains has been used up.

TABLE 2-6 Calculation of After-Tax Dividends

	Investor 1		Investor 2	
Dividends received		$1,000		$1,000
Gross-up: ½ of dividend received		500		500
Total subject to tax		1,500		1,500
Federal tax (gross)	at 28%	420	at 39%	585
Dividend tax credit: 75% of the gross-up		375		375
Net federal tax payable		45		210
Provincial tax: 0.44 of net federal tax		20		92
Total tax payable		$ 65		$ 302
Dividend after-tax:	(1,000–65) = $ 935		(1,000–302) = $ 698	
Effective overall tax rate on dividends (tax paid/dividends received)		6.5%		30.2%

The total marginal tax rate for Investor 1 is 40.3 percent (i.e. $0.28 \times 1.44 \times 100$) and the rate for Investor 2 is 56.2 percent (i.e. $0.39 \times 1.44 \times 100$). For Investor 1, the effective tax rate on dividend income due to the dividend tax credit falls from 40.3 to 6.5 percent. At the higher marginal tax rate, a reduction is still present from 56.2 to 30.2 percent, but the percentage reduction is much smaller. The declining benefit of the tax credit as marginal rates increase occurs because gross federal tax increases with the marginal rate, but the tax credit is fixed at a proportion of the gross-up.

An interesting example of the impact of the dividend tax credit can be seen in the successful $175 million Bell Canada convertible preferred issue sold in early April, 1978. The security was priced at $25, and based on the dividend per share of $1.96, it had a 7.84 percent yield. Of the total issue, only $40 to $50 million of orders were obtained from institutional buyers. This is much smaller than the usual 50 to 60 percent of an issue usually sold to institutions.

The disinterest of the institutional buyer and the interest of the retail market can be explained by the dividend tax credit. Since institutions are tax free, they do not obtain the tax credits. However, since individuals can obtain these credits, the after-tax dividend yield will depend on their federal marginal rate and the province in which they live. For example, for an Ontario resident at the 28 percent federal marginal tax rate, the after-tax yield would be 7.3 percent. To obtain this yield on a bond would require bond yields of approximately 12 percent. For an institution, the before-tax yield equals the after-tax yield, and with bond rates well above the preferred yield, the institutions were interested only to the extent of the conversion feature.

FORM OF ORGANIZATION

A taxpayer operating a business has the choice of two basic organizational forms. On the one hand, the business can be unincorporated and operate as either a *sole proprietorship* or a *partnership*. In the sole proprietorship, there is a sole owner who owns the assets and is responsible for all of the liabilities. If there is a default, the general creditors can take the personal assets of the proprietor if the assets of the business are insufficient to satisfy their claims. Under the partnership alternative, there is more than one owner, and typically, there is a formal agreement drawn up that specifies how the profits or losses will be shared. If this agreement is not present, the partners share profits or losses equally. In this case, also, the personal assets of the partners can be taken by unsatisfied general creditors. A variation on the partnership theme is called the *limited partnership.* Here there is a general partner that has all the rights and financial responsibilities of the partners in a regular partnership. However, certain other partners (a) cannot be involved in a managerial role, (b) must share profits on a pre-arranged basis, and (c) have their liability for the debts of the partnership limited to their original contribution. Such partners are called *limited partners* since their risk exposure is limited (i.e. having paid up fully for their interest in the company, they are not personally responsible for any unsatisfied claims of the creditors).

The second basic form of organization is the corporation which is a legal entity that can enter contracts and own property. In fact, the corporation is considered as a person for legal purposes. Incorporation can occur either under provincial or federal regulations. The owners of the corporation (i.e. the shareholders) have limited liability—their liability is restricted to the amount paid for the shares and there is no recourse to them by creditors of the corporation. In all provincial incorporations (except Alberta) and in federal incorporations, the company must have one of the following terms in its title: "limited", "incorporated", or "corporation" (or abbreviations of these words). In Alberta, only the term "limited" or its abbreviation, is permitted.

Should a company operate on an incorporated or unincorporated basis? There are a number of factors which must be considered in this decision. These factors can be grouped into two major areas—tax and non-tax factors.

Non-tax Factors

An important consideration is the existence of limited liability for incorporated business. The sole proprietorship risks his personal assets while the shareholder does not. However, for small, risky incorporated businesses, limited liability may be a fiction. Creditors, in an attempt to reduce their risk, will often require personal guarantees from the owners. If they do not ask for guarantees, they will increase the interest rates that the companies must pay.

Another consideration is that it may be easier to transfer ownership in an incorporated enterprise than in a sole proprietorship. This, however, will depend on the number of shares outstanding for the incorporated business and the size of the business.

Tax Factors

Unincorporated business income is taxed at the personal tax rates of the owners and not at corporate tax rates. Depending on the taxable income of the company and the applicability of such deductions as that for small businesses, there may be a clear preference for incorporation. In fact, active business income subject to the small business deduction is always better under the incorporated form of organization.

For an incorporated business, any unused capital losses are written off against capital income only; but for an unincorporated business, the unused capital loss can be applied against non-capital income as well as capital gains. However, there is a maximum deduction against non-capital income.

In an incorporated business, the shareholder(s) can be an employee(s) of the corporation and obtain benefits as tax-deductible expenses. In an unincorporated business, the owner can not obtain these tax deductible employee benefits.

There are a number of additional factors that would have to be included in the decision on whether to incorporate, but the final decision will depend on the particular circumstances. Nevertheless, it appears that, for a wide range of taxable income levels, incorporation has a number of benefits which can not be obtained by an unincorporated business.

SUMMARY

This chapter provides some basic background on the tax environment within which business firms operate. Whether we are looking at corporate or individual taxes, the final taxes payable are determined by calculating taxable income and applying the appropriate tax rate. The result is the value of taxes payable which is then reduced by the application of tax credits.

Corporate Taxes

In calculating taxable income for corporations, all sources of income must be included. These sources of income are from operations, dividends, and taxable capital gains. Taxable capital gains are equal to one half of the total capital gain. Capital losses, on the other hand, can be netted against capital gains, and if the result is a positive value, one half of the net is included in income as taxable capital gains. If the net value is negative, one half of the loss (the allowable capital loss) is applied to taxable gains one year back and as far in the future as necessary to absorb the loss.

Deductions from income to calculate taxable income include interest expense, dividends from taxable Canadian corporations and capital cost allowances. In addition, non-capital (operating) losses can be carried forward for five years and back one year.

The tax rates applied to taxable income reflect the basic federal corporate tax rate of 46 percent plus a provincial income tax element as well. The tax rates are affected by special deductions for corporate profits generated from manufacturing and processing operations and for small businesses. The final element in calculating taxes payable is the application of tax credits such as the investment tax credit.

Personal Income Tax

Just as in the calculation of corporate tax, all sources of income are included in taxable income. Unused capital losses can be applied to taxable capital gains in the preceeding year and, unlike corporations, applied for a maximum of $2,000 against income in that year. The unused capital losses can be applied forward until the remainder is absorbed. The effect of this is to tax capital gains at one half the individual tax rate. There is a $1,000 deduction for capital gains, interest and grossed-up dividends, as well as a dividend tax credit. This tax credit has an important impact on the after-tax dividend received by a shareholder. The impact depends on the marginal rate of the taxpayer.

The foregoing material on the Canadian tax system is not designed to transform the reader into a tax expert. However, it provides the essential elements to recognize the tax aspects of business financial problems and to develop an awareness of the types of problems that should be taken to tax specialists for further guidance. These tax basics will be referred to frequently throughout the text, because income taxes are often an important factor in business decisions.

QUESTIONS

2-1. a. If a depreciable asset's original cost is $100,000, what will be the undepreciated capital cost (UCC) of the asset at the end of 10 years when the capital cost rates are 10%, 15% and 20%?

b. What would be the maximum capital cost allowance (CCA) for the 10th year of this asset for each of the capital cost rates in Part a.?

2-2. The taxable income (losses are shown in parenthesis) of the D. Johnson Corp., formed in 19X3, is shown below:

19X3	$(250,000)
19X4	125,000
19X5	175,000
19X6	325,000
19X7	(125,000)

What is the corporate tax liability for each year? Assume the corporate tax rate is 48%.

2-3. The current undepreciated capital cost of a specific pool of assets is $1,300,000. The firm decides to sell from the pool an asset that originally cost $1,500,000. Calculate the amount of recaptured depreciation and capital gains, if any, and the value of the undepreciated capital cost of the pool after the sale under the following assumed proceeds from sale:

(i) $1 million.   (iii) $1.5 million.

(ii) $1.3 million.   (iv) $1.8 million.

2-4. A firm acquires an asset for $1 million on January 1, 19X9. It is added to a pool of assets that has an UCC balance as of the same date of $3 million. The firm has taxable income as of December 31, 19X9, before the deduction of CCA of $30 million. The capital cost rate applicable to this pool of assets is 6 percent. If the firm operates in Ontario and the asset is eligible for a 5 percent investment tax credit, calculate the total corporate tax payable.

2-5. The David Smith Bookstore has $25,000 of taxable income. If it were incorporated, would it have a lower tax liability? (Assume the business would be eligible for the small business deduction in Ontario if it is incorporated.) Assume a personal marginal federal tax rate of 32% for the owner, David Smith.

2-6. Assume that an investor who resides in Ontario receives $1,000 in dividend income and is subject to a 19 percent marginal federal tax rate. Calculate the tax on the dividend income for this individual assuming that the $1,000 interest, dividend exemption has been used up. If the tax paid is negative, interpret what this means.

2-7. If an individual is subject to a 28 percent marginal federal tax rate, what would be the total tax payable on $1,000 income from (i) dividends (ii) bond interest and (iii) capital gains. Assume the $1,000 exemption has been used up and the investor resides in Manitoba.

PROBLEMS

2-1. The T. Snyder Manufacturing Company Limited is a solely owned incorporated company resident in Ontario. The type of business Mr. Snyder operates permits the manufacturing and processing deduction to be used. If Mr. Snyder takes all of the after-tax profits out of the firm in dividends, what would Mr. Snyder's personal after-tax income be on the dividend income from the firm if his marginal federal tax rate is 32 percent and the company earns $30,000 before taxes?

2-2. The Maple Creek Mining Company Limited has an asset pool consisting of a group of assets which all belong to a single class. These assets have an original cost of $7.2 million. The accumulated capital cost allowance on the pool is $2.8 million. The company sold assets which originally cost $5 million for $7.5 million. Describe the effect on company taxes. How would the recapture and/or capital gains be treated for tax purposes? Assume the company has a marginal tax rate of 48 percent.

2-3. The Oak Leaf Snowplow Co. Ltd. had earnings before tax deductible expenses of $1 million in 19X7. Expenses, other than the CCA expense, were $500,000 during the year. The company's assets all fall into a single capital pool which had an UCC of $500,000 in that year. These assets were all in their fifth year of use during 19X7, and the capital cost rate for that asset class was 20 percent. On the last day of 19X7, the company sold some of its assets which had an original cost of $250,000 to the Big A Snow Plow Co. Ltd. for $280,000. The company then used the funds to buy new smaller equipment for $280,000. The corporate income tax rate is 48 percent and the capital gains will be treated in the usual way. Calculate the company's income after taxes in 19X7 if it had no carryback losses to take advantage of. What would be the impact on Oak Leaf's tax liability if, instead of purchasing the new snow plow's, the company paid out the $280,000 proceeds from the sale of the old equipment as a dividend to shareholders?

2-4. The Anne Erickson School of Languages is a collection of schools across Canada but the income from each school is taxable at the rate of the province in which it is earned. The company has a large building in the center of Edmonton, Alberta, which cost $400,000 ten years ago. The appropriate capital cost rate is 6 percent for this type of asset. Ms. Erickson has now sold the structure for $300,000 and purchased a new modern building for $1 million. Refer to the text for the appropriate tax rate for the province. What is the tax liability on the sale and what is the UCC on the pool after the purchase?

2-5.* Daisy Lewis borrowed $1,000 at 10 percent on November 31, 19X8, and used the funds to purchase 40 shares of Real Estate Growth Corp. On December 31, 19X8, the company paid a dividend of $20.00 per share and repurchased the outstanding shares at $5 per share. D. Lewis has $14,000 of other taxable income in 19X8.

    a. What will be the net effect of the above investment and stock repurchase on D. Lewis' tax liability?

    b. Was this investment profitable for D. Lewis? Assume that the dividend income was in excess of the $1,000 exemption; that she lived in Ontario; and that the interest expense can be ignored in the analysis.

    c. Would your answers to Parts a. and b. change if Lewis could use the $1,000 dividend exemption?

---

* * This problem is complicated and should be attempted only by students who have mastered the tax intricacies noted in the chapter.

Ratio Analysis

3

Planning is the key to the financial manager's success. Financial plans may take many forms, but any good plan must be related to the firm's existing strengths and weaknesses. The strengths must be understood if they are to be used to proper advantage, and the weaknesses must be recognized if corrective action is to be taken. For example, are inventories adequate to support the projected level of sales? Does the firm have too heavy an investment in accounts receivable, and does this condition reflect a lax collection policy? The financial manager can plan future financial requirements in accordance with the forecasting and budgeting procedures we will present in succeeding chapters, but the plan must begin with the type of financial analysis developed in this chapter.

BASIC FINANCIAL STATEMENTS

Because ratio analysis employs financial data taken from the firm's balance sheet and income statement, it is useful to begin this chapter with a review of these accounting reports. To illustrate the usefulness of the data in these reports, the financial statements of the Surrey Company Limited will be employed. The company is an established retailing operation in Canada with stores in eight of the ten provinces and is a respected merchandiser of car, home and office products. Originally a family business, the firm has grown to become a popular and widely-held company with annual sales of close to a billion dollars.

In order for the Surrey Company to remain in a competitive position, it is necessary for the financial officer of the company to scrutinize the financial accounts and review any changes over time in these accounts in order to ensure that the firm's financial good helath is maintained. At this point we will present the basic components of the financial statements, explain their purpose, and then examine certain ratios which will assist in the diagnosis of the health of the firm.

Balance Sheet

Surrey's balance sheet, given in Table 3-1, shows the value of the firm's assets, and of the claims on these assets, at two particular points in time, December 31, 19X6, and December 31, 19X7. The assets are arranged from top to bottom in order of decreasing liquidity; that is, assets toward the top of the column will be converted to cash sooner than those toward the bottom of the column. The top group of assets—cash, marketable securities, accounts receivable, and inventories, which are expected to be converted into cash within one year—is defined as *current assets.* Assets in the lower part of the statement—plant and equipment—are not expected to be converted to cash within one year; these are defined as *fixed assets.*

The right side of the balance sheet is arranged similarly. Those items toward the top of the Claims column mature, and must be paid off, relatively soon; those further down the column are due in the more distant future.[1] Current liabilities must be paid within one year; because the firm never has to "pay off" common shareholders, common shares and retained earnings represent "permanent" capital.

---

[1] In Chapter 2 we noted that, for tax purposes, the depreciation expense is the capital cost allowance (CCA) charge. However, for accounting and reporting in financial statements, depreciation may be calculated on a different basis—for example, by the straight-line method. During the early years of the asset's life, the CCA charge may exceed the accounting depreciation expense used for reporting purposes.

For a variety of reasons, none of which we will present, the Canadian Institute of Chartered Accountants suggests that, for reporting purposes, the tax expense should be calculated on the basis of the depreciation technique used for reporting purposes. This tax charge or expense is presented on the income statement and is composed of two parts: the first part is taxes currently payable, based on the CCA charge; and the second part is the difference between the tax expense and the taxes currently payable (these are called *deferred taxes).* In the early years of the asset's life, the taxes currently payable will be less than the tax expense on the income statement, and the deferred tax will be applied to a deferred tax account on the liability side of the balance sheet; this positive deferred tax occurs because the CCA expense exceeds the reported depreciation expense. In future years, taxes payable will exceed the tax expense, and the deferred tax account will be reduced.

A simple example may be useful at this point. Suppose a company has $500 in net income before taxes and depreciation. The depreciation charge for reporting purposes is $100; based on a 40 per cent tax rate, the income tax expense is $160 (i.e. before-tax income of $400 times the tax rate of 40 per cent). For tax purposes, the CCA charge is $200 and the taxes payable are $120 (i.e. taxable income of $300 times the tax rate of 40 per cent). The tax expense of $160 is composed of taxes currently payable of $120 plus deferred taxes of $40. This $40 will be added to the deferred tax account on the balance sheet.

The deferred tax account can be thought of as an interest free loan from the government. In our illustration, deferred taxes are excluded because they would present an unnecessary complication.

TABLE 3-1 Surrey Company Limited
Illustrative balance sheet (thousands of dollars)

Assets

	Dec. 31, 19X6	Dec. 31, 19X7
Current assets		
Cash	$ 30,000	$ 15,000
Receivables	250,000	230,000
Inventories	100,000	170,000
Total current assets	$380,000	$415,000
Property and Equipment		
Leasehold	10,000	12,000
Improvements	48,000	50,000
Equipment	110,000	130,000
Building	(33,000)	(42,000)
Less depreciation		
Land	37,000	41,000
Net property and equipment	$172,000	$191,000
Total assets	$552,000	$606,000

Claims on Assets

	Dec. 31, 19X6	Dec. 31, 19X7
Current liabilities		
Accounts payable	$ 45,000	$ 50,000
Loans, notes payable	32,000	39,000
Income taxes payable	2,000	2,000
Total current liabilities	$ 79,000	$ 91,000
Long-term debt		
Mortgage bonds	90,000	107,000
Sinking fund debentures	220,000	220,000
Total long-term debt	$310,000	$327,000
Shareholder's equity		
Capital stock	50,000	50,000
Retained earnings	113,000	138,000
Total net worth	$163,000	$188,000
Total claim on assets	$552,000	$606,000

Generally speaking, the right-hand side of the balance sheet displays the sources of funding for the assets employed on the left-hand side. The liabilities represent claims by the creditors, and common shares and retained earnings reflect the investment by the owners of the firm. Notice that the values of the liabilities and shareholders' equity do *not* represent market values.

Income Statement

Surrey's income statement is shown in Table 3–2. Sales are shown at the top of the statement; various costs, including income taxes, are deducted to arrive at the net income available to common shareholders. The figure on the last line represents earnings per share *(EPS)*, calculated as net income divided by number of shares outstanding.

Statement of Retained Earnings

Earnings may be paid out to shareholders as dividends, or retained and reinvested in the business. Shareholders like to receive dividends, of course, but if earnings are plowed back into the business, the value of the shareholders' position in the company increases. Later in the book we shall consider the pros and cons of retaining earnings versus paying them out in dividends, but for now we are simply interested in the effects of dividends and retained earnings on the balance sheet. For this purpose, accountants use the statement of retained earnings illustrated for Surrey in Table 3–3. Surrey earned $30 million during the year, paid $5,000,000 in dividends to shareholders and retained $25 million within the business. This appears both on the balance sheet and on the statement of retained earnings, where the earnings are $138,000,000 (i.e. $25 million more than the 19X6 year-end value).

Relationship among the Three Statements

It is important to recognize that the balance sheet is a statement of the firm's financial position *at a point in time*, whereas the income statement shows the results of operations *during an interval of time*. Thus, the balance sheet represents a snapshot of the firm's position on a given date, while the income statement is based on a flow concept, showing what occurred between two points in time.

The statement of retained earnings indicates how the retained earnings account on the balance sheet is adjusted between balance sheet dates. Since the company began operations, Surrey had retained a total of $113 million up to December 31, 19X6. Of the $30 million earned in 19X7, $25 million was retained. Therefore, the new retained earnings figure for 19X7 is $138 million as shown on the balance sheet.

When a firm retains earnings, it generally does so to expand the business —that is, to finance the purchase of assets such as plant, equipment, and inventories. As a result of operations in 19X7, Surrey has $25 million available for that purpose. Sometimes retained earnings will be used to build up the cash account, but *retained earnings as shown on the balance sheet are not cash.* Through the years they have been invested in bricks and mortar and other assets, so retained earnings as shown on the balance sheet are not "available" for anything. The earnings *for the current year* may be available for investment, but the *past retained earnings* have already been employed.

TABLE 3-2   Surrey Company Limited
Illustrative income statement
For year ended December 31, 19X7 (thousands of dollars)

Total revenue		$920,000
Cost of goods sold		710,000
Gross profit		210,000
Less: Operating expenses		
Selling	$52,000	
General administrative	26,000	
Lease payment on buildings	20,000	98,000
Gross operating income		112,000
Depreciation		9,000
Net operating income		103,000
Less: Other expenses		
Interest on notes payable	4,000	
Interest on mortgage	10,000	
Interest on debentures	24,000	38,000
Net income before taxes		65,000
Income taxes		35,000
Net income for year available to shareholders		$30,000
Earnings per share (EPS)		$ 2.61

TABLE 3-3   Surrey Company Limited
Statement of retained earnings
For year ended December 31, 19X7 (thousands of dollars)

Balance of retained earnings, December 31, 19X6	$113,000
Add: Net income, 19X7	30,000
	143,000
Less: Dividends to shareholders	5,000
Balance of retained earnings, December 31, 19X7	$138,000

Stated another way, the balance sheet item "retained earnings" simply shows how much of their earnings the shareholders, through the years, have elected to reinvest in the business. Thus, the retained earnings account shows the additional investment the shareholders as a group have made in the business, over and above their initial investment at the inception of the company and through any subsequent issues of stock.

BASIC TYPES OF FINANCIAL RATIOS

Each type of analysis has a purpose or use that determines the different relationships emphasized in the analysis. The analyst may, for example, be a banker considering whether or not to grant a short-term loan to a firm. Primarily, concern is in the firm's near-term, or liquidity, position, so stress is placed on ratios that measure liquidity. In contrast, long-term creditors place far more emphasis on earning power and on operating efficiency. They know that unprofitable operations will erode asset values and that a strong current position is no guarantee that funds will be available to repay a 20-year bond issue. Equity investors are similarly interested in long-term profitability and efficiency. Management is, of course, concerned with all those aspects of financial analysis—it must be able to repay its debts to long- and short-term creditors as well as earn profits for shareholders.

It is useful to classify ratios into four fundamental types:

1. *Liquidity ratios*, which measure the firm's ability to meet its maturing short-term obligations.
2. *Leverage ratios*, which measure the extent to which the firm has been financed by debt.
3. *Activity ratios*, which measure how effectively the firm is using its resources.
4. *Profitability ratios*, which measure management's overall effectiveness as shown by the returns generated on sales and investment.

Specific examples of each ratio are given in the following sections, where the Surrey case history is used to illustrate their calculation and use.

Liquidity Ratios

Generally, the first concern of the financial analyst is liquidity: Is the firm able to meet its maturing obligations? Surrey has debts totaling $91 million that must be paid within the coming year. Can these obligations be satisfied? Although a full liquidity analysis requires the use of cash budgets (described in Chapter 6), ratio analysis, by relating the amount of cash and other current assets to the current obligations, provides a quick and easy-to-use measure of liquidity. Two commonly used liquidity ratios are presented below.

Current Ratio   The current ratio is computed by dividing current assets by current liabilities. Current assets normally include cash, marketable securities, accounts receivable, and inventories; current liabilities consist of accounts payable, short-term notes payable, current maturities of long-term debt, accrued income taxes, and other accrued expenses (principally wages). The current ratio is the most commonly used measure of short-term solvency, since it indicates the extent to which the claims of short-term creditors are covered by assets that are expected to be converted to cash in a period roughly corresponding to the maturity of the claims.

The calculation of the current ratio for Surrey at year end, 19X7, is shown below.

$$\text{Current ratio} = \frac{\text{current assets}}{\text{current liabilities}} = \frac{\$415,000}{\$\ 91,000} = 4.56 \text{ times.}$$

$$\text{Industry average} = 1.78 \text{ times.}$$

The current ratio is well above the average for the industry, 1.78 times, and this may be of concern to the management. Since current assets are near maturity, it is quite likely that they could be liquidated at 22 percent of book value in order to satisfy current creditors.[2]

Although industry average figures are discussed in Table 3–4 in this chapter, it should be stated at this point that the industry average is not a magic number that all firms should strive to maintain. In fact, some very well managed firms will be above it, and other good firms will be below it. However, if a firm's ratios are very far removed from the average for its industry, the analyst must be concerned about why this variance occurs; that is, a deviation from the industry average should signal the analyst to check further.

The substantial discrepancy from the industry average could be a result of the combination of different types of companies in the merchandising industry category. Within this industry, there is a wide variation in current ratios for individual companies. Alternatively, the large current ratio may suggest that the firm should reduce its accounts receivable by reducing the credit sales to customers, or increase the accounts payable by taking greater advantage of credit offered to them by their suppliers.

Quick Ratio or Acid Test   The quick ratio is calculated by deducting inventories from current assets and dividing the remainder by current liabilities. Inventories are typically the least liquid of a firm's current assets and the assets on which losses are most likely to occur in the event of liquidation. Therefore, this measure of the firm's ability to pay off short-term obligations

---

[2](1/4.56) =.22 or 22 percent. Note that (.22) ($415,000,000) ≈ $91,000,000, the amount of current liabilities.

without relying on the sale of inventories is important.

$$\text{Quick, or acid test, ratio} = \frac{\text{current assets} - \text{inventory}}{\text{current liabilities}} = \frac{\$245,000,000}{\$\ 91,000,000}$$

$$= 2.69 \text{ times.}$$

$$\text{Industry average} = .82 \text{ times.}$$

The average quick ratio for the industry is .82, and consistent with the observation of the current ratio, Surrey is well above the industry average. It is clear from these two ratios that Surrey is in a highly liquid short-term position. All short-term liabilities can be paid off easily if the receivables can be liquidated at more than 33 percent of their book value. This is calculated by the following formula.

$$\frac{\text{current liabilities} - \text{cash}}{\text{receivables}} = \frac{\$\ 76,000,000}{\$230,000,000} = .33 \text{ or } 33\%$$

Leverage Ratios

Leverage ratios, which measure the funds supplied by owners as compared with the financing provided by the firm's creditors, have a number of implications. First, creditors look to the equity, or owner-supplied funds, to provide a margin of safety. If owners have provided only a small proportion of total financing, the risks of the enterprise are borne mainly by the creditors. Second, by raising funds through debt, the owners gain the benefits of maintaining control of the firm with a limited investment. Third, if the firm earns more on the borrowed funds than it pays in interest, the return to the owners is magnified. For example, if assets earn 6 percent and debt costs only 4 percent, there is a 2 percent differential accruing to the shareholders. Leverage cuts both ways, however; if the return on assets falls to 3 percent, the differential between that figure and the interest cost of debt must be made up from equity's share of total profits. In the first instance, where assets earn more than the interest cost of debt, leverage is favorable; in the second, it is unfavorable.

Firms with low leverage ratios have less risk of loss when the economy is in a recession, but they also have lower expected returns when the economy booms. Conversely, firms with higher leverage ratios run the risk of large losses but also have a chance of gaining high profits. The prospects of high returns are desirable, but investors are averse to risk. Decisions about the use of leverage, then, must balance higher expected returns against increased risk.[3]

[3]The problem of determining optimum leverage for a firm with given risk characteristics is examined extensively in Chapters 19 and 20.

In practice, leverage is approached in two ways. One approach examines balance sheet ratios and determines the extent to which borrowed funds have been used to finance the firm. The other approach measures the risks of debt by income statement ratios designed to determine the number of times fixed charges are covered by operating profits. These sets of ratios are complementary, and most analysts examine both leverage ratios.

Total Debt to Total Assets   The ratio of total debt to total assets, generally called the *debt ratio*, measures the percentage of total funds provided by creditors. Debt includes current liabilities and all bonds. Creditors prefer moderate debt ratios, since the lower the ratio, the greater the cushion against creditors' losses in the event of liquidation. In contrast to the creditors' preference for a low debt ratio, the owners may seek high leverage either (1) to magnify earnings or (2) because raising new equity means giving up some degree of control. If the debt ratio is too high, there is a danger of encouraging irresponsibility on the part of the owners. The stake of the owners can become so small that speculative activity, if it is successful, will yield a substantial percentage return to the owners. If the venture is unsuccessful, however, only a moderate loss is incurred by the owners because their investment is small.

$$\text{Debt ratio} = \frac{\text{total debt}}{\text{total assets}} = \frac{\$418,000,000}{\$606,000,000} = .6897 \text{ or } 68.97\%$$

$$\text{Industry average} = 67.75\%$$

Surrey's debt ratio of 68.97% means that the creditors have supplied that proportion of the company's total financing. Since Surrey's ratio is slightly greater than the industry average, Surrey's financial officer could consider the possibility of future financing problems. If new debt is issued to finance the acquisition of new assets, the debt ratio will increase and this could result in substantially higher interest rates; in fact, the higher ratio may cause a hardship on the existing shareholders.[4] Finally, Surrey may have to determine if they are approaching their debt capacity level for the given level of equity in the company. If so, future financing will require an equity component as well as debt.

Times Interest Earned   The times-interest-earned ratio is determined by dividing earnings before interest and taxes (gross income in Table 3–2) by the interest charges. The times-interest-earned ratio measures the extent to

---

[4]The ratio of debt to equity is also used in financial analysis. The debt to assets (D/A) and debt to equity (D/E) ratios are simply transformations of one another:

$$D/E = \frac{D/A}{1 - D/A} \quad \text{and} \quad D/A = \frac{D/E}{1 + D/E}.$$

Both ratios increase as a firm of a given size (total assets) uses a greater proportion of debt, but D/A rises linearly and approaches a limit of 100 percent while D/E rises exponentially and approaches infinity.

which earnings can decline without resultant financial embarrassment to the firm because of inability to meet annual interest costs. Failure to meet this obligation can bring legal action by the creditors, possibly resulting in bankruptcy. Note that the before-tax profit figure is used in the numerator. Because income taxes are computed after interest expense is deducted, the ability to pay current interest is not affected by income taxes.

$$\text{Times interest earned} = \frac{\text{gross income}}{\text{interest charges}}$$

$$= \frac{\text{profit before taxes} + \text{interest charges}}{\text{interest charges}}$$

$$= \frac{\$103,000}{\$\ 38,000} = 2.71 \text{ times.}$$

Industry average $= 2.65$ times.

Surrey's interest charges consist of three payments totalling $38 million (see Table 3–2). The firm's gross income available for servicing these charges is $103 million, so the interest is covered 2.71 times. Comparing this figure to the industry average indicates that Surrey has an adequate margin of safety. This ratio may suggest that the company should not try to finance a greater part of the company with debt than it has up to this time.[5]

Fixed Charge Coverage   This ratio is similar to the times-interest-earned ratio, but it is somewhat more inclusive in that it recognizes that many firms lease assets and incur long-term obligations under lease contracts.[6] As we show in Chapter 16, leasing has become quite widespread in recent years, making this ratio preferable to the times-interest-earned ratio for most financial analyses. "Fixed charges" are defined as interest plus annual long-term lease obligations, and the fixed charge coverage ratio is defined as follows:

[5]This average ratio is referred to as the *overall coverage* ratio, since it lumps all bonds into a single category. However, the user of financial ratios may want to distinguish among the classes of debt with different priorities in order to determine the interest coverage for each class. To do this the analyst would start with the highest priority bond, and since all earnings are available to pay interest on these bonds, interest coverage is calculated as earnings before taxes and total interest payments, divided by interest payments on bonds of the highest priority. The coverage for the second priority bonds must reflect the fact that, before interest payments can be made to bonds of lower priority, interest on high priority bonds must be paid. The best way to do this is to include in the interest coverage ratio, the interest payments on the bonds of the priority under consideration *plus* interest payments on all bonds of a higher priority. Since the earnings figure in this ratio remains constant, the interest coverage ratio falls as the priority of bonds under consideration falls.

[6]Generally, a long-term lease is defined as one extending at least 3 years into the future. Thus, rent incurred under a 1-year lease would not be included in the fixed charge coverage ratio, but rental payments under a 3-year or longer lease would be defined as fixed charges.

$$\text{Fixed charge coverage} = \frac{\overset{\text{profit}}{\text{before taxes}} + \overset{\text{interest}}{\text{charges}} + \overset{\text{lease}}{\text{obligations}}}{\text{interest charges} + \text{lease obligations}}$$

$$= \frac{\$65{,}000{,}000 + \$38{,}000{,}000 + \$20{,}000{,}000}{\$38{,}000 + \$20{,}000}$$

$$= \frac{\$123{,}000{,}000}{\$\ 58{,}000{,}000}$$

$$= 2.12 \text{ times.}$$

Industry average $= 2.18$ times.

Surrey's fixed charges are covered 2.12 times compared with the industry average of 2.18 times. The company again seems to be maintaining a reasonable ratio. Its fixed charge ratio is slightly below the industry average, whereas its interest coverage ratio is above the industry average. This suggests that the firm is using lease financing more heavily than the average firm in the industry. Considering that the debt ratio is slightly on the high side, and if we consider that leases are a form of debt,[7] then Surrey may be very close to its borrowing capacity.[8]

Activity Ratios

Activity ratios measure how effectively the firm employs the resources at its command. These ratios all involve comparisons between the level of sales and the investment in various asset accounts. The activity ratios presume that a "proper" balance should exist between sales and the various asset accounts—inventories, accounts receivable, fixed assets, and others. As we shall see in the following chapters, this is generally a good assumption.

Inventory Turnover   The inventory turnover is defined as sales divided by inventories.

$$\text{Inventory turnover} = \frac{\text{sales}}{\text{inventory}} = \frac{\$920{,}000{,}000}{\$120{,}000{,}000} = 5.41 \text{ times.}$$

Industry average $= 8.0$ times.

---

[7]The relationship of lease obligations, debt, and borrowing capacity are investigated in Chapter 16.

[8]A still more complete coverage ratio is the *debt service coverage ratio,* defined similarly to the fixed charge coverage except that mandatory annual payments to retire long-term debt (amortization payments, discussed in Chapter 16) are also included in the denominator. The ratio is not widely used, primarily because sinking fund obligations are not generally known to outside analysts. Moreover, it is difficult to develop industry averages for this ratio because of the absence of data. The information on lease obligations, in contrast, is almost always available in footnotes to financial statements.

Surrey's turnover of 5.41 times is significantly less than the industry average of 8.0 times. This suggests that Surrey is holding greater inventories than necessary; the excess inventory is, of course, unproductive and represents an investment with a low or zero rate of return. Surrey must also be concerned with the possibility that their inventory contains damaged or obsolete materials not actually worth their stated value. With the combination of the very high current ratio, lower quick ratio, and lower than average inventory turnover, it is a distinct possibility that some of the inventories are damaged or obsolete.

There are a number of problems that arise in calculating and interpreting the inventory turnover ratio. First, sales are at market prices and inventories are carried at cost. Thus, it would be more appropriate to use cost of goods sold in place of sales in the numerator of the formula. However, the cost-of-goods-sold information is not always shown separately in financial statements. In addition, most compilers of financial ratio statistics measure inventory turnover ratios based on sales. Thus, to permit comparability of the individual company and industry ratios, it is necessary to measure inventory turnover with sales in the numerator.

Second, the valuation of inventories may not be the same across firms in the same industry. Generally, the FIFO valuation method (first-in-first-out) is used. If, however, the LIFO method (last-in-first-out) is used, then older, lower-valued stocks may be included in the inventory, which could lead to a higher inventory turnover ratio.

The final problem lies in the fact that sales occur over the entire year, whereas the inventory figure is for one point in time. This makes it better to use an average inventory for the year, computed by adding the 12 end-of-month inventory figures and dividing by 12. If it is determined that the firm's business is highly seasonal, or if there has been a strong upward or downward sales trend during the year, it becomes essential to make some such adjustment. Since Surrey is in a highly seasonal type of business, management would need more information than is provided here to determine if this is an important problem.

Average Collection Period   The average collection period, which is a measure of the accounts receivable turnover, is computed in two steps: (1) annual sales are divided by 360 to get the average daily sales;[9] (2) daily sales are divided into accounts receivable to find the number of days' sales tied up in receivables. This is defined as the average collection period, because it represents the average length of time that the firm must wait after making

---

[9]Because information on credit sales is generally unavailable, total sales must be used. Since all firms do not have the same percentage of credit sales, there is a good chance that the average collection period will be somewhat in error. Also, note that for convenience, the financial community generally uses 360 rather than 365 as the number of days in the year for purposes such as these.

a sale before receiving cash. The calculations for Surrey show an average collection period of 90 days. This is well above the industry average of 30 days.

Step 1: $$\text{Sales per day} = \frac{\$920,000,000}{360} = \$2,555,000$$

Step 2: $$\text{Average collection period} = \frac{\text{receivables}}{\text{sales per day}} = \frac{\$230,000,000}{\$2,555,000} = 90 \text{ days.}$$

Industry average = 30 days.

This ratio is definitely unsatisfactory. It indicates that customers are not paying their bills promptly. One mitigating factor is that this ratio does not take into consideration the fact that some of the company's sales are on installment plans and the payments will be drawn out over several months. However, for simplication, the total revenue in the income statement includes interest earned on the delayed payments. The industry ratio includes some firms which deal mostly in cash sales. Even with these qualifications in the interpretation of the average collection period, it appears that the 90-day period for Surrey should be reduced.

For companies without installment sales, the average collection period can be evaluated by comparison with the terms on which the firm sells its goods. For example, if a company sells on terms that require payment within 30 days and the average collection period is 40 days, then it is clear that customers, on average, are not paying their bills on time. If the trend in the collection period over the past few years had been rising while the credit policy has not changed, this would be even stronger evidence that steps should be taken to expedite the collection of accounts receivable.

One nonratio financial tool should be mentioned in connection with accounts receivable analysis—the *aging schedule*, which breaks down accounts receivable according to how long they have been outstanding. For Surrey, the aging schedule is as follows.

Age of Accounts (days)	Percent of Total Value of Accounts Receivable
0-20	12
21-40	11
41-60	13
61-80	10
81-100	19
over 100	35
Total	100

It is still difficult, based on this information, to determine just how many of the company's customers are delaying their payments. We can see that the over-

100-days category has a large percentage of the total value of accounts receivable. Management should give serious attention to determining whether or not the 90-day collection period is due to installment sales. This potential problem for Surrey is emphasized by the industry collection period of 30 days.

Fixed Asset Turnover   The ratio of sales to fixed assets measures the turnover of plant and equipment.

$$\text{Fixed asset turnover} = \frac{\text{sales}}{\text{net fixed assets}} = \frac{\$920,000,000}{\$191,000,000}$$

$$= 4.82 \text{ times.}$$

$$\text{Industry average} = 7.48 \text{ times.}$$

The Surrey turnover of 4.82 times compares poorly with the industry average of 7.48 times. This indicates that the firm is not using its fixed assets to as high a percentage of capacity as are the other firms in the industry. This figure could be misleading if Surrey leases fewer of its buildings than other firms in the industry, since for the same level of sales as the average firm in the industry, the net fixed assets would be higher and the fixed asset turnover, lower.

Total Assets Turnover   The final activity ratio measures the turnover of all the firm's assets—it is calculated by dividing sales by total assets.

$$\text{Total assets turnover} = \frac{\text{sales}}{\text{total assets}} = \frac{\$920,000,000}{\$606,000,000} = 1.52 \text{ times.}$$

$$\text{Industry average} = 2.53 \text{ times.}$$

Again, the poor turnover figure, as compared to the industry average, implies that Surrey is not generating sufficient sales for the amount of assets employed. This problem is related to the poor turnover experienced with inventory. Sales should be increased, or some inefficient assets should be disposed of; or both steps should be taken.

Profitability Ratios

Profitability is the net result of a large number of policies and decisions. The ratios examined thus far reveal some interesting things about the way the firm is operating, but the profitability ratios give final answers about how effectively the firm is being managed.

Profit Margin on Sales   The profit margin on sales, computed by dividing net income after taxes by sales, gives the profit per dollar of sales.

$$\text{Profit margin on sales} = \frac{\text{net income after taxes}}{\text{sales}} = \frac{\$30,000,000}{\$920,000,000}$$

$$= 3.26\%$$

$$\text{Industry average} = 1.17\%$$

Surrey's profit margin is considerably above the industry average, indicating that their prices are relatively high or that their operating costs are relatively low; or both.

Return on Total Assets   The ratio of net profit to total assets measures the return on total investment in the firm, or the ROI, as it is frequently called.[10]

$$\text{Return on total assets} = \frac{\text{net income after taxes}}{\text{total assets}} = \frac{\$\ 30,000,000}{\$606,000,000} = 0.0495 \text{ or } 4.95\%.$$

$$\text{Industry average} = 2.97\%.$$

Surrey's return on assets is significantly above the industry average. This results from the high profit margin on sales which more than offsets the low turnover of total assets.

Return on Net Worth   The ratio of net profit after taxes to net worth measures the rate of return on the shareholders' investment.

$$\text{Return on net worth} = \frac{\text{net income after taxes}}{\text{net worth}} = \frac{\$\ 30,000}{\$188,000} = .1595 \text{ or } 15.95\%.$$

$$\text{Industry average} = 9.21\%.$$

The 15.95% return on book equity is well above the industry average. This return must be considered superior since Surrey's debt ratio is just slightly higher than the debt ratio for the industry. In a later section of this chapter, where the du Pont method of analysis is applied to the Surrey case, we will see why this is so.

---

[10] In calculating the return on total assets, it is sometimes desirable to add interest to net profits after taxes to form the numerator of the ratio. The theory here is that since assets are financed by both shareholders and creditors, the ratio should measure the productivity of assets in providing returns to both classes of investors. We have not done so at this point because the published averages we use for comparative purposes exclude interest. Later in this book, however, we do add back interest and use this revised ratio.

TABLE 3–4 Summary of Financial Ratio Analysis

Ratio	Formula for Calculation	Value for Surrey	Industry Average	Evaluation
Liquidity				
Current	$\dfrac{\text{current assets}}{\text{current liabilities}}$	4.56 times	1.78 times	Good, but should be investigated
Quick, or acid test	$\dfrac{\text{current assets} - \text{inventory}}{\text{current liabilities}}$	2.69 times	.82 times	Good, but should be investigated
Leverage				
Debt to total assets	$\dfrac{\text{total debt}}{\text{total assets}}$	68.97 percent	67.75 percent	Satisfactory
Times interest earned (interest coverage)	$\dfrac{\text{income before taxes plus interest charges}}{\text{interest charges}}$	2.71 times	2.65 times	Satisfactory
Fixed charge coverage	$\dfrac{\text{income available for meeting fixed charges}}{\text{fixed charges}}$	2.12 times	2.18 times	Satisfactory
Activity				
Inventory turnover	$\dfrac{\text{sales}}{\text{inventory}}$	5.41 times	7.96 times	Poor
Average collection period	$\dfrac{\text{receivables}}{\text{sales per day}}$	90 days	30 days	Poor
Fixed assets turnover	$\dfrac{\text{sales}}{\text{fixed assets}}$	4.82 times	7.48 times	Poor
Total assets turnover	$\dfrac{\text{sales}}{\text{total assets}}$	1.52 times	2.53 times	Poor
Profitability				
Profit margin on sales	$\dfrac{\text{net income after taxes}}{\text{sales}}$	3.26 percent	1.17 percent	Good
Return on total assets	$\dfrac{\text{net income after taxes}}{\text{total assets}}$	4.95 percent	2.97 percent	Good
Return on net worth	$\dfrac{\text{net income after taxes}}{\text{net worth}}$	15.95 percent	9.21 percent	Good

Summary of the Ratios

The summary of individual ratios in Table 3-4 outlines where management should be satisfied and where there are reasons to be concerned. Surrey does not have any liquidity problems; in fact, this high level of liquidity may be more than necessary. Liquid assets included in the liquidity ratios either do not earn any explicit rate of return (e.g. inventories, accounts receivable) or earn a very low after-tax rate of return (e.g. marketable securities). Surrey's large liquidity ratios indicate that, in the near term, the company is solvent, but this may be an error on the high side by management. The optimum amount of liquid assets may be at some lower level, and it is in the interest of the shareholders for the company to convert some of these assets into more productive and profitable uses.

The debt ratio, and the interest and fixed coverage ratios all confirm that Surrey is adequately debt financed without exposing the shareholders to unnecessary risk. Lease financing information is not provided at this point, but it should be recognized that this form of financing should be regarded as a substitute for debt financing since it generates a fixed claim on the earnings of the firm. Including lease obligations, Surrey may be at its optimal capital structure.

The activity ratios are Surrey's weakest point. As has already been cautioned, the comparisons with the industry may not be completely valid due to the financing of fixed assets via lease contracts. However, Surrey should consider rationalizing its fixed investments with a view to efficiency since it appears that the firm is not making the best use of its buildings and equipment. This could also be a sign of the start of a growth phase and the undercapacity may be only temporary. Investment occurs before returns, and in the long run, this situation will improve if properly managed.

The profitability ratios all confirm that this is a basically healthy company. If the activity ratios suggest an underutilization of assets, the profitability ratios suggest that the firm has been able to make use of its large size across the country to spread fixed costs and to purchase goods in sufficient quantities to maintain a higher than average gross margin. Given the fact that the company has a level of financial risk similar to the industry as a whole, Surrey is earning a superior return.

Trend Analysis

While the preceding ratio analysis gives a reasonably good picture of Surrey's operations for 19X7, it is incomplete in one important respect—it ignores the time dimension. The ratios are snapshots of the picture at one point in time, but there may be trends in motion that are in the process of rapidly eroding a relatively good present position. Conversely, an analysis of the ratios over the past few years may suggest that a relatively weak position is being improved at a rapid rate.

FIGURE 3-1   Illustration of Trend Analysis

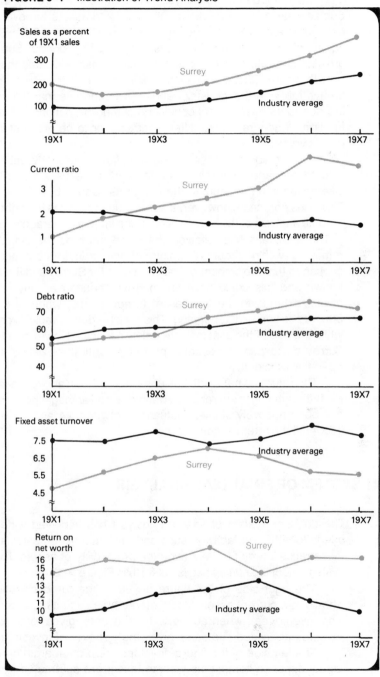

The method of trend analysis is illustrated in Figure 3-1 where graphs of Surrey's sales, current ratio, debt ratio, fixed assets turnover, and return on net worth are presented for the periods 19X1 to 19X7. The figures are compared with industry averages for the same period. Surrey's sales are growing at a rate faster than the industry, which indicates that Surrey is in a growth phase. Casual observation will show that the Surrey ratios have not always followed the industry trends. This suggests that the company trends are due to its own internal conditions and not to national influences affecting the firm. In general, these differences appear to be greatest in the two most recent years.

Surrey's liquidity position has become significantly out of line with the industry average. This reinforces the earlier discussion that the firm should take action soon to improve the use of its assets, both liquid and long term. This does not mean, however, that the industry ratio is the right one for Surrey —some analysis of the composition of the industry averages may be required.

The debt ratio has followed the same trend as the industry. Surrey has remained within about 10 points of the industry; but again, it must be cautioned that the amount of leased assets for Surrey and the industry are not known and this could have an important bearing on any comparison. This caveat extends to the fixed-asset turnover ratio, where it appears that the Surrey position is deteriorating. This may be due to rapid expansion in assets while the use of the assets is still below capacity. However, it is important that Surrey not expand its assets any further until the existing fixed assets are operating efficiently.

The return on net worth has consistently been above the industry average even though their debt ratio has been of a similar magnitude. The rate of return has been relatively stable, fluctuating between 14 and 16 percent. Only in 19X4 did the return exceed 16 percent.

DU PONT SYSTEM OF FINANCIAL ANALYSIS

The du Pont system of financial analysis has achieved wide recognition. It brings together the activity ratios and profit margin on sales and shows how these ratios interact to determine the profitability of assets. The nature of the system, modified somewhat, is set forth in Figure 3-2.

The right side of the figure develops the turnover ratio. That section shows how current assets (cash, marketable securities, accounts receivable, and inventories), when added to fixed assets, gives total investment. Total investment divided into sales gives the turnover of investment.

The left side of the figure develops the profit margin on sales. The individual expense items, plus income taxes, are subtracted from sales to produce net profits after taxes. Net profits divided by sales gives the profit

FIGURE 3-2 Modified du Pont System of Financial Control Applied to Surrey

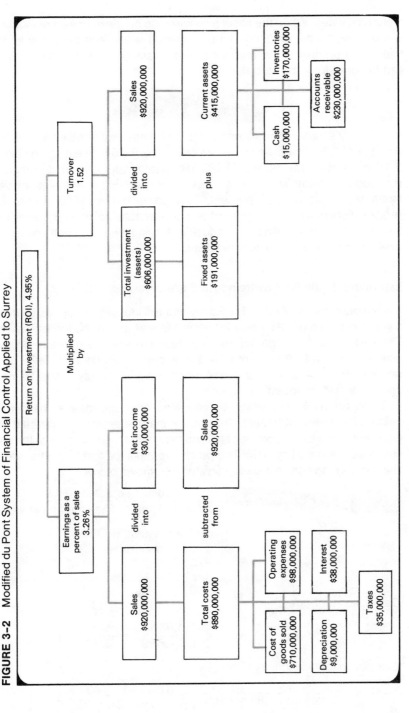

margin on sales. When the asset turnover ratio on the right side of Figure 3–2 is multiplied by the profit margin on sales developed on the left side of the figure, the product is the return on total investment (ROI) in the firm. This can be seen from the following formula:

$$\frac{sales}{investment} \times \frac{profit}{sales} = ROI.$$

Surrey's turnover was found to be 1.52 times as compared to an industry average of 2.53 times. Its margin on sales was 3.26 percent as compared to 1.17 percent for the industry. Multiplied together, turnover and profit margin produced a return on assets equal to 4.95 percent, a rate well above the industry average of 2.97 percent. To improve the return on assets would require management to improve the turnover ratio to bring it closer to the average in the merchandising industry. Tracing back through the du Pont system should help them with their task.

Extending the du Pont System to Include Leverage

Even though the debt ratios for Surrey and the industry are approximately the same, the return on net worth for Surrey is well above the industry average. The reason for this large difference is found in the rate of return on assets where Surrey's 4.95 percent is well in excess of the industry level of 2.97 percent. Thus, using the same amount of leverage, Surrey is able to magnify its superior rate of return on assets.

The return on net worth is calculated after the interest paid to debt holders has been subtracted. This means that the entire 4.95 percent return on assets goes to the common shareholders, even though some of the assets have been financed by debt. The precise formula for measuring the effect of financial leverage on shareholders' returns is shown below.

$$\text{Rate of return on net worth} = \frac{\text{return on assets (ROI)}}{\text{percent of assets financed by net worth}}$$

$$= \frac{\text{return on assets (ROI)}}{1.0 - \text{debt ratio}}.$$

Calculation for Surrey:

$$\text{Return on net worth} = \frac{4.95\%}{1.0 - .6897} = \frac{4.95}{.3103} = 15.95\%.$$

Calculation for the industry average:

$$\text{Return on net worth} = \frac{2.97\%}{1.0 - .6775} = \frac{2.97}{3.225} = 9.21\%.$$

This formula is useful for showing how financial leverage can be used to increase the rate of return on net worth.[11] For example, the combination of a low return on assets with a high debt ratio can result in a rate of return that is equal to, or even exceeds, a company with a high return on assets and a low debt ratio. But increasing returns on net worth by using more and more leverage causes the leverage ratios to rise higher and higher above the industry norms. Creditors resist this tendency, so there are limitations to the practice. Moreover, greater leverage increases the risk of bankruptcy and thus endangers the firm's shareholders.

RATES OF RETURN IN DIFFERENT INDUSTRIES

Would it be better to have a 5 percent margin on sales and a total asset turnover of 2 times, or a 2 percent sales margin and a turnover of 5 times? It makes no difference—in either case the firm has a 10 percent return on investment. Actually, most firms are not free to make the kind of choice posed in the above question. Depending on the nature of its industry, the firm *must* operate with more or fewer assets, and it will experience a turnover that depends on the characteristics of its particular line of business. In the case of a dealer in fresh fruits and vegetables, fish, or other perishable items, the turnover should be high—every day or two would be most desirable. In contrast, some lines of business require very heavy fixed investment or long production periods. A telecommunications utility with its heavy investment in buildings, switching systems, cable, etc. requires heavy fixed investment; a shipbuilder or an aircraft producer needs a long production period. Such companies necessarily have a low asset turnover rate but a correspondingly higher profit margin on sales.

If a grocery chain has a high turnover, and a chemical producer, with its heavy investment in fixed assets, a low turnover, would you expect to find differences in their profit margins on sales? In general, you would—the chemical producer should have a considerably higher profit margin to offset its lower turnover. Otherwise, the grocery business would be much more profitable than the chemical, investment would flow into the grocery industry, and profits in this industry would be eroded to the point where the rate of return was about equal to that in the chemical industry.

We know, however, that leverage must be taken into account when considering the rate of return on net worth. If the firms in one industry have a somewhat lower return on total assets but use slightly more financial leverage

---

[11]There are limitations on this statement—specifically, the return on net worth increases with leverage only if the return on assets exceeds the rate of interest on debt, after considering the tax deductibility of interest payments. This whole concept is explored in detail in Chapter 19, which is devoted entirely to financial leverage.

than do those in another industry, both sets of firms may end up with approximately the same rate of return on net worth.[12]

These points, which are all necessary for a complete understanding of ratio analysis, are illustrated in Table 3–5. There we see how turnover and profit margins interact with each other to produce varying returns on assets and also how financial leverage affects the returns on net worth. Crown Zellerbach, with its heavy fixed-asset investment, has a relatively low turnover; whereas Schneider Corporation, as a food processor, has a very high turnover ratio. But the rates of return on assets is not substantially different, since the profit margin on sales for Crown Zellerbach compensates for its low turnover. Finally, the rate of return on net worth for both companies is the same. This occurs because the higher debt ratio for Schneider compensates for their lower return on assets.

TABLE 3–5 Turnover, Profit Margins, and Returns on Net Worth

	Sales to Total × Assets (Times)	Profit to Sales (Percent)	Profit = to Total Assets (Percent)	Debt to Total Assets (Percent)	Profit to Net Worth[a] (Percent)
Crown Zellerbach Canada, Ltd. (Forest products)	1.39	5.63	7.84	38	12.7
Schneider Corp. (Food processing)	4.04	1.75	7.07	44	12.6

[a] The figures in this column may be found as

$$\text{Profit to net worth} = \frac{\text{profit to total assets}}{1 - \text{debt to total assets}}.$$

SOURCES OF COMPARATIVE RATIOS

The industry averages used in this chapter were obtained from a study published by McLeod Young Weir Limited. This study provides the historical aggregate balance sheet and income statement information, as well as selected ratios, for various industrial groupings in Canada. In addition, historical growth rates in some of the more important financial accounts and ratios are presented. The industry groups are based on the industry groupings on the Toronto Stock Exchange Index (TSE–300) and the inclusion of particular companies in the various groupings is not always straightforward. McLeod Young Weir Limited use the Financial Post Data Bank to build their survey results.

[12]The factors that make it possible for firms to use more leverage are taken up in Chapters 15 and 19. It may be stated now, however, that the primary factor favoring leverage is sales stability.

TABLE 3-6 McLeod Young Weir Ltd., Ratios 1976

Line of Business	Current Assets to Current Debt (times)	Fixed Charge Coverage (times)	Receivables Turnover (times)	Inventories Turnover (times)	Collection Period (days)	Operating Margin (percent)	Return on Invested Capital Post-tax (percent)	Return on Common Equity (percent)	Inventory to Working Capital (percent)	Working Capital to Long-term Debt (percent)	Working Capital to Sales (percent)	Long-term Debt to Invested Capital (percent)	Common Equity to Invested Capital (percent)	Debt to Common Equity at Book (percent)	Debt to Common Equity at Market (percent)	Payout Rate (percent)
Major Canadian Industries	1.74	2.44	7.69	5.70	46.80	14.01	9.19	11.30	112.21	60.39	15.63	32.56	49.61	65.63	61.23	41.68
Communications and Media	1.58	7.38	6.62	22.10	54.38	21.40	15.70	18.75	45.78	99.38	9.88	13.94	74.22	18.78	8.65	34.21
Consumer Products	1.95	2.68	11.29	5.03	31.89	7.21	10.30	10.85	122.22	190.88	16.27	23.62	62.22	37.39	42.75	45.07
Golds	7.28	a	32.51	10.23	11.07	27.84	14.17	9.76	9.12	a	107.11	a	145.29	a	a	25.81
Industrial Products	1.94	2.65	6.28	3.81	57.35	13.03	11.23	12.48	111.39	120.31	23.59	28.43	56.41	50.40	49.69	34.46
Management Companies	1.22	1.53	7.16	8.05	50.28	19.59	7.73	10.40	169.03	15.55	7.35	36.27	37.99	95.46	143.60	33.13
Merchandising	1.78	2.18	11.84	7.96	30.40	4.52	9.83	8.24	122.77	87.92	10.23	44.07	53.31	82.67	69.56	46.62
Metals and Minerals	2.03	2.42	6.15	3.71	58.55	16.71	7.94	8.88	104.57	85.24	25.79	28.58	54.43	52.51	44.10	54.59
Oil and Gas	1.83	4.69	5.69	7.95	63.25	19.72	11.32	15.06	73.53	88.41	17.11	21.61	62.37	34.65	24.70	30.87
Paper and Forest Products	2.12	2.03	7.37	4.76	48.87	11.11	6.56	6.80	101.57	86.03	20.68	31.22	47.18	66.17	77.10	41.31
Pipelines	1.28	1.52	8.15	29.41	44.15	21.49	8.37	10.67	69.40	6.32	4.90	53.02	33.10	160.19	131.21	82.20
Real Estate and Construction	1.57	6.49	5.78	26.91	62.30	9.59	14.03	15.44	31.77	470.89	11.85	6.28	82.76	7.59	10.15	28.25
Transportation	1.06	1.74	7.35	7.49	49.00	21.34	7.05	9.24	690.41	3.97	1.93	36.34	38.44	94.56	150.14	34.04
Utilities	1.12	1.97	8.35	12.90	43.13	33.28	8.21	11.84	284.14	3.08	2.73	44.39	32.75	135.53	148.30	58.43

a Company Reporting did not have any long-term debt.
Source McLeod Young Weir Ltd., Performance Summaries Major Canadian Industries Ltd., 1972-76.

Alternative sources of basic financial data and ratios are available. Dun and Bradstreet, Canada, Ltd. compile financial ratios for a large number of industries. These industries are defined in a more conventional manner. The publication is called *Key Business Ratios* and is derived from Revenue Canada data. Unfortunately, this taxation-based data source is not very current and the ratios may be dated. For example, the ratios presented in the 1976 Dun and Bradstreet report are based on 1973 tax statistics.

Statistics Canada gathers quarterly and annual data on all corporations in Canada. Balance sheet and income statement information is presented in aggregate form for all corporations as well as by industry sector and by size of firm. This data, however, is not very current since it is only produced every three years. At the beginning of 1978, the most current data available from Statistics Canada was for 1974. The financial community awaits with interest the delivery of some new data.

Instead of using the ratios as derived by the above-mentioned groups, the financial manager can derive the ratios from the basic firm data. This permits a definition of the industry that is satisfactory to the financial manager but not to the compilers of the financial ratios. This process of deriving ratios from basic data could be laborious and time consuming were it not for the services provided by two Canadian companies. These companies provide access to financial information on a large number of companies through computer tapes.

The first company is FRI Information Services Ltd. of Toronto and Montreal. This company provides its clients with an extensive data base, access to a computer, and sophisticated software packages to manipulate the data as required by the user. The second company is Financial Post Computer Services Ltd. Unlike FRI, Financial Post does not have its own computers or the programs necessary to manipulate the data. Its major service is the sale of data tapes. Some of the data, however, are available on a time sharing basis from a computer utility company.

USE OF FINANCIAL RATIOS IN CREDIT ANALYSIS

In this chapter we have discussed a rather long list of ratios and have learned what each ratio is designed to measure. Sometimes it will be unnecessary to go beyond a few calculations to determine that a firm is in very good or very bad condition, but often the analysis is equivalent to a detective-story investigation—what one ratio will not indicate, another may. Also, a relation vaguely suggested by one ratio may be corroborated by another. For these reasons, it is often useful to calculate a number of different ratios.

In numerous situations, however, a few ratios will tell the story. For example, a credit manager who has a great many invoices flowing across his desk each day may limit himself to three ratios as evidence of whether the prospective buyer of his goods will pay promptly: (1) He may use either the current or the quick ratio to determine how burdened the prospective buyer is with current liabilities; (2) he may use the debt to total assets ratio to determine how much of the prospective buyer's own funds are invested in the business; (3) he may use any one of the profitability ratios to determine whether or not the firm has favorable prospects. If the profit margin is high enough, it may justify the risk of dealing with a slow-paying customer— profitable companies are likely to grow and thus to become better customers in the future. However, if the profit margin is low in relation to other firms in the industry, if the current ratio is low, and if the debt ratio is high, a credit manager probably will not approve a sale involving an extension of credit.[13]

Of necessity, the credit manager is more than a calculator and a reader of financial ratios. Qualitative factors may override quantitative analysis. For instance, oil companies, in selling to truckers, often find that the financial ratios are poor, and if they based their decisions solely on financial ratios, they would not make sales. Or, to take another example, profits may have been low for a period, but if the customer understands why profits have been low and can remove the cause of the difficulty, a credit analyst may be willing to approve a sale. The decision is also influenced by the seller's own profit margin. If the selling firm is making a large profit on sales, it is in a better position to take credit risks than if its own margin is low. Ultimately, the credit manager must judge a customer with regard to his or her character and management ability, and intelligent credit decisions must be based on careful consideration of conditions in the selling firm as well as in the buying firm.

USE OF FINANCIAL RATIOS IN SECURITY ANALYSIS

We have emphasized the use of financial analysis by the financial manager and by outside credit analysts. However, this type of analysis is also useful in security analysis, that is, in the analysis of the investment merits of stocks and bonds. When the emphasis is on security analysis, the principal focus is on judging the long-run profit potential of the firm. Profitability is dependent in large part on the efficiency with which the firm is run; because financial analysis provides insights into this factor, it is useful to the security analyst.

In evaluating the risk of a bond, the analyst is interested in default risk; this risk includes not only the potential for bankruptcy, but also the chance that interest payments will be delayed. There are two agencies in Canada that assess this risk on bonds; the Canadian Bond Rating Service and the

[13]Statistical techniques have been developed to improve the use of ratios in credit analysis. One such development is the discriminant analysis model reported by Edward I. Altman ["Financial Ratios, Discriminant Analysis, and the Prediction of Corporate Bankruptcy," *Journal of Finance* 23 (September 1968)]. In his model, Altman combines a number of liquidity, leverage, activity, and profitability ratios to form an index of a firm's probability of going bankrupt. His model has predicted bankruptcy quite well one or two years in the future.

Dominion Bond Rating Service. Statistical techniques have been used to explain the ratings assigned by the rating services to the bonds of various companies. It has been determined that ratings are based on financial ratios that reflect risk of the bonds and profitability of the company. The ratios used are coverage, leverage, and return on investment among others. In an investigation of the bond ratings on long-term Canadian bonds, it was found that financial ratios were important in explaining the ratings. Of course, just as in credit analysis, considerations other than the values of the financial ratios are important in determining a bond rating. In fact, the one variable found to be most important in determining the bond rating was the size of the issue. This result was found in studies of both U.S. and Canadian ratings.

SOME LIMITATIONS OF RATIO ANALYSIS

Although ratios are exceptionally useful tools, they do have limitations and must be used with caution. Ratios are constructed from accounting data, and accounting data are subject to different interpretations and even to manipulation. For example, two firms may use different depreciation methods or inventory valuation methods; depending on the procedures followed, reported profits can be raised or lowered. Similar differences can be encountered in the treatment of research and development expenditures, pension plan costs, mergers, product warranties, and bad-debt reserves. Further, if firms use different fiscal years, and if seasonal factors are important, this can influence the comparative ratios. Thus, if the ratios of two firms are to be compared, it is important to analyze the basic accounting data upon which the ratios were based and to reconcile any major differences.

A financial manager must also be cautious when judging whether a particular ratio is "good" or "bad" and in forming a composite judgment about a firm on the basis of a set of ratios. For example, a high inventory turnover ratio could indicate efficient inventory management, but it could also indicate a serious shortage of inventories and suggest the likelihood of stock-outs. Further, there is nothing sacred about the industry average figures—after all, any management worth its salt will try to be better than average.

Ratios, then, are extremely useful tools. But as with other analytical methods, they must be used with judgment and caution, not in an unthinking, mechanical manner.

SUMMARY

Ratio analysis, which relates balance sheet and income statement items to one another, permits the charting of a firm's history and the evaluation of its present position. Such analysis also allows the financial manager to anticipate reactions of investors and creditors and thus gives a good insight into how attempts to acquire funds are likely to be received.

Basic Types of Ratios   Ratios are classified into four basic types: (1) liquidity, (2) leverage, (3) activity, and (4) profitability. Data from the Surrey Company were used to compute each type of ratio and to show how a financial analysis is made in practice. An almost unlimited number of ratios may be calculated, but in practice a limited number of each type is sufficient. We have discussed in this chapter what are probably the twelve most common ratios.

Use of Ratios   A ratio is not a meaningful number in and of itself—it must be compared with something before it becomes useful. The two basic kinds of comparative analysis are (1) trend analysis, which involves computing the ratios of a particular firm for several years and comparing the ratios over time to see if the firm is improving or deteriorating, and (2) comparisons with other firms in the same industry. These two comparisons are often combined in the graphic analysis illustrated in Figure 3–1.

du Pont System   The du Pont system shows how the return on investment is dependent upon asset turnover and the profit margin. The system is generally expressed in the form of the following equation:

$$\frac{\text{sales}}{\text{investment}} \times \frac{\text{profit}}{\text{sales}} = \text{ROI}.$$

The first term, investment turnover, times the profit margin equals the rate of return on investment. The kinds of actions we discussed in this chapter can be used to effect needed changes in turnover and the profit margin and thus improve the return on investment.

The du Pont system can be extended to encompass financial leverage and to examine the manner in which turnover, sales margins, and leverage all combine to determine the rate of return on net worth. The following equation is used to show this relationship:

$$\text{Rate of return on net worth} = \frac{\text{return on assets (ROI)}}{1.0 - \text{debt ratio}}.$$

Rates of Return in Different Industries   The extended du Pont system shows why firms in different industries—even though they have widely different turnovers, profit margins, and debt ratios—may end up with very similar rates of return on net worth. In general, firms dealing with relatively perishable commodities are expected to have high turnovers but low profit margins; firms whose production processes require heavy investments in fixed assets are expected to have low turnover ratios but high profit margins.

QUESTIONS

3-1. "A uniform system of accounts, including identical forms for balance sheets and income statements, would be a most reasonable requirement for securities commissions to impose on all publicly owned firms." Discuss.

3-2. We have divided financial ratios into four groups: liquidity, leverage, activity, and profitability. We could also consider financial analysis as being conducted by four groups of analysts: management, equity investors, long-term creditors, and short-term creditors.

    a. Explain the nature of each type of ratio.

    b. Explain the emphasis of each type of analyst.

3-3. Why can norms with relatively well-defined limits be stated in advance for some financial ratios but not for others?

3-4. How does trend analysis supplement the basic financial ratio calculations and their interpretation?

3-5. Why should the inventory turnover figure be more important to a grocery store than to a shoe repair store?

3-6. How can a firm have a high current ratio and still be unable to pay its bills?

3-7. "The higher the rate of return on investment (ROI), the better the firm's management." Is this statement true for all firms? Explain. If you disagree with the statement, give examples of instances in which it might not be true.

3-8. What factors would you, as a financial manager, want to examine if a firm's rate of return (a) on assets or (b) on net worth is too low?

3-9. Profit margins and turnover rates vary from industry to industry. What industry characteristics account for these variations? Give some contrasting examples to illustrate your answer.

3-10. Which relation would you, as a financial manager, prefer: (a) a profit margin of 10 percent and a capital turnover of 2, or (b) a profit margin of 20 percent and a capital turnover of 1? Can you think of any firm with a relation similar to b?

3-11. In calculating interest coverage, we use earnings before interest and taxes, and total interest payments. Suppose we wanted to calculate a coverage ratio for preferred shares outstanding. Since preferred shares are of lower priority, they are paid after payment to debt holders. If we use earnings before interest and taxes in the numerator, what do we use in the denominator to calculate the preferred coverage ratio?

PROBLEMS

3-1. General Steel Company Ltd. has $800,000 in current assets and $200,000 in current liabilities. How much can its short-term debt (notes payable) increase without violating a current ratio of 3 to 1? The funds from the additional notes payable will be used to increase inventory.

3-2. Geometric Poster Design Company Ltd. has $2.5 million of debt outstanding. There are two classes or priorities of this debt: $1.5 million first priority (senior) debt with an interest rate of 8 percent and $1 million junior priority debt with an interest rate of 10 percent. Earnings before interest and taxes are $3 million. Calculate the overall interest coverage ratio for Geometric and the interest coverage ratios appropriate for senior and junior debt (see footnote 5).

3-3. Complete the balance sheet and sales information (fill in the blanks) for the Fiske Company Ltd. using the following financial data:

Debt to net worth:	40 percent
Acid test ratio:	1.2
Total asset turnover:	2.0 times
Days' sales outstanding in accounts receivable:	30
Gross profit margin:	30 percent
Sales to inventory turnover:	4 times

Balance Sheet

Cash	$ _____	Accounts payable	$ _____
Accounts receivable	_____	Common shares	15,000
Inventory	_____	Retained earnings	33,000
Plant and equipment	_____		
Total Assets	_____	Total liabilities and capital	_____
Sales	_____	Cost of goods sold	_____

3-4. The following data were taken from the financial statements of the Coit Corporation Ltd. for the calendar year 19X7. The norms given below are industry averages for the furniture industry.

a. Fill in the ratios for Coit.

b. Indicate by comparison with the industry norms the possible errors in management policies reflected in these financial statements.

Coit Corporation Ltd.
Income statement
For year ended December 31, 19X7

Sales		$690,000
Cost of goods sold		
Materials	$260,000	
Labor	165,000	
Heat, light, and power	25,000	
Indirect labor	40,000	
Depreciation	15,000	505,000
Gross profit		$185,000
Selling expenses	$ 70,000	
General and administrative expenses	80,000	150,000
Operating profit		$ 35,000
Less: interest expense		6,050
Net profit before taxes		$ 28,950
Less: income taxes (assumed		
50% rate)		14,475
Net profit		$14,475

	Ratios	
Ratio	*Coit*	*Norm*
$\dfrac{\text{current assets}}{\text{current liabilities}}$	_____	2.5 times
$\dfrac{\text{debt}}{\text{total assets}}$	_____	35%
times interest earned	_____	7 times
$\dfrac{\text{sales}}{\text{inventories}}$	_____	9.9 times
average collection period	_____	33 days
$\dfrac{\text{sales}}{\text{total assets}}$	_____	2.2 times
$\dfrac{\text{net profit}}{\text{sales}}$	_____	3.2%
$\dfrac{\text{net profit}}{\text{total assets}}$	_____	7.0%
$\dfrac{\text{net profit}}{\text{net worth}}$	_____	10.7%

Coit Corporation Ltd.
Balance sheet
December 31, 19X7

Cash	$ 55,000	Accounts payable	$ 40,000
Receivables	70,000	Notes payable (5%)	55,000
Inventory	200,000	Other current liabilities	25,000
Total current assets	$325,000	Total current liabilities	$120,000
Net fixed assets	150,000	Long-term debt (6%)	55,000
		Net worth	300,000
Total assets	$475,000	Total claims on assets	$475,000

3-5. Griffin Supply Co. Ltd., a small manufacturer of surgical supplies and equipment, has been plagued with relatively low profitability in recent years. As a result, the board of directors replaced the president of the firm. The new president, Pat Roffman, asks you to make an analysis of the firm's financial position using the du Pont system. The most recent financial statements are reproduced below.

  a. Calculate some ratios which you feel would be useful in this case.

  b. Construct a du Pont chart of analysis for Griffin similar to the one in Figure 3–2.

  c. Do the balance sheet accounts or the income statement figures seem to be primarily responsible for the low profits?

  d. Which specific accounts seem to be most out of line in relation to other firms in the industry?

	Industry Average Ratios
Current ratio	2/1
Quick ratio	1/1
Debt to total assets	30%
Times interest earned	7 times
Fixed charge coverage	5 times
Inventory turnover	10 times
Average collection period	15 days
Fixed assets turnover	6 times
Total assets turnover	3 times
Net profit on sales	3%
Return on total assets	9%
Return on net worth	12.8%

Griffin Supply Company Ltd.
Balance sheet
December 31, 19X7
(thousands of dollars)

Cash		$ 450	Accounts payable	$ 450
Marketable securities		330	Notes payable (6%)	450
Net receivables		660	Other current liabilities	210
Inventories		1,590	Total current liabilities	$1,110
Total current assets		$3,030	Long-term debt (5%)	240
Gross fixed assets	$2,250		Total liabilities	$1,350
Less: depreciation	780		Common shares	$1,140
Net fixed assets		1,470	Retained earnings	2,010
			Total stockholders' equity	3,150
Total assets		$4,500	Total claims on assets	$4,500

Griffin Supply Company Ltd.
Income statement
For year ended December 31, 19X7
(thousands of dollars)

Net sales	$7,950	
Cost of goods sold	6,600	
Gross profit		$1,350
Operating expenses	$ 735	
Depreciation expense	120	
Interest expense	45	
Total expenses		900
Net income before tax		$ 450
Taxes 50%		225
Net income		$ 225

Impact of Inflation on Financial Ratios

 ## Appendix

Since the late 1960s, many countries have experienced a prolonged period of high inflation rates. Canada, unfortunately, has not been an exception to this inflationary experience. Attempts to control the increase in both consumer and wholesale prices included reductions in the growth of the money supply and the formation of the Anti-Inflation Board.

With this actual or threatened double-digit inflation, the accounting profession is addressing the question of the quality of information provided by accounting statements based on historical cost. In this appendix we will consider the impact of inflation on financial statements and the techniques that have been considered to adjust these statements.

INFLATION AND THE MEASUREMENT OF PROFITABILITY

In an economy experiencing a high rate of price increases, the measurement of profitability becomes complicated. The times at which assets are purchased have a great impact on accounting profitability measures and on taxation. For example, Firm A purchased its assets in Year 1 when their cost was $20,000,000; while Firm B purchased virtually identical assets 5 years later at a cost of $40,000,000. Let us assume that the assets will have an average 20-year life; that both firms use straight-line depreciation; that the income before taxes for both firms is $5,000,000 per year over the life of the assets; and that their tax rate is 50 percent.[1] Let us compare the financial profiles of the two companies.

	Firm A	Firm B
Income before taxes and depreciation	$5,000,000	$5,000,000
Less depreciation expense	-1,000,000	-2,000,000
Income before taxes	4,000,000	3,000,000
Taxes (at 50%)	2,000,000	1,500,000
Net income after taxes	2,000,000	1,500,000
Average return on investment	20%	7.5%

Since the cost of the assets will depreciate to zero over their 20-year lives, their average value is half the original cost. The net income after taxes is assumed to be constant for each year, so the average annual returns are 20 percent for Firm A and 7.5 percent for Firm B. But does Firm A really have a return almost three times greater than Firm B's? The *replacement* value of Firm A's assets is $40,000,000; and the current depreciation expense would be $2,000,000 per year, not $1,000,000. Is it correct for an investor to project Firm A's earning power into the future at 20 percent, or should the higher replacement cost of Firm A's assets, that are being used up, be taken into account? Should the tax-deductible depreciation expense for Firm A be $2,000,000 per year rather than $1,000,000?

There are no easy answers to these questions, which arise because of the changing values of assets. Some people feel that Firm A is gaining windfall profits because it is using assets that it was able to purchase at lower than current costs. Others argue that Firm A is paying excessive taxes, because the real depreciation expense should be doubled. The lesson for management is that it should not necessarily buy assets early to avoid inflation, because the assets may become obsolete if purchased too early or if better equipment becomes available before the excess assets are put into use.

There are a number of possible reasons for the rising costs of later investments. An overriding influence in recent years, of course, has been the high rate of general inflation. Thus, during a period of general inflation, the return on investment of two different businesses may vary greatly, simply due to the timing of their asset acquisitions. Even during periods when the rates of general price changes have been more moderate than those experienced in recent years, the timing of asset purchases can still affect profitability. There may, for example, be wide differences between the historical accounting

[1] We are looking at the reporting practices and not the calculation of the federal tax liability. The latter would require the use of capital cost allowance.

costs and the current replacement costs of assets. Current replacement costs may be lower if a high rate of absolescence in those assets has occurred. Or, the current replacement value of assets may greatly increase, in the absence of general inflation, because of productivity increases achieved by improvements at modest cost in the utilization of equipment (in this case, the manufacturer would have increased the price of the equipment because of its improved efficiency). In general, the net income earned by the firm should reflect the underlying replacement value of its assets. If this value is not adjusted, the resulting measures of return on investment may reflect a substantial distortion of true profitability levels.

INFLATION AND INVENTORY VALUATION METHODS

The divergence between economic and accounting measures of profitability results from the valuation of both fixed assets and inventories. During periods of inflation, the method of inventory valuation for income statements and balance sheets has a major impact on profitability measurement.

By comparing FIFO (first-in-first-out) and LIFO (last-in-first-out) inventory costing and valuation methods, Table 3A-1 illustrates the difficulty of obtaining a meaningful economic measure of profitability during a period of unstable prices. During such a period, Firms C and D each have two batches of inventory. The first batch of 100 units was acquired at a cost of $1 per unit; the second was acquired later at $1.50 per unit. Firm C uses the FIFO method, and Firm D uses the LIFO method. The income statement for Firm C shows that it sold 100 units at $5 apiece. Since Firm C uses the FIFO method, it has calculated the cost of goods sold (inventories used) as $100 (the cost of

TABLE 3A-1   Effects of FIFO and LIFO Inventory Costing and Valuation

Firm C (FIFO)			Firm D (LIFO)		
Income Statement			*Income Statement*		
Sales 100 (at $5)		$ 500	Sales 100 (at $5)		$500
Inventories used	$100		Inventories used	$150	
Other costs	300		Other costs	300	
Total costs		400	Total costs		450
Net income		$ 100	Net income		$ 50
Balance Sheet			*Balance Sheet*		
Inventories on hand		$ 150	Inventories on hand		$100
Other assets		850	Other assets		850
Total assets		$1,000	Total assets		$950
Return on assets		10%	Return on assets		5.3%

Note: Inventories for both companies are batch 1, 100 units at $1 per unit, for a total of $100; batch 2, 100 units at $1.50 per unit, for a total of $150.

batch 1). Since Firm D uses the LIFO method, it has calculated the cost of goods sold as $150 (the cost of batch 2). As a consequence, Firm C reports a net income of $100 and Firm D a net income of only $50.

However, the effects are reversed on the balance sheet, where Firm C carries batch 2 at $150 and Firm D carries batch 1 at $100. On this basis, Firm C reports total assets of $1,000 and Firm D $950. The return on assets is thus 10 percent for Firm C and 5.3 percent for Firm D.

During a period of rising price levels, the use of LIFO results in an expense item on the income statement that is closer to the current replacement cost of items taken from inventory. However, using LIFO also means that the balance sheet amount of inventory investment is carried at historical costs rather than current costs. Thus, although LIFO comes closer to a correct measure of *expenses* for the income statement, it results in an understatement of *investment* on the balance sheet, and hence, an overstatement of the measured profitability ratio. Conversely, if FIFO is used, the expense item on the income statement is understated and the balance sheet valuation of inventory is closer to current costs. The consequences are similar to those for depreciation based on historical acquisition costs versus current replacement costs.

This simple example illustrates the impact inflation has on reported financial results and, therefore, on financial ratios. Because of the lack of comparability among financial statements as a consequence of rising price levels, proposals have been made to modify accounting procedures in order to recognize that the traditional postulate of a stable measuring unit is no longer valid. In July, 1975, an Exposure Draft entitled "Accounting for Changes in the General Purchasing Power of Money" was issued by the Accounting Research Committee of the Canadian Institute of Chartered Accountants (CICA) for comment by December 31, 1975. The Exposure Draft suggested that historical cost financial statements be restated in units of purchasing power which do not strictly reflect the current or replacement value of the assets. There was no obligation on corporations to publish this type of information in their reports. The Committee's purpose in issuing the Draft was to stimulate discussion and experimentation in the area of inflation accounting in order to determine the type of information relevant for users of financial reports.

In August, 1976, a discussion paper entitled "Current Value Accounting" was issued which took a preliminary position on the technique to be used for inflation accounting and invited comments on this position. At the same time, action on the Exposure Draft was deferred until there had been further consideration of current value accounting. The preliminary position included the following proposals:

i) a combination of current value methods—replacement cost values for inventories, investments and fixed assets; net realizable values for marketable securities; and discounted cash flow for monetary assets and liabilities.

ii) income on a current value basis be charged with a provision for maintenance of the general purchasing power of invested capital.

iii) segregation in the income statement of realized and unrealized profits
(losses) and operating profits (losses) should be distinguished from holding
gains (losses) due to revaluations.

iv) current value accounting information should be supplemental to the historic
cost financial statements.

In December, 1976, the CICA withdrew its 1975 Exposure Draft which
means that no accounting recommendations on the subject will be forthcoming. However, there is some chance that a revised guideline for accounting
under inflation will be presented. This guideline will not be a proposal, but only
a suggestion as to the application of general price level techniques to be used
as supplementary information in financial statements.

The accounting profession in the United States has a position that is
similar to that in Canada. In December, 1974, the Financial Accounting
Standards Board (FASB) issued an exposure draft on a proposed statement
entitled "Financial Reporting in Units of General Purchasing Power". In June,
1976, the FASB announced that action was being deferred on the issuance of
a statement on its "Financial Reporting in Units of General Purchasing Power".
In April, 1978, the FASB recommended that the impact of inflation should be
disclosed as a supplement to financial statements without alterations in
traditional financial statements.

In 1976, the Securities and Exchange Commission (SEC) in the United
States issued a release which requires disclosure of replacement costs for
inventory items and depreciable plant from companies with $100 million or
more (at historical cost) of gross plant assets and with inventories constituting
10 percent or more of their total assets. Starting in 1977, the SEC now
requires additional details on the replacement costs of plant assets and
inventories. Any Canadian companies which are registrants of the SEC, and
meet the gross plant and inventory requirements, must abide by the SEC
reporting requirements.

It has been pointed out that, in a period of inflation, distortions result from
the use of the historical cost postulate. Assets are recorded at cost, but
revenue and other expense flows are in dollars of different purchasing power.
The amortization of fixed costs does not reflect the current cost of these
assets.[2] Furthermore, net income during periods when assets are held does
not reflect the effects of management's decision to hold the assets rather than
sell them. Since assets are not stated on the balance sheet at their current
values, the firm's financial position cannot be accurately evaluated. And when
assets are sold, gains or losses are reported during that period even though

---

[2]R.C. Thompson and Robert Koons, "Accounting for Changes in General Price Levels and Current Values,"
Modern Accountant's Handbook, ed. James D. Edwards and Homer A. Black (Homewood, Ill.: Dow Jones; Irwin,
1976), pp. 560-561.

these results reflect prior decisions to hold the assets.[3]

Many large Canadian companies have included a variety of "inflation adjusted" statements, and discussions about these adjustments, supplementary to their basic financial reports. In most cases, caveats were employed to emphasize the caution needed in the interpretation and use of this additional information. Those companies providing inflation adjusted information include Alcan Aluminum Ltd., Bell Canada Ltd., C.I.L., Falconbridge Nickel Mines Ltd., Imperial Oil Ltd., John Labatt Ltd. and Shell Canada Ltd.

PROCEDURES IN REPLACEMENT COST ACCOUNTING

In replacement cost accounting, two major categories of problems must be solved: (1) how to measure the current value of assets; and (2) how to measure income and financial position. Three methods of measuring the current value of assets have been identified: (a) current replacement cost; (b) net realizable value; and (c) present value of future cash flow (discounted cash flow).

Current replacement cost has been referred to as an entry value. It can be defined as the current cost of an identical asset, or of an asset equivalent in capacity and service. The SEC requirements mentioned earlier are not for current values in general, but for one specific measure of current values— replacement costs. Other measures of current value can be disclosed in addition to, but not as a substitute for, replacement costs.

However, for a company that liquidates by selling off its assets, the relevant measure of value is the net realizable value of the individual assets. In applying this approach, the only assets for which current market values are quoted are those that are continuously traded, such as marketable securities. Consequently, net realizable values are hardly relevant for a going concern in which liquidation is not contemplated.

The present value of future cash flow, or the discounted cash flow, method is considered by many to represent economic value. Its practical implementation requires dependable forecasts and selection of the applicable discount rates. Most companies continue to make new investments, seeking to add to the earning power of existing assets, and hence, it is difficult to segregate the future cash flows of the firm from its existing assets and new investments. Therefore, the discounted cash flow method, while widely and effectively used in evaluating individual investment projects, is more difficult to apply in valuing the physical assets of the firm as a whole.

It has been stated that, in judging the ability of a business to do the same kinds of things in the future as in the past and to pay dividends or to finance

---

[3]Sidney Davidson et al., *Financial Accounting* (Hinsdale, Ill.: Dryden Press, 1975), p. 441.

expansion without requiring new external financing, "replacement costs are perhaps the most useful measure of current value."[4] It might also be argued that the discounted cash flow method, when soundly applied, yields results consistent with the current replacement value method.

Once a measure of replacement costs have been achieved, the task of measuring income and financial position is considered. A number of concepts of income are involved. A simplified illustration presented by Falkenstein and Weil is reproduced in Table 3A-2, along with three concepts of income.

Pre-tax distributable income is defined as *revenues less expenses based on replacement costs.* It is a measure of income that can be distributed as taxes and returns to owners without impairing the firm's physical capacity to remain in business at current levels.

Realized income is *distributable income plus holding gains that have been realized during the period.* The realized holding gain is the replacement value of goods sold less their historical cost. The sum of the distributable income and the realized holding gain is the realized income. This is the same as the conventional measure of income based on the realization principle. Replacement cost data make it possible to separate distributable income and realized holding gains.

The sum of realized income plus unrealized holding gains has been called *economic income.* This view holds that an increase in the value of assets is economic income whether or not the asset has been sold. The economic measure of income has been defined as the income that can be consumed during the period while leaving the person or firm as well off at the end of the period as at the beginning. This leads to an emphasis on the physical capacity of the firm. Thus, a company is said to be as well off at the end of the period as at the beginning, only if it has sufficient physical assets to carry on the same level of business activity. Under this view, holding gains, whether realized or not, are tied up in the net assets required to conduct the operations of the firm at the current physical levels of activity. Thus, it might be more appropriate to label the third measure of income "realized plus unrealized income unadjusted for general purchasing power changes".

Taking distributable income as the most relevant measure of income, Falkenstein and Weil compare it with income as conventionally reported for the Dow-Jones Industrials for 1975. As conventionally reported, income approximated $14.5 billion. Using replacement costs, the cost of goods sold increased by $2.2 billion, and depreciation increased by $6.5 billion. Distributable income dropped to somewhat under $6 billion, representing 40 percent of the conventionally measured income.

While dividends were about 50 percent of conventional income, they were 127 percent of distributable income. Income taxes currently payable were 63

---

[4] A. Falkenstein and R.L. Weil, "Replacement Cost Accounting, *Financial Analysts' Journal* 33 (January–February 1977), pp. 47–48.

TABLE 3A-2 Simple Illustration of Replacement Cost Income Statement

Assumed Data		Acquisition Cost (Historical)	Replacement Cost
Inventory, 1/1/76		$ 900	$1,100
Inventory, 12/31/76		1,200	1,550
Cost of goods sold for 1976		4,000	4,500
Sales for 1976	$5,200		
Income Statement for 1976			
Sales			$5,200
Cost of goods sold, replacement cost basis			4,500
1. Distributable income			$ 700
Realized holding gains			500[a]
2. Realized income			$1,200
Unrealized holding gains			150[b]
3. Economic income			$1,350

[a] Realized holding gain during a period is replacement cost of goods sold less historical cost of goods sold; for 1976 the realized holding gain was $500 = $4,500 – $4,000.

[b] The total unrealized holding gain at any time is replacement cost of inventory on hand at that time less historical cost of that inventory. The unrealized holding gain during a period is the unrealized holding gain at the end of the period less the unrealized holding gain at the beginning of the period. The unrealized holding gain prior to 1976 was $200 = $1,100 – $900. The unrealized holding gain during 1976 was ($1,550 – $1,200) – ($1,100 – $900) = $350 – $200 = $150.

Source: A. Falkenstein and R.L. Weil, "Replacement Cost Accounting." *Financial Analysts' Journal* 33 (January–February 1977), p. 49. Reprinted by permission.

percent of pre-tax conventional income but almost 81 percent of distributable income. A wide variation among the individual companies reflected variations in the economic characteristics of their industries, the extent of their use of LIFO accounting methods, and other individual circumstances. Thus, the impact of inflation was different on individual companies.

The use of current replacement costs in calculating a distributable income measure can result in substantial changes in income as well as financial position. When economic changes are so large that current values of assets differ greatly from their historical values, major distortions may result if these changes are not taken into account in accounting procedures and practices.

GENERAL PURCHASING POWER REPORTING (GPPR)

Because both the realized and unrealized holding gains in the use of replacement accounting may simply reflect a declining value of the unit of account, more general adjustments are needed. These adjustments, which recognize that the assumption of a stable unit of account is no longer valid in most parts of the world, have resulted in proposals for General Purchasing Power Reporting (GPPR) along the lines of the December, 1974, FASB draft proposal in the U.S.

GPPR seeks to adjust the current value of nonmonetary items by using a general price index. It retains the historical cost basis of accounting but also adjusts it by a price index. That is, it adjusts original cost data to compensate for changes in the purchasing power of the dollar and in capital consumption expenses and then adjusts the value of goods sold from inventory. A new entry is introduced to financial reports: net holding gains on monetary items. Operationally, monetary and nonmonetary items must be separated in financial statements, and a price index must be selected. Cash, claims to cash, and claims on cash fixed in terms of dollars are designated as monetary items.

While the adjustments can be quite detailed, some simplifications can be made. When income and expenses are spread in a relatively uniform way throughout the year, a roughly accurate measure of monetary gain or loss can be calculated on the basis of the average balance of monetary items rather than on the transactions that created them. Consider the following balance sheets, for which the general price level rose 10 percent between the two balance sheet dates.

GPPR Company Balance Sheets for 19X1 and 19X2

	19X1	19X2
Monetary Assets		
Cash	$ 8,000	$ 10,000
Receivables	12,000	20,000
Nonmonetary Assets		
Inventories	30,000	40,000
Net fixed assets	50,000	60,000
Total assets	$100,000	$130,000
Monetary Liabilities		
Current liabilities	$ 10,000	$ 15,000
Deferred income taxes	2,000	3,000
Long-term debt	28,000	36,000
Net holding gains on monetary items		2,000
Nonmonetary Liabilities		
Net worth	60,000	74,000
Total claims	$100,000	$130,000

The net balance of monetary items was ($20,000) in 19X1 and ($24,000) in 19X2. The average net monetary liability was $22,000. The rate of inflation during the year was 10 percent. Hence, the value of the net monetary liability at the end of the year price index was $22,000 divided by 1.10, or $20,000; the constant dollar value of the net monetary liabilities decreased by $2,000; and the net holding gains on monetary items were $2,000.[5]

The broad significance of the two major forms of adjustments can be indicated by some aggregate measures that have been made. We have already seen the major impact of current replacement accounting on financial measures for the Dow-Jones Industrial Averages. We will illustrate further from some other aggregate measures.

Table 3A–3 shows the effects on selected financial ratios for U.S. non-financial corporations over the last 11 years of utilizing current value reporting versus conventional reporting. Note that debt to equity ratios of over 130 percent under conventional reporting fell to below 100 percent under current value reporting.

However, the operating income coverage of interest liability dropped from somewhat less than 2 to approximately 1. This is because the operating income to equity ratio dropped from about 12 percent to 6 percent in recent years. The ratio of taxes to operating income, which had been in the region of 42 percent under conventional reporting, rose to 60 percent or more under current value reporting.

This example from the United States illustrates how the use of current value reporting can have a substantial impact on ratios involving the operating performance and financial position of business firms. Given the substantial changes that have taken place in the Canadian economy during the past decade, and given that the inflation rate has been in the two-digit range, supplemental accounting information is necessary. Without taking into account changes in the purchasing power of the monetary unit, changes in the relative value of assets held by different business firms in the same industry, and the differential impact of change on different industries, conventional accounting reporting based on historical cost postulates can be seriously misleading. A reworking of financial ratio analysis based on current values therefore becomes a highly desirable check on financial ratio analysis that utilizes conventional accounting reports.

[5]See a similar illustration in Thompson and Koons, "Accounting for Changes," pp. 580–581.

TABLE 3A-3 Selected Financial Ratios for U.S. Nonfinancial Corporations

	Conventional Reporting				Current Value Reporting			
	Debt Equity (1)	Operating Income Interest Liability (2)	Operating Income Equity (3)	Taxes Operating Income (4)	Debt Equity (5)	Operating Income Interest Liability (6)	Operating Income Equity (7)	Taxes Operating Income (8)
1965	0.97	5.3	0.15	0.42	0.91	5.4	0.15	0.41
1966	1.02	4.8	0.15	0.42	0.92	4.4	0.14	0.42
1967	1.08	3.9	0.13	0.43	1.02	3.4	0.13	0.43
1968	1.14	3.7	0.14	0.47	0.96	3.0	0.12	0.49
1969	1.21	2.7	0.12	0.50	0.94	2.1	0.09	0.53
1970	1.28	1.8	0.09	0.49	1.01	1.4	0.07	0.57
1971	1.30	2.0	0.10	0.47	1.06	1.6	0.08	0.54
1972	1.29	2.2	0.11	0.44	1.07	1.9	0.09	0.48
1973	1.32	2.1	0.13	0.43	1.00	1.7	0.08	0.52
1974	1.36	1.8	0.13	0.42	0.95	0.9	0.05	0.77
1975	1.34	1.7	0.12	0.42	0.92	1.1	0.06	0.60

Source: R.W. Kepcke, "Current Accounting Practices and Proposals for Reform," *New England Economic Review*. Federal Reserve Bank of Boston (September/October 1976), p. 23.

Profit Planning

4

The preceding chapter described how ratios are used in financial analysis and showed how the basic ratios are related to one another. A major area of financial management involves a continuous review of these ratios to insure that no aspects of the firm's existing operations are getting out of control—this key element of the system of financial controls designed to maximize operating efficiency is discussed in Chapter 5. Still other tools are available to aid the financial manager in the planning and control process. Two of these—(1) break-even analysis, which is especially useful when considering plant expansion and new product decisions, and (2) the sources and uses of funds statement, which is an important aid in seeing how the firm has obtained funds and how these funds have been used—are discussed in this chapter.

BREAK-EVEN ANALYSIS

Break-even analysis is an analytical technique for studying the relations among fixed costs, variable costs, and profits. If a firm's costs were all variable, the problem of break-even volume would seldom arise; by having some variable and some fixed costs, the firm must suffer losses until a given volume has been reached.

Break-even analysis is a formal profit-planning approach based on established relations between costs and revenues. It is a device for determining the point at which sales will just cover total costs. If the firm is to avoid losses, its sales must cover all costs—those that vary directly with production and those that do not change as production levels change. Costs that fall into each of those categories are outlined in Table 4–1.

TABLE 4–1   Fixed and Variable Costs

Fixed Costs [a]	Direct or Variable Costs
Depreciation on plant and equipment	Factory labor
Rentals	Materials
Interest charges on debt	Sales commissions
Salaries of research staff	
Salaries of executive staff	
General office expenses	

[a] Some of these costs — for example, salaries and office expenses — could be varied to some degree; however, firms are reluctant to reduce these expenditures in response to temporary fluctuations in sales. Such costs are often called *semivariable* costs. In addition, costs that are fixed in the short-run become variable as the time period of analysis is extended. Since break-even analysis investigates the relationship between profits and sales given fixed and variable costs, it is a short-run analysis.

FIGURE 4–1   Break-even Chart

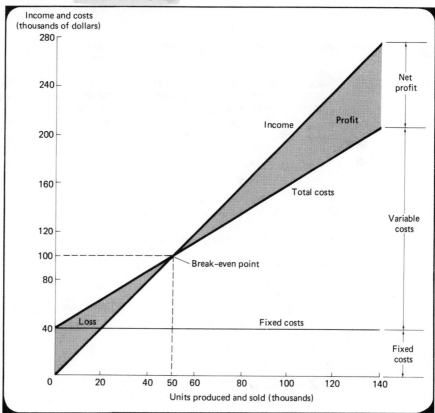

The nature of break-even analysis is depicted in Figure 4–1, the basic break-even chart. The chart is on a unit basis, with volume produced shown on the horizontal axis and costs and income measured on the vertical axis. Fixed costs of $40,000 are represented by a horizontal line; they are the same (fixed) regardless of the number of units produced. Variable costs are assumed to be $1.20 a unit. Total costs rise by $1.20, the amount of the variable costs, for each additional unit produced. Production is assumed to be sold at $2 a unit, so the total income is pictured as a straight line, which must also increase with production. The slope (or the rate of ascent) of the total-income line is steeper than that of the total-cost line. This must be true, because the firm is gaining $2.00 of revenue for every $1.20 paid out for labor and materials, the variable costs.

Up to the break-even point, found at the intersection of the total-income and total-cost lines, the firm suffers losses. After that point, the firm begins

TABLE 4–2 Relations among Units Sold, Total Variable Costs, Fixed Costs, Total Costs, and Total Income

A. Trial-and-error Calculations

Units Sold	Total Variable Costs	Fixed Costs	Total Costs	Sales	Net Profit (Loss)
20,000	$ 24,000	$40,000	$ 64,000	$ 40,000	$(24,000)
40,000	48,000	40,000	88,000	80,000	(8,000)
50,000	60,000	40,000	100,000	100,000	—
60,000	72,000	40,000	112,000	120,000	8,000
80,000	96,000	40,000	136,000	160,000	24,000
100,000	120,000	40,000	160,000	200,000	40,000
120,000	144,000	40,000	184,000	240,000	56,000
140,000	168,000	40,000	208,000	280,000	72,000

B. Algebraic Solution to Break-even Point

1. The break-even quantity is defined as that volume of output at which revenue is just equal to total costs (fixed costs plus variable costs).

2. Let:

   P = sales price per unit
   Q = quantity produced and sold
   F = fixed costs
   V = variable costs per unit.

3. Then:

   $P \cdot Q = F + V \cdot Q$
   $P \cdot Q - V \cdot Q = F$
   $Q(P - V) = F$

   $Q = \dfrac{F}{P - V}$ at break-even Q.

4. Illustration:

   $Q = \dfrac{\$40,000}{\$2.00 - \$1.20}$
   = 50,000 units.

to make profits. Figure 4–1 indicates a break-even point at a sales and cost level of $100,000 and a production level of 50,000 units.

More exact calculations of the break-even point can be derived algebraically or by trial and error. In section A of Table 4–2, profit and loss relations are shown for various levels of sales; in section B the algebraic calculations are carried out.

Nonlinear Break-even Analysis

In break-even analysis, linear (straight-line) relationships are generally assumed. Although introducing nonlinear relationships complicates matters slightly, it is easy enough to extend the analysis in this manner. For example, it is reasonable to think that increased sales can be obtained only if sales prices are reduced. Similarly, empirical studies suggest that the average variable cost per unit falls over some range of output and then begins to rise. These assumptions are illustrated in Figure 4–2. There we see a loss region when sales are low, then a profit region (and a maximum profit), and finally another loss region at very high output levels.

FIGURE 4–2   Nonlinear Break-even Chart

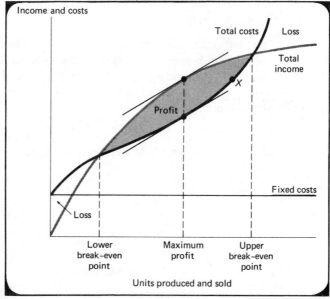

Note: The angle of a line from the origin to a point on the total-income line measures price (that is, total income/units sold = price), and a line from the origin to the total-costs curve measures cost per unit. It can be seen that the angle of the line to the income curve declines as we move toward higher sales, which means that price reductions are necessary to obtain higher unit sales volume. Unit costs (total costs/units produced) declines to point *X,* the tangency point of a line from the origin to the total-costs curve, then begins to rise.

The slopes of the total-costs and total-income lines measure marginal cost (MC) and marginal revenue (MR), respectively. At the point where the slopes of the two total curves are equal, MR = MC, and profits are at a maximum.

Although nonlinear break-even analysis is intellectually appealing, linear analysis is probably more appropriate for the uses to which it is put. Break-even charts allow focus to be placed on the key elements: sales, fixed costs, and variable costs. Even though linear break-even charts are drawn extending from *zero* output to very high output levels, no one who uses them would ordinarily be interested in or even consider the high and low extremes. In other words, users of break-even charts are really interested only in a "relevant range"; within this range linear functions are for the most part reasonably accurate.

An Example of Break-even Analysis: New Product Decision

Break-even analysis can be used in three separate but related ways:

1. To analyze a program to modernize and automate, where the firm would be operating in a more mechanized, automated manner and substituting fixed costs for variable costs. This topic is covered later in this chapter under the section on operating leverage.
2. To study the effects of a general expansion in the level of operations. This topic is covered in the section entitled "Break-even Point Based on Dollar Sales."
3. In new product decisions: How large must the sales volume on a new product be if the firm is to break even on the proposed project? This topic is illustrated in this section.

The textbook publishing business provides a good example of the effective use of break-even analysis for new product decisions. To illustrate, consider the hypothetical example of the analysis of the production costs of a college textbook as described in Table 4–3. The costs and revenues are graphed in Figure 4–3.

TABLE 4–3 Hypothetical Cost and Revenue Figures for a Textbook

Fixed costs	
Copy editing	$ 3,000
Art work	1,000
Type setting	36,000
Total fixed costs	$40,000
Variable costs per copy	
Printing and binding	$ 1.10
Bookstore discounts	2.00
Sales commissions	.25
Author's royalties	1.00
General and administrative costs	.50
Total variable costs per copy	$ 4.85
Sales price per copy	$10.00

FIGURE 4–3   Break-even Chart for a Hypothetical
Textbook

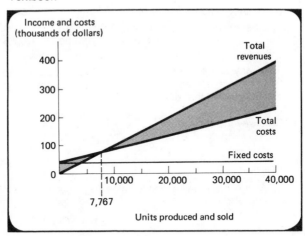

The fixed costs can be estimated quite accurately; the variable costs, most of which are set by contracts, can also be estimated precisely (and they are linear). The sales price is variable, but competition keeps prices within a sufficiently narrow range to make a linear total-revenue curve reasonable. Applying the formula, we find the break-even sales volume to be 7,767 copies.

Publishers know the size of the total market for a given book, the competition, and so forth. With these data as a base, they can estimate the possibility that sales of a given book will reach or exceed the break-even point. If the estimate is that they will not, the publisher may consider cutting production costs by spending less on art work and editing, using a lower grade of paper, negotiating with the author on royalty rates, and so on. In this particular business—and for new product decisions in many others—linear break-even analysis has proved itself to be a useful tool.

Break-even Point Based on Dollar Sales

Calculating break-even points on the basis of dollar sales instead of on units of output is frequently useful. The main advantage of this method, which is illustrated in Table 4–4, is that it enables one to determine a general break-even point for a firm that sells many products at varying prices. Furthermore, the procedure requires a minimum of data. Only three values are needed: sales, fixed costs, and variable costs. Sales and total-cost data are readily available from annual reports of corporations and from investment manuals. Total costs must then be segregated into fixed and variable components. The major fixed charges (rent, interest, depreciation, and general and administrative expenses) may be taken from the income statement. Finally, variable costs are calculated by deducting fixed costs from total costs.

TABLE 4–4 Calculation of Break-even Point Based on Dollar Sales

$$\text{Break-even point (sales volume)} = \frac{\text{total fixed costs}}{1 - \dfrac{\text{total variable costs}}{\text{total sales volume}}} = \frac{FC}{1 - \dfrac{VC}{S}}$$

Procedure

Take any sales level and use the related data to determine the break-even point. For example, assume that 20,000 units were actually produced and sold, and use the data related to that output in Table 4–2:

$$\text{Break-even point} = \frac{\$40,000}{1 - \dfrac{\$24,000}{\$40,000}} = \frac{\$40,000}{0.4} = \$100,000.$$

Rationale

1. At the break-even point, sales (S_B) are equal to fixed cost (FC) plus variable cost (VC):

$$S_B = FC + VC. \tag{4-1}$$

2. Because both the sales price and the variable cost per unit are assumed to be constant in break-even analysis, the ratio VC/S for *any* level of sales is also constant and may be found from the annual income statement.
3. Since variable cost is a constant percentage of sales, equation 4–1 can be rewritten as follows:

$$S_B = FC + \frac{VC}{S}(S_B)$$

$$S_B\left(1 - \frac{VC}{S}\right) = FC$$

$$S_B = \frac{FC}{1 - \dfrac{VC}{S}} \text{ at break-even } S.$$

Operating Leverage

To a physicist, leverage implies the use of a lever to raise a heavy object with a small force. To a layman, if a person has leverage, his smallest word or action can accomplish a lot. In business terminology, a high degree of leverage implies that a relatively small change in sales results in a large change in profits. We can divide leverage into two categories: (1) *financial leverage*, discussed briefly in Chapter 3 (and much more extensively in Chapter 19), and (2) *operating leverage,* the subject of this section.

Operating leverage refers to the impact on the net operating income of a firm, usually measured before taxes, from a given change in sales. As we shall demonstrate, the degree of operating leverage will depend on the importance of fixed operating costs in the firm's cost structure. The significance of the degree of operating leverage is clearly illustrated by Figure 4-4. Three firms, A, B, and C, with differing degrees of leverage, are contrasted. Firm A has a

FIGURE 4-4 Operating Leverage

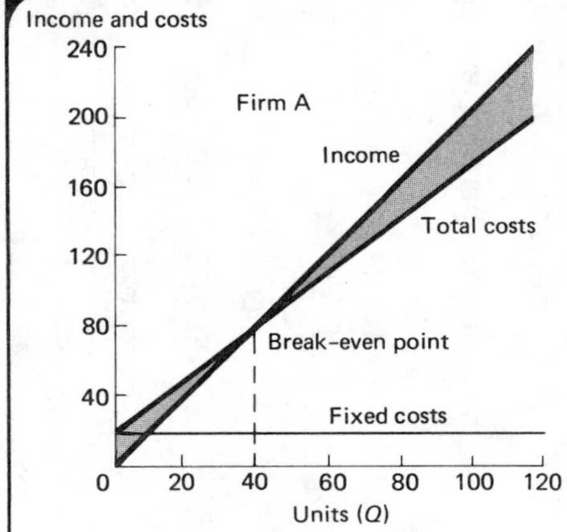

Firm A

Selling price = $2.00
Fixed costs = $20,000
Variable costs = $1.50 Q

Units sold (Q)	Sales	Costs	Profit
20,000	$ 40,000	$ 50,000	−$10,000
40,000	80,000	80,000	0
60,000	120,000	110,000	10,000
80,000	160,000	140,000	20,000
100,000	200,000	170,000	30,000
120,000	240,000	200,000	40,000

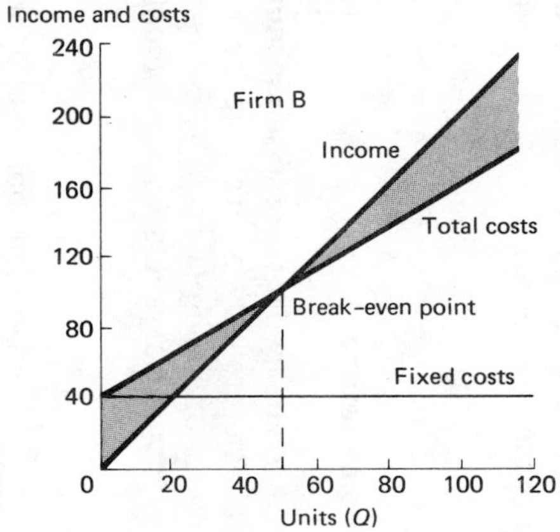

Firm B

Selling price = $2.00
Fixed costs = $40,000
Variable costs = $1.20 Q

Units sold (Q)	Sales	Costs	Profit
20,000	$ 40,000	$ 64,000	−$24,000
40,000	80,000	88,000	− 8,000
60,000	120,000	112,000	8,000
80,000	160,000	136,000	24,000
100,000	200,000	160,000	40,000
120,000	240,000	184,000	56,000

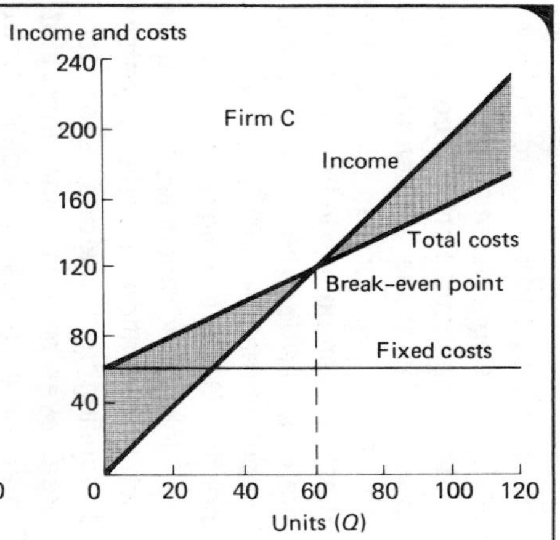

Firm C

Selling price = $2.00
Fixed costs = $60,000
Variable costs = $1.00 Q

Units sold (Q)	Sales	Costs	Profit
20,000	$ 40,000	$ 80,000	−$40,000
40,000	80,000	100,000	− 20,000
60,000	120,000	120,000	0
80,000	160,000	140,000	20,000
100,000	200,000	160,000	40,000
120,000	240,000	180,000	60,000

relatively small amount of fixed charges — it does not have much automated equipment, so its depreciation cost is low. Note, however, that A's variable-cost line has a relatively steep slope, denoting that its variable costs per unit are higher than those of the other firms. Firm B is considered to have a normal amount of fixed costs in its operations. It uses automated equipment (with which one operator can turn out a few or many units at the same labor cost) to about the same extent as the average firm in the industry. Firm B breaks even at a higher level of operations than does firm A. At a production level of 40,000 units, B is losing $8,000 but A breaks even.

On the other hand, firm C has the highest fixed costs. It is highly auto-mated, using expensive, high-speed machines that require very little labor per unit produced. With such an operation, its variable costs rise slowly. Because of the high overhead resulting from charges associated with the expensive machinery, firm C's break-even point is higher than that for either firm A or firm B. Once firm C reaches its break-even point, however, its profits rise faster than do those of the other firms.

Degree of Operating Leverage

Operating leverage can be defined more precisely in terms of the way a given change in volume affects profits. For this purpose we use the following definition: *The degree of operating leverage is defined as the percentage change in operating income that results from a percentage change in units sold.* Algebraically,

$$\text{Degree of operating leverage} = \frac{\text{percentage change in operating income}}{\text{percentage change in sales}}.$$

For firm B in Figure 4–4, the degree of operating leverage (OL_B) at 100,000 units of output is

$$\text{Degree of } OL_B = \frac{\dfrac{\Delta \text{profit}}{\text{profit}}}{\dfrac{\Delta Q}{Q}}$$

$$= \frac{\dfrac{\$56,000 - \$40,000}{\$40,000}}{\dfrac{120,000 - 100,000}{100,000}} = \frac{\dfrac{\$16,000}{\$40,000}}{\dfrac{20,000}{100,000}}$$

$$= \frac{40\%}{20\%} = \boxed{2.0}.$$

Here Δ profit is the increase in profit, Q is the quantity of output in units, and ΔQ is the increase in output. For this calculation, we assume an increase in volume from 100,000 to 120,000 units, but the calculated degree of OL would have been the same for any other increase from 100,000 units.

For linear break-even, a formula has been developed to aid in calculating the degree of operating leverage at any level of output, Q:[1]

$$\text{Degree of operating leverage at point } Q = \frac{Q(P - V)}{Q(P - V) - F} \quad (4-2)$$

$$= \frac{S - VC}{S - VC - F}. \quad (4-2a)$$

Here P is the price per unit, V is the variable cost per unit, F is fixed costs, S is total sales, and VC is total variable costs. Equation 4-2 expresses the relationship in terms of units, while equation 4-2a expresses it in terms of total dollar figures. Using the equations, we find firm B's degree of operating leverage at 100,000 units of output to be

$$OL_B \text{ at 100,000 units} = \frac{100,000(\$2.00 - \$1.20)}{100,000(\$2.00 - \$1.20) - \$40,000}$$

$$= \frac{\$200,000 - \$120,000}{\$200,000 - \$120,000 - \$40,000}$$

$$= \frac{\$80,000}{\$40,000} = \boxed{2.0}.$$

The two methods must, of course, give consistent answers.

Equation 4-2 can also be applied to firms A and C. When this is done, we find A's degree of operating leverage at 100,000 units to be 1.67 and that of C to be 2.5. Thus, for a 1 percent increase in volume, firm C, the company with the most operating leverage, will experience a profit increase of 2.5 percent; for the same 1 percent volume gain, firm A, the one with the least leverage, will have only a 1.67 percent profit gain. Of course, it must be stressed that operating leverage cuts both ways. Thus, for a 1 percent decrease in volume, firm B will have a decrease in net operating income of 2 percent; C a decrease of 2.5 percent; and A a decrease of 1.67 percent.

[1] Equation 4-2 is developed as follows:
The change in output is defined as ΔQ. Fixed costs are constant, so the change in profits is $\Delta Q(P - V)$, where P = price per unit and V = variable cost per unit. The initial profit is $Q(P - V) - F$, so the percentage change in profit is:

$$\frac{\Delta Q(P - V)}{Q(P - V) - F}.$$

The percentage change in output is $\Delta Q/Q$, so the ratio of the change in profits to the change in output is:

$$\frac{\frac{\Delta Q(P - V)}{Q(P - V) - F}}{\frac{\Delta Q}{Q}} = \frac{\Delta Q(P - V)}{Q(P - V) - F} \cdot \frac{Q}{\Delta Q} = \frac{Q(P - V)}{Q(P - V) - F}.$$

In summary, the calculation of the degree of operating leverage shows algebraically the same pattern that Figure 4–4 shows graphically—that the profits of firm C, the company with the most operating leverage, are most sensitive to changes in sales volume, while those of firm A, which has only a small amount of operating leverage, are relatively insensitive to volume changes. Firm B, with an intermediate degree of leverage, lies between the two extremes.[2]

The degree of operating leverage is an important ingredient in determining the **business risk** of a firm. Business risk is defined as the basic risk inherent in a firm's operations and is manifest in the variability of net operating income. Clearly, a company can influence the degree of business risk by its choice of the degree of operating leverage. Holding all other influences constant, the larger the degree of operating leverage, the greater will be the business risk. However, the underlying variability in sales volumes is another component in assessing business risk. The larger the degree of operating leverage, the greater will be the amplification of a change in sales on the net operating income. A regulated utility in the communications area, such as Bell Canada, may have a large degree of operating leverage, but due to the stability of sales, the business risk is not substantial. Conversely, a company with a small fixed cost component can still have high business risk if the basic sales volume has high variability.

The choice by a manufacturing firm of its production process is a decision that will be analyzed in the capital budgeting chapter. However, it should be obvious that the larger the potential market for the firm's products, the more likely the firm is to choose a production process with higher capital intensity, and hence a higher ratio of fixed to variable costs. In Canada, the size of the market is limited and the potential for using more capital intensive production techniques is reduced. Thus, a Canadian manufacturing company would choose a production process which has lower capital intensity and hence lower break-even sales volumes. A straight replication of the technology used by similar firms where the size of the market is larger, for example, in the United States, would result in high break-even sales levels, high operating leverage and lower profits.

However, if the potential market is large enough, high break-even production methods can be used. This is the case in the base metals and pulp and paper industries where, due to the export activities of the industries, the market has been expanded and production methods have become more efficient. In this case, higher break-even processes are used.

---

[2]The degree of operating leverage is a form of *elasticity concept* and, thus, is akin to the familiar price elasticity developed in economics. Since operating leverage is an elasticity, it varies depending upon the particular part of the break-even graph that is being considered. For example, in terms of our illustrative firms the degree of operating leverage is greatest close to the break-even point, where a very small change in volume can produce a very large percentage increase in profits simply because the base profits are close to zero near the break-even point.

FIGURE 4-5 Cash Break-even Analysis

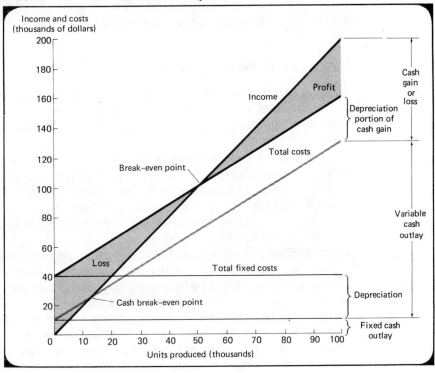

Cash Break-even Analysis

Some of the firm's fixed costs are noncash outlays, and for a period some of its revenues may be in receivables. The cash break-even chart for firm B, constructed on the assumption that $30,000 of the fixed costs from the previous illustration are depreciation charges and, therefore, a noncash outlay, is shown in Figure 4–5.[3] Because fixed cash outlays are only $10,000, the cash break-even point is at 12,500 units rather than 50,000 units, which is the profit break-even point.

Cash break-even analysis does not fully represent cash flows—for this a cash budget is required. But cash break-even analysis is useful because it provides a picture of the flow of funds from operations. A firm could incur a level of fixed costs that would result in losses during periods of poor business but large profits during upswings. If cash outlays are small, even during periods of losses the firm might still be operating above the cash break-even

[3]The nature of depreciation as a noncash charge is explained later in this chapter.

point. Thus, the risks of insolvency, in the sense of inability to meet cash obligations, would be small. This allows a firm to reach out for higher profits through automation and operating leverage.

Limitations of Break-even Analysis

Break-even analysis is useful in studying the relations among volume, prices, and costs; it is thus helpful in pricing, cost control, and decisions about alternative expansion programs. It has limitations, however, as a guide to managerial actions.

Linear break-even analysis is especially weak in what it implies about the sales possibilities for the firm. Any linear break-even chart is based on a constant sales price. Therefore, in order to study profit possibilities under different prices, a whole series of charts is necessary, one chart for each price. Alternatively, nonlinear break-even analysis can be used.

With regard to costs, break-even analysis is also deficient — the relations indicated by the chart do not hold at all outputs. As sales increase, existing plant and equipment are worked to capacity; both this situation and the use of additional workers and overtime pay cause variable costs to rise sharply. Additional equipment and plant are required, thus increasing fixed costs. Over a period, the products sold by the firm change in quality and quantity. Such changes in product mix influence the level and slope of the cost function. Finally, when using this analysis for a new product, it becomes necessary to allocate to this product the costs that are common to other products produced by the company. The allocation must be arbitrary and can affect the break-even point. Linear break-even analysis is useful as a first step in developing the basic data required for pricing and for financial decisions. But more detailed analysis, perhaps including nonlinear analysis, is required before final judgments can be made.

SOURCES AND USES OF FUNDS STATEMENT[4]

When a firm requests a loan, the bank's loan officer will doubtless pose these three questions: What has the firm done with the money it had? What will it do with the new funds? How will it repay the loan? The sources and uses statement helps provide answers to these questions, as well as to questions that other interested parties may have about the firm. This information may indicate that the firm is making progress or that problems are arising.

---

[4]The Canadian Institute of Chartered Accountants (CICA) recommends that this statement be referred to in the annual report as the Statement of Changes in Financial Position.

Depreciation as a Source of Funds*

Before going on to construct a sources and uses of funds statement, it is useful to pause and consider why, in financial analysis, we consider depreciation to be a source of funds. First, what is depreciation? In effect, it is an annual charge against income which reflects the cost of the capital equipment used in the production process. For example, suppose a machine with an expected useful life of 10 years and a 0 expected salvage value was purchased in 19X1 for $100,000. This $100,000 cost must be charged against production during those 10 years; otherwise, profits will be overstated. If the machine is depreciated by the straight-line method, the annual charge is $10,000. This amount is deducted from sales revenues, along with such other costs as labor and raw materials, to determine income. *However, depreciation is not a cash outlay — funds were expended back in 19X1, so the depreciation charged against income in 19X3 is not a cash outlay, as are labor or charges for raw materials.*

To illustrate the significance of depreciation in cash flow analysis, let us consider the Manitoba Chemical Company Limited, which has the following income statement for 19X3:

Sales	$300,000,000
Costs excluding depreciation	$270,000,000
Depreciation	10,000,000
Profit before tax	$ 20,000,000
Taxes	8,000,000
Profit after tax	$ 12,000,000

Assuming that sales are for cash and that all costs except depreciation are paid during 19X3, how much cash was available from operations to pay dividends, retire debt, or make investments in fixed or current assets or both? The answer is $22 million, the sum of profit after tax plus depreciation. The sales are all for cash, so the firm took in $300 million in cash money. Its costs other than depreciation were $270 million, and these were paid in cash, leaving $30 million. Depreciation *is not* a cash charge — the firm does not pay out the $10 million of depreciation expenses — so $30 million of cash money is still left after depreciation. Taxes, on the other hand, are paid in cash, so $8 million for taxes must be deducted from the $30 million gross operating cash flow, leaving a net cash flow from operations of $22 million. This $22 million is, of course, exactly equal to profit after tax plus depreciation: $12 million plus $10 million equals $22 million.

This example shows the rationale behind the statement that depreciation is a source of funds. However, we should note that without sales revenues,

*In this section we consider depreciation and the resulting cash flow as reported in the annual report. However, in Chapters 2 and 3 we noted that capital cost allowance is the depreciation expense used in calculating the actual tax liability. In our discussion of capital budgeting we argue that the appropriate cash flow to use is based on the capital cost allowance and not reported depreciation.

depreciation would *not* be a source of funds. If a strike idles the plant, the $300 million of sales revenues would vanish; cash flows from depreciation would evaporate.[5] Nevertheless, most firms do not suffer shutdowns for long periods, so normally a firm's depreciation does indeed constitute a source of funds as we use the term.

Sources and Uses Analysis

Several steps are involved in constructing a sources and uses statement. First, the changes in balance sheet items from one year to the next must be tabulated and then classified as either a source or a use of funds, according to the following pattern:

- *Source of funds:* (1) decrease in asset item or (2) increase in liability item
- *Use of funds:* (1) increase in asset item or (2) decrease in liability item.

Table 4–5 gives Manitoba Chemical's comparative balance sheets for 19X2 and 19X3, and also net changes in each item classified as to source or use.

TABLE 4–5 Manitoba Chemical Company, Limited
Comparative Balance Sheets and Sources and Uses of Funds
(millions of dollars)

	Dec. 31, 19X2	Dec. 31, 19X3	Sources	Uses
Cash	$ 10	$ 5	$ 5	
Marketable securities	25	15	10	
Net receivables	15	20		$ 5
Inventories	25	30		5
Gross fixed assets	150	180		30
Less: Accumulated depreciation[a]	(40)	(50)	10	
Net fixed assets	110	130		
Total assets	$185	$200		
Accounts payable	$ 10	$ 6		4
Notes payable	15	10		5
Other current liabilities	10	14	4	
Long-term debt	60	70	10	
Preferred shares	10	10	—	—
Common shares	50	50	—	—
Retained earnings	30	40	10	
Total claims on assets	$185	$200		

[a]The accumulated depreciation is actually a contra-asset that appears on the left side of the balance sheet. Note that it is deducted, not added, when totaling the column.

[5]This potential problem was brought to the authors' attention in connection with a project involving a financial plan for Communications Satellite Corporation. Comsat has very healthy projected cash flows that would seem able to support a substantial amount of debt. However, Comsat's revenues are derived almost entirely from three satellites (over the North Atlantic, Pacific, and Indian Oceans), and if these satellites failed it would take months to replace them. Thus, when we recognized the degree of uncertainty about these cash flows, we adjusted downward our estimates of how much debt Comsat could safely carry.

The next step in constructing a sources and uses statement involves (1) making adjustments to reflect funds derived from operations and (2) isolating changes in working capital (current assets minus current liabilities). These changes are reflected in the sources and uses statement shown in Table 4-6. Funds derived from operations equal net income of $12 million and deprecia- tion of $10 million is added back. In addition, long-term debt provided $10 million as a source of funds. The section for the use of funds shows that an increase of fixed assets required $30 million and a dividend payment used $2 million. Since net income and dividends are accounted for explicitly in the statement, the $10 million retained earnings shown in Table 4–5 is deleted from Table 4–6 to avoid double counting.

The third section in Table 4-6 presents the changes in the working capital component. Notice that Manitoba Chemical had no net change in working capital — the increases were exactly equal to the decreases. This was merely a coincidence; ordinarily there would be some change in working

TABLE 4-6   Manitoba Chemical Company Limited
Statement of Changes in Financial Position, 19X3
(millions of dollars)

Funds derived from:	
Operations	
Net income	$12
Depreciation	10
	22
Increase on long-term debt	10
Working capital decrease	—
	$32
Funds used for:	
Gross fixed asset expansion	$30
Dividends to shareholders	2
Working capital increase	—
	$32
Changes in working capital components:	
Reduction in cash	(5)
Sales of marketable securities	(10)
Increase in other current liabilities	(4)
Inventory investment	5
Increase in receivables	5
Reduction in notes payable	5
Reduction in accounts payable	4
Working capital increase (decrease)	$ 0

capital. If there was a working capital increase, the balance would be inserted as a use of funds; a decrease would be a source of funds.

What does this statement of sources and uses of funds tell the financial manager? It tells him or her that plant size was expanded and that fixed assets amounting to $30 million were acquired. Inventories and net receivables also increased as sales increased. The firm needed funds to meet working capital and fixed assets demands.[6]

Previously, Manitoba Chemical had been financing its growth through bank credit (notes payable). In the present period of growth, management decided to obtain some financing from permanent sources (long-term debt). It obtained enough long-term debt not only to finance some of the asset growth but also to pay back some of its bank credit and to reduce accounts payable. In addition to the long-term debt, funds were obtained from earnings and from depreciation charges. Moreover, the firm had been accumulating marketable securities in anticipation of this expansion program, and some were sold to pay for new buildings and equipment. Finally, cash had been accumulated in excess of the firm's needs and was also worked down. In summary, this example illustrates how the sources and uses of funds statement can provide both a fairly complete picture of recent operations and a good perspective on the flow of funds within the company.

Pro Forma Sources and Uses of Funds

A *pro forma*, or projected, sources and uses of funds statement can also be constructed to show how a firm plans to acquire and employ funds during some future period. In the next chapter we will discuss financial forecasting, which involves the determination of future sales, the level of assets necessary to generate these sales (the left side of the projected balance sheet), and the manner in which these assets will be financed (the right side of the projected balance sheet). Given the projected balance sheet and supplementary projected data on earnings, dividends, and depreciation, the financial manager can construct a pro forma sources and uses of funds statement to summarize his firm's projected operations over the planning horizon. Such a statement is obviously of much interest to lenders as well as to the firm's own management.

---

[6]This is a simplified example of the calculation of a sources and uses statement. A more complicated example would involve the use of accounts such as taxes payable, deferred income tax, unamortized bond discounts, etc. The basic technique to determine if year to year changes in these accounts are sources or uses is still appropriate. Finally, in real world examples the change in accumulated depreciation can differ from the depreciation charge shown on the income statement. To be consistent with CICA recommendations, the depreciation charge on the income statement is a source of funds and the gross change in fixed assets is calculated by adding back the depreciation charge to the net fixed assets at the end of the year and subtracting from this the net fixed assets at the end of the previous year. If the balance is positive, then gross fixed assets increased and were a use of funds.

SUMMARY

This chapter analyzes two important financial tools, *break-even analysis* and the *sources and uses of funds statement*, and the key concept of *operating leverage*.

Break-even Analysis   Break-even analysis is a method of relating fixed costs, variable costs, and total revenues to show the level of sales that must be attained if the firm is to operate at a profit. The analysis can be based on the number of units produced or on total dollar sales. It can also be used for the entire company or for a particular product or division. Further, with minor modifications, break-even analysis can be put on a cash basis instead of a profit basis. Ordinarily, break-even analysis is conducted on a linear, or straight-line, basis. However, this is not necessary—nonlinear break-even analysis is feasible and at times desirable.

Operating Leverage   Operating leverage is defined as the extent to which fixed costs are used in operations. The *degree of operating leverage,* defined as the percentage change in operating income that results from a specific percentage change in units sold, provides a precise measure of how much operating leverage a particular firm is employing. Break-even analysis provides a graphic view of the effects of changes in sales on profits; the degree of operating leverage presents the same picture in algebraic terms. Finally, the degree of operating leverage is an important element in evaluating the business risk of a company.

Sources and Uses of Funds Statement   The sources and uses of funds statement indicates where cash came from and how it was used. When a firm wishes to borrow funds, one of the first questions posed by the bank's loan officer is "What has the firm done with the money it had?" This question is answered by the sources and uses of funds statement. The information it provides may indicate that the firm is making progress or that problems are arising. Sources and uses data may also be analyzed on a *pro forma*, or projected, basis to show how a firm plans to acquire and employ funds during some future period.

Break-even analysis, operating leverage, and sources and uses statements are all fundamental concepts for the financial manager, and they are encountered time and time again throughout the remainder of this book.

QUESTIONS

4-1. What benefits can be derived from break-even analysis?

4-2. What is operating leverage? Explain how profits or losses can be magnified in a firm with a great deal of operating leverage as opposed to a firm without this characteristic.

4-3. What data are necessary to construct a break-even chart?

4-4. What is the general effect of each of the following changes on a firm's break-even point?

  a. An increase in selling price with no change in units sold.

  b. A change from the leasing of a machine for $5,000 a year to the purchase of the machine for $100,000. The useful life of this machine will be twenty years, with no salvage value. Assume straight-line depreciation.

  c. A reduction in variable labor costs.

4-5. Why is depreciation considered to be a source of funds?

4-6. A financial advisory service noted that during 1977 those companies which were automated, and hence capital intensive, appeared to have a poorer operating profit performance than companies which were more labor intensive. The conclusion drawn by the writer of the article was that increasing the capital intensity of an industry results in poorer financial performance. Comment on this conclusion.

PROBLEMS

4-1. For Mathis Industries the following relations exist: each unit of output is sold for $75; for output up to 25,000 units the fixed costs are $240,000; variable costs are $35 a unit.

  a. What is the firm's gain or loss at sales of 5,000 units? of 8,000 units?

  b. What is the break-even point? Illustrate by means of a chart.

  c. What is Mathis' degree of operating leverage at sales of 5,000 and 8,000 units?

  d. What happens to the break-even point if the selling price rises to $85? What is the significance of the change to financial management? Illustrate by means of a chart.

  e. What occurs to the break-even point if the selling price rises to $85 but variable costs rise to $45 a unit? Illustrate by means of a chart.

4-2. Win Corporation Ltd.'s only product is an oil additive for automobile engines. Win's 19X1 after tax profit was $60,000 on sales of $750,000. Its average tax rate is 40 percent. The oil additive sells for $5 per unit and has a variable cost of $4 per unit.

  a. What is Win's annual total fixed cost?

  b. What is its break-even point in units? in dollars?

  c. If Win's after tax profits increase by $30,000 to $90,000, when sales increase to 200,000 units, what is Win's degree of operating leverage at 150,000 units?

4-3. Use the data in 4-2 to answer the following.

What would be the effect on the break-even point of Win Corporation if:

  a. Fixed costs increase by $20,000.

  b. The average tax rate was 50 percent instead of 40 percent; after tax profits remain at $60,000. Sales and variable costs remain at $750,000 and $600,000, respectively, but fixed costs decline to $30,000.

  c. Unit variable costs increased $0.50 and fixed costs decreased by $5,000 to $45,000.

4-4. Digital Electronics Ltd. is considering developing a new miniature calculator. The quantity *(Q)* sold is a function of the price *(P)* where

$$Q = 2,000 - 50P.$$

Per unit variable costs are $10 and fixed costs are $10,000. Graphically determine the break-even point for the calculator in units and dollars.

4-5. The Timmins Tire Co. Ltd. is currently considering two possible mutually exclusive plant modernizations. Under the first, newer and more efficient machinery would be added; this would tend to reduce labor costs and, because of much less waste, raw material usage. The other alternative would involve a more extensive changeover in the plant to an entirely new process for forming and curing rubber. The second procedure would involve a more extensive investment in both plant and equipment, but it would result in larger savings in labor and materials costs.

The current sales level is about 76,500 units a year at a price of $40 each, but volume has fluctuated from year to year with changes in general economic conditions. The firm's management is primarily concerned with the extent to which profitability will be affected by each alternative project in relation to risk. (For current purposes, riskiness may be considered to be a function of the probability of not reaching the break-even point.) A break-down of costs for the current sales volume is given below, together with estimates of what each item would be after each of the modernization proposals.

Estimated Costs	Currently	Modernization I	Modernization II
Depreciation on plant and equipment	$513,000	$630,000	$787,500
Depreciation on building	288,000	360,000	468,000
Property taxes	36,000	45,000	63,000
Salary expense	639,000	693,000	778,500
Other fixed expenses	54,000	72,000	99,000
Factory labor	*8.18* 625,500	*6.12* 468,000	*3.53* 270,000
Raw materials	*5.88* 450,000	*4.94* 378,000	*3.53* 270,000
Variable selling expenses	*.94* 72,000	*.94* 72,000	*.94* 72,000

a. Determine the break-even point in units for the firm, assuming (1) no modernization is undertaken, (2) the first program is undertaken, and (3) the second program is undertaken.

b. Compute the degree of operating leverage at the current volume (76,500 units) for each of the three possibilities.

c. Compute profits for each alternative, assuming future sales of 76,500 units. Profits for each alternative at other sales levels have been calculated (to save you work) and are given below:

Unit Sales	Profits				
No Modernization		Modernization I		Modernization II	
65,000	$ 95,000	65,000	$ 20,000	65,000	$ (116,000)
90,000	720,000	90,000	720,000	90,000	684,000
100,000	970,000	100,000	1,000,000	100,000	1,004,000

d. Rank the alternatives in terms of potential riskiness.

e. How would the decision if and how to modernize be affected by the expectation of large fluctuations in future sales?

f. (To be worked at the option of the instructor.) Suppose we have estimated the following probability distribution for sales:

Probability	Sales (in Units)
.1	65,000
.3	76,500
.3	90,000
.3	100,000

Use this information to determine the expected values of the three alternative courses of action.

g. Which project is best? What factors would influence your decision?

4-6. The consolidated balance sheets for the Ashe Corporation at the beginning and end of 19X1 are shown below.

Ashe Corporation Ltd.
Balance Sheet
Beginning and end 19X1
(millions of dollars)

	Jan. 1	Dec. 31	Source	Use
Cash	$ 45	$ 21	_____	_____
Marketable securities	33	0	_____	_____
Net receivables	66	90	_____	_____
Inventories	159	225	_____	_____
Total current assets	$303	$336	_____	_____
Gross fixed assets	225	450	_____	_____
Less: reserve for depreciation	(78)	(123)	_____	_____
Net fixed assets	147	327	_____	_____
Total assets	$450	$663	_____	_____
	Jan. 1	Dec. 31	Source	Use
Accounts payable	$ 45	$ 54	_____	_____
Notes payable	45	9	_____	_____
Other current liabilities	21	45	_____	_____
Long-term debt	24	78	_____	_____
Common shares	114	192	_____	_____
Retained earnings	201	285	_____	_____
Total claims on assets	$450	$663	_____	_____

The company bought $225 million worth of fixed assets. The charge for current depreciation was $45 million. Earnings after taxes were $114 million, and the company paid out $30 million in dividends.

a. Fill in the amount of source or use in the appropriate column.

b. Prepare a percentage statement of sources and uses of funds.

c. Briefly summarize your findings.

Financial Forecasting

5

The planning process is an integral part of the financial manager's job. As we will see in subsequent chapters, long-term debt and equity funds are raised infrequently and in large amounts, primarily because the cost per dollar raised by selling such securities decreases as the size of the issue increases. Because of these considerations, it is important that the firm have a working estimate of its total needs for funds for the next few years. It is therefore useful to examine methods of forecasting the firm's overall needs for funds, and this is the subject of the present chapter.

CASH FLOW CYCLE

We must recognize that firms need assets to make sales; if sales are to be increased, assets must also be expanded. Growing firms require new investments—immediate investment in current assets and, as full capacity is reached, investment in fixed assets as well. New investments must be financed, and new financing carries with it commitments and obligations to service the capital obtained.[1] A growing, profitable firm is likely to require additional cash for investments in receivables, inventories, and fixed assets. Such a firm can, therefore, have a cash flow problem. The nature of this problem, as well as the cause and effect relationship between assets and sales, is illustrated in the following discussion, in which we trace the consequences of a series of transactions.

[1]"Servicing" capital refers to the payment of interest and principal on debt and to dividends and retained earnings (the cost of equity capital) on common shares.

Effects on the Balance Sheet

1. Two partners invest a total of $50,000 to create the Glamour Galore Dress Co. Ltd. The firm rents a plant; equipment and other fixed assets cost $30,000. The resulting financial situation is shown by Balance Sheet 1.

2. Glamour Galore receives an order to manufacture 10,000 dresses. The receipt of an order in itself has no effect on the balance sheet, but in preparation for the manufacturing activity, the firm buys $20,000 worth of cotton cloth on terms of net 30 days. Without additional investment by the owners, total assets increase by $20,000, financed by the trade accounts payable to the supplier of the cotton cloth.

BALANCE SHEET 1

Assets		Liabilities	
Current Assets		Capital stock	$50,000
Cash	$20,000		
Fixed Assets			
Plant and equipment	30,000		
Total assets	$50,000	Total liabilities and net worth	$50,000

After the purchase, the firm spends $20,000 on labor for cutting the cloth to the required pattern. Of the $20,000 total labor cost, $10,000 is paid in cash and $10,000 is owed in the form of accrued wages. These two transactions are reflected in Balance Sheet 2, which shows that total assets increase to $80,000. Current assets are increased; net working capital—total current assets minus total current liabilities—remains constant. The current ratio declines to 1.67, and the debt ratio rises to 38 percent. The financial position of the firm is weakening.

BALANCE SHEET 2

Assets		Liabilities	
Current Assets		Accounts payable	$20,000
Cash	$10,000	Accrued wages payable	10,000
Inventories		Total current liabilities	$30,000
Work in process		Capital stock	50,000
Materials	20,000		
Labor	20,000		
Total current assets	$50,000		
Fixed Assets			
Plant and equipment	30,000	Total liabilities and	
Total assets	$80,000	net worth	$80,000

3. In order to complete the dresses, the firm incurs additional labor costs of $20,000 and pays in cash. It is assumed that the firm desires to maintain a minimum cash balance of $5,000. Since the initial cash balance is $10,000, Glamour Galore must borrow an additional $15,000 from its bank to meet the wage bill. The borrowing is reflected in notes payable in Balance Sheet 3. Total assets rise to $95,000, with a finished goods inventory of $60,000. The current ratio drops to 1.4, and the debt ratio rises to 47 percent. These ratios show a further weakening of the financial position.

BALANCE SHEET 3

Assets		Liabilities	
Current Assets		Accounts payable	$20,000
Cash	$ 5,000	Notes payable	15,000
Inventory		Accrued wages payable	10,000
Finished goods	60,000		
Total current assets	$65,000	Total current liabilities	$45,000
Fixed Assets		Capital stock	50,000
Plant and equipment	30,000	Total liabilities and	
Total assets	$95,000	net worth	$95,000

4. Glamour Galore ships the dresses on the basis of the original order, invoicing the purchaser for $100,000 within 30 days. Accrued wages and accounts payable have to be paid now, so Glamour Galore must borrow an additional $30,000 in order to maintain the $5,000 minimum cash balance. These transactions are shown in Balance Sheet 4.

BALANCE SHEET 4

Assets		Liabilities	
Current Assets		Notes payable	$ 45,000
Cash	$ 5,000	Total current liabilities	$ 45,000
Accounts receivable	100,000	Capital stock	$ 50,000
Total current assets	$105,000	Retained earnings	40,000
Fixed Assets		Total net worth	$ 90,000
Plant and equipment	30,000	Total liabilities and	
Total assets	$135,000	net worth	$135,000

Note that in Balance Sheet 4, finished goods inventory is replaced by receivables, with the markup reflected as retained earnings. This causes the debt ratio to drop to 33 percent. Since the receivables are carried at the sales price, current assets increase to $105,000 and the current ratio rises to 2.3. Compared with the conditions reflected in Balance Sheet 3, most of the financial ratios show improvement. However, the absolute amount of debt is large.

Whether the firm's financial position is really improved depends upon the credit worthiness of the purchaser of the dresses. If the purchaser is a good credit risk, Glamour Galore may be able to borrow further on the basis of the accounts receivable.

5. The firm receives payment for the accounts receivable, pays off the bank loan, and is in the highly liquid position shown by Balance Sheet 5. If a new order for 10,000 dresses is received, it will have no effect on the balance sheet, but a cycle similar to the one we have been describing will begin.

BALANCE SHEET 5

Assets		Liabilities	
Current Assets		Capital stock	$50,000
Cash	$60,000	Retained earnings	40,000
Fixed Assets			
Plant and equipment	$30,000	Total liabilities and	
Total assets	$90,000	net worth	$90,000

6. The idea of the cash flow cycle can now be generalized. An order that requires the purchase of raw materials is placed with the firm. The purchase in turn generates an account payable. As labor is applied, work-in-process inventories build up. To the extent that wages are not fully paid at the time labor is used, accrued wages will appear on the liability side of the balance sheet. As goods are completed, they move into finished goods inventories. The cash needed to pay for the labor to complete the goods may make it necessary for the firm to borrow.

Finished goods inventories are sold, usually on credit, which gives rise to accounts receivable. As the firm has not received cash, this point in the cycle represents the peak in financing requirements. If the firm did not borrow at the time finished goods inventories were at their maximum, it may do so as inventories are converted into receivables by credit sales. Income taxes, which were not considered in the example, can add to the problem. As accounts receivable become cash, short-term obligations can be paid off.

FINANCING PATTERNS

The influence of sales on current asset levels has just been illustrated. Over the course of several cycles, the fluctuations in sales will be accompanied in most industries by a rising long-term trend. Figure 5–1 shows the consequences of such a pattern. Total permanent assets increase steadily in the form of current and fixed assets. Increases of this nature should be financed by long-term debt; by equity; or by "spontaneous" increases in liabilities, such as accrued taxes and wages and accounts payable, which naturally accompany increasing sales. However, temporary increases in assets can be covered by short-term liabilities. The distinction between temporary and permanent asset levels may be difficult to make in practice, but it is neither illusory nor unimportant. Short-term financing for the financing of long-term needs is dangerous. A profitable firm may become unable to meet its cash obligations if funds borrowed on a short-term basis have become tied up in permanent asset needs.

FIGURE 5–1   Fluctuating versus Permanent Assets

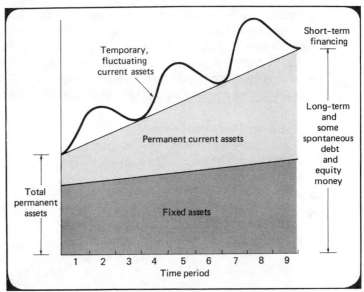

It is apparent from the preceding discussion that *the most important variable that influences a firm's financing requirements is its projected dollar volume of sales. A good sales forecast is an essential foundation for forecasting financial requirements.* In spite of its importance, we shall not go into sales forecasting here; rather, we simply assume that a sales forecast has been made, then estimate financial requirements on the basis of this forecast.[2]

[2]For a discussion of demand forecasting, see E. F. Brigham and J. L. Pappas, *Managerial Economics* (Hinsdale, Ill.: Dryden Press, 1976).

Short-Run Financial Forecasting

The principal methods of short-run financial forecasting are described in the following sections; we leave the more difficult problem of long-run forecasting to a subsequent section. The crucial element in financial forecasting, be it long or short run, is the appropriate use of historical information to generate reasonable forecasts. There are a number of methods available, ranging from the very naïve to the very sophisticated.

For short-run forecasting, the naïve techniques are surprisingly good.

PERCENT-OF-SALES METHOD

The simplest approach to forecasting financial requirements expresses the firm's needs in terms of the percentage of annual sales invested in each balance sheet item. As an example, consider the Moore Company Ltd. whose balance sheet as of December 31, 19X1, is shown in Table 5–1. The company's sales are running at about $500,000 a year, which is its capacity limit; the profit margin after tax on sales is 4 percent. During 19X1, the company earned $20,000 after taxes and paid out $10,000 in dividends, and it plans to continue paying out half of net profits as dividends. How much additional financing will be needed if sales expand to $800,000 during 19X2? The percent-of-sales method of calculating this figure is explain below.[3]

TABLE 5–1 The Moore Company Ltd.
Balance sheet
December 31, 19X1

Assets		Liabilities	
Cash	$ 10,000	Accounts payable	$ 50,000
Receivables	85,000	Accrued taxes and wages	25,000
Inventories	100,000	Mortgage bonds	70,000
Fixed assets (net)	150,000	Common shares	100,000
		Retained earnings	100,000
		Total liabilities and	
Total assets	$345,000	net worth	$345,000

First, isolate those balance sheet items that can be expected to vary directly with sales. In the case of the Moore Company, this step applies to each category of assets—a higher level of sales necessitates more cash for transactions, more receivables, higher inventory levels, and additional fixed

[3]We recognize, of course, that as a practical matter, business firms plan their needs in terms of specific items of equipment, square feet of floor space, and other factors, and not as a percentage of sales. However, the outside analyst does not have access to this information; the manager, even though he has the information on specific items, needs to check his forecasts in aggregate terms. The percent-of-sales method serves both these needs surprisingly well.

plant capacity. On the liability side, accounts payable as well as accruals may be expected to increase with increases in sales. Retained earnings will go up as long as the company is profitable and does not pay out 100 percent of earnings, but the percentage increase is not constant. However, neither common stock nor mortgage bonds would increase spontaneously with an increase in sales.

The items that can be expected to vary directly with sales are tabulated as a percentage of sales in Table 5–2. For every $1.00 increase in sales, assets must increase by $.69; this $.69 must be financed in some manner. Accounts payable will increase spontaneously with sales, as will accruals; these two items will supply $.15 of new funds for each $1.00 increase in sales. Subtracting the 15 percent for spontaneously generated funds from the 69 percent funds requirement leaves 54 percent. Thus, for each $1.00 increase in sales, the Moore Company must obtain $.54 of financing either from retained earnings or from external sources.

TABLE 5–2 The Moore Company Ltd.
Balance sheet items expressed as a percent of sales
December 31, 19X1
(percent)

Assets		*Liabilities*	
Cash	2.0	Accounts payable	10.0
Receivables	17.0	Accrued taxes and wages	5.0
Inventories	20.0	Mortgage bonds	na[a]
Fixed assets (net)	30.0	Common shares	na[a]
		Retained earnings	na[a]
		Total liabilities and	
Total assets	69.0	net worth	15.0

Assets as percent of sales	69.0
Less: Spontaneous increase in liabilities	15.0
Percent of each additional dollar of sales that must be financed	54.0

[a]Not applicable.

In the case at hand, sales are scheduled to increase from $500,000 to $800,000, or by $300,000. Applying the 54 percent developed in the table to the expected increase in sales leads to the conclusion that $162,000 will be needed.

Some of that need will be met by retained earnings. Total sales during 19X2 will be $800,000; if the company earns 4 percent after taxes on this volume, profits will amount to $32,000. Assuming that the 50 percent dividend payout ratio is maintained, dividends will be $16,000 and $16,000 will be retained. Subtracting the retained earnings from the $162,000 that was needed leaves a figure of $146,000—this is the amount of funds that must be obtained through borrowing or by selling new common stock.

This process may be expressed in equation form:[4]

$$\text{External funds needed} = \frac{A}{S}(\Delta S) - \frac{L}{S}(\Delta S) - MS_2(1-d).$$

Here

$\dfrac{A}{S}$ = assets that increase spontaneously with sales as a percent of sales

$\dfrac{L}{S}$ = those liabilities that increase spontaneously with sales as a percent of sales

ΔS = change in sales

M = profit margin

S_2 = *total sales projected for the year*

d = the dividend payout percentage.

For the Moore Company, then,

$$\text{External funds needed} = .69\,(300{,}000) - .15\,(300{,}000)$$
$$- .04\,(800{,}000)\,(.5)$$

$$= 54\,(300{,}000) - .02\,(800{,}000)$$

$$= \$146{,}000.$$

The $146,000 found by the formula method must, of course, equal the amount derived previously.

Notice what would have occurred if the Moore Company's sales forecast for 19X2 had been only $515,000, or a 3 percent increase. Applying the formula, we find the external funds requirements as follows:

$$\text{External funds needed} = .54\,(15{,}000) - .02\,(515{,}000)$$

$$= \$8{,}100 - \$10{,}300$$

$$= (\$2{,}200).$$

In this case, no external funds are required. In fact, the company will have $2,200 in excess of its requirements; it should therefore plan to increase dividends, retire debt, or seek additional investment opportunities. The example shows not only that higher levels of sales bring about a need for funds but also that while small percentage increases can be financed through retained earnings, larger increases cause the firm to go into the market for

---

[4]If the forecast is for more than one year, then the retained earnings part of the equation, $MS_2(1-d)$, must be modified to $MS_T(1-d)$, where S_T is total sales during the forecast period.

outside capital. In other words, a certain level of growth can be financed from internal sources, but higher levels of growth require external financing.[5]

An important assumption made when using the percent-of-sales method is that the relationship between the forecasted financial variables (e.g. inventories, current liabilities) and sales remains constant. In our example, we based the 19X2 forecast on the relationships obtained from the most recent balance sheet, 19X1. This may not be reasonable if this balance sheet has elements in it that are transitorily high or low. One method of circumventing this dilemma is to use an average of historical percent-of-sales relationships. This, however, may also result in serious distortions. As sales increase, firms become more efficient in their use of current assets. Thus, better inventory control techniques, for example, will result in inventories as a percent of sales decreasing as sales increase. This is demonstrated in Table 5-3 where inventories as a percent of sales have fallen from 44 percent in 1972 to 11 percent in 1977. Use of the average value of 22 percent would lead to serious distortions in the forecasted financial requirements.

The percent-of-sales method of forecasting financial requirements is neither simple nor mechanical, although an explanation of the ideas requires simple illustrations. Experience in applying the technique in practice suggests the importance of understanding (1) the basic technology of the firm and (2) the logic of the relation between sales and assets for the particular firm. If the firm decides to enter into fields in which technology is different, the historical relationship between assets and sales may not be relevant. A great deal of experience and judgment is required to apply the technique in actual practice.

SCATTER DIAGRAM, OR SIMPLE REGRESSION, METHOD

An alternative method used for forecasting financial requirements is the *scatter diagram,* or *simple regression,* method. A scatter diagram is a graphic representation of the historical relationship between a particular balance sheet item and sales. Proper use of the scatter diagram method requires practical, but not necessarily statistical, sophistication.

Table 5-3 and Figure 5-2 illustrate the use of the scatter diagram method in forecasting. As in all financial forecasting, the sales forecast is the starting point. The financial manager is given the sales forecast, or perhaps participates in formulating it. Suppose that data through 1977 is available and that a forecast of inventories for 1978 is needed, as indicated in Table 5-3. If the *simple regression* method is being used, a line is drawn through the points for 1972 through 1977, as shown in Figure 5-2. The line that fits the scatter

---

[5]At this point, one might ask two questions: "Shouldn't depreciation be considered as a source of funds, and won't this reduce the amount of external funds needed?" The answer to both questions is no. In the percent-of-sales method, we are implicitly assuming that funds generated through depreciation (in the sources and uses of funds sense) must be used to replace the assets to which the depreciation is applicable. Accordingly, depreciation does not enter the calculations in this forecasting technique; it is netted out.

of points in this example is a straight line. It is called the *line of best fit,* or the *regression line.* Of course, all points seldom fall exactly on the regression line, and the line itself may be curved as well as linear.[6]

If the percent-of-sales method had been used, some difficulties would have arisen immediately. Table 5–3 gives inventory as a percent of sales for 1972 through 1977. What relation should be used? The 44 percent for 1972? The 11 percent for 1977? Or some average of the relations? If the relation for 1977 had been used, a forecast of $38,500 for inventories in 1978 would have been made, compared with $34,000 by the scatter diagram method. That forecast is not a major error.

TABLE 5–3   Relationship between Inventory and Sales

Year	Sales	Inventory	Inventory as a Percent of Sales
1972	$ 50,000	$22,000	44
1973	100,000	24,000	24
1974	150,000	26,000	17
1975	200,000	28,000	14
1976	250,000	30,000	12
1977	300,000	32,000	11
1978 (estimated)	350,000	34,000	10
.	.	.	.
.	.	.	.
1982 (estimated)	500,000	40,000	8

The regression method is seen to be superior for forecasting financial requirements, but the differences are not substantial for short-run forecasting. When a firm is likely to have a base stock of inventory or fixed assets, the ratio of the item to sales declines as sales increase. In such cases, the percent-of-sales method can result in large errors.[7]

---

[6] In these illustrations, inventories are used as the item to be forecast. Much theory suggests that inventories increase as a square root of sales. This characteristic would tend to turn the regression line between inventories and sales slightly downward. Also, improvements in inventory control techniques would curve the line downward. However, the increased diversity of types, models, and styles tends to increase inventories. Applications by the authors' students of the regression method to hundreds of companies indicate that the linear straight-line relations frequently represent the line of best fit or, at worst, involve only a small error. If the line were in fact curved over, a curved line could be fitted to the data and used for forecasting purposes.

[7] The widespread use of the percentage method makes for lax control. It would be easy to reduce inventories below the $55,000 percent-of-sales forecast level and still be inefficient because the correct target amount is closer to $40,000.

FIGURE 5-2 Illustrative Relation between
Sales and Inventory

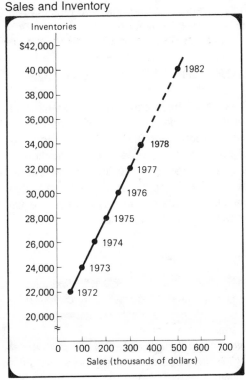

MULTIPLE REGRESSION METHOD

A more sophisticated approach to forecasting the firm's balance sheet items calls for the use of *multiple regression analysis.* In simple regression a particular balance sheet item, for example, inventory, was assumed to be a function of only one variable — sales. To generate a forecast of the inventory required, a forecast of sales was needed. In multiple regression it is assumed that the balance sheet item under analysis is related not only to sales but also to one or more additional variables called explanatory variables. For example, inventory may be related to sales, production levels, and other variables. The historical relationship of the balance sheet item and the explanatory variables is derived by means of statistical techniques. A forecast of the balance sheet item is obtained by using the statistical relationship and forecasts of the explanatory variables.

We shall not go into detail on the use of multiple regression analysis at this time. However, most computer installations have "canned" regression programs incorporated into their systems, making it extremely easy to use multiple regression techniques; multiple regression is widely used by at least the larger corporations.[8]

COMPARISON OF FORECASTING METHODS

Thus far we have considered three methods used in financial forecasting: (1) percent of sales, (2) scatter diagram, or simple linear regression, and (3) multiple regression. Each of these techniques uses historical data to obtain a relationship; the degree of sophistication of the relationship distinguishes the techniques from one another. To the extent that there are no major changes in the company's operations, a derived historical relationship can be useful for financial forecasting. In this section we will summarize and briefly compare these historical relationships.

Percent of Sales

The percent-of-sales method of financial forecasting is the simplest approach and it assumes that certain balance sheet items vary directly with sales; that is, that the ratio of a given balance sheet item to sales remains constant. The postulated relationship is shown in Figure 5–3. *Notice that the percent-of-sales method implicitly assumes a linear relationship that passes through the origin.* The slope of the line representing the relationship may vary, but the line always passes through the origin. Implicitly, the relationship is established by finding one point, or ratio, such as that designated as X in Figure 5–3, and then connecting this point with the origin. Then, for any projected level of sales, the forecasted level of the particular balance sheet item can be determined.

Scatter Diagram, or Simple Linear Regression

The scatter diagram method differs from the percent-of-sales method principally in that it does not assume that the line of relationship passes through the origin. Either by statistical or visual analysis, the relationship between the relevant balance sheet items and sales can be obtained. The greater the number of observations, the better the resulting relationship; again assuming that the underlying relationship has remained constant during the time period under analysis.

---

[8] In deriving a sales forecast, multiple regression is particularly useful. For example, sales of ski equipment will depend upon a number of variables; these include the general level of prosperity as measured by GNP or personal disposable income, population increases, weather conditions, advertising, etc.

FIGURE 5–3 Percent-of-sales

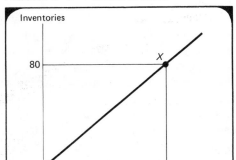

The scatter diagram method is illustrated in Figure 5–4, where the percent-of-sales relationship is also shown for comparison. The error induced by the use of the percent-of-sales method is represented by the gap between the two lines. At a sales level of 125, the percent-of-sales method would call for an inventory of 100 versus an inventory of only 90 using a scatter diagram forecast. *Notice that the error is very small if sales continue to run at approximately the current level, but the gap widens and the error increases as sales deviate in either direction from current levels, as they probably would if a long-run forecast was being made.*

FIGURE 5–4 Scatter Diagram, or Simple Linear Regression

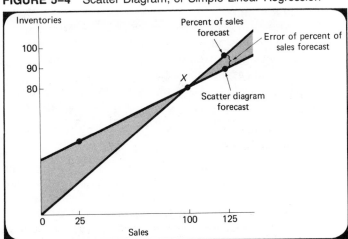

Multiple Regression

In a number of situations, the linear relationship may not be very good in explaining the historical observations of sales and the balance sheet items. One reason for a poor explanation is that the value of the balance sheet item under consideration, inventories, for example, may be determined by factors in addition to sales. Inventory levels are certainly influenced by work stoppages at the plants of suppliers. If a strike in the steel industry is anticipated, then a steel fabricator would stock up on steel products. Such hedge buying would cause actual inventories to be above the level forecast on the basis of sales projections. Then, assuming a strike does occur and continues for many months, inventories will be drawn down and may fall well below the expected level. Multiple regression techniques, which introduce additional variables (such as work stoppages) into the analysis, are employed to further improve financial forecasting.

However, in attempting to use multiple regression as a forecasting tool, it is necessary to have forecasts of the explanatory variables used in the analysis. Therefore, these variables should be amenable to forecasting.

The need to employ more complicated forecasting techniques varies from situation to situation. For example, the percent-of-sales method may be perfectly adequate for making short-run forecasts where conditions are relatively stable, while more sophisticated techniques may be deemed essential in more dynamic industries. As in all other applications of financial analysis, the cost of using more refined techniques must be balanced against the benefits of increased accuracy.

LONG-TERM FORECASTING

In long-term forecasting the firm is primarily interested in the fixed assets it intends to acquire and the profitability derived from these assets. Given that the firm has decided on its future investment plan, the firm must determine the financing requirements. To accomplish this, long-term forecasts of spontaneous assets and liabilities must be made, and profits from operations must be estimated. This is equivalent to a long-term forecast of the firm's income and balance sheets. Comparing the total asset requirements with the spontaneous sources of funds and cash flows from operations provides an estimate of the external funds required.

Long-term forecasting is much more difficult than short-term forecasting. First, the firm may undertake to manufacture products which are different from their existing products. This results in relationships between balance sheet items and sales that are different from historical relationships. Second, the firm is interested not only in the amount of external financing needed but also the timing. Since it is cheaper to make a large issue of securities than a number of smaller issues, the firm may want to finance debt requirements with short-term notes and then refinance those notes with a large, long-term bond issue. Third, a number of assumptions must be made to expedite the analysis; these include the dividend policy of the company and the long-run leverage ratio. Changes in dividend policy will alter the retained earnings for the company and thus the external requirements. Changes in the leverage ratio will alter the amount of funds raised through debt and equity. Finally, uncertainty is much greater in the long-run. The crucial variable in forecasting is the expected sales level. Based on a sales forecast, a number of the important balance sheet and income statement items can be derived. If sales differ substantially from the forecasted values, the forecasts of spontaneous funding and retained earnings may be wrong, and hence the external financing requirements would be incorrect. The longer the time period over which sales must be forecasted, the greater the uncertainty in the sales forecast.

Given these difficulties, how should the firm forecast its long-term financial requirements? The essence of long-term financial forecasting is the preparation of year-by-year forecasted financial statements. The first input is the forecast of fixed assets and the derived sales values for each forecast year. The spontaneous asset and liability values for the balance sheet can be forecast by using the percent-of-sales technique or the regression techniques discussed in the previous section. For long-term forecasting of these balance sheet items, the percent-of-sales technique is not very useful. If we return to Table 5–3 and Figure 5–2, we observe that, if the 1977 value of inventory as a percent of sales is used to forecast the inventory in 1982, a forecast of $55,000 would be obtained. This is in excess of the simple regression forecast for 1982 of $40,000. Thus, the preferred forecasting techniques will be more sophisticated so that a better representation of the underlying relationships can be obtained. Based on these balance sheet items and fore-casts of retained earnings obtained from income statements, the firm can determine its long-run external financing requirements.

Many large corporations and research departments of major underwriting companies have financial planning models. These models require as inputs the policy variables chosen by the firm such as dividend policy, the investment budget and sales forecasts. Based on these data and a number of statistical relationships between sales, balance sheet and income statement variables, year-by-year balance sheets are generated. From these balance sheets, the amount of external financing can be forecast. These models permit the company to simulate the impact of a number of policy decisions on external funds require-ments. If the company decides to change its dividend policy, for example, the model can determine the impact on the external funds requirements. In addition, the risk of the company's operations can be integrated into the analysis by considering various sales forecasts and their impact on external financing requirements. By looking at the variation in sales levels, the firm can determine what amount of external financing will be needed when sales are above or below average. This can permit a determination of the minimum and maximum external financing requirements and their timing.

Even though these models are very sophisticated, they can have serious deficiencies and should be used with caution. First, the models rely on relationships which may not be valid for the forecast period. Second, an important rule in using any model is "garbage in — garbage out". The quality of the forecasted external financing depends on the quality of the sales forecasts given the future investment plans. No model is powerful enough to turn bad inputs into good forecasts.

SUMMARY

Firms need assets to make sales; if sales are to be increased, assets must also be expanded. The first section of this chapter illustrates the relationship between sales and assets and shows how even a growing, profitable firm can have a cash flow problem.

The most important causal variable in determining financial requirements is a firm's projected dollar volume of sales; a good sales forecast is an essential foundation for forecasting financial requirements. The two principal methods used for making financial forecasts are (1) the percent-of-sales method and (2) the regression method. The first has the virtue of simplicity — the forecaster computes past relationships between asset and liability items and sales, assumes these same relationships will continue, and then applies the new sales forecast to get an estimate of the financial requirements.

The percent-of-sales method assumes that the ratios of balance sheet items to sales will remain constant, and thus it is useful for relatively short-run forecasting. The regression and scatter diagram techniques apply more sophisticated analyses to the historical data and they can be used either for long-run or short-run forecasting. In short-run forecasting, the percent-of-sales technique is likely to be acceptable, but for long-run forecasting the regression methods are preferable since they allow for non-constant balance sheet to sales relationships.

In long-run forecasting, the firm is interested in the timing of funds requirements as well as the amount. Based on long-range, fixed asset decisions, the analyst can derive forecasts of sales. These can be point or single estimates, or high-low-average estimates; the latter permit the introduction of uncertainty into the analysis. Based on assumptions of dividend policy and the debt-equity choice, the analyst can forecast balance sheets and income statements, and thus, external funds requirements. At a more sophisticated level, the firm can simulate different balance sheets and funds requirements by altering the assumptions in the analysis.

The tools and techniques we have discussed in this chapter are generally used in the following manner: As a first step, one of the long-range forecasting techniques is used to make a long-run forecast of the firm's financial requirements over a three- to five-year period. This forecast is then used to make the strategic financing plans during the planning period. Long lead times are necessary when companies sell bonds or stocks; otherwise financial managers might be forced to go into the market for funds during unfavorable periods.

In addition to the long-run strategic forecasting, the financial manager must also make accurate short-run forecasts to be sure that bank funds will be available to meet seasonal and other short-run requirements. We consider this topic in the following chapter.

QUESTIONS

5-1. What should be the approximate point of intersection between the sales-to-asset regression line and the vertical axis (*Y*-axis intercept) for the following: inventory, accounts receivable, fixed assets? State your answer in terms of positive, zero, or negative intercept. Can you think of any accounts that might have a negative intercept?

5-2. How does forecasting financial requirements in advance of needs assist the financial manager to perform his or her responsibilities more effectively?

5-3. Explain how a downturn in the business cycle could cause either a cash shortage for a firm or generate excess cash.

5-4. Explain this statement: "To a considerable extent, current assets represent permanent assets."

5-5. What advantages might a multiple regression technique have over a simple regression technique in forecasting sales? What might be some drawbacks in the actual use of this technique?

PROBLEMS

5-1. In 19X1, Brock Company Ltd.'s total assets were $1.9 million. Sales, which were $3.8 million, will increase by 20 percent in 19X2. The 19X1 ratio of assets to sales will be maintained throughout 19X2. Common shares amounted to $545,000 in 19X1, and retained earnings were $500,000. Debt will increase by 10 percent in 19X2, but common shares will remain unchanged; net profit after taxes will be 5 percent of sales and no dividends will be declared or paid. What amount of new financing will be needed in 19X2?

5-2. The Tobin Supply Company Ltd. is a wholesale steel distributor. It purchases steel in carload lots from more than twenty producing mills and sells to several thousand steel users. The items carried include sheets, plates, wire products, bolts, windows, pipe, and tubing.

The company owns two warehouses, each housing 15,000 m², and contemplates the erection of another warehouse of 20,000 m². The nature of the steel supply business requires that the company maintain large inventories to take care of customer requirements in the event of mill strikes or other delays.

In examining patterns from 19X1 through 19X6, the company found a rather consistent relation between the following accounts as a percent of sales.

Current assets	50%
Net fixed assets	20%
Accounts payable	5%
Other current liabilities, including accruals and provision for income taxes but not bank loans	5%
Net profit after taxes	2%

The company's sales for 19X7 were $3 million, and its balance sheet on December 31, 19X7, was as follows:

Tobin Supply Company Ltd., Balance sheet, December 31, 19X7

Current assets	$1,500,000	Accounts payable	$ 150,000
Fixed assets	600,000	Notes payable	300,000
		Other current liabilities	150,000
		Total current liabilities	$ 600,000
		Mortgage loan	100,000
		Common shares	250,000
		Retained earnings	1,150,000
Total assets	$2,100,000	Total liabilities and net worth	$2,100,000

The company expects its sales to increase by $200,000 each year. If this is achieved, what will its financial requirements be at the end of the five-year period? Assume that accounts not tied directly to sales (for example, notes payable) remain constant. Assume also that the company pays no dividends.

a. Construct a *pro forma* balance sheet for the end of the fifth year using "additional financing needed" as the balancing item.

b. What are the crucial assumptions made in your projection method?

5-3. One useful test, or guide, for evaluating a firm's financial structure in relation to its industry is by comparison with financial ratio composites for its industry. A new firm, or one contemplating entering a new industry, may use such industry composites as a guide to what its financial position is likely to approximate after the initial settling-down period.

The following data represent the ratios for the printing industry for 19X1.

Sales to net worth	4 times
Current debt to net worth	50%
Total debt to net worth	80%
Current ratio	2.2 times
Net sales to inventory	8 times
Average collection period	40 days
Fixed assets to net worth	70%

Creative Printers, Ltd., Pro forma balance sheet, December 31, 19X1

Cash	$_____	Current debt	$_____
Accounts receivable	_____	Long-term debt	_____
Inventory	_____	Total debt	_____
Current assets	_____	Net worth	_____
Fixed assets	_____	Total liabilities and	
Total assets	$_____	net worth	$_____

a. Complete the above *pro forma* balance sheet (round to nearest thousand) assuming Creative Printers' 19X1 sales are $3,200,000.

b. What does the use of the financial ratio composites accomplish?

c. What other factors will influence the financial structure of the firm?

5-4. The 19X3 sales of Kilburn Controls, Ltd. amounted to $12 million. Common shares and notes payable are constant. The dividend payout ratio is 60 percent. Retained earnings as shown on the December 31, 19X2, balance sheet were $124,000. The percent of sales in each balance sheet item that varies directly with sales are expected to be as follows:

Cash	4%
Receivables	16
Inventories	18
Net fixed assets	35
Accounts payable	12
Accruals	6
Profit rate (after taxes) on sales	2

a. Complete the balance sheet given on the following page.

b. Now suppose that in 19X4 sales increase by 5 percent over 19X3 sales. How much additional (external) capital will be required?

c. Construct the year-end 19X4 balance sheet. Assume that any required funds are borrowed as "notes payable."

d. What would happen to capital requirements under each of the following conditions? Answer in words, without calculations.

1. The profit margin went (i) from 2 percent to 6 percent? (ii) from 2 percent to 1 percent? Set up an equation to illustrate your answer.

2. The dividend payout rate (i) was raised from 60 percent to 90 percent? (ii) was lowered from 60 percent to 20 percent? Set up an equation to illustrate your answer.

3. Credit terms on sales were relaxed substantially.

e. Suppose now that the firm was started in 19X1 and that data for 19X1 and 19X2 are available, with sales levels of $1 million and $2 million respectively. If the percent-of-sales figures for these years are as shown in the following tabulations, what does this imply about the appropriateness of the percent-of-sales forecasting method for the various balance sheet accounts? (No calculations are required; discuss verbally.)

	19X1 Sales = $1 million	19X2 Sales = $2 million
Cash	5.0%	3.0%
Receivables	10.0	12.0
Inventories	20.0	15.0
Net fixed assets	37.0	32.0
Accounts payable	13.0	12.5
Accruals	4.0	4.5
Profit rate (after taxes) on sales	1.0	1.5

Kilburn Controls, Ltd., Balance sheet, December 31, 19X3

Cash	_____	Accounts payable	_____
Receivables	_____	Notes payable	630,000
Inventory	_____	Accruals	_____
Total current assets	_____		
Fixed assets	_____	Total current liabilities	_____
		Common shares	5,750,000
		Retained earnings	_____
Government securities	0	Total liabilities and	
Total assets	=======	net worth	=======

5-5. Jones Klein, Ltd., a large drug manufacturer, had the following balance sheet and income statement for 19X1. (Also shown is the industry norm for each item based on studies of the drug industry.) The industry norm for sales to assets is 1.5.

a. Given only the total sales figure of $606,300 and using the industry norm values, estimate the pro forma balance sheet and income statements for this company using the same format. Show liabilities and assets. (round to hundreds.)

b. For each item, compute the percent difference between actual and pro forma in the form (actual/pro forma) – 1.

c. Comment on the difference between the actual and pro forma account based on the industry norms.

Jones Klein, Ltd.
Balance Sheet as of December 31.

Assets			Liabilities		
	Firm	Norm		Firm	Norm
Cash and securities	$186,700	12.5%	Accounts payable	$ 33,400	10.0%
Receivables	125,100	22.8	Notes payable	77,700	8.0
Inventories	105,700	28.0	Other current		
Other current assets	9,900	1.2	liabilities	52,600	8.3
Total current assets	$427,400	64.5%	Total current liabilities	$163,700	26.3%
Net fixed assets	143,300	31.5			
Other tangible assets	16,200	4.0	Long-term debt	111,000	22.6
Total assets	$58,900	100.0%	Net worth	312,200	51.1
			Total claims on assets	$586,900	100.0%

Jones Klein, Ltd.
Income statement for Year Ended December 31.

	Firm	Norm
Sales	$606,300	100.0%
Cost of goods sold	228,000	60.2
Gross profit	378,300	39.8
Selling and administrative expense	269,800	21.6
Operating Income	108,500	18.2
Less interest expense	– 14,200	– 1.4
Net income before tax	94,300	16.8
Less federal income tax	– 30,600	– 8.4
Net income	$ 63,700	8.4%

5-6. A firm has the following relationships. The ratio of assets to sales is 60 percent. Liabilities that increase spontaneously with sales are 15 percent. The profit margin on sales after taxes is 5 percent. The firm's dividend payout ratio is 40 percent.

a. If the firm's growth rate on sales is 10 percent per annum, what percentage of the sales increase in any year must be financed externally?

b. If the firm's growth rate on sales increases to 20 percent per annum, what percentage of the sales increase in any year must be financed externally?

c. How will your answer to Part a. change if the profit margin increases to 6 percent?

d. How will your answer to Part b. change if the firm's dividend payout is reduced to 10 percent?

e. If the profit margin increases from 5 percent to 6 percent and the dividend payout ratio is 20 percent, at what growth rate in sales will the external financing requirement percentage be exactly zero?

Financial Planning and Control: Budgeting

In the preceding chapter we first examined the relationship between assets and sales. Then we considered several procedures the financial manager can use to forecast his requirements. In addition to his long-range forecasts, the financial manager is also concerned with short-term needs for funds. It is embarrassing for a corporate treasurer to "run out of money." Even though he may be able to negotiate a bank loan on short notice, his plight may cause the banker to question the soundness of the firm's management and, accordingly, to reduce the company's line of credit or raise the interest rate. Therefore, attention must be given to short-term budgeting, with special emphasis on cash forecasting, or *cash budgeting,* as it is commonly called.

The cash budget is, however, only one part of the firm's overall budget system. The nature of the budget system, and especially the way it can be used for both planning and control purposes, is also discussed in this chapter.

BUDGETING

A budget is simply a financial plan. A household budget itemizes the family's sources of income and describes how this income will be spent: so much for food, housing, transportation, entertainment, education, savings, and so on. Similarly, the federal budget indicates the government's income sources and allocates funds to defense, unemployment insurance, cultural programs, and the like. By the same token, a firm's budget is a plan detailing how funds will be spent on labor, raw materials, capital goods, and so on, and also how the funds for these expenditures will be obtained. Just as governmental budgets can be used as devices to insure that the various departments limit their expenditures to specified amounts, the corporate budget can also be used as a device for formulating the firm's plans and for exercising control over the various departments.

Budgeting is, thus, a management tool used for both *planning* and *control*. Depending on the nature of the business, detailed plans may be formulated for the next few months, the next year, the next five years, or even longer. A company engaged in, say, heavy construction is constantly extending bids that may or may not be accepted; it cannot, and indeed need not, plan as far ahead as an electric utility company. The electric utility can base its projections on population growth, which is predictable for five- to ten-year periods, and it *must* plan asset acquisitions years ahead because of the long lead times involved in constructing dams, nuclear power plants, and the like.

NATURE OF THE BUDGETING PROCESS

Fundamentally, the budgeting process is a method to improve operations; it is a continuous effort to specify what should be done to get the job completed in the best possible way. Corporate budgeting should not be thought of as a device for limiting expenditures: the budgeting process is a tool for obtaining the most productive and profitable use of the company's resources. The budget requires a set of performance standards, or targets, that can be compared to actual results; this process is called "controlling to plan." It is a continuous monitoring procedure, reviewing and evaluating performance with reference to the previously established standards.

Establishing standards requires a realistic understanding of the activities carried on by the firm. Arbitrary standards, set without a basic understanding of the minimum costs as determined by the nature of the firm's operations, can do more harm than good. Budgets imposed in an arbitrary fashion may represent impossible targets at the one extreme or standards that are too lax at the other. If standards are unrealistically high, frustrations and resentment will develop. If standards are unduly lax, costs will be out of control, profits will suffer, and morale will deteriorate. However, a set of budgets based on a clear understanding and careful analysis of operations can play an important, positive role for the firm.[1]

[1] The authors are familiar with one case where an unrealistic budget ruined a major national corporation in the U.S. Top management set impossible performance and growth goals for the various divisions. The divisions, in an effort to meet the sales and profit projections, expanded into high-risk product lines (especially real estate development ventures), employed questionable accounting practices that tended to overstate profits, and the like. Debt financing was emphasized in order to leverage earnings. Things looked good for several years, but eventually the true situation became apparent. Top management brought in a team of consultants in an attempt to correct the problems, but it was too late — the firm was beyond help. The interesting point, to us, is that the consultants traced the firm's difficulties *directly* back to the unrealistic targets that were established by top management without adequate consultation with the division managers.

Budgets can provide valuable guides to both high-level executives and middle-management personnel. Well-formulated and effectively developed budgets make subordinates aware that top management has a realistic understanding of the nature of the operations in the business firm, and such a budget can be an important communication link between top management and the divisional personnel whom they guide.

Budgets also represent planning and control devices that enable management to anticipate change and adapt to it. Business operations in today's economic environment are complex and are subject to heavy competitive pressures. In such an environment many kinds of changes take place. The rate of growth of the economy as a whole fluctuates, and these fluctuations affect different industries in a number of different ways. If a firm plans ahead, the budget and control process can provide management with a better basis for understanding the firm's operations in relation to the general environment. This increased understanding leads to faster reactions to developing events, thus increasing the firm's ability to perform effectively.

The budgeting process, in summary, improves internal coordination. Decisions for each product at every stage—at the research, engineering, production, marketing, personnel, and financial levels—all have an impact on the firm's profits. Planning and control is the essence of profit planning, and the budget system provides an integrated picture of the firm's operations as a whole. Therefore, the budget system enables the manager of each division to see the relation of his part of the enterprise to the totality of the firm. For example, a production decision to alter the level of work-in-process inventories, or a marketing decision to change the terms under which a particular product is sold, can be traced through the entire budget system to show its effects on the firm's overall profitability. The budgeting system is thus a most important financial tool.

Budget System

The overall nature of the budget process is outlined in Figure 6–1. Budgeting is a part of the total planning activity in the firm, so we must begin with a statement of corporate goals or objectives. The statement of goals (shown in the box at the top of the figure) determines the second section of the figure, the corporate long-range plan. Moving down the figure, we see that a segment of the corporate long-range plan includes a long-range sales forecast. This forecast requires a determination of the number and types of products that will be manufactured both at present and in the future years encompassed by the long-range plan: this is the product mix strategy.

Short-term forecasts and budgets are formulated within the framework of the long-range plan. For example, one might begin with a sales forecast covering six months or one year. The short-term sales forecast provides a basis for (and is dependent on) the broad range of policies indicated in the lower portion of Figure 6–1. *First,* there are manufacturing policies covering the choice of types of equipment, plant layout, and production-line arrangements. In addition, the kind of durability built into the products and their associated costs will be considered. *Second,* a broad set of marketing policies must be formulated. These relate to such items as the development of the firm's own sales organization versus the use of outside sales organizations; the number of salesmen, and the method by which they will be compensated; the forms of, types of, and amounts spent on advertising; and other factors. *Third* are the research and general management policies. Research policies relate to relative emphasis on basic versus applied research and the product areas emphasized by both types of research. *Fourth* are financial policies, the subject of this chapter. The four major policy sets must be established simultaneously, as each affects the other. We shall concentrate on financial control policies, but it is important to realize the interdependencies between financial and other policies.

FIGURE 6–1   Overall View of the Total Budgeting Process

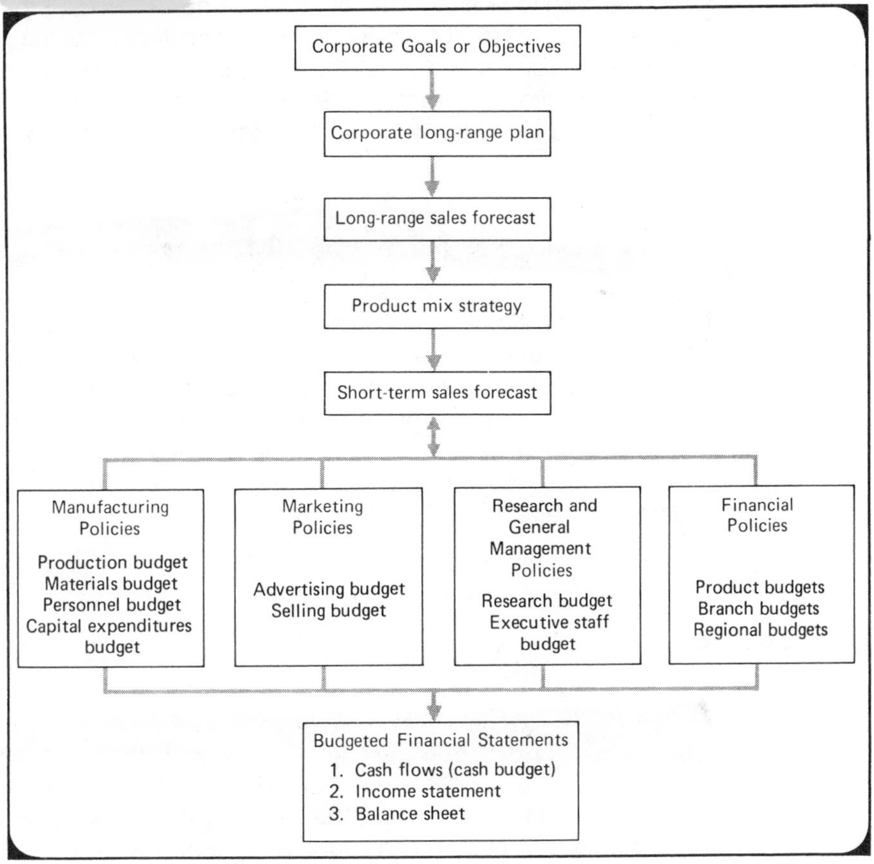

Financial Control Policies

Financial control policies include the organization and content of various kinds of financial control budgets. These include a budget for individual products and for every significant activity of the firm. In addition, budgets will be formulated to control operations at individual branch offices. Those budgets, in turn, are grouped and modified to control regional operations.

In a similar manner, policies established at the manufacturing, marketing, research, and general management levels give rise to a series of budgets. For example, the production budget will reflect the use of materials, parts, labor, and facilities; each of the major elements in a production budget is likely to have its own individual budget program. There will be a materials budget, a labor or personnel requirements budget, and a facilities or long-run capital expenditures budget. After the product is produced, the next step in the process will call for a marketing budget. Related to the overall process are the general office and executive requirements, which will be reflected in the general and administrative budget system.

The results of projecting all those elements of cost are reflected in the budgeted (also called "pro forma" or "projected") income statement. The anticipated sales give rise to the various types of investments needed to produce the products; these investments, plus the beginning balance sheet, provide the necessary data for developing the assets side of the balance sheet.

Those assets must be financed, and a cash flow analysis—the cash budget—is required. The cash budget indicates the combined effects of the budgeted operations on the firm's cash flows. A positive net cash flow indicates that the firm has ample financing. However, if an increase in the volume of operations leads to a negative cash flow, additional financing will be required. And that will lead directly to choices of financing, which is the subject of a considerable portion of the remainder of the book.

Since the structures of the income statement and the balance sheet have already been covered in Chapter 3, the rest of this section will deal with the two remaining aspects of the budgeting process—the cash budget and the concept of variable, or flexible, budgets.

CASH BUDGETING

The cash budget indicates not only the total amount of financing that is required but its timing as well. This statement shows the amount of funds needed month by month, week by week, or even on a daily basis; it is one of the financial manager's most important tools. Because a clear understanding of the nature of cash budgeting is important, the process is described by means of an example that makes the elements of the cash budget explicit.

Marvel Toy is a medium-sized toy manufacturer. Sales are highly seasonal, with the peak occurring in September when retailers stock up for the Christmas season. All sales are made on terms that allow a cash discount on payments made within 30 days; if the discount is not taken, the full amount must be paid in 60 days. However, Marvel, like most other companies, finds that some of its customers delay payment up to 90 days. Experience shows that on 20 percent of the sales, payment is made within 30 days; on 70 percent of the sales, payment is made during the second month after the sale; while on 10 percent of the sales, payment is made during the third month.

Marvel's production is geared to future sales. Purchased materials and parts, which amount to 70 percent of sales, are bought the month before the company expects to sell the finished product. Its own purchase terms permit Marvel to delay payment on its purchases for one month. In other words, if August sales are forecast at $30,000, then purchases during July will amount to $21,000, and this amount will actually be paid in August.

Wages and salaries, rent, and other cash expenses are given in Table 6–1. The company also has a tax payment of $8,000 coming due in August. Its capital budgeting plans call for the purchase in July of a new machine tool costing $10,000, payment to be made in September. Assuming the company needs to keep a $5,000 cash balance at all times and has $6,000 on July 1, what are Marvel's financial requirements for the period July through December?

The cash requirements are worked out in the cash budget shown in Table 6–1. The top half of the table provides a worksheet for calculating collections on sales and payments on purchases. The first line in the worksheet gives the sales forecast for the period May through January—May and June sales are necessary to determine collections for July and August. Next, cash collections are given. The first line of this section shows that 20 percent of the sales during any given month are collected that month. The second shows the collections on the prior month's sales—70 percent of sales in the preceding month. The third line gives collections from sales two months earlier—10 percent of sales in that month. The collections are summed to find the total cash receipts from sales during each month under consideration.

With the worksheet completed, the cash budget itself can be considered. Receipts from collections are given on the top line. Next, payments during each month are summarized. The difference between cash receipts and cash payments is the net cash gain or loss during the month; for July, there is a net cash loss of $4,200. The initial cash on hand at the beginning of the month is added to the net cash gain or loss during the month to yield the cumulative cash that will be on hand if no financing is done; at the end of July, Marvel Toy will have cumulative cash equal to $1,800. The desired cash balance, $5,000, is subtracted from the cumulative cash balance to determine the amount of financing that the firm needs if it is to maintain the desired level of cash. At the end of July we see that Marvel will need $3,200; thus, loans outstanding will total $3,200 at the end of July.

TABLE 6-1 Marvel Toy Company *Cash Budget*

	May	June	July	Aug.	Sept.	Oct.	Nov.	Dec.	Jan.
					Worksheet				
Sales (net of cash discounts)	$10,000	$10,000	$20,000	$30,000	$40,000	$20,000	$20,000	$10,000	$10,000
Collections									
First month (20%)		$ 2,000	$ 4,000	$ 6,000	$ 8,000	$ 4,000	$ 4,000	$ 2,000	$ 2,000
Second month (70%)		7,000	7,000	14,000	21,000	28,000	14,000	14,000	7,000
Third month (10%)			1,000	1,000	2,000	3,000	4,000	2,000	2,000
Total	$ 2,000	$ 9,000	$12,000	$21,000	$31,000	$35,000	$22,000	$18,000	$11,000
Purchases (70% of next month's sales)	$ 7,000	$14,000	$21,000	$28,000	$14,000	$14,000	$ 7,000	$ 7,000	
Payments (one month lag)		7,000	14,000	21,000	28,000	14,000	14,000	7,000	7,000
					Cash Budget				
Receipts									
Collections			$12,000	$ 21,000	$ 31,000	$ 35,000	$22,000	$18,000	$11,000
Payments									
Purchases			14,000	21,000	28,000	14,000	14,000	7,000	
Wages and salaries			1,500	2,000	2,500	1,500	1,500	1,000	
Rent			500	500	500	500	500	500	
Other expenses			200	300	400	200	200	100	
Taxes			—	8,000	—	—	—	—	
Payment on machine			—	—	10,000	—	—	—	
Total payments			$16,200	$ 31,800	$ 41,400	$ 16,200	$16,200	$ 8,600	
Net cash gain (loss) during month			$ (4,200)	$(10,800)	$(10,400)	$ 18,800	$ 5,800	$ 9,400	
Cash at start of month if no borrowing is done			6,000	1,800	(9,000)	(19,400)	(600)	5,200	
Cumulative cash (= cash at start plus gains or minus losses)			$ 1,800	$ (9,000)	$(19,400)	$ (600)	$ 5,200	$14,600	
Less: Desired level of cash			(5,000)	(5,000)	(5,000)	(5,000)	(5,000)	(5,000)	
Total loans outstanding to maintain $5,000 cash balance			$ 3,200	$ 14,000	$ 24,400	$ 5,600	—	—	
Surplus cash			—	—	—	—	$ 200	$ 9,600	

This same procedure is used in the following months. Sales will expand seasonally in August; with the increased sales will come increased payments for purchases, wages, and other items. Moreover, the $8,000 tax bill is due in August. Receipts from sales will go up too, but the firm will still be left with a $10,800 cash deficit during the month. The total financial requirements at the end of August will be $14,000—the $3,200 needed at the end of July plus the $10,800 cash deficit for August. Thus, loans outstanding will total $14,000 at the end of August.

Sales peak in September, and the cash deficit during this month will amount to another $10,400. The total need for funds through September will increase to $24,400. Sales, purchases, and payments for past purchases will fall markedly in October; collections will be the highest of any month because they reflect the high September sales. As a result, Marvel Toy will enjoy a healthy $18,800 cash surplus during October. This surplus can be used to pay off borrowings, so the need for financing will decline by $18,800, to $5,600.

Marvel will have another cash surplus in November, and this extra cash will permit the company to eliminate completely the need for financing. In fact, the company is expected to have $200 in surplus cash by the month's end, while another cash surplus in December will swell the extra cash to $9,600. With such a large amount of unneeded funds, Marvel's treasurer will doubtless want to make investments in some interest-bearing securities or put the funds to use in some other way.[2]

VARIABLE, OR FLEXIBLE, BUDGETS

Budgets are planned allocations of a firm's resources, based on forecasts for the future. Two important elements influence actual performance. One is the impact of external influences over which the firm has little or no control—developments in the economy as a whole and competitive developments in the firm's own industry. The second element, which is controllable by the firm, is its level of efficiency at a given volume of sales. It is useful to separate the impact of these two elements, as this separation is necessary for evaluating individual performances.

The essence of the variable budget system is to introduce flexibility into budgets by recognizing that certain types of expenditures will vary at different levels of output. Thus, a firm might have an alternative level of outlay budgeted for different volumes of operation—high, low, medium. One of management's responsibilities is to determine which of the alternative budgets should be in effect for the planning period under consideration.

---

[2]Types of investments for excess funds are discussed in Chapter 8.

The regression method, which we described in the preceding chapter in connection with financial forecasting, may also be used to establish the basis for flexible budgeting. The use of the concept can be illustrated by a specific example. Suppose that a retail store, the Hubler Department Store, has had the experience indicated by the historical data set forth in Table 6–2. It is apparent from the data that the number of employees the firm needs is dependent upon the dollar volume of sales that occurs during a month. This is seen more easily from a scatter diagram such as that in Figure 6–2. The freehand regression line is sloped positively because the number of employees increases as the volume of sales increases. The independent variable, dollar volume of sales, is called the *control variable*. Variations in the control variable cause changes in total expenses. The volume of sales

TABLE 6–2 Hubler Department Store
Relationship between Sales and Employees

Month	Sales (in millions of dollars)	Number of Employees
January	4	42
February	5	51
March	6	60
April	7	75
May	10	102
June	8	83
July	5	55
August	9	92

FIGURE 6–2 Scatter Diagram and Regression Line:
Hubler Department Store

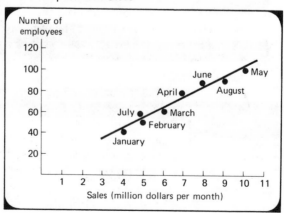

can be forecast, and the number of employees can be read from the regression chart. The relations are expressed in tabular form in Table 6–3. Given the forecast of sales, standards are provided for the expected number of employees and the weekly payroll.[3]

TABLE 6–3 Hubler Department Store
Budget Allowance

Sales (millions of dollars)	Number of Employees	Weekly Payroll Estimate (average wage, $100)
$ 6	62	$ 6,200
7	72	7,200
8	82	8,200
9	92	9,200
10	102	10,200
11	112	11,200

PROBLEMS OF BUDGETING

Four major problems are encountered when using budget systems. First, budgetary programs can grow to be so complete and so detailed that they become cumbersome, meaningless, and unduly expensive. Overbudgeting is dangerous.

Second, budgetary goals may come to supersede enterprise goals. A budget is a tool, not an end in itself. Enterprise goals by definition supersede subsidiary plans of which budgets are a part. Moreover, budgets are based on future expectations that may not be realized. There is no acceptable reason for neglecting to alter budgets as circumstances change. This reasoning is the core of the argument in favor of more flexible budgets.

Third, budgets can tend to hide inefficiencies by continuing initial expenditures in succeeding periods without proper evaluation. Budgets growing from precedent usually contain undesirable expenditures. They should not be used as umbrellas under which slovenly, inefficient management can hide. Consequently, the budgetary process must contain provision for reexamination of standards and other bases of planning by which policies are translated into numerical terms.

[3]Note that regression analysis provides even more flexibility in budgeting than do the high, medium, and low levels mentioned earlier. Also, it is possible to include *confidence levels* when using the regression method. For example, Table 6–3 shows that when volume is at $8 million, we expect to have 82 employees and a weekly payroll of $8,200. Although this relationship would probably not hold *exactly*, we might find that actual observations lie within 78 and 86 employees at this sales volume 95 percent of the time. Thus, 95 percent confidence levels would encompass the range 78–86. Similar ranges could be determined for other volumes; management might, as a matter of control policy, investigate whenever actual performances were outside this expected range.

Finally, case study evidence suggests that the use of budgets as a pressure device defeats their basic objectives. Budgets, if used as instruments of tyranny, cause resentment and frustrations, which in turn lead to inefficiency. In order to counteract this effect, it has been recommended that top management increase the participation of subordinates during the preparatory stages of the budgets.

USE OF FINANCIAL PLANS AND BUDGETS

Forecasts, or long-range plans, are necessary in all the firm's operations. The personnel department must have a good idea of the scale of future operations if it is to plan its hiring and training activities properly. The production department must be sure that the productive capacity is available to meet the projected product demand, and the finance department must be sure that funds are on hand to meet the firm's financial requirements.

The tools and techniques discussed in this and the preceding chapters are actually used in several separate, but related, ways. First, the percent-of-sales method or, preferably, the regression method is used to make a long-range forecast of financial requirements over a projected three- to five-year period. This forecast is then used to draw up the strategic financing plans during the planning period. The company might, for example, plan to meet its financial requirements with retained earnings and short-term bank debt during, say, 19X1 and 19X2, float a bond issue in 19X3, use retained earnings in 19X4, and finally sell an issue of common shares in 19X5. Fairly long lead times are necessary when companies sell bonds or stocks; otherwise, they might be forced to go into the market during unfavorable periods.

In addition to the long-run strategic planning, the financial manager must also make accurate short-run forecasts to be sure that funds will be available to meet seasonal and other short-run requirements. He might, for example, have a meeting with his bank's loan officer to discuss his company's need for funds during the coming year. Prior to the meeting, he would have his accountants prepare a detailed cash budget showing the need for money during each of the coming twelve months. The cash budget would show the maximum amount that would be needed during the year, how much would be needed during each month, and how cash surpluses would be generated at some point to enable the firm to repay the bank loan.

The financial manager would also have his firm's most recent, and its pro forma, balance sheets and income statements. He would have calculated the key financial ratios to show both his actual and his projected financial positions to the banker. If the firm's financial position is sound and if its cash budget appears reasonable, the bank will commit itself to make the required funds available. Even if the bank decides that the company's request is unreasonable and denies the loan request, the financial manager will have time to seek other sources of funds. While it might not be pleasant to have to look elsewhere for money, it is much better to know ahead of time that the loan request will be refused.

DIVISIONAL CONTROL IN A DECENTRALIZED FIRM

In our discussion of the du Pont system of financial control in Chapter 3, we considered its use for the firm as a whole rather than for different divisions or the operating subsidiaries of a single firm. However, the du Pont system, or some variation, can also be used to control the various parts of a multi-divisional firm.

For organizational reasons, many large firms are set up on a decentralized basis in which a division is responsible for a particular activity. A good example is Genstar Limited, a diversified operating company. Genstar has both division and wholly-owned subsidiaries operating in six major industry classifications: building materials, cement, housing and land development, construction, marine, chemicals and fertilizers. In many of these classifications, Genstar has more than one operating division (or subsidiary). Groups of divisions and/or subsidiaries are defined as *profit centers* or financial responsibility centers. Each profit center has its own investments — its fixed and current assets — and each is expected to earn an appropriate rate of return on its investment.

Corporate management controls the various operating divisions and subsidiaries by means of a variation of the du Pont system. Each operating entity is evaluated by the rate of return on net assets relative to a target level, where net assets are equal to total assets less non-interest bearing liabilities; this evaluation criterion is similar to the divisional rate of return on investment (ROI) used in the du Pont system. The target for each operating unit is determined through the planning process.

Each division manager is judged by his division's rate of return on net assets and is rewarded accordingly. Thus, each division in attempting to meet the target rate of return on its net assets is operating to maintain the total firm's rate of return on net assets at an appropriate level.

In addition to its use in managerial control, ROI can be used to allocate funds to the various divisions. Funds, obtained by the corporate entity, can be allocated to different divisions and subsidiaries on the basis of divisional ROI's, with divisions having high ROI's receiving more funds than those with low ROI's.[4]

Genstar uses a more sophisticated process to allocate the capital funds among the various divisions. The parent company has the responsibility for providing funds from corporate operations and also debt and equity raised in

---

[4]The point of this procedure is to increase the total firm's ROI. To maximize the overall ROI, marginal ROI's between divisions should be equalized.

the capital markets. The divisions present their projects to the head office; the cash flows and timing of these flows are considered in the calculation of the profitability of each project. If this profitability exceeds minimum standards considering the risk involved, then capital may be allocated to this project.[5] The divisional allocation is equal to the capital required for the accepted projects.

A number of problems may arise if ROI control is used without proper safeguards. Since the divisional managers are rewarded on the basis of their ROI performance, if their morale is to be maintained it is absolutely essential that the divisional managers feel that their divisional ROI does indeed provide an accurate measure of relative performance. But ROI is dependent on a number of factors in addition to managerial competence. Some of them are listed below.

1. *Depreciation:* ROI is very sensitive to depreciation policy. If one division is writing off assets at a relatively rapid rate, its annual profits and, hence, its ROI will be reduced.

2. *Book value of assets:* If an older division is using assets that have been largely written off, both its current depreciation charges and its investment base will be low. This will make its ROI high in relation to newer divisions.

3. *Transfer pricing:* In most corporations some divisions sell to other divisions. In Ford of Canada, for example, the assembly divisions purchase engines from another division. In such cases the prices at which goods are transferred between divisions has a fundamental effect on divisional profits and divisional ROI. If the transfer price of engines is set relatively high, then the assembly division will have a relatively low ROI and the engine division a relatively high ROI. If divisional managers are rewarded on the basis of ROI, it is easy to see how internal competition could become destructive.

4. *Time periods:* Many projects have long gestation periods—expenditures must be made for research and development, plant construction, market development, and the like; such expenditures will add to the investment base without a commensurate increase in profits for several years. During this period, a division's ROI could be seriously reduced; without proper constraints, its division manager could be improperly penalized. Especially when we recognize the frequency of personnel transfers in larger corporations, we can see that the timing problem could possibly cause managers to refrain from making long-term investments that are in the best interests of the firm.

5. *Industry conditions:* If one division is operating in an industry where conditions are favorable and rates of return are high, whereas another is in an industry suffering from excessive competition, such environmental differences may cause the favored division to look good and the unfavored

[5]The technique that Genstar is using is presented in detail in Chapter 11. The profitability of the project is called the project's internal rate of return and the cut-off rate is the cost of capital. This technique circumvents a number of problems associated with the use of a divisional ROI.

division to look bad, quite apart from any differences in their respective managers. Therefore, external conditions must be taken into consideration when appraising divisional ROI performance.

Because of the problems noted above, divisional ROI's must be supplemented with other criteria when evaluating performance. For example, a division's growth rate in sales, profits and market share have been utilized. In addition, expense and profit budgets are set by the head office along with a target ROI. Evaluation and control is obtained by comparison of actual performance of the division compared to the budget.

Chrysler of Canada has set up its divisional control in a very different way to avoid a number of the problems with ROI control. Instead of using the divisions as profit centers, they are cost centers where products are transferred at an accounting cost-based price that does not reflect a divisional profit. This removes the incentive to engage in internally destructive competition.

Although ROI control has been used with great success in both Canada and the United States, the system cannot be used in a mechanical sense by inexperienced personnel. As with most other tools, it is a good one if used properly; but it is a destructive one if misused.

EXTERNAL USES OF FINANCIAL FORECASTS AND BUDGETS

We have stressed the use of planning and budgeting for internal purposes, that is, to increase the efficiency of a firm's operations. With relatively minor modifications, those same tools and techniques can be used in both credit analysis and security analysis. For example, outside security analysts can make a forecast of a given firm's sales and, through the income statement and balance sheet relationships, can prepare pro forma (projected) balance sheets and income statements. Credit analysts can make similar projections to aid in estimating the likely need for funds by their customers and the likelihood that borrowers can make prompt repayment.

This kind of analysis has actually been conducted on a large scale in recent years. Complete stock market and financial statement data from the Toronto, Montreal, New York and American Stock Exchanges are provided by FRI Information Services Ltd. of Toronto and Montreal. In addition, FRI provides computer packages to access and manipulate the data. The Financial Post Computer Service sells computer tapes which include financial statement information and stock price data for a subsample of TSE companies. These services are used by a large number of companies such as investment dealers, pension fund managers, and all types of financial institutions. The applications of the data are usually sophisticated model building to evaluate company or fund performance or to forecast demands for future financing.

SUMMARY

A budget is a plan stated in terms of specific expenditures for specific purposes. It is used for both planning and control, its overall purpose being to improve internal operations, thereby reducing costs and raising profitability. A budgeting system starts with a set of performance standards, or targets. The targets constitute, in effect, the firm's financial plan. The budgeted figures are compared with actual results—this is the control phase of the budget system, and it is a critical step in well-operated companies.

Although the entire budget system is of vital importance to corporate management, one aspect of the system is especially important to the financial manager—the cash budget. The cash budget is, in fact, the principal tool for making short-run financial forecasts. Cash budgets, if used properly, are highly accurate and can pinpoint the funds that will be needed, when they will be needed, and when cash flows will be sufficient to retire any loans that might be necessary.

A good budget system will recognize that some factors lie outside the firm's control. Especially important here is the state of the economy and its effects on sales, and *flexible budgets* will be set up as targets for the different departments assuming different levels of sales. Also, a good system will insure that those responsible for carrying out a plan are involved in its preparation; this procedure will help guard against the establishment of unrealistic targets and unobtainable goals.

As a firm becomes larger, it is necessary for it to decentralize operations to some extent, and decentralized operations require some centralized control over the various divisions. The principal tool used for such control is the return on investment (ROI) method. There are problems with ROI control. But if care is taken in its use, the method can be quite valuable to a decentralized firm.

QUESTIONS

6-1. What use might a confidence interval scheme have in variable budgeting?

6-2. Why is a cash budget important even when there is plenty of cash in the bank?

6-3. What is the difference between the long-range financial forecasting concept (for example, the percent-of-sales method) and the budgeting concept? How might they be used together?

6-4. Assume that a firm is making up its long-run financial budget. What period should this budget cover—one month, six months, one year, three years, five years, or some other period? Justify your answer.

6-5. Why is a detailed budget more important to a large, multidivisional firm than to a small single-product firm?

6-6. Assume that your uncle is a major shareholder in a multidivisional firm that uses a naive ROI criterion for evaluating divisional managers and bases managers' salaries in large part on this evaluation. You can have the job of division manager in any division you choose. If you are a salary maximizer, what divisional characteristics would you seek? If, because of your "good performance," you become president of the firm, what changes would you make?

PROBLEMS

6-1. The Simms Company Limited is planning to request a line of credit from its bank. The following sales forecasts have been made for 19X1 and 19X2.[6]

May 19X1	$150,000
June	150,000
July	300,000
August	450,000
September	600,000
October	300,000
November	300,000
December	75,000
January 19X2	150,000

Collection estimates were obtained from the credit and collection department as follows: collected within the month of sale, 5 percent; collected the month following the sale, 80 percent; collected the second month following the sale, 15 percent. Payments for labor and raw materials are typically made during the month following the month in which these costs are incurred. Total labor and raw materials costs are estimated for each month as follows (payments are made the following month):

May 19X1	$ 75,000
June	75,000
July	105,000
August	735,000
September	255,000
October	195,000
November	135,000
December	75,000

General and administrative salaries will amount to approximately $22,500 a month; lease payments under long-term lease contracts will be $7,500 a month; depreciation charges are $30,000 a month; miscellaneous expenses will be $2,250 a month; income tax payments of $52,500 will be due in both September and December; and a progress payment of $150,000 on a new research laboratory must be paid in October. Cash on hand on July 1 will amount to $110,000, and a minimum cash balance of $75,000 should be maintained throughout the cash budget period.

a. Prepare a monthly cash budget for the last six months of 19X1.

[6] This problem is adapted from *Cases in Managerial Finance,* second edition, Case 5.

b. Prepare an estimate of required financing (or excess funds) for each month during the period, that is, the amount of money that the Simms Company will need to borrow (or will have available to invest) each month.

c. Suppose receipts from sales come in uniformly during the month (that is, cash payments come in 1/30th each day), but all outflows are paid on the fifth of the month. Would this have an effect on the cash budget; that is, would the cash budget you have prepared be valid under these assumptions? If not, what could be done to make a valid estimation of financing requirements?

6-2. Gulf and Eastern, Inc., is a diversified multinational corporation that produces a wide variety of goods and services, including chemicals, soaps, tobacco products, toys, plastics, pollution control equipment, canned food, sugar, motion pictures, and computer software.[7] The corporation's major divisions were brought together in the early 1960s under a decentralized form of management; each division was evaluated in terms of its profitability, efficiency, and return on investments. This decentralized organization persisted through most of the decade, during which Gulf and Eastern experienced a high average growth rate in total assets, earnings, and stock prices.

Toward the end of 1975, however, those trends were reversed. The organization was faced with declining earnings, unstable stock prices, and a generally uncertain future. This situation persisted into 1976, but during that year a new president, Lynn Thompson, was appointed by the board of directors. Thompson, who had served for a time on the financial staff of I.E. du Pont, used the du Pont system to evaluate the various divisions. All showed definite weaknesses.

Thompson reported to the board that a principal reason for the poor overall performance was a lack of control by central management over each division's activities. She was particularly disturbed by the consistently poor results of the corporation's budgeting procedures. Under that system, each division manager drew up a projected budget for the next quarter, along with estimated sales, revenue, and profit; funds were then allocated to the divisions, basically in proportion to their budget requests. However, actual budgets seldom matched the projections; wide discrepancies occurred and this, of course, resulted in a highly inefficient use of capital.

In an attempt to correct the situation, Thompson asked the firm's chief financial officer to draw up a plan to improve the budgeting, planning, and control processes. When the plan was submitted, its basic provisions included the following:

1. To improve the quality of the divisional budgets, the division managers should be informed that the continuance of wide variances between their projected and actual budgets would result in dismissal.

2. A system should be instituted under which funds would be allocated to divisions on the basis of their average return on investment (ROI) during the last four quarters. Since funds were short, divisions with high ROIs would get most of the available money.

3. Only about one-half of each division manager's present compensation should be received as salary; the rest should be in the form of a bonus related to the division's average ROI for the quarter.

4. Each division should submit to the central office for approval all capital expenditure requests, production schedules, and price changes. Thus the company would be *recentralized*.

[7]This problem is taken from *Cases in Managerial Finance,* second edition.

a. 1. Is it reasonable to expect the new procedures to improve the accuracy budget forecasts?

   2. Should all divisions be expected to maintain the same degree of accuracy?

   3. In what other ways might the budgets be made?

b. 1. What problems would be associated with the use of the ROI criterion in allocating funds among the divisions?

   2. What effect would the period used in computing ROI (that is, four quarters, one quarter, two years, and so on) have on the effectiveness of this method?

   3. What problems might occur in evaluating the ROI in the crude rubber and auto tires divisions? between the sugar products and pollution control equipment divisions?

c. What problems would be associated with rewarding each manager on the basis of his division's ROI?

d. How well would Thompson's policy of recentralization work in a highly diversified corporation such as this, particularly in light of her financial officer's three other proposals?

Working Capital Management

Part Two

In Part One, we analyzed the firm's operations in an overall, aggregate manner. Now we must examine the various aspects of the firm's financial picture in more detail. In Part Two, we focus on the top half of the balance sheet, studying current assets, current liabilities, and the interrelationship between these two sets of accounts. This type of analysis is commonly called *working capital management.*

In Chapter 7, we examine some general principles of overall working capital management. Then, in Chapter 8, we consider the determinants of current assets: cash, marketable securities, accounts receivable, and inventories. Finally, in Chapter 9, we discuss current liabilities, considering in some detail the principal sources and forms of short-term funds.

Working Capital Policy

7

Working capital refers to a firm's investment in short-term assets—cash, short-term securities, accounts receivable, and inventories. *Net working capital* is defined as current assets minus current liabilities. *Working capital management* refers to all aspects of the administration of both current assets and current liabilities.

No new theories or basic principles are involved in working capital management—rather, this phase of financial management simply requires the application of valuation concepts developed throughout the text. Current asset holdings should be expanded to the point where marginal returns on increases in such assets are just equal to the cost of capital required to finance these increases, while current liabilities should be used in place of long-term debt whenever their use lowers the average cost of capital.

IMPORTANCE OF WORKING CAPITAL MANAGEMENT

Working capital management includes a number of aspects that make it an important topic for study, and we will now consider some of them.

Time Devoted to Working Capital Management

Surveys indicate that the largest portion of a financial manager's time is devoted to the day-by-day internal operations of the firm; this may be appropriately subsumed under the heading "working capital management." Since so

141

much time is spent on working capital decisions, it is appropriate that the subject be covered carefully in managerial finance courses.

Investment in Current Assets

Characteristically, current assets represent almost one-half of the total assets of a business firm. Because they represent a large investment and because this investment tends to be relatively volatile, current assets are worthy of the financial manager's careful attention.

Importance for Small Firms

Working capital management is particularly important for small firms. A small firm may minimize its investments in fixed assets by renting or leasing plant and equipment, but there is no way it can avoid an investment in cash, receivables, and inventories. Therefore, current assets are particularly significant for the financial manager of a small firm. Further, because a small firm has relatively limited access to the long-term capital markets, it must necessarily rely heavily on trade credit and short-term bank loans, both of which affect net working capital by increasing current liabilities.

Relationship between Sales Growth and Current Assets

The relationship between sales growth and the need to finance current assets is close and direct. For example, if the firm's average collection period is forty days and if its credit sales are $1,000 a day, it will have an investment of $40,000 in accounts receivable. If sales rise to $2,000 a day, the investment in accounts receivable will rise to $80,000. Sales increases produce similar immediate needs for additional inventories and, perhaps, for cash balances. All such needs must be financed, and since they arise so quickly, it is imperative that the financial manager keep fully aware of developments in the working capital segment of the firm. Of course, continued sales increases will require additional long-term assets, which must also be financed. However, fixed asset investments, while critically important to the firm in a strategic, long-run sense, do not generally have the same urgency as do current asset investments.

ORIGINAL CONCEPT OF WORKING CAPITAL

The term "working capital" originated at a time when most industries were closely related to agriculture. Processors would buy crops in the fall, process them, sell the finished product, and end up just before the next harvest with relatively low inventories. Bank loans with maximum maturities of one year were used to finance both the purchase and the processing costs, and these loans were retired with the proceeds from the sale of the finished products.

The situation is depicted in Figure 7–1. There fixed assets are shown to be growing steadily over time, while current assets jump at harvest season, then decline during the year, ending at zero just before the next crop is harvested. Short-term credit is used to finance current assets, and fixed assets are financed with long-term funds. Thus, the top segment of the graph deals with working capital.

FIGURE 7–1 Fixed and Current Assets and Their Financing

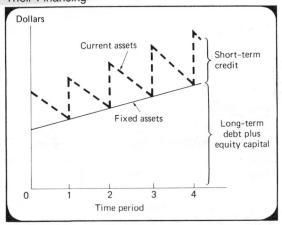

The figure represents, of course, an idealized situation—current assets build up gradually as crops are purchased and processed; inventories are drawn down less regularly; and ending inventory balances do not decline to zero. Nevertheless, the example does illustrate the general nature of the production and financing process, and working capital management consists of decisions relating to the top section of the graph—managing current assets and arranging the short-term credit used to finance them.

EXTENDING THE WORKING CAPITAL CONCEPT

As the economy became less oriented toward agriculture, the production and financing cycles of "typical" businesses changed. Although seasonal patterns still existed, and business cycles also caused asset requirements to fluctuate, it became apparent that current assets rarely, if ever, dropped to zero. This realization led to the development of the idea of "permanent current assets," diagrammed in Figure 7-2.

FIGURE 7–2   Fluctuating versus Permanent Assets

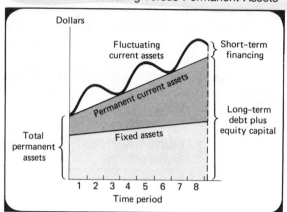

As Figure 7-2 is drawn, it maintains the traditional notion of the *matching principle* in which, to minimize both risk and financing costs, the firm should match the maturity of the liabilities to the length of time that the funds are needed. Therefore, short-term assets should be financed with short-term liabilities and both long-term assets and permanent current assets should be financed with long-term sources.

In Figure 7-2, fixed assets and permanent current assets are financed by long-term sources and the fluctuating current assets are financed with short-term sources. The pattern shown in Figures 7-1 and 7-2 is considered to be desirable since it minimizes both the risk to the firm and the financing costs. For example, suppose a firm borrows on a one year basis and uses the funds obtained to build and equip a plant. Cash flows from the plant (profits plus depreciation) are not sufficient to pay off the loan at the end of the year, so the loan must be refinanced. It is at this stage that the firm faces risk. First, there is the risk that the loan will be refinanced at interest rates higher than were expected to prevail when the borrowing occurred. Second, the lender may refuse to renew the loan. This would force the firm to search for new sources and to incur transaction costs. Had the plant been financed with long-term debt, the firm would face neither the risks noted above nor the added transaction costs, since cash flows would have been sufficient to retire the loan.

Alternatively, the firm could finance short-term assets with long-term sources of funds. In this instance, there will be periods when there is an excess of cash which will have to be invested in short-term securities. Since the rates paid by the firm on the long-term sources will exceed the investment in short-term securities, the firm will have lower profits than in cases where the matching principle is applied.

Thus, if a firm finances long-term assets with permanent capital and short-term assets with temporary capital, its financial risk is lower than it would be if long-term assets were financed with short-term debt or short-term assets were financed with long-term debt.

At the limit, a firm can attempt to match the maturity structure of its assets and liabilities exactly. A machine expected to last for five years could be financed by a five year loan; a building lasting twenty years could be financed by a twenty-year mortgage bond; inventory expected to be sold in twenty days could be financed by a twenty-day bank loan; and so forth. Actually, of course, uncertainty about the lives of assets prevents this exact maturity matching. We will examine this point in the following sections.

Figure 7–2 shows the situation for a firm that attempts to match asset and liability maturities exactly. Such a policy could be followed, but firms may follow other maturity-matching policies if they desire. Figure 7–3, for example, illustrates the situation for a firm that finances all its fixed assets with long-term capital but part of its permanent current assets with short-term credit.[1]

FIGURE 7–3   Fluctuating versus Permanent Assets

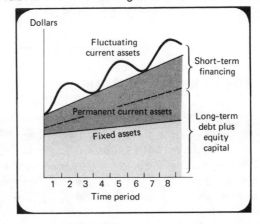

The dashed line could have even been drawn *below* the line designating fixed assets, indicating that all the current assets and part of the fixed assets are financed with short-term credit; this would be a highly aggressive, non-conservative position, and the firm would be very much subject to potential loan renewal problems and fluctuations in interest rates.

Alternatively, as in Figure 7–4, the dashed line could be drawn *above* the line designating permanent current assets, indicating that permanent capital is being used to meet seasonal demands. In this case, the firm uses a small amount of short-term credit to meet its peak seasonal requirements, but it also

[1] Firms generally have some short-term credit in the form of "spontaneous" funds — accounts payable and accruals (see Chapter 5). There are permanent levels of these spontaneous funds that constitute "free" capital; thus, virtually all firms employ at least some short-term credit at all times. In terms of the matching principle, the permanent spontaneous funds are considered long-term sources. We could modify the graphs to take these sources into account, but nothing is lost by simply abstracting from spontaneous funds, as we do.

meets a part of its seasonal needs by "storing liquidity" in the form of marketable securities during the off-season. The humps above the dashed line represent short-term financing; the troughs below the dashed line represent short-term security holdings.

FIGURE 7–4 Fluctuating versus Permanent Assets and Liabilities

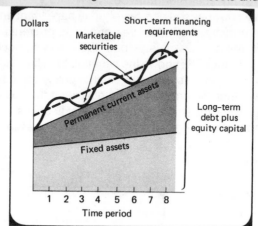

LONG-TERM VERSUS SHORT-TERM DEBT

The larger the percentage of funds obtained from long-term sources, the more conservative the firm's working capital policy. The reason for this, of course, is that during times of stress the firm may not be able to renew its short-term debt. This being so, why would firms ever use short-term credit (other than spontaneous credit)? Why not just use long-term funds? There are three primary answers to this question: flexibility, cost, and risk.

Flexibility

If the need for funds is seasonal or cyclical, the firm may not want to commit itself to long-term debt. Such debt can be refunded, provided the loan agreement includes a call or prepayment provision, but, even so, prepayment penalties can be expensive. Accordingly, if a firm expects its needs for funds to diminish in the near future, or if it thinks there is a good chance that such a reduction will occur, it may choose short-term debt for the flexibility it provides.

A cash budget is used to analyze the flexibility aspect of the maturity structure of the debt. To illustrate, suppose a company intends to finance a series of five-year projects by issuing debt. The debt retirement can be scheduled to the expected cash flows (profits plus depreciation) from the series of projects. A long-term bond issue would not be appropriate.

Cost of Long-Term versus Short-Term Debt

The cost aspect of the maturity decision involves *the term structure of interest rates,* or the relationship between the maturity of debt and the interest rate on the debt. Interest rates are frequently lower on short-term debt than on long-term debt. The graphic relationship between yield-to-maturity and term-to-maturity is called the *yield curve.*[2] In Figure 7-5, we present the yield curves for Government of Canada bonds and Bell Canada bonds as of August 11, 1978. The yield curve is that line which fits best the observations of yield-to-maturity and term-to-maturity. Not all of the bonds will plot on the yield curve, since they will have unique features which affect their yields.

The yield curve for Government of Canada bonds lies below that for Bell Canada and has the same general shape — short rates are slightly below long rates.

The yield-to-maturity on a corporate bond of a given maturity can be thought of as the risk-free rate on a Government bond at the same maturity

FIGURE 7-5 Yield Curve: Selected Bell Canada and Government of Canada Bonds as of August 11, 1978

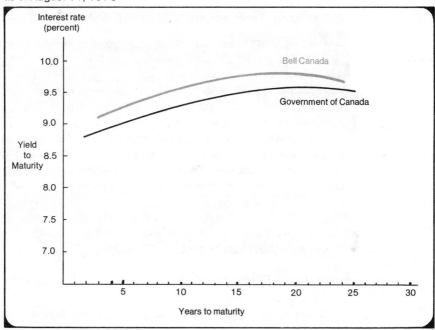

[2]A yield curve relates the yield-to-maturity to the term-to-maturity for a set of bonds that are equivalent in terms of default risk. Thus, a yield curve can be drawn for Government of Canada bonds or for Province of Quebec bonds or for companies of the same risk. However, putting all of these bonds on the same yield curve would be incorrect, since the groups do not have the same default risk.

plus a risk premium to reflect the risk of default on the corporate bond.[3] The risk premium need not be constant over the whole spectrum of yields-to-maturity. Therefore, the corporate yield curve should be above the Government bond yield curve, but not by a constant amount.

Suppose Bell Canada were interested in the yield it would have to pay on a new debt issue of a particular term-to-maturity. Clearly, the yields at which Bell can borrow will be related to the current yields on bonds outstanding of the same risk and term-to-maturity. The current yield curve for Bell bonds would demonstrate the pattern of yield- and term-to-maturity required on a new issue.

The yield curves presented in Figure 7 – 5 are relatively flat; more often short-term rates are considerably lower than long-term rates. However, there are times when the yield curve is downward sloping.[4] At such times, which almost always occur when both long-term and short-term rates are relatively high, short-term money costs more than long-term debt. Nevertheless, since short-term rates have *generally* been lower than long-term rates, a firm's capital will probably be less costly if it borrows short term rather than long term.

Risk of Long-Term versus Short-Term Debt

Even though short-term debt is generally less expensive than long-term debt, use of short-term debt subjects the firm to more risk than does long-term debt. This risk effect occurs for two reasons: (1) If a firm borrows on a long-term basis, its interest costs will be relatively stable over time, but if it borrows on a short-term basis, its interest expenses will fluctuate widely, at times going quite high. For example, from January to June 1974, the interest rate in finance company paper — a short-term (i.e. 90 day) borrowing rate — went from just under 9 percent to almost 12 percent. Early in 1975, the rate fell back to under 7 percent. Over the same period, Government of Canada, 91-day treasury bills went from 6.2 percent to 9 percent and fell back to 6.4 percent. (2) If a firm borrows heavily on a short-term basis, it may find itself unable to repay this debt or it may be in such a shaky financial position that the lender will not extend the loan; thus, the firm could be forced into bankruptcy. We elaborate on these risk factors in the following sections.

Interest Rate Fluctuations   Figure 7 – 6 shows the pattern of long-term and short-term interest rates from 1968 to 1977. The long-term rate is represented by the McLeod, Young, Weir, 10-Industrial bond average rate;

---

[3]The higher the default risk, the higher the interest rate lenders require on the loan. The difference between the Government of Canada bond rate and the rate the firms must pay for a given maturity is defined as the risk premium. The risk premium for Bell Canada is lower than that for a smaller, less seasoned borrower.

[4]In Chapter 18 we spell out these relationships in more detail and explain why yield curves can have these different shapes.

FIGURE 7-6 Plot of long-term Industrial Bonds and 90-day Finance Company Paper

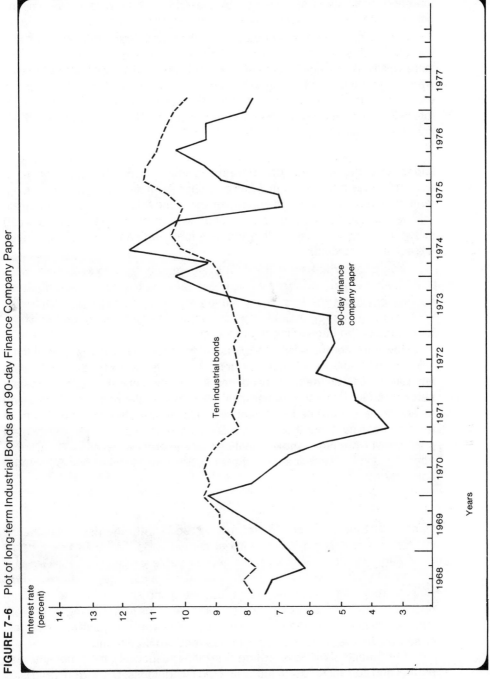

the short-term rate is represented by the rate on 90-day finance company paper.

Several points should be noted about the graph. *First,* both long-term and short-term rates generally rose over the period. *Second,* short-term rates are more volatile than long-term rates. *Third,* only during parts of 1973 and 1974 were long-term rates below short-term rates. This confirms the point we made earlier about the yield curve generally sloping upward: whenever the long-term rate in Figure 7 – 6 is above the short-term rate, the yield curve in Figure 7 – 5 must be upward sloping.

Impact of a Rise in Rates on Interest Expenses   Consider two firms, each with $100 million of debt; firm S has only short-term debt and firm L only long-term debt. Both are stable, mature companies: the total assets of each remain relatively constant from year to year, and the debt of each stays at the $100 million level. Finally, assume that the long-term and short-term interest rates are equal to 7 percent.

Firm S must "turn over" its debt every year, borrowing at the prevailing short-term interest rate. For simplicity, we assume that firm L's debt will not mature for twenty years, so that it's interest rate is fixed at 7 percent for the next twenty years regardless of what happens to either long-term or short-term rates in the intervening years.

Now consider the interest expense of the two firms one year later. Firm L still has $100 million of 7 percent debt, so its interest expense is $7 million annually. Firm S, on the other hand, has $100 million of debt that now costs 5 percent, so its interest expense has fallen to $5 million. If other costs and revenues have remained constant, firm L's profits after interest will have remained constant, but those of firm S will have risen sharply. The significant point is that while firm L *knows* what its future interest expenses will be, firm S does not, and this very absence of precise knowledge makes firm S the more risky one.

Danger of Being Unable to Refund   In addition to the risk of fluctuating interest charges, firm S faces another risk vis-à-vis firm L: S may run into temporary difficulties that prevent it from being able to refund its debt. Remember that when S's debt matures each year, the firm must negotiate new loans with its creditors. S must, of course, pay the going short-term rate, but suppose the loan comes up for renewal at a time when the firm is facing labor problems, a recession in demand for its products, extreme competitive pressures, or some other set of difficulties that has reduced its earnings.

The creditors will look at firm S's ratios, especially the times-interest-earned and current ratios, to judge its credit worthiness. S's current ratio is, of course, always lower than that of L, but in good times this will be overlooked—

if earnings are high, the interest will be well covered and lenders will tolerate a low current ratio. If, however, earnings decline, pulling down the interest coverage ratio, creditors will certainly reevaluate the credit worthiness of firm S. At the very least, because of the perceived increased riskiness of the company, creditors will raise the interest rate charged; at the extreme, they will refuse to renew the loan. In the latter event, the firm will be forced to raise the funds needed to pay off the loan by selling assets at bargain basement prices, borrowing from other sources at exorbitant interest rates, or, in the extreme, going bankrupt.

Example of the Risk-Return Tradeoff

Thus far we have seen that short-term debt is typically less costly than long-term debt, but that using short-term debt entails greater risk than does using long-term debt. Thus, we are faced with a tradeoff between risk and rate of return. Although we are not prepared to resolve the conflict between risk and rate of return at this point in the book, a further example will help to clarify the issues involved.

Table 7–1 illustrates the nature of the tradeoff. Here, we assume that the firm has $100 million of assets, one-half held as fixed assets and the other half as current assets, and that it will earn 15 percent before interest and taxes on total assets. The debt ratio has been set at 50 percent, but the policy issue of whether to use short-term debt, costing 6 percent, or long-term debt, costing 8 percent, has not been determined. Working through the relationships, we see that a conservative policy of using no short-term credit results in a rate of

TABLE 7–1 Effect of Maturity Structure of Debt on Return on Equity (Millions of dollars)

	Conservative	Average	Aggressive
Current assets	$ 50.00	$ 50.00	$ 50.00
Fixed assets	50.00	50.00	50.00
Total assets	$100.00	$100.00	$100.00
Short-term credit (6%)	—	25.00	50.00
Long-term debt (8%)	50.00	25.00	—
Current ratio	∞	2 : 1	1 : 1
Earnings before interest and taxes (EBIT)	15.00	15.00	15.00
Less interest	4.00	3.50	3.00
Taxable income	$ 11.00	$ 11.50	$ 12.00
Less taxes at 50%	5.50	5.75	6.00
Earnings on common shares	$ 5.50	$ 5.75	$ 6.00
Rate of return on book equity (%)	11.0	11.5	12.0

return on book equity of 11 percent, while the more aggressive policy of using only short-term credit boosts the rate of return to 12 percent.

What occurs when uncertainty is introduced into this example? We noted earlier that a firm which makes extensive use of short-term credit may find its earnings fluctuating widely. Suppose, for example, that there is a significant unexpected interest rate increase — a rise from 6 percent to 10 percent is not at all unrealistic given the recent historical experience. This rise would not affect the firm using the conservative policy, but it would increase the interest expense under the average policy to $4.5 million and under the aggressive policy to $5 million. The rates of return on equity for the three policies would consequently be 11.0 percent, 10.5 percent, and 10.0 percent, respectively — a reversal in relative ranking by rate of return. Of course, a decline in interest rates would have the opposite effect on the rates of return, but it should be clear that the variability of the return under an aggressive policy is more than that under a conservative policy.

Fluctuations in earnings before interest and taxes (EBIT) can pose even more severe problems—if EBIT declines, lenders may simply refuse to renew short-term debt or agree to renew it only at very high rates of interest. To illustrate this, suppose the EBIT of $15 million in Table 7–1 declines to only $5 million. Since the firm's ability to repay has diminished, creditors would certainly be reluctant to lend to it. This would cause creditors to require a higher return on their investment and, thus, raise the interest expense, which would, of course, jeopardize the firm's future even more and, at the same time, compound the effects of the declining EBIT on shareholder returns.

It is possible for the general level of interest rates to rise at the same time a firm's EBIT is falling, and the compound effects could cause the situation to deteriorate so much that the aggressive firm could not renew its credit at any interest rate. The result is bankruptcy.

Notice that if the firm follows a conservative policy of using all long-term debt, it need not worry about short-term, *temporary* changes either in the term structure of interest rates or in its own EBIT. Its only concern is with its long-run performance, and its conservative financial structure may permit it to survive in the short run to enjoy better times in the long run.

Extending the Example

These concepts can be incorporated into our example.[5] A firm has assets of $100 million and is considering the three financial structures, or policies, shown in Table 7–1. Management makes estimates of the future level of risk-

[5]This illustration uses the concept of a probability distribution, a topic discussed at some length in Chapter 12. A probability is the chance of an event occurring, or the odds on the occurrence of the event. The sum of the probabilities must equal 1.0, or 100 percent. The statistical aspects of this section may be omitted without loss of continuity if the statistical concepts are totally new.

less interest rates (the Treasury bill rate) and the level of EBIT for the coming year. Management knows that the firm's earnings for next year will be the prime determinant of the risk premium that will be added to the riskless rate.

Probability distributions for riskless rates and EBIT are given in Table 7–2. Assuming that the two probability distributions are independent of each other, we can determine the expected interest rate for the next year by the technique shown in Table 7–3. Column 1 gives the possible riskless rates of return. Column 2 gives the possible risk premiums, or the premiums investors require as compensation for making risky loans. Column 3 combines the riskless rates of interest with the risk premiums to give the possible rates of interest the firm may face. Column 4 gives the joint probabilities—the probability of the simultaneous occurrence of each possible riskless rate and risk premium. Column 5 gives the products of each joint probability multiplied by its associated interest rate; the sum of column 5 is the expected interest rate or 11.74 percent.

TABLE 7–2 Probability Distributions for Riskless Rates and EBIT

Treasury Bill Rate One Year Hence	
(i)	Probability
3%	.2
5	.3
7	.3
9	.2

EBIT for Next Year and Associated Risk Premiums Expected on Next Year's Renewal of Short-Term Credit		
EBIT	Risk Premium	Probability
(5.00) million	25.0%	.15
5.00	5.0	.20
15.00	2.0	.30
25.00	1.2	.20
35.00	1.0	.15

Since the expected value of the firm's short-term rate exceeds the long-term rate, 8 percent, the firm should probably use long-term rather than short-term financing. More important, however, is the fact that there is a 15 percent probability that the interest rate will be 28 percent or higher. Because total debt is $50 million, a 28 percent rate of interest would require an EBIT of $14 million to break even. But, at the time when this high rate is applied, EBIT would be *minus* $5 million, so the firm would run a loss before taxes of $19 million. This loss would reduce equity and increase the debt ratio, making the situation even more tense the next time the loan comes up for renewal. Good times might be just around the corner, but the aggressive firm, if its EBIT is subject to wide swings, may not survive until then.

Our example is unrealistic in that few firms will be able to actually generate the data needed to construct a table like Table 7–3. However, the events described are certainly *not* unrealistic, and the example does illustrate that the maturity structure of a firm's debt affects its overall risk. The example also shows that the risk tolerance of the firm with respect to the maturity composition of its liabilities depends to a large extent on the amount of risk already present in the firm owing to industry business risk, operating leverage, and overall financial leverage. It is important to keep the overall risk level of the firm within reasonable limits. Thus, a firm with high business risk should probably not use a very aggressive policy in its financial structure and especially not in its maturity structure, but a firm in a stable industry might use such a policy to advantage. Of course, the firm's asset maturity structure has a bear-

TABLE 7–3   Firm's Expected Interest Rate One Year Hence

i (1)	Risk Premium (2)	Interest Rate to Firm (3) = (1) + (2)	Joint Probability[a] (4)	Product (5) = (3) × (4)
3%	1.0%	4.0%	.030	.120%
	1.2	4.2	.040	.168
	2.0	5.0	.060	.300
	5.0	8.0	.040	.320
	25.0	28.0	.030	.840
5%	1.0	6.0	.045	.270
	1.2	6.2	.060	.372
	2.0	7.0	.090	.630
	5.0	10.0	.060	.600
	25.0	30.0	.045	1.350
7%	1.0	8.0	.045	.360
	1.2	8.2	.060	.492
	2.0	9.0	.090	.810
	5.0	12.0	.060	.720
	25.0	32.0	.045	1.440
9%	1.0	10.0	.030	.300
	1.2	10.2	.040	.408
	2.0	11.0	.060	.660
	5.0	14.0	.040	.560
	25.0	34.0	.030	1.020
			1.000	

Expected interest rate = 11.740%

[a]Joint probabilities are developed by multiplying the probabilities contained in Table 7–2 by each other. For example, the joint probability at the top of column 4 is the product .2 × .15 = .03; the second is the product .2 × .20 = .04; and so on. The expected value, or most likely interest rate, is found by multiplying the possible interest rates shown in column 3 by the joint probabilities given in column 4, then adding these products.

ing on its ability to employ short-term debt, and we cover this topic in the next section.

RELATIONSHIP OF CURRENT ASSETS TO SALES

In the chapters that deal with capital budgeting, we will see that capital budgeting decisions involve estimating the stream of benefits expected from a given project and then discounting these expected cash flows back to the present to find the present value of the project. Although current asset investment analysis is similar to fixed asset analysis in the sense that it also requires estimates of the effects of such investments on profits, it is different in three key respects. *First,* the time element is of vital importance in fixed asset analysis but not of much significance in current asset analysis; accordingly, compound interest and other aspects of the timing problem play a major role in capital budgeting but only a minor one in current asset analysis. *Second,* increasing the firm's current assets—especially cash and marketable securities—while holding constant expected production and sales reduces the riskiness of the firm, but it also reduces the overall return on assets. *Third,* although both fixed and current asset holdings are functions of *expected* sales, only current assets can be adjusted to *actual* sales in the short run; hence, adjustments to short-run fluctuations in demand lie in the domain of working capital management.

FIGURE 7–7   Relationship between Current Assets and Output

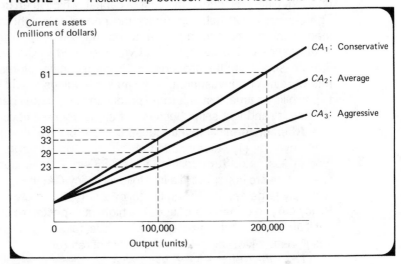

Some of these ideas are illustrated in Figure 7–7, which shows the short-run relationship between the firm's current assets and output. The firm's fixed assets are assumed to be $50 million, and they cannot be altered in response to short-run fluctuations in output. Three possible current asset policies are depicted. CA_1 represents a conservative policy: relatively large balances of cash and marketable securities are maintained, large "safety stocks" of inventories[6] are kept on hand, and the firm maximizes sales by adopting a "liberal" credit policy that causes a high level of accounts receivable. Policy CA_2 is somewhat less conservative than CA_1, while CA_3 represents a risky, aggressive policy.

Current asset holdings are highest at any output level under policy CA_1, lowest under CA_3. For example, at an output of 100,000 units, CA_1 calls for $33 million of current assets versus only $23 million for CA_3. If demand strengthens and short-run plans call for production to increase from 100,000 to 200,000 units, current asset holdings will likewise increase. Under policy CA_1, current assets rise to $61 million; under CA_3, the increase is to only $38 million. As we shall see in the following section, the more aggressive policy will lead to a higher expected rate of return, but it also entails greater risk.

Risk-Return Tradeoff for Current Asset Holdings

If it could forecast perfectly, a firm would hold *exactly* enough cash to make disbursements as required, *exactly* enough inventories to meet production and sales requirements, *exactly* the accounts receivable called for by an optimal credit policy, and no marketable securities unless the interest returns on such assets exceeded the cost of capital, which is an unlikely occurrence. The current asset holdings under the perfect foresight case would be the theoretical minimum for a profit-maximizing firm. Any larger holdings would, in the sense of the du Pont chart we described in Chapter 3, increase the firm's assets without a proportionate increase in its returns, thus lowering its rate of return on investment. Any smaller holdings would mean the inability to pay bills on time, lost sales and production stoppages because of inventory shortages, and lost sales because of an overly restrictive credit policy.

When uncertainty is introduced into the picture, current asset management involves (1) determination of the minimum required balances of each type of asset and (2) addition of a safety stock to account for the fact that forecasters are imperfect. If a firm follows policy CA_1 in Figure 7–7, it is adding relatively large safety stocks; if it follows CA_3, its safety stocks are minimal. Policy CA_3, in general, produces the highest expected returns on investment, but it also involves the greatest risk—that is, following this policy may actually result in the *lowest* actual or realized rate of return.

The effect of the three alternative policies on expected profitability is

---

[6]The concept of inventory safety stocks is discussed in Chapter 8.

illustrated in Table 7–4. Under the conservative policy, CA_1, the rate of return on assets before interest and taxes is 13.5 percent; the return rises to 15 percent for an average policy and to 17 percent for the risky, aggressive policy, CA_3. However, we know that CA_3 is the most risky policy, since lost sales, lost customer goodwill, and bad credit ratings caused by poor liquidity ratios could combine to bring the actual realized rate of return well below the anticipated 17 percent.

TABLE 7–4 Effects of Alternative Current Asset Policies on Rates of Return and Asset Turnover

	Conservative (CA_1)	Average (CA_2)	Risky (CA_3)
Sales			
Units	200,000	200,000	200,000
Dollars	$100,000,000	$100,000,000	$100,000,000
EBIT	$ 15,000,000	$ 15,000,000	$ 15,000,000
Current assets	$ 61,000,000	$ 50,000,000	$ 38,000,000
Fixed assets	50,000,000	50,000,000	50,000,000
Total assets	$111,000,000	$100,000,000	$ 88,000,000
Rate of return on assets (EBIT/assets)	13.5%	15.0%	17.0%

In the real world, things are considerably more complex than this simple example suggests. For one thing, different types of current assets affect both risk and returns differently. Increased holdings of cash do more to improve the firm's risk posture than a similar dollar increase in marketable securities, but idle cash penalizes earnings more severely than does the same investment in marketable securities. Generalizations become even more difficult when we move on to accounts receivable and inventories, because it becomes increasingly difficult to measure either the earnings penalty or the risk reduction that results from increasing the balances of these items beyond their theoretical minimums. In subsequent chapters, we consider determining the optimal balances of each type of current asset, where *optimal* is defined to include the theoretical minimum plus an optimal safety stock. First, however, we must complete our generalized discussion of working capital policy by combining current asset and current liability management.

WORKING CAPITAL POLICY: COMBINING CURRENT ASSET AND CURRENT LIABILITY MANAGEMENT

Table 7–5 illustrates the effect of working capital policy on expected returns and on risk as measured by the current ratio. A conservative policy calling for no short-term debt and large holdings of current assets results in a 9.6 percent expected after-tax return on equity and a very high current ratio. The actual return would probably be quite close to 9.6 percent. An aggressive policy, with minimal holdings of current assets and short-term rather than long-term debt, raises the expected return to 14 percent, but the current ratio under this policy is only .86, a dangerously low level for most industries. Simultaneously, the increasing risks associated with the aggressive policy might adversely affect stock market opinion about the company; therefore, even if working capital policy pushes rates of return up, the net effect still might be to lower stock prices.

Can we resolve this risk/return tradeoff to determine *precisely* the firm's optimal working capital policy, that is, the working capital policy that will maximize the value of existing common equity? In theory, the answer is yes, but in practice it is no. Determining the optimal policy would require detailed information on a complex set of variables, information that is unobtainable today. Progress is being made in the development of computer simulation models designed to help determine the effects of alterna-

TABLE 7–5 Effects of Working Capital Policy on the Rate of Return on Common Equity

	Conservative Long-Term Debt Large Investment in Current Assets (CA_1)	Average Average Use of Short-Term Debt; Average Investment in Current Assets (CA_2)	Aggressive All Short-Term Debt; Minimal Investment in Current Assets (CA_3)
Current assets	$ 61,000,000	$ 50,000,000	$ 38,000,000
Fixed assets	50,000,000	50,000,000	50,000,000
Total assets	$111,000,000	$100,000,000	$ 88,000,000
Current liabilities (6%)	—	$ 25,000,000	$ 44,000,000
Long-term debt (8%)	$ 55,500,000	$ 25,000,000	—
Total debt (debt/assets = 50%)	$ 55,500,000	$ 50,000,000	$ 44,000,000
Equity	55,500,000	50,000,000	44,000,000
Total liabilities and net worth	$111,000,000	$100,000,000	$ 88,000,000
Sales in dollars	$100,000,000	$100,000,000	$100,000,000
EBIT	$ 15,000,000	$ 15,000,000	$ 15,000,000
Less: interest	4,400,000	3,500,000	2,640,000
Taxable income	$ 10,600,000	$ 11,500,000	$ 12,360,000
Taxes (50%)	5,300,000	5,750,000	6,180,000
Earnings on equity	$ 5,300,000	$ 5,750,000	$ 6,180,000
Rate of return on equity	9.6%	11.5%	14.0%
Current ratio	a	2 : 1	.86

[a] Under policy CA_1, the current ratio is shown to be infinitely high. Actually, the firm would doubtless have some spontaneous credit, but the current ratio would still be quite high.

tive financial policy choices, including working capital decisions, but no one using such models would suggest that they can actually reach *optimal* solutions. We can, however, establish guidelines, or ranges of values, for each type of current asset, and we do have ways of examining the various types of short-term financing and their effects on the cost of capital. Because such information, used with good judgment, can be most helpful to the financial manager, we will consider these topics in the remaining chapters of Part Two.

SUMMARY

Working capital refers to a firm's investment in short-term assets—cash, short-term securities, accounts receivable, and inventories. *Gross working capital* is defined as the firm's total current assets; *net working capital* is current assets minus current liabilities. *Working capital management* involves all aspects of the administration of both current assets and current liabilities.

Working capital policy is concerned with two sets of relationships among balance sheet items. First is the policy question of the level of total current assets to be held. Current assets vary with sales, but the ratio of current assets to sales is a policy matter. If the firm elects to operate aggressively, it will hold relatively small stocks of current assets. This will reduce the required level of investment and increase the expected rate of return on investment. However, an aggressive policy also increases the likelihood of running out of cash or inventories or of losing sales because of an excessively tough credit policy.

The second policy question concerns the relationship between types of assets and the way these assets are financed. One policy calls for matching asset and liability maturities, financing short-term assets with short-term debt, and long-term assets with long-term debt or equity. If this policy is followed, the maturity structure of the debt is determined by the level of fixed versus current assets. However, short-term debt is frequently less expensive than long-term debt, so the expected rate of return may be higher if short-term debt is used. Offsetting this return advantage is the fact that large amounts of short-term credit increase the risks (1) of having to renew this debt at higher interest rates and (2) of not being able to renew the debt at all if the firm experiences difficulties.

Both aspects of working capital policy involve risk/return tradeoffs. In the following chapter, we examine methods used to determine the optimal levels of each type of current assets. Then, in Chapter 9, we examine alternative sources and forms of short-term credit.

QUESTIONS

7-1. How does the seasonal nature of a firm's sales influence the decision about the amount of short-term credit in the financial structure?

7-2. "Merely increasing the level of current asset holdings does not necessarily reduce the riskiness of the firm. Rather, the composition of the current assets, whether highly liquid or highly illiquid, is the important factor to consider." What is your reaction to this statement?

7-3. What is the advantage of matching the maturities of assets and liabilities?

7-4. There have been times when the term structure of interest rates has been such that short-term rates were higher than long-term rates. Does this necessarily imply that the best financial policy for a firm is to use all long-term debt and no short-term debt? Explain your answer.

PROBLEMS

7-1. Freund Corp. maintains a current ratio of 2.5 and current assets are a constant 30 percent of sales. Freund has $500,000 of long-term debt. Short-term loans are maintained at 75 percent of current liabilities. Sales forecasts for the next three years are as follows:

Year	Sales
1	$3,000,000
2	4,000,000
3	4,500,000

If all short-term notes can be obtained at an 8 percent interest rate, how much interest must Freund pay on its short-term notes in each of the next three years?

7-2. The Morgan Tile Corp. Ltd. is attempting to determine the optimal level of current assets for the coming year. Management expects sales to increase to approximately $1.2 million as a result of asset expansion presently being undertaken. Fixed assets total $500,000, and the firm wishes to maintain a 60 percent debt ratio. Morgan's interest cost is currently 8 percent on both short-term debt and long-term debt (which the firm uses in its permanent structure). Three alternatives regarding the projected current asset level are available to the firm: (1) an aggressive policy requiring current assets of only 45 percent of projected sales; (2) an average policy of 50 percent of sales as current assets; and (3) a conservative policy requiring current assets of 60 percent of sales. The firm expects to generate earnings before interest and taxes at a rate of 12 percent on total sales.

    a. What is the expected return on equity under each current asset level? (Assume a 50 percent tax rate.)

    b. In this problem, we have assumed that interest rates and the level of expected sales are independent of current asset policy. Is this a valid assumption?

    c. How would the overall riskiness of the firm vary under each policy? Discuss specifically the effect of current asset management on demand, expenses, fixed charge coverage, risk of insolvency, and so on.

7-3. Three companies — Aggressive, Between, and Conservative — have different working capital management policies as implied by their names. For example, Aggressive employs only minimal current assets and finances almost entirely with current liabilities and equity. This tight ship approach has a dual effect. It keeps total assets low, and this tends to increase return on assets. But for reasons such as stock-outs, total sales are reduced; and since inventory is ordered more frequently and in smaller quantities, variable costs are increased. Condensed balance sheets for the three companies are presented below.

Balance Sheets

	Aggressive	Between	Conservative
Current assets	$150,000	$200,000	$300,000
Fixed assets	200,000	200,000	200,000
Total assets	$350,000	$400,000	$500,000
Current liabilities (at 8%)	$200,000	$100,000	$ 50,000
Long-term debt (at 10%)	0	100,000	200,000
Total debt	$200,000	$200,000	$250,000
Equity	150,000	200,000	250,000
Total claims on assets	$350,000	$400,000	$500,000
Current ratio	0.75:1	2:1	6:1

The cost of goods sold functions for the three firms are as follows:

Cost of goods sold = Fixed costs + Variable costs
Aggressive:Cost of goods sold = $200,000 + 0.7 (sales)
Between:Cost of goods sold = $250,000 + 0.6 (sales)
Conservative:Cost of goods sold = $300,000 + 0.6 (sales)

A company with normal net working capital, such as Between, will sell $1 million a year when economic growth is average. If the economy is weak, sales for Between will be reduced by $100,000; if strong, sales will increase $100,000. In any given economic condition, Aggressive will sell $100,000 less than Between, and Conservative will sell $100,000 more. This is because of the working capital differences.

    a. Make out income statements for strong, average, and weak economies using the following pattern:

Sales
Less cost of goods sold
Earnings before interest and taxes (EBIT)
Less interest expense
Taxable income
Less taxes (at 50%)
Net income

    b. Compare the rates of return (EBIT/Assets and return on equity). Which company is best in a strong economy? in an average economy? in a weak economy?

    c. What considerations for management of working capital are indicated by this problem?

7-4. Indicate the effects of the transactions listed below on each of the following: total current assets, working capital, current ratio, and net profit. Use + to indicate an increase, – to indicate a decrease, and 0 to indicate no effect. State necessary assumptions and assume an initial current ratio of more than 1 to 1.

	Total Current Assets	Net Working Capital[a]	Current Ratio	Net Profit
1. Cash is acquired through issuance of additional common shares.	____	____	____	____
2. Merchandise is sold for cash.	____	____	____	____
3. Federal income tax due for the previous year is paid.	____	____	____	____
4. A fixed asset is sold for less than book value.	____	____	____	____
5. A fixed asset is sold for more than book value.	____	____	____	____
6. Merchandise is sold on credit.	____	____	____	____
7. Payment is made to trade creditors for previous purchases.	____	____	____	____
8. A cash dividend is declared and paid.	____	____	____	____
9. Cash is obtained through short-term bank loans.	____	____	____	____
10. Short-term notes receivable are sold at a discount.	____	____	____	____
11. A profitable firm increases its fixed assets depreciation allowance account.	____	____	____	____
12. Marketable securities are sold below cost.	____	____	____	____
13. Uncollectible accounts are written off against the allowance account.	____	____	____	____
14. Advances are made to employees.	____	____	____	____
15. Current operating expenses are paid.	____	____	____	____
16. Short-term promissory notes are issued to trade creditors for prior purchases.	____	____	____	____
17. Ten-year notes are issued to pay off accounts payable.	____	____	____	____
18. A wholly depreciated asset is retired.	____	____	____	____
19. Accounts receivable are collected.	____	____	____	____
20. A stock dividend is declared and paid.	____	____	____	____
21. Equipment is purchased with short-term notes.	____	____	____	____
22. The allowance for doubtful accounts is increased.	____	____	____	____
23. Merchandise is purchased on credit.	____	____	____	____
24. The estimated taxes payable are increased.	____	____	____	____

[a] *Net working capital* is defined as current assets minus current liabilities.

7-5. The Cane Card Co. Ltd. is attempting to project its financial requirements for the next ten-year period. The firm is a relative newcomer to the industry, having been in business only three years. Initially, the firm was totally unknown and found financing, particularly of a permanent nature, quite difficult to obtain. As a result, Cane was literally "forced" to structure the right-hand side of its balance sheet as follows:

Trade credit payable	$200,000
Short-term bank borrowing	240,000
Common equity	440,000
Total claims	$880,000

In the three years the firm has been very successful, increasing its total capitalization by $120,000 of retained earnings. It is now in a position where it could obtain a long-term loan for ten years from an insurance company at a rate of 11 percent in place of all or any of its present short-term borrowings. Alternatively, it could renew its existing $240,000 loan, or any part thereof, on a one-year loan from the bank at a rate of 9 percent.

George Groves, the financial vice-president, is considering three possible financing plans: (1) to renew the 1-year loan with the bank; (2) to borrow $240,000 from the insurance company; and (3) to borrow $120,000 from each. Groves has estimated short-term riskless rates, the premiums that Cane might have to pay over the riskless rate for three possible "states of the economy," and the probability of each possibility. The *average* rates that the firm would likely pay over the next ten years on its short-term borrowings are shown below.

State of Economy	Cane EBIT*	Riskless Rate	Cane Risk Premium	Joint Probability
Good	$300,000	4%	2%	.125
Good	300,000	6	2	.125
Average	160,000	6	4	.250
Average	160,000	8	4	.250
Bad	20,000	8	10	.125
Bad	20,000	10	10	.125

*Earnings before interest and taxes.

a. Assuming a 50 percent tax rate, compute expected profits under each of Groves' three alternative financing plans. (Ignore possible growth effects. The expected EBIT is $160,000 under each plan.)

b. On the basis of Groves' estimates, what is the worst profit that could result under each alternative? the best? (Assume no loss carry-back provision in the tax law.) Interpret your results and recommend a financing plan for Cane.

c. Is there anything to prevent Cane from refinancing its short-term debt with the insurance company, thus converting it to long-term debt, at some future date if and when the short-term rate to the firm becomes unreasonably high?

d. In both this problem and the example in the chapter, some very high interest rates were averaged into the computation of an expected short-term interest rate. If such rates would "ruin" a firm, can you see any problem with using them in this computation?

7-6. From a recent issue of the *Bank of Canada Review* or from any other convenient source:

a. Construct a yield curve for the most recent complete data for Government of Canada securities. Choose ten bonds which give as wide a range in term-to-maturity as possible.

b. Construct the yield curve for January, 1976, and January, 1977, again using ten Government bonds. Comment on any shifts you observe.

c. From the yield curve in part a. above, you will find that some bonds plot a substantial distance off the yield curve. These observations are referred to as outliers. Can you give any explanation why they are outliers?

d. Why does the yield curve show only Government of Canada bonds instead of including yields and terms to maturity on commercial paper and corporate bonds?

e. If you had constructed a yield curve for provincial government debt, where would it plot relative to the yield curve constructed for Government of Canada bonds?

Current Asset Management

8

In the preceding chapter we viewed working capital management in a general, overall sense. Now we focus our attention on the firm's investment in specific current assets, examining cash, marketable securities, accounts receivable, and inventories. According to a report on performance summaries of Canadian industries compiled by McLeod, Young, Weir Limited, current assets represented approximately 57 percent of manufacturing companies' total assets in 1976. Clearly, current asset management is an important subject.

CASH MANAGEMENT

Controlling the investment in current assets begins with cash management. Cash consists of the firm's holdings of currency and demand deposits, with demand deposits being by far the more important for most firms.

Why Hold Cash?

Businesses or individuals have three primary motives for holding cash: (1) the *transactions motive*, (2) the *precautionary motive*, and (3) the *speculative motive*.

Transactions Motive The transactions motive for holding cash is to enable the firm to conduct its ordinary business—making purchases and sales. In some lines of business, such as the utilities, where billings can be cycled throughout the month, cash inflows can be scheduled and synchronized closely with the need for the outflow of cash. Hence, we expect the cash-to-revenues ratio and cash-to-total-assets ratio for utility firms to be relatively low. In retail trade, by contrast, sales are more random, and a number of transactions may actually be conducted by physical currency. As a consequence, retail trade requires higher ratios of cash to sales and to total assets.

The seasonality of a business may give rise to a need for cash for the purchase of inventories. For example, raw materials may be available only during a harvest season, as in the food-canning business. Or sales may be seasonal, as are department store sales around the Christmas and the Easter holidays, giving rise to an increase in needs for cash.

Precautionary Motive   The precautionary motive relates primarily to the predictability of cash inflows and outflows. If predictability is high, less cash must be held against an emergency or any other contingency. Another factor that strongly influences the precautionary motive for holding cash is the ability to borrow additional cash on short notice when circumstances necessitate. Borrowing flexibility is primarily a matter of the strength of the firm's relations with banking institutions and other credit sources.

When interest rates are high, the firm will forego income by holding precautionary balances in the form of cash. Therefore, the precautionary motive for holding cash is actually satisfied in large part by holding near-money assets — short-term government obligations and the like.

Speculative Motive   The speculative motive for holding cash is to be ready for profit-making opportunities that may arise. For example, if the company expects short-term interest rates to increase, the amount of money held in cash will increase until interest rates have peaked. At this point, the firm will use the cash to purchase marketable securities. Although there are other situations in which a large, speculative holding of cash would be understandable, by and large, businesses do not accumulate cash for speculative purposes. Holding cash is more common among individual investors.

However, the cash and marketable securities balances may rise to rather sizable levels on a temporary basis as funds are accumulated to meet specific future needs. These "financing balances" are built up to meet cash requirements such as dividend and interest payments, bond repayments and investments in fixed assets.

Advantages of Adequate Cash: Specific Points

In addition to these general motives, sound working capital management requires maintenance of an ample amount of cash for several specific reasons. First, it is essential that the firm have sufficient cash to take trade discounts. A commonly encountered billing procedure, or term of trade, allows a 2 percent discount if the bill is paid within ten days, with full payment required in thirty days in any event. (This is usually stated as 2/10, net 30.) Since the net amount is due in thirty days, failure to take the discount means paying this extra 2 percent for using the money an additional twenty days. If one were to pay 2 percent for every twenty-day period over the year, there would be eighteen such periods:

$$18 = \frac{360 \text{ days}}{20 \text{ days}}.$$

This represents an annual interest rate of 36 percent.[1] Most firms have a cost of debt that is substantially lower than 36 percent.

Second, since the current and acid test ratios are key items in credit analysis, it is essential that the firm, in order to maintain its credit standing, meet the standards of the line of business in which it is engaged. A strong credit standing enables the firm to purchase goods from trade suppliers on favorable terms and to maintain its line of credit with banks and other sources of credit.

Using the knowledge about the general nature of cash flows presented in Chapter 5, the financial manager may be able to improve the inflow-outflow pattern of cash. If the financial manager can improve the synchronization of the cash flows, a smaller cash balance is required and funds are released for use in other areas. In addition, the faster the inflows are deposited in the bank, the sooner the company will earn interest on the cash or be able to use the funds for other purposes. In the following sections, we discuss some of the techniques that can be used to improve the cash flow pattern.

Synchronization of Cash Flows

An example of synchronization demonstrates how cash flows may be improved by more frequent requisitioning of funds by divisional offices from the firm's main or central office. Some Gulf Oil Corporation divisional field offices,

[1]The following equation may be used for calculating the cost, on an annual basis, of not taking discounts:

$$\text{Cost} = \frac{\text{discount percent}}{(100 - \text{discount percent})} \times \frac{360}{(\text{final due date} - \text{discount period})}.$$

The denominator in the first term, (100 − discount percent), equals the funds made available by not taking the discount. To illustrate, the cost of not taking a discount when the terms are 2/10, net 30 is computed.

$$\text{Cost} = \frac{2}{98} \times \frac{360}{20} = 0.0204 \times 18 = 36.72\%.$$

Notice that the calculated cost can be reduced by paying late. Thus if the illustrative firm pays in 60 days rather than the specified 30, the credit period becomes 60 − 10 = 50, and the calculated cost becomes

$$\text{Cost} = \frac{2}{98} \times \frac{360}{50} = 0.0204 \times 7.2 = 14.7\%.$$

In periods of excess capacity, some firms may be able to get away with late payments, but such firms may suffer a variety of problems associated with being a "slow-payer" account.

for instance, formerly requisitioned funds once or twice a week; now the treasurer's office insists on daily requisitions, thus keeping cash on tap as much as four days longer. On the basis of 20 offices, each requiring $1 million a week, these staggered requisitions free the equivalent of $10 million for one day each week. At 6 percent interest, this earns better than $84,000 a year.

Moreover, effective forecasting can reduce the investment in cash. The cash flow forecasting at CIT Credit Corporation illustrates this idea. An assistant treasurer forecasts planned purchases of automobiles by the dealers. He estimates daily the number of cars shipped to the 10,000 dealers who finance their purchases through CIT. He then estimates how much money should be deposited in banks that day to pay automobile manufacturers. On one day he estimated a required deposit of $6.4 million; the actual bill for the day was $6.397 million, a difference of one-tenth of 1 percent. Although such close forecasting cannot be achieved by every firm, the system enables CIT to economize on the amount of money it must borrow and thereby keeps interest expense to a minimum.

Expediting Collections

Another effective way of economizing on the amount of cash required is to reduce the delay from the time a billing is sent to the customer until the payment is deposited in the bank and available for company use.

If the firm makes sales across the country, then the regional divisions of the firm can be used as billing and collection centers. Since the customers are closer to these divisional offices than to the head office, the time that the bill and the payment are in the mails is reduced. Cheques are received at the regional office and then processed and deposited in the bank. Since both the head office and the divisions will bank at branches of the same bank, transfers of funds from the latter to the former are expedited. Based on the expected cash flow pattern of the division and its minimum required balance, head office can set up an automatic transfer of funds to itself, either by writing a cheque on the division's account or by having the bank do the transfer. To speed up the transfer of funds to head office, more sophisticated and costlier techniques are availabe.

In this discussion, we have assumed that, upon deposit of the cheque in the division's bank account, the company obtains use of the full amount of the deposit even though the funds have not been transferred from the customer's to the company's account; this is equivalent to the extension of short-term credit by the bank to the company. Although this is the normal arrangement, the bank does reserve the right to prevent the use of the funds until the cheque has been cleared and the funds are deposited in the company's account. The exercise of this option by the bank will depend on who issued the cheque, its size and other factors.

One delay that still remains is related to the time required to process the cheque before it can be deposited in the bank. To reduce this delay, a *lock box* plan can be used. If a firm makes sales in large amounts at great distances, it can establish a lock box in a post office located in the customer's area. The number of lock boxes used and their locations will depend on the concentration of the customers within the sales territory and the cost of operating the lock box. The customers are instructed to send their payments to the postal box in their area.

The bank picks up the cheques (usually more than once a day), deposits them in the company's bank account and informs the firm of the issuers of the cheques received and their amounts. The funds are available for the company's use and the actual processing of the payments by the company begins after the cheques are deposited. The lock box system is used by a number of companies; however, it is a costly technique and may not be a cost effective option for most companies.

Slowing Disbursements

Just as expediting the collection process conserves cash, slowing down disbursements accomplishes the same thing by keeping cash on hand for longer periods. One obviously could simply delay payments, but this involves equally obvious difficulties. Firms have, in the past, devised rather ingenious methods for "legitimately" lengthening the collection period on their own cheques. Since such practices are usually recognized for what they are, there are severe limits to their use.

One procedure that is rarely used, but is very effective in slowing down the expenditure of funds, is the use of drafts. While a cheque is payable upon demand, a draft must be transmitted to the issuer, who approves it and then deposits funds to cover it, after which it can be collected. Since there is a period of time required to clear the draft and transmit it to the issuer for approval, the company has extended the time that it has use of the funds before they must be paid out.

In the United States, AT&T presents an example of the creative use of the draft. "In handling its payrolls, for instance, AT&T can pay an employee by draft on Friday. The employee cashes the draft at his local bank, which sends it on to AT&T's New York bank. It may be Wednesday or Thursday before the draft arrives. The bank then sends it to the company's accounting department, which has until 3 p.m. that day to inspect and approve it. Not until then does AT&T deposit funds in its bank to pay the draft."[2]

Both banks and those who receive drafts dislike them—they represent an awkward, clumsy, costly anachronism in an age when computer transfer

[2]"More Firms Substitute Drafts for Checks to Pay, Collect Bills," *The Wall Street Journal* (August 29, 1971).

mechanisms are reducing the time and expense involved in transfers of funds.

Using Float

Float is defined as the difference between the balance shown in a firm's (or individual's) chequebook balance and the balance on the bank's books. Since payments to a firm are available for use as soon as they are deposited, cash inflows on the company's and bank's books will be identical. Therefore, float will reflect the difference between the value of cheques issued by the firm as reflected on its own books and the value of the cheques actually cleared and deducted from the company's balance at the bank. This should be recognized by anyone who has ever tried to reconcile a bank statement as the value of cheques outstanding. Suppose a firm writes, on average, cheques in the amount of $50,000 per day. If it takes approximately three days for these cheques to clear and be deducted from the firm's bank balance, the float is, on average, $150,000 (i.e. on any particular day, there will be $150,000 worth of cheques outstanding).

Any firm can make use of float to reduce the actual amount of cash held in the firm's account. In fact, for some firms, whereas their cash balance is positive at the bank, the actual cash balance is negative in their own accounts; the difference is the large amount of cheques outstanding. Some firms have indicated that they *never* have true positive cash balances. The degree to which float is used to reduce the firm's holding of cash balances will depend on the predictability of cash outflows and inflows.

Cost of Cash Management[3]

We have just described a number of procedures that may be used to hold down cash balance requirements. Implementing these procedures, however, is not a costless operation. How far should a firm go in making its cash operations more efficient? As a general rule, the firm should incur these expenses so long as their marginal returns exceed their marginal expenses.

For example, suppose that by establishing a lock-box system and increasing the accuracy of cash inflow and outflow forecasts, a firm can reduce its investment in cash by $1 million. Further, suppose that this project, based on its very low risk, has an opportunity cost of capital equal to the firm's borrowing rate of 12 percent. The steps taken have released $1 million and the capital costs required to finance this $1 million investment in cash are $120,000 per year. If the annual costs of the procedures necessary to release the $1 million are less than $120,000, the move is a good one; if the costs exceed $120,000, the greater efficiency is not worth the cost.[4] It is

---

[3]We are abstracting from the security aspects of cash management, that is, the prevention of fraud and embezzlement. These topics are better covered in accounting than in finance courses.

[4]This analysis of the investment in cash management is an application of capital budgeting techniques

clear that larger firms, with larger cash balances, can better afford to hire the personnel necessary to maintain tight control over their cash positions. Cash management is one element of business operations in which economies of scale are clearly present.

Very clearly, the value of careful cash management depends upon the costs of funds invested in cash, which in turn depend upon the current rate of interest. In the 1970s, with interest rates at high levels, firms are devoting more care than ever to cash management.

DETERMINING THE MINIMUM CASH BALANCE

Thus far we have seen that cash is held primarily for transactions purposes; the other traditional motives for holding cash, the speculative and precautionary motives, are today met largely by reserve borrowing power and by holdings of short-term marketable securities. Some minimum cash balance—which may actually be negative if float is used effectively—is required for transactions, and an additional amount over and above this figure may be held as a safety stock. For many firms the total of transactions balances plus safety stock constitutes the minimum cash balance, the point at which the firm either borrows additional cash or sells part of its portfolio of marketable securities. For many other firms, however, banking relationships require still larger balances.

Maintenance Balances

We have seen that banks provide a number of services to firms — they provide credit to firms until cheques have been cleared, operate lock-box plans, supply credit information, and the like. These services cost the bank money, so the bank must be compensated for rendering them.

Banks earn most of their income by lending money at interest, and most of the funds they lend are obtained in the form of deposits. If a firm maintains a deposit account with an average balance of $100,000, and if the bank can lend these funds at a return of $8,000, then the account is, in a sense, worth $8,000 to the bank. Thus, it is to the bank's advantage to provide services worth up to $8,000 to attract and hold the account.

Banks determine first the costs of the services rendered to their larger customers and then the average account balances necessary to provide enough income to compensate for these costs. These balances are defined as *maintenance balances* and are often maintained by firms instead of paying

(continued from page 170)
described in Chapter 11. In this simplified example, there are level annual costs of cash management. In a more complicated example, the costs may not be the same each year and a somewhat more involved analysis would be necessary.

cash service charges to the bank.[5]

Compensating balances are required by some bank loan agreements. During periods when the supply of credit is restricted and interest rates are high, banks frequently insist that borrowers maintain accounts that average some percentage of the loan amount — 10 percent is a typical figure — as a condition for granting the loan. *If the balance is larger than the firm would otherwise maintain,* then the effective cost of the loan is increased; the excess balance presumably "compensates" the bank for making a loan at a rate below what it could earn on the funds if they were invested elsewhere.[6]

The Bank Act requires that the borrower must agree to the use of compensating balances or they cannot be used in the loan agreement. Since the compensating balance is recognized by both the borrower and the lender as a method of increasing the interest rate, it is unlikely that a borrower would be able to remove the compensating balance provision while maintaining the stated rate on the loan.

Both maintenance and compensating balances could be established (1) as an *absolute minimum,* say $100,000, below which the actual balance must never fall, or (2) as a *minimum average balance,* perhaps $100,000, over some period, generally a month. The absolute minimum is a much more restrictive requirement, because the average amount of cash held during the month will be above $100,000 by the amount of transactions balances. The $100,000 in this case is "dead money" from the firm's standpoint. Under the minimum average, however, the balance could fall to zero one day provided it was $200,000 some other day, with the average working out to $100,000. Thus, the $100,000 in this case is available for transactions.

The minimum average balance technique is the one used to measure maintenance and compensating balances in Canada. In the U.S., the absolute minimum technique has been used, albeit sparingly, during periods of extremely high interest rates.

Minimum Cash Balance

The firm's minimum cash balance is set as the larger of (1) its transactions balances plus precautionary balances (that is, safety stocks) or (2) its required maintenance plus compensating balances. Statistics are not available on which factor is more important, but the Canadian and U.S. experience suggests that maintenance and compensating balance requirements generally dominate.[7]

---

[5]Banks are compensated for services rendered either by maintenance balances or by direct fees.

[6]The interest rate effect of compensating balances is discussed further in Chapter 9.

[7]This point is underscored by an incident that occurred at a professional finance meeting. A professor presented a scholarly paper that used operations research techniques to determine "optimal cash balances" for a sample of firms. He then reported that actual cash balances of the firms greatly exceeded their "optimal" balances, suggesting inefficiency and the need for more refined techniques. The discussant of the paper made her comments short and sweet. She reported that she wrote and asked the sample firms why they had so much cash; they uniformly replied that their cash holdings were set by compensating balance requirements. The model was useful to determine the optimal cash balance in the absence of

Overdraft System

Canada is one of a number of countries in which the banks use an overdraft system. In such a system, a depositer writes cheques in excess of the balance, and the bank automatically extends a loan to cover any shortage. The maximum amount of such loans and the interest cost of this line of credit must, of course, be established ahead of time. Since there are no maintenance or compensating balances in the account, the bank will charge a higher rate on the overdraft loan than on an equivalent loan to a company that has these balances.

MARKETABLE SECURITIES

Firms sometimes report sizable amounts of such short-term marketable securities as Treasury bills or bank certificates of deposit among their current assets. Why might marketable securities be held? The two primary reasons —as a substitute for cash and as a temporary investment—are considered in this section.

Substitute for Cash

Some firms hold portfolios of marketable securities in lieu of larger cash balances, liquidating part of the portfolio to increase the cash account when cash outflows exceed inflows. Data are not available to indicate the extent of this practice, but our impression is that it is not common. Most firms prefer to let their banks maintain such liquid reserves, with the firms themselves borrowing to meet temporary cash shortages.

Temporary Investment

In addition to using marketable securities as a buffer against cash shortages, firms also hold them on a strictly temporary basis. Firms engaged in seasonal operations, for example, frequently have surplus cash flows during part of the year, deficit cash flows during other months. (See Table 6–1 for an example.) Such firms may purchase marketable securities during their surplus periods, then liquidate them when cash deficits occur. Other firms, particularly in capital goods industries, where fluctuations are violent, attempt to accumulate cash or near-cash securities during a downturn in order to be ready to finance an upturn in business volume.

Firms also accumulate liquid assets to meet predictable financial requirements. For example, if a major modernization program is planned for the near

(continued from page 172)
compensating balance requirements, but it was precisely those requirements that determined actual balances. Since the model did not include compensating balances as a determinant of cash balances, its usefulness is questionable,

future, or if a bond issue is about to mature, the marketable securities portfolio may be increased to provide the required funds. Furthermore, marketable securities holdings are frequently large immediately preceding quarterly corporate tax payment dates.

Firms may also accumulate resources as a protection against a number of contingencies. When they make uninsurable product warranties, companies must be ready to meet any claims that may arise. Firms in highly competitive industries must have resources to carry them through substantial shifts in the market structure. A firm in an industry in which new markets are emerging—for example, foreign markets—needs to have resources to meet developments; these funds may be on hand for fairly long periods.

Criteria Used in Selecting Security Portfolios

Different types of securities, varying in risk of default, marketability, and length of maturity, are available. We will discuss some of the characteristics of these securities, and the criteria that are applied in choosing among them, here.

Risk of Default   The firm's liquidity portfolio is generally held for a specific, known need; if it should depreciate in value, the firm would be financially embarrassed. Further, most nonfinancial corporations do not have investment departments specializing in appraising securities and determining the probability of their going into default. Accordingly, the marketable securities portfolio is generally confined to securities with a minimal risk of default. However, the lowest risk securities also provide the lowest returns, so safety is bought at the expense of yield.

Marketability   The security portfolio is usually held to provide liquid reserves or to meet known needs at a specific time. In either case, the firm must be able to sell its holdings and realize cash on short notice. Accordingly, the securities held in the portfolio must be readily marketable.

Maturity   We shall see in Chapter 18 that the price of a long-term bond fluctuates much more with changes in interest rates than does the price of a similar short-term security. Further, as we saw in the last chapter, interest rates fluctuate widely over time. These two factors combine to make long-term bonds riskier than short-term securities for a firm's marketable security portfolio. However, partly because of this risk differential, higher yields are more frequently available on long-term than on short-term securities, so again risk-return tradeoffs must be recognized.

However, looking exclusively at the maturities of the securities held in this portfolio is not sufficient to determine the risk exposure. The other element that must be considered is the length of time that the funds will be invested.

Typically, funds are invested in marketable securities when they are temporarily not required for company operations. If the securities purchased have a maturity that is shorter than the time period over which the funds are idle, the firm is incurring the risk that the funds may have be re-invested at lower interest rates. Conversely, if the maturities of the securities are longer than this time period, there is risk that interest rates may increase and the securities will have to be liquidated when needed at reduced market values. These risks will be minimized only when the maturities of the securities purchased are equal to the time period for which the funds are surplus — this is known as a hedging or matching strategy. Since companies use their funds that are surplus for the short-term, the portfolios are generally composed of short-term securities.

Investment Alternatives

The main investment alternatives open to business firms are given in Table 8 - 1. Rates available on Government of Canada securities range from 7.24 percent on 90 day bills to 9.11 percent on 18 year bonds. High quality corporate issues range from approximately 7.4 percent on commercial paper and bankers' acceptances to 9.3 — 9.7 percent on long-term debt. Yields on common shares (discussed in Chapter 18) are too uncertain to warrant inclusion in the table.

TABLE 8 - 1   Alternative Marketable Securities for Investment

Money Market Securities	Approximate Maturities December 3, 1977	Approximate Yields to Maturity December 3, 1977
Treasury bills	90 days	7.24%
Treasury bills	182 days	7.39
Commercial paper	90 days	7.45
Bankers' acceptances	90 days	7.40
Government of Canada bonds	1 year	7.69
Government of Canada bonds	6 years	8.03
Government of Canada bonds	18 years	9.11
Government of Ontario bonds	20 years	9.11
Government of Quebec bonds	18 years	9.86
Corporate bonds — prime quality	16 - 18 years	9.3 - 9.7

Source: *The Financial Post,* December 3, 1977.

Depending on how long it is anticipated holding the funds, the financial manager decides upon a suitable maturity pattern for the holdings. The numerous alternatives can be selected and balanced in such a way that the manager obtains the maturities and risks appropriate to the financial situation of the firm. Commercial bankers, investment dealers, and brokers provide the

financial manager with detailed information on each of the forms of investments in the list. Because their characteristics change with shifts in financial
market conditions, it would be misleading to attempt to give detailed descriptions of these investment outlets here. The financial manager must keep up
to date on these characteristics, and should follow the principle of making
investment selections that offer maturities, yields, and risks appropriate to the
firm.

MANAGEMENT OF ACCOUNTS RECEIVABLE: CREDIT POLICY

The level of accounts receivable is determined by (1) the volume of credit
sales and (2) the average period between sales and collections. The average
collection period is partially dependent upon economic conditions—during
a recession or a period of extremely tight money, customers may be forced
to delay payment—but it is also dependent upon a set of controllable factors,
or *credit policy variables.* The major policy variables include (1) *credit standards,* or the maximum riskiness of acceptable credit accounts; (2) *credit
period,* or the length of time for which credit is granted; (3) *discounts* given
for early payment; and (4) the firm's *collection policy.* We first discuss each
policy variable separately and in qualitative rather than quantitative terms;
then we illustrate the interaction of these elements and discuss the actual
establishment of a firm's credit policy.

Credit Standards

If a firm makes credit sales to only the strongest of customers, it will never
have bad debt losses, and it will not incur much in the way of expenses for a
credit department. On the other hand, it will probably be losing sales, and the
profit foregone on these lost sales could be far larger than the costs it has
avoided. Determining the optimal credit standard involves equating the marginal costs of credit to the marginal profits on the increased sales.

Marginal costs include production and selling costs, but we may abstract
from these at this point and consider only those costs associated with the
"quality" of the marginal accounts, or *credit quality costs.* These costs include
(1) default, or bad debt losses; (2) higher investigation and collection costs;
and (3) if less credit-worthy customers delay payment longer than stronger
customers, higher costs of capital tied up in receivables.

Since credit costs and credit quality are correlated, it is important to be
able to judge the quality of an account. First, how should we define "quality"?
Perhaps the best way is in terms of the probability of default. These probability
estimates are, for the most part, subjective estimates, but credit rating is a

well-established practice, and a good credit manager can make reasonably accurate judgments of the probability of default by different classes of customers.

To evaluate the credit risk, credit managers consider the five C's of credit: character, capacity, capital, collateral, conditions. *Character* refers to the probability that a customer will *try* to honor his obligations. This factor is of considerable importance, because every credit transaction implies a *promise* to pay. Will the creditor make an honest effort to pay his debts, or is he likely to try to get away with something? Experienced credit men frequently insist that the moral factor is the most important issue in a credit evaluation.

Capacity is a subjective judgment of the ability of the customer. This is gauged by his past record, supplemented by physical observation of the customer's plant or store and business methods. *Capital* is measured by the general financial position of the firm as indicated by a financial ratio analysis, with special emphasis on the tangible net worth of the enterprise. *Collateral* is represented by assets that the customer may offer as a pledge for security of the credit extended to him. Finally, *conditions* refer to the impact of general economic trends on the firm or to special developments in certain areas of the economy that may affect the customer's ability to meet his obligations.

The five C's of credit represent the factors by which the credit risk is judged. Information on these items is obtained from the firm's previous experience with the customer, supplemented by a well-developed system of information-gathering groups. Two major sources of external information are available. The first is the work of the credit associations. By periodic meetings of local groups and by correspondence, information on experience with debtors is exchanged. For example, Credit Bureau Inc. assembles and distributes information of debtors' past performance. The reports show the paying record of the debtors and the industries from which they have bought.

The second source of external information is the work of the credit-reporting agencies, the best known of which is Dun & Bradstreet. Agencies that specialize in coverage of a limited number of industries also provide information. These agencies provide factual data that can be used by the credit manager in credit analysis; they also provide ratings similar to those on corporate bonds. An informal method of obtaining credit information is through the firm's bank. The bank can contact the bank of the potential debtor and obtain information on the loans outstanding and the bank's experience with the company in question.

An individual firm can translate its credit information into risk classes, grouped according to the probability of loss associated with sales to a customer. The combination of rating and supplementary information might lead to the following groupings of loss experience.

Risk Class Number	Loss Ratio (in percentages)
1	None
2	0–½
3	½–1
4	1–2
5	2–5
6	5–10
7	10–20
8	over 20

If the selling firm has a 20 percent margin over the sum of direct operating costs and all delivery and selling costs, and if it is producing at less than full capacity, it may adopt the following credit policies. It may sell on customary credit terms to groups 1 to 5; sell to groups 6 and 7 under more stringent credit terms, such as cash on delivery; and require advance payments from group 8. As long as the bad debt loss ratios are less than 20 percent, the additional sales are contributing something to overhead.

Statistical techniques, especially regression analysis and discriminant analysis,[8] have been used with some success in judging credit worthiness. These methods work best when individual credits are relatively small and a large number of borrowers are involved. Thus, they have worked best in retail credit, consumer loans, mortgage lending, and the like. As the increase in credit cards and similar procedures builds up, as computers are used more frequently, and as credit records on individuals and small firms are developed, statistical techniques promise to become much more important than they are today.[9]

Terms of Credit

The terms of credit specify the period for which credit is extended and the discount, if any, given for early payment. For example, as we saw earlier, if a firm's credit terms to all approved customers are stated as "2/10, net 30," then a 2 percent discount from the stated sales price is granted if payment is made within ten days, and the entire amount is due thirty days from the invoice date if the discount is not taken. If the terms are stated "net 60," this indicates that no discount is offered and that the bill is due and payable sixty days after the invoice date.

[8]Discriminant analysis is similar to multiple regression analysis, except that it partitions a sample into two components on the basis of a set of characteristics. The sample, for example, might be loan applicants at a consumer loan company. The components into which they are classified might be those likely to make prompt repayment and those likely to default. The characteristics might be such factors as whether the applicant owns his home, how long he has been with his employer, and so forth.

[9]It has been said that the biggest single deterrent to the increased automation of credit processes is George Orwell's classic book, *1984,* in which he described the social dangers of centralized files of information on individuals.

If sales are seasonal, a firm may use seasonal datings. For example, Garfields Limited, a Toronto based manufacturer of lady's knitwear, produces a line of clothes for each season. The spring line, for example, would be shipped in mid to late December on terms of "net 30, February 1 dating". This means that the effective invoice date is February 1, so that the full amount of the invoice must be paid at the end of February regardless of when the shipment was made. The use of seasonal dating results in short-run financing of the retailer's inventories by Garfields but there are some important benefits. Since the merchandise is shipped to the retailer sooner, there is a reduction in Garfields' storage costs. In addition, the early shipment allows the retailer to provide a complete display of the merchandise earlier in the season; this should have a beneficial effect on sales.

If sales are seasonal, a firm may use seasonal datings. Jensen, Inc., a bathing suit manufacturer, sells on terms of "2/10, net 30, May 1 dating." This means that the effective invoice date is May 1, so the discount may be taken until May 10, or the full amount must be paid on May 30, regardless of when the sale was made. Jensen produces output throughout the year, but retail sales of bathing suits are concentrated in the spring and early summer. Because of its practice of offering seasonal datings, Jensen induces some customers to stock up early, saving Jensen storage costs and also "nailing down sales."

Credit Period   Lengthening the credit period stimulates sales, but there is a cost to tying up funds in receivables. For example, if a firm changes its terms from net 30 to net 60, the average receivables for the year might rise from $100,000 to $300,000, with the increase caused partly by the longer credit terms and partly by the larger volume of sales. If the cost of capital needed to finance the investment in receivables is 8 percent, then the marginal cost of lengthening the credit period is $16,000 (= $200,000 × 8 percent). If the incremental profit (sales price minus all direct production, selling, and credit costs associated with the additional sales) exceeds $16,000, then the change in credit policy is profitable. Determining the optimal credit period involves locating that period where marginal profits on increased sales are exactly offset by the costs of carrying the higher amount of accounts receivable.

Cash Discounts   The effect of granting cash discounts may be analyzed similarly to the credit period. For example, if a firm changes its terms from "net 30" to "2/10, net 30," it may well attract customers who want to take discounts, thereby increasing gross sales. Also, the average collection period will be shortened, as some old customers will pay more promptly to take advantage of the discount. Offsetting these benefits is the cost of the discounts taken. The optimal discount is established at the point where costs and benefits are exactly offsetting.

Collection Policy

Collection policy refers to the procedures the firm follows to obtain payment of past-due accounts. For example, a letter may be sent to such accounts when the account is ten days past due; a more severe letter, followed by a telephone call, may be used if payment is not received within thirty days; and the account may be turned over to a collection agency after ninety days.

The collection process can be expensive in terms of both out-of-pocket expenditures and lost goodwill, but at least some firmness is needed to prevent an undue lengthening in the collection period and to minimize outright losses. Again, a balance must be struck between the costs and benefits of different collection policies.

Accounts Receivable versus Accounts Payable

Whenever goods are sold on credit, two accounts are created—an asset item entitled an *account receivable* appears on the books of the selling firm, and a liability item called an *account payable* appears on the books of the purchaser. At this point, we are analyzing the transaction from the viewpoint of the seller, so we have concentrated on the type of variables under his control. In Chapter 9, we will examine the transaction from the viewpoint of the purchaser. There we will discuss accounts payable as a source of funds and consider the cost of these funds vis-à-vis funds obtained from other sources.

Establishing a Credit Policy: An Illustration

Some profitability aspects of establishing a credit policy are illustrated in the following case example. The Wales Company is considering changes in its credit policies. A proposal has been made to relax these policies in order to increase sales and to expand the allowable discount terms in order to keep the investment in receivables unchanged.[10] The company has annual sales of $2.4 million under the present credit policy. Under a liberalized credit policy, sales will increase to $3 million; but the average collection period will increase from one to two months. The unit selling price is $10 and the unit variable cost $7. The firm's required return on investment is 20 percent. The change in discount policy will bring the collection period back to one month. Should the firm make the changes proposed?

In developing a solution, one issue that has to be faced is whether the investment in the additional receivables should be carried at the cost of investment as measured variable costs or at the sales value of the goods on which collections have not been made. There are two grounds for using the sales value. The first is that the alternative to having receivables is to have made the

---

[10]This example is based on Tirlochan S. Walia, "Explicit and Implicit Cost of Changes in the Level of Accounts Receivable," *Financial Management* Winter 1977, pp. 75-78. Other points not directly related to the discussion are found in two other papers in the same issue by Edward Dyl and by Joseph Atkins and Yong Kim.

sales. If the sales are made, they will necessarily be at sales value. While the actual costs are less than the sales value, the opportunity cost must include the sales value that has been lost by having the receivables. The second ground is that on a change in credit policy that results in collections instead of funds tied up in receivables, the increase in cash flow that otherwise would not occur is the actual cash sales receipts. Thus, in solving the problem, the lack of symmetry if sales value is not used will result in different answers depending whether the problem is solved in two steps or combined so that only the net change in receivables is considered. Under the correct procedure, the answer will be the same whether solved in two steps or one. The correct procedure with two steps is shown in Table 8 – 2.

TABLE 8 – 2   Two Analyses of Credit Policy Changes

	Existing Policy	Liberalized Policy
Annual sales	$2,400,000	$3,000,000
Additional sales	—	$ 600,000
Additional profits	—	$ 180,000 (0.3 × $600,000)
Level of receivables	$ 200,000	$ 500,000
Additional receivables	—	$ 300,000
Opportunity cost of additional receivables	—	$ 60,000 (0.2 × $300,000)
Net profit		$ 120,000

	Liberalized Policy	Discount Policy
Annual sales	$3,000,000	$3,000,000
Level of receivables	$ 500,000	$ 250,000
Reduction in receivables	—	$ 250,000
Return on funds released	—	$ 50,000 (0.2 × $250,000)
Cost of discount	—	$ 30,000 (0.02 × 0.5 × $3,000,000)
Net profit		$ 20,000

Each of the two changes in policy results in a gain to the firm. The liberalized credit policy adds $120,000 to net profits, and the change in discount policy adds $20,000 to net profits. The total benefit from the two policy changes is $140,000. Table 8 – 3 shows the calculations needed when the two policy changes are made simultaneously.

The effect of changing directly from the existing credit policy to an easier credit policy with a new discount policy is to increase annual net profits by $140,000. This is the same as when the two credit policy changes were considered in sequence. Thus, when a firm formulates a policy that shifts cash collections to receivables, the opportunity cost involved is the cash sales that otherwise would have increased cash inflows; and the relevant cost requires a consideration of the opportunity cost, not just the explicit cost of the additional investment in increased receivables.

Table 8 – 3   One-Step Analysis of Credit Policy Changes

	Existing Policy	Discount Policy
Annual sales	$2,400,000	$3,000,000
Additional sales	—	$ 600,000
Additional profits	—	$ 180,000 (0.3 × $600,000)
Level of receivables	$ 200,000	$ 250,000
Additional receivables	—	$ 50,000
Opportunity cost of additional receivables	—	$ 10,000 (0.2 × $50,000)
Cost of discount	—	$ 30,000 (0.02 × 0.5 × $3,000,000)
Net profit	—	$ 140,000

This kind of analysis requires that some very difficult judgments be made. Estimating the changes in sales and costs associated with changes in credit policies is, to say the least, a highly uncertain business. Second, even if the sales and cost estimates are reasonably accurate, there is no assurance that some other credit policy would not be even better. For instance, an easy credit policy that involved a different mix of the four policy variables might be superior to the one examined in Tables 8 – 2 and 8 – 3.

For both these reasons, firms usually move slowly toward optimal credit policies. One or two credit variables are changed slightly, the effect of the changes is observed, and a decision is made to change these variables even more or to retract them. Further, different credit policies are appropriate at different times, depending on economic conditions. Thus, credit policy is not a static, once-for-all-time decision. Rather, it is fluid, dynamic, and ever changing in its effort to reach a continually moving optimal target.

INVENTORY

Manufacturing firms generally have three kinds of inventories: (1) raw materials, (2) work in process, and (3) finished goods. The levels of *raw material inventories* are influenced by anticipated production, seasonality of production, reliability of sources of supply, and efficiency of scheduling purchases and production operations.

Work-in-process inventory is strongly influenced by the length of the production period, which is the time between placing raw material in production and completing the finished product. Inventory turnover can be increased by decreasing the production period. One means of accomplishing this is perfecting engineering techniques to speed up the manufacturing process. Another means of reducing work in process is to buy items rather than make them.

The level of *finished goods inventories* is a matter of coordinating production and sales. The financial manager can stimulate sales by changing credit terms or by allowing credit to marginal risks. Whether the goods remain on the books as inventories or as receivables, the financial manager has to finance them. Many times, firms find it desirable to make the sale and thus take one step nearer to realizing cash. The potential profits can outweigh the additional collection risk.

Our primary focus in this section is control of investment in inventories. *Inventory models* have been developed as an aid in this task and have proved extremely useful in minimizing inventory requirements. As our examination of the du Pont system in Chapter 3 showed, any procedure that can reduce the investment required to generate a given sales volume may have a beneficial effect on the firm's rate of return and hence on the value of the firm.

DETERMINANTS OF THE SIZE OF INVENTORIES

Although wide variations occur, inventory-to-sales ratios are generally concentrated in the 12-to-30 percent range, and inventory-to-total assets ratios are concentrated in the 16-to-30 percent range.

The major determinants of investment in inventory are the following: (1) level of sales, (2) length and technical nature of the production processes, and (3) durability versus perishability, or style factor, in the end product. Inventories in the tobacco industry, for example, are high because of the long curing process. Similarly, in the machinery-manufacturing industries, inventories are large because of the long work-in-process period. However, inventory ratios are low in coal mining and in oil and gas production because no raw materials are used and the goods in process are small in relation to sales. Because of the seasonality of the raw materials, average inventories are large in the canning industry.

With respect to durability and style factors, large inventories are found in the hardware and the precious-metals industries because durability is great and the style factor is small. Inventory ratios are low in baking because of the perishability of the final product. Inventories are low in printing because the items are manufactured to order and require negligible finished inventories.

Within limits set by the economics of a firm's industry, there exists a potential for improvement in inventory control from the use of computers and operations research. Although the techniques are far too diverse and complicated for a complete treatment in this text, the financial manager should be prepared to make use of the contributions of specialists who have developed effective procedures for minimizing the investment in inventory.

Illustrative of the techniques at this practical level is Esbe Scientific's inventory system. Since Esbe is a distributor of scientific equipment and laboratory supplies — it has upwards of 9,000 items — its investment in inventories is an important decision. The inventory system works in the following manner: upon the arrival of an order, a clerk processes the order and enters the customer's name, order number and quantities required. The computer keeps track of the number of units of each product still in inventory and compares this with the order point. When an order draws the stock below the order point, an entry is automatically triggered into the re-order file.

An interesting feature of this system is the ability to reserve certain products for customers who are on contract and have a standing order or periodic releases. This feature provides these customers with first claim on the particular product.

The computer system also has the added benefit of permitting analysis and control of inventories and sales. Products are ordered in batches and the cost of each batch is retained in the computer until the last unit associated with a batch is used; at this point the batch cost is deleted. In addition, sales by product and product group can be calculated for analytical purposes.

In the next section, we will investigate the optimal order point and the number of units that should be ordered from a distributor or manufactured by a producing company; this order size is called the economic ordering quantity (EOQ).

GENERALITY OF INVENTORY ANALYSIS

Managing assets of all kinds is basically an inventory problem—the same method of analysis applies to cash and fixed assets as applies to inventories themselves. First, a basic stock must be on hand to balance inflows and outflows of the items, with the size of the stock depending upon the patterns of flows, whether regular or irregular. Second, because the unexpected may always occur, it is necessary to have safety stocks on hand. They represent the little extra to avoid the costs of not having enough to meet current needs. Third, additional amounts may be required to meet future growth needs. These are anticipation stocks. Related to anticipation stocks is the recognition that there are optimum purchase sizes, defined as *economic ordering quantities.* In borrowing money, in buying raw materials for production, or in purchasing plants and equipment, it is cheaper to buy more than just enough to meet immediate needs.

With the foregoing as a basic foundation, we can develop the theoretical basis for determining the optimal investment in inventory, which is illustrated in Figure 8–1. Some costs rise with larger inventories—among these are warehousing costs, interest on funds tied up in inventories, insurance, obsolescence, and so forth. Other costs decline with larger inventories—these include the loss of profits resulting from sales lost because of running out of stock, costs of production interruptions caused by inadequate inventories, possible purchase discounts, and so on.

FIGURE 8 – 1 Determination of Optimum Investment in Inventory

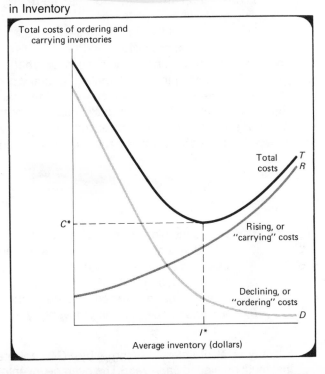

The costs that decline with higher inventories are designated by curve D in Figure 8–1; those that rise with larger inventories are designated by curve R. Curve T is the total of the R and D curves, and it represents the total cost of ordering and holding inventories. At the point where the absolute value of the slope of the R curve is equal to the absolute value of the slope of the D curve (that is, where *marginal* rising costs are equal to *marginal* declining costs), the T curve is at a minimum. This represents the optimum size of investment in inventory.

INVENTORY DECISION MODELS

The generalized statements in the preceding section can be made much more specific. In fact, it is usually possible to specify the curves shown in Figure 8–1, at least to a reasonable approximation, and actually to find the minimum point on the total cost curve. Since entire courses (in operations research programs) are devoted to inventory control techniques, and since a number of books have been written on the subject, we obviously cannot deal with inventory decision models in a very complete fashion. The model we illustrate, however, is probably more widely used—even by quite sophisticated firms—than any other, and it can be readily expanded to encompass any refinements one cares to make.

The costs of holding inventories—the cost of capital tied up, storage costs, insurance, depreciation, and so on—rise as the size of inventory holdings increases. Conversely, the cost of ordering inventories—the cost of placing orders, shipping and handling, quantity discounts lost, and so on—falls as the average inventory increases. The total cost of inventories is the summation of these rising and declining costs, or the *T* curve in Figure 8–1. It has been shown that, under reasonable assumptions, the minimum point on the *T* curve can be found by an equation called the EOQ formula:

$$EOQ = \sqrt{\frac{2FS}{CP}}.$$

Here

EOQ = the economic ordering quantity, or the optimum quantity to be ordered each time an order is placed.
F = fixed costs of placing and receiving an order.
S = annual sales in units.
C = carrying cost expressed as a percentage of inventory value.
P = purchase price per unit of inventory.

For any level of sales, dividing *S* by *EOQ* indicates the number of orders that must be placed each year. The average inventory on hand—the average balance sheet inventory figure—will be

$$\text{Average inventory} = \frac{EOQ}{2}.$$

The derivation of the EOQ model assumes (1) that usage is at a constant rate and (2) that delivery lead times are constant. In fact, usage is likely to vary considerably for most firms—demand may be unexpectedly strong for any number of reasons; if it is, the firm will run out of stock and will suffer sales losses or production stoppages. Similarly, delivery lead times will vary depending on weather, strikes, demand in the suppliers' industries, and so on. Because of these factors, firms add *safety stocks* to their inventory holdings, and the average inventory becomes

$$\text{Average inventory} = \frac{EOQ}{2} + \text{safety stock}.$$

The size of the safety stock will be relatively high if uncertainties about usage rates and delivery times are great, low if these factors do not vary greatly.[11]

[11] In the case of Esbe Scientific, certain products must be ordered from European manufacturers. Due to

Similarly, the safety stock will be larger if the costs of running out of stock are great. For example, if customer ill will would cause a permanent loss of business or if an elaborate production process would have to stop if an item were out of stock, then large safety stocks will be carried.[12]

USE OF EOQ MODEL: AN ILLUSTRATION

Let us assume that the following values are determined to be appropriate for a particular firm:

S = sales = 100 units.
C = carrying cost = 20 percent of inventory value.
P = purchase price = $1 per unit.
F = fixed cost of ordering = $10.

Substituting these values into the formula, we obtain

$$EOQ = \sqrt{\frac{2FS}{CP}}$$

$$= \sqrt{\frac{2 \times 10 \times 100}{0.2 \times 1}} = \sqrt{\frac{2000}{0.2}} = \sqrt{10,000}$$

$$= 100 \text{ units.}$$

If the desired safety stock is 10 units, then the average inventory (A) will be

$$A = \frac{EOQ}{2} + \text{safety stock}$$

$$= \frac{100}{2} + 10$$

$$= 60 \text{ units.}$$

Since the cost of purchasing or manufacturing inventory is $1 a unit, the average inventory in dollars will be $60 for this item.

Effects of Inflation on EOQ

During inflation, formal models such as the EOQ may lose applicability. As freight costs rise, the cost of placing an order may increase rapidly. Purchase prices may also rise abruptly and repeatedly. Therefore, the values used in the EOQ equation may not remain constant for any appreciable length of time. If

(continued from page 187)
the vicissitudes of the delivery systems, among other reasons, the delivery times may be very long. For these products, a large inventory would be important since an unexpected stock-out could not be met in the short-run.

[12]Formal methods have been developed to assist in striking a balance between the costs of carrying larger safety stocks and the cost of stock-outs (inventory shortages). A discussion of these models, whicn go beyond the scope of this book, can be found in most production textbooks.

so, the optimal order quantity will not remain fixed. Some companies will need greater flexibility in the timing of their orders than that afforded by the "automatic order point". This is because they may be able to buy marginal production at reduced prices. Also, certain companies may stockpile inventories. This takes advantage of the opportunity to purchase supplies before major price increases and provides protection against shortages. Therefore, during periods of inflation and tight money, a firm may need more flexible inventory management as it attempts to take advantage of bargains and to provide for future contingencies. The basic logic of the inventory model remains intact: some costs will rise with larger inventories, and others will fall. Although an optimum is still there to be found, it may change and require repeated discovery.

CASH MANAGEMENT AS AN INVENTORY PROBLEM

In our cash budgeting discussion in Chapter 6, we indicated that firms generally have minimum desired cash balances. Then, in discussing cash management, we considered the various factors that influence cash holdings. We did not, however, attempt to specify optimum cash balances, which can be found by the use of inventory type models such as those discussed above. Cash management, together with inventory controls, is the area of financial management where mathematical tools have proved most useful.

Sophisticated cash management models recognize the uncertainty inherent in forecasting both cash inflows and cash outflows. Inflows are represented, in effect, by the orders in our inventory model; they come principally from receipts, borrowing, and sales of securities. The primary carrying cost of cash is the opportunity cost of having funds tied up in non-earning assets (or in low-yielding near-cash items); the principal ordering costs are brokerage costs associated with borrowing funds or converting marketable securities into cash.

SUMMARY

In this chapter we focused attention on four types of current assets—cash, marketable securities, accounts receivable, and inventories. First, we examined the motives for holding cash and ways of minimizing the investment in cash. With this background, we considered the minimum cash balances a firm is likely to hold. This minimum will be the higher (1) of compensating plus maintenance balance requirements or (2) of transactions balances plus a safety stock.

Marketable securities are held as a substitute for "cash safety stocks" and as temporary investments while the firm is awaiting permanent investment of funds. "Safety stocks" are almost always held in low-risk, short-maturity securities; temporary investments are held in securities whose maturity depends upon the length of time before the funds are permanently employed.

The investment in accounts receivable is dependent (1) upon sales and (2) upon the firm's credit policy. The credit policy, in turn, involves four controllable variables: credit standards, the length of the credit period, cash discounts, and the collection policy. The significant aspect of credit policy is its effect on sales: an easy credit policy will stimulate sales but involves costs of capital tied up in receivables, bad debts, discounts, and higher collection costs. The optimal credit policy is one in which these costs are just offset by the profits on sales generated by the credit policy change.

Inventories—raw materials, work in process, and finished goods—are necessary in most businesses. Rather elaborate systems for controlling the level of inventories have been designed. These systems frequently use computers for keeping records of all the items in stock; an inventory control model that considers anticipated sales, ordering costs, and carrying costs can be used to determine EOQ's for each item.

The basic inventory model recognizes that certain costs (carrying costs) rise as average inventory holdings increase but that certain other costs (ordering costs and stock-out costs) fall as average inventory holdings rise. These two sets of costs make up the total cost of ordering and carrying inventories, and the EOQ model is designed to locate an optimal order size that will minimize total inventory costs.

QUESTIONS

8-1. How can better methods of communication reduce the necessity for firms to hold large cash balances?

8-2. "The highly developed financial system of Canada, with its myriad of different near-cash assets, has greatly reduced cash balance requirements by reducing the need for transactions balances." Discuss this statement.

8-3. Would you expect a firm with a high growth rate to hold fewer precautionary and speculative cash balances than a firm with a low growth rate? Explain.

8-4. Many firms that find themselves with temporary surplus cash invest these funds in Treasury bills. Since Treasury bills frequently have the lowest yield of any investment security, why are they chosen as investments?

8-5. Assume that a firm sells on terms of net 30 and that its accounts are, on the average, thirty days overdue. What will its investment in receivables be if its annual credit sales are approximately $720,000?

8-6. "It is difficult to judge the performance of many of our employees but not that of the credit manager. If he's performing perfectly, credit losses are zero; and the higher our losses (as a percent of sales), the worse his performance." Evaluate this statement.

8-7. Explain how a firm may reduce its investment in inventory by having its supplier hold raw materials inventories and its customers hold finished goods inventories. What are the limitations of such a policy?

8-8. What factors are likely to reduce the holdings of inventory in relation to sales in the future? What factors will tend to increase the ratio? What, in your judgment, is the net effect?

8-9. What are the probable effects of the following on inventory holdings?

   a. Manufacture of a part formerly purchased from an outside supplier.

   b. Greater use of air freight.

   c. Increase, from seven to seventeen, in the number of styles produced.

   d. Large price reductions to your firm from a manufacturer of bathing suits if the suits are purchased in December and January.

8-10. Inventory decision models are designed to help minimize the cost of obtaining and carrying inventory. Describe the basic nature of the fundamental inventory control model, discussing specifically the nature of increasing costs, decreasing costs, and total costs. Illustrate your discussion with a graph.

PROBLEMS

8-1. Hayes Associates Ltd. is short on cash and is attempting to determine if it would be advantageous for them to forego the discount on this month's purchases or to borrow funds to take advantage of the discount. The discount terms are 2/10, net 45. What is the maximum annual interest rate that Hayes Associates should pay on borrowed funds? Why? What are some of the intangible disadvantages associated with foregoing discount?

8-2. Scott, Ltd. currently has a centralized billing system located in Toronto. However, over the years their customers have gradually become less concentrated and now cover the whole country. On average, it requires five days from the time customers mail payments until Scott is able to receive, process, and deposit their payments. To shorten this time lag, Scott is considering installing a lock-box collection system. They estimate that they will be able to reduce the time lag from customer mailing to deposit by three and one-half days. Scott has a daily average collection of $700,000.

   a. What reduction in cash balances can Scott achieve by initiating the lock-box system?

   b. If Scott has an opportunity cost of 8 percent, how much is the lock-box system worth on an annual basis?

   c. What is the maximum monthly charge Scott can pay for the lock-box system?

8-3. Standard Distributors, whose sales are on a credit basis, makes a routine credit evaluation of all its customers at least once each year. It finds that this procedure allows it to rank its customers in categories from 1 to 5, in order of increasing risk. On the basis of past experience, the firm has found the following bad debt loss percentage and average collection period on the accounts in each category:

Category	Percentage Bad Debts	Average Collection Period
1	None	10 days
2	0.5	12
3	2.0	20
4	5.0	30
5	10.0	60

The firm's current credit policy is to extend unlimited credit to firms in categories 1 to 3, limited credit to firms in category 4, and no more credit to firms in category 5.

The result of this policy is that orders totaling $250,000 from category 4 firms and $750,000 from category 5 firms are turned down each year. If the firm makes a 9 percent gross profit margin on sales (gross profit on sales = sales less cost of goods sold) and has an opportunity cost on investments in receivables of 9 percent, what would be the net effect on profits of extending full credit to category 4? to category 5?

8-4. A firm issues cheques in the amount of $1 million each day and deducts them from its own records at the close of business on the day they are written. On average, the bank receives and clears (that is, deducts from the firm's bank balance) the cheques the evening of the fourth day after they are written; for example, a cheque written on Monday will be cleared on Friday afternoon. The firm's loan agreement with the bank requires it to maintain a $750,000 minimum average compensating balance; this is $250,000 greater than the cash safety stock the firm would otherwise have on deposit.

    a. Assuming that the firm makes deposits in the late afternoon (and the bank includes the deposit in the day's transactions), how much must the firm deposit each day to maintain a sufficient balance once it reaches a steady state?

    b. How many days of float does the firm carry?

    c. What ending daily balance should the firm try to maintain at the bank and on its own records?

    d. Explain how float can help increase the value of the firm's common stock. Use a partial balance sheet, and the du Pont system concept, in your answer.

8-5. Callaway Electronics Company is considering changing its credit terms from 2/15, net 30, to 3/10, net 45. All its sales are "credit sales," but 75 percent of the customers presently take the 2 percent cash discount; under the new terms this percentage is expected to decline to 65 percent. The average collection period is also expected to change under the new policy, from 17 days at present to 20 days under the new plan. (Note that these averages are heavily weighted with customers who pay within ten days.) Expected sales, before discounts are deducted, are $600,000 with the present terms, but $675,000 if the new terms are used. Assume that (1) Callaway earns a 12 percent profit margin after all costs, including credit costs, on present sales after a change in credit policy, (2) sales will have a 12 percent margin *before* incremental credit-associated costs, and (3) a 5 percent opportunity cost applies to the investment in receivables. Calculate

    a. the increase in gross profits

    b. the increase in discount costs

    c. the increased cost of carrying receivables

    d. the net change in pretax profits.

8-6. The following relations for inventory purchase and storage costs have been established for the Lomer Fabricating Corporation.

    1. Orders must be placed in multiples of 100 units.

    2. Requirements for the year are 300,000 units. (Use 50 weeks in a year for calculations.)

    3. The purchase price per unit is $3.

    4. Carrying cost is 25 percent of the purchase price of goods.

    5. Cost per order placed is $20.00.

    6. Desired safety stock is 10,000 units (on hand initially).

    7. Two weeks are required for delivery.

a. What is the economical order quantity?

b. What is the optimal number of orders to be placed?

c. At what inventory level should a reorder be made?

(Hint: the inventory level should be sufficient to cover the amount used during delivery, plus the safety stock.)

Major Sources and Forms of Short-Term Financing

9

In Chapter 7 we discussed the maturity structure of the firm's debt and showed how this structure can affect both risk and expected returns. However, a variety of short-term credits are available to the firm, and the financial manager must know the advantages and disadvantages of each. Accordingly, in the present chapter we take up the main forms of short-term credit, considering both the characteristics and the sources of this credit.

Short-term credit is defined as *debt originally scheduled for repayment within one year.* We discuss the three major sources of funds with short maturities in this chapter. Ranked in descending order by volume of credit supplied to business, the main sources of short-term financing are (1) trade credit between firms, (2) loans from commercial banks, and (3) commercial paper.

TRADE CREDIT[1]

In the ordinary course of events, a firm buys its supplies and materials on credit from other firms, recording the debt as an *account payable*. Accounts payable, or *trade credit*, as it is commonly called, is the largest single category of short-term credit, and it represents about 40 percent of the current liabilities of nonfinancial corporations. This percentage is somewhat larger for smaller

---

[1]In Chapter 8 we discussed trade credit from the point of view of minimizing investment in current assets. In the present chapter we look at "the other side of the coin," viewing trade credit as a *source* of financing rather than as a *use* of financing. In Chapter 8, the use of trade credit by our customers resulted in an asset investment called *accounts receivable*. In the present chapter, the use of trade credit gives rise to short-term obligations, generally called *accounts payable*.

firms; because small companies may not qualify for financing from other sources, they rely rather heavily on trade credit.

Trade credit is a *spontaneous* source of financing in that it arises from ordinary business transactions. For example, suppose a firm makes average purchases of $2,000 a day on terms of net 30. On the average it will owe 30 times $2,000, or $60,000, to its suppliers. If its sales, and consequently its purchases, double, accounts payable will also double to $120,000. The firm will have spontaneously generated an additional $60,000 of financing. Similarly, if the terms of credit are extended from thirty to forty days, accounts payable will expand from $60,000 to $80,000; thus, lengthening the credit period, as well as expanding sales and purchases, generates additional financing.

Credit Terms

The terms of sale, or *credit terms*, describe the payment obligation of the buyer. In the following discussion we outline the four main factors that influence the length of credit terms.

Economic Nature of Product Commodities with high sales turnover are sold on relatively short credit terms; the buyer resells the product rapidly, generating cash that enables him to pay the supplier. Groceries have a high turnover, but perishability also plays a role. The credit extended for fresh fruits and vegetables might run from five to ten days, whereas the credit extended on canned fruits and vegetables would more likely be fifteen to thirty days. Terms for items that have a slow retail turnover, such as jewelry, may run six months or longer.

Seller Circumstances Financially weak sellers must require cash or exceptionally short credit terms. For example, farmers sell livestock to meat-packing companies on a cash basis. In many industries, variations in credit terms can be used as a sales promotion device. Although the use of credit as a selling device could endanger sound credit management, the practice does occur, especially when the seller's industry has excess capacity. Also, a large seller could use his position to impose relatively short credit terms. However, the reverse appears more often in practice; that is, financially strong sellers are suppliers of funds to small firms.

Buyer Circumstances In general, financially sound retailers who sell on credit may, in turn, receive slightly longer terms. Some classes of retailers regarded as selling in particularly risky areas (such as clothing) receive extended credit terms, but they are offered large discounts to encourage early payment.

Cash Discounts   A cash discount is a reduction in price based on payment within a specified period. The costs of not taking cash discounts often exceed the rate of interest at which the buyer can borrow, so it is important that a firm be cautious in its use of trade credit as a source of financing—it could be quite expensive. If the firm borrows and takes the cash discount, the period during which accounts payable remain on the book is reduced. The effective length of credit is thus influenced by the size of discounts offered.

Illustrative Credit Terms   Credit terms typically express the amount of the cash discount and the date of its expiration, as well as the final due date. Earlier, we noticed that one of the most frequently encountered terms is 2/10, net 30. (If payment is made within ten days of the invoice date, a 2 percent cash discount is allowed. If the cash discount is not taken, payment is due thirty days after the date of invoice.) The cost of not taking cash discounts can be substantial, as shown here.[2]

Credit Terms	Costs of Credit if Cash Discount Not Taken (Percent)
1/10, net 20	36.36
1/10, net 30	18.18
2/10, net 20	73.44
2/10, net 30	36.72

CONCEPT OF "NET CREDIT"

Trade credit has double-edged significance for the firm. It is a source of credit for financing purchases, and it is a use of funds to the extent that the firm finances credit sales to customers. For example, if, on the average, a firm sells $3,000 of goods a day with an average collection period of forty days, at any balance sheet date it will have accounts receivable of approximately $120,000.

If the same firm buys $2,000 worth of materials a day and the balance is outstanding for twenty days, accounts payable will average $40,000. *The firm is extending net credit for $80,000, the difference between accounts receivable and accounts payable.*

Large firms and well-financed firms of all sizes tend to be net suppliers of trade credit; small firms and undercapitalized firms of all sizes tend to be net users of trade credit. It is impossible to generalize about whether it is better to be a net supplier or a net user of trade credit—the choice depends upon the firm's own circumstances and conditions, and the various costs and benefits of receiving and using trade credit must be analyzed as described here and in Chapter 8.

[2]The method of calculating the effective interest rate on accounts payable was described in Chapter 8.

Advantages of Trade Credit as a Source of Financing

Trade credit, a customary part of doing business in most industries, is convenient and informal. A firm that does not qualify for credit from a financial institution may receive trade credit because previous experience has familiarized the seller with the credit-worthiness of his customer. As the seller knows the merchandising practices of the industry, he is usually in a good position to judge the capacity of his customer and the risk of selling to him on credit. The amount of trade credit fluctuates with the buyer's purchases, subject to any credit limits that may be operative.

Whether trade credit costs more or less than other forms of financing is a moot question. Sometimes trade credit can be surprisingly expensive to the buyer. The user often does not have any alternative forms of financing available, and the costs to the buyer will be commensurate with the risks to the seller. But in some instances trade credit is used simply because the user does not realize how expensive it is. In such circumstances, careful financial analysis may lead to the substitution of alternative forms of financing for trade credit.

At the other extreme, trade credit may represent a virtual subsidy or sales promotion device offered by the seller. The authors know, for example, of cases where manufacturers quite literally supplied *all* the financing for new firms by selling on credit terms substantially longer than those of the new company. In one instance a manufacturer, eager to obtain a dealership in a particular area, made a loan to the new company to cover operating expenses during the initial phases and geared the payment of accounts payable to cash receipts. Even in such instances, however, the buying firm must be careful that it is not really paying a hidden financing cost in the form of higher product prices than could be obtained elsewhere. Extending credit involves a cost to the selling firm, and this firm may well be raising its own prices to offset the "free" credit it extends.

SHORT-TERM FINANCING BY COMMERCIAL BANKS

Commercial bank lending appears on the balance sheet as *notes payable* and is second in importance to trade credit as a source of short-term financing. Banks occupy a pivotal position in the short-term and intermediate-term money markets. Their influence is greater than appears from the dollar amounts they lend because the banks provide nonspontaneous funds. As the financing needs of the firm increase, it requests the banks to provide the additional funds. If the request is denied, often the alternative is to slow down the rate of growth or to cut back operations.

Characteristics of Loans from Commercial Banks

In the following sections, the main characteristics of lending patterns of commercial banks are briefly described.

Forms of Loans A bank loan is either a self-liquidating loan, such as the financing of a seasonal build up in inventory, or a loan needed for working capital; the latter loan will not be self-liquidating but must be repaid out of profits. The loan can be secured or unsecured and it has the following characteristics: the interest rate is set at the prime rate, which is the rate of interest given to the bank's prime risks, plus an additional amount which reflects the risk of the particular company. Since the prime rate can fluctuate over time, interest rates charged on loans are also flexible. Repayment of the loan can be made in a lump sum at maturity when the note is due, or in install- ments (i.e. amortized) throughout the life of the loan. Finally, the loan is a demand loan and thus is callable at the option of the bank at any time without penalty. Banks realize the problems that could be caused by the calling of a loan and thus do not use this option very frequently.

A *line of credit* is a formal understanding between the bank and the borrower concerning the maximum loan balance the bank will allow the borrower. For example, a bank loan officer may indicate to a financial manager that the bank regards the firm as "good" for up to $80,000 for the forthcoming year. Subsequently, the manager signs a promissory note for $15,000 for ninety days — he or she is said to be "taking down" $15,000 of the total line of credit. This amount is credited to the firm's chequing account at the bank. Before repayment of the $15,000, the firm may borrow additional amounts up to a total of $80,000. However, there is no legal requirement for the bank to extend credit up to the maximum; each time the firm wants to draw down additional amounts, the bank must agree to extend the additional credit.

Revolving credit, on the other hand, provides the firm with a commitment from the bank to extend credit up to a negotiated maximum amount for a given period of time.

When considering both revolving credit and a line of credit, there are additional fees that can be levied by the bank to increase the return to the bank without increasing the stated interest rate. The first is called a commit- ment fee and it is independent of the amount of credit used; the commitment fee is set at ½ to ¾ of 1 percent on the total line of credit. The second fee is a stand-by fee which is levied as a percent of the unused portion of the credit. In both cases, the fees are to compensate the bank for committing itself to the loan.

Maturity Commercial banks concentrate on the short-term lending market. The bulk of the loans, measured either by dollar volume or number of loans, is short-term. Term loans (loans with maturities longer than one year) have not been very important in the past. However, the chartered banks have been providing these loans to meet the competitive pressures of some foreign banks operating in Canada.

Security Almost all of the loans provided by the Canadian banking system are secured. In some instances, foreign banks will provide unsecured loans. The forms of security are described later in this chapter.

Compensating Balances   On large accounts, banks typically require that a regular borrower maintain an average chequing account balance equal to approximately 10 percent of the monthly usage. These balances, which are called *compensating balances,* are a method of raising the effective interest rate on a loan. For example, if a firm raises $90,000 as a loan, but must maintain a 10 percent compensating balance, it must borrow $100,000 to obtain the required $90,000. If the stated interest rate is 5 percent, the effective interest cost is actually 5.6[3] percent — the $5,000 annual interest cost divided by the amount of the loan, $90,000. These compensating balances are, of course, added to any maintenance balances (discussed in Chapter 8) that the firm's bank may require.

Cost of Commercial Bank Loans   On unsecured loans, the stated interest rate will depend on the risk of the loan being made. For loans to large, stable companies, the banks will charge the prime rate; this has ranged from 11 percent at the end of 1974 to 8.25 percent at the end of August, 1977. The prime rate fluctuates with movements in interest rates on short-term government bonds. If the borrower has more risk than prime risk companies, the interest cost will equal prime plus a specific increment to reflect the risk of the loan. There is little variation in the stated rates on unsecured loans since companies whose operations are risky do not obtain unsecured loans — the loans are either secured or the companies borrow from non-bank financial intermediaries.

The effective cost of unsecured loans is very difficult to calculate. The bank has a number of variables that it can manipulate to influence the true interest cost. For example, the charging of commitment fees, compensating balances, and stand-by fees can be used to alter the effective cost of a loan. Thus, a company may obtain a loan at prime, but the effective cost may be equal to prime plus 3 percent when all of the other fees are considered.

"Regular" Interest   Determination of the effective, or true, rate of interest on a loan depends on the stated rate of interest and the method of charging interest used by the lender. If the interest is paid at the maturity of the loan, the stated rate of interest is the effective rate of interest. For example, on a $10,000 loan for one year at 5 percent, the interest is $500:

$$\text{"Regular" loan, interest paid at maturity:} \quad \frac{\text{interest}}{\text{borrowed amount}} = \frac{\$500}{\$10,000} = 5\%.$$

[3]Note, however, that the compensating balance is generally set as a minimum monthly *average;* if the firm would maintain this average anyway, the compensating balance requirement does not entail higher effective rates.

This method of paying interest is used very infrequently for short-term loans.

Discounted Interest   If the bank deducts the interest in advance (*discounts* the loan), the effective rate of interest is increased. On the $10,000 loan for one year at 5 percent, the discount is $500, and the borrower obtains the use of only $9,500. The effective rate of interest is 5.3 percent versus 5 percent on a "regular" loan:

$$\text{Discounted loan: } \frac{\text{interest}}{\text{borrowed amount} - \text{interest}} = \frac{\$500}{\$9,500} = 5.3\%.$$

Installment Loan   If the loan is repaid in 12 monthly installments but the interest is calculated on the original balance, then the effective rate of interest is even higher. The borrower has the full amount of the money only during the first month, and by the last month he has already paid eleven-twelfths of the loan. Thus our hypothetical borrower pays $500 for the use of about half the amount he receives. The amount received is $10,000 or $9,500, depending upon the method of charging interest, but the *average* amount outstanding during the year is only $5,000 or $4,750. If interest is paid at maturity, the approximate effective rate on an installment loan is calculated as follows:

$$\text{Interest rate on original amount of installment loan } = \frac{\$500}{\$5,000} = 10\%.$$

Under the discounting method, the effective cost of the installment loan would be approximately 10.5 percent:

$$\text{Interest rate on discounted installment loan } = \frac{\$500}{\$4,750} = 10.53\%.$$

Even though this method of calculating interest is not used for business loans, it is presented as an example of the impact on the effective interest cost of a loan as a result of the specific terms of the loan; other examples were commitment fees and compensating balances.

COMMERCIAL PAPER

Commercial paper consists of promissory notes of *large* firms and is sold primarily to other business firms, insurance companies, pension funds, and banks. Although the amounts of commercial paper outstanding are much smaller than bank loans outstanding, this form of financing has grown rapidly in recent years.

The major issuers of commercial paper are the sales finance and consumer loan companies, but non-financial corporations have increased their use of this financing vehicle. From 1971 to 1976, the amount of commercial paper outstanding grew 16 percent a year for the sales finance and consumer loan companies and 13 percent a year for non-financial corporations. At the end of August, 1977, commercial paper outstanding for the former group was $3300 million and $1968 million for the latter.

Commercial paper is traded in the money market by investment dealers who purchase the paper at a discount and then sell it or hold it in inventory. The evolution of an active money market in which trading of a number of short-term negotiable notes takes place was an important condition for the existence of substantial activity in the commercial paper market.

Maturity, Cost and Security

Maturities of commercial paper generally vary from one day to one year, with an average of approximately five months. In addition, commercial paper can be issued on a demand basis. The rates on prime commercial paper vary but are generally about ¼ to 1¼ percent below the prime rate. Since compensating balances are not required for commercial paper, the effective cost differential is still wider.[4]

Non-financial commercial paper is not secured by any property or assets of the issuer. However, the issuer usually has an unused line of credit sufficient to cover the amount of the commercial paper outstanding.

Use

The use of the money market for commercial paper is restricted to a comparatively small number of concerns that are very good credit risks. The proceeds of the issue are used to finance short-term working capital needs for the non-financial corporate user. The paper is issued with a minimum denomination of $50,000 and interest is paid either at a stated rate or on a discount basis.

Appraisal of Use

The commercial paper market has some significant advantages. (1) It permits the broadest and the most advantageous distribution of paper. (2) It provides more funds at lower rates than do other methods. (3) The borrower avoids the inconvenience and expense of financing arrangements with a number of institutions, each of which requires a compensating balance. (4) Publicity and prestige accrue to the borrower as his product and his paper become

---

[4]However, this factor is offset to some extent by the fact that firms issuing commercial paper are sometimes required by commercial paper dealers to have unused bank lines of credit to back up their outstanding commercial paper, and fees must be paid on these lines.

more widely known. (5) The commercial paper dealer frequently offers valuable advice to his clients. (6) Finally, the company has access to funds when financial institutions are restricting the supply of credit.

A basic limitation of the commercial paper market is that the size of the funds available is limited to the excess liquidity that corporations, the main suppliers of funds, may have at any particular time. Another disadvantage is that a debtor who is in temporary financial difficulty receives little consideration because commercial paper dealings are impersonal. Bank relations, on the other hand, are much more personal; a bank is much more likely to help a good customer weather a temporary storm than is a commercial paper dealer.[5]

BANKER'S ACCEPTANCE

A banker's acceptance is a bill of exchange drawn by a borrowing firm on its bank. The bank, by accepting the bill, agrees to pay the amount shown on the bill when it is presented at the bank for payment on the due date. The borrowing corporation takes the bill and sells it to an investment dealer. Since there is no interest rate stated on the bill, the investment dealer will purchase it at a discount. The banker's acceptance, just like commercial paper, will be traded in the money market. Since a banker's acceptance has been considered a loan or an advance, the bank can ask for the normal forms of security to ensure that there will be funds available in the company's account when the banker's acceptance is presented for payment. In addition, the acceptance is considered as part of the line of credit used by the company.

Maturity and Cost

Although the maximum maturity for a banker's acceptance is 180 days, the usual maturity is a maximum of 90 days and a minimum of 30 days. These bills are issued in multiples of $100,000 and a commission, called a stamping fee, of three-quarters of 1 percent of the issue is charged to the borrower by the bank. The effective rate of interest is calculated as the sum of the costs of the issue (i.e. the commission plus the discount on the sale to the investment

---

[5] This point was emphasized dramatically in the aftermath of the Penn-Central bankruptcy in the U.S. Penn-Central has a large amount of commercial paper which went into default and embarrassed corporate treasurers who had been holding the paper as part of their liquidity reserves. Immediately after the bankruptcy, the commercial paper market dried up to a large extent, and some companies that had relied heavily on this market found themselves under severe liquidity pressure as their commercial paper matured and could not be refunded. Chrysler, for example, had to seek bank loans of over $500 million because it could not sell commercial paper for a time. Without adequate bank lines, Chrysler might well have been forced into bankruptcy itself, even though it was basically sound, because of the "Penn-Central panic." Incidentally, the Federal Reserve Board recognized that many other firms would be in the same position as Chrysler, so the Fed expanded bank reserves in order to enable the banking system to take up the slack caused by the withdrawal of funds from the commercial paper market.

dealer) divided by the proceeds obtained by the issuer from the investment dealer.

For example, on a $10,000,000 issue the stamping fee is $75,000. If the interest rate on outstanding acceptances is 8 percent, then the proceeds to the issuer are $9,259,259. The effective interest rate is 8.8 percent. The interest rate on outstanding banker's acceptances is usually ½ to 1 percent below the prime rate. However, when including the stamping fee, the effective cost of the acceptance will increase.

Only large companies with good credit risks use banker's acceptances. The effective interest costs are usually below the prime rate.

USE OF SECURITY IN SHORT-TERM FINANCING

Given a choice, it is ordinarily better to borrow on an unsecured basis, as the bookkeeping costs of secured loans are often high. However, it frequently happens that a potential borrower's credit rating is not sufficiently strong to justify the loan. If the loan can be secured by the borrower's putting up some form of collateral to be claimed by the lender in the event of default, then the lender may extend credit to an otherwise unacceptable firm. Similarly, a firm that could borrow on an unsecured basis may elect to use security if it finds that this will induce lenders to quote a lower interest rate.

Several different kinds of collateral can be employed—marketable stocks or bonds, land or buildings, equipment, inventory, and accounts receivable. Marketable securities make excellent collateral, but few firms hold portfolios of stocks and bonds. Similarly real property (land and buildings) and equipment are good forms of collateral, but they are generally used as security for long-term loans. The bulk of secured short-term business borrowing involves the pledge of short-term assets—accounts receivable or inventories.

When considering security for short-term, chartered bank financing, the Bank Act specifies the procedures to be followed and the forms of security that can be used. Section 88 of the Bank Act specifies that, for manufacturing companies, banks may lend on the security of inventories, both current and future. Although the company need not relinquish control of the inventory under a Section 88 loan, the bank has the rights and powers identical to those it would have obtained had a direct form of security on the inventory, such as a warehouse receipt, been used.

Alternative methods of securing inventories, other than through Section 88, can be used by the banks. In the case of non-manufacturing companies, these alternatives *must* be used.

Finally, accounts receivable can be used as security for bank loans. In fact, lending on the security of receivables is by far the most common form of lending.

The simplicity and administrative ease with which security under Section

88 is handled is not duplicated for the non-bank use of personal property as security. For example, in Ontario a number of statutes dealing with personal property as security had unnecessary differences and cumbersome registration procedures. In the United States, a related problem existed with respect to the uniformity of state laws dealing with the use of security. The solution there was the passage in all states of the Uniform Commercial Code which standardized and simplified the procedure for the establishment of loan security.

The Province of Ontario has now passed The Personal Property Security Act, which was modelled on the Uniform Commercial Code. This Act will simplify the registration procedure through the use of a computerized registry and replace a number of existing statutes.

FINANCING ACCOUNTS RECEIVABLE

Accounts receivable financing involves either the *pledging or assignment of receivables* or the *selling of receivables (factoring).* The *assignment of accounts receivable* is characterized by the fact that the lender not only has a lien on the receivables, but also has recourse to the borrower (seller); if the person or the firm that bought the goods does not pay, the selling firm must take the loss. In other words, the risk of default on the accounts receivable assigned remains with the borrower. Also, the buyer of the goods is not ordinarily notified about the assigning of the receivables. The financial institution that lends on the security of accounts receivable is generally either a chartered bank, a large industrial finance company or a factoring company.

Factoring, or selling accounts receivable, involves the purchase of accounts receivable by the lender without recourse to the borrower (seller). The buyer of the goods is notified of the transfer and makes payment directly to the lender. Since the factoring firm assumes the risk of default on bad account, it must do the credit checking. Accordingly, factors provide not only money but also a credit department for the borrower.

Most factoring companies began their operations servicing the textile industry, but they are currently diversifying their activities into other areas such as footwear and data processing. At the end of 1977, there were eight factoring companies which accounted for most of the industry's volume and the top four companies had in excess of 75 percent of the volume. Currently, chartered banks are not allowed to engage directly in factoring activities. However, three banks (and an investment dealer) are involved in factoring through ownership in factoring companies. In 1978, the pending Bank Act revisions made it seem likely that chartered banks would be permitted to enter the factoring industry directly.

Incidentally, the factoring companies not only serve as factors but also engage in commercial financing through loans against receivables. Thus, depending on the circumstances and the wishes of the borrower, the factor can provide either form of receivables financing.

Procedure for Pledging Accounts Receivable

The financing of accounts receivable is initiated by a legally binding agreement between the seller of the goods and the financing institution. The agreement sets forth in detail the procedures to be followed and the legal obligations of both parties. Once the working relation has been established, the seller periodically takes a batch of invoices to the financing institution. The lender reviews the invoices and makes an appraisal of the buyers. Invoices of companies that do not meet the lender's credit standards are not accepted for pledging. The financial institution seeks to protect itself at every phase of the operation. Selection of sound invoices is the essential first step in safeguarding the financial institution. If the buyer of the goods does not pay the invoice, the lender still has recourse against the seller of the goods. However, if many buyers default, the seller may be unable to meet his obligation to the financial institution.

Additional protection is afforded the lender in that the loan will generally be for less than 100 percent of the pledged receivables; for example, the factoring company may advance the selling firm 80 percent of the amount of the pledged (or assigned) receivables, whereas a bank would advance 50 percent.

Procedure for Factoring Accounts Receivable

The procedure for factoring is somewhat different from that for pledging. Again, an agreement between the seller and the factor is made to specify legal obligations and procedural arrangements. When the seller receives an order from a buyer, a credit approval slip is written and immediately sent to the factoring company for a credit check. If the factor does not approve the sale, the seller generally refuses to fill the order. This procedure informs the seller, prior to the sale, about the buyer's credit-worthiness and acceptability to the factor. If the sale is approved, shipment is made and the invoice is stamped to notify the buyer to make payment directly to the factoring company.

The factor performs three functions in carrying out the normal procedure as outlined above: (1) credit checking, (2) lending, and (3) risk bearing. The seller can select various combinations of these functions by changing provisions in the factoring agreement. For example, a small or a medium-sized firm can avoid establishing a credit department. The factor's service might well be less costly than a department that may have excess capacity for the firm's credit volume. At the same time, if the firm uses part of the time of a non-credit specialist to perform credit checking, lack of education, training, and experience may result in excessive losses.

The seller may utilize the factor to perform the credit-checking and risk-taking function, but not the lending function. This is referred to as *maturity factoring* and is useful for companies with adequate working capital and a desire to eliminate the credit department and the associated credit risk. The following procedure is carried out on receipt of a $10,000 order. The factor checks and approves the invoices. The goods are shipped on terms of net 30. Payment is made to the factor, who remits to the seller. But assume that the factor has received only $5,000 by the end of the credit period. He must still remit $10,000 to the seller (less his fee, of course). If the remaining $5,000 is never paid, the factor sustains a $5,000 loss. The fee ranges from ⅛ of 1 percent to 1½ percent of sales.

Next, consider classical factoring in which the factor performs a lending function by making payment in advance of collection. Upon proof of the shipment of goods, the factor immediately advances up to 90 percent of the invoice amount to the seller even though the payment is not due for 30 days. The 10 percent hold-back is a reserve established by the factor to cover disputes between seller and buyer on such issues as damaged goods, goods returned to the seller by the buyer, and failure to make outright sale of goods. This hold-back is paid to the selling firm when the factor collects on the account.

Suppose $10,000 of goods is shipped; the seller receives $9,000 immediately and an account receivable of $1,000 is set up to reflect the hold-back. Since the factor is checking the credit of the buyer and bearing the credit risk, a fee of ⅛ of 1 percent of sales is charged; in this example, this fee is $87.50. In addition, the interest expense is set at 2 to 2½ percent above prime on the amount advanced. In this example, the interest rate is 10.5 percent a year and the interest expense for the month is $78.75.[6]

The seller's accounting entry is as follows:

Cash	$8,833.75	
Interest expense	78.75	
Factoring commission	87.50	
Reserve: due from factor on collection of account	1,000.00	
Accounts receivable		$10,000

Factoring is normally a continuous process instead of the single cycle described above. The seller of the goods receives orders; he transmits the

---

[6] Since the interest is only for one month, we take one-twelfth of the stated rate, 10.5 percent, and multiply this by the $9,000 invoice price:

$$\frac{1}{12} \times 0.105 \times \$9,000 = \$78.75.$$

purchase orders to the factor for approval; on approval, the goods are shipped; the factor advances the money to the seller; the buyers pay the factor when payment is due; and the factor periodically remits any excess reserve to the seller of the goods. Once a routine is established, a continuous circular flow of goods and funds takes place between the seller, the buyers of the goods, and the factor. Thus, once the factoring agreement is in force, funds from this source are *spontaneous*.

Cost of Receivables Financing

Accounts receivable assigning and factoring services are convenient and advantageous, but they can be costly. For factoring, a fee of ⅞ of 1 percent to 1½ percent of sales is charged for the credit-checking and credit-risk bearing functions. If a loan is made by the factor, the cost of money is 2 to 2½ percent over prime.

Both factoring companies and banks will lend short-term on the assignment of accounts receivable. Interest costs for this form of financing from factoring companies range from 5½ to 8 percent over prime. This very high premium reflects the fact that there is no service charge for credit administration.

Finally, factoring companies will also lend money on an assignment of receivables where credit management is undertaken; payment is made to the factor but the factor does not assume credit risk. In this case, the commission is 1¼ percent of sales and the interest cost is 2 to 2½ percent over prime on the money lent.

Evaluation of Receivables Financing

It cannot be said categorically that accounts receivable financing is always either a good or a poor method of raising funds for an individual business. Among the advantages is, first, the flexibility of this source of financing. As the firm's sales expand and more financing is needed, a larger volume of invoices is generated automatically. Because the dollar amounts of invoices vary directly with sales, the amount of readily available financing increases. Second, receivables or invoices provide security for a loan that a firm might otherwise be unable to obtain. Third, factoring provides the services of a credit department that might otherwise be available to the firm only under much more expensive conditions.

Accounts receivable financing also has disadvantages. First, when invoices are numerous and relatively small in dollar amount, the administrative costs involved may render this method of financing inconvenient and expensive. Second, the firm is using a highly liquid asset as security. For a long time, accounts receivable financing was frowned upon by most trade creditors. In fact, such financing was regarded as confession of a firm's unsound financial position. It is no longer regarded in this light, and many sound firms engage in receivables pledging or factoring. However, the traditional attitude causes some trade creditors to refuse to sell on credit to a firm that is factoring or pledging its receivables, on the grounds that this practice removes one of the most liquid of the firm's assets and, accordingly, weakens the position of other creditors.

Future Use of Receivables Financing

We might make a prediction at this point—in the future, accounts receivable financing will increase in relative importance. Computer technology is rapidly advancing toward the point where credit records of individuals and firms can be kept in computer memory units. Systems have been devised so that a retailer can have a unit on hand that, when an individual's magnetic credit card is inserted into a box, gives a signal that his credit is "good" and that a bank is willing to "buy" the receivable created when the store completes the sale. The cost of handling invoices will be greatly reduced over present-day costs because the new systems will be so highly automated. This will make it possible to use accounts receivable financing for very small sales, and it will reduce the cost of all receivables financing. The net result will be a marked expansion of accounts receivable financing.

INVENTORY FINANCING

A substantial volume of credit is secured by business inventories. For manufacturing companies, chartered banks have the option of lending under Section 88 or using the direct forms of inventory security. When given the choice, both banks and borrowers prefer the former because of the lower administrative costs. However, for companies that are ineligible for Section 88 lending, direct forms of inventory security are required. These include the floating charge debenture (also known as a blanket inventory lien), and the infrequently used trust receipts and warehouse financing. These methods of using inventories as security are discussed below.

Floating Charge Debenture

A floating charge debenture provides a claim to all assets currently owned, or subsequently acquired, which are not already covered by a fixed charge. Since the bank does not have direct control of the assets under this debenture, it must protect its loan from an erosion of the security. Therefore, the debentures have trust indentures with specific covenants designed to protect the bank. Examples of these covenants include quarterly financial reports and restrictions on some financial decisions. If the borrower is in default, the floating charge "crystallizes" and becomes a fixed charge on any assets remaining at the time of the crystallization. Since the security at the point of default will depend on the assets under the floating charge, the debenture specifies, in detail, the rights of the company to issue more fixed or floating charges to other lenders which have a priority higher than the bank's floating charge.

Trust Receipts

We will now turn to the trust receipt. A trust receipt is an instrument acknowledging that the borrower holds the goods in trust for the lender. When trust receipts are used, the borrowing firm, on receiving funds from the lender, conveys a trust receipt for the goods. The goods can be stored in a public warehouse or held on the premises of the borrower. The trust receipt provides that the goods are held in trust for the lender or are segregated in the borrower's premises on behalf of the lender, and proceeds from the sale of goods held under trust receipts are transmitted to the lender at the end of each day. Automobile dealer financing is the best example of trust receipt financing.

One defect of trust receipt financing is the requirement that a trust receipt must be issued for specific goods. For example, if the security is bags of coffee beans, the trust receipts must indicate the bags by number. In order to validate its trust receipts, the lending institution would have to send a man to the premises of the borrower to see that the bag numbers are correctly listed. Furthermore, complex legal requirements of trust receipts require the attention of a bank officer. Problems are compounded if borrowers are widely separated geographically from the lender. To offset these inconveniences, *warehousing* is coming into wide use as a method of securing loans with inventory.

Warehouse Financing

Like trust receipts, warehouse financing uses inventory as security. A *public warehouse* represents an independent third party engaged in the business of storing goods. Sometimes a public warehouse is not practical because of the bulkiness of goods and the expense of transporting them to and from the borrower's premises. *Field warehouse* financing represents an economical method of inventory financing in which the warehouse is established at the place of the borrower. To provide inventory supervision, the lending institution employs a third party in the arrangement, the field warehousing company. This company acts as the control (or supervisory) agent for the lending institution.

Field warehousing is illustrated by a simple example. Suppose a potential borrower has stacked iron in an open yard on his premises. A field warehouse can be established if a field warehousing concern places a temporary fence around the iron and erects a sign stating: "This is a field warehouse supervised and conducted by the Lawrence Warehousing Corporation." These are minimal conditions, of course.

The example illustrates the two elements in the establishment of a warehouse: (1) public notification of the field warehouse arrangement and (2) supervision of the field warehouse by a custodian of the field warehouse concern. When the field warehousing operation is relatively small, the second condition is sometimes violated by hiring an employee of the borrower to supervise the inventory. This practice is viewed as undesirable by the lending institution, because there is no control over the collateral by a person independent of the borrowing concern.[7]

The field warehouse financing operation is described best by a specific illustration. Assume that a tomato canner is interested in financing his operations by bank borrowing. The canner has sufficient funds to finance 15 to 20 percent of his operations during the canning season. These funds are adequate to purchase and process an initial batch of tomatoes. As the cans are put into boxes and rolled into the storerooms, the canner needs additional funds for both raw materials and labor.

Because of the canner's poor credit rating, the bank decides that a field warehousing operation is necessary to secure its loans. The field warehouse is established, and the custodian notifies the lending institution of the description, by number, of the boxes of canned tomatoes in storage and under his control. Thereupon the lending institution establishes for the canner a deposit on which he can draw. From this point on, the bank finances operations. The canner needs only enough cash to initiate the cycle. The farmers bring more tomatoes; the canner processes them; the cans are boxed, and the boxes are put into the field warehouse; field warehouse receipts are drawn up and sent to the bank; the bank establishes further deposits for the canner on the basis of the receipts; the canner can draw on the deposits to continue the cycle.

Of course, the canner's ultimate objective is to sell the canned tomatoes. As the canner receives purchase orders, he transmits them to the bank, and the bank directs the custodian to release the inventories. It is agreed that, as remittances are received by the canner, they will be turned over to the bank. These remittances by the canner pay off the loans made by the bank.

Typically, a seasonal pattern exists. At the beginning of the tomato har-

---

[7]This absence of independent control was the main cause of the breakdown that resulted in the huge losses connected with the loans to the Allied Crude Vegetable Oil Company headed by Anthony (Tino) DeAngelis. American Express Field Warehousing Company hired men from Àllied's staff as custodians. Their dishonesty was not discovered because of another breakdown—the fact that the American Express touring inspector did not actually take a physical inventory of the warehouses. As a consequence, the swindle was not discovered until losses running into the hundreds of millions of dollars had been suffered. See Norman C. Miller, *The Great Salad Oil Swindle* (Baltimore, Md.: Penguin Books, 1965), pp. 72–77.

vesting and canning season, the canner's cash needs and loan requirements begin to rise and reach a maximum by the end of the canning season. It is hoped that, just before the new canning season begins, the canner has sold a sufficient volume to have paid off the loan completely. If for some reason the canner has had a bad year, the bank may carry him over another year to enable him to work off his inventory.

Acceptable Products   In addition to canned foods, which account for about 17 percent of all field warehouse loans, many other product inventories provide a basis for field warehouse financing. Some of these are miscellaneous groceries, which represent about 13 percent; lumber products, about 10 percent; and coal and coke, about 6 percent.

These products are relatively nonperishable and are sold in well-developed, organized markets. Nonperishability protects the lender if he should have to take over the security. For this reason a bank would not make a field warehousing loan on perishables such as fresh fish. However, frozen fish, which can be stored for a long time, can be field warehoused. An organized market aids the lender in disposing of an inventory that it takes over. Banks are not interested in going into the canning or the fish business. They want to be able to dispose of an inventory within a matter of hours and with the expenditure of a minimum amount of time.

Cost of Financing   The fixed costs of a field warehousing arrangement are relatively high; such financing is therefore not suitable for a very small firm. If a field warehouse company sets up the field warehouse itself, it will typically set a minimum charge of about $1,000 a year, plus about 1 or 2 percent of the amount of credit extended to the borrower. Furthermore, the financing institution will charge from 8 to 12 percent interest. The minimum size of an efficient field warehousing operation requires an inventory of about $100,000.

Appraisal   The use of field warehouse financing as a source of funds for business firms has many advantages. First, the amount of funds available is flexible because the financing is tied to the growth of inventories, which in turn is related directly to financing needs. Second, the field warehousing arrangement increases the acceptability of inventories as loan collateral. Some inventories would not be accepted by a bank as security without a field warehousing arrangement. Third, the necessity for inventory control, safekeeping, and the use of specialists in warehousing has resulted in improved warehouse practices. The services of the field warehouse companies have often saved money for the firm in spite of the costs of financing mentioned above. The field warehouse company may suggest inventory practices which reduce the labor that the firm has to employ, and reduce inventory damage and loss as well.

The major disadvantage of a field warehousing operation is the fixed cost element, which reduces the feasibility of this form of financing for small firms.

OTHER SECURITY

Chattel Mortgage

This is a mortgage of personal or movable property such as an automobile or machinery and equipment. The goods are left with the borrower until there is a default at which point they become the property of the lender. Chartered banks are permitted to use this form of security.

Personal Guarantee

Due to the existence of limited liability, a creditor is not able to attach personal property of the debtor if a loan is in default. One way around this problem, especially for loans to small companies, is to have the principal shareholders (and perhaps their spouses if they have a direct interest in the company) sign a personal guarantee of the loan. This guarantees the repayment of the loan, both principal and interest, up to a stated maximum amount.

SUMMARY

Short-term credit is defined as debt originally scheduled for repayment within one year. This chapter has discussed the three major sources of short-term credit—trade credit between firms, loans from commercial banks, and commercial paper—as well as methods of securing this credit.

Trade Credit   Trade credit, represented by accounts payable, is the largest single category of short-term credit and is especially important for smaller firms. Trade credit is a *spontaneous source of financing* in that it arises from ordinary business transactions; as sales increase, so does the supply of financing from accounts payable.

Bank Credit   Bank credit occupies a pivotal position in the short-term money market. Banks provide the marginal credit that allows firms to expand more rapidly than is possible through retained earnings and trade credit; to be denied bank credit often means that a firm must slow its rate of growth.

Bank interest rates are quoted in two ways — regular compound interest, and discount interest. Regular interest needs no adjustment — it is "correct" as stated. Discount interest requires a small upward adjustment to make it comparable to regular compound interest rates.

Commercial Paper   Bank loans are personal in the sense that the financial manager meets with the banker, discusses the terms of the loan with him, and reaches an agreement that requires direct and personal negotiation. Commercial paper, however, although it is physically quite similar to a bank loan, it is sold in a broad, impersonal market. A British Columbia firm might, for example, sell commercial paper to a manufacturer in Ontario.

Only the very strongest firms are able to use the commercial paper markets—the nature of these markets is such that the firm selling the paper must have a reputation so good that buyers of the paper are willing to buy it without any sort of credit check. Interest rates in the commercial paper market are the lowest available to business borrowers.

Banker's Acceptance This bill is a mixture between a bank loan and commercial paper. The bank guarantees that the funds will be available when the acceptance is presented at the maturity date. In this sense, it is an advance or a loan. However, the acceptance is sold and traded in the money market like commercial paper. The cost of funds is comparable to that in the commercial paper market and only large, very stable companies use this form of financing.

Use of Security in Short-Term Financing The most common forms of collateral used for short-term credit are inventories and accounts receivable. Accounts receivable financing can be done either by *assigning the receivables* or by selling them outright, frequently called *factoring.* When the receivables are pledged, the borrower retains the risk that the person or firm who owes the receivable will not pay; in factoring, this risk is typically passed on to the lender. Because the factor takes the risk of default, he will typically investigate the purchaser's credit; therefore, the factor can perform three services—a lending function, a risk-bearing function, and a credit-checking function. When receivables are pledged, the lender typically performs only the first of these three functions. Consequently, factoring is generally quite a bit more expensive than is pledging accounts receivable.

If the company meets certain requirements, then inventories can be used as collateral under a Section 88 loan. If the company does not meet the requirements for a Section 88 loan, then other methods of using inventories for security must be used. These include floating charge debentures and the infrequently used field warehouse financing or trust receipts. The trust receipt technique is particularly inconvenient where borrowers and lenders are widely separated geographically. As an alternative, field warehousing is used to provide security to the lender. Under a field warehousing arrangement, the inventory is under the physical control of a warehouse company which releases the inventory only on order from the lending institution. Only products which are traded in organized markets, are non-perishable and standardized are acceptable for use in field warehousing arrangements.

QUESTIONS

9-1. It is inevitable that firms will obtain a certain amount of their financing in the form of trade credit, which is, to some extent, a free source of funds. What are some other factors that lead firms to use trade credit?

9-2. "Commercial paper interest rates are always lower than bank loan rates to a given borrower. Nevertheless, many firms perfectly capable of selling commercial paper employ higher cost bank credit." Discuss the statement, indicating (a) why commercial paper rates are lower than bank rates and (b) why firms might use bank credit in spite of its higher cost.

9-3. "Trade credit has an explicit interest rate cost if discounts are available but not taken. There are also some intangible costs associated with the failure to take discounts." Discuss.

9-4. A large manufacturing firm that had been selling its products on a 3/10, net 30 basis changed its credit terms to 1/20, net 90. What changes might be anticipated on the balance sheets of the manufacturer and of its customers?

9-5. The availability of bank credit is more important to small firms than to large ones. Why is this so?

9-6. What factors should a firm consider in selecting its primary bank? Would it be feasible for a firm to have a primary deposit bank (the bank where most of its funds are deposited) and a different primary loan bank (the bank where it does most of its borrowing)?

9-7. Indicate whether each of the following changes would raise or lower the cost of a firm's accounts receivable financing, and why this occurs:

    a. The firm eases up on its credit standards in order to increase sales.

    b. The firm institutes a policy of refusing to make credit sales if the amount of the purchase (invoice) is below $100. Previously, about 40 percent of all invoices were below $100.

    c. The firm agrees to give recourse to the finance company for all defaults.

    d. The firm, which already has a recourse arrangement, is merged into a larger, stronger company.

    e. A firm without a recourse arrangement changes its terms of trade from net 30 to net 90.

9-8. Would a firm that manufactures specialized machinery for a few large customers be more likely to use some form of inventory financing or some form of accounts receivable financing? Why?

9-9. "A firm that factors its accounts receivable will look better in a ratio analysis than one that discounts its receivables." Discuss.

9-10. Why would it not be practical for a typical retailer to use field warehousing?

9-11. List an industry, together with your reasons for including it, that might be expected to use each of the following forms of credit:

    a. field warehousing

    b. factoring

    c. accounts receivable discounting

    d. trust receipts

    e. none of these.

PROBLEMS

9-1. What is the equivalent annual interest rate that would be lost if a firm failed to take the cash discount under each of the following terms?

 a. 1/15, net 30
 b. 2/10, net 60
 c. 3/10, net 60
 d. 2/10, net 40
 e. 1/10, net 40.

9-2. Dixon Associates Limited is negotiating with a bank for a $100,000, one-year loan. The bank has offered Dixon the following three alternatives:

 a. A 12 percent interest rate, no compensating balance, and interest due at the end of the year.

 b. A 10 percent interest rate, a 20 percent compensating balance, and interest due at the end of the year.

 c. A 9 percent interest rate, a 15 percent compensating balance, and the loan is discounted.

If Dixon wishes to minimize the effective interest rate, which alternative would they choose?

9-3. Wagner Industries is having difficulty paying its bills and is considering foregoing its trade discounts on $100,000 of accounts payable. As an alternative, Wagner can obtain a sixty-day note with a 12 percent annual interest rate. The note is discounted. Trade credit terms are 2/10, net 70.

 a. Which alternative has the lower effective cost?

 b. If trade discounts are not taken, what conclusions may outsiders draw?

9-4. Supreme Catsup Co. Ltd. is considering the following two alternatives for financing next year's canning operations:

 a. Establishing a $1,000,000 line of credit with a 12 percent annual interest rate on the used portion and a 1 percent commitment fee rate on the unused portion. A $150,000 compensating balance is required at all times on the entire $1 million line.

 b. Use field warehousing to finance $850,000 of inventory. Financing charges are a flat fee of $500, plus 2 percent of the maximum amount of credit extended, plus a 10 percent annual interest rate on all outstanding credit. Supreme has $150,000 of funds available for inventory financing, so financing requirements will be equal to the expected inventory level minus $150,000.

All financing is done on the first of the month and is sufficient to cover the value of the inventory at the end of the month. Expected inventory levels are as follows:

Month	Amount	Month	Amount
July	$ 150,000	January	$600,000
August	400,000	February	450,000
September	600,000	March	350,000
October	800,000	April	225,000
November	1,000,000	May	100,000
December	750,000	June	0

Which financing plan has the lowest cost? (Hints: Borrowing under bank loan in July equals $150,000 and in December $750,000; under the field warehouse plan, July borrowings are zero and December borrowings are $600,000.)

9-5. Collins Manufacturing needs an additional $100,000. The financial manager is considering two methods of obtaining this money: a loan from a commercial bank or through a factoring arrangement.

The bank charges 8 percent per annum interest, discount basis. A 12 percent compensating balance is also required.

The factor is willing to purchase Collins' accounts receivable and to advance the amount purchased, less a 3 percent factoring commission on the invoices purchased each month. (All sales are on 30 day terms). An 8 percent annual interest rate will be charged on the total invoice price and deducted in advance. Also, with the factoring agreement, Collins can eliminate its Credit Department and reduce credit expenses by $2,000 per month. Bad debt losses of 1 percent on the factored amount can also be avoided.

    a. How much should the bank loan be for in order to net $100,000? How much accounts receivable should be factored to net $100,000?

    b. What are the effective interest rates, and the annual total dollar costs, including credit department expenses and bad debt losses, associated with each financing arrangement?

    c. Discuss some considerations other than cost that may influence management's decision between factoring and a commercial bank loan.

9-6. Fair Deal Co. Ltd. estimates that due to the seasonal nature of their business they will require an additional $200,000 of cash for the month of November. Fair Deal has three options available to provide the needed funds.

    a. Establish a one year line of credit for $200,000 with a commercial bank. The commitment fee would be .5 percent and the interest charge on the used funds would be 10 percent per annum. The minimum time that the funds may be used is thirty days.

    b. Forego the November trade discount of 2/10, net 40 on $200,000 of accounts payable.

    c. Issue $200,000 of sixty-day commercial paper at an 8 percent per annum interest rate. Since the funds only are required for thirty days, the excess funds ($200,000) are invested in 7 percent per annum marketable securities for the month of December. The total transaction fee on purchasing and selling the marketable securities is 1/2 of 1 percent of the fair value.

Which financing arrangement results in the lowest cost?

Decisions Involving Long-Term Assets

Part Three

In Part Two, we dealt with the top portion of the firm's balance sheet—the current assets and liabilities. Now, in Part Three, we move down to the lower left side of the statement, focusing on the decisions involved in fixed asset acquisitions.

In Chapter 10 we discuss the concepts of compound interest and the time value of money, important subjects in all long-term financial decisions. Capital budgeting—the planning of expenditures whose returns will extend beyond one year—is covered in Chapter 11. Uncertainty about both the costs and the returns associated with a project is introduced in Chapter 12; since projects differ in riskiness, that chapter develops methods of analysis which can be used to incorporate risk into the decision-making process.

The Interest Factor
in Financial Decisions

Investing in fixed assets should, logically, be taken up at this point. However, the long-term nature of fixed investments makes it necessary to consider first the theory of compound interest—the "math of finance." Compound interest is essential to an understanding of capital budgeting, the topic of the following chapter, and interest rate theory is also an integral part of several other topics taken up later in the text. Financial structure decisions, lease versus purchase decisions, bond refunding operations, security valuation techniques, and the whole question of the cost of capital are some other subjects that cannot be understood without a knowledge of compound interest.

Many people are afraid of the subject of compound interest and simply avoid it. It is certainly true that many successful businessmen—even some bankers—know essentially nothing of the subject. However, as technology advances, as more and more engineers become involved in general management, and as modern business administration programs turn out more and more highly qualified graduates, this "success in spite of yourself" pattern will become more and more difficult to achieve. Furthermore, a fear of compound interest relationships is quite unfounded—the subject matter is simply not that difficult. Almost all problems involving compound interest can be handled satisfactorily with only a few basic formulas.

COMPOUND VALUE

A person deposits $1,000 in a savings account at a chartered bank that pays 4 percent interest compounded annually. How much will the saver have at the end of one year? To treat the matter systematically, let us define the following terms:

$$P_0 = \text{principal, or beginning amount at time 0.}$$

$$i = \text{interest rate.}$$

$$I = \text{total dollar amount of interest earned.}$$

$$P_n = \text{principal value at the end of } n \text{ periods.}$$

When n equals 1, P_n may be calculated as follows:

$$P_1 = P_0 + I$$
$$= P_0 + P_0 i \qquad (10\text{--}1)$$
$$= P_0 (1 + i).$$

Equation 10–1 shows that the ending amount (P_1) is equal to the beginning amount (P_0) times the factor $(1 + i)$. In the example, where $P_0 =$ $1,000, $i = 4$ percent, and n is one year, P_n is determined as follows:

$$P_1 = \$1,000(1.0 + .04) = \$1,000(1.04) = \$1,040.$$

Multiple Periods

If the person leaves the $1,000 on deposit for five years, to what amount will it have grown at the end of that period? Equation 10–1 can be used to construct Table 10–1, which indicates the answer. Note that P_2, the balance at the end of the second year, is found as follows:

$$P_2 = P_1 (1 + i) = P_0 (1 + i)(1 + i) = P_0 (1 + i)^2.$$

Similarly, P_3, the balance after three years, is found as

$$P_3 = P_2 (1 + i) = P_0 (1 + i)^3.$$

TABLE 10–1 Compound Interest Calculations

Period	Beginning Amount	×	$(1 + i)$	=	Ending Amount (P_n)
1	$1,000		1.04		$1,040
2	1,040		1.04		1,082
3	1,082		1.04		1,125
4	1,125		1.04		1,170
5	1,170		1.04		1,217

In general, P_n, the compound amount at the end of any year n, is found as

$$P_n = P_0 (1 + i)^n. \qquad (10\text{--}2)$$

Equation 10-2 is the fundamental equation of compound interest. Note that Equation 10-1 is simply a special case of Equation 10-2, where $n = 1$.

While it is necessary to understand the derivation of Equation 10-2 in order to understand much of the material in the remainder of this chapter (as well as material to be covered in subsequent chapters), the concept can be applied quite readily in a mechanical sense. Tables have been constructed for values of $(1 + i)^n$ for wide ranges of i and n. Table 10-2 is illustrative, while Table A-1, in Appendix A at the end of the book, is a more complete table.

TABLE 10-2 Compound Value of $1 (*CVIF*): $CVIF = (1 + i)^n$

Period	1%	2%	3%	4%	5%	6%	7%	8%	9%	10%
1	1.010	1.020	1.030	1.040	1.050	1.060	1.070	1.080	1.090	1.100
2	1.020	1.040	1.061	1.082	1.102	1.124	1.145	1.166	1.188	1.210
3	1.030	1.061	1.093	1.125	1.158	1.191	1.225	1.260	1.295	1.331
4	1.041	1.082	1.126	1.170	1.216	1.262	1.311	1.360	1.412	1.464
5	1.051	1.104	1.159	1.217	1.276	1.338	1.403	1.469	1.539	1.611
6	1.062	1.126	1.194	1.265	1.340	1.419	1.501	1.587	1.677	1.772
7	1.072	1.149	1.230	1.316	1.407	1.504	1.606	1.714	1.828	1.949
8	1.083	1.172	1.267	1.369	1.477	1.594	1.718	1.851	1.993	2.144
9	1.094	1.195	1.305	1.423	1.551	1.689	1.838	1.999	2.172	2.358
10	1.105	1.219	1.344	1.480	1.629	1.791	1.967	2.159	2.367	2.594
11	1.116	1.243	1.384	1.539	1.710	1.898	2.105	2.332	2.580	2.853
12	1.127	1.268	1.426	1.601	1.796	2.012	2.252	2.518	2.813	3.138
13	1.138	1.294	1.469	1.665	1.886	2.133	2.410	2.720	3.066	3.452
14	1.149	1.319	1.513	1.732	1.980	2.261	2.579	2.937	3.342	3.797
15	1.161	1.346	1.558	1.801	2.079	2.397	2.759	3.172	3.642	4.177

Letting *CVIF* ($\equiv$ compound value interest factor) $= (1 + i)^n$, Equation 10-2 may be written as $P_n = P_0 (CVIF)$. It is necessary only to go to an appropriate interest table to find the proper interest factor. For example, the correct interest factor for the illustration given in Table 10-1 can be found in Table 10-2. Look down the Period column to 5, then across this row to the appropriate number in the 4 percent column to find the interest factor, 1.217. Then, using this interest factor, we find the compound value of the $1,000 after five years as

$$P_n = P_0 (CVIF) = \$1,000(1.217) = \$1,217.$$

Notice that this is precisely the same figure that was obtained by the long method in Table 10-1.

Graphic View of the Compounding Process: Growth

Figure 10–1 shows how the interest factors for compounding increase, or grow, as the compounding period increases. Curves could be drawn for any interest rate, including fractional rates; we have plotted curves for 0 percent, 5 percent, and 10 percent. The curves in the graph were plotted from data taken from Table 10–2.

FIGURE 10–1   Relationship between Compound Value Interest Factors, Interest Rates, and Time

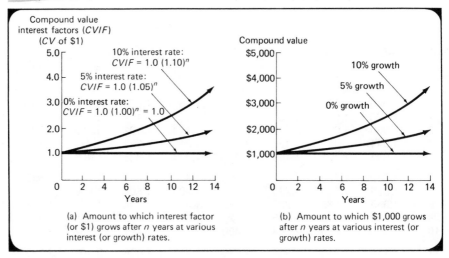

(a) Amount to which interest factor (or $1) grows after n years at various interest (or growth) rates.

(b) Amount to which $1,000 grows after n years at various interest (or growth) rates.

Figure 10–1 shows how $1 (or any other sum) grows over time at various rates of interest. The higher the rate of interest, the faster the rate of growth. The interest rate is, in fact, the growth rate: If a sum is deposited and earns 5 percent, then the funds on deposit grow at the rate of 5 percent per year.

PRESENT VALUE

Suppose you are offered the alternative of either $1,217 at the end of five years or X dollars today. There is no question but that the $1,217 will be paid in full (perhaps the payer is the Canadian government); having no current need for the money, you would deposit it with a savings association paying 4 percent interest. (Four percent is defined to be your "opportunity cost.") How small must X be to induce you to accept the promise of $1,217 five years hence?

Table 10–1 shows that the initial amount of $1,000 growing at 4 percent a year yields $1,217 at the end of five years. Thus, you should be indifferent in your choice between $1,000 today and $1,217 at the end of five years. *The $1000 is defined as the present value of $1,217 due in five years when the applicable interest rate is 4 percent.* It should be noted that the subscript zero in the term P_0 indicates the present. Hence present value quantities may be identified by either P_0 or PV.

Finding present values (or *discounting,* as it is commonly called) is simply the reverse of compounding, and Equation 10–2 can readily be transformed into a present value formula.

$$\text{Present value} = P_0 = \frac{P_n}{(1+i)^n} = P_n\left[\frac{1}{(1+i)^n}\right]. \qquad (10\text{–}3)$$

Tables have been constructed for the term in brackets for various values of i and n; Table 10–3 is an example. A more complete table, Table A–2, is found in Appendix A at the end of the book. For the illustrative case being considered, look down the 4 percent column in Table 10–3 to the fifth row. The figure shown there, 0.822, is the present value interest factor (*PVIF*) used to determine the present value of $1,217 payable in five years, discounted at 4 percent.

$$P_0 = P_5(PVIF)$$
$$= \$1,217(0.822)$$
$$= \$1,000.$$

TABLE 10–3 Present Values of $1 (*PVIF*): $PVIF = \dfrac{1}{(1+i)^n} = \dfrac{1}{CVIF}$

Period	1%	2%	3%	4%	5%	6%	7%	8%	9%	10%	12%	14%	15%
1	.990	.980	.971	.962	.952	.943	.935	.926	.917	.909	.893	.877	.870
2	.980	.961	.943	.925	.907	.890	.873	.857	.842	.826	.797	.769	.756
3	.971	.942	.915	.889	.864	.840	.816	.794	.772	.751	.712	.675	.658
4	.961	.924	.889	.855	.823	.792	.763	.835	.708	.683	.636	.592	.572
5	.951	.906	.863	.822	.784	.747	.713	.681	.650	.621	.567	.519	.497
6	.942	.888	.838	.790	.746	.705	.666	.630	.596	.564	.507	.456	.432
7	.933	.871	.813	.760	.711	.665	.623	.583	.547	.513	.452	.400	.376
8	.923	.853	.789	.731	.677	.627	.582	.540	.502	.467	.404	.351	.327
9	.914	.837	.766	.703	.645	.592	.544	.500	.460	.424	.361	.308	.284
10	.905	.820	.744	.676	.614	.558	.508	.463	.422	.386	.322	.270	.247

Graphic View of the Discounting Process

Figure 10–2 shows how the interest factors for discounting decrease as the discounting period increases. The curves in the figure were plotted from data taken from Table 10–3; they show that the present value of a sum to be received at some future date decreases (1) as the payment date is extended further into the future and (2) as the discount rate increases. If relatively high discount rates apply, funds due in the future are worth very little today; even at relatively low discount rates, funds due in the distant future are not worth much today. For example, $1,000 due in ten years is worth $247 today if the discount rate is 15 percent, but it is worth $614 today at a 5 percent discount rate. Similarly, $1,000 due in ten years at 10 percent is worth $386 today, but at the same discount rate $1,000 due in five years is worth $621 today.[1]

FIGURE 10–2 Relationship between Present Value Interest Factors, Interest Rates, and Time

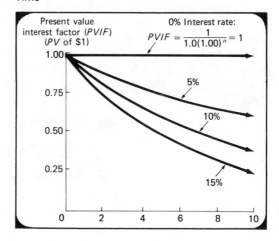

COMPOUND VALUE VERSUS PRESENT VALUE

Because a thorough understanding of compound value concepts is vital in order to understand the remainder of both this chapter and the book, and because compound interest gives many students trouble, it will be useful to examine in more detail the relationship between compounding and discounting.

Notice that Equation 10–2, the basic equation for compounding, was developed from the logical sequence set forth in Table 10–1: the equation merely presents in mathematical form the steps outlined in the table. The present value interest factor ($PVIF_{i,n}$) in Equation 10–3, the basic equation for discounting or finding present values, was found as the *reciprocal* of the

---

[1]Notice that Figure 10–2 is *not* a mirror image of Figure 10–1. The curves in Figure 10–1 approach ∞ as n increases; in Figure 10–2, the curves approach zero, not − ∞, as n increases.

compound value interest factor ($CVIF_{i,n}$) for the same i, n combination:

$$PVIF_{i,n} = \frac{1}{CVIF_{i,n}}.$$

For example, the *compound value* interest factor for 4 percent over five years is seen in Table 10–2 to be 1.217. The *present value* interest factor for 4 percent over five years must be the reciprocal of 1.217:

$$PVIF_{4\%, 5 \text{ years}} = \frac{1}{1.217} = .822.$$

The *PVIF* found in this manner must, of course, correspond with the *PVIF* shown in Table 10–3.

The reciprocal nature of the relationship between present value and compound value permits us to find present values in two ways—by multiplying or by dividing. Thus, the present value of $1,000 due in five years and discounted at 4 percent may be found as

$$P_0 = PV = P_n (PVIF_{i,n}) = P_n \left[\frac{1}{1+i}\right]^n = \$1,000(.822) = \$822,$$

or

$$P_0 = PV = \frac{P_n}{CVIF_{i,n}} = \frac{P_5}{(1+i)^n} = \frac{\$1,000}{1.217} = \$822.$$

In the second form, it is easy to see why the present value of a given future amount (P_n) declines as the discount rate increases.

To conclude this comparison of present and compound values, compare Figures 10–1 and 10–2. Notice that the vertical intercept is at 1.0 in each case, but compound value interest factors rise while present value interest factors decline. The reason for this divergence is, of course, that present value factors are reciprocals of compound factors.

COMPOUND VALUE OF AN ANNUITY

An annuity is defined as a series of payments of a fixed amount for a specified number of years. Each payment occurs at the end of the year.[2] For example, a promise to pay $1,000 a year for three years is a three-year annuity. If you were to receive such an annuity and were to deposit each annual payment in a savings account paying 4 percent interest, how much would you have at the end of three years? The answer is shown graphically

[2] Had the payment been made at the beginning of the period, each receipt would simply have been shifted back one year. The annuity would have been called an *annuity due;* the one in the present discussion, where payments are made at the end of each period, is called a *regular annuity* or, sometimes, a *deferred annuity.*

in Figure 10–3. The first payment is made at the end of year 1, the second at the end of year 2, and the third at the end of year 3. The last payment is not compounded at all; the next to the last is compounded for one year; the second from the last for two years; and so on back to the first, which is compounded for $(n - 1)$ years. When the compound values of each of the payments are added, their total is the sum of the annuity. In the example, this total is $3,122.

FIGURE 10–3 Graphic Illustration of an Annuity: Compound Sum

	End of year 0	1	2	3
Payments		$1,000	$1,000	$1,000
			→	1,040
		→		1,082
			Compound sum	$3,122

Expressed algebraically, with S_n defined as the compound sum, R as the periodic receipt, n as the length of the annuity, and $CVIF_a$ as the compound value interest factor for an annuity, the formula for S_n is

$$\begin{aligned} S_n &= R(1+i)^{n-1} + R(1+i)^{n-2} + \cdots + R(1+i)^1 + R(1+i)^0 \\ &= R[(1+i)^{n-1} + (1+i)^{n-2} + \cdots + (1+i)^1 + (1+i)^0] \\ &= R[CVIF_a]. \end{aligned}$$

The expression in brackets, $CVIF_a$, has been given values for various combinations of n and i. An illustrative set of these annuity interest factors is given in Table 10–4; a more complete set may be found in Table A–3 in Appendix A. To find the answer to the three-year, $1,000 annuity problem, simply refer

TABLE 10–4 Sum of an Annuity of $1 for n Years ($CVIF_a$): $CVIF_a = \dfrac{(1+i)^n - 1}{i}$

Period	*1%*	*2%*	*3%*	*4%*	*5%*	*6%*	*7%*	*8%*
1	1.000	1.000	1.000	1.000	1.000	1.000	1.000	1.000
2	2.010	2.020	2.030	2.040	2.050	2.060	2.070	2.080
3	3.030	3.060	3.091	3.122	3.152	3.184	3.215	3.246
4	4.060	4.122	4.184	4.246	4.310	4.375	4.440	4.506
5	5.101	5.204	5.309	5.416	5.526	5.637	5.751	5.867
6	6.152	6.308	6.468	6.633	6.802	6.975	7.153	7.336
7	7.214	7.434	7.662	7.898	8.142	8.394	8.654	8.923
8	8.286	8.583	8.892	9.214	9.549	9.897	10.260	10.637
9	9.369	9.755	10.159	10.583	11.027	11.491	11.978	12.488
10	10.462	10.950	11.464	12.006	12.578	13.181	13.816	14.487

to Table 10–4, look down the 4 percent column to the row for the third year, and multiply the factor 3.122 by $1,000. The answer is the same as the one derived by the long method illustrated in Figure 10–3:

$$S_n = R \times CVIF_a \qquad (10-4)$$

$$S_3 = \$1,000 \times 3.122 = \$3,122.$$

Notice that $CVIF_a$ for the sum of an annuity is always *larger* than the number of years the annuity runs.

PRESENT VALUE OF AN ANNUITY

Suppose you were offered the following alternatives: a three-year annuity of $1,000 a year or a lump-sum payment today. You have no need for the money during the next three years, so if you accept the annuity you would simply deposit the receipts in a savings account paying 4 percent interest. How large must the lump-sum payment be to make it equivalent to the annuity? The graphic illustration shown in Figure 10–4 will help explain the problem.

FIGURE 10–4 Graphic Illustration of an Annuity: Present Value

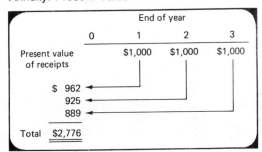

The present value of the first receipt is $R[1/(1 + i)]$; the second is $R[1/(1 + i)]^2$; and so on. Defining the present value of an annuity of n years as A_n, and with $PVIF_a$ defined as the present value interest factor for an annuity, we may write the following equation:

$$A_n = R\left[\frac{1}{1+i}\right]^1 + R\left[\frac{1}{1+i}\right]^2 + \cdots + R\left[\frac{1}{1+i}\right]^n$$

$$= R\left[\frac{1}{(1+i)} + \frac{1}{(1+i)^2} + \cdots + \frac{1}{(1+i)^n}\right] \qquad (10-5)$$

$$= R[PVIF_a].$$

Again, tables have been worked out for the $PVIF_a$, the term in the brackets. Table 10–5 is illustrative; a more complete table is found in Table A–4 in Appendix A. From Table 10–5, the $PVIF_a$ for a three-year, 4 percent annuity is found to be 2.775. Multiplying this factor by the $1,000 annual receipt gives $2,775, the present value of the annuity. This figure departs from the long-method answer shown in Figure 10–4 only by a rounding difference:

$$A_n = R \times PVIF_a \qquad\qquad (10\text{–}6)$$

$$A_3 = \$1,000 \times 2.775$$

$$= \$2,775.$$

Notice that $PVIF_a$ for the *present value* of an annuity is always *less* than the number of years the annuity runs, whereas $CVIF_a$ for the *sum* of an annuity is *larger* than the number of years. Also, notice that the $PVIF_a$ factor for any year n can be obtained by summing the $PVIF$ factors from 1 to n, that is,

$$PVIF_a = \sum_{t=0}^{n} PVIF.$$

To illustrate, if $n = 3$ and $i = 10\%$, then, from Table 10–3, we obtain $PVIF$ values, sum them, and find they differ from the $PVIF_a$ factor in Table 10–5 only by a rounding error: $PVIF_a = .909 + .826 + .751 = 2.486.$

TABLE 10–5   Present Value of an Annuity of $1: $PVIF_a = \dfrac{1 - \dfrac{1}{(1+i)^n}}{i}$

Period	1%	2%	3%	4%	5%	6%	7%	8%	9%	10%
1	0.990	0.980	0.971	0.962	0.952	0.943	0.935	0.926	0.917	0.909
2	1.970	1.942	1.913	1.886	1.859	1.833	1.808	1.783	1.759	1.736
3	2.941	2.884	2.829	2.775	2.723	2.673	2.624	2.577	2.531	2.487
4	3.902	3.808	3.717	3.630	3.546	3.465	3.387	3.312	3.240	3.170
5	4.853	4.713	4.580	4.452	4.329	4.212	4.100	3.993	3.890	3.791
6	5.795	5.601	5.417	5.242	5.076	4.917	4.766	4.623	4.486	4.355
7	6.728	6.472	6.230	6.002	5.786	5.582	5.389	5.206	5.033	4.868
8	7.652	7.325	7.020	6.733	6.463	6.210	6.971	5.747	5.535	5.335
9	8.566	8.162	7.786	7.435	7.108	6.802	6.515	6.247	5.985	5.759
10	9.471	8.983	8.530	8.111	7.722	7.360	7.024	6.710	6.418	6.145

ANNUAL PAYMENTS TO ACCUMULATE A FUTURE SUM

Thus far in the chapter all the equations have been based on Equation 10–2. The present value equation merely involves a transposition of Equation 10–2, and the annuity equations merely take the sum of the basic compound interest equation for different values of n. We now examine some additional modifications of the equations.

Suppose we want to know the amount of money that must be deposited at 5 percent for each of the next five years in order to have $10,000 available to pay off a debt at the end of the fifth year. Dividing both sides of Equation 10–4 by $CVIF_a$, we obtain

$$R = \frac{S_n}{CVIF_a}.$$

Looking up the sum of an annuity interest factor for five years at 5 percent in Table 10–4 and dividing that figure into $10,000, we find

$$R = \frac{\$10,000}{5.526} = \$1,810.$$

Thus, if $1,810 is deposited each year in an account paying 5 percent interest, at the end of five years the account will have accumulated $10,000. We will employ this procedure in later chapters when we discuss sinking funds set up to provide for bond retirements.

ANNUAL RECEIPTS FROM AN ANNUITY

Suppose that on September 1, 19X1, you receive an inheritance of $7,000. The money is to be used for your education and is to be spent during the academic years beginning September 19X2, 19X3, and 19X4. If you place the money in a bank account paying 4 percent annual interest and make three equal withdrawals at each of the specified dates, how large can each withdrawal be to leave you with exactly a zero balance after the last one has been made?

The solution requires application of the present value of an annuity formula, Equation 10–6. Here, however, we know that the present value of the annuity is $7,000, and the problem is to find the three equal annual payments when the interest rate is 4 percent. This calls for dividing both sides of Equation 10–6 by $PVIF_a$ to make Equation 10–7.

$$A_n = R \times PVIF_a \qquad (10\text{–}6)$$

$$R = \frac{A_n}{PVIF_a}. \qquad (10\text{–}7)$$

The interest factor ($PVIF_a$) is found in Table 10–5 to be 2.775; substituting this value into Equation 10–7, we find the three equal annual withdrawals to be $2,523 a year:

$$R = \frac{\$7,000}{2.775} = \$2,523.$$

This particular kind of calculation is used frequently in setting up insurance and pension plan benefit schedules; a good example is the calculation of the maximum annuity payments to individuals who register in a Registered Retirement Savings Plan. It is also used to find the periodic payments necessary to retire a loan within a specified period. For example, if you want to retire a $7,000 bank loan, bearing interest at 4 percent on the unpaid balance, in three equal annual installments, the amount of each payment is $2,523. In this case, you are the borrower, and the bank is "buying" an annuity with a present value of $7,000.

PRESENT VALUE OF A PERPETUITY

A *perpetuity* is defined as a series of payments of a fixed amount that continue forever; each payment is made at the end of the year. The perpetuity, then, is equivalent to a perpetual annuity. Because of its very simple mathematical solution, perpetuities are used frequently in theoretical finance literature and in a large number of numerical illustrations of theoretical results. The real world applications of this concept are limited to the valuation of perpetual bonds—a topic covered in Chapter 18. Until recently, the Government of Canada had a perpetual bond outstanding.

Suppose you are offered, today, the option to purchase a perpetuity that will pay you $1,000 per year, forever. Since we are safe in ruling out immortality, assume that you will give the perpetuity as an inheritance. The opportunity cost for investments of this risk, as of today, is 6 percent. What is the maximum price that you would pay for this perpetuity?

Let P_∞ be the present value of the perpetual stream of receipts; R the annual receipts, and i the opportunity cost. The present value is written in Equation 10–8 below.

$$P = R\left(\frac{1}{1+i}\right) + R\left(\frac{1}{1+i}\right)^2 + \ldots + R\left(\frac{1}{1+i}\right)^n + \ldots$$

$$= \frac{R}{1+i}\left(1 + \frac{1}{1+i} + \left[\frac{1}{1+i}\right]^2 + \ldots\right)$$

$$= \frac{R}{i}$$

(10–8)

The first line of Equation 10–8 shows that the present value is the sum of the discounted periodic receipts. This equation is rewritten in the second line; the entries within the large parentheses represent the sum of an infinite geometric series.[3] The final result is presented on the third line. In the

[3]In order to move from the second to the third line of Equation 10–8, the reader must be familiar with the concept of a geometric progression. A geometric progression is a series of numbers where any number is

example, the maximum amount that should be paid for this perpetuity is $16,667 (i.e. $1,000/.06).

Annual Receipts from a Perpetuity

An individual decides that, upon retirement, she will cash in her retirement savings plan and purchase a perpetuity that will be left to her children after her death. What is the maximum annual receipt that she can obtain given that the retirement fund has $60,000 and the interest rate is 6 percent?

Equation 10-8, can be rewritten, if both sides are multiplied by i, as:

$$R = P_\infty \times i$$

where R is the maximum annual perpetual receipt. In this example, $P = $60,000$, $i = 6$ percent and $R = $3,600$ (i.e. $60,000 \times .06$). Therefore, this individual can purchase a perpetuity today for $60,000 that will pay $3,600 per year in perpetuity beginning one year from today.

DETERMINING INTEREST RATES

In many instances the present values and cash flows associated with a payment stream are known, but the interest rate involved is not known. Suppose a bank offers to lend you $1,000 today if you sign a note agreeing to pay the bank $1,217 at the end of five years. What rate of interest would you be paying on the loan? To answer the question we must use Equation 10-2:

$$P_n = P_0 (1 + i)^n = P_0 (CVIF). \qquad (10\text{-}2)$$

Simply solve for $CVIF$, then look up this value of $CVIF$ in Table 10-2 (or A-1) under the row for the fifth year:

$$CVIF = \frac{P_5}{P_0} = \frac{\$1,217}{\$1,000} = 1.217.$$

Looking across the row for the fifth year, we find the value 1.217 in the 4 percent column; therefore, the interest rate on the loan is 4 percent.

Precisely the same approach is taken to determine the interest rate implicit in an annuity. For example, suppose a bank will lend you $2,775 if you sign a note in which you agree to pay the bank $1,000 at the end of each of

---

equal to the previous number times a constant factor. Let the initial value be a and the factor be g. Then the second number is ag; the third number is ag^2, etc. The sum of an infinite geometric progression is $a/1-g$. In our example, $a = 1$ and $g = 1/1 + i$.

Thus, Equation 10-8 is rewritten as:

$$P = \frac{R}{1+i} \left(\frac{1}{1 - 1/1 + i} \right)$$
$$= \frac{R}{1+i} \left(\frac{1+i}{i} \right)$$
$$= \frac{R}{i}.$$

PART THREE – DECISIONS INVOLVING LONG-TERM ASSETS

the next three years. What interest rate is the bank charging you? To answer the question, solve Equation 10–6 for $PVIF_a$, then look up $PVIF_a$ in Table 10–5 or (A–4):

$$A_n = R \times PVIF_a \qquad (10\text{–}6)$$

$$PVIF_a = \frac{A_3}{R} = \frac{\$2,775}{\$1,000} = 2.775.$$

Looking across the third-year row, we find the factor 2.775 under the 4 percent column; therefore the bank is lending you money at 4 percent.

PRESENT VALUE OF AN UNEVEN SERIES OF RECEIPTS

Recall that the definition of an annuity includes the words *fixed amount*—in other words, annuities deal with constant, or level, payments or receipts. Although many financial decisions do involve constant payments, many important decisions are concerned with uneven flows of cash. In particular, the kinds of fixed asset investments dealt with in the following chapter very frequently involve uneven flows. Consequently, it is necessary to expand our analysis to deal with varying payment streams. Since most of the applications call for present values, not compound sums or other figures, this section is restricted to the present value *(PV)*.

To illustrate the calculating procedure, suppose someone offers to sell you a series of payments consisting of $300 after one year, $100 after two years, and $200 after three years. How much would you be willing to pay for the series, assuming the appropriate discount rate (interest rate) is 4 percent? To determine the purchase price, simply compute the present value of the series; the calculations are worked out in Table 10–6. The receipts for each year are shown in the second column; the discount factors (from Table 10–3) are given in the third column; and the product of these two columns, the present value of each individual receipt, is given in the last column. When the individual present values in the last column are added, the sum is the present value of the investment, $558.90. Under the assumptions of the example, you should be willing to pay this amount for the investment.

Table 10–6 Calculating the Present Value of an Uneven Series of Payments

Period	Receipt	×	Interest Factor (PVIF)	=	Present Value (PV or P_0)
1	$300		.962		$288.60
2	100		.925		92.50
3	200		.889		177.80
				PV of investment	$558.90

Had the series of payments been somewhat different—say $300 at the end of the first year, $200 at the end of the second year, then eight annual payments of $100 each—we would probably want to use a different procedure for finding the investment's present value. We could, of course, set up a calculating table such as Table 10–6, but because most of the payments are part of an annuity we can use a short cut. The calculating procedure is shown in Table 10–7, and the logic of the table is diagrammed in Figure 10–5.

FIGURE 10–5 Graphic Illustration of Present Value Calculations for an Uneven Series of Payments That Includes an Annuity

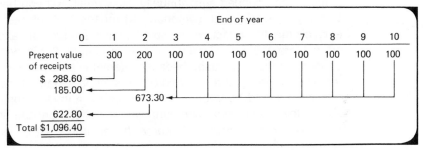

Section 1 of Table 10–7 deals with the $300 and the $200 received at the end of the first and second years respectively; their present values are found to be $288.60 and $185. Section 2 deals with the eight $100 payments. In part (a), the value of a $100, 8-year, 4 percent annuity is found to be $673.30. However, the first receipt under the annuity comes at the end of the third year, so it is worth less than $673.30 today. Specifically, it is worth the present value of $673.30, discounted back two years at 4 percent, or $622.80; this calculation is shown in part (b) of section 2.[4] When the present values of the first two payments are added to the present value of the annuity component, the sum is the present value of the entire investment, or $1,096.40.

Table 10–7 Calculating Procedure for an Uneven Series of Payments That Includes an Annuity

1. *PV* of $300 due in 1 year = $300(0.962) =	$ 288.60
PV of $200 due in 2 years = $200(0.925) =	185.00
2. *PV* of eight-year annuity with $100 receipts	
(a) *PV* at beginning of year 3: $100(6.733) = $673.30	
(b) *PV* of $673.30 = $673.30(0.925) =	622.80
3. *PV* of total series =	$1,096.40

[4]The present value of the annuity portion, $622.80, could also have been found by subtracting the *PVIF* for a two-year annuity from the *PVIF$_a$* for a ten-year annuity, then multiplying the result by $100.

SEMIANNUAL AND OTHER COMPOUNDING PERIODS[5]

In all the examples used thus far, it has been assumed that returns were received once a year, or annually. For example, in the first section of the chapter, dealing with compound values, it was assumed that funds were placed on deposit in a savings and loan association and grew by 4 percent a year. However, suppose the advertised rate had been 4 percent compounded *semiannually*. What would this have meant? Consider the following example.

You deposit $1,000 in a bank savings account and receive a return of 4 percent compounded semiannually. How much will you have at the end of one year? Semiannual compounding means that interest is actually paid each six months, a fact taken into account in the tabular calculations in Table 10–8. Here, the annual interest rate is divided by 2, but twice as many compounding periods are used because interest is paid twice a year. Comparing the amount on hand at the end of the second six-month period, $1,040.40, with what would have been on hand under annual compounding, $1,040, shows that semiannual compounding is better from the standpoint of the saver. *This result occurs, of course, because interest is earned on interest more frequently.*

Table 10–8 Compound Interest Calculations with Semiannual Compounding

Period	Beginning amount (P_0)	×	$(1 + i)$	=	Ending amount (P_n)
1	$1,000.00		(1.02)		$1,020.00
2	1,020.00		(1.02)		1,040.40

General formulas can be developed for use when compounding periods are more frequent than once a year. To demonstrate this, Equation 10–2 is modified as follows:

$$P_n = P_0(1 + i)^n. \qquad (10\text{–}2)$$

$$P_n = P_0\left(1 + \frac{i}{m}\right)^{mn} \qquad (10\text{–}9)$$

Here, m is the number of times per year compounding occurs. When banks compute daily interest, the value of m is set at 365, and Equation 10-9 is applied.

The interest tables can be used when compounding occurs more than once a year. Simply divide the nominal, or stated, interest rate by the number of times compounding occurs, and multiply the years by the number of compounding periods per year. For example, to find the amount to which $1,000

---

[5]This section can be omitted without loss of continuity.

will grow after five years if semiannual compounding is applied to a stated 4 percent interest rate, divide 4 percent by 2 and multiply the five years by 2. Then look in Table 10–2 (or Table A–1) under the 2 percent column and in the row for the tenth period. You find an interest factor of 1.219. Multiplying this by the initial $1,000 gives a value of $1,219, the amount to which $1,000 will grow in five years at 4 percent compounded semiannually. This compares with $1,217 for annual compounding.

The same procedure is applied in all the cases covered—compounding, discounting, single payments, and annuities. To illustrate semiannual compounding in finding the present value of an annuity, for example, consider the case described in the above section, Present Value of an Annuity: $1,000 a year for three years, discounted at 4 percent. With annual compounding (or discounting) the interest factor is 2.775, and the present value of the annuity is $2,775. For semiannual compounding look under the 2 percent column and in the year-6 row of Table 10–5, to find an interest factor of 5.601. This is now multiplied by half of $1,000, or the $500 received each six months, to get the present value of the annuity, $2,800. The payments come a little more rapidly —the first $500 is paid after only six months (similarly with other payments), so the annuity is a little more valuable if payments are received semiannually rather than annually.

By letting m approach infinity, Equation 10-9 can be modified to the special case of *continuous compounding*. Continuous compounding is extremely useful in theoretical finance, and it also has practical applications. For example, some banks and savings associations pay interest on a continuous basis.

EFFECTIVE INTEREST RATES

If compounding occurs more than once a year, the *stated* or *nominal annual rate of interest* is not equal to the *true* or *effective annual interest rate.* The effective rate is that annual interest rate that will produce the same future value as obtained by compounding more frequently than once a year.

If the initial amount invested (P_0) is $1, then the future value after 1 year, with compounding more than once a year, is obtained from Equation 10-9, where $n = 1$.

$$P_1 = P_0 \left(1 + \frac{i}{m}\right)^m = \left(1 + \frac{i}{m}\right)^m$$

But the same future value could be obtained by compounding once a year at the effective rate of interest, i^*. This equivalence is shown in Equation 10-10.

$$\left(1 + \frac{i}{m}\right)^m = 1 + i^* \tag{10-10}$$

Subtracting 1 from both sides of Equation 10-10 results in the effective interest rate as a function of the nominal annual rate and the number of compounding periods.

$$i^* = \left(1 + \frac{i}{m}\right)^m - 1$$

For example, in Table 10-9 we present the effective interest rate for a number of compounding periods and the nominal annual interest rates of 6 and 12 percent.

TABLE 10-9 Effective Interest Rates

Annual Nominal Rate, i	Number of Compounding Periods per year, m				
	1	2	3	6	Infinite[a]
6%	6%	6.09%	6.12%	6.15%	6.18%
12%	12%	12.36%	12.49%	12.62%	12.75%

[a]This is continuous compounding and the effective rate is calculated as $e^i - 1$.

As an example, consider the 6 percent nominal rate compounded every four months. Substituting into the equation for the effective rate, we obtain:

$$i^* = \left(1 + \frac{.06}{3}\right)^3 - 1 \quad = (1 + .02)^3 - 1$$

Using Table 10-2, we find that the compound value of $1 at 2 percent for 3 periods is 1.061. The effective interest rate is 6.1 percent.[6]

There are two important observations from Table 10-9. First, for a given nominal rate, the effective rate of interest increases as the number of compounding periods per year increase. Second, the effective rate increases at a decreasing *rate*. The biggest impact is the change from annual to semi-annual compounding. Increasing the number of compounding periods per year does not have as large an impact on the effective annual interest rate.

A SPECIAL CASE OF SEMIANNUAL COMPOUNDING: BOND VALUES[7]

Most bonds pay interest semiannually, so semiannual compounding procedures are appropriate for determining bond values. To illustrate, suppose a particular bond pays interest in the amount of $30 each six months, or $60 a year. The bond will mature in ten years, paying $1,000 (the "principal") at that time. Thus, if you buy the bond you will receive an annuity of $30 each six months, or twenty payments in total, plus $1,000 at the end of ten years (or twenty six-month periods). What is the bond worth, assuming that the appropriate market discount (or interest) rate is (A) 6 percent; (B) higher than 6 percent, say 8 percent; and (C) lower than 6 percent, say 4 percent?

[6]The entries in Table 10-9 differ from the results obtained from the use of the CVIF tables because the latter present one less significant digit.

[7]This section may be omitted without loss of continuity.

PART A: 6% discount rate.

Step 1. You are buying an annuity plus a lump sum of $1,000.

Find the PV of the interest payments:

1. Use $i/m = 6\%/2 = 3\%$ as the "interest rate."
2. Look up the $PVIF_a$ in Table A–4 for 20 periods at 3 percent, which is 14.877.
3. Find the PV of the stream of interest payments:

$$PV \text{ of the interest} = \$30 \ (PVIF_a)$$
$$= \$30(14.877) = \$446.$$

Step 2. Find the PV of the $1,000 maturity value:

1. Use $i/m = 6\%/2 = 3\%$ as the "interest rate."[8]
2. Look up the PVIF in Table A–2 for twenty periods at 3 percent, which is .554.
3. Find the PV of that value at maturity:

$$PV \text{ of the maturity value} = \$1,000(PVIF)$$
$$= \$1,000(.554) = \$554.$$

Step 3. Combine the two component PV's to determine the value of the bond:

Bond value = $446 + $554 = $1,000.

PART B: 8% discount rate. Repeating the process, we have

Step 1. $8\%/2 = 4\% =$ the "interest rate."

$PVIF_a$ from Table A–4 = 13.59.

PVIF from Table A–2 = .456.

Step 2. Bond value = $30(13.59) + $1,000(.456)

$$= \$408 + \$456$$
$$= \$864.$$

Notice that the bond is worth less when the going rate of interest for investments of similar risk is 8 percent than when it is 6 percent. At a price of $864, this bond provides an annual rate of return of 8 percent; at a price of $1,000, it provides an annual return of 6 percent. If 6 percent is the "going rate of return" on a bond of a given degree of risk, then whenever interest rates in the economy rise to the point where bonds of this degree of risk have an 8 percent return, the price of our bond will decline to $864, at which price it will yield the competitive rate of return, 8 percent.

---

[8]This question is sometimes raised: "Why not discount the $1,000 at 6% over 10 years rather than at 3 percent for 20 six-month periods?" The answer is that the same compounding rate should be used for different elements in a cash flow stream. Six percent compounded semiannually (3 percent each six months) is different from 6 percent annually so for consistency the $1,000 must be discounted at 3 percent over twenty periods. Alternatively, from Table 10-9, it is seen that the effective annual rate for 6 percent compounded semi-annually is 6.09 percent. The $1,000 could be discounted at this effective rate for 10 years. However, the present value must be identical to that obtained from semi-annual discounting. In any case, bonds are priced in the market as we have calculated, so for consistency with the "real world" our procedure must be followed.

PART C: 4% discount rate. Using the same process produces the following results:

Step 1. 4 percent/2 = 2 percent = the "interest rate."
$PVIF_a$ from Table A–4 = 16.351.
PVIF from Table A–2 = .673.

Step 2. Bond value = $30(16.351) + $1,000(.673)
= $491 + $673 = $1,164.

The bond is worth *more* than $1,000 when the going rate of interest is less than 6 percent, because then it offers a yield higher than the going rate. Its price rises to $1,164, where it provides a 4 percent annual rate of return. This calculation illustrates the fact that when interest rates in the economy decline, the prices of outstanding bonds rise.

APPROPRIATE COMPOUNDING OR DISCOUNTING RATES

Throughout the chapter, assumed compounding or discounting rates have been used in the examples. Although we will cover the subject in depth later in the book, it is useful at this point to give some idea of what the appropriate interest rate for a particular investment might be.[9]

The starting point is, of course, the general level of interest rates in the economy as a whole. This level is set by the interaction of supply-and-demand forces, with demand for funds coming largely from businesses, individual borrowers, and the federal government when it is running a deficit. Funds are supplied by individual and corporate savers and, under the control of the Bank of Canada, by the creation of money by banks. Depending on the relative levels of supply and demand the basic pattern of interest rates is determined.

There is no one rate of interest in the economy—rather, there is, at any given time, an array of different rates. The lowest rates are found on the safest investments, the highest rates on the most risky ones. Usually, there is less risk on investments that mature in the near future than on longer term investments, so higher rates are usually associated with long-term investments. There are other factors that affect interest rate differentials (also called "yield" differentials), but a discussion of these factors is best deferred until later in the book.

A person faced with the kinds of decisions considered in this chapter must accept the existing set of interest rates found in the economy. If he or she has money to invest, the person could invest in short-term, Government of Canada securities and incur no risk whatever. However, one will generally have to accept a relatively low yield on the investment. If a person is willing to

[9]For convenience, in this chapter we speak of "interest rates," which implies that only debt is involved. In later chapters this concept is broadened considerably, and the term "rate of return" is used in lieu of "interest rate."

accept a little more interest-rate risk, one can invest in longer-term, government securities which usually have a higher yield. The investor may be willing to accept default risk, and thus purchase high-grade, long-term corporate bonds which will be priced to give a higher rate of return than long-term government securities. If the investor is willing to accept still more risk, he or she can move into common shares where the return (dividends plus capital gains) on investment is more variable, but expected to be higher. Other alternatives include bank and trust company deposits, lower-grade corporate bonds, mortgages, apartment houses, land held for speculation, and so on.

Risk Premiums

With only a limited amount of money to invest, one must pick and choose among investments; the final selection involves a tradeoff between risk and expected returns. Suppose, for example, that you are indifferent between a five-year government bond yielding 4 percent a year, a five-year corporate bond yielding 5 percent, and a share of stock on which you can expect a 6 percent return. Given this situation, you can take the government bond as a riskless security, and you attach a 1 percent risk premium to the corporate bond and a 2 percent risk premium to the share of stock. Risk premiums, then, are the added returns that risky investments must command over less risky ones if there is to be a demand for risky assets. The concept of the risk premium is discussed in detail in Chapter 18.

Opportunity Costs

Although there are many potential investments available in the economy at any given time, a particular individual actively considers only a limited number of them. After making adjustments for risk differentials, the various alternatives are ranked from the most attractive to the least. Then, presumably, our investor puts his or her available funds in the most attractive investment. If a new investment is being offered, one must compare it with the best of the existing alternatives with the same level of risk. If the investor accepts the new investment, he or she must give up the opportunity of investing in the best of the old alternatives with the same level of risk as the new investment. *The yield on the best of the alternatives of similar risk is defined as the opportunity cost of investing in the new alternative.* For example, suppose you have funds invested in a bank time deposit that pays 6 percent. Now suppose that someone offers you another investment of equal risk. To make the new investment, you must withdraw funds from the bank deposit; therefore *6 percent is defined as the opportunity cost of the new investment.* You could determine the interest rate on the new investment (using Equation 10–2); if the new investment yields more than 6 percent, then make the switch. We have stressed the idea that an opportunity cost for a given investment must reflect the risk of the investment. Therefore, if an investor has placed $1,000 in a time deposit at 6 percent and has the option to invest in a short-term corporate security, the opportunity cost of the new investment is *not* 6 percent, because the risks are not equivalent. The interest rates used in the examples throughout this chapter were all determined as opportunity costs available to the person in the example. This concept is also used in the following chapter, where we consider business decisions on investments in fixed assets, or the *capital budgeting decision*.

SUMMARY

A knowledge of compound interest and present value techniques is essential to an understanding of many important aspects of finance: capital budgeting, financial structure, security valuation, and many other topics. The basic principles of compound interest, together with the most important formulas used in practice, were described in this chapter:

Compound Value:

$$P_n = P_0(1 + i)^n.$$

Present Value (*PV*):

$$P_0 = P_n\left[\frac{1}{(1 + i)^n}\right].$$

Compound Value of an Annuity:

Compound value = $CVIF_a \times$ annual receipt.

Present Value of an Annuity:

PV of annuity = $PVIF_a \times$ annual receipt.

Present Value of a Perpetuity:

PV of perpetuity = $\dfrac{1}{\text{interest rate}} \times$ annual receipt.

Effective Annual Rate:

$$i^* = \left(1 + \frac{i}{m}\right)^m - 1$$

Other Uses of the Basic Equations   The basic interest formulas can be used in combination to find such things as the present value of an uneven series of receipts. The formulas can also be transformed to find (1) the annual payments necessary to accumulate a future sum, (2) the annual receipts from a specified annuity, (3) the periodic payments necessary to amortize a loan, and (4) the interest rate implicit in a loan contract.

Appropriate Interest Rate   The appropriate interest rate to be used is critical when working with compound interest problems. The true nature of the interest rates to be used when working with business problems can be understood only after the chapters dealing with the cost of capital have been examined; this chapter concluded with a brief discussion of some of the factors that determine the appropriate rate of interest for a particular problem—the risk of the investment and the investor's opportunity cost of money.

QUESTIONS

10-1. What kinds of financial decisions require explicit consideration of the interest factor?

10-2. Compound interest relations are important for decisions other than financial ones. Why are they important to marketing managers?

10-3. Would you rather have an account in a chartered bank that pays 7 percent interest compounded semiannually or 7 percent interest compounded daily? Why? (Calculate the effective annual rates on each option.)

10-4. For a given interest rate and a given number of years, is the interest factor for the sum of an annuity larger or smaller than the interest factor for the present value of the annuity?

10-5. Suppose you are examining two investments, A and B. Both have the same maturity, but A pays a 6 percent return and B yields 5 percent. Which investment is probably riskier? How do you know it is riskier?

PROBLEMS

10-1. Which amount is worth more at 7 percent: $1,000 today or $2,000 after ten years?

10-2. At an annual growth rate of 8 percent, how long does it take a sum to double?

10-3. a. What amount would be paid for a $1,000, fifteen-year bond that pays $30 interest semiannually ($60 a year) and is sold to yield 10 percent, compounded semiannually?

b. What would be paid if the bond is sold to yield 6 percent?

c. What would be paid if semiannual interest payments are $45 and the bond is sold to yield 8 percent?

10-4. You are offered a stream of $150 per year in perpetuity. The current interest rate is 8 percent.

a. What is the price you would pay for this perpetuity today?

b. Would the price you pay be different if there was a probability that the payments may not be met in every future year?

c. What price would you pay for the same payment stream if you purchased it one year later? Assume that the interest rate remains at 8 percent.

10-5. On December 31, Craig Fields buys a building for $60,000, payable 15 percent down and the balance in 20 equal annual installments that are to include principal plus 10 percent compound interest on the declining balance. What are the equal installments?

10-6. Having proven yourself to be a superior student, your university offers you a choice between an outright gift of $2,000 or a $10,000 interest-free loan to be paid back in five equal annual installments of $2,000 each. Which alternative would represent the optimal choice for you?

10-7. The Scott Company Ltd. is establishing a sinking fund to retire an $800,000 mortgage that matures on December 31, XX15. The company plans to put a fixed amount into the fund each year for fifteen years. The first payment will be made on December 31, XX01, the last on December 31, XX15. The company anticipates that the fund will earn 8 percent a year. What annual contributions must be made to accumulate the $800,000 as of December 31, XX15?

10-8. You have just purchased a newly issued $1,000, five-year Dot Company Ltd. bond for $1,000. This bond pays $40 in interest payments semiannually ($80 a year); call this bond A. You are also negotiating the purchase of a $1,000, five-year Dot Company Ltd. bond which returns $25 in semiannual interest payments and has five years remaining before it matures; call this bond B.

a. What is the "going rate of return" on bonds of the risk and maturity of Dot Company's bonds?

b. What should you be willing to pay for bond B?

c. How would your answer for the value of bond B change if bond A had paid $20 in semiannual interest instead of $40, but still sold for $1,000? The second bond still pays $25 semiannually and $1,000 at the end of five years.

10-9. You need $66,132 at the end of twenty years. You know that the best you can do is to make equal payments into a bank account on which you can earn 5 percent interest compounded annually.

a. What amount must you plan to pay annually to achieve your objective? The first payment is to be made at the end of the first year.

b. Instead of making annual payments, you decide to make one lump-sum payment today. To achieve your objective of $66,132 at the end of the twenty-year period, what should this sum be? You can still earn 5 percent interest compounded annually on your account.

10-10. You can buy a note at a price of $10,250. If you buy the note, you will receive five annual payments of $2,500, the first payment to be made one year from today. What rate of return, or yield, does the note offer?

10-11. You can buy a bond for $1,000 that will pay no interest during its 5-year life but will have a value of $1,276 when it matures. What rate of interest will you earn if you buy the bond and hold it to maturity?

10-12. A bank agrees to lend you $1,000 today in return for your promise to pay the bank $1,419 six years from today. What rate of interest is the bank charging you?

10-13. If earnings in 1979 were $2.16 a share, while ten years earlier, in 1969, they were $1, what has been the annual rate of growth in earnings?

10-14. The Hudson Company Ltd.'s sales last year were $1 million.

a. Assuming that sales grow 15 percent a year, calculate sales for each of the next five years.

b. Plot the sales projections.

c. If your graph is correct, your projected sales curve is nonlinear. If it had been linear, would this have indicated a constant, increasing, or decreasing percentage growth rate?

10-15. You are considering two investment opportunities, A and B. A is expected to pay $300 a year for the first ten years, $500 a year for the next fifteen years, and nothing thereafter. B is expected to pay $1,000 a year for ten years, and nothing thereafter. You find that alternative investments of similar risk yield 7 percent and 16 percent for A and B respectively.

a. Find the present value of each investment. Show calculations.

b. Which is the more risky investment? Why?

c. Assume that your rich uncle will give you your choice of investments without cost to you, and that (1) you must hold the investment for its entire life (cannot sell it) or (2) you are free to sell it at its going market price. Which investment would you prefer under each of the two conditions?

10-16. The Hudson Company Ltd.'s common shares paid a dividend of $1 last year. Dividends are expected to grow at a rate of 15 percent for each of the next five years.

a. Calculate the expected dividend for each of the next five years.

b. Assuming that the first of these five dividends will be paid one year from now, what is the present value of the five dividends? Given the riskiness of the dividend stream, 15 percent is the appropriate discount rate.

c. Assume that the price of the shares will be $20 five years from now. What is the present value of this "terminal value?" Use a 15 percent discount rate.

d. Assume that you will buy the share, receive the five dividends, then sell the share; how much should you be willing to pay for it?

e. Do not do any calculations for this question, but explain in words what would happen to the share price (1) if the discount rate declined because the riskiness of the equity declined or (2) if the growth rate of the dividend stream increased.

10-17. The Pettway Printing Company Limited is considering the purchase of a new press that will provide the following net cash flow (or profit) stream:

Year	
1	$10,000
2	20,000
3	30,000
4	40,000
5	50,000
6	60,000

a. What is the present value of the profit stream, using a 10 percent discount rate?

b. If the press costs $100,000, should Pettway Printing purchase it?

Capital Budgeting Techniques

Capital budgeting involves the entire process of planning expenditures whose returns are expected to extend beyond one year. The choice of one year is arbitrary, of course, but it is a convenient cutoff point for distinguishing between kinds of expenditures. Obvious examples of capital outlays are expenditures for land, buildings, and equipment, and for permanent additions to working capital associated with plant expansion. An advertising or promotion campaign, or a program of research and development, is also likely to have an impact beyond one year, so they too can be classified as capital budgeting expenditures.

Capital budgeting is important for the future well-being of the firm: it is also a complex, conceptually difficult topic. As we shall see later in this chapter, the optimum capital budget—the level of investment that maximizes the present value of the firm—is simultaneously determined by the interaction of supply and demand forces under conditions of uncertainty. Supply forces refer to the supply of capital to the firm, or its *cost of capital schedule.* Demand forces relate to the investment opportunities open to the firm, as measured by the *stream of revenues* that will result from an investment decision. *Uncertainty* enters the decision because it is impossible to know exactly either the cost of capital or the stream of revenues that will be derived from a project.

To facilitate an exposition of the investment decision process, we have broken the topic down into its major components. In this chapter, we consider the capital budgeting process and the techniques generally employed by reasonably sophisticated business firms. Here our focus is on the time factor, and the compound interest concepts covered in the preceding chapter are

242

used extensively. Uncertainty is explicitly and formally considered in Chapter 12, and the cost of capital concept is developed and related to capital budgeting in Chapters 18 through 20, after a discussion of the sources and forms of long-term capital in Chapters 13 through 17.

SIGNIFICANCE OF CAPITAL BUDGETING

A number of factors combine to make capital budgeting perhaps the most important decision with which financial management is involved. Further, all departments of a firm—production, marketing, and so on—are vitally affected by the capital budgeting decisions, so all executives, no matter what their primary responsibility, must be aware of how capital budgeting decisions are made. In addition, the determination of the information required to use the capital budgeting techniques forces a careful analysis of the expected costs and benefits of a number of projects. These points are discussed in this section.

Long-Term Effects

First and foremost, the fact that the results continue over an extended period means that the decision maker loses some flexibility. He or she must make a commitment into the future. For example, the purchase of an asset with an economic life of ten years requires a long period of waiting before the final results of the action can be known.

Asset expansion is fundamentally related to expected future sales. A decision to buy or to construct a fixed asset that is expected to last five years involves an implicit five-year sales forecast. Indeed, the economic life of a purchased asset represents an implicit forecast for the duration of the economic life of the asset. Hence, failure to forecast accurately will result in overinvestment or underinvestment in fixed assets.

An erroneous forecast of asset requirements can result in serious consequences. If the firm has invested too much in assets, it will incur unnecessarily heavy expenses. If it has not spent enough on fixed assets, two serious problems may arise. First, the firm's equipment may not be sufficiently modern to enable it to produce competitively. Second, if it has inadequate capacity, it may lose a portion of its share of the market to rival firms. To regain lost customers typically requires heavy selling expenses, price reductions, or both.

Raising Funds

Another reason for the importance of capital budgeting is that asset expansion typically involves substantial expenditures. Before a firm spends a large amount of money, it must make the proper plans—large amounts of funds are not available automatically. A firm contemplating a major capital expenditure program may need to arrange its financing several years in advance to be sure of having the funds required for the expansion.

A SIMPLIFIED VIEW OF CAPITAL BUDGETING

Capital budgeting is, in essence, an application of a classic proposition from the economic theory of the firm: namely, a firm should operate at the point where its marginal revenue is just equal to its marginal cost. When this rule is applied to the capital budgeting decision, marginal revenue is taken to be the percentage rate of return on investments, while marginal cost is the firm's marginal cost of capital. It will be demonstrated in Chapter 20 that the firm's cost of capital is a marginal cost derived as a long-run weighted average of the required yields on the various sources of funds that the firm intends to use.

A simplified version of the concept is depicted in Figure 11–1(a). Here the horizontal axis measures the dollars of investment during a year, while the vertical axis shows both the percentage cost of capital and the rate of return on projects. The projects are denoted by boxes—project A, for example, calls for an outlay of $3 million and promises a 17 percent rate of return; project B requires $1 million and yields about 16 percent; and so on. In Figure 11–1(b), the concept is generalized to show smoothed investment opportunity schedules *(IRR),* and three alternative schedules are presented.[1]

FIGURE 11–1   Illustrative Capital Budgeting Decision Process

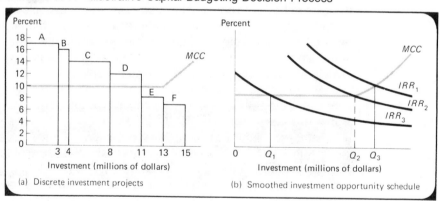

(a) Discrete investment projects

(b) Smoothed investment opportunity schedule

---

[1]The investment opportunity schedules measure the rate of return on each project. The rate of return on a project is generally called the *internal rate of return* (*IRR*). This is why we label the investment opportunity schedules *IRR*. The process of calculating the *IRR* is explained later in this chapter.

The curve *MCC* designates the marginal cost of capital, or the cost of each additional dollar acquired for purposes of making capital expenditures. As it is drawn in 11–1(a), the marginal cost of capital is constant at 10 percent until the firm has raised $13 million, after which the marginal cost of capital curve turns up.[2] To maximize profits, the firm should accept projects A through D, obtaining and investing $11 million, and reject E and F.

Notice that three alternative investment opportunity schedules are shown in 11–1(b). IRR_1 designates relatively many good investment opportunities, while IRR_3 designates relatively few good projects. The three different curves could be interpreted as applying either to three different firms or to one firm at three different times. As long as the *IRR* curve cuts the *MCC* curve to the left of Q_2—for example, at Q_1—the marginal cost of capital is constant. To the right of Q_2—for example, at Q_3—the cost of capital is rising. Therefore, if investment opportunities are such that the *IRR* curve cuts the *MCC* curve to the right of Q_2, the *actual* marginal cost of capital (a single point) varies depending on the *IRR* curve. In this chapter we generally *assume* that the *IRR* curve cuts the *MCC* curve to the left of Q_2, thus permitting us to assume that the cost of capital is constant. This assumption is relaxed in Chapter 20, where we show how the *MCC* varies with the amount of funds raised during a given year.

APPLICATION OF THE CONCEPT

At the applied level, the capital budgeting process is much more complex than the preceding example suggests. Projects do not just appear; a continuing stream of good investment opportunities results from hard thinking, careful planning, and, often, large outlays for research and development. Moreover, some very difficult measurement problems are involved: the sales and costs associated with particular projects must be estimated, frequently for many years into the future, in the face of great uncertainty. Finally, some difficult conceptual and empirical problems arise over the methods of calculating rates of return and the cost of capital.

Businessmen are required to take action, however, even in the face of the kinds of problems described; this requirement has led to the development of procedures that assist in making optimal investment decisions. One of these procedures, forecasting, was discussed in Chapter 5; uncertainty is discussed in formal terms in the next chapter; and the important subject of the cost of capital is deferred to Chapter 20. The essentials of the other elements of capital budgeting are taken up in the remainder of this chapter.

---

[2]The reasons for assuming this particular shape for the marginal cost of capital curve are explained in Chapter 20.

Investment Proposals

Aside from the actual generation of ideas, the first step in the capital budgeting process is to assemble a list of the proposed new investments, together with the data necessary to appraise them. Although practices vary from firm to firm, proposals dealing with asset acquisitions are frequently grouped according to the following four categories:

1. Replacements.
2. Expansion: additional capacity in existing product lines.
3. Expansion: new product lines.
4. Other (for example, pollution control equipment).

These groupings are somewhat arbitrary, and it is frequently difficult to decide the appropriate category for a particular investment. In spite of such problems, the scheme is used quite widely and, as we shall see, with good reason.

Ordinarily, replacement decisions are the simplest to make. Assets wear out or become obsolete, and they must be replaced if production efficiency is to be maintained. The firm has a very good idea of the cost savings to be obtained by replacing an old asset, and it knows the consequences of non-replacement. All in all, the outcomes of most replacement decisions can be predicted with a high degree of confidence.

An example of the second investment classification is a proposal for adding more machines of the type already in use, or the opening of another branch in a city-wide chain of food stores. Expansion investments are frequently incorporated in replacement decisions. To illustrate, an old, inefficient machine may be replaced by a larger and more efficient one.

A degree of uncertainty—sometimes extremely high—is clearly involved in expansion, but the firm at least has the advantage of examining past production and sales experience with similar machines or stores. When it considers an investment of the third kind, expansion into new product lines, little if any experience data are available on which to base decisions. To illustrate, when Union Carbide decided to develop the laser for commercial application, it had very little idea of either the development costs or the specific applications to which lasers could be put. Under such circumstances, any estimates must at best be treated as very crude approximations.

The "other" category is a catchall and includes intangibles; an example is a proposal to boost employee morale and productivity by installing a music system. Mandatory pollution control devices, which must be undertaken even though they produce no revenues, are another example of the "other" category. Major strategic decisions such as plans for overseas expansion, or mergers, might also be included here, but more frequently they are treated separately from the regular capital budget.

ADMINISTRATIVE DETAILS

The remaining aspects of capital budgeting involve administrative matters. Approvals are typically required at higher levels within the organization as we move away from replacement decisions and as the sums involved increase. One of the most important functions of the board of directors is to approve the major outlays in a capital budgeting program. Such decisions are crucial for the future well-being of the firm.

The planning horizon for capital budgeting programs varies with the nature of the industry. When sales can be forecast with a high degree of reliability for ten to twenty years, the planning period is likely to be correspondingly long; electric utilities are an example of such an industry. Also, when the product-technology developments in the industry require an eight-to-ten-year cycle to develop a new major product, as in certain segments of the aerospace industry, a correspondingly long planning period is necessary.

After a capital budget has been adopted, payments must be scheduled. Characteristically, the finance department is responsible for scheduling payments and for acquiring funds to meet payment schedule requirements. The finance department is also primarily responsible for cooperating with the members of operating divisions to compile systematic records on the uses of funds and the uses of equipment purchased in capital budgeting programs. Effective capital budgeting programs require such information as the basis for periodic review and evaluation of capital expenditure decisions—the feedback and control phase of capital budgeting, often called the "post audit."

In Canada, there are a number of companies that are subsidiaries of multi-national companies. Since the multi-national operates to maximize the market value of its equity, considerations of the tax laws and operating costs in each country in which it operates are important. Based on these inputs, the multi-national may make decisions for a particular operating subsidiary that are different than would be made if the company were independent. Thus, the parent organization may provide the operating subsidiaries with the funds for capital expenditures and the cost of capital that should be used. However, the capital budgeting analysis will still be important within the subsidiary since cash flow information will still be required to make investment decisions.

The foregoing represents a brief overview of the administrative aspects of capital budgeting; the analytical problems involved are considered next.

CAPITAL BUDGETING ANALYSIS: CHOOSING AMONG ALTERNATIVE PROPOSALS

In most firms there are more proposals for projects than the firm is able or willing to finance. Some proposals are good, others are poor, and methods must be developed for distinguishing between the good and the poor. Essentially, the end product is a ranking of the proposals and a cutoff point for determining how far down the ranked list to go.

In part, proposals are eliminated because they are *mutually exclusive.* Mutually exclusive proposals are alternative methods of doing the same job. If one piece of equipment is chosen to do the job, the others will not be required. Thus, if there is a need to improve the materials handling system in a chemical plant, the job may be done either by conveyer belts or by fork trucks. The selection of one method of doing the job makes it unnecessary to use the others. They are mutually exclusive items.

Independent items are pieces of capital equipment that are being considered for different kinds of projects or tasks that need to be accomplished. For example, in addition to the materials handling system, the chemical firm may need equipment to package the end product. The work would require a packaging machine, and the purchase of equipment for this purpose would be independent of the equipment purchased for materials handling. Finally, projects can be *contingent* or *interdependent*. For these projects, the choice of one requires the choice of the other. For example, suppose the chemical company is considering the purchase of a machine to produce a new product. However, a specially designed packaging system is required if the new product project is to be accepted. It would be incorrect to consider the new product and the packaging system as independent projects. Instead, the projects are interdependent and must be combined and evaluated as a single project.

To distinguish among the many items that compete for the allocation of the firm's capital funds, a ranking procedure must be developed. This procedure requires, first, calculating the estimated benefits from the use of equipment and, second, translating the estimated benefits into a measure of the advantage of the purchase of the equipment. Thus, an estimate of benefits is required, and a method for converting the benefits into a ranking measure must be developed.

IMPORTANCE OF GOOD DATA

Most discussions of measuring the cash flows associated with capital projects are relatively brief, but it is important to emphasize *that in the entire capital budgeting procedure, probably nothing is of greater importance than a reliable estimate of the cost savings or revenue increases that will be achieved from the prospective outlay of capital funds.* The increased output and sales revenue resulting from expansion programs are obvious benefits. Cost reduction benefits include changes in quality and quantity of direct labor; in amount and cost of scrap and rework time; in fuel costs; and in maintenance expenses, down time, safety, flexibility, and so on. So many variables are involved that it is obviously impossible to make neat generalizations. However, this should not minimize the crucial importance of the required analysis of the benefits derived from capital expenditures. Each capital equipment expenditure must be examined in detail for possible *additional* or *incremental* costs and savings.

All the subsequent procedures for ranking projects are no better than the data input—the old saying, "garbage in, garbage out," is certainly applicable to capital budgeting analysis. Thus, the data assembly process is not a routine clerical task to be performed on a mechanical basis. It requires continuous monitoring and evaluation of estimates by those competent to make such evaluations—engineers, accountants, economists, cost analysts, and other qualified persons.

After the incremental costs and benefits have been estimated, they are utilized for ranking alternative investment proposals. How this ranking is accomplished is our next topic.

RANKING INVESTMENT PROPOSALS

The point of capital budgeting—indeed, the point of all financial analysis—is to make decisions that will maximize the current market price of the firm's common equity, or equivalently, to make decisions that will maximize the market value of the equity of the shareholders outstanding before the investment decision was made. The capital budgeting process is designed to answer two questions: (1) Which of several mutually exclusive investments should be selected? (2) How many projects, in total, should be accepted?

Among the many methods used for ranking investment proposals, three are discussed here:[3]

1. *Payback method (or payback period):* number of years required to return the original investment.
2. *Net present value (NPV) method:* present value of future returns discounted at the appropriate cost of capital, minus the cost of the investment.
3. *Internal rate of return (IRR) method:* interest rate which equates the present value of future returns to the investment outlay.

Future returns are, in all cases, defined as the net profits after taxes, plus depreciation, that result from a project. In other words, returns are synonymous with net cash flows from investments. Since the firm and its shareholders are interested in the actual amount of taxes paid and not the amount

[3] A number of "average rate of return" methods have been discussed in the literature and used in practice. These methods are generally unsound and, with the widespread use of computers, completely unnecessary. We discussed them in earlier editions, but they are deleted from this edition.

presented on the books, the depreciation charge will equal the charge for capital cost allowances, and the after tax net profits reflect the deduction of capital cost allowances for income tax purposes. The nature and characteristics of the three methods are illustrated and explained next. To make these explanations more meaningful, the same data are used to illustrate each procedure.

Payback Method

Assume that two projects are being considered by a firm. Each requires an investment of $1,000. The firm's marginal cost of capital is 10 percent.[4] The net cash flows from investments A and B are shown in Table 11–1.

TABLE 11–1 Net Cash Flows: Profit after Taxes Plus Charge for Capital Cost Allowance

Year	A	B
1	$500	$100
2	400	200
3	300	300
4	100	400
5		500
6		600

The *payback period* is the number of years it takes a firm to recover its original investment from net cash flows. Since the cost is $1,000, the payback period is two and one-third years for project A and four years for project B. To use this technique, the company specifies a target payback period and compares the payback period of the project to the target. If the target is a three-year payback period, project A would be accepted, but project B would be rejected.

Although the payback period is very easy to calculate, it can lead to incorrect decisions. As the illustration demonstrates, it ignores cash flows beyond the payback period. If the project is one maturing in later years, the use of the payback period can lead to the selection of less desirable investments. Projects with longer payback periods are characteristically those involved in long-range planning—developing a new product or tapping a new market. These are just the strategic decisions which do not yield their highest returns for a number of years. This means that the payback method may be

[4]The cost of capital can be viewed as the minimum acceptable rate of return required on a project of a given level of risk. The cost of capital is based on market data and reflects the opportunity cost of investors—both debt and equity. If the firm cannot earn this opportunity cost, it should not invest in the project. Thus, if investors require a 10 percent cost of capital for projects of a certain level of risk, the opportunity cost is 10 percent.

biased against the very investments that are most important to a firm's long-run success.

Recognition of the longer period over which an investment is likely to yield savings points up another weakness in the use of the payback method for ranking investment proposals: its failure to take into account the time value of money. To illustrate, consider two assets, X and Y, each costing $300 and each having the following cash flows:

Year	X	Y
1	200	100
2	100	200
3	100	100

Each project has a two-year payback; hence, each would appear equally desirable. However, we know that a dollar today is worth more than a dollar next year, so project X, with its faster cash flow, is certainly more desirable.

The use of the payback period is sometimes defended on the grounds that returns beyond three or four years are fraught with such great uncertainty that it is best to disregard them altogether in a planning decision. However, that is clearly an unsound procedure. Some investments with the highest returns are those which may not come to fruition for eight to ten years. The new product cycle in industries involving advanced technologies may not have a payoff for eight or nine years. Furthermore, even though returns that occur after three, four, or five years may be highly uncertain, it is important to make a judgment about the likelihood of their occurring. To ignore them is to assign a zero probability to these distant receipts. This can hardly produce the best results.

Another defense of the payback method is that a firm which is short of cash must necessarily give great emphasis to a quick return of its funds so that they may be put to use in other places or in meeting other needs. However, this does not relieve the payback method of its many shortcomings, and there are better methods for handling the cash shortage situation.[5]

A third reason for using payback is that, typically, projects with faster paybacks have more favorable short-run effects on earnings per share. Firms that use payback for this reason are sacrificing future growth for current accounting income, and in general such a practice will not maximize the value of the firm. The discounted cash flow techniques discussed in the next section, if used properly, automatically give consideration to the present earnings versus future growth tradeoff and strike the balance that will maximize the firm's value.

Also, the payback method is sometimes used simply because it is so easy to apply. If a firm is making many small capital expenditure decisions,

[5]We interpret a cash shortage to mean that the firm has a high opportunity cost for its funds and a high cost of capital. We would consider this high cost of capital in the internal rate of return method or the net present value method, thus taking account of the cash shortage.

the costs of using more complex methods may outweigh the benefits of possibly "better" choices among competing projects. However, it is essential that the companies be aware of the shortcomings of the payback method and the costs that are imposed on shareholders by the use of the technique.

Finally, many firms use payback in combination with one of the discounted cash flow procedures described below. The *NPV* or *IRR* method is used to appraise a project's profitability, while the payback is used to show how long the initial investment will be at risk; that is, payback is used as a risk indicator. Recent surveys in the United States have shown that when larger firms use payback in connection with major projects, it is almost always used in this manner.

Net Present Value Method

As the flaws in the payback method were recognized, people began to search for methods of evaluating projects that would recognize that a dollar received immediately is preferable to a dollar received at some future date. This recognition led to the development of *discounted cash flow (DCF) techniques* to take account of the time value of money. One such discounted cash flow technique is called the "net present value method," or sometimes simply the "present value method." *To implement this approach, find the present value of the expected net cash flows of an investment, discounted at the cost of capital, and subtract from it the initial cost outlay of the project.*[6] If the net present value is positive, the project should be accepted; if negative, it should be rejected. If the two projects are mutually exclusive, the one with the higher net present value should be chosen.

The equation for the net present value (*NPV*) is[7]

$$NPV = \left[\frac{R_1}{(1 + k)^1} + \frac{R_2}{(1 + k)^2} + \cdots + \frac{R_N}{(1 + k)^N} \right] - C \qquad (11-1)$$

$$= \sum_{t=1}^{N} \frac{R_t}{(1 + k)^t} - C.$$

---

[6] If costs are spread over several years, this must be taken into account. Suppose, for example, that a firm bought land in 1974, erected a building in 1975, installed equipment in 1976, and started production in 1977. One could treat 1974 as the base year, comparing the present value of the costs as of 1974 to the present value of the benefit stream as of that same date.

[7] The second equation is simply a shorthand expression in which sigma (Σ) signifies "sum up" or add the present values of N profit terms. If $t = 1$, then $R_t = R_1$ and $1/(1 + k)^t = 1/(1 + k)^1$; if $t = 2$, then $R_t = R_2$ and $1/(1 + k)^t = 1/(1 + k)^2$; and so on, until $t = N$, the last year the project provides any profits. The symbol $\sum_{t=1}^{N}$ simply says "go through the following process: Let $t = 1$ and find the *PV* of R_1; then let $t = 2$ and find the *PV* of R_2. Continue until the *PV* of each individual profit has been found; then add the *PV*s of these individual profits to find the *PV* of the asset."

Here R_1, R_2, and so forth, represent the net cash flows; k is the marginal cost of capital; C is the initial cost of the project; and N is the project's expected life.

The net present values of projects A and B are calculated in Table 11–2. Project A has an *NPV* of $80, while B's *NPV* is $400. On this basis, both should be accepted if they are independent, but B should be the one chosen if they are mutually exclusive.[8]

TABLE 11–2 Calculating the Net Present Value *(NPV)* of Projects with $1,000 Cost

	Project A			Project B		
Year	Net Cash Flow	PVIF (10%)	PV of Cash Flow	Net Cash Flow	PVIF (10%)	PV of Cash Flow
1	$500	.91	$ 455	$100	.91	$ 91
2	400	.83	332	200	.83	166
3	300	.75	225	300	.75	225
4	100	.68	68	400	.68	272
5				500	.62	310
6				600	.56	336
	PV of inflows		$1,080			$1,400
	Less: cost		– 1,000			– 1,000
	NPV		$ 80			$ 400

When a firm takes on a project, the value of the firm will increase by an amount equal to the present value of the cash flows. Thus, if the *NPV* of a project is positive, the increase in the value of the firm is greater than the amount of funds needed to finance the investment. The *NPV* reflects the gain accruing to the shareholders existing before the investment decision was made. In our example, the value of the firm will increase by $1,080 and the existing shareholders will gain $80 if project *A* is undertaken; if project *B* is accepted, the increase in the value of the firm is $1,400 and $400 accrues to the existing shareholders. Viewing the alternatives in this manner, it is easy to see why *B* is preferred to *A*, and it is also easy to see the logic of the *NPV* approach.

---

[8] In making a decision on mutually exclusive projects, it is best to compare projects of equal lives. If one project has cash flows that extend for a longer period, a comparison of the alternatives requires an assumption of what will be done with the cash flows over the period between the cessation of the shorter and the longer projects. This timing difference is not crucial if:

 i) the difference in the lifetime is small;
 ii) the difference occurs far out in the future—for example, one project lasts 20 years, the other 25; or
 iii) it is assumed that the cash flows from the shorter lived project are re-invested at the cost of capital.

Internal Rate of Return Method

The internal rate of return *(IRR)* is defined as the *interest rate that equates the present value of the expected future cash flows, or receipts, to the initial cost outlay.* The equation for calculating the internal rate of return is

$$\frac{R_1}{(1 + r)^1} + \frac{R_2}{(1 + r)^2} + \cdots + \frac{R_N}{(1 + r)^N} - C = 0$$

$$\sum_{t=1}^{N} \frac{R_t}{(1 + r)^t} - C = 0. \qquad (11\text{--}2)$$

Here we know the value of C and also the values of $R_1, R_2, \ldots, R_N$, but we do not know the value of r. Thus, we have an equation with one unknown, and we can solve for the value of r. Some value of r will cause the sum of the discounted receipts to equal the initial cost of the project, making the equation equal to zero, and that value of r is defined as the internal rate of return; that is, the solution value of r is the *IRR*.

Notice that the internal rate of return formula, Equation 11–2, is simply the *NPV* formula, Equation 11–1, solved for that particular value of k that causes the *NPV* to equal zero. In other words, the same basic equation is used for both methods, but in the *NPV* method the discount rate *(k)* is specified and the *NPV* is found, while in the *IRR* method the *NPV* is specified to equal zero and the value of r that forces the *NPV* to equal zero is found.

The internal rate of return may be found by trial and error. First, compute the present value of the cash flows from an investment, using an arbitrarily selected interest rate. (Since the cost of capital for most firms is in the range of 10–15 percent, projects will hopefully promise a return of at least 10 percent. Therefore, 10 percent is a good starting point for most problems.) Then compare the present value so obtained with the investment's cost. If the present value is higher than the cost figure, try a higher interest rate and go through the procedure again. Conversely, if the present value is lower than the cost, lower the interest rate and repeat the process. Continue until the present value of the flows from the investment is approximately equal to its cost. *The interest rate that brings about this equality is defined as the internal rate of return.*[9]

This calculation process is illustrated in Table 11–3 for projects A and B. First, the 10 percent interest factors are obtained from Table A–2 at the end of the book. These factors are then multiplied by the cash flows for the corresponding years, and the present values of the annual cash flows are

---

[9]In order to reduce the number of trials required to find the internal rate of return, it is important to minimize the error at each iteration. One reasonable approach is to make as good a first approximation as possible, then to "straddle" the internal rate of return by making fairly large changes in the interest rate early in the iterative process. In practice, if many projects are to be evaluated or if many years are involved, one would not work out the calculations by hand but would use a computer. Computational techniques have been developed to enable us to find the *IRR* in three or four trials.

placed in the appropriate columns. For example, the *PVIF* of .91 is multiplied by $500, and the product, $455, is placed in the first row of column A.

The present values of the yearly cash flows are then summed to get the investment's total present value. Subtracting the cost of the project from this figure gives the net present value. As the net present values of both investments are positive at the 10 percent rate, increase the rate to 15 percent and try again. *At this point the net present value of investment A is approximately zero, which indicates that its internal rate of return is approximately 15 percent. Continuing, B is found to have an internal rate of return of approximately 20 percent.*

TABLE 11–3 Finding the Internal Rate of Return

				Cash Flows (R_t Values)		
				Year	R_A	R_B
	C = Investment = $1,000			1:R_1 = $500		$100
				2:R_2 = 400		200
				3:R_3 = 300		300
				4:R_4 = 100		400
				5:R_5 =		500
				6:R_6 =		600

	10 Percent			15 Percent			20 Percent		
		Present Value			Present Value			Present Value	
Year	PVIF	A	B	PVIF	A	B	PVIF	A	B
1	0.91	455	91	0.87	435	87	0.83	415	83
2	0.83	332	166	0.76	304	152	0.69	276	138
3	0.75	225	225	0.66	198	198	0.58	174	174
4	0.68	68	272	0.57	57	228	0.48	48	192
5	0.62		310	0.50		250	0.40		200
6	0.56		336	0.43		258	0.33		198
Present value		1,080	1,400		994	1,173		913	985
Net present value = $PV - C$		80	400		(6)	173		(87)	(15)

What is so special about the particular interest rate that equates the cost of a project with the present value of its receipts? To illustrate, suppose a firm obtains all its capital by borrowing from a bank, and the interest cost of this debt is 6 percent. If the internal rate of return on a particular project is calculated to be 6 percent, the same as the cost of capital, then the firm would be able to invest in the project, use the cash flow generated by the investment to pay off the principal and interest on the bank loan, and come out exactly even on the transaction. If the internal rate of return exceeds 6 percent, the project would be profitable; if the internal rate of return is less than 6 percent, taking on the project would result in losses. It is this "break-even" characteristic that makes us interested in the internal rate of return.

Assuming that the firm uses a cost of capital of 10 percent, the internal rate of return criterion states that, if projects A and B are independent, both should be accepted—they both do better than "break even." If they are mutually exclusive, B ranks higher and should be accepted, while A should be rejected.

A more complete illustration of how the internal rate of return would be used in practice is given in Table 11–4. Assuming a 10 percent cost of capital, the firm should accept projects 1 through 7, reject projects 8 through 10, and have a total capital budget of $10 million.

TABLE 11–4 The Prospective-Projects Schedule

Nature of Proposal	Amount of Funds Required	Cumulative Total	IRR
1. Purchase of leased space	$2,000,000	$ 2,000,000	23%
2. Mechanization of accounting system	1,200,000	3,200,000	19
3. Modernization of office building	1,500,000	4,700,000	17
4. Addition of power facilities	900,000	5,600,000	16
5. Purchase of affiliate	3,600,000	9,200,000	13
6. Purchase of loading docks	300,000	9,500,000	12
7. Purchase of tank trucks	500,000	10,000,000	11
			10% cutoff
8. Installation of conveyor system	200,000	10,200,000	9
9. Construction of new plant	2,300,000	12,500,000	8
10. Purchase of executive aircraft	200,000	12,700,000	7

IRR for Level Cash Flows

If the cash flows from a project are level, or equal in each year, then the project's internal rate of return can be found by a relatively simple process. In essence, such a project is an annuity: the firm makes an outlay, C, and receives a stream of cash flow benefits, R, for a given number of years. The *IRR* for the project is found by applying Equation 10–6, discussed in Chapter 10.

To illustrate, suppose a project has a cost of $10,000 and is expected to produce cash flows of $1,627 a year for ten years. The cost of the project, $10,000, is the present value of an annuity of $1,627 a year for ten years, so applying Equation 10–6 we obtain

$$\frac{Cost}{R} = \frac{\$10,000}{\$1,627} = 6.146 = PVIF_a.$$

Looking up $PVIF_a$ in Table A–4, across the ten-year row, we find it (approximately) under the 10 percent column. Accordingly, 10 percent is the IRR on the project. In other words, 10 percent is the value of r that would satisfy Equation 11–2 when R is constant at \$1,627 for ten years and C is \$10,000. This procedure works only if the project has constant annual cash flows; if it does not, the IRR must be found by trial and error or by using a computer.

BASIC DIFFERENCES BETWEEN THE *NPV* AND *IRR* METHODS[10]

As noted above, the NPV method (1) accepts all independent projects whose NPV is greater than zero and (2) ranks mutually exclusive projects by their NPV's, selecting the project with the higher NPV according to Equation 11–3:

$$NPV = \sum_{t=1}^{N} \frac{R_t}{(1+k)^t} - C. \tag{11-3}$$

The IRR method, on the other hand, finds the value of r that forces the NPV of Equation 11–4 to equal zero:

$$NPV = \sum_{t=1}^{N} \frac{R_t}{(1+r)^t} - C = 0. \tag{11-4}$$

The IRR method calls for accepting independent projects where r, the internal rate of return, is greater than k, the cost of capital, and for selecting among mutually exclusive projects depending on which has the higher IRR.

It is apparent that the only structural difference between the NPV and IRR methods lies in the discount rates used in the two equations—all the values in the equations are identical except for r and k. Further, we can see that if $r > k$, then $NPV > 0$.[11] *Accordingly, the two methods give the same accept-reject decisions for specific projects—if project J is acceptable under the* NPV *criterion, it is also acceptable if the* IRR *method is used.*

This relationship between the NPV and IRR criteria is presented graphically in Figure 11–2 where we consider project A from the previous section. On the vertical axis, the net present value is plotted, and on the horizontal axis, the cost of capital. The relationship between the NPV and the cost of capital is called the *present value profile*. When the cost of capital is equal to zero, the

---

[10] This section is relatively technical and may be omitted on a first reading without loss of continuity.

[11] This can be seen by noting that $NPV = 0$ if and only if $r = k$:

$$NPV = \sum_{t=1}^{N} \frac{R_t}{(1+k)^t} - C = \sum_{t=1}^{n} \frac{R_t}{(1+r)^t} - C = 0,$$

If $r > k$, then $NPV > 0$, and if $r < k$, then $NPV < 0$. We should also note that, under certain conditions, there may be more than one root to Equation 11–4, hence multiple IRRs are found. See Appendix 10A of *Managerial Finance* for a more detailed discussion of the multiple root problem.

net present value is the simple summation of the cash flows, i.e. $300.

FIGURE 11-2 Relationships of *NPV* and *IRR Criteria*

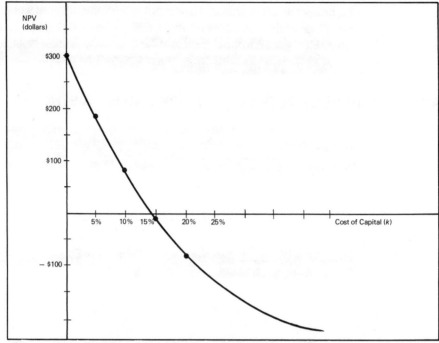

As the cost of capital increases, the cash flows further in the future have a lower and lower weight in the net present value. At a cost of capital of 5 percent, *NPV* is $180; at 10 percent, $80; at 15 percent, $-6; and at 20 percent, -$87. For project *A,* as the cost of capital increases, the lower limit for *NPV* is -$1,000 (the initial outlay). Notice that at approximately 15 percent, the *NPV* is zero and this is the *IRR* of the project.

If the cost of capital is 10 percent, the *NPV* is positive and the project should be accepted. The same accept decision is generated by the *IRR* criterion, since the *IRR* (15 percent) is greater than the cost of capital (10 percent). If the cost of capital is greater than the *IRR,* the *IRR* criterion says reject; this is consistent with the negative *NPV* which requires a reject decision.

However, under certain conditions the *NPV* and *IRR* methods can *rank* projects differently, and if mutually exclusive projects are involved or if capital is limited, then rankings can be important. The conditions under which different rankings can occur are as follows:

1. The cost of one project is larger than that of the other.
2. The timing of the projects' cash flows differ. For example, the cash flows of one project may increase over time, while those of the other decrease, or the projects may have different expected lives.

The first point can be seen by considering two mutually exclusive projects, L and S, of greatly differing sizes. Project S calls for the investment of $1.00 and yields $1.50 at the end of one year. Its *IRR* is 50 percent, and at a 10 percent cost of capital its *NPV* is $0.36. Project L costs $1 million and yields $1.25 million at the end of the year. Its *IRR* is only 25 percent, but its *NPV* at 10 percent is $113,625. The two methods rank the projects differently: $IRR_S > IRR_L$, but $NPV_L > NPV_S$. This is, of course, an extreme case, but whenever projects differ in size, the *NPV* and the *IRR* can give different rankings.[12]

The effect of differential cash flows is somewhat more difficult to understand, but it can be illustrated by an example. Consider two projects, A and B, whose cash flows over their three-year lives are given below:

	Cash Flow from Project	
Year	A	B
1	$1,000	$ 100
2	500	600
3	100	1,100

Project A's cash flows are higher in the early years, but B's cash flows increase over time and exceed those of A in later years. Each project costs $1,200, and their *NPV*s, discounted at the specified rates, are shown below:

	NPV	
Discount Rate	A	B
0%	$ 400	$ 600
5	300	400
10	200	200
15	100	50
20	50	(85)
25	(25)	(175)
30	(100)	(250)

In Figure 11–3, the net present value profiles of projects *A* and *B* are plotted. As can be seen in this figure, the *IRR* for project *A* is 22 percent and for *B*, 17 percent. Because its largest cash flows come late in the project's life, when the discounting effects of time are most significant, *B's NPV* falls rapidly as the discount rate rises. However, since *A's* cash flows come early, when the impact of higher discount rates is not so severe, its *NPV* falls less rapidly as interest rates increase.

Notice that from the *IRR* rankings, project *A* is preferred to project *B*, since *A* has the higher internal rate of return. However, if the cost of capital is less than 10 percent, project *B* has a higher *NPV* than *A*. In this case, the *IRR* and *NPV* rankings are inconsistent. We can generalize these results: *When-*

---

[12] Projects of different size *could* be ranked the same by the *NPV* and *IRR* methods; that is, different sizes do not necessarily mean different rankings.

ever the NPV profiles of two projects cross one another, a conflict will exist if the cost of capital is below the cross-over rate. For our illustrative projects, no conflict would exist if the firm's cost of capital exceeded 10 percent, but the two methods would rank *A* and *B* differently if *k* is less than 10 percent.

Figure 11–3 Net Present Value Profile

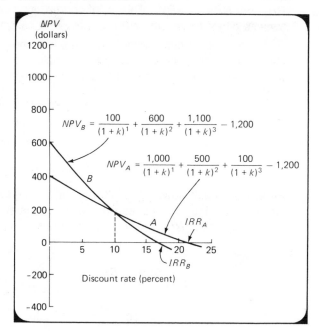

WHICH RANKING TECHNIQUE, *NPV* OR *IRR*, SHOULD BE USED?

How should conflicts between the *NPV* and *IRR* methods be resolved; for example, when the *NPV* and *IRR* methods yield conflicting rankings, which of two mutually exclusive projects should be selected? Assuming that management is seeking to maximize the value of the firm, the correct decision is to select the project with the higher *NPV*. After all, the *NPV*s measure the projects' contributions to the value of the equity, so the one with the higher *NPV* must be contributing more. *This line of reasoning leads to the conclusion that firms should, in general, use the NPV method for evaluating capital investment proposals.*[13] Recognizing this point, sophisticated firms generally rely on the *NPV* method. These firms often calculate (by computer) both the *NPV* and the *IRR,* but they rely on the *NPV* when conflicts arise among mutually exclusive projects.

---

[13]The question of *why* the conflict arises is an interesting one. Basically, it has to do with the reinvest-

CAPITAL BUDGETING PROJECT EVALUATION

Thus far the problem of measuring net cash flows—the benefits used in the present value calculations above—has not been dealt with directly. This matter will now be discussed and a few simple examples given. To facilitate an understanding of the basic concepts, we have opted to make as few complicating assumptions as possible. In the real world, the applications of the techniques become more difficult due to the tax implications of the investment decisions. We will begin with a very simple expansion decision example and complicate the analysis with a replacement decision in which the tax implications become more important. It is our intention to provide a framework for the analysis of capital budgeting problems; this will permit the analysis of more complicated problems with complex tax implications.

Expansion Decision

The Caligari Cabinet Company Limited anticipates an increase in demand for one of its products. In order to meet this demand, a new cutting and finishing machine costing $10,000 must be purchased. The machine will last five years and it will be sold at the beginning of the sixth year.[14] Based on forecasted sales levels, it is expected to generate an increase in net operating income, before taxes, of $3,500 per year for five years. It is anticipated that when the machine is sold for scrap, the CCA pool will still have assets in it. The capital cost rate applicable for CCA calculations is 20 percent. Taxes are at a 40 percent rate; the salvage value is expected to be equal to the undepreciated capital cost for the sixth year of $3,277; and the firm's after-tax cost of capital is 10 percent. Should Caligari Cabinet buy this new machine?

The decision process requires five steps: (1) estimate the cash outlay attributable to the project; (2) determine the incremental after-tax cash flows; (3) find the present value of these cash flows; (4) add the present value of the impact of the expected salvage value to the present value of the cash flows; and (5) see whether the *NPV* is positive or whether the *IRR* exceeds the cost of capital. These steps are explained further in the following sections.

ment of cash flows—the *NPV* method implicitly assumes reinvestment at the marginal cost of capital *(MCC)*, while the *IRR* method implicitly assumes reinvestment at the internal rate of return. For a value-maximizing firm, reinvestment at the *MCC* is the better assumption. The rationale is as follows: A value-maximizing firm will expand to the point where it accepts all projects yielding more than the *MCC* (these projects will have *NPV* > 0). How these projects are financed is irrelevant—the point is, they will be financed and accepted. Now consider the question of the cash flows from a particular project; if these cash flows are reinvested, at what rate will reinvestment occur? All projects that yield more than the cost of capital have already been accepted; thus, these cash flows can only be invested in physical assets yielding *less than* the *MCC*, or else be used in lieu of other capital with a cost of *MCC*. A rational firm will take the second alternative, so reinvested cash flows will save the firm the cost of capital. This means, in effect, that cash flows are reinvested to yield the cost of capital, which is the assumption implicit in the *NPV* method. For a detailed discussion see Appendix 10A in *Managerial Finance*.

[14]In Chapter 2, it was noted that if an asset is sold in a particular year, the CCA charge for that year is lost. Thus, to obtain a CCA deduction in the fifth year, we assume that the machine is sold in the beginning of the sixth year.

Estimated Cash Outlay   In an expansion decision, the estimation of the outlay is straight-forward. Since there is no replacement of existing equipment, any tax complications caused by the proceeds of sale of old equipment are not present. For Caligari, the cost of the machine, including any installation costs, is $10,000, and this is the net outflow used in the analysis.

If additional working capital is required as a result of the capital budgeting decision, this factor must be taken into account. The amount of incremental *net* working capital (additional current assets required as a result of the expansion, minus any spontaneous funds generated by the expansion) is estimated and added to the initial cash outlay. This factor is found more frequently in expansion decisions than in cost-reducing replacement decisions. We assume that there is no additional working capital required in the Caligari example.

After-Tax Net Cash Flows   The benefits and costs used in the investment decision analysis must be measured on an incremental or marginal basis. This will reflect the additional costs and revenues that will be generated if the project is undertaken. In analysing the impact of a project, it is incorrect to include in the analysis any existing costs that are being allocated to this particular project. These costs would have to be met whether the project is accepted or not, and hence, should have no influence on the decision. For example, suppose a project will use some excess space in an existing factory and the accounting department has decided to allocate a portion of the factory rent as an annual cost to the project. Since this project did not result in an increase in factory rent, the allocation of the rent should not be included in the investment analysis. There are some instances where the identification of all the incremental costs is difficult; however, the technique discussed is based on their proper identification. In our example, it is assumed that all the costs and benefits are incremental.

In Table 11–5, Part (a), we present a calculation of the annual, incremental, after-tax net cash flows. The after-tax net cash flow is equal to the after-tax income plus the amount deducted for capital cost allowances (CCA). The CCA allowances for the project must be based on the incremental impact of the purchase on the pool of assets. For example, in all five years, the operating income before tax is $3,500 and the incremental impact on the pool is equal to the book value of the asset of $10,000[15]. In the first year the CCA deduction is $2,000, leaving after-tax income at $900. The net cash flow for the year is $2,900 i.e. the sum of the after-tax income plus the CCA charge. In Part (b) of the same table, the calculation of the CCA value for each year is provided along with the UCC balance before and after the deduction of the

---

[15]The original capital cost of the asset on which CCA deductions are based reflects the full cost to the company of acquiring the asset. These costs include legal, accounting, engineering and other fees necessary to acquire the property. If the asset is purchased outside of Canada, the Canadian dollar equivalent as of the date of purchase is used as the original capital cost.

annual CCA charge.

Based on the net cash flows and the present value factors for each period, a present value net cash flow could be calculated. However, there is an easier technique available to calculate the present value of the net cash flows. This technique also allows more flexibility in solving problems with more difficult tax implications.

TABLE 11–5(a)   Calculation of After-Tax Net Cash Flows

	Year 1	Year 2	Year 3	Year 4	Year 5
Operating income before tax	$3,500	$3,500	$3,500	$3,500	$3,500
CCA charge	2,000	1,600	1,280	1,024	819
	1,500	1,900	2,220	2,476	2,681
Tax: 40 percent	600	760	888	990	1,072
After-tax income	900	1,140	1,332	1,486	1,609
Net cash flow– After-tax	$2,900	$2,740	$2,612	$2,510	$2,428

TABLE 11–5(b)   Calculation of CCA and UCC by Year

Year	UCC: base for calculation of CCA charge	CCA	UCC: after deduction of CCA
1	$10,000	$2,000	$8,000
2	8,000	1,600	6,400
3	6,400	1,280	5,120
4	5,120	1,024	4,096
5	4,096	819	3,277
6	3,277		

From Table 11–5(a) we found the after-tax net cash flow for each year by determining after-tax income and adding the CCA deduction. However, the after-tax cash flow in any year can be written as the sum of two components. The first component is the after-tax operating income (i.e. revenues less expenses) from the project; this is calculated as if there were no deduction for CCA. The second term is the tax saving due to the deduction of the CCA expense. The formula for the after-tax net cash flow in year j is written in Equation 11–5 where t refers to the corporate tax rate.

$$\begin{pmatrix} \text{After-tax net} \\ \text{cash flow} \end{pmatrix}_j = \left[\begin{pmatrix} \text{Operating} \\ \text{income} \end{pmatrix}_j - CCA_j \right](1-t) + CCA_j$$

or $\quad \begin{pmatrix} \text{After-tax net} \\ \text{cash flow} \end{pmatrix}_j = \begin{pmatrix} \text{Operating} \\ \text{income} \end{pmatrix}_j (1-t) + t\ CCA_j$

$$(11\text{-}5)$$

In the first year of the project being considered, the after-tax net cash flow is $2,900 (see Table 11–5(a)). Using Equation 11–5 above, the after-tax net cash flow is:

$$\begin{pmatrix} \text{After-tax Net} \\ \text{Cash Flow} \end{pmatrix}_1 = 3,500(1-0.4) + 0.4(2,000)$$

$$= 2,100 + 800$$

$$= \$2,900$$

It would appear that, to use this technique, the after-tax cash flows for each year must be estimated and then the present value of each calculated; this appears to be as much work as needed in deriving the figures in Table 11–5(a). However, we will demonstrate in the following section that there are some simplifications available.

Finding the Present Value of the Cash Flow Based on Equation 11–5, the after-tax cash flow in any year has two components—the after-tax operating income and the tax saving due to the CCA deduction. The present value of the after-tax cash flow is equal to the present value of the after-tax operating income, plus the present value of the tax savings. In calculating the first quantity, we note that the after-tax operating income will be constant over the five years and equal to $2,100 per year (i.e. $3,500(1 - 0.4)). Using the *PVIF* factor of 3.791 for a five year annuity at 10 percent, the present value of the after-tax operating income is $7,961.

The calculation of the present value of the tax saving can be simplified by using the formula presented in Equation 11–6.[16] The present value of the tax saving is written as:

$$PV_{\text{tax saving}} = \frac{tC_0 d}{k+d} - \frac{tdS}{k+d} \times \frac{1}{(1+k)^N} \qquad (11\text{-}6)$$

where t is the tax rate,
  C_0 is the cost of the asset as included in the asset pool,
  d is the capital cost rate,
  k is the cost of capital,
  S is the salvage value, and
  N is the time when the asset is sold.

[16] The derivation of Equation 11–6 is presented in the Appendix to this chapter.

The first term in this equation reflects the present value of the tax savings as if the asset were never sold and all future tax savings accrued to the project in question. However, after five years, the asset is to be sold and the book value of the pool will be reduced by the proceeds of sale. The future tax savings lost due to the sale are based on the amount by which the book value of the pool is reduced i.e. the salvage value. Thus, the second term measures the present value of the lost tax savings due to the sale.

In our example, the variables in the equation have the following values:

$$C_0 = \$10,000 \qquad d = 0.2 \qquad N = 5 \qquad t = 0.4$$
$$k = 10 \text{ percent} = \text{cost of capital} \qquad S = \$3,277$$

$$PV_{\text{tax saving}} = \frac{0.4(10,000)0.2}{0.1 + 0.2} - \frac{(0.4)(0.2)(3277)}{0.1 + 0.2} \times \frac{1}{(1.1)^5}$$

$$\doteq \$2,667 - \$543$$

$$= \$2,124$$

The present value of the after-tax cash flow is $10,085 which is the sum of the present values of the after-tax operating income ($7,961) and the tax savings ($2,124).

Salvage Value   The new machine has an estimated sale price at the beginning of the sixth year of $3,277. Since this is an incremental flow, its present value must be included in the analysis. The present value of an inflow of $3,277 due in five years is $2,035, found as $3,277 × 0.621. If working capital had been required and included in the initial cash outlay, this amount would be added to the salvage value of the machine because the working capital will be recovered if and when the project is abandoned.

Determining the Net Present Value   The project's net present value is found as the sum of the present values of the inflows, or benefits, less the outflows, or costs:

Inflows:	PV of annual benefits	$10,085
	PV of salvage value, new machine	2,035
Less:	net cash outflow, or cost	(10,000)
	Net present value (NPV)	$ 2,120

Since the NPV is positive, the project should be accepted.

A Complication Introduced by the Expected Salvage Value

In the example, it was assumed that the salvage value was equal to the undepreciated capital cost of $3,277. However, suppose the analyst believes the salvage value will be equal to $5,000. The first adjustment that must be made reflects the impact on the present value of the salvage value. In this example, the present value of the salvage value becomes $3,105. The second impact on the analysis is through the present value of the tax savings. Using Equation 11-6 with the new salvage value of $5,000, we calculate the present value of the tax saving to be $1,839.

$$PV_{\text{tax saving}} = \frac{tC_0\,d}{k+d} - \frac{tdS}{k+d} \times \frac{1}{(1+k)^N}$$

$$= 2,667 - \frac{(0.4)\,(0.2)\,5,000}{0.1 + 0.2} \times \frac{1}{(1.1)^5}$$

$$= 2,667 - 828$$

$$= \$1,839$$

This present value is less than the value calculated in the previous example. The reason is that, in this example, the pool is reduced by a larger amount, and hence, the present value of the lost tax savings are greater.

This method of handling the expected salvage value is consistent with the concept that the project must bear all incremental costs and benefits. The fact that there is a very high salvage value means that future CCA charges will be lower, since the pool has been lowered. This reduction is a direct result of the project and must be reflected in the net present value of the project.[17]

REPLACEMENT DECISION

The analysis presented above is sufficiently general to apply to replacement decision problems as well. However, replacement decisions have a number of interesting complications. The first wrinkle is that in a replacement decision the acceptance of a project, say the purchase of a new truck, requires the sale of

[17]When evaluating a capital expenditure, in many cases the analyst does not have a good estimate of the salvage value. The best estimate to use, as of the date of the project evaluation, could be the undepreciated capital cost of the asset at the termination date of the project. Of course, when the asset is actually sold, the proceeds may be different than the UCC. This difference will have an impact on the value of the pool, and hence, an impact on the future tax savings from CCA charges. However, this impact is not reflected in the current net present value analysis. Only the expected salvage value, not the actual salvage value, is of importance in the NPV analysis.

the existing asset. Thus, the inflows and outflows associated with accepting the new project must be incremental. For example, if the new truck has operating costs of $3,000 per year and the old $3,500, the incremental savings in operating costs is $500. Second, the sale of the old asset has an impact on the incremental book value of the new asset that will be used to calculate the future tax savings.

In the simple replacement example to follow the problems noted above are highlighted. Since calculation of the present values of the net cash flows and salvage values has been covered, the analysis of these factors will be brief.

The Widget Division of Casino Inc., a profitable, diversified manufacturing company, purchased a machine five years ago at a cost of $7,500. The machine had an expected life of fifteen years at the time of purchase and an estimated salvage value equal to $264. The machine is included in an asset pool in which the maximum capital cost rate is 20 percent and the company intends to use the maximum allowed. Currently, the undepreciated capital cost (i.e. at the beginning of the sixth year after purchase) is $2,458 ($7,500 × $(1 - 0.2)^5 = \$2,458$). The division manager reports that she can purchase a new machine for $12,000 (including installation) which, over its ten-year life will expand sales from $10,000 to $11,000 a year. Further, it will reduce labor and raw materials usage sufficiently to cut annual operating costs from $7,000 to $5,000. The new machine has a maximum capital cost rate of 20 percent; an estimated salvage value of $1,300; and the sale at that time will not eliminate the asset pool. The old machine's current market value is $1,000. Taxes are at a 40 percent rate and Casino's after-tax cost of capital is 10 percent. Should Casino purchase the new machine?

Using the same approach as in the previous example, we will consider the component parts of the investment decision analysis.

Estimated Cash Outlay   The net initial cash outlay will be evaluated assuming that the new machine is accepted. Under this assumption, the amount paid for the asset, including installation, is $12,000. However, acceptance of the new machine requires the sale of the old machine for $1,000. Thus, the net cash outlay is equal to $11,000.

Annual Benefits   Table 11–6 presents the calculations of the after-tax operating income per year, with and without the new machine. In addition, the incremental impact of accepting the new machine is calculated in Column 3.

The calculation of the tax saving from the CCA deduction will depend on the book value of the asset for tax purposes. If the new machine is not purchased, the book value of the asset is equal to the UCC value of $2,458 and the tax savings are based on this value. However, if the new machine is purchased, the book value of the new machine for tax purposes will reflect the deduction of the sale proceeds of the old machine and the addition of the cost

TABLE 11–6   Calculation of After-Tax Operating Income

	(1) Without New Machine	(2) With New Machine	(3) (2) – (1) Difference (Δ)
Sales	$10,000	$11,000	$1,000
Operating costs	7,000	5,000	-2,000
Operating income	3,000	6,000	3,000
Taxes (40 percent)	1,200	2,400	1,200
After-tax operating income	$ 1,800	$ 3,600	$1,800

of the new machine. Since we are interested in incremental effects, we must isolate the impact on the book value of the pool of assets when the new machine is purchased.

The calculation of the book value of the new machine for tax purposes (assuming the sale of the asset does not eliminate the pool) is presented in Table 11–7. In general, the book value of the new machine will equal the book value of the asset before the sale, plus the cost of the new asset, minus the proceeds of the sale of the old asset.

TABLE 11–7   Calculation of Book Value of New Machine for Tax Purposes

	New Machine
UCC book value—old machine	$ 2,458
Cost of new machine	12,000
	$14,458
Less: sale proceeds	1,000
Book value—new machine	$13,458

In this example, the sale price of $1,000 is less than the UCC of the old machine of $2,458. Therefore, this difference is added to the book value of the new machine and results in CCA expenses and tax savings that are higher than those if the old machine were sold at the UCC value of $2,458.

Present Value of the Cash Flows

As in the previous example, the present value of the net cash flows will be composed of two components. The first component is the present value of the after-tax operating income. For the old machine, the after-tax operating income is $1,800 per year for ten years. Using the annuity factor, we find the present value to be $11,061. For the new machine, the present value of the after-tax operating income of $3,600 per year for ten years is $22,122.

The second component is the present value of the tax savings for the old and new machine. To find these values, we use the formula presented in Equation 11–6 and substitute the appropriate values for the variables. For the old machine, the initial value (C_0) is $2,458; the UCC at the time of the decision; and the salvage value is $264. This results in a present value of the tax savings equal to $628. For the new machine, the present value of the tax savings is $3,455 based on an initial book value for tax purposes of $13,458 (from Table 11–7) and a salvage value of $1,300.[18]

Salvage Value In this decision, the present value of the expected salvage value of both the new and the old machine must be determined. The present values are $102 for the old machine and $501 for the new.

Determining the Net Present Value In Table 11–8(a) below, the present values of all the cash flows and salvage values are summarized and the incremental impact of buying the new machine is calculated. It is found that the sum of these incremental present values is $14,287.

TABLE 11–8(a) Comparative Present Values With and Without the New Investment

Present Value of:	(1) With Old Machine	(2) With New Machine	(3) (2) – (1) Difference (Δ)
(i) After-tax operating income	$11,061	$22,122	$11,061
(ii) Tax savings	683	3,455	2,827
(iii) Salvage value	102	501	399
Total present value of inflows	$11,846	$26,078	$14,287

TABLE 11–8(b) Calculation of Net Present Value

Inflows:	Present value of incremental inflows (from Part a, column 3)	$14,287
Less:	Net cash outflow, or cost	11,000
	Net present value *(NPV)*	$ 3,287

In assessing whether the project should be accepted, the present value of the incremental inflows associated with accepting the new machine is compared to the cost if the new machine is accepted. This comparison is

---

[18] The calculation of the present value of the tax savings for the new machine is:

$$PV_{\text{tax saving}} = \frac{tC_0 d}{k+d} - \frac{tdS}{k+d} \times \frac{1}{(1+k)^N}$$

$$= \frac{0.4\,(13,458)\,0.2}{0.1 + 0.2} - \frac{(0.4)\,(0.2)\,(1,300)}{0.1 + 0.2} \times \frac{1}{(1.1)^{10}}$$

$$= \$3,455$$

found in Table 11–8(b) where it is found that the *NPV* is positive and the new machine should be accepted.

SUMMARY OF CASH FLOWS

Table 11–9 summarizes the budgeting decision process used in the replacement decision example. The first step is to calculate the project cost which reflects the investment in the new equipment, minus the receipts from the sale of the old machine. Next, the annual incremental benefits from taking the new

TABLE 11–9   Worksheet for Capital Budgeting Project Evaluation—Casino Inc.

1. Project Cost, or Initial Outflows Required to Undertake Project	
Investment in new equipment	$12,000
Receipt from sale of old machine	(1,000)
Total project cost	$11,000
2. Calculation of Annual Benefits	
Change in Sales	$ 1,000
Less: change in costs	(2,000)
Change in operating income	$ 3,000
Less: taxes at 40 percent	1,200
Change in after-tax operating income	$ 1,800
(a) Present value of after-tax operating income Change in cash flow times interest factor	
$1,800 × 6.145 =	$11,061
(b) Present value of change in tax savings	2,827
Present value of benefits	$13,888
3. Present Value of Difference in Expected Salvage	
Expected difference in present value of salvage value	
$501 – $102 =	$ 399
4. Net Present Value	
PV of inflows: after-tax operating income	$11,061
tax savings	2,827
salvage	399
	$14,287
Less: Project cost	11,000
NPV	$ 3,287

machine are calculated and their present value is determined. The present value of the annual benefits is calculated as the sum of the present value of the after-tax operating income, which does not include a deduction for CCA, plus the present value of the tax savings from CCA deductions. The present value of the tax savings includes an adjustment to the book value base for CCA charges due to the sale of the old machine at a price below the UCC value and the expected salvage value. The present value of the benefits is $13,888.

We now find the present value of the incremental salvage value if the new machine is taken. This present value equals $399.

The final step is to sum up the present values of the inflows and then deduct the project cost of $11,000 to determine the *NPV* of $3,287 in the example. Since the *NPV* is positive, the project should be accepted.

CAPITAL RATIONING

Ordinarily, firms operate as illustrated in Figure 11–1 above; that is, they take on investments to the point where the marginal returns from investment are just equal to their estimated marginal cost of capital. For firms operating in this way, the decision process is as described above—they make those investments having positive net present values, reject those whose net present values are negative, and choose between mutually exclusive investments on the basis of the higher net present value. However, a firm will occasionally set an absolute limit on the size of its capital budget for any one year that is less than the level of investment it would undertake on the basis of the criteria described above.

The principal reason for such action is that some firms are reluctant to engage in external financing (borrowing, or selling common equity). One management, recalling the plight of firms with substantial amounts of debt in the 1930s, may simply refuse to use debt. Another management, which has no objection to selling debt, may not want to sell equity capital for fear of losing some measure of voting control. Still others may refuse to use any form of outside financing, considering both safety and control to be more important than additional profits.

Other reasons for capital rationing exist. One possibility is that the unit evaluating the investment decisions is a division or a subsidiary of a large company. The parent provides the unit with a fixed dollar amount for capital expenditures which must be allocated among the competing projects. Another possibility is that the market is very pessimistic in its evaluation of the prospective benefits of an investment project and the funds are withheld.

These are all cases of capital rationing, and they result in limiting the rate of expansion to a slower pace than would be dictated by "purely rational value maximizing behavior".[19] It is important to recognize that capital rationing is very

[19]We should make three points here. First, capital rationing should not be confused with high yields on

likely to be a short-run problem. If the management of a firm decides to limit its investment budget, and hence not accept profitable projects, the firm will become a target for a takeover or the management will face opposition at the annual shareholders' meeting. From a competitive point of view, a company cannot arbitrarily limit its capital budget while its competitors do not. This places the competitors in an advantageous position.

Project Selection under Capital Rationing

How should projects be selected under conditions of capital rationing? First, note that under conditions of true capital rationing, the firm's value is not being maximized—if management was maximizing, then it would move to the point where the marginal project's *NPV* was zero, and capital rationing as defined would not exist. So, if a firm uses capital rationing, it has ruled out value maximization. The firm may, however, want to maximize value *subject to the constraint that the capital ceiling is not exceeded.* Following constrained maximization behavior will, in general, result in a lower value than following unconstrained maximization, but some type of constrained maximization may produce reasonably satisfactory results. Linear programming is one method of constrained maximization that has been applied to capital rationing. To our knowledge, this method has not been widely applied, but much work is going on in the area, and linear programming may, in the future, prove useful in capital budgeting.[20] If the capital rationing is expected to occur for more than one period, the linear programming solution is particularly useful. If, however, the constraint is for a single period, the solutions are not as complicated.

If a financial manager faces short-run capital rationing, and if the constraint cannot be lifted, what should be done? The manager's objective should be to choose, from all of the available projects, that subset of projects that maximizes the aggregate *NPV* subject to the capital constraint. Satisfactory results can be obtained by ranking projects by their net present value per dollar of initial cost[21]. Starting at the top of this list of projects, the company takes projects of successively lower rank until the available funds have been exhausted.

---

securities issued to finance the investments. The high yields will be reflected in the cost of capital and will thus reduce the number of projects accepted. Second, a decision to hold back on expansion may not be irrational from the viewpoint of a solely owned firm in which the owner wishes to relax and concentrate on enjoying what has already been earned. Of course, if the owner could sell the firm for a higher price due to the expansion, and then relax, the reduced expansion may be irrational. However, the reduced activity would be inappropriate for a publicly owned firm. Third, firms sometimes set a limit on capital expenditures, not because of a shortage of funds, but because of limitations on other resources, especially managerial talent. A firm might feel, for example, that its personnel development program is sufficient to handle an expansion of no more than 10 percent a year, and then set a limit on the capital budget to insure that expansion is held to that rate. This is not capital rationing —rather, it involves a downward reevaluation of project returns if growth exceeds some limit; that is, expected rates of return are, after some point, a decreasing function of the level of expenditure.

[20]For a further discussion of programming approaches to capital budgeting, see Appendix 10A in *Managerial Finance.*

[21]Rankings can also be based on the *IRR* of the project.

However, no investment with a negative *NPV* per unit cost (i.e. a negative *NPV*) should be undertaken.

Why do we rank projects based on the *NPV* per dollar of initial cost instead of *NPV*? In a capital rationing situation, the manager is interested in obtaining the most efficient use of the limited capital available. The *NPV* per dollar of initial cost reflects the scarcity of investment funds by putting a premium on lower cost projects. For example, in a non-capital rationing situation, two projects with the same *NPV* would have the same rank; this ranking would be independent of the initial cost. If we were to rank the two projects in a capital rationing situation, the project with the lower initial cost would be ranked higher, since the same *NPV* is obtained with a smaller investment.

A firm might, for example, have the investment opportunities shown in Table 11–10 and only $6 million available for investment. In this situation, the firm has ranked the projects from highest to lowest *NPV* per dollar of project cost and takes each project in turn in order to meet the constraint. The firm would probably accept projects 1 through 4 and project 6; ending with a capital budget of 5.9 million and a cumulative *NPV* of $2.6 million. Under no circumstances should it accept projects 8, 9, or 10 as they all have negative net present values.

TABLE 11–10   The Prospective Projects Schedule

	(1) Project's Initial Cost	*(2)* PV of Benefits	*(3)* Project's NPV	*(3)/(1)* Ratio NPV to Project's Cost
Nature of Proposal				
1. Purchase of leased space	$2,000,000	3,200,000	$1,200,000	0.60
2. Mechanization of accounting system	1,200,000	1,740,000	540,000	0.45
3. Modernization of office building	1,500,000	2,070,000	570,000	0.38
4. Addition of power facilities	900,000	1,125,000	225,000	0.25
5. Purchase of affiliate	3,600,000	4,248,000	648,000	0.18
6. Purchase of loading docks	300,000	342,000	42,000	0.14
7. Purchase of tank trucks	500,000	540,000	40,000	0.08
8. Installation of conveyor system	200,000	186,000	– 14,000	– 0.07
9. Construction of new plant	2,300,000	2,093,000	– 207,000	– 0.09
10. Purchase of executive aircraft	200,000	128,000	– 72,000	– 0.36

INFLATION AND CAPITAL BUDGETING

Over the decade of the 1960s, inflation was not a serious problem. The rate of inflation, as measured by the Consumer Price Index, averaged 2.7 percent per year. In this environment, inflation was not an issue in capital budgeting. Most capital budgeting analyses ignored the impact of inflation and the resulting decisions were not greatly distorted. However, since the late 1960s the inflationary problem has become much more serious. Although Canada has not reached the hyper-inflation rates of Brazil, Chile, or even Italy, the average annual rate for the period 1970 to 1977 was 7.5 percent per annum; for 1971 the inflation rate was 2.8 percent and for 1977, 8.0 percent.

In this environment, the distortions to capital investment decisions would be severe if inflationary trends were ignored. In this section, we present one method that incorporates inflationary expectations into the analysis. The first problem for the financial manager is to estimate the expected cash flows from the capital expenditure. The expected net cash flow that is appropriate in any period should take into consideration the expected rate of inflation from the date of the investment decision to the date of the net cash flow. To do this, the financial manager should obtain a forecast of the expected rate of inflation. These forecasts, available from government and private sources, are based either on very sophisticated statistical models, or sometimes merely on the forecaster's intuition. However, it may not be sufficient to argue that the net cash flows from the project will be expected to grow at this expected rate of inflation. Each component in the net cash flow may grow at a rate that is related, but not equal to, the inflation rate. For example, revenues may be expected to grow at a rate that is 10 percent higher than the inflation rate and operating costs, 10 percent less. Thus, the net cash flow need not necessarily grow at the expected rate of inflation. The relationship of the growth rate of the components of the cash flow and the inflation rate can be derived from historical relationships. If these are not available, then the analyst may be forced to assume that the cash flows grow at a rate identical to expected inflation.

Consider the following simplified example. Assume that a project costs $400, and beginning one year from today, it is expected to yield $100 per year for five years if there were no inflation expected. Economists are forecasting an inflation rate of 8 percent. Based on past experience, this firm's net cash flows grow at a rate which is 75 percent of the inflation rate. Therefore, the net cash flows are expected to grow at 6 percent per year. Finally, assume that there are no taxes[22] and there is no salvage value.

The expected cash flow at the end of the first year is $106; this is equal to the $100, as if there were no inflation, times the 6 percent inflation rate. At the end of the second year, the expected cash flow is $112.36; this is obtained by having the cash flow of $100 grow by two years of expected inflation i.e. $100 $(1.06)^2$. The cash flows for the third, fourth, and fifth year are $119.10, $126.25 and $133.82, respectively. In each year the expected cash flow must be adjusted for the inflation that is expected to occur.

The next problem is to determine the appropriate discount rate to use. If this project were risk-free, the discount rate would be the market determined rate on medium-term government bonds. Since investors in government bonds want to protect themselves from the reduction in purchasing power due to

---

[22]In a tax world, the tax savings would be based both on the book value of the asset acquired, which is independent of the inflation rate, and on the expected salvage value.

expected inflation, the discount rate will reflect the market's expectations of inflation. Thus, the higher the expected rate of inflation, the higher will be the interest rate on bonds. But risk free bonds are just one financial instrument out of many; each instrument will have a different risk. In order to induce an investor to hold a risky asset, not only must the yield compensate the investor for the added risk, but also the expected rate of inflation. Since the cost of capital reflects the market's opportunity cost for a project of a given risk, no adjustment to the discount rate is necessary since the expectations of the inflation rate are already reflected.

In our example, we assume that the discount rate is 10 percent. The present value of the cash flows at this discount rate is $448.03. With an initial cost of $400, the net present value is $48.03 and the project should be accepted.

SUMMARY

Capital budgeting, which involves commitments for large outlays whose benefits (of drawbacks) extend well into the future, is of the greatest significance to a firm. Decisions in these areas will, therefore, have a major impact on the future well-being of the firm. This chapter focused on how capital budgeting decisions can be made more effective in contributing to the health and growth of a firm. The discussion stressed the development of systematic procedures and rules for preparing a list of investment proposals, for evaluating them, and for selecting a cutoff point. The chapter emphasized that one of the most crucial phases in the process of evaluating capital budget proposals is obtaining a dependable estimate of the benefits that will be obtained from undertaking the project. It cannot be overemphasized that the firm must allocate the making of these judgements to competent and experienced personnel.

Determining Cash Flows   The cash inflows from an investment consist of the incremental profit after taxes, plus the incremental capital cost allowance. An alternative definition of cash inflows which was used extensively in this chapter is the sum of after-tax operating income, plus the tax saving from capital cost allowances. The cash outflow is the cost of the investment. If the project involves a replacement decision, the scrap value of the replaced machine must be deducted from the cost of the new machine.

Ranking Investment Proposals   Three commonly used procedures for ranking investment proposals were discussed in the chapter:

Payback is defined as the number of years required to return the original investment. Although the payback method is used frequently, it has serious conceptual weaknesses, because it ignores the facts (1) that some receipts come in beyond the payback period and (2) that a dollar received today is more valuable than a dollar received in the future.

Net present value (NPV) is defined as the present value of future returns, discounted at the cost of capital, minus the cost of the investment. The *NPV* method overcomes the conceptual flaws noted in the use of the payback method.

Internal rate of return (IRR) is defined as the interest rate that equates the present value of future returns to the investment outlay. The IRR method, like the *NPV* method, meets the objections to the payback approach.

In most cases, the two discounted cash flow methods give identical answers to these questions: Which of two mutually exclusive projects should be selected? How large should the total capital budget be? However, under certain circumstances conflicts may arise. Such conflicts are caused by the fact that the *NPV* and *IRR* methods make different assumptions about the rate at which cash flows may be reinvested, or the opportunity cost of cash flows. In general, the assumption of the *NPV* method (that the opportunity cost is the cost of capital) is the correct one. Accordingly, our preference is for using the *NPV* method to make capital budgeting decisions.

Inflation To incorporate inflation in the analysis requires a forecast of the expected net cash flow for each period; these flows reflect the impact of the expected rate of inflation. The discount rate does not need any adjustment, since it is a market determined rate and will include the market's expectations of the inflation rate. The project is then evaluated with the *NPV* rule.

QUESTIONS

11-1. The primary importance of capital budgeting is to ensure that the firm maximizes the market value of its common equity. Why does the net present value rule method achieve this goal?

11-2. A firm has $100 million available for capital expenditures. Suppose project A involves the purchase of $100 million of grain, shipping it overseas, and selling it within a year at a profit of $20 million. The project has an *IRR* of 20 percent, an *NPV* of $20 million, and *it will cause earnings per share (EPS) to rise within one year.* Project B calls for the use of the $100 million to develop a new process, acquire land, build a plant, and begin processing. Project B, which is not postponable, has an *NPV* of $50 million and an *IRR* of 30 percent, but the fact that some of the plant costs will be written off immediately, combined with the fact that no revenues will be generated for several years, means that accepting project B will *reduce* short-run *EPS*.

a. Should the short-run effects on *EPS* influence the choice between the two projects?

b. How might situations such as the one described here influence a firm's decision to use payback as a screening criterion?

11-3. Are there conditions under which a firm might be better off if it chooses a machine with a rapid payback rather than one with the largest rate of return?

11-4. What are the most critical problems that arise in calculating a rate of return for a prospective investment?

11-5. What is capital rationing? Why might it exist for a firm? What dangers does a firm face if it arbitrarily limits its investment budget?

11-6. Would it be beneficial for a firm to review its past capital expenditures and capital budgeting procedures? Why?

11-7. The text suggests a technique for including inflation in the capital budgeting analysis. What adjustments should and should not be made to the capital budgeting technique to include inflation?

11-8. In evaluating the present value of the benefits accruing from an investment decision, the expected salvage value has two important influences. Describe these influences.

11-9. Describe the steps that must be taken in the capital budgeting process in the case of a replacement decision.

11-10. Fiscal and monetary policies are tools used by the government to stimulate the economy. Explain, using the analytical devices developed in this chapter, how each of the following might be expected to stimulate the economy by encouraging investment.

  a. A speed-up in the tax allowable depreciation, such as the use of a two-year write-off of the cost of an asset.

  b. A reduction in interest rates.

  c. An investment tax credit of 5 percent of the capital cost of assets.

PROBLEMS

11-1. The Windsor Corporation is currently reviewing two projects which are mutually exclusive investments. The first investment would require an outlay of $1 million and would yield an annual net cash flow after taxes of $150,000 per year. The second investment opportunity involves an outlay of $700,000 and produces a net cash flow after tax of $105,000 per year. Both projects are in the same risk class which requires a cost capital of 12 percent. Both projects are expected to last for 18 years. What are the net present values and internal rates of return for each project? Which project should be chosen?

11-2. Each of two mutually exclusive projects involves an investment of $6,000. After-tax cash flows are $4,000 a year for two years for project S and $1,600 a year for six years for project L.

  a. Compute the present value of each project if the firm's cost of capital is 0 percent, 6 percent, 10 percent, 20 percent.

  b. Compute the internal rate of return for each project.

  c. Graph the present values of the two projects, putting *NPV* on the *Y*-axis and the cost of capital on the *X*-axis.

  d. Could you have determined the *IRR* of the projects from your graph? Explain.

  e. Which project would you select, assuming no capital rationing and a constant cost of capital of (1) 8 percent, (2) 10 percent, (3) 12 percent? Explain.

  f. If capital was severely rationed, which project would you select?

11-3. Rocky Mountain Ski Enterprise Ltd. (RMSE) is considering the replacement of its ski tow equipment with a more sophisticated chair lift facility. The present equipment cost $200,000 five years ago and the capital cost rate applied to calculate the capital cost allowance is 8 percent. The existing equipment has a further life of 15 years when it would be scrapped for $10,000. The new installation would last for 15 years at which time it could be sold for $150,000. The capital cost of the new chair lift is $600,000, but if the existing towing equipment is sold today, it would provide $50,000 towards the new outlay. The lift has a capital cost rate of 8 percent.

The management of RMSE foresee that the new chair lift would raise revenues from the current $700,000 per year to $1,200,000 per year. Operating costs would also increase from $350,000 to $400,000 per year. The corporate tax rate is 46 percent and the cost of capital is 12 percent. Should RMSE install the new chair lift? Prepare a worksheet similar to that illustrated in Table 11-9.

11-4. The Skylar Co. Ltd. operates a chain of garden centers. Their central greenhouse and nursery requires modernization. A contracting firm has provided management with estimates of the costs of doubling their greenhouse capacity. For an $800,000 outlay now, the building would be enlarged and new climate controlling equipment would be installed. This would increase annual running costs by $160,000. Staff would have to be augmented to provide additional customer and delivery service to the regional retial centers at a cost of $130,000 per year. Projected increased revenues would be $500,000 per year before taxes. The project would last for 15 years and have no scrap value. The building is in a pool where a 5 percent capital cost allowance rate is used. The corporate tax rate is 46 percent.

a. To the nearest full percent, at what discount rate will Skylar Co. be indifferent to going ahead with the project?

b. If the cost of capital is 12 percent, at what level of revenues would management be indifferent to the investment?

c. Calculate the net present value of the project if the cost of capital is 12 percent.

11-5. J.D.P. Associates is a group of consulting financial analysts. They publish a monthly newsletter that reviews the current Canadian economic state, stock and bond market trends, and possible future market developments. Due to budget constraints, the funds available for investment this year are limited to $120,000. Three projects are being considered. Each is an investment in a printing press that would produce a good quality publication, but the capacities of each would be different. From the few facts and figures management has projected that there are some extra costs and revenues from increasing their distribution.

	Press A	Press B	Press C
Year 0	- $90,000	- $70,000	- $50,000
1	+ 50,000	+ 23,000	+ 15,000
2	+ 40,000	+ 23,000	+ 15,000
3	+ 20,000	+ 23,000	+ 15,000
4	+ 10,000	+ 23,000	+ 15,000
5	+ 5,000	+ 23,000	+ 15,000

a. If the firm's cost of capital is 16 percent, which of the presses should be acquired?

b. If we consider presses B and C as one possible investment, graph the net present values of presses A and B + C with the *NPV* on the *Y*-axis and the cost of capital on the *X*-axis. Which project would be preferred at a discount rate of 18 percent, A or B + C; and which would be preferred at a discount rate of 10 percent?

11-6. The Winfield Company Ltd. is using a machine whose original cost was $72,000. The machine is 2 years old and has a current market value of $16,000. The asset is being depreciated for book purposes over a 12 year original life. The salvage value is expected to be zero. The asset belongs in the pool that has a depreciation rate for CCA purposes of 30 percent. The tax rate is 50 percent and the pool has a book value of $500,000.

Management is contemplating the purchase of a replacement which costs $75,000 and has an estimated salvage value of $10,000. The new machine will have a greater capacity, and annual sales are expected to increase from $1 million to $1.01 million, or by $10,000. Operating efficiencies with the new machine will also produce expected savings of $10,000 a year. The cost of capital is 8 percent, a 50 percent tax rate is applicable, and the company's total annual operating costs are $800,000. This asset belongs in the same pool for CCA purposes as the old machine.

  a. Should the firm replace the asset?

  b. Would your decision change if the capital cost rate applicable to the pool had been 15 percent?

  c. How would your decision be affected if a second new machine is available that costs $140,000, has a $20,000 estimated salvage value, and is expected to provide $25,000 in annual savings over its 10 year life? It also increases sales by $10,000 a year. (There are now three alternatives: (1) keep the old machine, (2) replace it with a $75,000 machine, or (3) replace it with a $140,000 machine.) This third asset falls in the same CCA pool as the other two and the applicable CCA rate is 30 percent.

  d. Disregarding the changes in part b—that is, under the original assumption that one $75,000 replacement machine is available— how would your decision be affected if a new generation of equipment is expected to be on the market in about 2 years that will provide increased annual savings and have the same cost, asset life, and salvage value?

  e. How would your decision be affected if the asset lives of the various alternatives were not the same?

11-7. The Elmwood Company Ltd. is considering the purchase of a new machine tool to replace an obsolete one. Assume that the machine being used for the operation has both a market value and book value for capital cost purposes equal to zero; it is in good working order and will last, physically, for at least an additional 15 years. The proposed machine will perform the operation so much more efficiently that Elmwood engineers estimate that labor, material, and other direct costs of the operation will be reduced by $4,500 a year if it is installed. The proposed machine costs $24,000 delivered and installed, and its economic life is estimated to be 15 years with zero salvage value. The company expects to earn 12 percent on its investment after taxes (12 percent is the firm's cost of capital). The tax rate is 50 percent and the capital cost rate for tax purposes is 30 percent.

  a. Should Elmwood buy the new machine?

  b. Assume that the book value of the old machine for CCA purposes had been $6,000, and that it had no sale value. How do these assumptions affect your answer?

c. Change part b to give the old machine a market value of $4,000.

d. Change part b to assume that the annual saving would be $6,000. (The change in part c is not made; the machine is not sold for $4,000.)

e. Rework part a assuming the relevant cost of capital is now 6 percent. What is the significance of this? What can be said about parts b, c, and d under this assumption?

f. In general, how would each of the following factors affect the investment decision, and how should each be treated?

1. The expected life of the existing machine decreases.

2. Capital rationing is imposed on the firm.

3. The cost of capital is not constant but is rising.

4. Improvements in the equipment to be purchased are expected to occur each year, and the result will be to increase the returns or expected savings from new machines over the saving expected with this year's model for every year in the foreseeable future.

Derivation of the Present Value of Tax Savings

 Appendix

Derivation of the Present Value of Tax Savings

A crucial component in the capital budgeting analysis is the calculation of the present value of tax savings derived from capital cost allowances. Although the present value of the after-tax net cash flows could be calculated directly, problems that arise from the expected salvage value are easier to handle by calculating the present value of the net cash flow as the sum of the present values of after-tax operating income and tax savings.

Let C_0 be the original capital cost of the asset,

d be the maximum capital cost rate for the class,

CCA_j be the capital cost allowances applied in year j,

UCC_j be the undepreciated capital cost on which the capital cost allowance for year j is calculated,

t be the company's tax rate, and

k be the opportunity cost of capital.

The tax saving from capital cost allowances is equal to the capital cost allowance taken in the year, times the tax rate $(tCCA_j)$. Since the asset is never fully used up, the tax savings occur in perpetuity. The present value of the tax savings is presented in Equation A11–1 below.

$$PV_{\text{tax saving}} = \frac{tCCA_1}{1+k} + \frac{tCCA_2}{(1+k)^2} + \frac{tCCA_2}{(1+k)^3} + \dots \qquad \text{(A11-1)}$$

$$= \frac{t}{1+k}\left[CCA_1 + \frac{CCA_2}{1+k} + \frac{CCA_3}{(1+k)^2} + \dots\right] \qquad \text{(A11-2)}$$

To solve for this present value, it is necessary to write the capital cost allowances in every year as a function of a set of fixed and given variables. In the first year, CCA_1 is equal to the original cost of the asset times the cost rate.

$$CCA_1 = C_0 d$$

The undepreciated capital cost for the second year is the original value, less the CCA charge for year 1.

$$UCC_2 = C_0 - CCA_1$$
$$= C_0 - C_0 d$$
$$= C_0(1-d) \qquad \text{(A11-3)}$$

In year 2, the CCA charge is equal to the capital cost rate, times the undepreciated capital cost.

$$CCA_2 = dUCC_2$$
$$= dC_0(1-d) \quad \text{(from A11-3)} \qquad \text{(A11-4)}$$

The undepreciated capital cost for the third year is the undepreciated capital cost for the second year less the CCA taken for the year.

$$UCC_3 = UCC_2 - CCA_2$$

Substituting the expression from Equation A11-3 for UCC_2 and from A11-4 for CCA_2, we obtain equation A11-5.

$$UCC_3 = C_0(1-d) - dC_0(1-d)$$
$$= C_0(1-d) \qquad \text{(A11-5)}$$

We are now in a position to generalize these expressions. For any year j, the undepreciated capital cost can be written as follows.

$$UCC_j = C_0(1-d)^{j-1} \qquad \text{(A11-6)}$$

This expression requires input of C_0, d, and j; all of which are given.

The generalization of the CCA charge is straight-forward. The CCA in any year j will be equal to the cost rate, times the undepreciated capital cost for that year.

$$CCA_j = dUCC_j \qquad \text{(A11-7)}$$

Substituting the expression for UCC_j from Equation A11-6 into A11-7, we obtain the following expression.

$$CCA_j = dC_0 (1-d)^{j-1} \qquad (A11-8)$$

The ground work has been set for the solution of the present value of the tax savings. Equation A11-2 can be re-written as equation A11-9 with the substitution of the appropriate expression for CCA_j from equation A11-8.

$$PV_{\text{tax saving}} = \frac{t}{1+k}\left[dC_0 + \frac{dC_0(1-d)}{1+k} + \frac{dC_0(1-d)^2}{(1+k)^2} + \dots\right]$$

$$= \frac{tdC_0}{(1+k)}\left[1 + \frac{1-d}{1+k} + \left(\frac{1-d}{1+k}\right)^2 + \dots\right] \qquad (A11-9)$$

The expression in the square brackets in Equation A11-9 is the sum of an infinite geometric series beginning with the value 1. Each factor is obtained by multiplying the previous value by the fixed value $\frac{1-d}{1+k}$. The summation of this series is $\frac{1+k}{k+d}$. Substituting this into Equation A11-9, we obtain the following expression for the present value of the tax savings.

$$PV_{\text{tax saving}} = \frac{tdC_0}{1+k}\left[\frac{1+k}{k+d}\right]$$

$$= \frac{tdC_0}{k+d} \qquad (A11-10)$$

The simplification in finding the present value occurs because all of the subsequent values for the CCA charges can be derived from the original cost of the asset and the cost rate applied to the asset.

The above analysis has been presented under the assumption that the asset will never be sold. Suppose, however, that when the asset is purchased it is expected to be sold after N years for a salvage value of S dollars. If the asset were not sold, the present value of the tax savings is equal to the expression in Equation A11-10. However, with the sale of the asset, all of the capital cost allowances from year $N + 1$ are lost. But, since the value of the pool is reduced by the sale proceeds, the lost CCA charges will depend on the salvage value.

The present value of the lost tax savings is written as follows.

$$PV_{\text{lost}} = \frac{1}{(1+k)^N}\left[\frac{tCCA_{N+1}}{1+k} + \frac{tCCA_{N+2}}{(1+k)^2} + \dots\right] \qquad (A11-11)$$

The expression in the square brackets is the sum of an infinite geometric progression beginning in period $N + 1$. The expression $\frac{1}{(1+k)^N}$ converts this infinite sum to a present value as of the acquisition date. The CCA in period $N + 1$ is equal to the proceeds of sale times the cost rate, d. Hence, all of the lost tax savings can be written in terms of the salvage value, S.

$$CCA_{N+1} = dS$$

$$CCA_{N+2} = dS (1 - d)$$

$$CCA_{N+3} = dS (1 - d)^2$$

Substituting these expressions into Equation A11–11 and solving for the sum of the infinite geometric series, we obtain the following expression for the present value of the lost tax savings.

$$PV_{lost} = \frac{tdS}{k + d} \times \frac{1}{(1 + k)^N} \tag{A11-12}$$

The present value of the tax savings obtained from the purchase and eventual sale of this asset is equal to the present value of the tax savings, as if the asset were held forever, less the lost tax savings based on the salvage value of the asset. This expression is presented in Equation A1–13.

$$PV_{tax\ saving} = \frac{tdC_0}{k + d} - \frac{tdS}{k + d} \times \frac{1}{(1 + k)^N} \tag{A11-13}$$

Since it is the salvage value that is deducted from the book value of the pool, this is the incremental impact that must be used in evaluating the lost tax savings.

Investment Decisions under Uncertainty

12

In order to develop the theory and methodology of capital budgeting in a systematic manner, the "riskiness" of alternative projects was not treated explicitly in the preceding chapter; in effect, we assumed that the projects were riskless. However, since investors and financial managers are risk averters, risk considerations should be taken into account when making investment decisions.

In this chapter we will be concerned with two major issues; the evaluation of risk for a project and the integration of this risk into the actual investment decision procedure.

Evaluating a project and assuming that there is no risk is dangerous at best and downright misleading at worst. Thus, the financial literature has been grappling with the problems of introducing risk into investment decisions. Most of these analyses are based on sophisticated mathematical and statistical treatments. Unfortunately, the use of these techniques is not currently feasible in business situations because (1) vital statistical information is unavailable, and (2) the theoretical concepts have not yet been worked out completely. Clearly, we cannot ignore risk, but we are reluctant to take a formal, mathematical approach to the subject in an introductory textbook. Therefore, we chart a middle course by presenting the essential elements of decision making under uncertainty at an intuitive level.

RISK IN FINANCIAL ANALYSIS

The riskiness of an asset is defined in terms of the likely variability of future

285

returns from the asset. For example, if one buys a $1 million short-term government bond expected to yield 5 percent, then the return on the investment, 5 percent, can be estimated quite precisely, and the investment is defined as relatively risk free. However, if the $1 million is invested in the stock of a company just being organized to prospect for uranium in Central Africa, then the probable return cannot be estimated precisely. The rate of return on the $1 million investment could range from minus 100 percent to some extremely large figure, and because of this high variability, the project is defined as relatively risky. Similarly, sales forecasts for different products of a single firm might exhibit differing degrees of riskiness. For example, Union Carbide might be quite sure that sales of its Eveready batteries will range between 50 and 60 million for the coming year, but be highly uncertain about how many units of a new laser measuring device will be sold during the year.

Risk, then, is associated with project variability—the more variable the expected future returns, the riskier the investment. However, we can define risk more precisely, and it is useful to do so. This more precise definition requires a step-by-step development, which constitutes the remainder of this section.

Probability Distributions

Any investment decision—or, for that matter, almost *any* kind of business decision—implies a forecast of future events that is either explicit or implicit. Ordinarily, the forecast of annual cash flow is a single figure, or *point estimate,* frequently called the "most likely" or "best" estimate. For example, one might forecast that the cash flows from a particular project will be $500 a year for three years.

How good is this point estimate; that is, how confident is the forecaster of the predicted return? Is it very certain, very uncertain, or somewhere in between? This degree of uncertainty can be defined and measured in terms of the forecaster's *probability distribution*—the probability estimates associated with each possible outcome. In its simplest form, a probability distribution could consist of just a few potential outcomes. For example, in forecasting cash flows, we could make an optimistic estimate, a pessimistic estimate, and a most likely estimate; or, alternatively, we could make high, low, and "best guess" estimates. We might expect our high, or optimistic, estimate to be realized if the national economy booms, our pessimistic estimate to hold if the economy is depressed, and our best guess to occur if the economy runs at a normal level. These ranges are illustrated in Table 12–1. The figures in the table represent some improvement over our earlier best-guess estimate of $500, as additional information has been provided. However, some critical information is still missing: How likely is it that we will have a boom, a recession, or normal economic conditions? If we have estimates of the probabilities of these events, we can develop a weighted average cash flow estimate and a measure of our degree of confidence in this estimate. This point is explored in the next section.

TABLE 12–1 Expected Cash Flows under Different Economic Conditions

State of the Economy	Cash Flows
Recession	$400
Normal	500
Boom	600

Risk Comparisons

To illustrate how the probability distribution concept can be used to compare the riskiness of alternative investment projects, suppose we are considering two investment decisions each calling for an outlay of $1,000 and each expected to produce a cash flow of $500 a year for three years. (The best-estimate cash flow is $500 a year for each project). If we assign a discount rate of 10 percent to each project, we can use the methods developed in the preceding chapter to estimate each project's net present value:

$$NPV = \$500 \times 2.487 - \$1,000$$

$$= \$1,243.50 - \$1,000$$

$$= \$243.50 \text{ for each project.}$$

The projects have the same expected returns; does this mean that they are equally desirable? Remember that we are interested in choosing that project (or set of projects) which will maximize the stock price of the firm. Therefore, when we reflect on the desirability of projects, we must be concerned with the way the market will view the projects. To determine whether the projects are equally desirable, we need to know whether the projects are also equally risky, since "desirability" depends upon the expected returns given the level of risk.

Let us suppose that project A calls for the replacement of an old machine used in normal operations by a more efficient one, and the benefits are labor and raw material savings that will result. Project B, on the other hand, calls for the purchase of an entirely new machine to produce a new product, the demand for which is highly uncertain. The replacement machine (project A) will be used more, hence savings will be greater, if demand for the product is high. Expected demand for the new product (project B) is also greatest when the economy is booming.

We stated above that the expected annual returns from each project are

$500. Let us assume that these figures were developed in the following manner:

1. First, we estimate project returns under different states of the economy as in Table 12–2. Tables of this kind are typically referred to as *payoff matrices.*

TABLE 12–2   Payoff Matrix for Projects A and B

State of the Economy	Annual Cash Flows	
	Project A	Project B
Recession	$400	$ 0
Normal	500	500
Boom	600	1,000

2. Next, we estimate the likelihood of different states of the economy. Assume our economic forecasts indicate that, given current trends in economic indicators, the chances are 2 out of 10 that a recession will occur, 6 out of 10 that the economy will be normal, and 2 out of 10 that there will be a boom.

3. Redefining the word "chance" as *probability,* we find that the probability of a recession is $2/10 = .2$, or 20 percent; the probability of normal times is $6/10 = .6$, or 60 percent; and the probability of a boom is $2/10 = .2$, or 20 percent. Notice that the probabilities add up to 1.0, or 100 percent: $.2 + .6 + .2 = 1.0$, or 100 percent.

TABLE 12–3   Calculation of Expected Values

State of the Economy (1)	Probability of This State's Occurring (2)	Outcome if This State Occurs (3)	(2) × (3) (4)
Project A			
Recession	0.2	$ 400	$ 80
Normal	0.6	500	300
Boom	0.2	600	120
	1.0	Expected value =	$500
Project B			
Recession	0.2	$ 0	$ 0
Normal	0.6	500	300
Boom	0.2	1,000	200
	1.0	Expected value =	$500

4. Finally, in Table 12–3 we calculate weighted averages of the possible returns by multiplying each dollar return by its probability of occurrence. When column 4 of the table is summed, we obtain a weighted average of the outcomes for each alternative under various states of the economy; this weighted average is defined as the *expected value* of the cash flows from the project. It need not, of course, be equal to the project's outcome for a normal state of the economy, although it is in this case.

We can graph the results shown in Table 12–3 to obtain a picture of the variability of actual outcomes; this is shown in the bar charts in Figure 12–1. The height of each bar signifies the probability that a given outcome will occur. The range of probable outcomes for project A is from $400 to $600, with an average or *expected value* of $500. The expected value for project B is also $500, but the range of possible outcomes is from $0 to $1,000.

FIGURE 12–1 Relationship between the State of the Economy and Project Returns

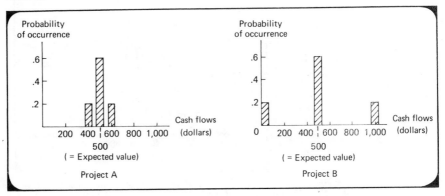

Project A

Project B

Continuous Distributions Thus far we have assumed that only three states of the economy can exist: recession, normal, and boom. Actually, of course, the state of the economy could range from a deep depression, as in the early 1930s, to a fantastic boom; and there are an unlimited number of possibilities in between. Suppose we had the time and patience to assign a probability to each possible state of the economy (with the sum of the probabilities still equaling 1.0) and to assign a monetary outcome to each project for each state of the economy. We would have a table similar to Table 12–3 except that it would have many more entries for "Probability" and "Outcome if this state occurs." These tables could be used to calculate expected values as shown above, and the probabilities and outcomes could be graphed as the continuous curves presented in Figure 12–2. Here we have changed the assumptions so that there is zero probability that project A will yield less than $400 or more than $600, and so that there is zero probability that project B will yield less than $0 or more than $1,000.

Figure 12–2 is a graph of the *probability distributions* of returns on projects A and B. In general, the tighter the probability distribution, or, alternatively stated, the more peaked the distribution, the lower the risk on a project. The tighter the probability distribution, of course, the more likely it is that the actual outcome will be close to the expected value. Since project A has a relatively tight probability distribution, its *actual* profits are likely to be closer to the *expected* $500 than are those of project B.

FIGURE 12–2   Probability Distribution Showing Relationship between the State of the Economy and Project Returns

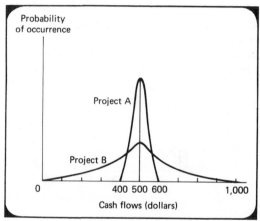

Note: The assumptions regarding the probabilities of various outcomes have been changed from those in Figure 12–1. The probability of obtaining *exactly* $500 was 60 percent in Figure 12–1; in Figure 12–2 it is nearly zero, because here there are many possible outcomes instead of just three. With continuous distributions as in Figure 12–2, it is more appropriate to ask, "What is the probability of obtaining *at least* some specified value?" than to ask what the probability is of obtaining exactly that value. This cumulative probability is equal to the area under the probability distribution curve up to the point of interest.

Risk versus Uncertainty

Sometimes a distinction is made between *risk* and *uncertainty*. When this distinction is made, risk is associated with those situations in which a probability distribution of the returns on a given project can be estimated; uncertainty is associated with those situations in which insufficient evidence is available even to estimate a probability distribution. We do not make this distinction; risk and uncertainty are used synonymously in this chapter.

We do, however, recognize that probability distributions of expected returns can themselves be estimated with greater or lesser precision. In some instances, the probability distribution can be estimated *objectively* with statistical techniques. For example, a large oil company may be able to estimate from past recovery data the probability distribution of recoverable oil reserves in a given field. When statistical procedures can be used, risk is said to be measured by *objective probability distributions.* There are, however, many situations in which statistical data cannot be used. For example, a company considering the introduction of a totally new product will have some idea about the required investment outlay, the demand for the product, the production costs, and so forth. These estimates will not, however, be determined by statistics; they will be determined subjectively and are defined as *subjective probability distributions.*

Measuring Risk: The Standard Deviation

Risk is a difficult concept to grasp, and a great deal of controversy has surrounded attempts to define and measure it. However, a common definition of risk, and one that is satisfactory for our purposes, is stated in terms of probability distributions such as those presented in Figure 12–2: *The tighter the probability distribution of expected future returns, the smaller the risk of a given project.* According to this definition, project A is less risky than project B because the actual return for A should be closer to the expected return than is true for B.

To be most useful, our measure of risk should have some definite value —we need a *measure* of the tightness of the probability distribution of project returns. One such measure, and the one we shall use, is the *standard deviation,* the symbol for which is σ, read "sigma." The smaller the standard deviation, the tighter the probability distribution and, accordingly, the lower the riskiness of the project.[1] Project A's standard deviation is found to be $63.25;

[1] The standard deviation of a distribution is found as follows:

1. Calculate the expected value of the distribution:

$$\text{Expected value} = \overline{R} = \sum_{i=1}^{n} (R_i P_i). \qquad (12\text{–}1)$$

Here R_i is the return associated with the ith outcome; P_i is the probability of occurrence of that ith outcome; and $\overline{R}$, the expected value, is a weighted average of the various possible outcomes, each weighted by the probability of its occurrence. (See Table 12–3.)

2. Subtract the expected value from each possible outcome to obtain a set of deviations about the expected value:

$$\text{Deviation}_i = R_i - \overline{R}.$$

3. Square each deviation, multiply the squared deviation by the probability of occurrence for its related outcome, and sum these products to obtain the *variance* of the probability distribution:

$$\text{Variance} = \sigma^2 = \sum_{i=1}^{n} (R_i - \overline{R})^2 P_i. \qquad (12\text{–}2)$$

4. The standard deviation is found by obtaining the square root of the variance:

$$\text{Standard deviation} = \sigma = \sqrt{\sum_{i=1}^{n} (R_i - \overline{R})^2 P_i}. \qquad (12\text{–}3)$$

that of project B is $316.20. Other projects available to the firm could be eval-uated for riskiness in similar fashion, thus providing the financial manager with information on both the risk (σ) and the expected profitability *(NPV* or *IRR)* of capital projects.

FIGURE 12–3 Probability Distributions of Two Investments with Different Expected Returns

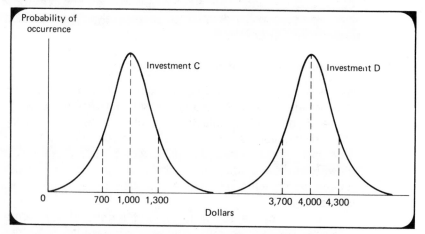

Measuring Risk: The Coefficient of Variation

Certain problems can arise when the standard deviation is used as a measure of risk. To illustrate, consider Figure 12–3, which shows the probability dis-tributions for investments C and D. Investment C has an expected return of $1,000 and a standard deviation of $300. Investment D also has a standard deviation of $300, but its expected return is $4,000. The likely percentage

---

5. Calculation of the standard deviation for project A:
  a. The expected value, or the mean, was found in Table 12–3 to be $500.

  b.

R_i – $\overline{R}$	= $(R_i - \overline{R})$	$(R_i - \overline{R})^2$	$(R_i - \overline{R})^2 P_i$
400 – 500	– 100	10,000	(10,000)(.2) = 2,000
500 – 500	0	0	(0)(.6) = 0
600 – 500	+ 100	10,000	(10,000)(.2) = 2,000

$$\sigma_A^2 = 4,000$$

$$\sigma_A = \sqrt{\sigma_A^2} = \sqrt{4,000} \doteq \$63.25.$$

  c. By the same procedure, we find project B's standard deviation to be $316.20. Since B's standard deviation is larger, it is the riskier project.

If a probability distribution is normal (symmetrically bell shaped), the *actual outcome* will lie within ± 1 stan-dard deviation of the *expected value* 68 percent of the time.

deviation from the mean of investment C is considerably higher than that from the mean of investment D, or, put another way, C has more risk *per dollar of return* than D. On this basis, it is reasonable to assign a higher degree of risk to investment C than to investment D even though they have identical standard deviations.

The best procedure for eliminating this problem is to divide the standard deviation (σ) by the mean expectation ($\overline{R}$) to obtain the *coefficient of variation* (*v*):

$$v = \frac{\sigma}{\overline{R}}.$$

For investment C, we divide the $300 standard deviation by the $1,000 mean expectation, obtaining .30 as the coefficient of variation; investment D's coefficient of variation is calculated to be .075. Henceforth, we shall use the coefficient of variation to compare the riskiness of alternative investments whenever the standard deviation might be misleading. In general, the coefficient of variation should be used when appraising returns stated in dollars, since there is a need to adjust the standard deviation by the size of the cash flow. However, if the returns are stated as percentage rates of return, the adjustment for size has already been made in the rate of return calculation. Therefore, the standard deviation can be used as the risk measure.

Riskiness over Time

We can also use Figure 12–2 above to consider the riskiness of a stream of receipts over time. Visualize, for example, investment A as being the expected cash flow from a particular project during year 1, and investment B as being the expected cash flow from the *same* project in the tenth year. The expected return is the same for each of the two years, but the subjectively estimated standard deviation (hence the coefficient of variation) is larger for the more distant return. In this case, riskiness is *increasing over time.*

Figure 12–4 may help to clarify the concept of increasing riskiness over time. Figure 12–4(a) simply shows the probability distribution of expected cash flows in two years—years 1 and 10. The distribution is flatter in year 10, indicating that there is more uncertainty about expected cash flows in distant years. Figure 12–4(b) represents a three-dimensional plot of the expected cash flows over time and their probability distributions. The probability distributions should be visualized as extending out from the page. The dashed lines show the standard deviations attached to the cash flows of each year; the fact that these lines diverge from the expected cash flow line indicates that riskiness is increasing over time. If risk was thought of as being constant over time—that is, if the cash flow in a distant year could be estimated equally as well as the cash flow of a close year—then the standard deviation would be constant and the boundary lines would not diverge from the expected cash flow line. The fact that the standard deviation is increasing over time, while the expected return is constant, would, of course, cause the coefficient of variation to increase similarly.[2]

FIGURE 12–4   Risk as a Function of Time

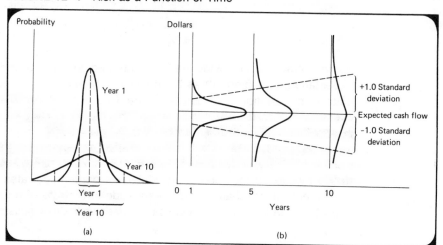

PORTFOLIO RISK

When considering the riskiness of a particular investment, it is frequently useful to consider the relationship between the investment in question and other existing assets or potential investment opportunities. For example, in Chapter 6 we discussed Genstar Limited in the context of decentralized decision making. Genstar is a diversified company which has a number of operating divisions that are involved in markets which are subject to different influences. For example, the marine and residential construction divisions are very likely to be influenced by rather different factors, although it is possible that the performances of the divisions are related through a common relationship with the general economy.

In some instances firms will choose to invest or operate in different

[2]If risk does change over time, then the investment analysis must take this into consideration. However, it has been demonstrated by Robichek and Myers, *Optimal Financing Decisions* (Englewood Cliffs, N.J., Prentice Hall, 1965) that using a constant discount rate in the net present value calculation actually implies that risk increases over time. Thus, the net present value, constant discount rate technique adjusts for this problem. If risk is decreasing over time, then the discount rate in the net present value calculation must be adjusted downward for the future cash flows.

industries so as to diversify their risk; the basis of this diversification is the cyclical patterns of the cash flows (or rates of return) from the different products or divisions. For example, a company whose earnings are very strongly related to the health of the overall economy may invest in a product line for which the earnings (or rates of return) are either independent of the economy, or if possible, move in an opposite (i.e. counter-cyclical) direction. By undertaking these types of investment decisions, management has decided to diversify the risk of the earnings stream of the company. This management behavior is equivalent to choosing a portfolio of assets such that the resulting earnings stream will have a more stable pattern than that in a firm that is involved exclusively in the production of any one of the products. This portfolio approach implies that it is possible to choose a number of products to include in the corporate portfolio such that the risk (i.e. standard deviation) of the returns on the corporate portfolio are less than the sum of the risks on the returns from the individual assets.[3] The diversification effect is the reduction in risk by combining the assets.

It must be emphasized that diversification need not always result in a reduction in risk. Suppose a bank decides to purchase a wildcat drilling company. The standard deviation of the new company may be greater than the standard deviation of the bank operations alone. However, it is possible that the risk can be lower. In addition, if diversification exists, the risk of the sum will be less than the sum of the risks when the operations are considered separately.

The degree of diversification will depend on the correlation of the earnings from each product or division. In our discussion we will assume that

FIGURE 12-5   Relationship of Returns on Two Hypothetical Products

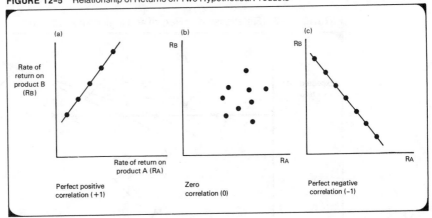

³ These conclusions obviously hold also for portfolios of financial assets—stocks and bonds. In fact, the basic concepts of portfolio theory were developed specifically for common stocks by Harry Markowitz and were first presented in his article, "Portfolio Selection," *Journal of Finance*, 7, no. 1 (March 1952), 77–91. The logical extension of portfolio theory to capital budgeting calls for considering firms as having "portfolios of tangible assets."

the company is deciding whether to add product B and how large an invest-ment should be made in this product. Product B has both a higher risk and higher expected return than the existing product A. The important variable in investigating diversification is the correlation coefficient between the returns on the products. The correlation coefficient, which lies between the limits of −1 and +1, measures the intensity and direction of the co-movement of the returns on the products. If the correlation coefficient is +1, there is perfect positive correlation—as shown in Figure 12–5, Panel a. In this instance the return on B can be predicted exactly by knowing the return on A. If there is a perfect positive relationship between the returns, then the returns on the products plot exactly on a straight line. In this case there can be no diversifica-tion gains. When the return on product A is above its average value, not only will the return on B be above its average, but we will know its value exactly.

As the correlation coefficient moves toward zero, there is still a positive relationship, but its intensity becomes smaller and smaller. When the correla-tion coefficient is zero—Figure 12–5, Panel (b)—there is no relationship between the rates of return on the two products. Thus, when the return on A is above its average, the return on B can be either above or below its mean. This lack of association results in diversification. In fact, as long as there is not perfect correlation, there is some diversification.

If the correlation coefficient is negative, then there is a negative associa-tion between the returns on the products. The more negative the correlation coefficient, the greater the intensity of the negative relationship. In fact, at the limit of −1, it is possible to build a portfolio of two products that eliminates risk entirely. Panel C in Figure 12–5 presents the plot for perfect negative correlation.

FIGURE 12-6   Relationship of Return and Risk on a Portfolio

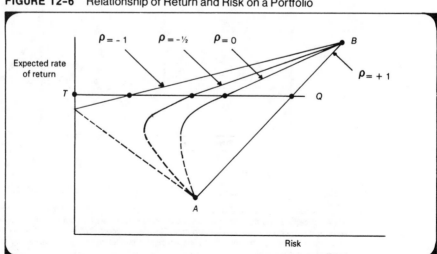

Although we will not derive the results, the impact on the portfolio rate of return and risk is presented in Figure 12-6.

The expected rate of return on the portfolio is plotted on the vertical axis and risk is plotted on the horizontal axis. A portfolio of products A and B is obtained by investing different dollar amounts in each product. At either extreme, the portfolio can be composed of either product A or B. Let ρ be the correlation coefficient. When $\rho = +1$, there is a straight line relationship between A and B. As ρ moves away from 1, the line joining A and B becomes more curved.[4] At the extreme of $\rho = -1$, there is a straight line between B and a point in the expected return axis *(T)*. In this case, it is possible to reduce risk entirely since the expected return, *T,* can be obtained with zero risk.

To show the importance of diversification, consider the expected return equal to *T*. If $\rho = 1$, the risk-return point is *Q*. As the correlation coefficient moves further away from 1, the same expected return is obtained but the overall risk is reduced. This is the diversification effect.

This diversification effect is enhanced as the number of products in the portfolio increase. This is true as long as the correlation is not equal to $+1$. For example, if the correlation is zero, the larger the number of projects the firm takes on, the smaller will be the variability in its overall rate of return for a given level of expected return.

We can summarize the arguments on portfolio risk that have been presented thus far:

(1) If *perfectly negatively correlated* projects are available; then, by choosing the amounts to invest in each project correctly, risk can be completely eliminated. Perfect negative correlation is, however, almost never found in the real world.

(2) If *uncorrelated* projects are available in sufficient numbers, then diversification can reduce risk significantly.

(3) If alternative projects are perfectly positive in correlation, then diversification does not reduce risk at all.

(4) The degree of diversification depends on the correlation coefficient. As long as the projects are not perfectly positive in correlation, there is potential for diversification. The diversification effect increases as the correlation coefficient moves away from $+1$ and approaches -1.

In fact, most projects are *positively* correlated but not *perfectly* correlated. The degree of intercorrelation among projects depends upon economic factors, and these factors are usually amenable to analysis. Returns on investments in projects closely related to the firm's basic products and markets will ordinarily be highly correlated with returns on the remainder of the firm's

---

[4]The curve between points A and B is called the efficient set of portfolios that can be built by using A and B. However, not all of the curve is efficient. If the investor can obtain a higher rate of return for the same risk or the same rate of return for a lower risk, he will do it. This occurs on the dashed part of the efficient sets. The dashed part of the curve is inefficient and would never be chosen by an investor.

assets, and such investments will not generally diversify the firm's risk. However, investments in other product lines and in other geographic markets may have a low degree of correlation with other components of the firm and may, therefore, reduce overall risk. Accordingly, if an asset's returns are not too closely related to the firm's other major assets (or, better still, are negatively correlated with other investments), this asset is more valuable to a risk-averting firm than is a similar asset whose returns are positively correlated with the bulk of the assets. It has been argued that this fact was one of the driving forces behind the trend toward conglomerate mergers during the 1950s and 1960s.

The important question to answer is whether it is profitable from the shareholders point of view for the company to undertake these diversification investment decisions. If a particular project's return is uncorrelated with the returns on existing assets, should the firm accept the project just for its risk-reduction benefits, or should these benefits be ignored and the only criterion for choice be the profitability of the project?

There are a number of issues that must be taken into account when we consider the importance of accepting projects for their risk-reduction benefit. First, when one company acquires another in a different business, there is always a danger that the acquiring firm will not know how to run the acquired firm and the end result will be low and unstable earnings. Second, we have ignored the possibility that investors have available to them the ability to diversify their own portfolios. The shareholder could have built a portfolio of an equivalent level of risk as the overall company by purchasing securities of the companies that have been combined. If the shareholder can achieve the same diversification as the company at a lower cost, then there is no benefit from corporate diversification.

There is one potential benefit from corporate diversification. To the extent that corporate diversification reduces risk, the default risk on the bonds of the company is reduced. This should be reflected in lower interest rates on new debt, and perhaps higher stock prices.[5]

The final problem occurs in relating the risk of a particular project to the risk of the existing assets. If two companies have different assets, then the risk of an asset appears to depend on the assets of the company in question. However, if the risk of an asset is based, not on the portfolio of assets held by a particular company, but on a market portfolio; then each company would view the risk of the asset in the same way. This is the basis of capital asset pricing theory;[6] however, this is a topic which can not be investigated in an

---

[5]This potential increase in stock price is considered in Chapter 20 where we investigate valuation and bankruptcy costs.

[6]In capital asset pricing theory, risk is measured by considering the comovement of the rates of return on an asset with the rates of return on a market portfolio consisting of all assets. This risk is referred to as systematic or non-diversifiable risk. The rate of return on an individual asset (or security) is composed of firm specific effects (i.e. strikes, new product developments) and systematic effects. The latter refer to impacts on the rate of return due to economy-wide influences. The firm-specific effects can be diversified away if an investor holds

introductory textbook. In our analysis in the remainder of the chapter, we will assume that the risk of a project can be measured by the standard deviation of return.

ALTERNATIVE METHODS OF TREATING RISK

Throughout this book we have stressed that all decisions made by the company, be they financial or investment decisions, must be of value to the current shareholders, i.e. the stock price of the company must increase. Since investors are risk averse, the implication of trying to meet the goal of stock price maximization is that the financial manager should measure and introduce risk in decision making in exactly the same way that investors do.

For example, if a firm takes an action that increases its risk level—then the stock price will fall, all other things being equal. However, if the financial manager requires that the risky project yield an expected rate of return based on the market's (i.e. investors') required compensation given the project's risk, then the stock price will *not* fall.

The definition of risk should, of course, include the coefficient of variation of returns on a project and any portfolio effect of the project on the risk of the company. For simplification, in this section we shall assume that a project's risk is defined in terms of its coefficient of variation.

Several different approaches to risk will be considered. Of these approaches, only one is consistent with the stock price maximization goal; this approach, called the risk-adjusted discount rate method, uses discount rates based on the market's required yield for a project of a given risk level. The other approaches are more informal methods of dealing with risk and they permit the financial manager to introduce personal, as opposed to the market's, risk aversion into the decision. These informal methods are unlikely to be optimal, but they may be of some use in determining risk for projects in which the company has had little or no previous experience.

Risk-Adjusted Discount Rates

The best procedure for taking risk into account calls for making adjustments to the discount rate, k. Risk-adjusted discount rates are based on *investors' tradeoff functions* between risk and return. For example, suppose a firm

---

a large portfolio of assets (or securities). The systematic risk measure is called *beta*. Beta measures the volatility of the rate of return on the asset relative to a change in the rate of return on the market portfolio. If beta equals 1, the risk of the asset is equal to the risk of the market portfolio. Assets which have volatility greater than the market have beta values greater than 1. If beta equals zero, the asset and the market portfolio are unrelated and the asset has zero risk. The standard deviation includes variation in the rate of return due to both firm specific and systematic influences. Since the former can be diversified away, the standard deviation is not the appropriate measure of risk for a particular asset or security under capital asset pricing theory.

determines that investors in the market are willing to trade between risk and expected return as shown in Figure 12–7. The upward sloping line is defined as a *market indifference curve, or a risk-return tradeoff function.*[7] The investors in the market are indifferent to a riskless asset with a sure 5 percent rate of return, a moderately risky asset with a 7 percent expected return, and a very risky asset with a 15 percent expected return. As risk increases, higher and higher returns on investment are required to compensate investors for the additional risk.

FIGURE 12–7   Hypothetical Relationship between Risk and Rate of Return

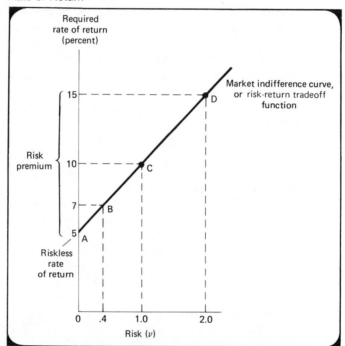

The difference between the required rate of return on a particular risky asset and the rate of return on a riskless asset is defined as the *risk premium* on the risky asset. In the hypothetical situation depicted in Figure 12–7, the riskless rate is assumed to be 5 percent; a 2 percent risk premium is required to compensate for a coefficient of variation of .4, and a 10 percent risk premium is attached to an investment with a coefficient of variation as high as 2.0. The average investor is indifferent between risky investments B, C, and D, and the riskless asset A.

[7]This risk-return tradeoff function is discussed in more detail in Chapter 18.

Suppose that the firm's current activities are such that the risk measure on existing earnings is equal to 1.0. The required rate of return or discount rate would be 10 percent; this is plotted on the risk-return tradeoff at point C. Suppose the firm is contemplating an investment project which has a risk value of 2.0. Based on this market tradeoff function, the required rate of return on this project should be 15 percent. The required rate of return is an opportunity cost, and its use as a cut-off rate implies that the company should obtain an expected rate of return on the investment equal to returns on alternative investments of equivalent risk. If the expected rate of return on the project is 12 percent, then the project should be rejected since the firm should earn 15 percent for projects of this level of risk. Conversely, if the expected rate of return from the project were 18 percent, the firm should accept the project since all the market requires for projects of this risk is 15 percent; the added 3 percent will accrue to the equity holders in the company.

One important lesson from this analysis is that the average cost of capital for the firm, i.e. that cost of capital which reflects the overall risk of the existing assets, cannot in general be used as the cost of capital for investment decisions. The average cost of capital should be used only if the project has the same cash-flow risk as the overall firm.[8] Obviously, the average cost of capital will change over time since new projects accepted by the firm will have an impact on the overall company cash-flow risk.

How does the financial manager determine the cost of capital for projects of a particular level of risk? Quite obviously, if the risk-return relationship were available, the determination of the discount rate is trivial. Even though there have been important developments in measuring this tradeoff function, it is only fair to say that these developments have not solved enough problems to make the techniques operational. The alternative approach is to measure the discount rate on firms that have cash-flow risk characteristics equivalent to the project under consideration.[9] For example, if a firm was contemplating the development of a publishing division, then the cost of capital of a publishing company could be used. In some cases, it will be difficult to find a company that has identical cash-flow risk. In this case, the cost of capital for companies with risk levels surrounding the project risk can be used. This will bracket the appropriate cost of capital and the analysis using these values will still be helpful in making investment decisions.

If the project under consideration is riskier (or less risky) than the overall company cash-flow risk and the project is very small relative to the size of the existing assets in the company, then the firm may be able to ignore the risk differences and evaluate the project using the overall cost of capital. However,

[8]For example, suppose there is a project with risk equal to 2.0 and an expected rate of return of 14 percent. Based on the risk-adjusted discount rates, this project would be rejected. But if the average cost of capital of 10 percent were used, the project would be accepted. Therefore, incorrect decisions can be made by inappropriate use of the overall average cost of capital.

[9]The technique of measuring the cost of capital is discussed in detail in Chapter 20. It will be noted in that chapter that the companies must be equivalent in financial structure as well as in cash-flow risk.

if the firm is in a growth phase and is contemplating a large number of these small projects, then the impact on the firm can be substantial. Using the overall cost of capital for all of the projects will result in accepting above-average risk projects when they should have been rejected or rejecting below-average risk projects when they should have been accepted.

Using Risk-Adjusted Discount Rates: An Illustration We can illustrate the use of risk-adjusted discount rates with an example. The Walter Watch Co. Ltd. is considering the manufacture of two mutually exclusive types of watchbands. One band is specifically designed for Walter watches and cannot be used with those of other manufacturers; the other is adaptable to a wide variety of watches, both Walter's and those of competitive watch companies. The expected investment outlay for design, engineering, production setup, and so on, is $100,000 for each alternative. Expected cash inflows are $20,000 a year for eight years if the bands are usable only with Walter watches (project A), and $22,000 a year for eight years if the bands can be used with a wide variety of watches (project B). However, because of its captive market, the standard deviation of expected annual returns from project A is only $3,000, while that of project B is $20,000. Based on the market's risk-return tradeoff, Walter Watch's management uses a 10 percent cost of capital for project A and 14 percent for project B. Which project should be selected?

We can calculate the risk-adjusted *NPV* for each project as follows:

$$NPV_A = \$20,000 \ (IF \text{ for eight-year, 10\% annuity}) - \$100,000$$
$$= \$20,000 \ (5.335) - \$100,000$$
$$= \$6,700.$$
$$NPV_B = \$22,000 \ (IF \text{ for eight-year, 14\% annuity}) - \$100,000$$
$$= \$22,000 \ (4.639) - \$100,000$$
$$= \$2,058.$$

Project B would have had the higher *NPV* if both projects had been evaluated at the same cost of capital, but when different discount rates are used to account for risk differentials, the analysis indicates that Walter Watch should choose the less risky alternative of manufacturing bands for its own watches.

Informal Method

A common method of dealing with risk is on a strictly informal basis. For example, the net present values based on single-valued estimates of annual returns (using the firm's average cost of capital or a long-term risk free rate) might be calculated. The decision maker would recognize that some projects are riskier than others. If the net present values of two mutually exclusive projects are reasonably close to each other, the less risky one is chosen. The extent by which the *NPV* of the riskier project must exceed that of the less risky project before the riskier project will be selected is not specified—the decision rules are strictly internal to the decision maker.

This approach may be formalized slightly by presenting the decision maker with both the mean expectation and the coefficient of variation of the *NPV*s. These provide an objective estimate of risk, but a choice is still made among risky projects in an unspecified manner, using judgment factors that have not been reduced to a formal basis. Since this technique does not incorporate the market's risk-return tradeoff, the decisions may be less than optimal, i.e. there can not be the maximum positive impact on the stock price.

Sensitivity Analysis

The *NPV* of a project will, in the final analysis, depend upon such factors as quantity of sales, sales prices, input costs, and the like. If these values turn out to be favorable—that is, if output and sales prices are high, and costs are low—then profits, the realized rate of return, and the actual *NPV* will be high, and conversely if poor results are experienced. Recognizing these causal relationships, analysts often calculate projects' *NPV*s under alternative assumptions, then see just how sensitive *NPV* is to changing conditions. One example that recently came to the authors' attention involves a fertilizer company that was comparing two alternative types of phosphate plants. Fuel represents a major cost, and one plant uses coal, which may be obtained under a long-term, fixed-cost contract, while the other uses oil, which must be purchased at current market prices. Considering present and projected future prices, the oil-fired plant looks better—it has a considerably higher *NPV*. However, oil prices are volatile, and if prices rise by more than the expected rate, this plant will be unprofitable. The coal-fired plant, on the other hand, has a lower *NPV* under the expected conditions, but this *NPV* is not sensitive to changing conditions in the energy market. The company finally selected the coal plant because the sensitivity analysis indicated it to be less risky.

Monte Carlo Simulation Analysis

Sensitivity analysis as practiced by the fertilizer company described above is informal in the sense that no probabilities are attached to the likelihood of various outcomes. Monte Carlo *simulation analysis* represents a refinement which does employ probability estimates. In this section we first describe how *decision trees* can be used to attach probabilities to different outcomes, and then we illustrate how full-scale computer simulation can be employed to analyze major projects.

Decision Trees   Most important decisions are not made once-and-for-all at one point in time. Rather, decisions are made in stages. For example, a petroleum firm considering the possibility of expanding into agricultural chemicals might take the following steps: (1) spend $100,000 for a survey of supply-demand conditions in the agricultural chemical industry; (2) if the survey results are favorable, spend $500,000 on a pilot plant to investigate production methods; and (3) depending on the costs estimated from the pilot study and the demand potential from the market study, either abandon the project, build a large plant, or build a small one. Thus, the final decision actually is made in stages, with subsequent decisions depending on the results of previous decisions.

The sequence of events can be mapped out like the branches of a tree, hence the name *decision tree.* As an example, consider Figure 12–8. There it is assumed that the petroleum company has completed its industry supply-demand analysis and pilot plant study, and has determined that it should proceed to develop a full-scale production facility. The firm must decide whether to build a large plant or a small one. Demand expectations for the plant's products are 50 percent for high demand, 30 percent for medium demand, and 20 percent for low demand. Depending upon demand, net cash flows (sales revenues minus operating costs, all discounted to the present) will range from $8.8 million to $1.4 million if a large plant is built, and from $2.6 million to $1.4 million if a small plant is built.

FIGURE 12–8   Illustrative Decision Tree

Action (1)	Demand conditions (2)	Probability (3)	Present value of cash flows (4)	Less Initial Cost (5)	Possible *NPV* [(4) – (5)] (6)	Column (6) times Column (3) (7)
	high	.5	$8,800,000	$5,000,000	$3,800,000	$1,900,000
	medium	.3	$3,500,000	$5,000,000	($1,500,000)	($450,000)
Build big plant: invest $5 million	low	.2	$1,400,000	$5,000,000	($3,600,000)	($720,000)
Decision point					Expected *NPV*	$730,000
Build small plant: invest $2 million	high	.5	$2,600,000	$2,000,000	$600,000	$300,000
	medium	.3	$2,400,000	$2,000,000	$400,000	$120,000
	low	.2	$1,400,000	$2,000,000	($600,000)	($120,000)
					Expected *NPV*	$300,000

Note: The figures in column 4 are the annual cash flows from operations—sales revenues minus cash operating costs—discounted at an appropriate rate.

The initial costs of the large and small plants are shown in column 5; when these investment outlays are subtracted from the *PV* of cash flows, the result is the set of possible *NPV*s shown in column 6. One, but only one, of these *NPV*s will actually occur. Finally, we multiply column 6 by column 3 to obtain column 7, and the sums in column 7 give the expected *NPV*s of the large and small plants.

Because the expected *NPV* of the larger plant ($730,000) is larger than that of the small plant ($300,000), should the decision be to build the large plant? Perhaps, but not necessarily. Notice that the range of outcomes is greater if the large plant is built, with the possible *NPV*s (column 4 in Figure 12–7 minus the investment cost) varying from $3.8 million to *minus* $3.6 million. However, a range of only $600,000 to minus $600,000 exists for the small plant. Since the required investments for the two plants are not the same, we must examine the coefficients of variation of the net present value possibilities in order to determine which alternative actually entails the greater risk. The coefficient of variation for the large plant's present value is 4.3, while that for the small plant is only 1.5.[10] Thus, risk is greater if the decision is to build the large plant.

Computer Simulation

The concepts embodied in decision tree analysis can be extended to computer simulation. To illustrate the technique, let us consider a proposal to build a new textile plant. The cost of the plant is not known for certain, although it is expected to run about $150 million. If no problems are encountered, the cost can be as low as $125 million, while an unfortunate series of events— strikes, unprojected increases in materials costs, technical problems, and the like—could result in the investment outlay running as high as $225 million.

Revenues from the new facility, which will operate for many years, will depend on population growth and income in the region, competition, developments in synthetic fabrics research, and textile import quotas. Operating costs will depend on production efficiency, materials and labor cost trends and the like. Since both sales revenues and operating costs are uncertain, annual profits are also uncertain.

Assuming that probability distributions can be assigned to each of the major cost and revenue determinants, a computer program can be constructed to simulate what is likely to happen. In effect, the computer selects one value at random from each of the relevant distributions, combines it with other values selected from the other distributions, and produces an estimated profit and net

---

[10]Using Equation 12–3 and the data on possible returns in Figure 12–7, the standard deviation of returns for the larger plant is found to be $3.155 million, and that for the smaller one is $458,260. Dividing each of these standard deviations by the expected returns for their respective plant size gives the coefficients of variation.

present value or rate of return on investment.[11] This particular profit and rate of return occur, of course, only for the particular combination of values selected during this trial. The computer goes on to select other sets of values and to

FIGURE 12-9   Simulation for Investment Planning

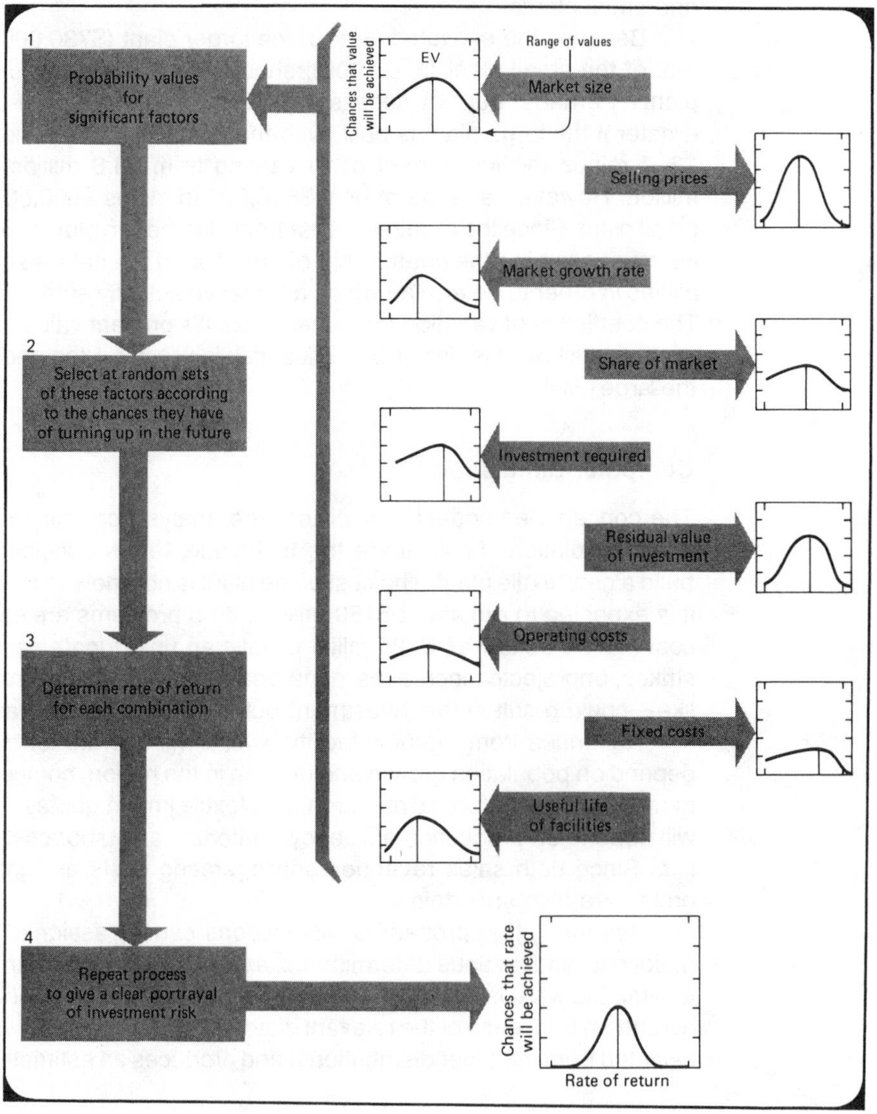

[11]If the variables are not independent, then conditional probabilities must be employed. For example, if demand is weak, then both sales in units and sales prices are likely to be low, and these interrelationships must be taken into account in the simulation.

compute other profits and rates of return repeatedly, for perhaps several hundred trials. A count is kept of the number of times each rate of return is computed, and when the computer runs are completed, the frequency with which the various rates of return occurred can be plotted as a frequency distribution.

The procedure is illustrated in Figures 12-9 and 12-10.[12] Figure 12-9 is a flow chart outlining the simulation procedure described above while Figure 12-10 illustrates the frequency distribution of rates of return generated by such a simulation for two alternative projects, X and Y, each with an expected cost of $20 million. The expected rate of return on investment X is 15 percent, and that of investment Y is 20 percent. However, these are only the *average* rates of return generated by the computer; simulated rates range from -10 percent to +45 percent for investment Y and from 5 to 25 percent for investment X. The standard deviation generated for X is only 4 percentage points— 68 percent of the computer runs had rates of return between 11 and 19 percent—while that for Y is 12 percentage points. Clearly, then, investment Y is riskier than investment X.

The computer simulation has provided us with both an estimate of the expected returns on the two projects and an estimate of their relative risks. A decision about which alternative should be chosen can now be made, preferably by using the risk-adjusted discount rate method but perhaps in a judgmental, informal manner.

FIGURE 12-10   Expected Rates of Return on
Investments X and Y

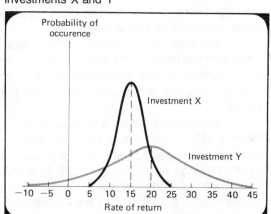

[12] The methodology illustrated in Figure 12-9 was developed in an article by David B. Hertz, "Risk Analysis in Capital Investment," *Harvard Business Review* (January–February 1964), 95-106.

However, computer simulation is not always feasible for risk analysis. The technique involves obtaining probability distributions about a number of variables—investment outlays, unit sales, product prices, input prices, asset lives, and so on—and a fair amount of programming and machine-time costs. Therefore, full-scale simulation is not generally worthwhile except for large and expensive projects, such as major plant expansions or new-product decisions. In those cases, however, when a firm is deciding whether to accept a major undertaking involving millions of dollars, computer simulation can provide valuable insights into the relative merits of alternative strategies.

SUMMARY

Two facts of life in finance are (1) that investors are averse to risk and (2) that at least some risk is inherent in most business decisions. Given investor aversion to risk and differing degrees of risk in different financial alternatives, it is necessary to consider risk in financial analysis.

Our first task is to define what we mean by risk; our second task is to measure it. The concept of *probability* is a fundamental element in both the definition and the measurement of risk. A *probability distribution* shows the probability of occurrence of each possible outcome, assuming a given investment is undertaken. The mean, or weighted average, of the distribution is defined as the *expected value* of the investment. The *coefficient of variation* of the distribution or, sometimes, the *standard deviation,* both of which measure the extent to which actual outcomes are likely to vary from the expected value, are used as measures of risk.

Under most circumstances, more distant returns are considered to be more risky than near-term returns. Thus, the standard deviation and coefficient of variation for distant cash flows are likely to be higher than those for cash flows expected relatively soon, even when the cash flows are from the same project.

In appraising the riskiness of an individual capital investment, not only the variability of the expected returns of the project itself but also the correlation between expected returns on this project and the remainder of the firm's assets must be taken into account. This relationship is called the *portfolio or diversification effect* of the particular project. Portfolio effects exist as long as the returns from a project are not perfectly positively correlated with the returns on the firm's existing assets. The weaker the positive correlation, or the stronger the negative correlation; the more important become the portfolio effects. Portfolio effects, along with a number of other benefits of diversification, may be an important explanation of a firm's efforts to diversify into products not closely related to the firm's main line of business.

Risk differentials are frequently dealt with in a strictly informal manner.

However, as firms become increasingly sophisticated, greater and greater efforts are being expended to deal with risk in a formal manner. When risk is treated formally, the most common technique is the *risk-adjusted discount rate method,* which increases the cost of capital used to discount more risky projects' returns. To use this method, the firm must first estimate investors' *risk-return tradeoff function,* then use this estimate to develop *risk premiums* for the riskier projects. Although some judgment is necessary when implementing this concept, more and more firms are deciding that these attempts to account for risk are better than no attempts at all.

Decision-making under uncertainty, especially for large projects, is facilitated by two other analytical techniques: *decision trees* and *simulation analysis.* Decision trees map out the sequence of events in a decision problem, helping a firm to trace events through time and to examine the complex set of probabilities. Computer simulation is used to generate frequency distributions of possible outcomes *(stochastic simulation)* or to determine the effects of changes in various operating conditions *(sensitivity analysis).*

QUESTIONS

12-1. Define the following terms, using graphs to illustrate your answers wherever feasible:
    a. risk
    b. uncertainty
    c. probability distribution
    d. expected value
    e. standard deviation
    f. coefficient of variation
    g. portfolio effects
    h. risk-adjusted discount rate

12-2. The probability distribution of a less risky expected return is more peaked than that of a risky return. What shape would the probability distribution have (1) for completely certain returns and (2) for completely uncertain returns?

12-3. Project A has an expected return of $500 and a standard deviation of $100. Project B also has a standard deviation of $100 but an expected return of $300. Which project is the more risky? Why?

12-4. Assume that residential construction and industries related to it are counter-cyclical to the economy in general and to steel in particular. Does this negative correlation between steel and construction-related industries necessarily mean that a hypothetical financial institution which derives most of its income from residential mortgages and whose profitability tends to vary with construction levels, would be less risky if it diversified by acquiring a steel distributor?

12-5. "The use of the market indifference curve concept illustrated in Figure 12–7 as a basis for determining risk-adjusted discount rates is all right in theory, but it cannot be applied in practice. Investors' reactions to risk cannot be measured precisely, so it is actually impossible to construct a set of risk-adjusted discount rates for different classes of investment." Comment on this statement.

12-6. What is the value of decision trees in managerial decision making?

12-7. In computer simulation, the computer makes a large number of "trials" to show what the various outcomes of a particular decision might be if the decision could be made many times under the same conditions. In practice, the decision will be made only once, so how can simulation results be useful to the decision-maker?

12-8. Using Figure 12–7, demonstrate that using the overall cost of capital for projects with risk less than that for existing assets may lead to incorrect investment decisions.

PROBLEMS

12-1. An investment proposal has been analyzed and the following information has been established.

Cash Flow	
Probability	Amount
.3	$15,000
.5	20,000
.2	25,000

The outlay is $100,000, the expected life is ten years, and your cost of capital is 12 percent. Assume zero salvage.

    a. Calculate the expected NPV and expected IRR.

    b. Calculate the probability that the investment will be a good one, i.e., have NPV > O.

12-2. The Rowan Co. Ltd. is faced with two mutually exclusive investment projects. Each project costs $4,500 and each has an expected life of three years. Annual net cash flows from each project begin one year after the initial investment is made and have the following probability distributions.

	Probability	Cash Flow
Project A:	2	$ 4,000
	.6	4,500
	.2	5,000
Project B:	.2	0
	.6	4,500
	.2	12,000

Rowan has decided to evaluate the riskier project at a 12 percent rate and the less risky project at a 10 percent rate.

    a. What is the expected value of the annual net cash flows from each project?

    b. What is the risk-adjusted *NPV* of each project?

    c. If it were known that project B was negatively correlated with other cash flows of the firm, while project A was positively correlated, how would this knowledge affect your decision?

12-3. Your firm is considering the purchase of a tractor. It has been established that this tractor will cost $32,000, will produce revenues in the neighborhood of $10,000 (before tax), and will be depreciated via straight line to zero in eight years. The board of directors, however, had a heated debate as to whether the tractor could be expected to last eight years. Specifically, Wayne Brown insisted that he knew of some which had lasted five years only. Tom Miller agreed with Wayne but argued that it was more likely that the tractor would give eight years of service. Wayne agreed. Finally, Ralph Evans said he had seen some last as long as ten years. Given this discussion, the board asked you to prepare a sensitivity analysis to ascertain how important the uncertainty about the life of the tractor is. Assume a 40 percent tax rate on both income and capital loss, zero salvage value, and a cost of capital of 10 percent. For simplicity, also assume that the straight line depreciation charge is the depreciation for tax purposes.

12-4. You have an investment opportunity for which the outlay as well as cash flows are uncertain. Careful analysis has produced the following subjective probability assessments.

Outlay		Annual Cash Flow	
Probability	Amount	Probability	Amount
.4	$80,000	.2	$14,000
.3	100,000	.5	16,000
.2	120,000	.3	18,000
.1	140,000		

Let your cost of capital be 12 percent, life expectancy ten years, and zero salvage.
   a. Construct a decision tree for this investment to show probabilities, payoffs, and expected NPV.
   b. Calculate the expected NPV, again using expected cash flow and expected outlay.
   c. What is the probability of and the NPV of the worst possible outcome?
   d. What is the probability of and the NPV of the best possible outcome?
   e. Compute the probability that this will be a good investment.

12-5. Suppose that the life of the investment in problem 12–4 is also uncertain, and that you have secured the following subjective probability assessment for the life of the investment. .

Investment Life	
Probability	Years
.2	8
.6	10
.2	12

   a. Calculate the expected NPV incorporating this new information. Explain why this is the same as before.
   b. Show how to draw an expanded decision tree with this information, but do not fill in all the numbers.

Sources and Forms of Long-Term Financing

Part Four

In the introductory section, we analyzed the firm in an overall, aggregate sense. Next, in Part Two, we considered the top half of the balance sheet, analyzing current assets, current liabilities, and the interactions between the two. Then, in Part Three, we moved to the lower left side of the balance sheet, examining the process by which firms decide on investments in fixed assets. Now, in Part Four, we move to the lower right side of the balance sheet, to consider the various types of long-term funds available to the firm when it seeks long-term external capital.

Chapter 13 presents an overview of the capital markets, explaining briefly certain institutional material without which no basic finance course is complete. Chapter 14 analyzes the financial characteristics of common shares; Chapter 15 examines bonds and preferred shares; Chapter 16 analyzes term loans and leases; and Chapter 17 discusses the nature and use of warrants and convertibles. This institutional background is essential for an understanding of Part Five, Financial Structure and the Cost of Capital, where we take up the question of the optimal mix of long-term funds.

The Market for Long-Term Securities

SECURITY MARKETS

There are two basic types of security markets—the *organized exchanges,* typified by the Toronto Stock Exchange, and the less formal *over-the-counter markets.*[1] Since the organized exchanges have actual physical market locations and are easier to describe and understand, we shall consider them first. With this foundation it will be easier to comprehend the nature of the over-the-counter market.

Organized Security Exchanges

The organized security exchanges are tangible, physical entities. Each of the larger ones occupies its own building, has specifically designated members, and has an elected governing body—its board of governors. Members are said to have "seats" on the exchange, although everybody stands up. These seats, which are bought and sold, represent the right to trade on the exchange.

In 1969, seats on the Toronto Stock Exchange (TSE) traded for $125,000. The record high price of $140,000 per seat was obtained in 1959; in November, 1977, a seat was traded for $17,000.

---

[1]Some stocks are sold through organized exchanges while others are traded over the counter. Bonds, typically, are traded in over-the-counter markets by investment dealers who may hold an inventory of the bonds; however, the Montreal Stock Exchange is currently experimenting in listing and trading bonds. There is also a "private" market in which the borrowing firm goes directly to the lending institution; this is called the "private placement" market. The primary instrument used in this market is the term loan, described in Chapter 16.

Most of the larger stock brokerage firms own seats on the exchanges and designate one of the officers of the firm as a member of the exchange.

Like other markets, a security exchange facilitates communication between buyers and sellers. For example, Wood Gundy Limited, (one of the larger brokerage firms) might receive an order to buy 100 shares of Bell Canada stock from a customer in its Vancouver office. Simultaneously, a brokerage house in Montreal might receive an order from a customer wishing to sell 100 shares of Bell. Each broker would communicate to its firm's representative on the TSE. Other brokers throughout the country would also communicate their buy and sell orders to their representatives on the exchange. The exchange members with *sell orders* offer the shares for sale and they are bid for by the members with *buy orders*. Thus, the exchanges operate as *auction markets*.[2]

There are five organized stock exchanges on which securities can be traded. The largest of these exchanges, based on any measure of size, is the Toronto Stock Exchange, and for this reason we will refer to its operations in our discussions. Many brokerage firms have seats on more than one stock exchange. In addition, a particular security which requires a wide distribution will be listed on more than one exchange. Therefore, in the example above, the broker in Montreal could trade the Bell Canada shares on the Montreal Stock Exchange (MSE) if the stock was listed on this exchange and the broker was a member of the exchange. If the stock is listed in more than one market, brokers will check these markets to ensure that their clients receive the best price.

Some companies, in attempting to open up new sources for equity capital, have listed their stock on the New York Stock Exchange (NYSE) or the American Exchange (AMEX). Since the shares of a company are sometimes listed on more than one stock exchange[3] (domestic or international), is it possible for the prices of the firm's shares to be different from one stock exchange to another? Any price differential must be transitory, since a share of stock is a claim to the earnings of a company regardless of where the stock is traded and two assets with identical attributes must ultimately sell for the same price.

To demonstrate that this is correct, consider the case of multiple listing of shares in Canada where the price of a share of Bell Canada stock on the Montreal Stock Exchange (MSE) is greater than the price per share of Bell on the TSE. In this case, an investor (or broker) could buy 100 shares of stock on the TSE, sell the 100 shares at a higher price on the MSE and make a profit

[2]This discussion is not intended to describe the trading process of the TSE or other organized exchanges. However, one important point to note is that the brokerage houses buy and sell securities as agents for their customers. The specialist, as found on the NYSE, attempts to provide a market for the securities in which he or she specializes by dealing as a principal from the specialist's own inventory of shares. The specialist is not an important element on the Canadian exchanges.

[3]As of August 31, 1977, there were 18 Canadian issues traded on the NYSE; 41 issues on the AMEX; and 16 issues were traded over the counter in the U.S. market. There were 57 issues that were listed on both the TSE and the MSE.

equal to the price differential less the transaction costs. Since there is no risk in this operation and no money need be invested, the process (called *arbitrage*) of buying in one market and selling in another will continue as long as there is a profit to be made after transaction costs. But the purchase of shares in the lower priced market will place upward pressure on the stock price in that market, and the sale of the same shares in the higher priced market will place downward pressure on the stock price in that market; thus tending to equalize the differential. There are brokerage firms that specialize in this arbitrage function.

The process of international arbitrage is identical and will result in the share prices of a company's stock tending to be identical in the Canadian and foreign markets after adjustment for exchange rates. For example, suppose the stock price of a particular company on the NYSE is $10 U.S.; the exchange rate on that day is $1 U.S. to $1.10 Canadian and the price of the same stock on the TSE is $12. An arbitrageur could buy the stock on the NYSE for $10 U.S. and sell it on the TSE for $12 Canadian, or an equivalent of $10.90 U.S. The arbitrageur gets back the original $10 U.S. and has made a profit of $0.90 U.S. This arbitrage activity will continue as long as the process results in profits for the arbitrageur, after consideration of transaction costs in exchange rates and brokerage fees.

Special procedures are available for handling large blocks of securities. For example, if Bell Canada, whose stock is already listed on the TSE, plans to sell a new issue of stock, the exchange has facilities that make it easier for the market to absorb the new issue. Similarly, if a large mutual fund or pension fund wants to sell a large block of a listed stock, procedures are available that facilitate the sale without putting undue pressures on the stock price.

Stock Market Reporting

Securities that are traded on the organized security exchanges are called *listed securities,* and are distinguished from other securities, known as *unlisted securities.* (Unlisted securities are traded in the over-the-counter market, which is discussed below.)

Quite a lot of information is available dealing with transactions among listed securities, and the very existence of this information reduces the uncertainty inherent in security investments. This reduction of uncertainty, of course, makes listed securities relatively attractive to investors, and it lowers the cost of capital to firms. We will not delve deeply into the matter of financial reporting—this is more properly the field of investment analysis—but it is useful to explain the reporting system used by the Toronto Stock Exchange.

Figure 13-1 is an excerpt from the stock market page of the *Globe and Mail's* "Report on Business" of September 25, 1978. Common shares and all traded preferred shares are listed alphabetically, the first being the preferred

FIGURE 13-1 Stock Market Transactions
Quotations for September 25, 1978, prepared by the Toronto Stock Exchange

1978					*Days*			
High	*Low*	*Stock*	*Div*	*High*	*Low*	*Close*	*Ch'ge*	*Vol*
290	171	A.G.F.M.	0.20	270	255	260		1300
6⅞	455	Abacus	.04	480	465	480	+ 20	5743
19⅛	10⅛	Abitibi	1.00	$17½	17⅛	17⅜	+ ¼	30842
56	52¾	Abitbi 10	5.00	$55¼	55¼	55¼		1700
14	11	Acklands	.48	$13	13	13		400
155	81	Action Trd		120	120	120	+ 5	5000
100	30	Adanac M		49	43	49	+ 12	5000
11	5¾	Affon Min		$11	10¼	11	+ ⅝	3350
6⅞	425	Agnico E		$6⅞	6½	6¾	+ ⅛	14650
205	120	Ahed C		180	180	180		1000
135	75	Akaitcho	p .05	94	88	94	+ 3	5100
95	53	Albany		60	59	60	+ 1	5000
18⅝	14⅝	Alt Energy		$17¼	17⅛	17¼	+ ⅛	5700
16⅜	14	Alta Gas A	.82	$15⅜	15¼	15¼	- ⅛	22770
29½	27⅜	Alta G 9.76	2.44	$28¼	28¼	28¼	+ ¼	2480
27⅛	25¼	Alta G 7.60	1.90	$26½	26½	26½	+ ¼	150
39¼	24⅛	Alcan	1.40	$36⅞	36⅜	36⅞	+ ⅜	12200
32	29	Alcan pr	1.70	$29¼	29¼	29¼		100
24	15⅝	Algo Cent	.84	$20¼	20¼	20¼		100

shares of A. G. F. Management, a management and distribution company for mutual funds. The two columns at the left show the highest and lowest prices at which the stocks have traded during the year; A. G. F. M. has traded in the range $2.90 to $1.71. The next major column after the company's abbreviated name is the dividend per share expected in the year; A.G.F.M. is expected to pay $.20 a share in 1978.

Between the name and dividend columns can be found various symbols and numbers. These entries give additional information about specific issues and are described in the legend which always accompanies the stock market quotations. For example, the lower case letter "p" is the symbol used to denote a preferred share. Most of these entries refer to dividends and they can best be understood after our discussion of this topic in Chapter 21.

Following the dividend column are the high and low prices for the day and the closing price.[4] On September 25, 1978, A. G. F. Management traded at $2.60; Agnico Eagle Mines Limited, shown as Agnico E in Figure 13-1, traded as high as $6⅞ (i.e. $6.875) and as low as $6.50; the last trade was at $6.75. The column headed "Ch'ge" gives the change from the closing price on the previous day. For A.G.F. Management, the close on September 22, (a Friday) was $2.60; since Agnico Eagle was up ⅛ or $0.125, the close on the

[4] Every week the *Financial Post* publishes a weekly stock market report for all five Canadian stock exchanges. This includes weekly high and low prices, week-ending closing (or latest) prices, net change in price and weekly trading volume. In addition, this report presents high-low prices for the previous 53 weeks; the indicated dividend rate in dollars; the indicated dividend yield (the dividend divided by the week-end stock price); the P/E ratio—the current stock price divided by the last twelve months earnings; and earnings per share for the latest interim report and the latest fiscal year.

previous day must have been $6 ⅝ or $6.625. The last column presents the volume of trading for the day; 1300 shares of A. G. F. M. were traded on September 25.

Benefits Provided by Security Exchanges

Organized security exchanges are said to provide important benefits to businesses in at least three ways.

1. Security exchanges facilitate the investment process by providing a marketplace in which to conduct transactions efficiently and relatively inexpensively. Investors are thus assured that they will have a place in which to sell their securities, if they decide to do so. The increased liquidity thus provided by the exchanges makes investors willing to accept a lower rate of return on securities than they would otherwise require. This means that exchanges lower the cost of capital to businesses.

2. By providing a market, exchanges create an institution in which continuous transactions test the values of securities. The purchases and sales of securities record judgments on the values and prospects of companies and their securities. Companies whose prospects are judged favorably by the investment community will have higher values, thus facilitating new financing and growth.

3. The securities markets aid in the digestion of new security issues and facilitate their successful flotation.

These benefits are important, but not all firms are in a position to utilize the exchanges. Such firms can, however, get many of the same benefits by having their securities traded in the over-the-counter market.

OVER-THE-COUNTER SECURITY MARKETS

In contrast to the formal security exchanges, the over-the-counter market is a nebulous, intangible organization. Perhaps an explanation of the name "over the counter" will help clarify exactly what this market is. The exchanges operate as auction markets—buy and sell orders come in more-or-less simultaneously, and the exchanges are used to match these orders. But if a stock is traded less frequently, perhaps because it is the stock of a new or a small firm, few buy and sell orders come in, and matching them within a reasonable length of time would be difficult. To avoid this problem, brokerage firms maintain an inventory of the stocks. They buy when individual investors wish to sell, and sell when investors want to buy. At one time the inventory of securities was kept in a safe, and when bought and sold, the stocks were literally passed "over the counter."

Today, over-the-counter markets are defined as all facilities that provide for security transactions not conducted on the organized exchanges. These facilities consist primarily (1) of the relatively few brokers who hold inventories of over-the-counter securities and who are said to "make a market" in these securities and (2) of the many other brokers who act as agents in bringing these dealers together with investors. The dealers who make a market in a particular stock will, upon request, quote a price at which they are willing to buy the stock (the "bid" price) and a price at which they will sell shares (the "asked" price). The spread between bid and asked prices represents the dealer's mark-up, or profit.

All bond transactions take place in the over-the-counter market. The reason for this is that bonds typically are traded among the large financial institutions, for example, life insurance companies and pension funds, which deal in very large blocks of securities. It is relatively easy for the over-the-counter bond dealers to arrange the transfer of large blocks of bonds among the relatively few holders of the bonds. It would be impossible to conduct similar operations in the stock market among the many thousands of large and small shareholders.[5]

The Investment Dealers Association of Canada (IDA) provides daily high and low prices and volumes in unlisted mines and industrials. For listed industrials that do not trade on a particular day, bid and ask prices are supplied to the IDA by a brokerage firm. The bid and ask for non-traded mines and oils are supplied by the Broker-Dealers Association of Ontario.

DECISION TO LIST STOCK

The exchanges have certain requirements that firms must meet before their stock can be listed—these requirements relate to size of company, number of years in business, earnings record, number of shares outstanding and their market value, and the like. In general, requirements become more stringent as we move from the smaller exchanges to the TSE.

---

[5]During the 1960s and 1970s two new kinds of market were developed—the so-called "third market" and "fourth market." The third market refers to trades of large blocks of listed stocks off the floor of the exchange, with a brokerage house acting as an intermediary between two institutional investors. The fourth market refers to direct transfers of blocks of shares among institutional investors without an intermediary broker. These trends have lead to a drastic restructuring of the security markets, in the United States. In addition, an options market has been developed wherein investors (or speculators) trade in options to purchase Canadian shares. This market has been in existence since June, 1975, on the Montreal Stock Exchange and since March, 1976, on the TSE. These markets are in an embryonic stage. As of the end of October, 1976, there were only 26 Canadian stocks on which options could be written—of these, 7 options are listed exclusively on the TSE, 12 exclusively on the MSE and 7 are jointly listed. To illustrate option trading, on November 4, 1977, Imperial Oil Ltd. stock closed on the TSE at $18.50. One could buy an option to acquire 100 shares of Imperial Oil at

The firm itself makes the decision to seek to list or not to list its securities on an exchange. Typically, the stocks of new and small companies are traded over the counter—there is simply not enough activity to justify the use of an auction market for such stocks. As the company grows, establishes an earnings record, expands the number of shares outstanding, and increases its list of shareholders, it may decide to apply for listing on one or more of the organized exchanges. Typically, if the company is non-Ontario based, it will list on a smaller exchange in its province of operation. As the firm becomes larger and the size of its financing requirements increases, a listing on the TSE will be sought. Since the TSE is the largest exchange, there will be more liquidity, and perhaps a larger market, for the stock if it is listed on this exchange.

Assuming a company qualifies, many people believe that listing is beneficial both to it and to its shareholders. Listed companies receive a certain amount of free advertising and publicity, and their status as a listed company enhances their prestige and reputation. This probably has a beneficial effect on the sales of the products of the firm, and it probably is advantageous in terms of lowering the required rate of return on the common shares. Investors respond favorably to increased information, increased liquidity, and increased prestige; by providing investors with these services in the form of listing their companies' stocks, financial managers lower their firms' costs of capital.

Of course, these benefits must be balanced against the added costs associated with maintaining a stock exchange listing. These include the costs of preparing financial reports as required by the securities exchange, and the maintenance of certain financial ratios and distribution of share holdings.

INVESTMENT DEALERS

In our economy, saving is generally done by one group of persons while real investment is done by another. (Real investment refers to the demand for funds to purchase plant, equipment and inventory, and not to the buying of securities). Mechanisms have evolved to assist in the efficient transfer of funds between savers and investors. Basically, the investor issues a financial instrument which is purchased by savers. In the banking system, this transfer of funds is indirect since the money used to purchase the financial instruments (i.e. demand loans or notes) has been deposited by savers. However, this is not the only mechanism by which savers' funds can be channelled to firms wishing to acquire plant and equipment and to hold inventories. The firms

---

$17.50 per share before the end of May, 1978, at an option price of $2.50 per share (this is called a *call option* since the shares can be *called* by the holder of the option). If the option were purchased and exercised immediately, the total per-share cost would be $20 (i.e. $2.50 for the call plus $17.50 for the stock). But the stock could be purchased in the marketplace for $18.50. Therefore, there is a premium of $1.50 being paid for the option. If Imperial Oil goes up by more than $1.50 before the exercise date on the option, the option purchaser makes a profit. If not, he loses the amount invested in the option.

could issue securities, either debt or equity, and sell them directly to savers. But this requires that firms have a well-organized selling organization and knowledge of the current conditions in the securities markets. It is more efficient for investment dealers to perform these functions, and thus the distribution of new securities issues is performed by this group. In this section we are interested in how investment dealers assist in the channelling of funds. We will see that new securities of individual companies are purchased by the investment dealer and then sold to the savers. The investment dealer performs the functions of underwriting, distributing securities, and giving advice and counsel.

In the United States, the term "investment banker" is used to describe the individual or company that performs the functions noted above. This term is misleading since the investment banker is neither an investor nor a banker who takes deposits. In Canada, the term investment banker is not used. We refer to these securities firms as *investment dealers;* this is a general term which includes firms that trade securities, provide research, underwrite and distribute securities and operate as fiscal agents by providing advice and counsel. However, for this discussion we are not interested in the first two functions.

Alternatively, we could refer to these firms as underwriters. However, an underwriter need not be an investment dealer and would not provide the other functions associated with the investment dealer function. With the lack of a generally accepted descriptive title, we will use the terms investment dealer and underwriter interchangeably.

Underwriting

Underwriting is the insurance function of bearing the risks of adverse price fluctuations during the period in which a new issue of securities is being distributed. The nature of the underwriting function of the investment dealer can best be conveyed by an example. A business firm needs $10 million. It selects an investment dealer, conferences are held, and the decision is made to issue $10 million of bonds. An underwriting agreement is drawn up; on a specific day, called the *closing date,* the investment dealer presents the company with a cheque for $10 million (less commission). In return, the investment dealer receives bonds in denominations of $1000 each which he sells to the public.

The company receives the $10 million about three to four weeks after the prospectus for the issue has been cleared through all of the securities commissions. Often the investment dealer has sold the issue by this time. However, it can take the investment dealer six weeks or longer to sell the bonds. If, in the interim, the bond market collapses, the investment dealer will be carrying the risk of loss on the sale of the bonds.

Fortunately for the underwriters, there have not been any dramatic instances of a bond market collapse in Canada in which the underwriters had a large loss. In the United States, an example of the costs of a bond market collapse is the 1974 issue of New Jersey Sporting Arena bonds which dropped in value to $140 per $1000 bond during the underwriting period; this cost the underwriters an estimated $8 million. However, the issuing firm does not need to be concerned about the risk of market price fluctuations while the investment dealer is selling the bonds. The firm has received its money. *One fundamental economic function of the investment dealer, then, is to underwrite the risk of a decline in the market price between the time the issue is cleared through all the securities commissions and is ready to be sold, and the time the bonds are placed in the hands of their ultimate buyers.* For this reason, the investment dealer is often called an *underwriter:* he or she is an underwriter of risk during the distribution period. In the following sections we will note the terms under which underwriters can relieve themselves of their liability to purchase the issue. This limits their underwriting risk exposure and the potential loss in the underwriting.

Distribution

The second function of the investment dealer is marketing new issues of securities. The investment dealer is a specialist who has a staff and dealer organization to distribute securities. The dealer can, therefore, perform the physical distribution function more efficiently and more economically than could an individual corporation. Sporadically, whenever it wished to sell an issue of securities, each corporation would find it necessary to establish a marketing or selling organization. This would be a very expensive and ineffective method of selling securities. The investment dealer has a permanent, trained staff and dealer organization continually available to distribute the securities. In addition, the investment dealer's reputation for selecting good companies and pricing securities fairly builds up a broad clientele over a period, further increasing the ease with which securities can be sold.

Advice and Counsel

Since the investment dealer is engaged in the origination and sale of securities, through experience he or she becomes an expert in advising about terms and characteristics of securities that will appeal to investors. The advice and guidance of the investment dealer in determining the characteristics and provisions of securities so that they will be successfully marketed is valuable. Furthermore, the reputation of the investment dealer as a seller of the securities depends upon the subsequent performance of the securities. Therefore, the dealer will often sit on the boards of directors of firms whose securities he has sold. In this way he is able to provide continuing financial counsel and to increase the firm's probability of success.[6]

UNDERWRITING OPERATIONS

The best way to gain a clear understanding of the underwriting function is to trace the history of a new issue of securities. Accordingly, in this section we describe the steps necessary to issue new securities.

Preunderwriting Conferences

First, the members of the issuing firm, the underwriter (or underwriters) and legal counsel for all parties hold preunderwriting conferences at which they discuss the amount of capital to be raised, the type of security to be issued, and the general terms of the issue.

Memoranda will be written by the treasurer of the issuing company to the firm's directors and other officers, describing alternative proposals suggested at the conferences. Meetings of the board of directors of the issuing company will be held to discuss the alternatives and to attempt to reach a decision.

A number of meetings are required to prepare the preliminary prospectus which must be filed with the appropriate provincial securities commission, e.g. the Ontario Securities Commission. This prospectus must give full disclosure of all important developments that will materially affect the company. In addition, all of the convenants, if it is a bond issue, are presented. The preliminary prospectus reflects the agreement of all parties on the terms of the issue and is a draft of the final prospectus with only the size of the issue, price, underwriter commission and sinking fund requirements omitted. A public accounting firm will be called upon to make an audit of the issuing firm's financial situation, and they will also assist in the preparation of the financial statements for the preliminary prospectus. From the start of the process to the signing of the final draft of the preliminary prospectus will take approximately four weeks. During this period the underwriter(s) and the issuer have not signed a contract.

Registration Period

The registration period for a new security issue runs from the time that the preliminary prospectus has been filed with the securities commissions to the time

---

[6]It has been suggested that an underwriter who accepts a seat on the board of directors may be faced with a conflict of interest. First, any new security issue will go to the existing underwriter even though it may be to the company's advantage to search for a new underwriter. Second, the firm and the underwriter will encounter some very hard negotiating on the terms of new security issues. The underwriter who is also a member of the board of the company cannot serve both parties. Therefore, many underwriters have declined direct involvement in a board of directors but continue to provide advice.

that the final prospectus has been cleared and the underwriters can offer the securities for sale. The length of time that a security issue is in registration varies widely, depending on the particulars of the issue. Ideally, it should take approximately four weeks.

Preliminary Prospectus

When the preliminary prospectus is signed, it is filed with the appropriate provincial securities commission. A preliminary prospectus must be filed in each province in which the underwriter intends to sell the securities. The statutes in Ontario set a 21-day or 15-business day waiting period (which, in practice, may be lengthened or shortened by the securities commission) during which time the commission staff analyzes the preliminary prospectus to determine if there are any omissions or misrepresentations of fact. Each commission may file deficiencies to the preliminary prospectus or ask for additional information from the issuing company or the underwriter.

After all the deficiencies have been received, the underwriter attempts to satisfy the requested changes. It usually takes about two days, but in some cases the deficiencies are more severe and the time required to amend the prospectus is longer. Once these deficiencies are satisfied, the underwriter is ready to prepare the final draft of the prospectus and submit it for final clearance by the securities commission(s). The final draft will include all pricing information and the size of the underwriter's discount. Only after each provincial securities commission has cleared the final prospectus can the underwriter offer the securities for sale in the various provinces.

Final Prospectus and Final Clearance

After all deficiencies noted by the securities commissions have been resolved, the final prospectus is prepared. The underwriters and the issuing company meet late in the business day and reach a final decision on the price of the issue. This pricing decision is based on the closing market for the day. The next morning, the final prospectus is signed and filed with the various securities commissions. Hopefully, on the same day, final clearance is given by the commission and the company can begin to sell the securities.

In addition to signing the prospectus, the parties sign the underwriting agreement; this document specifies the terms and conditions under which the issue will be purchased from the company by the underwriters. Any breach or failure to comply with the terms and conditions permits the underwriter to terminate its obligation to purchase the shares.

Finally, the underwriting agreement specifies the date on which the underwriter must purchase the security issue from the issuer. This date is referred to as the *closing date* and is approximately three to four weeks after final clearance.

Pricing the Issue

The actual price that the underwriter pays the issuer is not usually determined until the final clearance of the prospectus. Speed of clearance is crucial in this phase, since the longer the period between setting the price and the final clearance, the greater the probability that the market will change.

In a new issue of bonds or preferred shares, the price is based on the closing yields in the market. On an issue of common shares for a company with stock outstanding, the price is based on the closing price on the final clearance date. On the closing date, the issuing firm receives an amount equal to this price, less the underwriter's commission.

The preceding pricing arrangements hold, of course, only for additional offerings of the shares of firms whose existing stock is currently traded. When a company "goes public" for the first time, the underwriter and the firm will negotiate a price in accordance with the valuation principles described in Chapter 18.

The investment dealer incurs less underwriter's risk if the security issue is priced under the market. For a new equity issue, this means that, after the shares are issued, the stock price will increase and result in a capital gain for the investor. For a bond or preferred issue, this means that, based on the issue price, the yield on the new securities is greater than the yield on securities outstanding of the same risk. Thus, there will be a large demand for these securities. On the other hand, however, the issuer of the securities wants as high a price as possible for the new issue. Therefore, some conflict of interest on price arises between the investment dealer and the issuer. If the issuer is financially sophisticated and makes comparisons with similar security issues, the investment dealer is forced to price at the market level.

The type of underwriting described above is referred to as a *firm underwriting,* since the company has received a firm commitment from the underwriter to a predetermined amount of money. This is not the only method that investment dealers use to distribute new securities. For high risk companies, the underwriter may act as an agent for the company; the underwriter does not insure the company against market fluctuation risk but uses its best efforts to sell the issue. This method of selling new securities is called *best efforts* underwriting. In this chapter we consider firm underwriting exclusively.

The sequence and timing of the events in the preparation of the final prospectus are presented in Figure 13–2.

DISTRIBUTION: UNDERWRITING SYNDICATE

The process that we have been describing usually begins when a company has decided that it needs capital from outside sources and approaches an underwriter. The underwriter is usually the same one that handled the company's previous securities issues. The two parties discuss the sources of

FIGURE 13-2 Sequence and Timing of Events in Preparation of a Prospectus

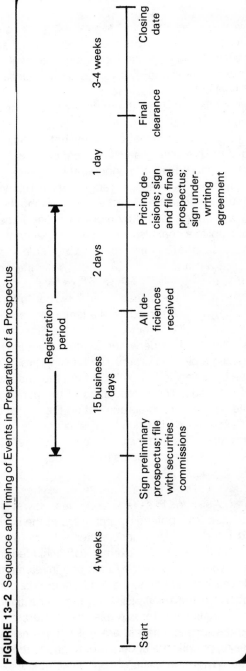

capital that could be raised and what particular source is to be used in this financing.

It is unusual for a security issue to have only a single underwriter. The common pattern is for two or three investment dealers to act as underwriters, with one of them taking the lead or the managing underwriter position. The lead underwriter is the one most heavily involved in the negotiations leading to the preliminary and final prospectuses. However, the other underwriters are kept abreast of the negotiations, may attend meetings and make suggestions concerning the various terms of the issue. For some issues there are two underwriters that operate as co-managers; they both attend meetings and assist in the drafting of the preliminary and final prospectuses.

The impetus to have more than one underwriter originates from the issuing company. For a number of reasons, ranging from repayment for past services rendered to the introduction of a little rivalry among the underwriters, companies feel they are better served by more than one underwriter. Since the underwriting group splits a commission that is independent of the number of underwriters, it is to their monetary advantage to be a sole underwriter.

If the issue is large and there is a risk of price fluctuations, the underwriter(s) will not want to accept the full liability to purchase and sell the whole issue. The usual situation is for the managing underwriter to form a syndicate to spread the underwriting risk. A syndicate is a temporary association for the purpose of carrying out a specific objective. During the preparation of the preliminary prospectus, the lead underwriter invites investment dealers to express interest in joining a banking group. The banking group accepts some of the risk of the issue by agreeing to purchase from the underwriting group a certain proportion of the issue. The composition of the banking group is not firm until they sign the banking-group agreement on the day of the final clearance. However, their expression of strong interest is usually a clear indication of their ultimate participation. The underwriters do not sell the total issue to the banking group but keep a share for themselves. Thus, the underwriters are members of the banking group.

During the registration period, the underwriters and the other members of the banking group are not allowed to sell the securities. However, expressions of interest can be obtained from potential purchasers of the issue. To prevent duplication of selling effort, the lead underwriter will approach a group of approximately 100 institutions on the *exempt list;* included in this list are banks, life insurance companies, pension funds and investment counsellors. Armed with the preliminary prospectus, the lead underwriter determines the interest of the members of the exempt list. At the same time, the banking group is contacting retail institutions for expressions of interest.

Although the expressions of interest are not commitments to purchase the issue, this canvassing permits the underwriter to gauge the acceptability of the terms of the issue. When the issue obtains final clearance, the banking group and lead underwriter check with their clients to determine if, based on the final terms, their interest still exists. However, a firm sale is not made until the final prospectus is delivered to the client (usually two days after final clearance), and a two day period elapses during which the purchasers may change their minds.

The expressions of interest from the exempt list is loosely referred to as the amount of the issue that is pre-sold. The interest from the exempt list is called the *institutional book* and on a bond issue, this is approximately 50 percent of the issue. For a preferred share issue, "the book" is usually smaller. On a new equity issue, the expressions of interest typically come from the banking-underwriting group's clients and not as much from institutions.

The final group in the underwriting syndicate is the selling group. Invitations to join the selling group are made by the banking group, although both underwriters and banking group members can sell the securities to the ultimate purchasers. Members of the selling group purchase the securities from members of the banking group and are expected to resell the securities at the issue price. As of the date of the final clearance, the selling group members sign a selling-group agreement which lasts from 30 to 90 days.

The purpose of forming a selling group is to encourage a rapid and, if required, widely-dispersed sale of the securities. For some issues there is no selling group. Sales are made by the banking group and any sales to exempt institutions by the lead underwriter are made on behalf of the whole banking group. Finally, even though the selling group buys the securities from the banking group, the selling group does not accept any liability for the issue. Thus, if the issue is unsold, the liability rests with the banking group.

The underwriting agreement specifies the conditions under which the underwriters are no longer bound to take the issue, and hence, when they are protected from unexpected events. The first condition obtains if there is an order issued which restricts the trading or distribution of the issue. The second occurs, if, before the fourth day after final clearance, there is a change which seriously affects, or will affect, the financial markets or the company's business. This is called the "market out" clause. Finally, if during the distribution period there is any material change that makes the final prospectus incorrect or misleading, then a new filing will be required and the "market out" clause again becomes applicable.

Price Restrictions

Both the banking and the selling group agree to sell to the ultimate purchasers at the issue price. The lead underwriter may break these price restrictions at any time after the distribution period begins. In fact, the lead underwriter has the right to look at the records of the banking group to determine if the price restrictions are being maintained. The purpose of the price restriction is to protect the members of the banking group against a member that sells all of its allotment below the issue price. For example, suppose the issue price is $100 but, during the distribution period, an increase in interest rates has lowered the bond price below $100. The lead underwriter does not want to be placed in a position in which he and other members of the banking group cannot sell any securities at the issue price because another member(s) is selling its allotment below the issue price. However, if all the members adhere to the price restrictions, they may be saddled with a stagnant issue. In this instance, the price restrictions will be lifted; the price will fall below the issue price; and the issue will be sold. In this case, the commission to the banking group will be reduced; and the market might even have fallen enough to force the banking group to incur a loss – the issue is sold on the market at a price that is less than the price at which the buying group purchased the securities from the underwriters.

Commissions

Commissions are specified in the banking- and selling-group agreements. The gross-underwriting spread, per bond, is the difference between the issue price and the proceeds to the company. The banking group purchases its allotment from the underwriting group at a specified price; this gives the underwriters their commission. The banking group then sells to the exempt list, to the selling group, and to their own customers at set prices; this determines the banking group commission. Finally, the sale of the issue by the selling group at the issue price results in the selling group commission.

As an example, consider a $50 million bond issue selling at par $100 with a gross underwriting spread of $2. The total commission to be spread among the participants in the underwriting group is $1,000,000.

TABLE 13-1   Commission Structure on a Bond Issue[a]

	Face Value ($ million)	Number of Bonds (in thousands)	Amount Paid ($ million)	Price Per Bond
1. Underwriter obtains securities from company	50.0	500	49.000	$ 98.00
2. Issue sold to banking group	50.0	500	49.200	$ 98.40
3. Banking group sells to				
Exempt list	24.0	240	24.000	100.00
Selling group	2.5	25	2.475	99.00
Own customers	23.5	235	23.500	100.00
4. Selling group sell to own customers	2.5	25	2.500	100.00

[a] This example is taken from *Canadian Investment Finance – Part I Corporate Finance,* Canadian Securities Institute, 1976.

From this table the size of the commissions to each group can be estimated. The underwriters obtain a commission of $.40 per bond sold to the banking group or a total of $200,000. This commission is split among the underwriting group on the basis of a negotiated agreement. The lead under-writer will obtain a larger share in compensation for the additional duties per-formed. Next, the banking group as a whole obtains a commission equal to the difference between the price at which the bonds were purchased from the underwriter and the prices at which they are sold. A full commission of $1.60 per bond (i.e. $100.00–98.40) is obtained from sales to exempt-list clients and their own customers. On sales to the selling group, the commission is $.60 per bond (i.e. $99–$98.40). The total commission to the banking group is $775,000. Finally, the commission to the selling group is $1 per bond (i.e. they buy the bonds at $99. and sell them at $100.), or $25,000 in total.

The distribution of the total commission is presented in Table 13–2 below.

TABLE 13–2 Distribution of Total Commission

	Commission Per Bond	Number of Bonds Sold (in thousands)		Commission
Underwriter	$ .40	500		$ 200,000
Banking group on sales to:				
Exempt list	1.60	240	$384,000	
Selling group	.60	25	15,000	
Own customers	1.60	235	376,000	
Total				775,000
Selling group				
Sales to own customers	1.00	25		25,000
Total Commission				$1,000,000

The amount allocated to each member of the banking group, including the underwriters, depends on the proportion of the issue sold by each member. To determine the actual commission to each member, the net proceeds on hand after all issue expenses are removed are multiplied by participation of each banking group member.

It must be emphasized that the commission structure in this example is based on sales of the issue to the ultimate purchaser at the issue price. If the issue is sold at a price below the issue price, the commissions will be reduced.

MARKET STABILIZATION

During the period of distribution, the lead underwriter is authorized through the banking group agreement to buy and sell the securities of the issue in the open market or otherwise. The lead underwriter may be either long or short in the security up to a specified limit. (An underwriter has taken a long position if some portion of the issue is retained and not sold; a short position is one in which the underwriter has sold more securities than were issued.) The aim of the purchase or sale of securities is to prevent a large cumulative downward movement in the price of the security, which would result in losses for all members of the underwriting group.

It has been charged that pegging the price during the offering period constitutes a monopolistic price-fixing arrangement. The investment dealer would reply that not to stabilize the price would increase underwriters' risk, and hence, the underwriting commission would have to increase accordingly. However, the important question is whether purchases by the underwriter can keep the price from falling. If this security is but one of thousands of other securities with similar characteristics, then the investment dealer does not have much power to maintain the price. In this case, purchases would result in a large inventory of the issue at market prices less than the issue price. This results in a large loss to the underwriting group. Unfortunately, there is no empirical evidence on the ability of underwriters to stabilize the market.

ISSUE COSTS[7]

The cost of selling new issues of securities is put into perspective in Table 13-3, where the issue costs measured as the gross underwriter spread relative to the net proceeds, are presented for issues of common and preferred shares and for bonds. The *gross underwriting spread* refers to the difference between the issue price and the proceeds of the issue to the company; this difference goes to the underwriter to cover out-of-pocket costs as well as a compensation for underwriting risk. This table is based on a submission in 1962 by the Investment Dealers Association to the Porter Commission. Although the data are somewhat old, the rankings of the issue costs by type of issue and the relationship of these issue costs to the issue size are still appropriate. Two important generalizations can be drawn from this table:

1. Issue costs for common shares are greater than for preferred shares, and the costs of both are greater than the issue costs for bonds.
2. The issue costs as a percentage of the net proceeds are greater for small issues than for large ones.

---

[7]The costs associated with a new issue of securities are also referred to as flotation costs.

TABLE 13-3 Issue Costs (costs set as average gross underwriter discount as a percent of net proceeds)*

Size of Issue		Type of Issue		
		Debt	Preferred Shares	Equity
Under $3 million	average	4.62	6.05	8.43
	median	4.90	4.77	9.09
	range	1.00–10.00	3.50–11.10	2.00–14.00
Over $3 million	average	2.82	4.75	6.98
	median	2.85	4.00	6.38
	range	.50–5.00	3.50–6.50	5.00–10.00

*Source: Submission by IDA to Porter Commission, June 1962. The usual estimate of these costs is the underwriter discount divided by the gross proceeds. This would result in smaller issue costs. If we let d be the issue costs as reported in the IDA submission, then issue costs as, usually reported, can be calculated as $d/(1+d)$.

What are the reasons for these relationships? The explanations are found in the amount of underwriting risk involved in the issue and in the job of physical distribution. Bonds are generally bought in large blocks by a relatively few institutional investors, whereas stocks are bought by a large number of individuals. For this reason, the distribution and marketing expenses for common and preferred shares are greater. Since the gross-underwriting spread must cover these expenses, the spreads will be higher for a stock issue than a bond issue. Similarly, since stock prices are more volatile than bond prices, underwriting risks are larger for stock than for bond issues, and the underwriting spreads reflect the added risk.

The explanation for the variation in cost with the size of issue is also easily found. In the first place, certain fixed expenses are associated with any distribution of securities: the underwriting investigation, the preparation of the prospectuses, legal fees, and so forth. Since these expenses are relatively large and fixed, their percentage of the total cost of an issue runs high on small issues. Second, small issues are typically those of relatively less well known firms, so underwriting expenses may be larger than usual because the danger of omitting vital information is greater. Furthermore, the selling job is more difficult: sales representatives must exert greater effort to sell the securities of a less well known firm. Finally, small firms tend to be riskier in terms of price volatility, and thus a large underwriting spread is required. For these reasons, issue costs are relatively high for small issues.

Suppose that a particular company makes a number of common share issues of the same size over a given time period. Even if the risk characteristics of the security remain constant, there is no reason to believe that the gross underwriting spread will be identical for each issue. The size of this spread will depend on the state of the stock market at the time of the issue. If the market is extremely volatile, then the underwriting risk will be greater, and therefore, the underwriting spread will be larger. Conversely, a stable market will result in a smaller spread.

Issue costs are also influenced by whether the issue is a "rights offering"; and if it is, by the extent of the underpricing[8]. If rights are used, if the issue is purchased from the issuer by the underwriter, and if the underpricing is substantial, then the investment dealer bears little risk of being unable to sell the shares. Further, very little selling effort will be required in this situation. These factors combine to enable a company to issue new equity to its own shareholders at a relatively low issue cost. As the underpricing decreases, the underwriter risk increases and so does the gross underwriting spread.

Instead of bearing any risk in the rights issue, the underwriter could issue the equity through a rights offering on a "best efforts" basis. Since the underwriter does not purchase the issue from the issuer, there is no underwriting risk and the gross underwriting spread is at a minimum.

PRIVATE PLACEMENT MARKET

Up to this point the discussion has dealt primarily with issues of debt, preferred shares or equity in which fairly stringent prospectus requirements must be met. In these cases, the underwriter purchases the issue from the firm, sells it to the ultimate purchaser, and bears the risk of adverse market fluctuations. However, the private placement market provides an alternative method of issuing longer-term debt and/or preferred shares. Under a private placement, the investment dealer (or private placement specialist) does not purchase the issue and resell it but acts only as an agent. This means that the dealer approaches a number of prospective clients and discusses the terms and conditions of the issue. If the client, usually an institution, shows some interest but is still reluctant there can be some tailoring of the terms of the issue.

There are a number of reasons why the private placement market has become a more important source of funds. First, the costs of the issue are cheaper. Since the issue is not sold to the public but to a "knowledgeable" institution, no prospectus is required. A private placement memorandum is prepared, but the reporting requirements are much less demanding than those required for a public offering. In addition, the underwriting discount is much smaller, since the investment dealer is not underwriting the issue but is using his or her "best efforts". Second, there is a greater degree of flexibility in the issue, because the investment dealer and the ultimate purchaser can negotiate the terms directly. As an example of this flexibility, there have been a number of unique financial instruments used in the private placement market. A good example is the floating preferred share for which the dividend payment floats a fixed number of percentage points above the prime rate. Therefore, if

---

[8]"Rights offerings" involve the sale of shares to existing shareholders. This topic is discussed extensively in Chapter 14.

prime increases (falls), the dividend payment increases (falls) by the same amount. Finally, those issues that are not large enough to require a public issue can be placed in this market.

There are two shortcomings to the use of the private placement market. First, the yields required are slightly higher than yields needed on a comparable underwritten public issue. This reflects the lack of marketability typical of a privately placed issue. Second, the issuing company bears market fluctuation risks, because the investment dealer is acting only as an agent. Presumably, the lower commission paid should compensate the company for this risk.

REGULATION OF SECURITY TRADING

The operations of investment dealers, securities exchanges, and over-the-counter markets described in the previous sections of this chapter are influenced to a high degree by securities regulation. In the United States, securities regulation is a federal matter administered by a federal agency known as the Securities and Exchange Commission (SEC). Canada, however, is very different. Securities regulation is a provincial responsibility, and when a security issue is to be sold in a number of provinces, each provincial regulatory body must review the issue. The existence of a number of regulatory bodies can cause problems, especially if the regulations are different in every province. Currently, each province licenses brokers and dealers operating within the province and regulates securities transactions.

In our brief discussion of securities regulation, we will concentrate on the regulations in Ontario since the TSE is the major exchange in Canada and securities issued there must meet the requirements of the Ontario Securities Act. In addition, the four Western Provinces have followed the lead of the Ontario Securities Commission (OSC) and generally have the same provisions in their securities acts.

The financial manager is affected by these securities acts for several reasons: (1) corporate officers can be subject to personal liabilities; (2) the laws affect the ease and costs of financing, and they also affect the behavior of the money and capital markets in which the corporation's securities are sold and traded; and (3) investors' willingness to buy securities may be influenced by the existence of safeguards provided by these laws.

The two basic reasons for securities regulation are the protection of the individual investor and the efficient allocation of capital by means of capital markets. Both of these goals are achieved through the techniques of full, continuing, and timely disclosure and control of individuals who are permitted to operate in the securities industry.

Full Disclosure

It is obvious that full disclosure assists an individual investor in making a well-informed decision. This disclosure requirement is intended to assist individual investors and the disclosure requirements on new issues directed to the institutional investor with access to professional advice are much less onerous. For example, on a private placement issue, a memorandum is required which has much easier disclosure requirements.

There are two approaches that a securities commission can take with respect to the full disclosure requirement. If we consider the example of a new issue, the first approach would require full and complete disclosure of all material information. The securities commission does not comment on the quality of the issue, but considers that the investor is sufficiently informed to make an investment decision. The Ontario Securities Act also has a withdrawal provision consistent with the full disclosure provisions. The purchaser can rescind the contract to purchase up to 90 days after the date of receipt of the prospectus or the contract date, whichever is later, if there were material errors or omissions in the prospectus.

The alternative approach is to argue that full disclosure is not sufficient —the prospectus may not be accepted by the commission or severe conditions may be laid down which must be met. This results in a paternalistic attitude which is a remnant of the repealed "Blue Sky" laws which required new issues to be approved by a government official. This paternalistic attitude has been found in the handling of new issues of penny mining stocks. Also, the fact that a purchaser has up to two business days after the receipt of the prospectus to withdraw from the purchase contract without needing *any* reason is another example of the desire to protect the investor.

Continuing Disclosure

In attempting to improve the efficiency of the capital markets the Kimber Report[9] recommended that ongoing disclosure by companies whose securities were traded was essential. The recommendations were incorporated in the Ontario Securities Act of 1966; they included restrictions on and reporting requirements for, insider trading, regular financial reporting, mandatory solicitation of proxies, and provision of information circulars to shareholders prior to the annual meeting. It is somewhat surprising that most of these provisions, which are found in the U.S. Securities Exchange Act of 1934, were introduced to the Ontario Act in 1966 and not in the prior revision of the Ontario Securities Act in 1945.

[9]Report of the Attorney General's Committee on Securities Legislation in Ontario (the "Kimber Report"), Toronto, 1965.

Timely Disclosure

Whereas continuing disclosure requires the availability of information on an ongoing basis, timely disclosure is concerned with the availability of information in the case of unusual or episodic events. An example introduced in 1966 is the regulation and disclosure requirements for take-over bids for either cash or securities. In 1968, both the TSE and the Ontario Securities Commission introduced policies concerned with timely disclosure in an attempt to prevent insiders from making trading profits from their access to private information. In a recent development, the OSC has emphasized the requirement by requiring companies to disclose to the Chairman of the Commission, on a confidential basis, future developments which may have an impact on their securities. The purpose of this policy is to assist the Commission in its monitoring of market trading.

Control of Participants

In 1928, an act was passed in Ontario which dealt mainly with the control of individuals trading in securities. This act required registration of brokers and dealers. The Attorney General had broad discretion to deny registration, and somewhat more limited discretion to cancel existing registration. Conduct that was deemed to be fraudulent was identified and penalties for fraudulent acts were specified.

Currently, registration conditions are quite detailed. In addition, supervision of those registered to trade in securities has increased.

APPRAISAL OF REGULATION OF SECURITY TRADING

Why should security transactions be regulated? It can be argued that a great body of relevant information is required to make an informed judgment of the value of a security. In addition, the securities markets provide a means for allocating capital. If there is information available, these markets will reflect this information, and hence the allocation function will be improved. Social well-being requires that efficient markets be promoted.

Based on the increased disclosure requirements and the more stringent control of participants in the market, it is clear that more information is now available to the individual investor. However, this does not necessarily imply that society is better off. The greater disclosure requirements in a prospectus has increased the time and expense involved in the issuing of securities by companies. Since investors can sue for damages if a prospectus is untrue or materially incomplete, the company has an incentive to incur significant costs to prepare the prospectus. In addition, the timely disclosure requirements may impose costs on a company. Suppose that a company is considering a take-over bid. A premature disclosure of the terms may erode the competitive position of the company. Harmful results may also occur if contemplated events are disclosed but do not occur.

A final cost is the opportunity loss incurred when the securities commission takes a paternalistic attitude toward new issues. Even though the securities commission might refuse to accept a prospectus and thus abort the issue, fully informed investors may have still been willing to risk an investment in the company. A very strict attitude by a commission can limit the access to capital through the markets, and hence retard the growth of an industry.

The regulations are powerless to prevent investors from investing in unsound ventures or to prevent stock prices from increasing rapidly during booms or falling greatly during periods of pessimism. Some economists have argued that the requirements for increased information have been of great value in preventing fraud and gross misrepresentations and also in reducing gyrations in stock prices. However, this conclusion is not universally accepted.[10]

SUMMARY

Securities are traded both on *exchanges* and in the *over-the-counter market.* The stocks of larger industrial and utility companies are generally listed on an exchange; stocks of small industrial firms, and almost all bonds are traded over the counter. From the standpoint of the financial manager, listing on an exchange seems advantageous for seasoned issues. The over-the-counter market may aid in the seasoning process until the security can meet the requirements for listing.

The investment dealer provides services to both the seller and the buyer of new securities. The dealer helps plan the issue, underwrites it, and handles the job of selling the issue to the ultimate investor. The cost of this service to the issuer is related to the magnitude of the total job the dealer must perform to place the issue. The investment dealer must also look to the interests of the brokerage's customers; if these investors are not satisfied with the dealer's products, they will deal elsewhere.

Issue costs are lower for bonds, higher for preferred shares, and highest for common shares. Larger companies have lower issue costs than smaller ones for each type of security, and most companies can cut their stock issue costs by issuing the new securities to shareholders through an underwritten rights offerings. (Rights offerings are discussed in Chapter 14.)

The financial manager should be familiar with the laws regulating the issuance and trading of securities, because they influence the manager's

---

[10] An excellent discussion of these issues is found in H.G. Manne (ed.), *Economic Policy and the Regulation of Corporate Securities,* American Enterprise Institute for Policy Research, 1969, Part III.

liabilities and affect financing methods and costs. Regulation of securities trading seeks (1) to provide information that investors can utilize as a basis for judging the merits of securities and (2) to promote an efficient securities market. The laws do not, however, prevent either the purchase of unsound issues or wide price fluctuations. The tools of regulation are disclosure, prevention of manipulation of prices and the exercise of controls over certain trading activities. Whether securities regulation has been effective in improving the efficiency of the capital markets is a topic that has generated substantial debate. Some economists argue that it has and that the confidence of the public in the securities markets has been increased. Other economists believe that securities regulation has generated more costs than benefits.

QUESTIONS

13-1. State several advantages to a firm that lists its stock on a major stock exchange.

13-2. Would you expect the cost of capital of a firm to be affected if it changed its status from one traded over the counter to one traded on the Toronto Stock Exchange? Explain.

13-3. Evaluate the following statement: The fundamental purpose of provincial security laws dealing with new issues is to prevent investors, principally small ones, from sustaining losses on the purchase of stocks.

13-4. Suppose two firms were each selling $10 million of common shares. The firms are similar—that is, they are of the same size, are in the same industry, have the same leverage, and have other similarities—except that one is publicly owned and the other is closely held. Would their issue be the same? If they are different, state the probable relationships. If the issue were $10 million of bonds, would your answer be the same?

13-5. Define these terms: brokerage firm, underwriting group, selling group, and investment dealer.

13-6. Each month the Ontario Securities Commission publishes a report on the transactions made by the insiders of listed firms in their own companies' equity securities. Why do you suppose the OSC makes this report?

13-7. Two large companies just received the net proceeds from their equity issues. One of the companies is in the steel industry and the issue costs were 8 percent of the gross proceeds. These costs are less than on an issue of comparable size undertaken five years before. The second company is a regulated utility and had issue costs of 5 percent of the gross proceeds.

Discuss the factors that could explain why (1) the issue costs are different for the two firms, and (2) why the current issue costs for the first firm are less than they were five years ago.

13-8. Before entering a formal agreement, investment dealers investigate quite carefully the companies whose securities they underwrite; this is especially true of the issues of firms going public for the first time. Since the dealers do not themselves plan to hold the securities but plan to sell them to others as soon as possible, why are they so concerned about making careful investigations? Does your answer to the question have any bearing on the fact that underwriting is a very difficult field to "break into"?

13-9. If competitive bidding was required on all security offerings, would issue costs be higher or lower? Would the size of the issuing firm be material in determining the effects of required competitive bidding?

13-10. Since investment dealers price new issues in relation to outstanding issues, should a spread exist between the yields on the new and the outstanding issues? Discuss this matter separately for stock issues and bond issues.

13-11. What problems are raised by the increasing purchase of equities by institutional investors?

PROBLEMS

13-1. Your firm is planning to sell $1.5 million of bonds with a fifteen-year term to maturity. The going rate on debt of this quality and maturity will be 10 percent. However, total costs of the underwriting have been estimated to be 10.5 percent of gross proceeds. Calculate the cost of this debt to your firm. (Hint: Let the coupon rate be 10 percent so the bonds will sell at face value, then solve for the IRR which will make the future payments on the bond equal to face value less 10.5 percent, i.e., to $895 per bond.)

13-2. If your firm were to sell preferred shares in the amount of $1.5 million, the total issue expense would be about 11.5 percent of gross proceeds. If the going rate on preferred shares of the same quality as your firm's is 12 percent, what will be the effective cost of the preferred share issue? Assume the stock will remain outstanding in perpetuity.

13-3[11]**.** In March 1975, three executives of the Hughes Aircraft Company, one of the largest privately owned corporations in the world, decided to break away from Hughes and to set up a company of their own. The principal reason for this decision was capital gains; Hughes Aircraft stock is all privately owned, and the corporate structure makes it impossible for executives to be granted stock purchase options. Hughes' executives receive substantial salaries and bonuses, but this income is all taxable at normal tax rates, and no capital gains opportunities are available.

The three men, Jim Adcock, Robert Goddard, and Rick Aiken, have located a medium-size electronics manufacturing company available for purchase. The stock of this firm, Baynard Industries, is all owned by the founder, Joseph Baynard. Although the company is in excellent shape, Baynard wants to sell it because of his failing health. A price of $5.7 million has been established, based on a price/earnings ratio of 12 and annual earnings of $475,000. Baynard has given the three prospective purchasers an option to purchase the company for the agreed price; the option is to run for six months, during which time the three men are to arrange financing with which to buy the firm.

Adcock has consulted with Jules Scott, a partner in the New York investment banking firm of Williams Brothers and an acquaintance of some years' standing, to seek his assistance in obtaining the funds necessary to complete the purchase. Adcock, Goddard, and Aiken each have some money available to put into the new enterprise, but they need a substantial amount of outside capital. There is some possibility of borrowing part of the money, but Scott has discouraged this idea. His reasoning is, first, that Baynard Industries is already highly leveraged, and if the purchasers were to borrow additional funds, there would be a very severe risk that they would be unable to service

---

[11]This case study is taken from E.F. Brigham, Timothy J. Nantell, Robert T. Aubey, and Richard H. Pettway, *Cases in Managerial Finance,* 2nd ed. (New York: Holt, Rinehart and Winston, Inc., 1974).

this debt in the event of a recession in the electronics industry. Although the firm is currently earning $475,000 a year, this figure could quickly turn into a loss in the event of a few canceled defense contracts or cost miscalculations.

Scott's second reason for discouraging a loan is that Adcock, Goddard, and Aiken plan not only to operate Baynard Industries and seek internal growth but also to use the corporation as a vehicle for making further acquisitions of electronics companies. This being the case, Scott believes that it would be wise for the company to keep any borrowing potential in reserve for use in later acquisitions.

Scott proposes that the three partners obtain funds to purchase Baynard Industries in accordance with the figures shown in Table P13–1.

TABLE P13–1 Baynard Industries

Price paid to Joseph Baynard			$5,700,000
(12 × $475,000 earnings)			
Authorized shares		5,000,000	
Initially issued shares		1,125,000	
Initial distribution of shares:			
Adcock	100,000 shares at $1.00		$ 100,000
Goddard	100,000 shares at $1.00		100,000
Aiken	100,000 shares at $1.00		100,000
Williams Brothers	125,000 shares at $7.00		875,000
Public stockholders	700,000 shares at $7.00		4,900,000
	1,125,000		$6,075,000
Underwriting costs: 5% of $4,900,000		$245,000	
Legal fees, and so on, associated with issue		45,000	$ 290,000
			$5,785,000
Payment to Joseph Baynard			5,700,000
Net funds to Baynard Industries			$ 85,000

Baynard Industries would be reorganized with an authorized 5,000,000 shares, with 1,125,000 to be issued at the time the transfer takes place and the other 3,875,000 to be held in reserve for possible issuance in connection with acquisitions. Adcock, Goddard, and Aiken would each purchase 100,000 shares at a price of $1 a share, the par value. Williams Brothers would purchase 125,000 shares at a price of $7. The remaining 700,000 shares would be sold to the public at a price of $7 a share.

Williams Brothers' underwriting fee would be 5 percent of the shares sold to the public, or $245,000. Legal fees, accounting fees, and other charges associated with the issue would amount to $45,000, for a total underwriting cost of $290,000. After deducting the underwriting charges and the payment to Baynard from the gross proceeds of the stock sale, the reorganized Baynard Industries would receive funds in the amount of $85,000 which would be used for internal expansion purposes.

As a part of the initial agreement, Adcock, Goddard, and Aiken each would be given options to purchase an additional 80,000 shares at a price of $7 a share one year from now. Williams Brothers would be given an option to purchase an additional 100,000 shares at $7 a share in one year.

a. What is the total underwriting charge, expressed as a percentage of the funds raised by the underwriter? Does this charge seem reasonable in the light of published statistics on the cost of floating new issues of common stock?

b. Suppose that the three men estimate the following probabilities for the firm's stock price one year from now:

Price	Probability
$ 1	.05
$ 5	.10
$ 9	.35
13	.35
17	.10
21	.05

Assuming Williams Brothers exercises its options, calculate the following ratio (ignore time-discount effects):

$$\frac{\text{Total proceeds to Williams Brothers}}{\text{Funds raised by underwriter}}$$

Disregard Williams Brothers' profit on the 125,000 shares it bought outright at the initial offering. Comment on the ratio.

c. Are Adcock, Goddard, and Aiken purchasing their stock at a "fair" price? Should the prospectus disclose the fact that they would buy their stock at $1 a share, whereas public stockholders would buy their stock at $7 a share?

d. Would it be reasonable for Williams Brothers to purchase its initial 125,000 shares at a price of $1.

e. Do you foresee any problems of control for Adcock, Goddard, and Aiken?

f. Would the expectation of an exceptionally large need for investment funds next year be a relevant consideration in deciding on the amount of funds to be raised now?

Common Shares

14
Common equity, or if unincorporated firms are being considered, partnership or proprietorship interests, constitutes the first source of funds to a new business and the base of support for borrowing by existing firms. Accordingly, our discussion of specific forms of long-term financing will begin with an analysis of common shares.

APPORTIONMENT OF INCOME, CONTROL, AND RISK

The nature of equity ownership depends upon the form of the business or organization. The central problem revolves around an apportionment of certain rights and responsibilities among those who have provided the funds necessary for the operation of the business.

The rights and responsibilities attaching to equity consist of positive considerations—income potential and control of the firm—and negative considerations—loss potential, legal responsibility, and personal liability.

General Rights of Holders of Common Shares

A business in Canada can be incorporated either provincially or federally. The decision will depend on the relative severity of the requirements for incorporation and, more importantly, whether the firm intends to operate in more than one province. If the company expects its operations to be in more than one province, the federal incorporation route is usually taken although this is not necessary.

The rights of the holders of common shares in a business corporation are established by the requirements in the jurisdiction in which the company is incorporated. There are a number of differences depending on the jurisdiction described. In this discussion we will present the rights that are common to all jurisdictions. Where there are important differences, we will note these.

Collective Rights   Certain collective rights are usually given to the holders of common shares. Some of the more important rights allow shareholders (1) to amend the articles of incorporation; (2) to adopt and amend bylaws; (3) to elect the directors of the corporation; (4) to authorize the sale of fixed assets; (5) to enter into mergers and amalgamations; (6) to change the amount of authorized common and preferred shares; (7) to alter the rights and restrictions attached to the common shares; and (8) to create a right of exchange of other shares into common shares.

Specific Rights   Holders of common shares also have specific rights as individual owners. (1) They have the right to vote in the manner prescribed by the corporate charter. (2) They may sell their share certificates, their evidence of ownership, and in this way transfer their ownership interest to other persons. (3) They have the right to inspect the corporate books.[1] (4) They have the right to require the company to purchase their shares at an appraised price if the company takes certain prescribed actions. This appraisal right protects the dissenting shareholders from decisions of the majority in cases where, for example, amendments of some of the articles of incorporation will alter the rights of common shares, and/or the business itself. (5) They have the right to share residual assets of the corporation on dissolution; however, the holders of common shares are last among the claimants to the assets of the corporation.

Apportionment of Income

Two important positive considerations are involved in equity ownership: income and control. The right to income carries risks of loss. Control also involves responsibility and liability. In an individual proprietorship, using only funds supplied by the owner, the owner has a 100 percent right to income and control and to loss and responsibility. As soon as the proprietor incurs debt, however, he has entered into contracts that place limitations on his complete freedom to control the firm and to apportion the firm's income.

In a partnership, these rights are apportioned among the partners in an agreed manner. In the absence of a formal agreement, a division is made by

---

[1]Obviously, a corporation cannot have its business affairs disturbed by allowing every shareholder to go through any record that he or she would like to inspect. A corporation could not wisely permit a competitor who happened to buy shares to look at all the corporation records. There must be, and there are, practical limitations to this right.

law. In a corporation, more significant issues arise concerning the rights of the owners.

Apportionment of Control

Through the right to vote, holders of common shares have legal control of the corporation. As a practical matter, however, in many corporations the principal officers constitute all, or a majority of, the members of the board of directors. In such circumstances the board of directors may be controlled by the management, rather than vice versa. Management control, or control of a business by other than its owners, results. However, numerous examples demonstrate that shareholders can reassert their control if they are dissatisfied with the policies of the corporation. Proxy battles, with the aim of altering corporate policies, have occurred, and firms whose managers are unresponsive to shareholders' desires are subject to takeover bids by other firms.

As receivers of residual income, holders of common shares are frequently referred to as the ultimate entrepreneurs in the firm. They are the ultimate owners, and they have the ultimate control. Presumably the firm is managed on behalf of its owners, the holders of common shares, but there has been much dispute about the actual situation. The point of view has been expressed that the corporation is an institution with an existence separate from the owners', and that the corporation exists to fulfill certain functions for shareholders as only one among other important groups, such as workers, consumers, and the economy as a whole. This view may have some validity, but it should also be noted that ordinarily the officers of a firm are also large shareholders. In addition, more and more firms are relating officers' compensation to the firm's profit performance, either by granting executives share purchase options or by giving bonuses. Finally officers of the company want to maintain their mobility and marketability. They will be able to do this only if they are successful in their existing job; success is measured in terms of corporate earnings and stock prices. Thus, by means of direct and indirect pressures, managers' personal goals are consistent with those of the shareholders — to increase the firm's earnings and stock price.

Apportionment of Risk

Another consideration involved in equity ownership is risk. Because, on liquidation, holders of common shares are last in the priority of claims, the portion of capital they contribute provides a cushion for creditors if losses occur on dissolution. The equity-to-total-assets ratio indicates the percentage by which assets may shrink in value on liquidation before creditors will incur losses.

For example, compare two corporations, A and B, whose balance sheets are shown in Table 14–1. The ratio of equity to total assets in corporation A is 80 percent. Total assets would therefore have to shrink by 80 percent before creditors would lose money. By contrast, in corporation B the extent by which assets may shrink in value on liquidation before creditors lose money is only 40 percent.

TABLE 14–1 Balance Sheets for Corporations A and B

Corporation A			Corporation B		
	Debt	$ 20		Debt	$ 60
	Equity	80		Equity	40
Total assets $100	Total claims $100		Total assets $100	Total claims $100	

COMMON SHARE FINANCING

Before undertaking an evaluation of common share financing, it is desirable to describe some of its additional important characteristics. These topics include (1) the nature of voting rights, (2) the nature of the preemptive right, and (3) variations in the forms of common shares.

Nature of Voting Rights

For each common share owned, the holder has the right to cast one vote at the annual meeting of shareholders of the corporation or at such special meetings as may be called. In general, decisions are decided by majority vote.

Proxy Provision in provincial legislation is made for the temporary transfer of the right to vote by an instrument known as a *proxy*. The transfer is limited in its duration, typically for a specific occasion such as the annual meeting of shareholders. At the time of the solicitation of the proxy, the management must supply to the shareholders a circular which contains specified information; this circular must be filed with the provincial securities commission. Specific forms for the proxy and disclosure requirements are stated by provincial legislation for a number of reasons. First, if the proxy machinery is left wholly in the hands of management, there is a danger that the incumbent management will be self-perpetuated. Second, if it is made easy for minority groups of shareholders and opposition shareholders to oust management, there is danger that they may gain control of the corporation for temporary advantages or to place their friends in management positions.

Cumulative Voting   In voting for directors, the usual rule is a majority vote. However, there has been an analysis of cumulative voting for revision of both the Ontario and Federal Corporations Acts. The Ontario and Federal Acts permit the use of cumulative voting as long as there are specific provisions in the articles or by-laws. The Alberta and British Columbia Acts do not mention cumulative voting specifically, but this voting would be allowed if included in the articles. In the United States, cumulative voting is required in twenty-two states and permissible in eighteen.

Cumulative voting permits multiple votes for a single director. For example, suppose six directors are to be elected. The owner of 100 shares can cast 100 votes for each of the six openings. Cumulatively, then, he has 600 votes. When cumulative voting is permitted, the shareholder may accumulate his votes and cast 600 votes for *one* director, instead of 100 each for *six* directors. Cumulative voting is designed to enable a minority group of shareholders to obtain some voice in the control of the company by electing at least one director to the board.

The nature of cumulative voting is illustrated by use of the following formula:

$$r = \frac{d \times S}{D + 1} + 1. \qquad (14\text{--}1)$$

Here,

r = number of shares required to elect a desired number of directors,

d = number of directors shareholder desires to elect,

S = total number of common shares outstanding and entitled to vote, and

D = total number of directors to be elected.

The formula may be made more meaningful by an example. The ABC Company will elect six directors. There are fifteen candidates and 100,000 shares entitled to vote. If a group desires to elect two directors, how many shares must it have?

$$r = \frac{2 \times 100,000}{6 + 1} + 1 = 28,572. \qquad (14\text{--}2)$$

Observe the significance of the formula. Here, a minority group wishes to elect one-third of the board of directors. They can achieve their goal by owning less than one-third the number of shares of stock.[2]

Alternatively, assuming that a group holds 40,000 shares of stock in this company, how many directors would it be possible for the group to elect, fol-

---

[2] Note also that at least 14,287 shares must be controlled to elect one director. As far as electing a director goes, any number less than 14,287 constitutes a useless minority.

lowing the rigid assumptions of the formula? The formula can be used in its present form or can be solved for d and expressed as

$$d = \frac{(r-1)(D+1)}{S}. \qquad (14\text{--}3)$$

Inserting the figures, the calculation would be

$$d = \frac{39{,}999 \times 7}{100{,}000} = 2.8. \qquad (14\text{--}4)$$

The 40,000 shares could elect two and eight-tenths directors. Since directors cannot exist as fractions, the group can elect only two directors.

As a practical matter, suppose that in the above situation the total number of shares is 100,000. Hence 60,000 shares remain in other hands. The voting of all the 60,000 shares may not be concentrated. Suppose the 60,000 shares (cumulatively, 360,000 votes) not held by our group are distributed equally among ten candidates, 36,000 shares held by each candidate. If our group's 240,000 votes are distributed equally for each of six candidates, we could elect all six directors even though we do not have a majority of the stock.

Actually, it is difficult to make assumptions about how the opposition votes will be distributed. What is shown here is a good example of game theory. One rule in the theory of games is to assume that your opponents will do the worst they can do to you and to counter with actions to minimize the maximum loss. This is the kind of assumption followed in the formula. If your opposition concentrates its votes in the optimum manner, what is the best you can do to work in the direction of your goal? Other plausible assumptions can be substituted if there are sufficient facts to support alternative hypotheses about the behavior of the opponents.

Preemptive Right

The preemptive right gives the existing holders of common shares the first option to purchase additional issues of common shares in proportion to their existing holdings. There is no preemptive right unless specified in the articles of incorporation. The preemptive right is permitted by the Alberta, Ontario and Federal Acts. The British Columbia Act permits the preemptive right for public companies and requires it for private companies. Under the existing Bank Act, banks must include the preemptive right in their articles of incorporation.

The purpose of this right is twofold. First, it protects the power of control of present shareholders. If it were not for this safeguard, the management of a corporation under criticism from shareholders could prevent shareholders from removing it from office by issuing a large number of additional shares at a very low price and purchasing those shares itself. Management would thereby secure control of the corporation to frustrate the will of the current shareholders.

The second, and by far the more important, protection that the preemptive right affords shareholders regards dilution of value. For example, assume that 1,000 common shares, each with a price of $100, are outstanding, making the total market value of the firm $100,000. An additional 1,000 shares are sold at $50 a share, or for $50,000, thus raising the total market value of the firm to $150,000. When the total market value is divided by the new total shares outstanding, a value of $75 a share is obtained. Thus, selling common shares at below market value will dilute the price of the stock and will be detrimental to present shareholders and beneficial to those who purchased the new shares. The preemptive right prevents such occurrences. This point is discussed at length later in this chapter.

Authorized, Issued, and Outstanding

The company's articles of incorporation specify the authorized number of shares; this is the maximum number of shares that can be issued. The articles can be amended so as to increase the authorized number of shares, but this requires a vote. To add flexibility most companies will set the authorized number of shares in excess of the amount needed in the short-run. As the shares are sold, they become *issued.* The outstanding shares reflect the number of shares actually held by shareholders. This will be less than the issued number of shares only when the company has repurchased shares.

Classified Common Shares[3]

Up to this point in the discussion we have considered common equity as a homogeneous class. However, common equity can be separated into different classes in which each class has different rights. There are two general ways in which common shares can be classified. The first technique distinguishes between common shares with special provisions or restrictions. For example, the class A share may have no voting rights, but a claim on dividends in advance of the regular common shares. If the dividends are in arrears, the class A shareholders have a vote. In essence, this class of common equity is a form of *preferred or preferrence shares.*

[3] Accountants also use the term "par value" to designate an arbitrary value assigned when stock is sold. When a firm sells newly issued stock, it must record the transaction on its balance sheet. For example, suppose a newly created firm commences operations by selling 100,000 shares at $10 a share, raising a total of $1 million. This $1 million must appear on the balance sheet, but what will it be called? One choice would be to assign the stock a "par value" of $10 and label the $1 million "common shares". Another choice would be to assign a $1 par value and show $100,000 ($1 par value times 100,000 shares) as "common shares" and $900,000 as "contributed surplus". Still another choice would be to disregard the term "par value" entirely — that is, use no par value stock—and record the $1 million as "common shares". This is the route taken under the Federal Act, since the use of par value has been abolished. Under provincial acts where par value continues to be permitted, there is a potential problem if par value shares are issued. With a stated par value, subsequent share issues can not be sold at less than par value. To ensure flexibility in financing, companies are setting the par value as low as possible—in the limit, no par value. More and more firms are adopting the procedure of abolishing the term "par value". Because there are quite enough useful concepts and terms in accounting and finance, we heartily applaud the demise of useless ones such as this.

The second general type of classification occurs because of the ability of companies to pay tax-deferred dividends. The common equity of the company is classified into two types of shares which are convertible one into the other and are ranked equally with respect to dividends and voting rights. The major difference is that one class obtains ordinary taxable dividends and the other class receives tax-deferred dividends.[4] Stelco, Molson, Labatts and the Toronto Star are just a few of the companies that have tax-deferred common shares. With the latest budget revisions, the tax-deferred dividend will be phased out by December 31, 1978, at which point the two classes of common shares will be identical.

The existence of the various classes of stocks has led to a confusing share structure. In Table 14–2 we present the share structure for Molson Companies Limited as of December 31, 1977.

TABLE 14–2 Molson Companies Limited, Capital Stock Structure, December 31, 1977

Class	Authorized Shares	Issued and Outstanding	Con-vertible Into	Terms	Tax Deferred	Voting	Preference
A	15,000,000	8,306,600	D	1 for 1	No	Only as a class to elect three directors	Dividend of 20% per annum
B	7,000,000	4,647,300	C	1 for 1	No	Yes	None
C	7,000,000	436,800	B	1 for 1	Yes	Yes	None
D	7,000,000	301,400	A	1 for 1	Yes	Same as class "A"	Same as class "A"

Molson has four classes of common shares. Classes A and D are convertible as are classes B and C. Looking first at classes B and C, we see that these two classes differ only as to the existence of the tax-deferred right for class C. However, neither of these classes have any preferences. Classes A and D have a preference and differ only with respect to the tax deferred dividend.

Classes A and B are not tax deferred; class A has a preference for dividends and restricted voting rights. With the removal of the tax-deferred dividend, both classes C and D would disappear and Molson's equity structure will become less complex.

[4] These dividends are not taxable immediately in the hands of the shareholders. The tax-deferred dividend reduces the cost base of the shares, and thus, when the shares are sold, a larger capital gain (or smaller capital loss) will be incurred. With the dividend tax credit, only investors in high marginal tax brackets would buy the share of the tax-deferred class.

EVALUATION OF COMMON SHARES AS A SOURCE OF FUNDS

Thus far, the chapter has covered the main characteristics of common shares, frequently referred to as equity shares. By way of a summary of the important aspects of common shares, we now appraise this type of financing from the standpoint of the issuer.

From Viewpoint of Issuer

Advantages   First, common shares do not entail fixed charges. If the company generates sufficient earnings, it can pay common share dividends. In contrast to bond interest, however, there is no legal obligation to pay dividends. Second, common shares carry no fixed maturity date. Third, since common shares provide a cushion against losses for creditors, the sale of common shares increases the credit-worthiness of the firm. Fourth, common shares may at times be sold more easily than debt. Common shares appeal to certain investor groups for two reasons: (1) they carry a higher expected return than do preferred shares or debt of the same company, and (2) they provide the investor with a better hedge against inflation than do straight preferred shares or bonds because they represent the ownership of the firm. Ordinarily, common shares increase in value when the value of real assets rises during an inflationary period.

Disadvantages   First, the sale of common shares extends voting rights or control to the additional shareowners who are brought into the company. For this reason, among others, additional equity financing is often avoided by small and new firms. The owner-managers may be unwilling to share control of their companies with outsiders.

Second, common shares give more owners the right to share in income. The use of debt may enable the firm to utilize funds at a fixed low cost, whereas common shares give equal rights to new shareholders to share in the net profits of the firm.

Third, as we saw in Chapter 13, the costs of underwriting and distributing common shares are usually higher than those of underwriting and distributing preferred shares or debt. Issue costs for selling common shares are characteristically higher because (1) costs of investigating an equity security investment are higher than investigating the feasibility of a comparable debt security, and (2) stocks are more risky, which means equity holdings must be diversified, which in turn means that a given dollar amount of new stock must be sold to a greater number of purchasers than the same amount of debt.

Fourth, common share dividends are not deductible as an expense for calculating the corporation's income subject to the federal income tax, but bond interest is deductible. The impact of this factor is reflected in the relative cost of equity capital vis-a-vis debt capital.

USE OF RIGHTS IN FINANCING

If, as with the chartered banks, the preemptive right is contained in a particular firm's articles, then it must offer any new common shares to existing shareholders. If the articles do not prescribe a preemptive right, the firm has a choice of making the sale to its existing shareholders or to an entirely new set of investors. If the sale is to the existing shareholders, the share issue is called a *rights offering.* Each shareholder is issued an option to buy a certain number of the new shares, and the terms of the option are contained on a piece of paper called a *right.* Each shareholder receives one right for each share of stock he owns. The advantages and disadvantages of rights offerings are described in this section.

THEORETICAL RELATIONSHIPS

Several issues confront the financial manager who is deciding on the details of a rights offering. The various considerations can be made clear by the use of illustrative data on Canadian Maritime Company Limited, whose balance sheet and income statement are given in Table 14–3.

TABLE 14-3 Canadian Maritime Company Ltd., Financial Statements Before Rights Offering

Partial balance sheet

	Total debt, 5%	$ 40,000,000
	Common shares	10,000,000
	Retained earnings	50,000,000
Total assets $100,000,000	Total liabilities and capital	$100,000,000

Partial income statement

Total earnings	$10,000,000
Interest on debt	2,000,000
Income before taxes	8,000,000
Taxes (50% assumed)	4,000,000
Earnings after taxes	4,000,000
Earnings per share (1,000,000 shares)	$4
Market price of stock (price/earnings ratio of 25 assumed)	$100

Maritime earns $4 million after taxes and has 1 million shares outstanding, so earnings per share are $4. The stock sells at 25 times earnings, or for

$100 a share. The company plans to raise $10 million of new equity funds through a rights offering and decides to sell the new stock to shareholders for $80 a share. The questions now facing the financial manager are

1. How many rights will be required to purchase a share of the newly issued stock?
2. What is the value of each right?
3. What effect will the rights offering have on the price of the existing stock?

We will now analyze each of these questions.

Number of Rights Needed to Purchase a New Share

Maritime plans to raise $10 million in new equity funds and to sell the new shares at a subscription price of $80 per share. Dividing the subscription price into the total funds to be raised gives the number of shares to be issued:

$$\text{Number of new shares} = \frac{\text{funds to be raised}}{\text{subscription price}} = \frac{\$10,000,000}{\$80}$$

$$= 125,000 \text{ shares.}$$

The next step is to divide the number of new shares into the number of previously outstanding shares to get the number of rights required to sub-scribe to one share of the new stock. Note that shareholders always get one right for each share of stock they own:

$$\frac{\text{Number of rights needed to}}{\text{buy a share of the stock}} = \frac{\text{old shares}}{\text{new shares}} = \frac{1,000,000}{125,000} = 8 \text{ rights.}$$

Therefore, a shareholder will have to surrender eight rights plus $80 to receive one of the newly issued shares. Had the subscription price been set at $95 a share, 9.5 rights would have been required to subscribe to each new share; if the price had been set at $10 a share, only one right would have been needed. Notice that given the total amount of funds to be raised, the higher the subscription price, the larger the number of rights needed to purchase a new share. Equivalently, the higher the subscription price the fewer the number of new shares that will be issued.

Value of a Right

It is clearly worth something to be able to buy, for less than $100, a share of stock selling for $100. The right provides this privilege, so the right must have a value. To see how the theoretical value of a right is estab-lished, we continue with the example of Canadian Maritime, assuming that it will raise $10 million by selling 125,000 new shares at $80 a share.

First, notice that the *market value* of the old stock was $100 million: $100 a share times 1 million shares. (The book value is irrelevant.) When the firm sells the new stock, it brings in an additional $10 million. As a first approximation, we assume that the market value of the common shares increases by exactly this $10 million. Actually, the market value of all the common shares will go up by more than $10 million if investors think the company will be able to invest these funds at a yield substantially in excess of the cost of equity capital, but it will go up by less than $10 million if investors are doubtful of the company's ability to put the new funds to work in the near future at yields below the cost of equity capital.

Under the assumption that all rights will be exercised and that the market value reflects the new funds brought in, the total market value of the common shares after the new issue will be $110 million. Dividing this new value by the new total number of shares outstanding, 1.125 million, we obtain a new market value of $97.78 a share. Therefore, we see that after the financing has been completed, the price of the common shares will have fallen from $100 to $97.78.

Since the rights give the shareholders the privilege of buying for only $80 a share of stock that will end up being worth $97.78, thus saving $17.78, is $17.78 the value of each right? The answer is "no", because eight rights are required to buy one new share; we must divide $17.78 by 8 to get the value of each right. In the example each one is worth $2.22.

Ex Rights

Maritimes' rights have a very definite value, and this value accrues to the holders of the common shares. But what happens if stock is traded during the offering period? Who will receive the rights, the old owners or the new? The standard procedure calls for the company to set a "holder-of-record date", then for stock to go *ex rights* two business days prior to the holder-of-record date. If the stock is sold prior to the ex rights date, the new owner will receive the rights; if it is sold on or after the ex rights date, the old owner will receive them. For example, on October 15, Maritime might announce the terms of the new financing, stating the rights will be mailed out on December 1 to shareholders of record as of the close of business on November 15. Anyone buying the old stock on or before November 12 will receive the rights; anyone buying the stock on or after November 13 will *not* receive the rights. Thus, November 13 is the *ex rights date;* before November 13 the stock sells *rights on.* In the case of Maritime, the *rights-on price* is $100, the *ex rights price* is $97.78.

Theoretical Value of a Right

Rights On   Equations have been developed for determining the value of rights without going through all the procedures described above. While the stock is still selling rights on, the value at which the rights will sell when they are issued can be found by use of the following formula:

$$\frac{\text{Value of}}{\text{one right}} = \frac{\text{market value of stock, rights on} - \text{subscription price}}{\text{number of rights required to purchase one share plus 1}}.$$

$$R = \frac{M_0 - S}{N + 1}. \qquad (14\text{–}5)$$

Here

M_0 = the rights-on price of the stock

S = the subscription price

N = the number of rights required to purchase a new share of stock

R = the value of one right.

Substituting the appropriate values for Canadian Maritime, we obtain

$$R = \frac{\$100 - \$80}{8 + 1} = \frac{\$20}{9} = \$2.22.$$

This agrees with the value of the rights we found by the long procedure.

Ex Rights Suppose you are a shareholder in Canadian Maritime. The stock is selling ex rights for $97.78 a share. How can you calculate the theoretical value of a right? Simply using the following formula, which follows the logic described in preceding sections, you can determine the value of each right to be $2.22:

$$\frac{\text{Value of}}{\text{one right}} = \frac{\text{market value of stock, ex rights} - \text{subscription price}}{\text{number of rights required to purchase one share}}.$$

$$R = \frac{M_e - S}{N}. \qquad (14\text{–}6)$$

$$R = \frac{\$97.78 - \$80}{8} = \frac{\$17.78}{8} = \$2.22.$$

Here M_e is the ex rights price of the stock.[5]

[5] We developed Equation 14–6 directly from the verbal explanation given in the above section, "Value of a Right." Equation 14–5 can then be derived from Equation 14–6 as follows:

1. Note that

$$M_e = M_0 - R. \qquad (14\text{–}7)$$

(continued on page 354)

Instead of holding the rights and exercising them to purchase new shares, the investor can sell the rights through the stock exchange. Rights are traded on the exchange and published quotations of the trading activity are readily available. The market value of a right exceeds the theoretical value as calculated by Equation 14–6. The difference between the market and theoretical values of the right narrows as the final date to exercise the rights approaches. The reason for this difference in market and theoretical values is that when purchasing a right, the investor obtains an option to purchase a security at a fixed price. If the price of the stock increases, the price of the right increases as well. However, the percentage increase in the value of the right is much larger than the percentage increase in the value of the stock. Thus, the investor, when purchasing a right, is buying the chance to have a very large percentage increase in his or her investment.

As an example of the difference in market and theoretical values for a right, consider the Canadian Imperial Bank of Commerce rights issue. This issue permits the shareholder to purchase one new share at $24 on the basis of 1 share for each 8 shares held, i.e. 1 new share is obtained by 8 rights plus $24. The theoretical value of this right as of May 29, 1978 is $0.48 and the market value is $0.66. The theoretical value is calculated using Equation 14–6 with the following data:

$$M = 28\,\tfrac{7}{8}, S = \$24, N = 8 \qquad R = \frac{27.875 - 24}{8} = \$0.48$$

EFFECTS ON POSITION OF SHAREHOLDERS

A shareholder has the choice of exercising rights or selling them. If the shareholder has sufficient funds and desires to buy more shares of the company's stock, the shareholder will exercise the rights. If he or she does not have the money or does not want to buy more stock, then the rights can be sold. In either case, provided the formula value of the rights holds true, the shareholder will neither benefit nor lose by the rights offering. This statement can be

---

2. Substitute Equation 14–7 into Equation 14–6, obtaining

$$R = \frac{M_0 - R - S}{N}. \qquad (14\text{–}8)$$

3. Simplify Equation 14–8 as follows, ending with Equation 14–5. This completes the derivation.

$$RN = M_0 - R - S$$
$$RN + R = M_0 - S$$
$$R(N + 1) = M_0 - S \qquad (14\text{–}5)$$
$$R = \frac{M_0 - S}{N + 1}.$$

made clear by considering the position of an individual shareholder in Canadian Maritime.

The shareholder had eight shares of stock before the rights offering. The eight shares had a market value of $100 per share, so the shareholder's wealth in the equity of Canadian Maritime was $800. If he or she exercises the right, the owner now has nine shares of Maritime equity, which after the rights offer, has a value of $97.78 per share. The market value of the holdings is now $880. However, to purchase the additional share, the investor had to exercise the right at $80. Thus, the wealth of the investor is equal to the market value of the equity after the rights issue, less the investment to purchase the new share, i.e. $800. Therefore, if the investor exercises the right, the investor's wealth is not impaired.

Alternatively, if the eight rights are sold and each right has a value of $2.22, the investor would receive $17.78 in cash. But the original eight shares now have a market price of $97.78 a share. The $782.22 market value of the stock plus the $17.78 in cash is the same as the original $800 market value of the eight shares of stock. Thus, if the investor sells the rights, the investor's wealth is not effected by a rights issue. Therefore, from a theoretical point of view, the shareholder neither benefits nor loses from the sale of additional shares of stock through rights. In fact, since the market value of a right exceeds the theoretical value, it is obvious that an investor cannot be hurt by the rights issue if the investor sells the rights. If the rights are not sold, a decision has been made to forego the added income from selling them at above their theoretical value for the chance to play the option. Of course, if the owner forgets to exercise or sell the rights, or if brokerage costs of selling the rights are excessive, then a shareholder can suffer a loss. But, in general, the issuing firm makes special efforts to minimize brokerage costs, and adequate time is given to enable the shareholder to take some action, so losses are minimal.

STOCK SPLIT EFFECT [6]

We have demonstrated in the previous section that the investor is not hurt in a rights issue, even though the stock price falls when the stock sells *ex rights.* The decrease in the *ex rights* price will depend on the difference between the current market price and the subscription price. For example, in the Canadian Maritime example, where the subscription price was set at $80, the *ex rights* price was $97.78. If the subscription price were set at $10, the theoretical value of a right would be $45 and the *ex rights* price is $55. In both cases, the total amount of funds obtained is $10,000,000, so that the impact on the

[6] Stock splits are discussed in Chapter 21. Basically, a stock split is simply the issuance of additional shares to existing shareholders for *no* additional funds. Stock splits "divide the pie into more pieces". Thus, the overall market value of the equity will not change, but the per-share stock value will fall.

value of the equity must be identical. The different *ex rights* prices have no effect on the wealth of the investor but are a result of dividing the pie into more and more pieces.

For example, at a subscription price of $80 there will be 125,000 new shares issued. But at a $10 subscription price, 1,000,000 new shares are needed to raise $10 million. The latter case divides the pie into more pieces, and hence, the value per piece is lower. The stock-split effect is related directly to the difference between the stock price and the subscription price. When the two are equal, there is no stock-split effect.

There is a common error, made by some financial writers, that a rights issue is detrimental to existing shareholders since the stock price falls, *ex rights*. We can see that this conclusion is false and that the rights issue is not more detrimental than a stock split.[7]

Relation between Market Price and Subscription Price

We can now investigate the factors influencing the use of rights and, if the rights are used, the level at which the subscription price will be set. The articles of incorporation of Canadian Maritime permit it to use rights or not, depending on whether it judges their use to be advantageous to the company and its shareholders. The financial vice-president of the company is considering three alternative methods of raising the additional sum of $10 million.

Alternative 1 Maritime could sell to the public through underwriters additional shares at approximately $100 a share, the company netting approximately $96 a share; thus, it would need to sell 105,000 shares in order to cover the underwriting commission.

Alternative 2 The company could sell additional shares through rights, using underwriters and paying a commission of 1 percent on the total dollar amount of the stock sold plus an additional ¾ percent on all shares unsubscribed and taken over by the underwriters. The subscription price has been set at $80 per share. Thus, 125,000 additional shares would be offered through rights. With eight rights, an additional share could be purchased at $80.

This is called an underwritten rights issue, since any shares not subscribed to by the exercise of rights are sold to the underwriters and subjected to the ¾ percent additional commission.

Alternative 3 The company could sell additional shares through rights at $10 a share. Underwriters would not be employed at all. The number of additional shares of stock to be sold would be one million. For each right held,

---

[7] One interesting complication is the impact on the dividends and earnings per share. Just as an adjustment is made in the per share financial variables for a stock split, the same adjustment for the stock-split effect should be made for a rights issue.

existing shareholders would be permitted to buy one share of the new stock.

Under alternative 1, underwriters are used and rights would not be utilized at all. In this circumstance the underwriting commision, or issue cost, is approximately 4 percent. In alternative 2, where rights are used with a 20 percent discount, the underwriting commission is reduced, because the discount removes much of the risk of not being able to sell the issue. The underwriting commission consists of two parts — 1 percent on the original issue and an additional ¾ of 1 percent commission on all shares the underwriters are required to take over and sell. Thus, the actual commission will range somewhere between 1 percent and 1¾ percent. Under alternative 3, the subscription price is $10 a share. With such a large concession, the company does not need to use underwriters at all, because the rights are certain to have value and to be either exercised or sold. Which of the three alternatives is superior?

Alternative 1 will provide a wider distribution of the securities sold, thus lessening any possible control problems. Also, it provides assurance from the underwriters that the company will receive the $10 million involved in the new issue. The company pays for these services in the form of underwriting charges. The stock price after the issue will be slightly below $100 to reflect the diluting impact of the underwriting costs.

Under alternative 2, by utilizing rights, the company reduces its underwriting expenses. There is also a reduction in the unit price per share, from $100 to $97.78 a share. Moreover, some shareholders may neither exercise nor sell their rights, thus suffering a loss. Existing shareholders will buy some of the new shares, so the distribution is likely to be less wide. Because of the underwriting contract, the firm, under alternative 2, is also assured of receiving the funds sought. Finally, it has been argued that investors like the opportunity of purchasing additional shares through rights offerings and that the use of rights offerings increases "shareholder loyalty".

Alternative 3 involves no underwriting expense, and it results in a substantial decrease in the unit price of shares. Initially, however, the shares will be less widely distributed. Note that alternative 3 has a large stock-split effect, which results in a much lower final stock price per share. Some people feel that there is an optimal stock price—one that will produce a maximum total market value of the shares—and that this price is generally in the range of $30 to $60 a share. If this is the feeling of Maritime's directors, they may believe that alternative 3 permits them to reach this more desirable price range, while at the same time reducing issue costs. However, since the rights have a substantial value, any shareholder who fails either to exercise or sell them would suffer a serious loss.

The three alternatives are summarized in Table 14-4. The alternative that is most advantageous depends upon the company's needs. If the company is strongly interested in a wider distribution of its securities, alternative 1 is preferable. If it is more interested in reducing the underwriting cost and the unit price of its shares and believes that the lower unit price will induce wider distribution of its shares, alternative 3 will be chosen. If the company's needs are moderate in both directions, alternative 2 may offer a satisfactory compromise. Whether rights will be used and the level of the subscription price both depend upon the needs of the company at a particular time.

TABLE 14-4 Summary of Three Methods of Raising Additional Money

	Advantages	Disadvantages
Alternative 1	1. Wider distribution 2. Certainty of receiving funds	1. High underwriting costs
Alternative 2	1. Smaller underwriting costs 2. Lower unit price of shares 3. Certainty of receiving funds 4. Increase shareholder loyalty	1. More narrow distribution 2. Losses to forgetful shareholders
Alternative 3	1. No underwriting costs 2. Substantial decrease in unit price of shares 3. Increase shareholder loyalty 4. Increase probability of exercised rights	1. More narrow distribution 2. Severe losses to forgetful shareholders

Exercise of Rights

Interestingly enough, it is expected that in most cases a small percentage of shareholders may neglect to exercise their rights or to sell them. Of course, the probability that shareholders will exercise their rights will depend directly on the value of these rights.

Market Price and Subscription Price

Setting the subscription price is an important consideration, since this gives value to the rights. The subscription price must be set so that, even with a fall in the stock price of the company, the rights will still be exercised. On the expiry date of the rights issue, the rights will be exercised; and consequently, the firm will receive its funds only if the market price exceeds the subscription price. To increase the probability that this will happen, the subscription price is set well below the current market price.

Measured from the registration date for the new issue of the security, the average percentage by which the subscription prices of new issues were below their market prices has been about 15 percent in recent years.

Examples of price concessions of 40 percent or more are observed in a small percentage of issues, but the most frequently encountered discounts are from 10 to 20 percent. The larger price concessions would be given on issues which have very volatile stock prices. Conversely, regulated utilities and banks have much more stable stock prices, and the discounts on issues by these types of companies are much lower.

Effect on Subsequent Behavior of Market Price of Stock

It is often stated that new issues of stock through rights will depress the price of the existing common shares of the company. To the extent that a subscription price in connection with the rights offering is lower than the market price, there will be a "stock-split effect" on the market price of the common shares. With the prevailing market price of Maritimes' stock at $100 and a $10 subscription price, the new market price will probably drop to about $55. However, as we have seen, this is not an important issue.

The crucial question is whether, because of the rights offering, the actual new market price will be $55 or lower or higher. Again, empirical analysis of the movement in stock prices during rights offerings indicates that generalization is not practical. What happens to the market price of the stock ex rights and after the rights trading period depends upon the prospects of the issuing company.

SUMMARY

In this chapter, a number of characteristics of common share financing have been presented. The advantages of different forms and conditions of external financing have been described. The purpose of the descriptive background material has been to provide a basis for making sound decisions when financing by common shares is being considered as a possible alternative.

The chapter also discussed some important variables the financial manager must consider when deciding whether the new equity issue should be accomplished through rights or a new outside equity issue. In either case, the price of the stock after the issue will depend on the investors' expectations of the profitability of the investment of the proceeds from the equity issue.

If the financial manager has decided that a rights issue is the best method, then there are still a number of important decisions to be made. Rights offerings may be used effectively by financial managers to increase the goodwill of shareholders. If the new financing associated with the rights represents a sound decision—one likely to result in improved earnings for the firm—a rise in stock values will probably result. The use of rights will permit shareholders to preserve their positions or to improve them.

Because the rights offering is directed to existing shareholders, it may be possible to reduce the issue costs.

A major decision for financial managers in a rights offering is to set the subscription price, or the amount of the concession, from the existing market price of the stock. Formulas reflecting the static effects of a rights offering indicate that neither the shareholders nor the company benefits or loses from the price changes. The rights offering has the effect of a stock split. The level set for the subscription price will, to a great degree, reflect the objectives and effects of a stock split.

The subsequent price behavior of the rights and the common shares in the associated new offering will reflect the earnings and dividends prospects of the company, as well as the underlying developments in the securities markets. The new financing associated with the rights offering may be an indicator of prospective growth in the sales and earnings of the company. The stock-split effects of the rights offering may be used to alter the company's dividend payments. The effects of these developments on the market behavior of the rights and the securities before, during, and after the rights trading period will reflect the expectations of investors toward the outlook for earnings and dividends per share.

QUESTIONS

14-1. What percentage could total assets shrink in value on liquidation before creditors incur losses in each of the following cases:
   a. Equity to total asset ratio, 50 percent?
   b. Debt to equity ratio, 50 percent?
   c. Debt to total asset ratio, 40 percent?

14-2. How many shares must a minority group own in order to assure election of two directors if nine new directors will be elected and 200,000 shares are outstanding? Assume cumulative voting exists.

14-3. Should the preemptive right entitle shareholders to purchase convertible bonds before they are offered to outsiders?

14-4. It is frequently stated that the primary purpose of the preemptive right is to allow individuals to maintain their proportionate share of the ownership and control of a corporation. Just how important do you suppose this consideration is for the average shareholders of a firm whose shares are traded on the Toronto Stock Exchange? Is the preemptive right likely to be of more importance to shareholders of closely held firms?

14-5. How would the success of a rights offering be affected by a declining stock market?

14-6. What are some of the advantages and disadvantages of setting the subscription price on a rights offering substantially below the current market price of the stock?

14-7. Is a firm likely to get wider distribution of shares if it sells new stock through a rights offering or directly to underwriters? Why would a company be interested in getting a wider distribution of shares?

PROBLEMS

14-1. The Rolley Company Ltd. needs to raise $10 million in common shares. The price per share is now $50 for Rolley. Underwriters have informed you that they will price the new issue at $48 per share to make sure it moves out. Further, total expenses of 7.2 percent of gross proceeds will be required in the issue of this stock. How many shares of Rolley should be sold to net the firm $10 million after underpricing and issuing expenses?

14-2. The common shares of Irving Development Company Ltd. are selling for $55 on the market. The shareholders are offered one new share at a subscription price of $25 for every five shares held. What is the value of each right?

14-3. Office Equipment Co. Ltd.'s common shares are priced at $72 a share on the market. Notice is given that shareholders may purchase one new share at a price of $40 for every seven shares held. You hold 120 shares at the time of notice.

    a. At approximately what price will each right sell on the market?

    b. Why will this be the approximate price?

    c. What effect will the issuance of rights have on the original market price? Why?

14-4. Shawn has 300 shares of Piper Industries Ltd. The market price per share is $75. The company now offers shareholders one new share to be purchased at $60 for every four shares held.

    a. Determine the value of each right.

    b. Assume that Shawn (1) uses 80 rights and sells the other 220, or (2) sells 300 rights at the market price you have calculated. Prepare a statement showing the changes in her position under the above assumptions.

14-5. Abacus Company Ltd. has the following balance sheet and income statement:

The Abacus Company Ltd.

Balance Sheet before Rights Offering	Total debt (6%)	$ 7,000,000
	Common shares (100,000 shares)	3,000,000
	Retained earnings	4,000,000
Total assets $14,000,000	Total liabilities and capital	$14,000,000

Income Statement before Rights Offering

Earning rate: 12% on total assets

Total earnings	$ 1,680,000
Interest on debt	420,000
Income before taxes	$ 1,260,000
Taxes (50% rate assumed)	630,000
Earnings after taxes	$ 630,000
Earnings per share	$ 6.30
Dividends per share (56% of earnings)	$ 3.53
Price/earnings ratio	15 times
Market price per share	$94.50

Abacus plans to raise an additional $5 million through a rights offering. The additional funds will continue to earn 12 percent. The price/earnings ratio is assumed to remain at 15 times, dividend payout will continue to be 56 percent, and the 50 percent tax rate will remain in effect. (Do not attempt to use the formulas given in the chapter for this problem. Additional information is given here which violates the "other things constant" assumption inherent in the formula.)

    a. Assuming subscription prices of $25, $50, and $80 a share:

        1. How many additional shares of stock will have to be sold?

        2. How many rights will be required to purchase one new share?

        3. What will be the new earnings per share?

        4. What will be the new market price per share?

        5. What will be the new dividend per share if the dividend payout ratio is maintained?

    b. What is the significance of your results?

14-6. The Freezer-Mate Food Co. Ltd. is principally engaged in the business of growing, processing, and marketing a variety of frozen vegetables and is a major company in this field. High-quality products are produced and marketed at premium prices.

Food Processing Industry Financial Ratios

Current ratio	2.2 times
Sales to total assets	2.0 times
Sales to inventory	5.6 times
Average collection period	22.0 days
Current debt/total assets	25–30%
Long-term debt/total assets	10–15%
Preferred/total assets	0.5%
Net worth/total assets	60–65%
Profits to sales	2.3%
Net profits to total assets	4.0%
Profits to net worth	8.4%
Expected growth rate of earnings and dividends	6.5%

Freezer-Mate Food Company Ltd.
Consolidated balance sheet
March 31, 19X5* (in million of dollars)

Current assets	$141	Accounts payable	$12	
Fixed plant and equipment	57	Notes payable	36	
Other assets	12	Accruals	15	
		Total current liabilities		$ 63
		Long-term debt, 5%		63
		Preferred shares		9
		Common shares (par $6)	$12	
		Retained earnings	63	
		Net worth		75
Total assets	$210	Total claims on assets		$210

*The majority of harvesting activities do not begin until late April or May.

During each of the past several years the company's sales have increased and the needed inventories have been financed from short-term sources. The officers have discussed the idea of refinancing their bank loans with long-term debt or common shares. A stock issue of 310,000 shares sold at this time (present market price $72 a share) would yield $21 million after expenses. This same sum could be raised by selling twelve-year bonds with an interest rate of 8 percent and a sinking fund to retire the bonds over their twelve-year life. (See statements.)

a. Should Freezer-Mate Food refinance the short-term loans? Why?

b. If the bank loans should be refinanced, what factors should be considered in determining which form of financing to use? (This question should not be answered in terms of precise cost of capital calculations. Rather, a more qualitative and subjective analysis is appropriate. The only calculations necessary are some simple ratios. Careful interpretation of these ratios is necessary, however, to understand and discuss the often complex, subjective judgment issues involved.)

Freezer-Mate Food Company Ltd.
Consolidated statement of income
Year ended March 31 (in millions of dollars)

	19X2	19X3	19X4	19X5
Net sales	225.0	234.6	292.8	347.1
Cost of goods sold	146.1	156.6	195.3	230.4
Gross profit	78.9	78.0	97.5	116.7
Other expenses	61.8	66.0	81.0	88.5
Operating income	17.1	12.0	16.5	28.2
Other income (net)	(3.3)	(4.2)	(5.7)	(9.3)
Earnings before tax	13.8	7.8	10.8	18.9
Taxes	7.2	3.3	5.4	9.6
Net profit	6.6	4.5	5.4	9.3
Preferred dividend	0.3	0.3	0.3	0.3
Earnings available to common shares	$ 6.3	$ 4.2	$ 5.1	$ 9.0
Earnings per share	$ 3.15	$ 2.10	$ 2.55	$ 4.50
Cash dividends per share	1.29	1.44	1.59	1.80
Price range for common shares				
High	$ 66.00	$ 69.00	$ 66.00	$ 81.00
Low	30.00	42.00	51.00	63.00

Fixed Income Securities: Debt and Preferred Shares

15

There are many classes of fixed income securities: long term and short term, secured and unsecured, marketable and nonmarketable, participating and nonparticipating, senior and junior, and so on.

Different classes of investors favor different classes of securities, and tastes change over time. An astute financial manager knows how to "package" securities at a given point in time to make them most attractive to the most potential investors, thereby keeping the cost of capital to a minimum. This chapter deals with the two most important types of long-term, fixed income securities—bonds and preferred shares.

INSTRUMENTS OF LONG-TERM DEBT FINANCING

For an understanding of long-term forms of financing, we need some familiarity with technical terminology. The discussion of long-term debt therefore begins with an explanation of several important instruments and terms.

Bond

Most people have had some experience with short-term promissory notes. A *bond* is simply a long-term promissory note, usually secured by a specific or fixed charge on present or future real property.[1]

---

[1] *Real property* is defined as real estate—land and buildings. *Personal property* is defined as anything else; including equipment, inventories, furniture, etc.

Mortgage

A *mortgage* represents a pledge of designated property for a loan. This long-term financing is provided by life insurance companies, pension funds and trust companies on the security of real estate. Under a *mortgage bond*, the corporation pledges certain real property as security for the bond.[2] The pledge is a condition of the loan. The security of this mortgage is not necessarily found in the ability to liquidate the asset, but in the earning power of the asset.

Debenture

A *debenture* is a long-term bond that may be secured or unsecured. If it is secured, the security is a floating charge against all assets that are not specifically pledged. If it is unsecured, the debenture holder relies totally upon the earning power of the assets.

Serial Bonds and Debentures

These are bonds that are made redeemable in blocks at fixed times in the future. This is equivalent to a number of separate bond issues each with different maturity dates but all issued at the same time.

Indenture

Since a bond is a long-term promissory note, a long-term relation between the borrower and lender is established in a document called a *trust indenture* or a *trust deed.* When it is a matter of an ordinary sixty- or ninety-day promissory note, few new developments are likely to occur in the life or affairs of the borrower to endanger repayment. The lender looks closely at the borrower's current position, because current assets are the main source of repayment. A bond, however, is a long-term contractual relationship between the issuer of the bond and the bondholders; over such an extended period the bondholder has cause to worry about a number of things. These include the possibility of new security issues with a priority to interest and principal payments equal to, or higher than, their existing bonds; a reduction in the value of the security pledged for the bond; and changes in the risk characteristics of the firm's assets. The trust indenture specifies certain terms and conditions that are attached to the bond to protect the bondholder.

In the ordinary common share or preferred share certificate or agreement, the details of the contractual relation can be summarized in a few para-

---

[2] There is also the *chattel mortgage,* which is secured by personal property, but this is generally an intermediate-term instrument.

graphs. The trust indenture, however, may be a document of several hundred pages covering a large number of factors that will be important to the contractual parties. It discusses the form of the bond and the instrument. It provides a complete description of property pledged. It specifies the authorized amount of the bond issue. It contains protective clauses, or *restrictive covenants,* which are detailed and which usually include limits on indebtedness, restrictions on dividends, and a sinking fund provision. Generally a minimum current ratio requirement, as well as provisions for redemption or call privileges, are also added.

Trustee

Not only is a bond of long duration, but the issue is also likely to be of substantial size. Before the rise of the large aggregations of savings through insurance companies or pension funds, no single buyer was able to buy an issue of such size. Bonds were therefore issued in denominations of $1,000 each and were sold to a large number of purchasers. To facilitate communication between the issuer and the numerous bondholders, another device was instituted, the trustee, who is the representative of the bondholders. The trustee is presumed to act at all times for the protection of the bondholders and on their behalf. The trustee is chosen by the bondholders and is usually a department of a trust company. The trustee has the responsibility to ensure that the borrowing corporation lives up to the obligations it assumed under the terms of the trust deed. In addition, if the borrower fails to meet the conditions in the trust deed, the trustee must exercise the rights given to it under the provisions of the trust deed. Thus, the trustee is responsible for taking appropriate action on behalf of the bondholders if the corporation defaults on the payment of principal or interest, for example.

Until very recently, there was no legislation that defined the rights, terms and powers of the trustee. In fact, trust deeds included a clause which protected the trustee from liability if the trustee made a mistake in good faith. In 1970, the Business Corporations Act of Ontario was amended to include sections dealing specifically with the duties and responsibilities of trustees appointed under the terms of a trust indenture for public debt issues.[3] These changes resulted from the default on debts of the Atlantic Acceptance Corporation Limited and the Prudential Finance Corporation.[4] It was recognized that the usual trust indenture provisions did not protect the investors. Both the British Columbia and Canadian Business Corporations Acts were amended to include provisions governing the role of trustees under trust indentures.

[3]The provisions of the new sections are not applicable to private placements, since it was felt that institutions are sufficiently sophisticated to protect themselves on the loans that they make.

[4]The Trust Indenture Act of 1939 in the U.S. was passed in order to give more protection to bondholders. The impetus for this legislation was the spate of corporate bond defaults in the early 1930s in which trustees did not act in the best interests of the bondholders. For example, trustees did not conserve the assets of the corporations effectively.

Call Provision

A *call provision* gives the issuing corporation the right to call in the bond for redemption. The bonds may be callable immediately after issue, or after a pre-determined number of years, as set in the bond contract. If it is used, the call provision generally states that the company must pay an amount greater than the par value of the bond, with this additional sum being defined as the *call premium.* The call premium is typically set equal to one year's interest if the bond is called during the first year after it becomes callable, with the premium declining at a constant rate each year thereafter. For example, the call premium on a $1,000 par value, twenty-year, 8 percent bond that can be called immediately after issue would generally be $80 if called during the first year, $76 if called during the second year (calculated by reducing the $80, or 8 percent, premium by one-twentieth), and so on.

The call privilege is valuable to the firm. As interest rates decrease, the market value of the outstanding bonds will increase. If the firm wants to refinance some of its outstanding, high coupon interest rate debt, it can use the call provision. The bonds can be repurchased at the call prices, which are less than the market prices, and new debt can be issued at the lower interest rates. This refunding decision will be analyzed later in this chapter.

If the call provision is of potential benefit to the company, it must be potentially detrimental to the investor, especially if the bond is issued in a period when interest rates are thought to be cyclically high. To protect them-selves, the bondholders of a callable bond will ask for a higher interest rate. Therefore, the interest rate on a new issue of callable bonds will exceed that on a new issue of noncallable bonds. The difference in interest rates will depend on the probability that the bonds will be called and on the expected life of the bond until it is called.

Sinking Fund

A *sinking fund* is a provision that facilitates the orderly retirement of a bond issue. Typically, the sinking fund provision requires the firm to buy and retire a portion of the bond issue each year. Sometimes the stipulated sinking fund payment is tied to sales or earnings of the current year, but usually it is a mandatory fixed amount. If it is mandatory, a failure to meet the sinking fund payment causes the bond issue to be thrown into default and could lead the company into bankruptcy. Obviously, then, a sinking fund can constitute a dangerous cash drain on the firm. Without a sinking fund provision, the bond-holders are exposing themselves to the risk that, at the maturity date, the company will not have sufficient liquid assets from normal operations to repay the principal; or that the company will not have access to capital markets to issue debt or equity securities to repay the principal.

There are two types of sinking funds that can be used. The first, called a *general sinking fund,* invests the sinking fund payment in securities, usually government bonds, that will mature at the same time as the bond issue. The second, and more common, is the *specific sinking fund* in which the payment is invested in the particular issue concerned. The firm is given the right to handle a specific sinking fund in either of two ways. (1) It may call a certain percentage of the bonds at a stipulated price each year—usually par plus accrued interest—and the actual bonds to be called, which are numbered serially, are determined by a lottery. (2) It may spend the funds provided by the sinking fund payment to buy the bonds on the open market. The firm will do whichever results in the greatest reduction of outstanding bonds for a given expenditure. Therefore, if interest rates have risen (and the price of the bonds has fallen), the firm will choose the open market alternative. If interest rates have fallen and bond prices have risen, the company will elect to use the option of calling bonds.

It must be recognized that the call provision of the sinking fund may at times work to the detriment of bondholders. If, for example, the bond carries a 7 percent interest rate, and if yields on similar securities are 4 percent, the bond will sell for well above par. A sinking fund call at par would thus greatly disadvantage some bondholders. On balance, securities that provide for a sinking fund and continuing redemption are likely to be offered initially on a lower yield basis than are securities without such a fund. Since sinking funds provide additional protection to investors, sinking fund bonds are likely to sell initially at higher prices; hence, they have a lower cost of capital to the issuer.

Funded Debt

Funded debt is simply long-term debt. When a firm is said to be planning to "fund" its floating debt, it will replace short-term securities by long-term securities. Funding does not imply placing money with a trustee or other repository; it is simply part of the jargon of finance and means "long term".

Retractable Bonds

The bondholder has the opportunity to sell the bonds back to the issuer at the par value of the bond at a specified time before the maturity date; these conditions are stipulated in the bond contract. The holder must give the issuer advance notice of his or her intention to sell the bond. This retractable feature is a form of option available to the bondholder which is equivalent to permitting the bondholder to reduce the maturity of the bond. As an example, consider Trizec Corporation Ltd. which issued $25 million, 10½ percent senior debentures on April 5, 1978, which would mature June 1, 1998. The bonds include a retractable feature which permit the bondholder to sell the bond back to Trizec on June 1, 1988. If the bondholder elects to use this feature, the maturity of the bond is reduced. Notice of intention to exercise this option must be made after September 1, 1987, and before December 1, 1987.[5]

This retractable feature is of benefit to bondholders if interest rates have increased above the coupon rate. For example, if before December 1, 1987, interest rates exceed the 10½ percent on the Trizec issue, then the price of the bond will be below par. If the bondholder were to sell, a capital loss would result. By exercising the retraction option, the bondholder can sell the bonds without incurring a capital loss and use the proceeds to invest in higher yielding bonds. This retraction feature is the bondholder's analogue to the corporation's inclusion of the call feature.

Extendible Bonds

Extendible bonds are short-term bonds which provide the bondholder with the option to exchange the short-term debt for a similar amount of long-term debt, on or before a specified date, at an interest rate determined at the date of the original issue. Thus, the extendible bond provides the option to increase the maturity of the debt. This option will be exercised only if, at the date when the option must be exercised, the interest rates on new debt are less than the interest rate on the debt that could be obtained from using the extendible feature. Just as in retractable bonds, this option has the potential to be of value to the bondholder, and hence, the yield on an extendible bond should be lower than on a similar bond without the extendible feature.

SECURED BONDS

Secured long-term debt may be classified according to (1) the priority of claims, (2) the right to issue additional securities, and (3) the scope of the lien.

Priority of Claims

A *senior* or *first mortgage bond* has prior claim on assets and earnings. A *junior mortgage bond* is a subordinated lien, such as a second or third mortgage; and it has a claim or lien junior to others.

Right to Issue Additional Securities

Mortgage bonds may also be classified with respect to the right to issue additional obligations pledging already encumbered property.

In the case of a *closed-end mortgage,* a company may not sell additional bonds, beyond those already issued, secured by the property specified in the

---

[5]The Trizec bond permits the company to increase the rate of interest payable after June 1, 1988, provided notice of the increase has been given on or before December 15, 1987.

mortgage. For example, assume that a corporation with plant and land worth $5 million has a $2 million mortgage on these properties. If the mortgage is closed end, no more bonds having first liens on this property may be issued. Thus a closed-end mortgage provides greater security to the bond buyer. The ratio of the amount of the senior bonds to the value of the property will not be increased by subsequent issues.

If the bond indenture is silent on this point, it is called an *open-end mortgage*. Its nature may be illustrated by referring to the example cited above. Against property worth $5 million, bonds of $2 million are sold. If an additional first mortgage bond of $1 million is subsequently sold, the property has been pledged for a total of $3 million of bonds. If, on liquidation, the property sold for $2 million, the original bondholders would receive 67 cents on the dollar. If the mortgage had been closed end, they would have been fully paid.

Most characteristic is the *limited open-end mortgage*. Its nature may be indicated by continuing the example. A first mortgage bond issue of $2 million, secured by the property worth $5 million, is sold. The indenture provides that an additional $1 million worth of bonds—or an additional amount of bonds up to 60 percent of the original cost of the property—may be sold. Thus, the mortgage is open only up to a certain point.

Scope of the Lien

Bonds may also be classified with respect to the scope of their lien. When a *specific lien* exists, the security for a first mortgage or a second mortgage is a specifically designated property. A lien is granted on certain specified property. On the other hand, a *blanket mortgage* pledges all real property currently owned by the company. Real property includes only land and those things affixed thereto, so a blanket mortgage would not be a mortgage on cash, accounts receivables, or inventories because these items are personal property. A blanket mortgage gives more protection to the bondholder than does a specific mortgage because it provides a claim on all real property owned by the company.

UNSECURED BONDS

Debentures

A *debenture* is an unsecured bond and, as such, provides no lien on specific property as security for the obligation. Debenture holders are therefore general creditors whose claim is protected by property not otherwise pledged. The advantage of debentures from the standpoint of the issuer is that property is left unencumbered for subsequent financing. However, in practice the use of debentures depends on the nature of the firm's assets and its general credit strength.

If the credit position of a firm is exceptionally strong, it can issue debentures—it simply does not need specific security. However, the credit position of a company may be so weak that it has no alternative to the use of debentures—all its property may already be encumbered. Currently, Bell Canada is issuing debentures to obtain the debt financing it requires. However, Bell Canada does have first mortgage bonds outstanding which are secured by a first mortgage and a floating charge. Due to some covenants in the first mortgage bond indenture that restricted Bell's flexibility to issue new first mortgage bonds, Bell closed the first mortgage indenture and issues only debentures under a more flexible trust indenture. Bell is a sufficiently strong company that it does not have to provide specific security for its debt issues.

Debentures are also issued by companies in industries where it would

TABLE 15–1 Illustration of Bankruptcy Payments to Senior Debt, Other Debt, and Subordinated Debt

Financial Structure	Book Value (1)	Percent of Total Debt (2)	Initial Allocation (3)	Actual Payment (4)	Percent of Original Claim Satisfied (5)
I. $200 available for claims on liquidation					
Bank debt	$200	50%	$100	$150	75%
Other debt	100	25	50	50	50
Subordinated debt	100	25	50	0	0
Total debt	$400	100%	$200	$200	50%
Net worth	300				0
Total	$700				29%
II. $300 available for claims on liquidation					
Bank debt	$200	50%	$150	$200	100%
Other debt	100	25	75	75	75
Subordinated debt	100	25	75	25	25
Total debt	$400	100%	$300	$300	75%
Net worth	300				0
Total	$700				43%

Steps: 1. Express each type of debt as a percentage of total debt (column 2).
2. Multiply the debt percentages (column 2) by the amount available, obtaining the initial allocations shown in column 3.
3. The subordinated debt is subordinate to bank debt. Therefore, the initial allocation to subordinate debt is added to the bank debt allocation until it has been exhausted or until the bank debt is finally paid off. This is given in column 4.

not be practical to provide a lien through a mortgage on fixed assets. Examples of such an industry would be the large mail order houses and the finance companies, which characteristically do not have large fixed assets in relation to their total assets. The bulk of their assets is in the form of inventory or receivables, neither of which is satisfactory security for a mortgage lien.

Subordinated Debentures

The term "subordinate" means below or inferior. Thus, *subordinated debt* has claims on assets after unsubordinated debt in the event of liquidation. Debentures may be subordinated to designated notes payable—usually bank loans—or to any or all other debt. In the event of liquidation or reorganization, the debentures cannot be paid until senior debt *as named in the indenture* has been paid. Senior debt typically does not include trade accounts payable. How the subordination provision strengthens the position of senior-debt holders is shown in Table 15–1.

Where $200 is available for distribution, the subordinated debt has a claim on 25 percent of $200, or $50. However, this claim is subordinated only to the bank debt (the only senior debt) and is added to the $100 claim of the bank. As a consequence, 75 percent of the bank's original claim is satisfied.

Where $300 is available for distribution, the $75 allocated to the subordinated debt is divided into two parts: $50 goes to the bank and the other $25 remains for the subordinated debt holders. In this situation, the senior bank debt holders are fully paid off, 75 percent of other debt is paid, and the subordinated debt receives only 25 percent of its claim.

Subordination is frequently required. Alert credit managers of firms supplying trade credit, or chartered bank loan officers, typically will insist upon subordination, particularly where debt is owed to the principal shareholders or officers of a company. Also, convertible bonds are virtually always subordinated; in this case, they are subordinated to all the firm's other debt.

Preferred shares, in comparison to subordinated debt, suffer from the disadvantage that preferred share dividends are not deductible as an expense for tax purposes. The interest on subordinated debentures is an expense for tax purposes. Some people have referred to subordinated debentures as being much like a special kind of preferred shares, the dividends of which are deductible as an expense for tax purposes. Subordinated debt has therefore become an increasingly important source of corporate capital.

The reasons for the use of subordinated debentures are clear. They offer tax advantages over preferred shares,[6] yet they do not restrict the ability of the borrower to obtain senior debt, as would be the case if all debt sources

---

[6]The introduction of the dividend tax credit has reduced the benefit of debt over preferred shares. With the very favorable treatment of preferred dividends, individuals will purchase preferred shares at much lower, before-personal-tax yields. Thus, the dividend yield cost of preferreds has decreased.

were on an equal basis.

Subordinated debentures are further stimulated by periods of tight money when chartered banks may require a greater equity base for short-term financing. Subordinated debentures provide a greater equity cushion for loans from chartered banks or other forms of senior debt. The use of subordinated debentures also illustrates the development of hybrid securities that emerge to meet changing situations that develop in the capital market.

Income Bonds

Income bonds typically arise from corporate reorganizations, and these bonds pay interest only if there is sufficient net income or profit to meet the obligation. Because the company, having gone through reorganization, has been in difficult financial circumstances, interest is not a fixed charge; the principal, however, must be paid when due. Income bonds are not very common in Canada. In the United States, a number of income bonds resulted from re-organizations of railroad companies.

Income bonds are like preferred shares in that management is not required to pay interest if it is not earned. However, they differ from preferred shares in that, if interest has been earned, management is required to pay it. Since the interest payment is out of profits and is not a fixed charge, the payment is treated as a dividend payment and is *not* deductible for income tax purposes. In order to qualify as an income bond, there must be no fixed element in the interest payment.

Since the income bond is basically a risky obligation from the point of view of the payment of interest, it is usually issued on a secured basis. This security can cover either just the principal repayment, or the interest as well. If the security covers the latter, court decisions in the United States have found that the income bondholder can effectively define income and expenses. However, it is usual for the bond indenture to define profits in the former case as well.

Some income bonds have cumulative interest payments (if interest is not paid it "accumulates" and can be paid at some future date). However, the accumulated interest payments can be paid only out of profits earned during the maturity of the income bond.

Income bonds may contain sinking fund provisions to provide for their retirement. The payments to the sinking funds range between ½ and 1 percent of the face amount of the original issue. Because the sinking fund payments are typically dependent on earnings, a fixed-cash drain on the company is avoided.

Some income bonds have been issued with convertible features. There are sound reasons for their being convertible if they arise out of a reorganization. Creditors who receive income bonds in exchange for defaulted obligations have a less desirable position than they had previously. Since they have received something based on an adverse and problematical forecast of the future of the company, it is appropriate that if the company should prosper, income bondholders should be entitled to participate. When income bonds are issued in situations other than reorganization, the convertibility feature is a "sweetener" likely to make the issue more attractive to prospective bond buyers.

Finally, income bonds do not have voting rights when they are issued. Sometimes bondholders are given the right to elect one, two, or some specified number of directors if interest is not paid for a certain number of years.

Foreign Currency Bonds

For a number of Canadian corporations and all levels of government, the capital market in which bonds can be issued has expanded beyond the geographical boundaries of Canada. The bond market has become international and a Canadian corporation can now issue debt that is denominated in a foreign currency with principal and interest payments made in that currency. Given that the financial manager wants to issue bonds in a foreign currency, the next decision is to determine which of two types of markets to use. The first market is called the *foreign bond market* and the bond is issued to investors in a particular country in the currency of that country. The interest rate on the bonds will be based on the investors' domestic rate. For example, a Canadian company might sell bonds in German Deutchmarks, but the bulk of these foreign borrowings are placed in the United States. Canadian governments are very active in this market, and corporate debt sold in the U.S. is issued mainly, but not exclusively, by regulated utilities.

The second market in which the foreign currency bond can be sold is called the *Eurobond market*. This market is based in Europe and includes bonds sold to investors in a foreign country, denominated in a currency other than the domestic currency of the investor. For example, a Canadian company can sell Eurobonds denominated in U.S. dollars to investors in Germany. The principal and interest payments are made in U.S. dollars and the investor, in turn, can convert these payments to domestic currency if he or she wishes.

Advantages The issuer of foreign currency bonds has the following advantages:

1. Some companies require a large amount of debt financing. To the extent that the Canadian capital market cannot handle these issues, the international bond market opens up new pools of funds.
2. There is the potential for an interest rate savings, since the foreign currency borrowings are related to the lower interest rates in the foreign countries, relative to Canada, after adjusting for the current exchange rate.

3. Companies with sales in foreign countries can reduce exchange rate risk by borrowing in the foreign currencies in which their sales are made.[7]

Disadvantage   The major disadvantage of foreign currency borrowing is the exchange rate risk incurred by the borrowing company. Since the bond is denominated in a foreign currency, fluctuations in exchange rates will be reflected in the actual amount of Canadian dollars necessary to service the interest payments and to repay the principal. For example, suppose U.S. bond rates are 8½ percent, Canadian rates are 10 percent, and the exchange rate is $1 U.S. = $1.10 Canadian. Then an issue in U.S. dollars at 8½ percent requires a Canadian payment of $93.50 per $1000 bond. This is less than the $100 interest payment required if the bond were issued in Canada.

However, exchange rates fluctuate and this can either increase or reduce the Canadian dollar cost to service the interest payments fixed in terms of the foreign currency. For example, suppose that the exchange rate became $1 U.S. = $1.20 Canadian. Then, to service the $85.00 U.S. interest payment per $1000 bond requires $102.00 Canadian; the interest expense on the debt has increased. This, in fact, is what happened to a number of provincial and corporate borrowers in late 1978. Obviously, financial managers are aware of this risk and require a sufficiently large differential in yields between the foreign currency and the Canadian interest rates to compensate for this risk.

CHARACTERISTICS OF LONG-TERM DEBT

From Viewpoint of Holder

Risk   Debt is favorable to the holder because it gives him priority both in earnings and in liquidation. Debt also has a definite maturity and is protected by the covenants of the indenture.

Income   The bondholder has a fixed return; except in the case of income bonds, interest payments are not contingent on the level of earnings of the company. However, debt does not participate in any superior earnings of the company, and gains are limited in magnitude. Note particularly that bondholders suffer during periods of *unanticipated* inflation. A twenty-year, 10 percent bond pays $100 of interest (per $1000 of par value) each year. Since investors try to protect themselves from expected inflation, the 10 percent coupon includes the market's expectation of the inflation rate. If inflation is greater than anticipated, then the purchasing power of the $100 payment is

---

[7]One investment dealer has suggested that the growth of the Eurobond market is a result of the desire by corporate financial managers to visit Geneva or other European financial centers.

eroded more than was expected, and this causes a loss in real value to the bondholder.[8] Frequently, long-term debt is callable. If bonds are called, the investor receives funds that must be reinvested to be kept active. Alternatively, bonds can be extendible or retractable. These are options that are exercised by the bondholder and result in a lengthening or a shortening of the maturity date of the original debt instrument.

Control   The bondholder usually does not have the right to vote. However, if the bonds go into default, then bondholders will, in effect, take control of the company.

An overall appraisal of the characteristics of long-term debt indicates that for the investor it is good from the standpoint of risk, has limited advantages with regard to income, and is weak with respect to control.

From Viewpoint of Issuer

Advantages   The issuer of a bond has the following advantages.

1. The cost of debt is definitely limited. Bondholders do not participate in superior profits if earned.
2. Not only is the cost limited, but the expected yield is lower than the cost of common equity to the same company.
3. The owners of the corporation do not share their control when debt financing is used.
4. Except for income bonds, the interest payments on debt are a tax-deductible expense.
5. Flexibility in the financial structure of the corporation may be achieved by inserting a call provision in the bond indenture.

Disadvantages   Following are the disadvantages to the bond issuer.

1. Debt is a fixed charge; there is greater risk if the earnings of the company fluctuate because the corporation may be unable to meet these fixed charges.
2. As we will see in Chapter 18, higher risk brings higher capitalization rates on equity earnings. In addition, the increasing debt levels may increase the probability of default and the associated costs of bankruptcy. Thus, even though leverage can be favorable and raises earnings per share, the increased probability of default, along with the higher capitalization rate, may drive down the value of the common shares.
3. Debt usually has a definite maturity date. Because of the fixed maturity date, the financial officer must make provision for repayment of the debt.

---

[8]Recognizing this fact, investors demand higher interest rates during inflationary periods. This point is discussed at length in Chapter 18.

4. Since long-term debt is a commitment for a long period, it involves risk; the expectations and plans on which the debt was issued may change. The debt may prove to be a burden, or it may prove to have been advantageous. For example, if income, employment, the price level, and interest rates all fall greatly, the assumption of a large amount of long-term debt may prove to have been an unwise financial policy. U.S. railroads are always given as an example in this regard. They were able to meet their ordinary operating expenses during the 1930s but were unable to meet the heavy financial charges they had undertaken earlier, when the prospects for the railroads looked more favorable than they turned out to be.

5. In a long-term contractual relationship, the indenture provisions are likely to be much more stringent than they are in a short-term credit agreement. Hence the firm may be subject to much more disturbing and crippling restrictions in the indenture of a long-term debt arrangement than would be the case if it had borrowed on a short-term basis or had issued common shares.

6. There is a limit on the extent to which funds can be raised through long-term debt. Generally accepted standards of financial policy dictate that the debt ratio shall not exceed certain limits. These standards of financial prudence set limits or controls on the extent to which funds may be raised through long-term debt. When debt gets beyond these limits, its cost rises rapidly.

Bond Ratings

The important element in determining the yield on bonds is the risk of default. This default risk is more general than the extreme case of bankruptcy; it includes instances where interest payments are not met in full when they are due. In deciding whether or not to purchase a debt instrument, the potential bondholder evaluates the risk of default and decides whether the promised yield on the bond is sufficient to compensate for the risk.

In the United States, Moodys, and Standard and Poors are the two agencies which evaluate the default risk on bonds and provide a rating consistent with their perceptions of the default risk. In Canada, the Canadian Bond Rating Services (CBRS) was formed to rate bonds of Canadian companies. This rating service, like the U.S. services, has three general rating categories: A, B and C. Bonds in the A category have a long history of earnings and asset protection, and it is expected that the protection afforded to the bondholder will be maintained in the future. Within this A category, there are three rankings—A^{++}, A^+, and A. The first is the highest quality, and as the protection afforded to the bondholder falls, the rating falls. For example, Bell Canada has two classes of debt. The first mortgage bonds have an A^{++} rating, and the general debentures (with somewhat lower protection) have an A^+ rating. The top rating in the B category, B^{++}, is given to bonds that are of medium or average credits and are considered investment quality. The B$^+$ rating reflects protection to bondholders which is modest or unstable. The lowest rate in this category, B, is given to companies which lack most qualities for long-term investment; protection to bondholders is poor and the operating conditions of the companies are volatile. Finally, a C rating is given to speculative bonds.[9]

There has been considerable research to identify those variables that appear to be important in explaining the ratings assigned to the debt of various companies. The variables that have been identified include company size, earnings instability, leverage, interest coverage and subordination. These studies have investigated both U.S. and Canadian ratings. Finally, short-term corporate paper is also rated by CBRS and by the Dominion Bond Rating Service.

To the extent that bond ratings capture differences in default risk, there should be observed differentials in yields to maturity between different rating categories. In Figure 15–1, the yields are presented for long-term corporate bonds by rating category and Government of Canada bonds from mid-1976 to mid-1978. As expected, Governments have the lowest yields, whereas the highest risk category, B^{++}/BBB, have the highest yields. The yields on the other rating categories reflect the default risk in each category.

FIGURE 15-1   Recently Issued/Actively Traded Long Term Corporate Bonds by Rating Category

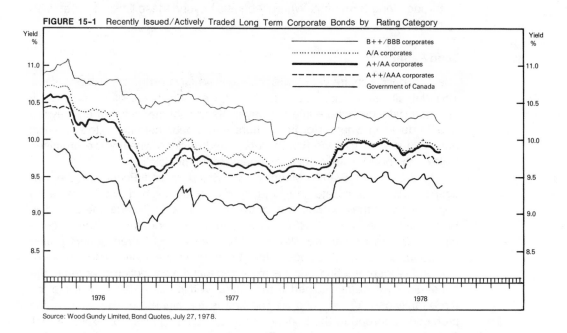

Source: Wood Gundy Limited, Bond Quotes, July 27, 1978.

[9]The description of the protection from default and the investment quality of the bonds classified in the different categories is based on the discussion in the CBRS manual.

DECISIONS ON USE OF LONG-TERM DEBT

When a number of alternative methods of long-term financing are under consideration, the following conditions favor the use of long-term debt:

1. Sales and earnings are relatively stable, or a substantial increase in future sales and earnings is expected to provide a significant benefit from the use of leverage.
2. The market has expectations that there will be an increase in the price level; however, the financial manager has expectations that the price level will increase more than is expected by the market. Under this condition, it is advantageous for the firm to incur debt that will be repaid with cheaper dollars.
3. The existing debt ratio is relatively low for the line of business.
4. Management thinks the price of the common shares in relation to that of bonds is temporarily depressed.
5. Sale of common shares would involve problems of maintaining the existing control pattern in the company.

Decisions about the use of debt may also be considered in terms of the average cost of capital curve as developed in Chapter 20. There we will see that firms have optimal capital structures, or perhaps optimal ranges, and that the average cost of capital is higher than it need be if the firm uses a non-optimal amount of debt. The factors listed above all relate to the optimal debt ratio: Some cause the optimal ratio to increase; others cause it to decrease.

Whenever the firm is contemplating raising new outside capital and is choosing between debt and equity, it is implicitly making a judgment about its actual debt ratio in relation to the optimal ratio. For example, consider Figure

FIGURE 15-2 The Longstreet Co. Ltd.'s Average Cost of Capital Schedule

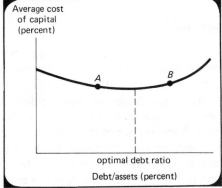

15-2, which shows the assumed shape of the Longstreet Co. Ltd.'s average cost of capital schedule. If Longstreet is planning to raise outside capital, it must make a judgment about whether it is presently at point *A* or point *B*. If it decides that it is at *A*, it should issue debt; if it believes that it is at *B*, the decision should be to sell new common shares. This, of course, is a judgment decision, but all the factors discussed in this chapter must be considered when the decision is being made. This subject is discussed further in Chapter 20.

NATURE OF PREFERRED SHARES

The term "preferred share" is not used in either the Ontario or Canada Business Corporations Acts. In the former Act, there are a number of different classes of shares permissible; one of which must be common shares with voting rights. If the corporation has more than one class of shares, the other classes can be called preference shares if they have some preference or right over common shares. Note, however, that the preference or right is broader than just a prior claim to dividend payments. In the Canada Business Corporation Act, the firm may have different classes of shares and each class has different privileges, restrictions and conditions. Although at least one class must have voting rights, this need not be the common shares.

Contrary to the letter of the two acts referred to above and consistent with our attempt to highlight concepts, we will use the term "preferred share" to refer to that class of shares with the following three basic attributes:

(i) non-voting under normal circumstances;

(ii) preference on payment of either dividends or assets (in the event of liquidation), or both; and

(iii) claims and rights behind all bondholders.

This section will investigate these attributes as well as other "bells and whistles" added to alter the risk and expected return attached to the preferred shares.

Hybrid Form

The hybrid nature of preferred shares becomes apparent when we try to classify it in relation to bonds and common shares. The priority feature and the (generally) fixed dividend indicate that preferred shares are similar to bonds. Payments to the preferred shareholders are limited in amount so that the common shareholders receive the advantages (or disadvantages) of leverage. However, if the preferred dividends are not earned, the company can forgo paying them without danger of bankuptcy. In this characteristic, preferred shares are similar to common shares. Moreover, failure to pay the stipulated dividend does not cause default of the obligation, as does failure to pay bond interest.

Debt and Equity   In some types of analysis, preferred shares are treated similarly to debt. For example, if the analysis is being made by a *common shareholder* considering the earnings fluctuations induced by fixed-charge securities, preferred shares would be treated like debt. Suppose, however, that the analysis is by a *bondholder* studying the firm's vulnerability to *failure* brought on by declines in sales or in income. Since the dividends on preferred shares are not a fixed charge in the sense that failure to pay them would represent a default of an obligation, preferred shares represent a cushion. They provide an additional equity base. From the point of view of *shareholders,* they are a leverage-inducing instrument much like debt. From the point of view of *creditors,* they constitute additional net worth. Preferred shares may therefore be treated either as debt or as equity, depending on the nature of the problem under consideration.[10]

MAJOR PROVISIONS OF PREFERRED SHARE ISSUES

Because the possible characteristics, rights, and obligations of any specific security vary so widely, a point of diminishing returns is quickly reached in a descriptive discussion of different kinds of securities. As economic circumstances change, new kinds of securities are manufactured. The possibilities are numerous. The kinds and varieties of securities are limited chiefly by the imagination and ingenuity of the managers formulating the terms of the security issues. It is not surprising, then, that preferred shares can be found in a variety of forms. We will now look at the main terms and characteristics in each case and examine the possible variations in relation to the kinds of situations or circumstances in which they could occur.

Priority in Assets and Earnings

Many provisions in a preferred share certificate are designed to reduce risk to the purchaser in relation to the risk carried by the holder of common shares. Preferred shares usually have priority with regard to earnings and assets. Two provisions designed to prevent undermining these preferred share priorities are often found. The first states that, without the consent of the holders of the preferred shares, there can be no subsequent sale of securities having a piror or equal claim on earnings, and no conversion of shares from a class with a lower priority to a class with priority equal to or greater than the priority on the preferred shares. The second provision is an attempt to prevent the company from dissipating the assets through dividend payments to common equity. These negative covenants on dividend distribution require a minimum level of retained earnings before common share dividends are permitted to be paid. In

---

[10]Accountants generally include preferred shares in the equity portion of the capital structure. But preferred is *very different* from common equity.

order to assure the availability of liquid assets that may be converted into cash for the payment of dividends, the maintenance of a minimum current ratio may also be required.

Par Value

Unlike common shares, preferred shares usually have a par value, and this value is a meaningful quantity. First, it establishes the amount due to the preferred shareholders in the event of liquidation. Second, the preferred dividend is requently stated as a percentage of the par value. For example, British Columbia Telephone has a 10.16 percent cumulative preferred share with a par value of $25. The annual dividend to be paid on the preferred share is $2.54. On many preferred shares, dividends are stated in dollar amounts rather than as a percent of par value.

Cumulative Dividends

Unless there is an explicit statement in the indenture to the contrary, dividends on preferred shares are *cumulative*—all past preferred dividends must be paid before common dividends may be paid. The cumulative feature is therefore a protective device. If the preferred shares were not cumulative, preferred and common share dividends could be passed by for a number of years. The directors of the company could then vote a large dividend on the common shares, but only the stipulated payment to preferred. Suppose the preferred shares with a par value of $100 carried a 7 percent dividend. Suppose the company did not pay dividends for several years so that it accumulated funds that would enable it to pay in total about $50 in dividends. It could pay one $7 dividend to each preferred share and a $43 dividend to each common share. Obviously, this device could be used to evade the preferred position that the holders of preferred shares have tried to obtain. The cumulative feature prevents such evasion.[11]

Large arrearages on preferred shares would make it difficult to resume dividend payments on common shares. To avoid delays in beginning common share dividend payments again, a compromise arrangement with the holders of common shares is likely to be worked out. A package offer is one possibility; for example, a recapitalization plan may provide for an exchange of shares. The arrearage will be wiped out by the donation of common shares with a value equal to the amount of the preferred dividend arrearage, and the holders of preferred shares are thus given an ownership share in the corporation. In addition, resumption of current dividends on the preferred may be promised. Whether these provisions are worth anything depends on the future earnings prospects of the company.

[11]Note, however, that compounding is absent in most cumulative plans. In other words, the arrearages themselves earn no return.

The advantage to the company of substituting common shares for dividends in arrears is that it can start again with a clean balance sheet. If earnings recover, dividends can be paid to the holders of the common shares without making up arrearages to the holders of preferred shares. The original common shareholders, of course, will have given up a portion of their ownership of the corporation.

Convertibility

A substantial proportion of the preferred shares that have been issued in recent years are convertible into common shares. For example, one share of a particular preferred could be convertible into 2.5 shares of the firm's common shares at the option of the preferred shareholder. The nature of convertibility is discussed in Chapter 17.

Use of Series

The company may from time to time want to issue more preferred shares. Given that conditions in the capital market change, both the preferences and the dividends on these subsequent issues of preferred shares may be different than was found in the original issue. To eliminate the costs of calling a shareholders meeting to ratify the terms of the new issue, the company can make use of the *series provision*. For a given class of shares, there is an authorized amount of capital. As the company requires new issues within this class, each issue will be designated as a series. Each series issue may differ with respect to the dividend payment and certain preferences—for example, conversion, compulsory redemption, and so on. However, all series within the class must have the same overall creditor position. If the company wishes to issue a preferred share with a higher priority than the existing preferreds, it must create a new class of shares which requires the vote of the classes junior to this class.

As an example, Canadian Utilities Limited has a class of preferred shares denoted "Series Second Preferred Shares". Of the 3,952,000 shares authorized, there were series A and B outstanding as of July 31, 1977, with 2,752,000 shares issued. The company issued the remaining shares as Series C within the same overall class. This class of shares ranks lower in priority than the First Preferred Shares class with respect to dividends and distribution on liquidation.

Some Additional Provisions

Some of the other provisions occasionally encountered in preferred shares include the following.

Voting Rights   Sometimes preferred shares are given the right to vote for directors. When this feature is present, it generally permits the preferred shareholders to elect a *minority* of the board, say three out of nine directors. The voting privilege becomes operative only if the company has not paid the preferred dividend for a specified period, for example, six, eight, or ten quarters, or the dividend arrearage is greater than a specified dollar amount.

Sinking Fund   Some preferred issues have a sinking fund requirement. When they do, the sinking fund ordinarily calls for the purchase and retirement of a given percentage of the preferred shares each year.

Maturity   Preferred shares almost never have maturity dates on which they must be retired. However, if the issue has a sinking fund, this effectively creates a maturity date, since some of the shares are retired under the sinking fund provision.

Participation   The conditions on a preferred share may provide for participation with the common shares in any dividends after there has been a dividend payment to the common equal to that paid to the preferred. The terms under which this participation takes place must be specified in the articles of incorporation. In addition, there may be participation with the common in the liquidation of a company.

Redemption   The issuing corporation has the right, if specified, to call in the preferred shares for redemption; this is the same as for bonds. If the stock has a par value, the redemption terms are set as a premium above par value; the maximum premium is 20 percent. For some issues, the redemption premium decreases over time. For example, the Canadian Utilities Limited issue, with a $25 par value is redeemable on or after November 15, 1982, at the option of the company at $26.00. However, the redemption price falls, and after November 15, 1987, there is no premium on redemption. If the preferred shares have no par value, the terms under which the stock can be redeemed must be written into the contract. Before redemption can occur, all current dividends and those in arrears must be paid.

Purchase for Cancellation   To add flexibility in their financing plans, the company may add a provision which permits the purchase of shares for cancellation directly from the shareholders. The maximum prices for these purchases are set equal to the redemption price (or prices). Unlike the redemption provision, the company does not have the power to force the sale; shareholders need not accept the offer. This provision is not the same as the repurchase of shares through the market; the repurchase of preferred shares is permitted in some jurisdictions. Share repurchase will be considered in Chapter 21.

EVALUATION OF PREFERRED SHARES

From Viewpoint of Issuer

An important advantage of preferred shares from the viewpoint of the issuer is that, in contrast to bonds, the obligation to make fixed interest payments is avoided. Also, a firm wishing to expand because its earning power is high may obtain higher earnings for the original owners by selling preferred shares with a limited return rather than by selling common equity.

Advantages   By selling preferred shares, the financial manager avoids the provision of equal participation in earnings that the sale of additional common shares would require. Preferred shares also permit a company to avoid sharing control through participation in voting. In contrast to bonds, it enables the firm to conserve mortgagable assets. Since preferred shares typically have no maturity and no sinking fund, they are more flexible than bonds.

Disadvantages   Characteristically, preferred shares must be sold on a higher yield basis than that for bonds.[12] Preferred share dividends are not deductible as a tax expense, a characteristic that makes their cost differential very great in comparison with that of bonds. As we shall see in Chapter 20, the after-tax cost of debt is approximately half the stated coupon rate for profitable firms. The cost of preferred, however, is the full percentage amount of the preferred dividend. This fact should have a dampening effect on the use of preferred shares.[13]

From Viewpoint of Investor

In fashioning securities, the financial manager needs to consider the investor's point of view. Frequently it is asserted that preferred shares have so many disadvantages both to the issuer and to the investor that they should never be issued. Nevertheless, preferred shares are issued in substantial amounts.

Advantages   Preferred shares provide the following advantages to the

---

[12]Historically, a given firm's preferred shares generally carried higher rates than its bonds because of the greater risk inherent in preferred shares from the holder's viewpoint. However, the fact that inter-corporate dividends are tax free and that the dividend tax credit makes dividends very attractive to investors with low marginal federal tax rates has lead to an increased demand for preferred shares, and hence lower yields. In recent years, high-grade preferreds have sold on a lower yield basis than high-grade bonds. For example, as of August 11, 1978, B.C. Telephone's, 4½ percent preferred was selling to yield 7.6 percent, whereas the debt of the same company yielded from 9.3 to 9.8 percent depending on the maturity of the debt issue. Thus, bond yields were well in excess of preferred yields. The tax treatment on dividends accounted for this differential. However, the *after-tax yield* to the investor was greater on the preferred shares than on the bonds.

[13]However, it must be remembered that the purchaser of debt must pay taxes on the interest payments at regular income tax rates which are in excess of the rate on dividends or capital gains. This higher tax liability should be reflected in a higher before-tax interest rate on debt. This will offset, somewhat, the gain through the deductibility of interest payments in the calculation of corporate tax.

investor. (1) Preferred shares provide reasonably steady income. (2) Preferred shareholders have a preference over common shareholders in liquidation; numerous examples can be cited where the prior-preference position of holders of preferred shares saved them from losses incurred by holders of common shares. (3) Many corporations like to hold preferred shares as investments, because dividends received by a corporation from taxable Canadian corporations are tax free. (4) The dividend tax credit can be applied to the dividends on preferred shares. Depending on the individual's marginal federal tax rate, the dividend tax credit can result in a low effective tax rate on dividends. This will increase the attractiveness of preferred shares among investors with low marginal tax rates.

Disadvantages   Preferred shares also have some disadvantages to investors. (1) Although the holders of preferred shares bear a substantial portion of ownership risk, their returns are limited. (2) The shares have no legally enforceable right to dividends. (3) Accrued dividend arrearages are seldom settled in cash comparable to the amount of the obligation that has been incurred.

It has been observed that price fluctuations on preferred shares are far greater than those in bonds, but yields on bonds are frequently higher than those of preferred shares. Is this observation consistent with the basic concept in finance that higher risks require higher returns? As expected, the answer is yes! The investor is interested in the after-tax yield and the risk-return relationship will hold for after-tax yields. Since preferred dividends result in a lower tax liability to the investor (due to the dividend tax credit or due to tax-free intercorporate dividends) than interest payments on debt, the before-tax yields can easily have the observed relationship, while the after-tax yields have the relationship consistent with the risk-return tradeoff.

Recent Trends

The preferred treatment that dividends receive under Canadian tax legislation has created an interest in preferred shares, both convertible and non-convertible issues. Along with this tax induced interest, there has been a number of preferred shares with *unusual* (often called "creative" by the investment community) provisions. These preferred shares are called *term preferred shares,* and we will describe a number of the more interesting terms attached to increase their marketability. The thrust of these new provisions is to reduce the maturity of the preferred share to be of benefit to the holder of the shares; the usual preferred share has no fixed maturity date.

First, there is the preferred share that is redeemable at the option of the holder after a specified date. This feature gives the holder an option to sell the preferred share back to the company at the par value as of some particular date. Thus, if interest rates increase, the yield on new issues of preferreds will increase and the price on older issues will fall. The holder is protected against this fall in price, since the share can be sold back to the company at par and re-invested at the new, higher interest rates. This feature is the holder's equivalent to the issuer's call feature. Second, preferred shares are issued with set maturity dates. Thus, they become equivalent to bonds, since there is an expected return-to-holder on the principal. The dividend payment stream on the preferred share is riskier than the interest payments on a bond of equivalent years outstanding. Third, a new instrument called the floating rate preferred share has been issued; primarily through the private placement market. The dividend rate on the preferred share is tied to a particular interest rate series, and fluctuations in this series are reflected in the dividend payment. This type of preferred share can be thought of as an issue which has a very short maturity. In essence, the preferred share issue reflects current yields and is, in effect, called and re-issued at a new rate every time there is a change in interest rates.

The rise of the term preferred issue has coincided with increases in the inflation rate and in uncertainty in the inflation rate. If investors knew that the inflation rate was going to be high and *stable* in the future, there would be no problem in adjusting yields on all financial instruments to take this into consideration. However, with increased uncertainty as to the future inflation rate, investors have asked for higher yields on long-term financial instruments that set a fixed payout—such as bonds and conventional preferreds. The reduction of the maturity of the preferred shares by the various terms noted above has shifted the risk of unexpected inflation rates, and hence interest rate fluctuations, from the investor to the company. These new term preferred shares should have lower yields than conventional preferred shares, since the inflation risk exposure is less.

DECISION MAKING ON USE OF PREFERRED SHARES

We can now distill the circumstances favoring the use of preferred shares from the foregoing analysis. As a hybrid security, the use of preferred shares is favored by conditions that fall between those favoring the use of common shares and those favoring the use of debt.

When a firm's profit margin is high enough to more than cover preferred share dividends, it will be advantageous to employ leverage. However, if the firm's sales and profits are subject to considerable fluctuations, the use of debt with fixed interest charges may be unduly risky. Preferreds may offer a happy compromise. The use of preferred shares will be strongly favored if the firm already has a debt ratio that is high in relation to the reference level maximum for the line of business.

Relative costs of alternative sources of financing are always important considerations. If the capital market is operating properly, there is a relationship between risk and expected return on all types of securities that is determined by investors. Thus, there are no bargains to be obtained by issuing one form of security if its cost is low relative to other securities. All yield differences are related to investors' evaluations of the differences in risk. However, management may believe that the yields (or costs) of one of the security types is out of line and that the firm should, therefore, issue a particular type of security. Thus, if management and their underwriters believe, for example, that the market has over-reacted in its evaluation of the dividend tax credit and that yields on preferreds are transitorily low, then the firm should issue preferred shares on the basis of relative cost.

Preferred shares may also be the desired form of financing whenever the use of debt would involve excessive risk, but the issuance of common shares would result in problems of control for the dominant ownership group in the company. These non-cost considerations are usually most important in determining the amount of preferred shares a firm should have in its capital structure.

RATIONALE FOR DIFFERENT CLASSES OF SECURITIES

At this point the following questions are likely to come to mind: Why are there so many different forms of long-term securities? Why would anybody ever be

FIGURE 15-3 Risk and Expected Returns on Different Classes of Securities, the Longstreet Co. Ltd.

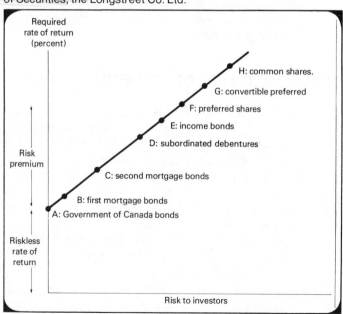

willing to purchase subordinated bonds or income bonds? The answers to both questions may be made clear by reference to Figure 15–3. The now familiar tradeoff function is drawn to show the risk and the expected returns for the various securities of the Longstreet Co. Ltd. for a particular holding period—say, one year. Longstreet's first mortgage bonds are slightly more risky than Government of Canada bonds and sell at a slightly higher expected return. The second mortgage bonds are yet more risky and have a still higher expected return. Subordinated debentures, income bonds , and preferred shares all are increasingly risky and have increasingly higher expected returns. Longstreet's common shares, the riskiest security the firm issues, have the highest expected return of any of its offerings.

Why does Longstreet issue so many different classes of securities? Why not just offer one type of bond plus common shares? The answer lies in the fact that different investors have different risk-return tradeoff preferences, so if its securities are to appeal to the broadest possible market, Longstreet must offer securities that appeal to as many investors as possible. Used wisely, a policy of selling differentiated securities can lower a firm's overall cost of capital below what it would be if it issued only one class of debt and common shares.

REFUNDING A BOND OR PREFERRED SHARE ISSUE

As has been noted in this chapter, a firm can protect itself against reductions in interest rates by inserting a call feature as one of the terms of a bond or preferred share issue. If interest rates fall, the company can sell a new issue with a lower interest rate and use the proceeds of the issue to retire the high interest rate issue. This is called a *refunding operation.*[14]

The decision to refund a security issue is analyzed in much the same manner as a capital budgeting expenditure. The costs of refunding—the "investment outlay"—include (1) the call premium paid for the privilege of calling the old issue and (2) the issue costs incurred in selling the new issue. The annual receipts, in the capital budgeting sense, are the interest payments that are saved each year; for example, if interest expense on the old issue is $1 million while that on the new issue is $700,000, the $300,000 saving constitutes the annual benefits.

In analyzing the advantages of refunding, the net present value method is the recommended procedure—discount the future interest savings back to the present and compare the discounted value with the cash outlays associated with the refunding. What discount rate should be used for the refunding decision? Since the benefits of the refunding operation are relatively

---

[14]For a good discussion of refunding, see O. D. Bowlin, "The Refunding Decision", *Journal of Finance,* (March, 1966), pp. 55-68.

safe—their safety is equivalent to the default risk on the bond or preferred shares involved—the discount rate should reflect the discount rate required by investors who invest in a cash flow of the riskiness noted. Since a bond (preferred shares) refunding operation will be fully financed by debt (preferred shares), *the appropriate discount rate is the after-tax cost of the new debt (preferred shares) and not the average cost of capital.*

To illustrate a bond refunding decision, consider a company that has outstanding a $60 million, twenty-five year bond issue carrying an 8 percent interest rate. This issue, which was sold five years ago, is callable at $1060 per $1000 of par value. Investment dealers have assured the company that it could sell an additional $60 to $70 million worth of twenty-year bonds at an interest rate of 6 percent. (To make the example simple, we will assume that the bonds are sold at par and that there are no sinking fund provisions.)[15] In addition, the underwriting discount on the new issue amounts to $2 million. To ensure that funds required to pay off the old debt will be available, the new bonds will be sold one month before the old issue is called; thus, for one month, interest must be paid on two issues. Predictions are that interest rates are unlikely to fall below 6 percent.[16] Finally, it is assumed that the firm will issue debt to pay for the investment outlay; the discount rate used to calculate the present value will be the after-tax interest rate on the new debt. Should the company refund the $60 million worth of bonds? The following steps outline the decision process.

Step 1. What is the investment outlay required to refund the issue?

a. Call premium:

$$.06 \times \$60,000,000 = \$3,600,000$$

The call premium of 6 percent is *not* a tax-deductible expense.

b. Underwriting discount:

Although the company is refunding $60 million of outstanding debt, the proceeds of the issue are $58 million. The $2 million underwriting discount is not a tax-deductible expense and the full value must be financed by some means.

---

[15]If the new bonds are issued at a discount from par, all or a portion of the discount is a tax deductible expense, not at the time of issue, but when the principal on the bond is paid. If the price of the bond and the coupon payments meet certain restrictions, the full amount of the discount is deductible; otherwise, only a portion of the discount is deductible. This provision is an attempt to stop companies from issuing bonds with very small coupons, and hence, "deep" discounts from the par value and deducting immediately from income the full amount of the discount. In effect, the deep discount permits the company to deduct the interest payments from income at the issue date, as opposed to the years in which interest is actually paid. If a sinking fund is present, the analysis would require inclusion of the sinking fund payments.

[16]The firm's management has estimated that interest rates will probably rise to center on 7 percent in the near future, with a standard deviation of ¾ percent. This implies that there is only a 9 percent chance (1.33 standard deviations from the mean) of future rates falling below 6 percent.

c. Issue costs:

Legal, accounting and printing costs are tax-deductible expenses for the issuing company.

Before tax: $200,000.
After-tax: $200,000 × (1 – tax rate) = 200,000 × .5 = $100,000.
With a corporate tax rate of 50 percent, the after-tax issue costs are $100,000.

d. Additional interest:[17]

One month "extra" interest on new issue, after taxes:

Dollar amount × $\frac{1}{12}$ of 6% × (1 – tax rate) = monthly interest cost.
$60,000,000 × .005 × .5 = $150,000

e. Total after tax investment:

The total investment outlay required to refund the bond issue is:

Call premium	$3,600,000
Underwriting discount	2,000,000
Issue costs	100,000
Additional Interest	150,000
	$5,850,000

Step 2. What are the annual savings?

a. Interest on existing bond after taxes:

$60,000,000 × .08 × .5 = $2,400,000

b. Interest on new bond after taxes:

$60,000,000 × .06 × .5 = $1,800,000

c. Savings $ 600,000

Step 3. What is the present value of the savings?

If we assume that the investment is financed with debt, then the after-tax discount rate to be used is 3 percent.[18]

a. Twenty-year *PV* of annuity factor at 3 percent:
14.877

[17]If the proceeds from the new issue are invested in short-term securities for one month, as they typically will be, this reduces the effect of the "extra" interest.
[18]The cost of capital is developed in detail in Chapter 20. There we will see (1) that the cost of capital

(continued on page 392)

b. *PV* of $600,000 a year for twenty years:

$$14.877 \times \$600,000 = \$8.926,200$$

Step 4. Conclusion.

Since the present value of the receipts ($8,926,200) exceeds the required investment ($5,850,000), the issue should be refunded.

Since the refunding operation is advantageous to the firm, it must be disadvantageous to the bondholders. With a reduction in interest rates, the market value of the bond increases to reflect the gain to the existing bondholders—they have a bond which pays 8 percent, whereas the market requires only 6 percent. However, the call premium forces the bondholder to give up the bond for a premium over par value which is less than the market value of the bond and to re-invest the proceeds in a bond with a lower interest rate. This points out the danger of the call provision to bondholders and explains why, at any given time, bonds without a call provision command higher prices (sell for lower yields) than callable bonds.

SUMMARY

Bonds   A *bond* is a long-term promissory note. A *mortgage bond* is secured by real property. An *indenture* is an agreement between the firm issuing a bond and the numerous bondholders, represented by a *trustee.*

Secured long-term debt differs with respect to (1) the priority of claims, (2) the right to issue additional securities, and (3) the scope of the lien provided. These characteristics determine the amount of protection provided to the bondholder by the terms of the security. Giving the investor more security will induce him to accept a lower yield but will restrict the future freedom of action of the issuing firm.

The main classes of unsecured bonds are (1) *debentures,* (2) *subordinated debentures,* and (3) *income bonds.* Holders of debentures are unsecured general creditors. Subordinated debentures are junior in claim to bank loans. Income bonds are similar to preferred shares in that interest is paid only when earned.

The characteristics of long-term debt determine the circumstances under which it will be used when alternative forms of financing are under analysis. The cost of debt is limited, but it is a fixed obligation. Bond interest is an ex-

increases as the riskiness of the firm increases and (2) that there is a cost of debt, a cost of equity, and an "average cost of capital," which is a weighted average of the cost of debt and equity. Also, we will see that the relevant cost of debt is an *after-tax cost,* calculated as follows:

After-tax cost of debt = (interest rate) (1 – tax rate).

This calculation recognizes that interest is tax deductible, so the federal government, in effect, bears a portion of the cost of debt.

pense deductible for tax purposes. Debt carries a maturity date and may require sinking fund payments to prepare for extinguishing the obligation. Indenture provisions are likely to include restrictions on the freedom of action of the management of the firm.

The nature of long-term debt encourages its use under the following circumstances:

1. Sales and earnings are relatively stable.
2. Profit margins are adequate to make leverage advantageous.
3. A rise in profits or the general price level is expected.
4. The existing debt ratio is relatively low.
5. Common share price/earnings ratios are low in relation to the levels of interest rates.
6. Control considerations are important.
7. Cash flow requirements under the bond agreement are not burdensome.
8. Restrictions of the bond indenture are not onerous.

Although seven of the eight factors may favor debt, the eighth can swing the decision to the use of equity capital. The list of factors is, thus, simply a check list of things to be considered when deciding on bonds versus stocks; the actual decision is based on a judgment about the relative importance of the several factors. There has been substantial growth in the use of corporate bonds denominated in foreign currencies. These bonds are issued either in the foreign bond market or the Eurobond market.

Preferred Shares The *characteristics of preferred shares* vary with the requirements of the situation under which they are issued. However, certain patterns tend to remain. Preferred shares usually have priority over common shares with respect to earnings and claims on assets in liquidation. Preferred shares are usually cumulative; they have no maturity but are sometimes callable. They are typically nonparticipating and have only contingent voting rights.

The advantages to the issuer are limited dividends and no maturity. These advantages may outweigh the disadvantages of higher cost and the nondeductibility of the dividends as an expense for tax purposes. However, the dividend tax credit can be applied to preferred dividends, and this will result in companies paying lower yields on preferred shares.

Companies sell preferred shares when they seek the advantages of financial leverage but fear the dangers of the fixed charges on debt in the face of potential fluctuations in income. If debt ratios are already high or if the costs of common share financing are relatively high, the advantages of preferred shares will be reinforced.

The use of preferred shares has not been very significant, since preferred dividends are not deductible for income tax purposes while bond interest payments are deductible. In recent years, changes in the taxation of dividends has introduced a new interest in both convertible and straight preferred issues. In addition, term preferred shares have become very popular. Term preferred shares have provisions which reduce their maturity so as to be of potential benefit to the preferred shareholder. This is in contrast to the straight preferred share which has no fixed maturity date.

Refunding   If a bond or a preferred share issue was sold when interest rates were higher than they are at present, and if the issue is callable, it may be profitable to call the old issue and refund it with a new, lower cost issue. An analysis similar to capital budgeting is required to determine whether a refunding operation should be undertaken.

QUESTIONS

15-1. A sinking fund is set up in one of two ways:
  a. The corporation makes annual payments to the trustee, who invests the proceeds in securities (frequently government bonds) and uses the accumulated total to retire the bond issue on maturity.
  b. The trustee uses the annual payments to retire a portion of the issue each year, either by calling a given percentage of the issue by a lottery and paying a specified price per bond or buying bonds on the open market, whichever is cheaper. Discuss the advantages and disadvantages of each procedure from the viewpoint of both the firm and the bondholders.

15-2. Since a corporation often has the right to call bonds at will, do you believe individuals should be able to demand repayment at any time they desire? If individuals are given this right, what will happen to the yield on bonds?

15-3. Consider two bonds that are issued today at par by the same company and are identical in all their provisions except that the first bond is callable in 2 years and the second bond is callable in 10 years. Would both bonds have the same interest rate?

15-4. Great Western 4¾ percent income bonds due in 2020 are selling for $770, while the company's 4¼ percent first mortgage bonds due in 2005 are selling for $945. Why would the bonds with the lower coupon sell at a higher price? (Each has a $1,000 par value.)

15-5. When a firm sells bonds, it must offer a package acceptable to potential buyers. Included in this package of terms are such features as the issue price, the coupon interest rate, the term to maturity, any sinking fund provisions, and other features. The package itself is determined through a bargaining process between the firm and the investment dealer(s) who will handle the issue. What particular features would you, as a corporate treasurer, be especially interested in having, and which would you be most willing to give ground on, under each of the following conditions:
  a. You believe that the economy is near the peak of a business cycle.
  b. Long-run forecasts indicate that your firm may have heavy cash inflows in relation to cash needs during the next five to ten years.
  c. Your current liabilities are presently low, but you anticipate raising a considerable amount of funds through short-term borrowing in the near future.

15-6. Index-linked bonds are bonds whose interest rates are linked to the consumer price index. Discuss the advantages and disadvantages to a corporation of issuing these inflation-proof index bonds.

15-7. If preferred share dividends are passed over for several years, the preferred shareholders are frequently given the right to elect several members of the board of directors. In the case of bonds that are in default on interest payments, this procedure is not followed. Why does this difference exist?

15-8. Preferred shares are found in almost all industries, but one industry is the really dominant issuer of preferred shares. What is this industry, and why are firms in it so disposed to using preferred shares?

15-9. If the corporate income tax was abolished, would this raise or lower the amount of new preferred shares issued?

15-10. Investors buying securities have some expected or required rate of return in mind. Which would you expect to be higher, the required rate of return (before personal taxes) on preferred shares or that on common shares (a) for individual investors with high federal marginal tax rates and (b) for corporate investors?

15-11. Do you think the before personal tax required rate of return is higher or lower on very high grade preferred shares or on bonds (a) for individual investors with high federal marginal tax rates and (b) for individual investors with low federal marginal tax rates?

15-12. For purposes of measuring a firm's leverage, should preferred shares be classified as debt or as equity? Does it matter if the classification is being made (a) by the firm itself, (b) by creditors, or (c) by equity investors?

15-13. It was noted that the important variables in determining bond ratings were size, earnings instability, leverage, interest coverage, and subordination. Describe how these variables should affect default risk, and hence, bond ratings.

PROBLEMS

15-1. Several years ago your father purchased a farm adjacent to his existing farm. The deal was financed partly by a long-term mortgage loan. This loan requires payments of $21,909 per year for 20 more years (this includes interest and principal) and has a contract interest rate of 10 percent. Your father is considering refunding the loan because current rates for similar loans have dropped to 8 percent. He is hesitant to refund the mortgage, however, because there is a prepayment penalty of six-months interest on the unpaid balance. Further, it will require about 4 percent of the loan amount for set-up fees for a new loan. Because of other writeoffs, your father pays no income taxes. Should your father refund the loan? (Hint: Begin by finding the unpaid balance of the existing loan, which is equal to the present value of the remaining payments, discounted at the contract interest rate.)

15-2. Three years ago your firm issued some eighteen-year bonds with 10.5 percent coupon rates and a 10 percent call premium. You have just called these bonds. The bonds originally sold at their face value of $1,000.

    a. Compute the realized rate of return for investors who purchased these bonds when they were issued.

    b. Given the rate of return in (a), did investors welcome the call? Explain.

15-3. Lemming Limited has a $300,000 long-term bond issue outstanding. This debt has an additional fifteen years to maturity and bears a coupon interest rate of 9 percent. The firm now has the opportunity to refinance the debt with fifteen-year bonds at a rate of 7 percent. Further declines in the interest rate are not anticipated. The bond redemption premium (call premium) on the old bond would be $15,000; issue costs on the new would be $16,000. If tax effects are ignored, should the firm refund the bonds?

15-4. In late 19X5, Sweet Gas Pipeline Co. Ltd. of Alberta sought to raise $6 million to refinance present preferred share issues at a lower rate. The company could sell additional debt at 6 percent, preferred shares at 5.34 percent, or common equity at $90 a share. How should the company raise the money? Relevant financial information is provided below.

(This question should not be answered in terms of precise cost of capital calculations. Rather, a more qualitative and subjective analysis is appropriate. The only calculations necessary are some simple ratios. Careful interpretation of these ratios is necessary, however, to understand and discuss the often complex, subjective judgment issues involved.)

Pipeline Utilities Financial Ratios

Current ratio (times)	1.0
Interest earned (before taxes) (times)	4.0
Sales to total assets (times)	0.3
Average collection period (days)	28.0
Current debt/total assets (percent)	5–10
Long-term debt/total assets (percent)	45–50
Preferred/total assets (percent)	10–15
Common equity/total assets (percent)	30–35
Earnings before interest and taxes to total assets (percent)	5.9
Profits to common equity (percent)	10.1
Expected growth in earnings and dividends (percent)	4.6

Sweet Gas Pipeline Co. Ltd.
Balance sheet, July 31, 19X5
(in millions of dollars)

Cash	$ 0.75	Current liabilities	$ 3.00
Receivables	1.50	Long-term debt, 3.5%	27.00
Material and supplies	1.20	Preferred shares, 5.60%	6.00
Total current assets	$ 3.45	Common shares, $25 par value	11.25
		Contributed surplus	6.60
Net property	56.55	Retained earnings	6.15
Total assets	$60.00	Total claims	$60.00

Sweet Gas Pipeline Co. Ltd.
Income statement for year ended July 31, 19X5
(in millions of dollars)

Operating revenues	$18.9000
Operating expenses	12.5000
Earnings before interest and taxes	$ 6.4000
Interest deduction	.9450
Earnings before taxes	$ 5.4550
Income taxes at 50%	2.7275
Earnings after taxes	$ 2.7275
Preferred dividends	.3360
Net income available to common	$ 2.3915
Earnings per share	$ 5.31
Dividends per share	$ 4.25

15-5. Shepard Electronics is planning a capital improvement program to provide greater efficiency and versatility in its operations. It is estimated that by mid-19X6 the company will need to raise $200 million. Shepard is a leading electronics producer with an excellent credit rating.

You are asked to set up a program for obtaining the necessary funds. Using the following information, indicate the best form of financing. Some items you should include in your analysis are profit margins, relative costs, control of the voting stock, cash flows, ratio analysis, and *pro forma* analysis.

Shepard's common stock is selling at $64 a share. The company could sell debt (twenty-five years) at 8.0 percent or preferred shares at 8.5 percent.

Electronics Industry Financial Ratios

Current ratio (times)	2.1
Sales to total assets (times)	1.8
Coverage of fixed charges (times)	7.0
Average collection period (days)	42.0
Current debt/total assets (percent)	20–25
Long-term debt/total assets (percent)	10.0
Preferred/total assets (percent)	0–5
Net worth/total assets (percent)	65–70
Profits to sales (percent)	3.3
Profits to total assets (percent)	6.0
Profits to net worth (percent)	9.5
Expected growth rate in earnings and dividends	5.3

Shepard Electronics Limited
Consolidated balance sheet, December 31, 19X5
(in millions of dollars)

Assets		
Current	$ 760	
Other investments	140	
Properties (net)	1,140	
Prepaid expenses	40	
Total assets		$2,080
Liabilities		
Current	$ 320	
Long-term debt, 5.5%	180	
Total liabilities		$ 500
Common shares, equity, $10 par	$ 320	
Contributed surplus	300	
Retained earnings	880	
Reserves	80	
Total net worth		1,580
Total liabilities and net worth		$2,080

Shepard Electronics Limited
Consolidated income statement
For years ended December 31, 19X3, 19X4, and 19X5
(in millions of dollars)

	19X3	*19X4*	*19X5*
Sales	$2,440	$1,820	$2,160
Other income	20	20	20
Total	$2,460	$1,840	$2,180
Cost and expenses	2,120	1,600	1,920
Income before taxes	$ 340	$ 240	$ 260
Federal income tax	172	120	128
Net income	$ 168	$ 120	$ 132
Cash dividends	92	92	92
Interest on long-term debt	$ 7	$ 8.8	$ 10
Depreciation	$ 80.0	$ 64.0	$ 68.0
Shares outstanding (widely held)		40,000,000	

Term loans and leases

Intermediate-term financing is defined as *debt originally scheduled for repayment in more than one year but in less than ten years.* Anything shorter is a current liability and falls in the class of short-term credit, while obligations due in ten or more years are thought of as long-term debt. This distinction is arbitrary, of course—we might just as well define intermediate-term credit as loans with maturities of one to five years. However, the one-to-ten year distinction is commonly used, so we shall follow it here.

The major forms of intermediate-term financing include (1) *term loans* and (2) *lease financing.*

TERM LOANS

A term loan is a business loan with a maturity of more than one year. These loans are used to finance the more permanent financing needs of a corporation which can range from financing operating equipment to "hard core" borrowing. This latter term refers to that portion of short-term borrowings from a bank which is not paid off by the borrower but is repeatedly renewed. The bank, having identified this hard-core portion, requests that the short-term borrowing be converted to a term loan. Generally, term loans are retired by systematic repayments (often called *amortization payments*) over the life of the loan, although there are exceptions to the rule. Security, usually in the form of a chattel mortgage on equipment, is often employed. In addition, there can be loan agreements which require the borrowing company to meet certain financial and reporting constraints.

399

From this brief description of term loans, it appears that they are very similar to bonds. However, unlike bonds which are underwritten by investment dealers, term loans are negotiated directly between borrower and lender—just as in the private placement market. The by-passing of the investment dealer is a rational decision for the participants in a term loan. First, the size of the loan is usually not very large and the per dollar underwriting costs of an issue would be very high. These costs would reflect the direct or out-of-pocket costs, along with the costs involved in preparing a detailed prospectus and the time delays until the prospectus is cleared through the securities commissions. In addition, the direct negotiation route adds flexibility to the loan contract so that the particular interests of both borrowers and lenders can be included.

The primary sources of term loans are banks, both foreign and Canadian owned, life insurance companies and specialized term lending organizations. Bank loans are generally restricted to maturities of between one and five years, while insurance companies make the bulk of their term loans for between ten and fifteen years. Thus, many insurance company term loans are long-term, not intermediate-term, financing. Sometimes, when relatively large loans are involved, banks and insurance companies combine to make a loan, with the bank taking the short maturities and the insurance company taking the long maturities. In addition, a number of governmental agencies provide term loans; these agencies include the Ontario Development Corporation and the Federal Business Development Bank. There are also term loans provided under the Small Business Loans Act.

Term loans can be put into two different categories based on the method by which the interest rate is determined on the loan. On the one hand, there are variable interest rate term loans used by the chartered banks. On the other hand, there are fixed interest rate term loans which are chiefly used by the foreign banks, insurance companies and other financial intermediaries. However, before investigating the differences between these two types of term loans, we will review an important feature common to all term loans—the *loan agreement*.

Loan Agreements

In addition to taking security on term loans, the financial institutions attempt to protect themselves in other ways. A major advantage of a term loan for a borrower is that the funds can be used for an extended period. However, this benefit for the borrower can be a potential problem for the lender. On a short-term loan, say 90 days, since the bank has the option to renew or not to renew the loan, the financial situation of the borrower can be re-examined quite frequently. If it has deteriorated unduly, the loan officer simply does not renew the loan. On a term loan, the financial institution is committed for a number of years and interim renewals of the loan are impossible. However, the financial institution will want to be kept aware of the financial position of the borrower and would not wish the borrower to undertake new debts or investment decisions that will have a detrimental impact on repayment of the loan. To this end, the lender establishes a set of protective covenants in the loan agreement; these covenants are very similar to the covenants in bond or preferred share trust indentures. They require the company to take certain actions and to refrain from taking others. As long as the borrower satisfies the covenants there is no problem; if, however, the borrower is in violation of one or more of the provisions, the borrower is in default and the lender has the legal right to ask for immediate repayment of the loan. This is the most drastic action that the lender could take; alternatively, the lender may not call for repayment but work with the borrower to remove the problems.

There are a large number of covenants that can be included in a loan agreement. We will give a brief description of a few of the more important ones.

Current Ratio and Working Capital   The current ratio must be maintained at some specified level, say 2½ to 1 or 3 to 1, depending upon the borrower's line of business. Working capital must also be maintained at some minimum level. The purpose of these provisions is to insure that the borrower has sufficient liquidity to meet the term loan payments; but the working capital restriction should not be set so high that the firm has an excess amount held in unproductive liquid assets.

Additional Long-Term Debt   Typically, there are prohibitions against incurring additional long-term indebtedness or indebtedness with a claim on earnings equal, or prior, to the claim of the term loan, except with the permission of the lender. Furthermore, the lender does not ordinarily permit the pledging of assets. The loan agreement may also prohibit the borrower from assuming any contingent liabilities, such as guaranteeing the indebtedness of a subsidiary. Finally, the loan agreement probably restricts the borrower from circumventing these provisions by signing long-term leases beyond specified amounts.

Management   The loan agreement may require that any major changes in the composition of management personnel be approved by the lender. The loan agreement may also require life insurance on the principals or key people in the business. In addition, the loan agreement may provide for the creation of a voting trust, or a granting of proxies for a specified period, to ensure that the management of the company will be under the control of the group on which the lender has relied when making the loan.

Financial Statements   The lender will require the borrower to submit periodic financial statements for review.

The list presented above is not intended to be exhaustive, but the provisions noted provide a good indication of the potential restrictions on management's flexibility due to covenants in a loan agreement. The ultimate set of covenants in the loan agreement will be a result of the relative bargaining strengths and skills of the borrower and lender.

Types of Term Loans

Variable Rate Term Loans   The variable rate term loan is the conventional form of term loan used by the Canadian chartered banks. The interest rate charged by the banks floats at a set number of percentage points above prime. For example, a standard variable rate loan would run from 3 to 5 years, for a $200,000 maximum. The interest rate differential over the prime rate is negotiable, but the most common current level is three percentage points above prime. The longer the term of the loan, the higher the premium required over the prime rate. Since a term loan typically embodies certain conditions, any failure to meet these conditions will result in the note being repayable on demand.

The chartered banks in using this form of the term loan are engaging in a matching strategy. The liabilities of the banks are very short-term; that is, the banks' savings and demand deposits have interest rates which can be changed with altered credit market conditions. Thus, the true maturity of these liabilities is very short, since every time interest rates change, the interest rates on liabilities are altered. Thus, to reduce risk, the banks' assets should be short-term. The true maturity of a variable rate term loan is very short since, as the prime rate increases, the term loan interest rate increases as well. This is equivalent to a new term loan issued at the new rate.

In setting up a term loan, a repayment schedule is determined. Monthly payments are calculated which will amortize the principal over the term of the loan. For example, a 5 year term loan for $200,000 would have equal monthly principal payments of $3,333 (i.e. $200,000 divided by 60 months). In some instances, the monthly payments are determined so that the principal is not fully repaid and the final payment is large. This final payment, which is called a *balloon payment*, may be refinanced by the lending institution.

Amortization forces the borrower to retire the loan slowly, thus protecting both the lender and borrower against the possibility that the borrower will not make adequate provisions for retirement during the life of the loan. Finally, the interest payable on the variable rate term loan is calculated on the monthly unpaid balance. In some instances, interest is calculated on the quarterly unpaid balance.

Fixed Rate Term Loans   The alternative type of term loan sets an interest rate that is fixed for the duration of the loan. This type of loan is used by the subsidiaries of U.S. banks, insurance companies and specialized term lending companies such as Roy Nat.[1] The fixed rate term loan has all of the character-

[1]Currently, Roy Nat Limited is beginning to make a limited number of variable rate term loans.

istics of a privately placed bond issue.

Institutions that lend through term loans typically have liabilities that are of much longer duration than those of the chartered banks, and thus the matching strategy permits lending on longer terms.

Repayment Schedule

The repayment schedule is based on the concept of a steady amortization of the loan over the life of the loan. The borrower's payments on the loan are usually the same amount over the life of the loan and blend both principal repayment and an interest payment into each installment. Finally, the amortization schedule is geared to the productive life of the equipment and payments are made from cash flows resulting from the use of the equipment.

To illustrate how the amortization schedule is determined, let us assume that a firm borrows $1,000 on a ten-year loan, that interest is computed at 5 percent on the declining balance, and that the principal and interest are to be paid in ten equal installments. What is the amount of each of the ten annual payments? To find this value we must use the present value concepts developed in Chapter 10.

First, notice that the lender advances $1,000 and receives in turn a ten-year annuity of R dollars each year. In the section headed Annual Receipts from an Annuity in Chapter 10, we saw that these receipts could be calculated as

$$R = \frac{A_n}{PVIF_a},$$

where R is the annual receipt, A_n is the present value of the annuity, and $PVIF_a$ is the appropriate interest factor found either in Table 10–5 or in Appendix Table A–4. Substituting the $1,000 for A_n and the interest factor for a ten-year 5 percent annuity, or 7.722, for $PVIF_a$, we find

$$R = \frac{\$1,000}{7.722} = \$130.$$

Therefore, if our firm makes ten annual installments of $130 each, it will have retired the $1,000 loan and provided the lender a 5 percent return on his investment.

Table 16–1 breaks down the annual payments into interest and repayment components and, in the process, proves that level payments of $130 will, in fact, retire the $1,000 loan and give the lender his 5 percent return. This breakdown is important for tax purposes, because the interest payments are deductible expenses to the borrower and taxable income to the lender.

TABLE 16–1   Term-loan Repayment Schedule

Year	Total Payment	Interest[a]	Amortization Repayment	Remaining Balance
1	$ 130	$ 50	$ 80	$920
2	130	46	84	836
3	130	42	88	748
4	130	38	92	656
5	130	34	96	560
6	130	28	102	458
7	130	23	107	351
8	130	18	112	239
9	130	13	117	122
10	130	8	122	0
	$1,300	$300	$1,000	

[a]Interest for the first year is 0.05 × $1,000 = $50; for the second year, 0.05 × $920 = $46; and so on.

One interesting development in term lending is the entrance by Canadian chartered banks into fixed rate term lending. The actual involvement in fixed rate term loans depends on the particular chartered bank. For a number of banks, the maximum term is 5 years and, based on the standard term loan maximum of $200,000, the interest rate charged (as of May, 1978) is 12 to 12½ percent. However, both duration and interest rates on the loans are negotiable; some banks will lend for longer than 5 years, whereas others will go for 2 years on a fixed rate basis and finance the remaining terms—say, 3 years—with a variable rate loan.

Given that interest rates on the chartered banks' liabilities fluctuate in response to credit conditions and that interest rates on fixed rate term loans are determined for the length of the loan, it is surprising that chartered banks have entered this market and exposed themselves to risks from mismatching.[2] One explanation for their involvement is the competition of foreign banks operating in Canada who provide fixed rate term loans as one of their normal products. There are a number of these international banks operating through affiliated companies in Canada—for example, the Dresdner Bank of Frankfurt, the Mitsui Bank of Tokyo and CMB Holdings Limited, an affiliate of Chase Manhattan Bank. Currently, these banks are financing trade between their country of origin and Canada. However, direct competition with Canadian banks has arisen in lending funds to the Canadian subsidiaries of foreign companies. This competition is in terms of interest rate cutting, cash flow loans and a reduced reliance on direct security for loans. The U.S. bank affiliates

[2]In fact, as the chartered banks enter this market more heavily, it is very likely that their use of term deposits will increase since this will provide better matching. Banks *do* have some long-term liabilities such as debentures and common shares, but as of the end of 1977, the long-term sources of funds were approximately 5 percent of total liabilities.

have had substantial experience with fixed rate term loans and are more familiar with cash flow loans, the use of loan agreements and covenants, rather than on the direct use of security in lending.

Some recommendations in the draft legislation for the new Bank Act suggest that the international banks be permitted to seek a bank charter; this would place them under the same federal regulations as Canadian chartered banks and would permit them to accept deposits. However, these banks would have corporate, and not individual, lending as their primary concern. In addition, there would be a limit, both on the size of each bank, individually, and on the aggregate size of the banks relative to the size of the market. There will be no requirement that all foreign bank affiliates obtain a bank charter. However, those that do not will be constrained by other provisions. Thus, based on the draft suggestions, there will be some significant changes in the structure of banking in Canada. Whether these changes will promote or constrain competition among foreign-owned and Canadian banks is a topic that has been vigorously debated by business, academics and government and there appears to be no consensus.

LEASE FINANCING

Firms are generally interested in obtaining the services provided by real estate and equipment. These services can be obtained either through a purchase of these assets or by means of a lease. Under the lease alternative, a contractual arrangement is set up under which the owner of the asset (the lessor) permits a second party (the lessee) to use the services of the asset for a specified period of time in exchange for a series of payments. Ownership of the leased asset remains with the lessor and the lessee can only purchase the asset at the expiry of the lease if that option was specified in the lease contract.

Leasing first came to prominence with real estate assets—land and buildings. Currently, it is possible to lease virtually any kind of fixed asset. Examples of assets that are leased include airplanes, shopping centers, shoe manufacturing equipment and even cranes for construction purposes.

It may appear from the discussion to follow that "lessors" are a homogeneous group. This impression is useful for describing the techniques of leasing; however, the leasing "industry" is composed of a large number of very different participants. The major group involved in this industry are the financial institutions. Life insurance companies, trust companies and some pension funds are involved heavily as lessors. Due to constraints in the current Bank Act, the chartered banks cannot be involved directly in leasing activities. However, the banks are involved indirectly by having financial interests in leasing companies; for example as of the end of 1977, the Royal Bank owned 42 percent of Roy Nat Ltd., and the Bank of Montreal owned 50 percent of Canada Dominion Leasing Corporation. When the legislation for the new Bank

Act is passed, the chartered banks will be permitted to operate directly in the leasing industry.

In addition to the above group, the leasing industry includes independent companies and partnerships of individuals in high tax brackets. The tax savings from CCA deductions are more valuable to these investors than to the lessee companies and there may be benefits to both parties.

Conceptually, leasing is quite similar to borrowing, since both require fixed contractual payments over a stated term. Just as in debt contracts, failure to make lease payments can cause insolvency, and in the event of bankruptcy, the lessor repossesses the asset and has a claim to the missed lease payments. Since leasing can be viewed as a form of debt financing, it provides financial leverage, thereby increasing both the risk and expected return to the equity investor. The presence of the fixed lease payments will also add risk to those creditors whose claims are subordinate to the lease payments.

Both academic and practitioner interest in leasing has increased since the early 1970s. This interest has resulted in the resolution of a number of the major issues involved in the evaluation of leasing contracts. Unfortunately, there are still a few unresolved issues. Our analysis of the leasing problem has been taken from the leasing literature[3] and we have taken the most reasonable approach. The analysis in this chapter will be from the lessee's point of view; we are interested in assisting the financial manager in deciding whether a lease, or an alternative financing package consisting of an equivalent amount of debt, should be used.

Sale and Leaseback

Under a sale and leaseback arrangement, a firm owning land, buildings, or equipment sells the property at approximately market value to a financial institution or independent leasing company and simultaneously executes an agreement to lease the property back for a specified period under specific terms. If real estate is involved, the financial institution is generally a life insurance company; if the property consists of equipment and machinery, the financial institution could be an insurance company, a finance company or a specialized leasing company.

Note that the seller, or *lessee,* immediately receives the purchase price put up by the buyer, or *lessor.* At the same time, the seller-lessee retains the use of the property while the buyer-lessor retains ownership, and hence a claim on the residual value from the asset.

Under a mortgage loan arrangement, the financial institution would receive a series of equal payments just sufficient to amortize the loan and to provide the lender with a specified rate of return on the investment. The nature

[3]The analysis in this chapter is based on a paper by M.J. Gordon, "General Solution to the Buy or Lease Decision", *Journal of Finance* (March 1974), 245-50.

of the calculations was described above in the section on term loans. Under a sale and leaseback arrangement, the lease payments are set up in exactly the same manner—the payments are sufficient to return the full purchase price to the lessor, in addition to providing it with a rate of return on its investment.

Operating Leases

Operating leases include both financing and maintenance services. IBM is one of the pioneers of the operating lease contract; computers and office copying machines, together with automobiles and trucks, are the primary types of equipment involved in operating leases; the acquisition of telephone services is a more common example of an operating lease. These leases ordinarily call for the lessor to maintain and service the leased equipment, and the costs of this maintenance are built into the lease payments.

Another important characteristic of the operating lease is the fact that it is frequently not fully amortized. In other words, the payments required under the lease contract are *not* sufficient to recover the full cost of the equipment. Obviously, however, the lease contract is written for considerably less than the expected life of the leased equipment, and the lessor expects to recover the cost either in subsequent renewal payments or on disposal of the leased equipment.

A final feature of the operating lease is that it frequently contains a cancellation clause giving the lessee the right to cancel the lease and return the equipment before the expiration of the basic lease agreement. This is an important consideration for the lessee, for it means that the equipment can be returned if technological developments render it obsolete, or if there is no longer any need for it.

Financial Leases

A financial lease permits a company to obtain the services of an asset that it did not previously own. The firm that intends to use the equipment selects the specific item it requires and negotiates the price and delivery terms with the manufacturer or the distributor. Then, the user company arranges with a leasing company or financial institution to buy the equipment from the manufacturer or the distributor, and the user firm simultaneously executes an agreement to lease the equipment from the financial institution.

The lease contract will specify the terms and conditions of the lease. Typically, the lease cannot be cancelled (or can be cancelled only upon agreement of both lessor and lessee). The length of the lease is specified and will depend upon the expected economic life of the asset. In most cases, the lease payments result in full amortization of the lessor's investment plus a rate of return on the unamortized annual balance. The lessee is generally given an option either to renew the lease at a reduced rental on expiration of the original lease or to purchase the asset from the lessor at a stated price. Finally, the contract will specify which of the parties has the responsibility for the payment for repairs and maintenance, taxes, insurance, and other expenses. If the lessee is responsible for these costs, the lease is called a *net lease*. If the lessor maintains the asset and pays the insurance, it is called a *maintenance lease*.

Financial leases are almost the same as sale and leaseback arrangements; the only difference is that the lease equipment is new and the lessor buys it from a manufacturer or a distributor instead of from the user-lessee. A sale and leaseback may, then, be thought of as a special type of financial lease.

Leverage Equipment Lease

This type of lease is relatively new and introduces a third party into the leasing arrangement. The analysis of this lease from the lessee's point of view is no different than the financial lease, since the lessee must make a series of lease payments. However, the procedure to finance the lessor's investment is more complicated.

The leveraged equipment lease arises after the potential user has arranged for a manufacturer to produce a required type of equipment. The user invites a number of financial institutions to submit tenders for the financing of the equipment and the tender with the lowest financing cost to the user is usually awarded the contract. A typical contract would have the client of the financial institution, called the investor, providing a portion, say 20 percent, of the price of the asset. The other 80 percent is financed by other parties such as the financial institution. The investor obtains ownership of the asset and arranges a series of lease payments with the lessee.

The important question for the investor-lessor is whether the capital cost allowance on the full cost of the asset can be used for tax purposes. If the investor is ultimately liable for the remaining 80 percent loan, then the Department of National Revenue has ruled that the full capital cost allowance is available. If, however, the other parties providing the 80 percent can look only to the equipment and the lessee for the security of the funds invested, then the capital cost allowance available to the investor would not include the 80 percent of that cost financed by other parties. While this complication of the leveraged lease does not affect the analysis of leasing from the lessee's point of view, it is of crucial interest to the lessor!

TAX IMPLICATIONS OF A LEASE

The full amount of annual lease payments is deductible for federal income tax purposes *provided that the tax authorities agree that a particular contract is a genuine lease and not simply an installment loan called a lease i.e. a disguised sale.* This is particularly important for a lease which provides an option to the lessee to purchase the leased equipment for a fixed amount of money at the end of the lease period. There are instances where a very low option price resulted in an interpretation of the contract as a time-payment purchase and not a lease.

If the option is exercised, the exercise price becomes the capital cost of the asset and the lessee is permitted to claim capital cost allowances on that amount. If the lease permits the application of the lease payments as part payment of the cost of the assets, the resulting capital cost of the asset to the lessee is the purchase price less the partial payments.

One highly touted benefit of a lease is the fact that the cost of land can be amortized in lease payments. This permits the amortization of this cost for federal income tax purposes—this benefit would not be available if the asset were purchased since land cannot be depreciated for tax purposes. Of course, there are a number of offsetting impacts to this "benefit". First, the firm that leases does not own the land, and hence has given up the value at the end of the lease. Second, the degree of competition among potential lessors and lessees can result in a sharing of these tax benefits.

ACCOUNTING IMPLICATIONS

We have argued that lease financing is equivalent to a form of debt and that it should be considered a liability of the firm. The lease payments are equivalent to the payments of principal and interest on a term loan and, thus, will have an impact on financial risk and the yield that equity holders require.

Lease financing has been referred to as "off the balance sheet" financing, because the liability generated by the lease is not reflected on the balance sheet. Current accounting practice in Canada requires the disclosure of particulars of long-term lease obligations in a note on the financial statements. Thus, the balance sheet and some financial ratios that are derived from balance sheet items will be distorted.

For example, consider the balance sheets of two hypothetical firms, A and B in Table 16-2.

TABLE 16-2 Balance Sheet Effects of Leasing

	Before Asset Increase				*After Asset Increase*					
	Firms A and B				*Firm A*				*Firm B*	
Assets	$100	Debt	$ 50	Assets	$200	Debt	$150	Assets	$100	Debt	$ 50
		Equity	50			Equity	50			Equity	50
	$100		$100		$200		$200		$100		$100

Initially, the balance sheets of both firms are identical and they both have debt ratios of 50 percent. Next, they each decide to acquire assets costing $100. Firm A borrows $100 to make the purchase, so an asset and a liability go on its balance sheet and its debt to total asset ratio is increased to 75 percent. Firm B leases the equipment. The lease may call for fixed charges as high, or even higher, than the loan and the obligations assumed under the lease can be equally or more dangerous to other creditors. However, the debt ratio remains at 50 percent.

This illustration has emphasized the weakness in the debt ratio—if two companies are being compared and if one leases a substantial amount of equipment, then the debt ratio as we calculate it does not accurately show their relative leverage positions. And there are other ratios that can be affected by the accounting treatment of leases; the asset turnover ratio, the rate of return on assets, and the interest coverage ratios will also be distorted under lease financing. It is for this very reason that we have suggested that a total fixed charges ratio, which includes lease payments, is a better measure of coverage than the times interest earned ratio. As an example, it was noted in Chapter 3 that the Surrey Company and the industry ratios may have been distorted due to the existence of substantial lease obligations.

Some accountants have argued that lease payments should be capitalized at an appropriate discount rate and the resulting liability be shown on the balance sheet along with the amortized value of the asset. The impact of this suggestion is to make the balance sheet more representative of the actual leverage existing in the company; this will permit creditors and equity holders to determine their risk exposure based on the fixed lease payments. In the United States, financial leases which meet certain conditions *must* be capitalized and included in the balance sheet. Based on the contents of an exposure draft issued in 1977, the Canadian Institute of Chartered Accountants appears to be moving toward the U.S. position.

EVALUATION OF LEASES

To evaluate whether or not a company should use lease financing, the net cost of leasing must be compared with the net cost of the alternative method of acquiring the use of the asset. In a typical case, a firm contemplating the acquisition of new equipment must also think about how to finance the equipment—no well managed firm will ever have idle cash just sitting around. If the firm is considering the use of a lease, then the alternative financing arrangement is to purchase the equipment by using a term loan secured by the equipment. Therefore, we are not deciding whether or not to purchase the asset *but* what financing method should be used—a lease or an equivalent loan.

Since the costs from either alternative occur over time, our decision criterion will be: *choose that option for which the present value of net after-tax costs is a minimum.*

Consider the costs associated with the lease option. The after-tax costs associated with the lease option are (i) maintenance costs, if any; (ii) lease payments; (iii) the purchase price of the asset if there is an option to purchase at the termination of the lease; and (iv) the tax shields associated with the capital cost allowance if the firm exercises its option to purchase the asset. This last item is a benefit from the lease contract and reduces the net after-tax cost of the lease. The present value of the after-tax cost of the lease is presented below where PV denotes present value.

$$PV\binom{\text{net cost}}{\text{of lease}} = PV\binom{\text{after-tax}}{\text{lease payments}} + PV\binom{\text{maintenance}}{\text{costs}} + PV\binom{\text{option}}{\text{price}}$$

$$- PV\binom{\text{tax savings from CCA deductions}}{\text{if option to purchase is exercised}} \qquad \textbf{16–1}$$

Notice that the present value of the tax savings has a negative sign since it reduces the net cost.

The next step is to identify the present value of the after-tax, borrow-to-purchase alternative. If the firm accepts the lease alternative, it gives up the tax shields generated by the CCA deduction if the asset is purchased in exchange for a set of lease payments which are fully deductible for tax purposes. Implicit in the lease payment is a financing charge which becomes tax deductible, since the lease payment is tax deductible. However, this tax saving from the financing charge can be obtained if the asset is financed with debt, since the interest payments on debt are tax deductible. Therefore, to neutralize this financing benefit and make the alternatives comparable, we assume that the purchase of the asset would be financed with a debt issue at the firm's current interest rate on debt. The value of the debt issue would equal the cost of the asset and the debt would be amortized over the time period equal to the length of the lease. The stream of total payments—the sum of principal and interest payments—should have the same pattern as the lease payments. Thus, if the lease payments are equal in every period, the total payments will be equal as well. The after-tax costs of this loan will be the principal plus interest payment, less the tax savings from the interest deductible for tax purposes.[4]

The present value of the borrow-to-purchase alternative is given below in Equation 16–2.

$$PV\binom{\text{after-tax cost;}}{\text{borrow-to-purchase}} = PV\binom{\text{after-tax cost of}}{\text{equivalent loan}} + PV\binom{\text{after-tax main-}}{\text{tenance costs}}$$

$$- PV\binom{\text{tax savings from}}{\text{CCA deductions}} - PV\binom{\text{salvage or}}{\text{residual value}} \qquad \textbf{16–2}$$

[4]If the total payment is $150 of which $100 is principal and $50 is interest and the tax rate is 40 percent, the after-tax payment is $150 — (.4) 50 = $130.

Notice that the last two terms are cash benefits from the purchase alternative and are identical to those that we investigated in the capital budgeting chapter. Thus, the complications when the salvage price is different from the undepreciated capital cost at the salvage date must be considered as well.[5]

The best way to demonstrate this evaluation is to use an example from which all unnecessary tax implications have been removed. Assume that the Tennis Elbow Racket Club Ltd. is contemplating the acquisition of a ball machine costing $1,000. The club can borrow the $1,000 at 5 percent to be repaid in 10 equal installments of $130 each, or lease the machine for lease payments of $150 a year for ten years. Assume that the machine will be used for ten years at which time there is expected to be no salvage value. The machine belongs to that capital cost class pool which has a maximum CCA rate of 20 percent. If the firm leases the equipment, there is no option to purchase the asset. The maintenance cost of $20 per year is included in the lease payment but must be paid explicitly if the asset is purchased. Finally, assume that the first lease payment occurs one year after the lease begins (the usual practice is to pay the first payment at the start of the lease period).

Note that the decision to acquire the machine is not at issue here—this decision was made previously as part of the capital budgeting process. We are concerned with the technique to use to finance the acquisition of the use of the asset. However, if the effective cost of the lease is substantially lower than the cost of debt—and, as explained later in this chapter, this could occur for a number of reasons, including the ability to obtain more debt financing if leasing is employed—then the cost of capital used in capital budgeting would have to be recalculated and, perhaps, projects formerly deemed unacceptable might become acceptable.[6]

The comparison of the alternatives in this problem is presented in Table 16–3. Columns 1 through 4 present the payment schedule for the borrow-to-purchase option; notice that this section is identical to the schedule shown in Table 16–1 for a term loan. Column 5 presents the tax savings obtained from the deductibility of interest payments. With a tax rate of 40 percent, the tax saving is the interest payment times the tax rate. The after-tax cost of the loan for each year is presented in Column 6. It is calculated as the total loan payment (Column 1 = Column 2 + Column 3) less the tax savings (Column 5). The after-tax maintenance cost is presented in Column 7; with a 40 percent tax rate, the after-tax maintenance cost is $20 times .6 or $12. Since there is no salvage value, there is no entry for the present value of this benefit. The final input to the borrow-to-purchase alternative is the present value of the tax savings from CCA deductions. The formula for this quantity when there is a zero salvage value was presented in Chapter 11 and is written as:

[5] The reader will have noted that if we inserted the present value of the after-tax revenues in both Equations 16–1 and 16–2, we would be calculating the net present value of the lease and the net present value of a purchase financed with debt.

[6] An alternative approach to the lease-versus-purchase decision calls for analyzing the *NPV* of a project if the asset is leased versus the *NPV* if it is purchased.

$$PV\left(\genfrac{}{}{0pt}{}{\text{tax}}{\text{savings}}\right) = \frac{C_0 td}{r + d}.$$

where C_0 = initial cost
d = capital cost rate
t = tax rate
r = applicable cost of capital.

The yearly cost if the asset is leased is presented in Column (8) of Table 16-3. This column is the after-tax lease payment of $90, which equals the lease payment of $150 times $1-t$ (that is, .6). Notice that the other terms in the present value of lease cost Equation 16-1 have been omitted since there are no maintenance costs borne by the lessee and no purchase option.

The final issue is the choice of an appropriate discount rate to calculate the present values of all the cash flows. This is one of the areas in which there is still some controversy. However, it appears from the current literature that there has been a resolution of this problem. To convert to present values, we

TABLE 16-3   Comparison of Cost of Leasing Versus Borrowing-to-Purchase

			Cost of Borrowing-to-Purchase					Cost of Lease
			Equivalent Loan					
	(1)	(2)	(3)	(4)	(5)	(6)	(7)	(8)
Year	Total payment	Interest	Amortization payment	Remaining balance	Tax saving (.4) × interest	(2) + (3) – (5) After-tax net cost of loan	After-tax maintenance cost (.6) × $20	After-tax cost of lease = (1 – .4) × lease payment
1	130	50	80	$920	$20.00	$110.00	$12	$90
2	130	46	84	836	18.40	111.60	12	90
3	130	42	88	748	16.80	113.20	12	90
4	130	38	92	656	15.20	114.80	12	90
5	130	34	96	560	13.60	116.40	12	90
6	130	28	102	458	11.20	118.80	12	90
7	130	23	107	351	9.20	120.80	12	90
8	130	18	112	239	7.20	122.80	12	90
9	130	13	117	122	5.20	124.80	12	90
10	130	8	122	0	3.20	126.80	12	90
Present value of the sum of the yearly costs						$905.33[a]	$93[b]	$695[c]

[a] Each payment is discounted by the appropriate discount factor based on a 5 percent discount rate.
[b] The present value of this 10 year annuity of $12 per year is $12 times the annuity factor of 7.722 for a 5 percent discount rate.
[c] Using the 10 year annuity factor of 7.722 and the annual payment of $90 the present value is $90 × 7.722 = $695.

will use a discount rate which is equal to the interest rate on the company's debt—5 percent. We have chosen this rate because the cash flows that are being considered in the analysis are relatively risk free and the cost of capital applicable to a risk free stream is the interest rate on the company's debt.[7]

The resulting present values are presented in Table 16–4. The present value of the after-tax lease costs at a 5 percent discount factor is $695. For the borrow-to-purchase alternative, the total after-tax cost is $678; this is the sum of the after-tax cost of the equivalent loan of $905 plus the after-tax maintenance cost of $93.00, less the present value of the tax savings from CCA deductions of $320. From this comparison, the borrow-to-purchase option is preferable to the lease since the former is $17 cheaper than the latter.

TABLE 16–4 Comparative Costs—Leasing versus Borrow-to-Purchase (discount rate equals before-tax cost of debt)

Leasing:	
Present value of after-tax lease costs	$695
Borrow-to-purchase:	
Present value of	
i) after-tax net cost of equivalent loan	$905
ii) after-tax maintenance cost	93
	$998
Less: present value of tax savings	(320)
Net cost:	$678

Modifications to Account for Other Factors

In this section, we will determine whether certain modifications of our analysis will result in a preference for leasing over borrowing-to-purchase. The

[7]As noted in Chapter 12, and as we discuss in still greater detail in Chapter 20, the appropriate discount rate to apply to an expected future cash flow depends upon the riskiness of the cash flow: cash flows known with relative certainty should be discounted at comparatively low rates, and conversely for risky cash flows. Applying this logic to lease analysis leads to the conclusion that each cash flow stream involved in a lease-versus-borrow-to-purchase decision (for example, the loan payment, maintenance cost, and so on) should be analyzed to determine its degree of risk, then discounted at an appropriate rate. The loan payment and lease payment schedules, which are contractual obligations and must be paid to avoid bankruptcy, are relatively certain streams and should be discounted at low rates. The maintenance expense (unless set by contract) is more uncertain and should be discounted at a higher rate, while the tax savings are somewhat uncertain and should be discounted at a higher rate. In our analysis, we have discounted the tax savings from capital cost allowance at the interest rate on the company's debt. Thus, we are assuming that this cash flow is as risky as the debt of the company. There are additional uncertainties in the tax savings derived from changes in tax rates and CCA provisions. The salvage value is probably the least certain cash flow, so it should be discounted at a still higher rate.

We do not extend our example to show variable discount rates, but to do so would involve the following steps: (1) assign a risk-adjusted discount rate to each cash flow stream, (2) find the present value of each stream, (3) add up the present value cash flows associated with leasing and with buying, and (4) determine the *NPV* advantage to leasing or borrowing. For an excellent discussion of all this, see R. S. Bower, "Issues in Lease Financing," *Financial Management,* Winter 1973, 25–34.

modifications are both quantitative and qualitative. The former will have an impact on the net costs of leasing or borrowing-to-purchase and will be included in our evaluation techniques. The qualitative factors, on the other hand, have been used to confer benefits to leasing. An example of this factor is the added borrowing capacity obtained through the use of leasing.

Quantitative Factors: Accelerated Write-Off

As noted in Chapter 2, accelerated write-off provisions exist for manufacturing and processing machinery and for certain types of pollution reduction and energy conservation assets. Under the accelerated write-off provisions, the book value of the asset for tax purposes is written off in 2 years. In the first year, the maximum claim for CCA is 50 percent of the capital cost with the remaining undepreciated capital cost written off in the second year.

The obvious impact of this accelerated write-off is to increase the present value of the tax savings from CCA deductions. This will reduce the present value of the after-tax cost of borrowing-to-purchase, and at first, would appear to make leasing less attractive.[8] However, this assumes that there is no impact on the lease payments from the accelerated write-off provisions; and this is unlikely to be true since the leasing market and the capital market are competitive. The accelerated write-off is available to the lessor and competition among lessors will force tax advantages such as this to be shared between lessor and lessee. Thus, any opportunities available to equipment owners must be reflected in the competitive system of rates charged by leasing companies. It cannot, therefore, be stated categorically that borrowing-to-purchase is preferable to leasing if there are accelerated write-off provisions; the choice will depend on the amount of the tax saving obtained by the lessor that is passed on to the lessee through lower lease payments.

Another provision which has the same impact on the present value of the cost of borrowing-to-purchase as the accelerated write-off provision is the investment tax credit. Assets which meet certain requirements qualify for this tax credit. The amount of the credit that can be used in the year of acquisition of the asset is governed by the rules noted in Chapter 2, and the impact of this credit is to reduce the amount of federal tax payable. Therefore, when evaluating the present value of the after-tax cost of borrowing to purchase, the after-tax net cost of the loan (Table 16–3, Column 6) for a particular year must be reduced by the amount of the tax credit applied in that year. In addition, the tax savings from capital cost allowances must be adjusted, since the capital cost of the asset is reduced by the full value of the investment tax credit.

As noted in the discussion of the accelerated write-off provision, the presence of competition among lessors should result in reduced lease payments. These lower lease payments will reflect the sharing of the benefit of

---

[8]One minor complication occurs when the asset is sold. At this point, UCC is zero and thus there is recaptured depreciation which will be taxed as regular income if there are no other assets in the pool.

the tax reduction accruing to the owner of the asset between the lessor and lessee.

Residual Value

One important point that must be mentioned in connection with leasing is that, unless there is a purchase provision given to the lessee, the lessor owns the property at the expiration of the lease. The value of the property at the end of the lease is called the *residual value.* Superficially, it would appear that where residual values are large, owning will be less expensive than leasing. However, even this obvious advantage of owning is subject to substantial qualification. On owned equipment, the obsolescence factor may be so large that it is doubtful whether residual values will be of a great order of magnitude. If residual values appear favorable, competition between leasing companies and other financial sources, as well as competition among leasing companies themselves, will force leasing rates down to the point where the potential of residual values are fully recognized in the leasing contract rates. Thus, the existence of residual values of equipment is not likely to result in materially lower costs of owning. However, in connection with decisions whether to lease or to own land, the obsolescence factor is not involved except to the extent of deterioration in areas with changing population or use patterns. If the lessor and the lessee have different expectations concerning the expected value of the land at the end of the lease period, there will be a preference by the user firm either to lease or to purchase. For example, suppose the user firm believes that the land (or, in fact, any asset) will have a lower residual value at the end of the lease period than the lessor expects. The user firm thus believes that the current price of the land is too high and the rate of return obtained from owning and obtaining the salvage value is very low. In this instance, the user firm may decide to lease the asset. Conversely, if the user believes that the residual value is greater than that expected by the lessor, then the asset is underpriced in their view and the user firm will buy the asset.

Thus it is difficult to generalize about whether residual value considerations are likely to make the effective cost of leasing higher or lower than the cost of owning. The results depend on whether the user firm has expectations of residual values that differ from the market as a whole. In evaluating the lease and borrow-to-purchase options, the user company's expectations of the residual value will be incorporated directly into the borrow-to-purchase option—see Equation 16–2.

Qualitative Factors

Rapid Obsolescence   Another popular notion is that leasing costs will be lower because of the rapid obsolescence of some kinds of equipment. It is argued that by having a lease with a very short life, the risk of obsolescence can be shifted to the lessor—the lessee does not have to bear the risk of holding an obsolete asset. Unfortunately, this argument is not very persuasive. The lessor will not bear this obsolescence risk without appropriate compensation through a higher return. Thus, the lease payments will reflect the high rate of obsolescence and the lessee pays for this risk. In general, it might be argued that neither residual values nor obsolescence rates can affect the cost of owning versus leasing.

In connection with leasing, however, it is possible that certain leasing companies may be better equipped to handle the obsolescence problem than the lessee. If the lease equipment becomes obsolete to one user, it is possible that the leasing company may find other companies for which this equipment is still useful. The lessor is equipped to engage in this redirection of assets among user companies. If the user company purchased the asset and it became obsolete, it might be very costly for them to find other companies who could make use of the equipment. The lessor company reduces the economic cost of obsolescence by increasing the effective residual value of the equipment. Part of this benefit will be passed along to the lessee by means of reduced lease payments. Therefore, leasing may be preferred to an outright purchase, since the economic costs of obsolescence are lower.

Possibly other institutions that do not combine financing and other specialist functions, such as manufacturing, reconditioning, servicing, and sales, may, in conjunction with financing institutions, perform the overall functions as efficiently and at as low cost as do integrated leasing companies. However, this is a factual matter depending upon the relative efficiency of the competing firms in different lines of business and different kinds of equipment. To determine which combination of methods results in the lower costs, an analysis along the lines of the pattern outlined in Table 16–3 is required.

Increased Credit Availability The reporting practices for leases on annual reports has been described in a previous section. It was noted that these reporting practices do not directly reflect the fact that leasing is an alternative to debt financing. It has been alleged by some proponents of leasing that based on this "off the balance sheet" financing, the borrowing capacity of a firm is improved. From first principles we would argue that a lease is equivalent to a debt issue, since both financing vehicles require a set of fixed payments. If the borrowing capacity of a firm is equal to $10 million and the firm has $5 million of debt outstanding, it can issue either additional debt equal to $5 million *or* lease obligations with an equivalent loan value of $5 million. Therefore, the lease alternative has no differential impact on debt capacity.

However, suppose that credit analysts, although aware of the lease obligations from the notes on the financial statements, put a value on the lease obligations less than the equivalent loan if debt were issued. In this case, the firm will be able to use lease financing but *not* reduce the potential amount of debt financing by the same dollar amount. In the example above, there is $5 million of borrowing capacity. If the firm issues lease obligations with an equivalent loan value of $2.5 million, the firm may be able to issue more than $2.5 million in debt.[9] In this case, the borrowing capacity has increased.

If borrowing capacity is increased by using lease financing, it is unlikely to be a result of the current reporting practices for lease obligations. It is not that difficult for an analyst to find the capitalized value of the lease obligations and to revise the financial ratios to reflect the lease obligations. Any increased borrowing capacity resulting from lease financing must result from a perceived difference between equivalent dollar values of the lease obligations and debt.

Implicit Interest Rates Higher in Leasing   The statement is frequently made that leasing always involves higher interest rates. This argument may be true, but it does not consider why the interest rates may be higher and if these higher rates have an impact on the lease or buy decision.

If an asset is financed by means of a lease, the restrictions on the firm's actions are not very demanding as compared to a bond issue in which the trust indenture specifies constraints on dividends, new investments, future leases, etc. In addition, bonds can have claims to earnings senior to all other financial instruments. These constraints reduce risk, and hence interest rates. Leases, on the other hand, do not usually have these covenants. If they do exist, they are less restrictive. Moreover, lease obligations are subordinate to debt. Therefore, the risk on lease financing may be higher and a higher interest rate is required. Any interest rate differentials between leasing and borrowing will reflect the differential risk of the financial instruments. Second, it is difficult to separate the money costs of leasing from the other services that may be embodied in a leasing contract. If, because of its specialized operations, the leasing company can perform nonfinancial services such as maintenance of the equipment at a lower cost than the lessee or some other institution can perform them, then the effective cost of leasing may be lower than for funds obtained from borrowing or other sources. The efficiencies of performing specialized services may thus enable the leasing company to operate by charging a lower total cost than the lessee would have to pay for the package of money plus services on any other basis.

SUMMARY

Intermediate-term financing is defined as any liability originally scheduled for repayment in more than one year but in less than ten years. Anything shorter is a current liability, while obligations due in ten or more years are thought of

---

[9] An interesting variation of the credit availability argument has been forwarded by a Canadian subsidiary of a U.S. company. The parent has a requirement that expenditures by the subsidiary above a certain cut-off dollar amount must be cleared through the parent, and so new debt issues or funds requested from the parent would likely be scrutinized. However, if the subsidiary leases the assets and the lease payments are less than the cut-off amount, no clearance is needed. Thus, leasing provided additional credit to the subsidiary. Needless to say, the parent eventually "plugged" this loophole in their operating rules.

as long-term debt. The major forms of intermediate-term financing include (1) *term loans* and (2) *lease financing.*

Term Loans   A term loan is a business credit with a maturity of more than one year but of less than fifteen years. There are exceptions to the rule, but generally, term loans are retired by systematic repayments (amortization payments) over the life of the loan. Security, generally in the form of a chattel mortgage on equipment, is often employed; the larger, stronger companies are able to borrow on an unsecured basis. Chartered banks and life insurance companies are the principal suppliers of term loan credit. Chartered banks and life insurance companies grant term loans.

The interest notes on a term loan can be set a certain number of percentage points above the prime rate and will fluctuate with changes in the prime rate. Alternatively, the interest rate charged can be fixed for the duration of the loan. The former technique is used by Canadian financial institutions, whereas the latter is more popular with Canadian subsidiaries of foreign banks, insurance companies and specialized term lending institutions. The interest cost of term loans, like rates on other credits, varies with the size of the loan and the strength of the borrower. Current rates on variable rate term loans are three to five percentage points above prime, while on fixed rate loans, the interest rates are 12 to 12½ percent.

Another aspect of term loans is the series of *protective covenants* contained in most loan agreements. The lender's funds are tied up for a long period, and during this time the borrower's situation can change markedly. For protection, the lender will include in the loan agreement stipulations that the borrower will maintain the current ratio at a specified level, limit acquisitions of additional fixed assets, keep the debt ratio below a stated amount, and so on. These provisions are necessary from the lender's point of view, but they necessarily restrict the borrower's actions.

Lease Financing   Leasing has long been used in connection with the acquisition of real estate assets. In recent years, it has been extended to a wide variety of equipment.

Three different forms of lease financing were considered: (1) sale and leaseback, in which a firm owning land, buildings, or equipment sells the property and simultaneously executes an agreement to lease the property for a specified period under specific terms; (2) operating leases which include both financing and maintenance services, are often cancellable, and call for payments under the lease contract which may not fully recover the cost of the equipment; and (3) financial leases, which do not provide for maintenance services, are not cancellable, and do fully amortize the cost of the leased asset during the basic lease contract period.

To understand the possible advantages and disadvantages of lease financing, the cost of leasing an asset must be compared with the cost of borrowing to purchase the same asset. In the absence of major tax advantages, whether or not leasing is advantageous turns primarily on the firm's ability to acquire funds by other methods. Leasing may provide an advantage by increasing the overall availability of nonequity financing to the firm. However, a financial lease contract is very similar to a straight-debt arrangement and uses some of the firm's debt-carrying ability.

QUESTIONS

16-1. "The type of equipment best suited for leasing has a long life in relation to the length of the lease, is a removable, standard product that could be used by many different firms, and is easily identifiable. In short, it is the kind of equipment that could be repossessed and sold readily. However, we would be quite happy to write a ten-year lease on paper towels for a firm such as General Motors." Discuss the statement.

16-2. Leasing is often called a hedge against obsolescence. Under what conditions is this actually true?

16-3. Is leasing in any sense a hedge against inflation for the lessee? for the lessor?

16-4. One alleged advantage of leasing is that it keeps liabilities off the balance sheet, thus making it possible for a firm to obtain more leverage than it otherwise could. This raises the question of whether or not both the lease obligation and the asset involved should be capitalized and shown on the balance sheet. Discuss the pros and cons of capitalizing leases and the related assets.

16-5. A firm is seeking a term loan from a bank. Under what conditions would it want a fixed interest rate, and under what condition would it want the rate to fluctuate with the prime rate?

16-6. Under what conditions would a "balloon note," or loan that is not fully amortized, be advantageous to a borrower?

PROBLEMS

16-1. The Lawton Co. Ltd. is faced with the decision whether to purchase or to lease a new fork-lift truck. The truck can be leased on a five-year contract for $2,300 a year, or it can be purchased for $6,990. The lease includes maintenance and service. The salvage value of the truck five years hence is $1,890. The company uses a capital cost rate on trucks of 30 percent. If the truck is owned, service and maintenance charges (a deductible cost) would be $500 a year. The company can borrow at 9 percent for amortized term loans. It has a 48 percent marginal tax rate.

    a. Which method of acquiring the use of equipment should the company choose?

    b. What factors could alter the results indicated by the quantitative analysis based on the above facts?

    c. Explain how you chose your discount rate or rates, emphasizing risk differentials and before-tax versus after-tax costs.

16-2. The Scott Brothers Department Store is considering a sale and leaseback of its major property, consisting of land and a building, because it is thirty days late on 80 percent of its accounts payable. The recent balance sheet of Scott Brothers is shown below. Profit before taxes in 19X5 is $36,000; after taxes, $19,800.

Scott Brothers Department Store Ltd.
Balance sheet
December 31, 19X5
(thousands of dollars)

Cash	$ 288	Accounts payable	$1,440
Receivables	1,440	Bank loans, 8%	1,440
Inventories	1,872	Other current liabilities	720
Total current assets	$3,600	Total current debt	$3,600
Land	$1,152	Common shares	1,440
Building	720	Retained earnings	720
Fixtures and equipment	288		
Net fixed assets	2,160		
Total assets	$5,760	Total claims	$5,760

Annual depreciation charges on a straight line basis for accounting and tax purposes are $57,600 a year on the building and $72,000 a year on the fixtures and equipment. The land and building could be sold for a total of $2.8 million. The annual net rental will be $240,000.

a. How much capital gains tax will Scott Brothers pay if the land and building are sold? (Assume all capital gains are taxed at the capital gains tax rate: that is, disregard such items as recapture of depreciation, tax preference treatment, and so on.)

b. Compare the current ratio before and after the sale and leaseback if the after-tax net proceeds are used to "clean up" the bank loans and to reduce accounts payable and other current liabilities.

c. If the lease had been in effect during 19X5, what would Scott Brothers' profit for 19X5 have been?

d. What are the basic financial problems facing Scott Brothers? Will the sale and leaseback operation solve them?

Warrants and Convertibles

17 Thus far in the discussion of long-term financing, we have examined the nature of common shares, preferred shares, various types of debt, and leasing. We have also seen how offering common shares through the use of rights can facilitate low issue costs. In this chapter, we see how the financial manager, through the use of warrants and convertibles, can make a company's securities attractive to an even broader range of investors. Since warrants and convertibles are being used more frequently, it is important to understand the characteristics of these two types of securities and the conditions under which their use is most beneficial to the company.

WARRANTS

A *warrant* is an option to purchase a stated number of shares of stock at a specified price called the *exercise price*. Warrants are usually attached to an issue of debt, preferred shares or sometimes common shares.[1] The warrants are detachable from their associated security issue and can be traded or exercised by the investor. For example, Consolidated-Bathurst Limited has warrants outstanding that give the warrant holder the right to purchase one share of Consolidated-Bathurst at an exercise price of $20 for each warrant held. If and when these warrants are exercised, it is equivalent to a new stock issue with the proceeds of the issue equal to the exercise price. Warrants

---

[1]Late in 1976, Bell Canada sold a portion of their stock holdings of Northern Telecom through a secondary issue. Associated with this issue were 2.6 million warrants to purchase Bell Canada stock at $46 any time before June 30, 1977. As of this expiration date, 99.8% of the warrants were exercised.

422

generally expire on a certain date—Consolidated-Bathurst's warrants expired on November 15, 1978—although some warrants have perpetual lives.

Theoretical Value of a Warrant

Warrants have a calculated or theoretical value, and an actual value (a price that is determined in the marketplace). The theoretical value is found by use of the following equation:

$$\begin{array}{c}\text{Theoretical}\\ \text{value}\end{array} = \left(\begin{array}{c}\text{market price of}\\ \text{common shares}\end{array}\right) - \left(\begin{array}{c}\text{exercise}\\ \text{price}\end{array}\right) \times \left(\begin{array}{c}\text{number of shares each}\\ \text{warrant entitles owner}\\ \text{to purchase}\end{array}\right) .$$

For instance, a Consolidated-Bathurst warrant entitles the holder to purchase common shares at $20 a share. If the market price of the common shares is $27.50, the formula price of the warrant may be obtained as follows:

$$(\$27.50 - \$20) \times 1.0 = \$7.50$$

The formula will result in a negative theoretical value when the stock is selling for less than the exercise price. For example, if the stock is selling for $18, the formula value of a warrant is minus $2. This makes no sense, so we define the theoretical value to be zero when the stock is selling for less than the exercise price.

Notice also that for this warrant, when the stock price is greater than the exercise price, an increase of $1 in the stock price results in an increase of $1 in the theoretical value of the warrant.

Actual Price of a Warrant

Generally, warrants sell above their theoretical values. When Consolidated-Bathurst stock was selling for $27.50, the warrants had a theoretical value of $7.50 but were selling at a price of $10.00. This represented a premium of $2.50 above the theoretical value.

In Figure 17-1, the hypothetical relationship of theoretical and market values for warrants is presented. This figure shows the impact of an increase in the price of the company's stock when all other variables such as interest rates, time left until the exercise date and the variability of the stock price are held constant. At any stock price below $20, the theoretical value of the warrant is zero, but the market value is positive. The actual market price of the warrant lies above the theoretical value at each assumed stock price. Notice, however, that the premium of market over theoretical value declines as the price per share of the common shares increases.[2]

[2] The size of the premium at a given stock price will depend on the actual value of the variables assumed to be constant. For example, if the basic risk of the stock increases, the premium will increase; if the time left to maturity decreases, the premium will decrease.

For example, when the common sold for $20 and the warrants had a zero theoretical value, their actual price was $2.25, which was also equal to the premium. As the price of the stock rose, the theoretical value of the warrants matched the increase dollar for dollar, but for a while the market price of the warrant climbed less rapidly and the premium declined. The premium was $2.25 when the stock sold for $20 a share, but it declines as the stock price rises to $40-$50 a share. Beyond this point, the premium seems to be constant.

FIGURE 17-1 Theoretical and Market Value of Consolidated Bathurst Warrants at Different Stock Prices

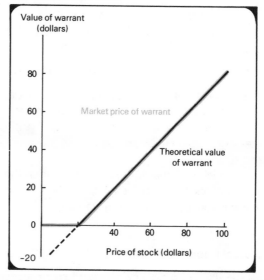

Why do you suppose this pattern exists? Why should the warrant ever sell for more than its theoretical value, and why does the premium decline as the price of the stock increases? The answer lies in the speculative appeal of warrants—they enable an investor to gain a high degree of personal leverage when buying securities. To illustrate, suppose Consolidated-Bathurst warrants always sold exactly at their theoretical value and that you are thinking of investing in the company's common shares at a time when they are selling for $25 each. If you buy a share and the price rises to $50 in a year, you have made a $25 capital gain or a 100 percent rate of return. However, had you purchased the warrants at their theoretical value of $5, the capital gain would still be $25 but the investment would have been $5; this results in a 500 percent rate of return. At the same time, your total loss potential with the warrant is limited to $5, while the potential loss from the purchase of the stock is $25. Thus, if the stock falls in value by more than $5, the warrant has provided protection since the loss is limited to the $5 investment in the warrant. The huge capital gains potential, combined with the loss limitation, is clearly worth something—the exact amount it is worth to investors is the amount of the premium.[3]

But why does the premium decline as the price of the stock rises? The answer is that both the leverage effect and the loss protection feature decline at high stock prices. For example, if you are thinking of buying the stock at $75 a share, the theoretical value of the warrant is $55. If the stock price doubles to $150, the theoretical value goes from $55 to $130.

While the capital gain on both the stock and the warrant is $75, the percentage rate of return on the stock is 100 percent and on the warrant, 136 percent; this is a substantial reduction from the 500 percent rate of return on the warrant associated with a 100 percent rate of return on the stock when the stock price was $25. Moreover, notice that the loss potential on the warrant is much greater when the warrant is selling at high prices. In addition, the loss protection is not very important if it is highly unlikely that the stock price will fall below $20.

These two factors, the declining leverage impact and the increasing danger of losses, explain why the premium diminishes as the price of the common shares rises.

Use of Warrants in Financing

In the past, warrants have generally been used by small, rapidly growing firms as "sweeteners" when selling either debt or preferred shares. Such firms are frequently regarded by investors as being highly risky. Their bonds could be sold (1) if the firms were willing to accept extremely high rates of interest and very restrictive indenture provisions, or (2) if warrants were issued along with the bonds, or (3) if the bonds were convertible. Warrants have a long history on the Toronto Stock Exchange; in 1939 there were five warrants listed. Their use has increased since then, and as seen in their use by Bell Canada in an issue of Northern Telecom stock, warrant financing is no longer restricted to a particular risk segment of the stock market.[4]

Giving warrants along with bonds (and preferred shares) enables investors to share in the company's growth, if it does, in fact, grow and prosper; therefore, investors are willing to accept a lower bond interest rate and less restrictive indenture provisions. A bond with warrants has some

---

[3]However, a $5 decline in the stock price from $25 produces only a 20 percent loss if the stock is purchased, and a 100 percent loss if the warrant is purchased.

[4]In 1961, there were 14 warrants listed in the TSE. The number increased and peaked at 16 in 1969. As of the end of 1975, there was 1 warrant outstanding. The decline in the use of warrants from 1970 on coincides with the decline in stock prices and new common equity issues. As the stock market picks up, the use of warrants will again probably increase.

characteristics of debt and some characteristics of equity. It is a hybrid security that provides the financial manager with an opportunity to expand the mix of securities and to appeal to a broader group of investors.

Warrants can also bring in additional funds. The exercise price is generally set 15 to 20 percent above the market price of the stock at the time of the bond issue.[5] If the firm does grow and prosper, and if its stock price rises above the option price at which shares may be purchased, warrant holders will surrender their warrants and buy stock at the stated price. There are several reasons for this. First, warrant holders will *surely* surrender warrants and buy stock if the warrants are about to expire with the market price of the stock above the option price. Second, warrant holders will *voluntarily* surrender and buy as just mentioned as the company raises the dividend on the common shares. No dividend is earned on the warrant, so it provides no current income. However, if the common shares pay a high dividend, they provide an attractive dividend yield. This induces warrant holders to exercise their option to buy the stock. Third warrants sometimes have *stepped-up option prices.* For example, suppose a company has warrants outstanding with an option price of $25 until December 31, 19X9, at which time the option price rises to $30. If the price of the common share is over $25 just before December 31, 19X9, many warrant holders will exercise their option before the stepped-up price takes effect.

One desirable feature of warrants is that they generally bring in additional funds only if such funds are needed. If the company grows and prospers, causing the price of the stock to rise, the warrants are exercised and bring in needed funds. If the company is not successful and cannot profitably employ additional money, the price of its stock will probably not rise sufficiently to induce exercise of the options.[6]

CONVERTIBLES

Convertible securities are bonds or preferred shares that are exchangeable under specified terms and conditions into common shares at the option of the holder. The most important of the special features relates to how many shares

---

[5]In July, 1977, Abacus Cities Limited, a real estate company with markets in Alberta and British Columbia attempted to list its shares on the Toronto Stock Exchange; the shares were already listed on the Alberta exchange. In October, 1977, the company withdrew its application for listing. The problem that Abacus faced was the novelty of the warrant issued in conjunction with a new preferred share issue. One warrant could be exchanged for one new share of Abacus but the option price was not fixed; it floated with the price of the common. In certain exercise periods, the warrant could be exercised at a minimum of $4 plus half the difference between this base price of $4 and a three month weighted average of Abacus' stock price during a six month period before the exercise date. It was the variability of the exercise price that appeared to present a problem to the Ontario Securities Commission. (See "Report on Business", *Globe and Mail,* January 14, 1978, p. B13, for a full discussion of the problem.)

[6]Suppose the warrants are exercised at the expiry date when the stock price is in excess of the exercise price. If the firm had made a new stock issue at this time instead of issuing warrants, the same amount of money would have been obtained by issuing fewer shares. This negative impact of warrant financing—called the *dilution effect*—will be offset by the lowered coupon rate obtained on the debt or preferred issue due to the sweetener effect of the warrant.

of stock a convertible holder receives if he converts. This feature is defined as the *conversion ratio,* which gives the number of common shares the holder of the convertible receives when the security is surrendered on conversion. Related to the conversion ratio is the *conversion price,* or the effective price paid for the common shares when conversion occurs.

Upon conversion, the convertible security is replaced in the capital structure by new equity and no new funds are provided to the company. This differs from a bond issued with warrants, since the exercise of the warrants brings in new equity funds and the bonds remain in the capital structure.

The relationship between the conversion ratio and the conversion price is illustrated by Chieftan Development Co. Ltd. convertible preferreds, issued in 1976 at a $50 par value. At any time prior to October 1, 1981, a convertible preferred holder can turn in preferred shares and receive in their place 3.846 common shares for each preferred share. Since the par value is $50 and the holder can receive 3.846 common shares, the price paid for a common share measured in terms of par value, is $13:

$$\text{Conversion price} = \frac{\text{par value of convertible security}}{\text{shares received}} = \frac{\$50}{3.846} = \$13.$$

The conversion price and the conversion ratio are established at the time the convertible bond or preferred is sold. Generally, these values are fixed for the life of the bond, although sometimes a stepped-up conversion price is used. Chieftan's convertible preferred has a conversion ratio that declines from the 1981 value until 1986. Thus, the conversion price increases to $15.50 until 1984 and to $18.50 until 1986. This feature is a means of inducing investors to convert their convertible security earlier. Another technique is to make the convertible securities callable at the option of the company.

Another factor that may cause a change in the conversion price and ratio is a standard feature of almost all convertibles—the clause protecting the convertible against dilution from stock splits, stock dividends, and the sale of common shares at low prices (as in a rights offering). The typical provision states that no common shares can be sold at a price below the conversion price and that the conversion price must be lowered (and the conversion ratio raised) by the percentage amount of any stock dividend or split. For example, if Chieftan has a two-for-one split, the conversion ratio would automatically be adjusted to 7.69 and the conversion price lowered to $6.50. If this protection was not contained in the contract, a company could completely thwart conversion by the use of stock splits and dividends. Warrants are similarly protected against dilution.

Like warrant option prices, the conversion price is characteristically set from 15 to 20 percent above the prevailing market price of the common shares at the time the convertible issue is sold. Exactly how the conversion price is established can best be understood after examining some of the reasons why firms use convertibles.

Advantages of Convertibles

Convertibles offer advantages to corporations as well as to individual investors. The most important of these advantages are discussed below.

As a *"sweetener" when selling debt.* A company can sell debt with lower interest rates and fewer restrictive covenants by giving investors a chance to share in potential capital gains. Convertibles, like bonds with warrants, offer this possibility. In addition, convertibles offer investors downside protection. Even if the capital gains do not materialize, the investor has a relatively safe coupon income. The value of the convertible cannot go below the market value of a bond (or preferred) offering the same coupon income.

To sell common shares at prices higher than those currently prevailing. Many companies actually want to sell common shares, not debt, but feel that the price of the stock is temporarily depressed. Management may believe, for example, that the current market price does not fully reflect the increase in earnings expected from the introduction of a new product. However, they expect the market to revise its expectations upward of the company's profitability and this should increase the company's stock price. To sell stock now would require giving up more shares to raise a given amount of money than management thinks is necessary. However, setting the conversion price 15 to 20 percent above the present market price of the stock will require giving up 15 to 20 percent fewer shares when the bonds are converted than would be required if stock, instead of the convertible, was sold.

Notice, however, that management is counting on the stock price's rising above the conversion price to make the bonds actually attractive in conversion. If the stock price does not rise and conversion does not occur, then the company has a "hung" convertible and the debt remains in the capital structure.

Notice, however, that management is counting on the stock price's rising above the conversion price to make the bonds actually attractive in conversion. If the stock price does not rise and conversion does not occur, then the company is saddled with debt.

How can the company be sure that conversion will occur when the price of the stock rises above the conversion price? Characteristically, convertibles have a provision that gives the issuing firm the opportunity of calling the convertible at a specified price. Suppose the conversion price is $50, the conversion ratio is 20, the market price of the common shares has risen to $60, and the call price on the convertible bond is $1,050. If the company calls the bond (by giving the usual notification), bondholders can either convert into common shares with a market value of $1,200 or allow the company to redeem the bond for $1,050. Naturally, bondholders prefer $1,200 to

$1,050, so conversion occurs. The call provision therefore gives the company a means of forcing conversion, provided that the market price of the stock is greater than the conversion price.

To meet short-run financing constraints. Suppose a company wants a particular ratio of equity to total capital in the long run but must issue either debt or preferred shares in the short run to obtain needed funds. The use of a convertible security is particularly useful in this instance, since conversion will increase the equity ratio. In addition, issue costs will be minimized by using the convertible, since the costs are incurred in the current period only. If debt is issued and refinanced later with equity, issue costs will be incurred twice along with refunding costs.

Disadvantages of Convertibles

From the standpoint of the issuer, convertibles have a possible disadvantage. Although the convertible bond does give the issuer the opportunity to sell common shares at a price 15 to 20 percent higher than it could otherwise be sold, if the common shares greatly increase in price, the issuer may find that it would have been better to have waited and simply sold the common shares. Further, if the company truly wants to raise equity capital and if the price of the stock declines after the bond is issued, then it is stuck with debt.

DECISIONS ON USE OF WARRANTS AND CONVERTIBLES

The Winchester Co. Ltd., an electronic circuit and component manufacturer with assets of $12 million, illustrates a typical case where convertibles are useful.

Winchester's profits have been depressed as a result of its heavy expenditures on research and development for a new product. This situation has held down the growth rate of earnings and dividends; the price/earnings ratio is only 18 times, as compared with an industry average of 22. At the current $2 earnings per share and *P/E* of 18, the stock is selling for $36 a share. The Winchester family owns 70 percent of the 300,000 shares outstanding, or 210,000 shares. It would like to retain majority control but cannot buy more stock.

The heavy R & D expenditures have resulted in the development of a new type of printed circuit that management believes will be highly profitable. Five million dollars is needed to build and equip new production facilities, and profits will not start to flow into the company for some eighteen months after construction on the new plant is started. Winchester's debt amounts to $5.4 million, or 45 percent of assets, well above the 25 percent industry average. Present debt indenture provisions restrict the company from selling additional debt unless the new debt is subordinate to that now outstanding.

Investment dealers inform J. H. Winchester, Jr., the financial vice-president, that subordinated debentures cannot be sold unless they are convertible or have warrants attached. Convertibles or bonds with warrants can be sold with a 5 percent coupon interest rate if the conversion price or warrant option price is set at 15 percent above the present market price of $36, or at $41 a share. Alternatively, the investment dealers are willing to buy convertibles or bonds with warrants at a 5½ percent interest rate and a 20 percent conversion premium, or a conversion (or exercise) price of $43.50. If the company wants to sell common shares directly, it can net $33 a share.

Which of the alternatives should Winchester choose? First, note that if common shares are used, the company must sell 151,000 shares ($5 million divided by $33). Combined with the 90,000 shares held outside the family, this amounts to 241,000 shares versus the Winchester holdings of 210,000, so the family will lose majority control if common shares are sold.

If the 5 percent convertibles or bonds with warrants are used and the bonds are converted or the warrants are exercised, 122,000 new shares will be added. Combined with the old 90,000, the outside interest will then be 212,000, so again the Winchester family will lose majority control. However, if the 5½ percent convertibles or bonds with warrants are used, then after conversion or exercise only 115,000 new shares will be created. In this case the family will have 210,000 shares versus 205,000 for outsiders; absolute control will be maintained.

In addition to assuring control, using the convertibles or warrants also benefits earnings per share in the long run—the total number of shares is less because fewer new shares must be issued to get the $5 million, so earnings per share will be higher. Before conversion or exercise, however, the firm has a considerable amount of debt outstanding. Adding $5 million raises the total debt to $10.4 million against new total assets of $17 million, so the debt ratio will be over 61 percent versus the 25 percent industry average. This could be dangerous. If delays are encountered in bringing the new plant into production, if demand does not meet expectations, if the company should experience a strike, if the economy should go into a recession—if any of these things occur—the company will be extremely vulnerable because of the high debt ratio.

In the present case, the decision was made to sell the 5½ percent convertible debentures. Two years later, earnings climbed to $3 a share, the P/E ratio to 20, and the price of the stock to $60. The bonds were called, but, of course, conversion occurred. After conversion, debt amounted to approximately $5.5 million against total assets of $17.5 million (some earnings had been retained), so the debt ratio was down to a more reasonable 31 percent.

Convertibles were chosen rather than bonds with warrants for the following reason. If a firm has a high debt ratio and its near-term prospects are favorable, it can anticipate a rise in the price of its stock and thus be able to call the bonds and force conversion. Warrants, on the other hand, have a stated life, and even though the price of the firm's stock rises, the warrants may not be exercised until near their expiration date.[7] If, subsequent to the favorable period (during which convertibles could have been called), the firm encounters less favorable developments and the price of its stock falls, the warrants may lose their value and may never be exercised. The heavy debt burden will then become aggravated. Therefore, the use of convertibles gives the firm greater control over the timing of future capital structure changes. This factor is of particular importance to the firm if its debt ratio is already high in relation to the risks of its line of business.

REPORTING EARNINGS IF CONVERTIBLES OR WARRANTS ARE OUTSTANDING

Before closing the chapter, we should note that firms with convertibles or warrants outstanding are required to report earnings per share in two ways: (1) *primary EPS,* which in essence is earnings available to common shares divided by the number of shares actually outstanding, and (2) *fully diluted EPS,* which shows what EPS would be if all warrants had been exercised or convertibles converted prior to the reporting date. For firms with large amounts of option securities outstanding, there can be a substantial difference between the two EPS figures. The purpose of the provision is, of course, to give investors a more accurate picture of the firm's true profit position.

SUMMARY

Both warrants and convertibles are forms of options used in financing business firms. The use of such long-term options is encouraged by an economic environment combining prospects of both boom or inflation and depression or deflation. The senior position of the securities protects against recessions. The option feature offers the opportunity for participation in rising stock prices.

Both the convertibility privilege and warrants are used as "sweeteners." The option privileges they grant may make it possible for small companies to sell debt or preferred shares that otherwise could not be sold. For both large and small companies, the "sweeteners" result in lower costs of the securities sold. In addition, the options provide for the future sale of the common shares at prices higher than could be obtained at present. The options thereby permit

---

[7]To our knowledge, no company has ever issued a "callable" warrant, that is, one that the issuer would call for exercise under specific conditions. We recently recommended to a company that it consider issuing perpetual, but callable, warrants. These could be called to force exercise if the price of the stock exceeded the exercise price by, say, 30 percent; they would otherwise have no expiration date. Such warrants would probably be viewed with favor by investors afraid of warrants that might expire valueless, and they would still give the company control over the warrants similar to that over convertibles.

the delayed sale of common shares at more favorable prices.

The conversion of bonds by their holders does not ordinarily bring additional funds to the company. The exercise of warrants will provide such funds. The conversion of securities will result in reduced debt ratios. The exercise of warrants will strengthen the equity position but will still leave the debt or preferred shares on the balance sheet. In comparing the use of convertibles to senior securities carrying warrants, a firm with a high debt ratio should choose convertibles. A firm with a moderate or low debt ratio may employ warrants.

In the past, larger and stronger firms tended to favor convertibles over bonds with warrants, so most warrants have been issued by smaller, weaker concerns. However, large companies are using warrants more frequently, and we anticipate that warrants will come into increasing use in the years ahead.

QUESTIONS

17-1. Why do warrants typically sell at prices greater than their theoretical values?

17-2. Why do convertibles typically sell at prices greater than their theoretical values (the higher of the conversion value or straight-debt value)? Would you expect the percentage premium on a convertible bond to be more or less than that on a warrant? (The percentage premium is defined as the market price minus the theoretical value, divided by the market price.)

17-3. What effect does the trend in stock prices (subsequent to issue) have on a firm's ability to raise funds (a) through convertibles and (b) through warrants?

17-4. If a firm expects to have additional financial requirements in the future, would you recommend that it use convertibles or bonds with warrants? Why?

17-5. If a firm increases its dividend payout ratio (dividends/earnings), how would this affect each of the following?
   a. The value of long-term warrants.
   b. The likelihood that convertible bonds will be converted.
   c. The likelihood that warrants will be exercised.

17-6. Evaluate the following statement: "Issuing convertible securities represents a means by which a firm can sell common shares at a price above the existing market."

17-7. Why do corporations often sell convertibles on a rights basis?

17-8. Suppose that, as of the conversion date, the stock price of the company is less than the conversion price of a convertible bond. Since conversion does not occur, the company is faced with a hung convertible. Discuss how you would find the value of this convertible at some date after the conversion date.

PROBLEMS

17-1. A convertible bond has a face value of $1,000; it has a 10 percent coupon rate and is convertible into stock at $50, i.e., each bond can be exchanged for twenty shares. The current price of the stock is $43 per share.

a. If the price per share grows at 6 percent per year for five years, what will the approximate conversion value be at that time?

b. If dividends on the stock are presently $2 per share, and if these also grow at 6 percent per year, would bondholders convert after five years or would they tend to hold onto their bonds?

c. If the bonds are callable at a 10 percent premium, about how much would you lose per bond if the bonds were called before you converted? (Assume the same conversion value as in part a above, after five years).

17-2. Warrants attached to a bond entitle the bondholder to purchase one share of stock at $10 per share. Compute the approximate value of a warrant if:

   a. The market price of the stock is $9 per share.

   b. Market price of the stock is $12 per share.

   c. Market price of the stock is $15 per share.

   d. Now each warrant entitles you to purchase two shares at $10, and the current price of a share of stock is $15 per share.

17-3. Garrett Lumber Co. Ltd.'s capital consists of 10,000 shares of common shares and 5,000 warrants, each good to buy two shares of common at $55 a share. The warrants are protected against dilution (that is, the subscription price is adjusted downward in the event of a stock dividend or if the firm sells common shares at less than the $55 exercise price). The company issues rights to buy one new share of common at $50 for every two shares held. With the stock selling rights on at $62, compute:

   a. The theoretical value of the rights before the stock sells ex rights.

   b. The new subscription price of the warrant after the rights issue.

17-4. The Williston Manufacturing Co. Ltd. was planning to finance an expansion in the summer of 19X5. The principal executives of the company were agreed that an industrial company such as theirs should finance growth by means of common shares rather than by debt. However, they felt that the price of the company's common shares did not reflect its true worth, so they were desirous of selling a convertible security. They considered a convertible debenture but feared the burden of fixed interest charges if the common shares did not rise in price to make conversion attractive. They decided on an issue of convertible preferred shares.

The common shares were currently selling at $28 each. Management projected earnings for 19X5 at $2 a share and expected a future growth rate of 10 percent a year. It was agreed by the investment dealers and the management that the common shares would sell at 18 times earnings, the current price/earnings ratio.

   a. What conversion price should be set by the issuer?

   b. Should the preferred shares include a call-price provision? Why?

17-5. Copy Right Duplicator Ltd., has the following balance sheet:

BALANCE SHEET 1

Current assets	$125,000	Current debt (free)	$ 50,000
Net fixed assets	125,000	Common shares, par value $2.	50,000
		Retained earnings	150,000
Total assets	$250,000	Total claims	$250,000

a. The firm earns 18 percent on total assets before taxes (assume a 50 percent tax rate). What are earnings per share? Twenty-five thousand shares are outstanding.

b. If the price/earnings ratio for the company's stock is 16 times, what is the market price of the company's stock?

c. What is the book value of the company's stock?

In the following few years, sales are expected to double and the financing needs of the firm will double. The firm decides to sell debentures to meet these needs. It is undecided, however, whether to sell convertible debentures or debentures with warrants. The new balance sheet would appear as follows:

BALANCE SHEET 2

Current assets	$250,000	Current debt	$100,000
Net fixed assets	250,000	Debentures	150,000
		Common shares, par value $2	50,000
		Retained earnings	200,000
Total assets	$500,000	Total claims	$500,000

The convertible debentures would pay 7 percent interest and would be convertible into forty common shares for each $1,000 debenture. The debentures with warrants would carry an 8 percent coupon and entitle each holder of a $1,000 debenture to buy twenty-five shares of common at $50.

d. Assume that convertible debentures are sold and all are later converted. Show the new balance sheet, disregarding any changes in retained earnings.

BALANCE SHEET 3

		Current debt	_____
		Debentures	_____
		Common shares, par value $2	_____
		Paid-in capital	_____
		Retained earnings	_____
Total assets	_____	Total claims	_____

e. Complete the firm's income statement after the debentures have all been converted:

INCOME STATEMENT 1

Net income after all charges except debenture interest and before taxes (18% of total assets)	_____
Debenture interest	_____
Federal income tax, 50%	_____
Net income after taxes	_____
Earnings per share after taxes	_____

f. Now, instead of convertibles, assume that debentures with warrants were issued. Assume further that the warrants were all exercised. Show the new balance sheet figures.

BALANCE SHEET 4

	Current debt		_____
	Debentures		_____
	Common shares, par value $2		_____
	Paid-in capital		_____
	Retained earnings		_____
Total assets	=======	Total claims	=======

g. Complete the firm's income statement after the debenture warrants have all been exercised.

INCOME STATEMENT 2

Net income after all charges except debenture interest and before taxes	_____
Debenture interest	_____
Taxable income	_____
Federal income tax	_____
Net income after taxes	_____
Earnings per share after taxes	_____

17-6. The Link Printing Co. Ltd. has grown rapidly during the past five years. Recently its commercial bank has urged the company to consider increasing permanent financing. Its bank loan under a line of credit has risen to $175,000, carrying 7 percent interest. Link has been thirty to sixty days late in paying trade creditors.

Discussions with an investment dealer have resulted in the suggestion to raise $350,000 at this time. Investment dealers have assured Link that the following alternatives will be feasible (issue costs will be ignored):

Alternative 1: Sell common shares at $7.
Alternative 2: Sell convertible bonds at a 7 percent coupon, convertible into common shares at $8.
Alternative 3: Sell debentures at a 7 percent coupon, each $1,000 bond carrying 125 warrants to buy common shares at $8.

Additional information is given below.

Link Printing Company Ltd. balance sheet

		Current liabilities	$315,000
		Common shares, par $1.00	90,000
		Retained earnings	45,000
Total assets	$450,000	Total liabilities and capital	$450,000

Link Printing Company Ltd. income statement

Sales	$900,000
All costs except interest	810,000
Gross profit	$ 90,000
Interest	10,000
Profit before taxes	$ 80,000
Taxes at 50%	40,000
Profits after taxes	40,000
Shares	90,000
Earnings per share	$0.44
Price/earnings ratio	17 ×
Market price of stock	$7.48

Larry Rinehart, the president, owns 70 percent of the common shares of Link Printing Company and wishes to maintain control of the company. Ninety thousand shares are outstanding.

a. Show the new balance sheet under each alternative. For alternatives 2 and 3, show the balance sheet after conversion of the debentures or exercise of warrants. Assume that one-half the funds raised will be used to pay off the bank loan and one-half to increase total assets.

b. Show Rinehart's control position under each alternative, assuming that he does not purchase additional shares.

c. What is the effect on earnings per share of each alternative, if it is assumed that profits before interest and taxes will be 20 percent of total assets?

d. What will be the debt ratio under each alternative?

e. Which of the three alternatives would you recommend to Rinehart and why?

Financial Structure and the Use of Leverage

Part Five

In Part Four, we examined the major sources and forms of long-term external capital, considering the market for long-term securities and the principal types of securities—common and preferred shares, bonds, term loans, leases, convertibles, and warrants. We compared the advantages and disadvantages of these different instruments and considered some of the factors that financial managers keep in mind as they decide which form of financing to use at a specific time. Now, in Part Five, we examine the long-term financing decision in a somewhat different manner, searching for the *optimal* financial structure, or the financial structure that simultaneously minimizes the firm's cost of capital and maximizes the market value of its common shares. As we shall see, financing decisions and investment decisions are interdependent— the optimal financing plan and the optimal level of investment must be determined simultaneously—so Part Five also serves the important function of integrating the theory of capital budgeting and the theory of capital structure.

Part Five contains four chapters: First, Chapter 18, Valuation and Rates of Return, examines the way risk and return interact to determine value. Next, Chapter 19, Financial Structure and the Use of Leverage, highlights the manner in which debt not only generally increases expected earnings, but also increases the firm's risk position. Chapter 20, The cost of Capital, draws on the two preceding chapters to establish the firm's optimal capital structure as well as its cost of capital. Finally, in Chapter 21, Dividend Policy and Internal Financing, we analyze the decision of whether to pay out earnings in the form of dividends or to retain earnings for reinvestment in the business, and we show the interrelationship between capital budgeting and cost of capital.

Valuation and Rates of Return

18

One of the financial manager's principal goals is to maximize the value of the firm's common shares; accordingly, an understanding of the way the market values securities is essential to sound financial management. Also, the rate of return concepts developed in this chapter are used extensively in Chapters 19 and 20, where we analyze the optimal capital structure and show how to calculate a marginal cost of capital for use in capital budgeting.

DEFINITIONS OF VALUE

While it may be difficult to ascribe monetary returns to certain kinds of assets —works of art, for instance—the fundamental characteristic of business assets is that they give rise to income flows. Sometimes these flows are easy to determine and measure—the interest return on a bond is an example. At other times, the cash flows attributable to the asset must be estimated, as was done in Chapters 11 and 12 with capital budgeting. Regardless of the difficulties of measuring income flows, it is the prospective income from business assets that gives them value.

Liquidating Value versus Going-Concern Value

Several different definitions of "value" exist in the literature and are used in practice, with different ones being appropriate at different times. The first distinction that must be made is that between liquidating value and going-concern value. *Liquidating value* is defined as the amount that could be realized if an asset or a group of assets (the entire assets of a firm, for example) were sold separately from the organization that had been using them. If the owner of a machine shop decided to retire, he might auction off his inventory and equipment, collect his accounts receivable, then sell his land and buildings to a grocery wholesaler for use as a warehouse. The sum of the proceeds from each category of assets would be the liquidating value of the assets. If his debts are subtracted from this amount, the difference would represent the liquidating value of his ownership in the business.

On the other hand, if the firm is sold as an operating business to a corporation or to another individual, the purchaser would pay an amount equal to the *going-concern value* of the company. If the going-concern value exceeded the liquidating value, the difference would represent the value of the organization as distinct from the value of the assets.[1]

Book Value versus Market Value

We must also distinguish between *book value,* or the accounting value at which an asset is carried, and *market value,* the price at which the asset can be sold. If the asset in question is a firm, it actually has two market values—a liquidating value and a going-concern value. Only the higher of the two is generally referred to as *the* market value.

For common shares, which are of primary concern in this chapter, book value of equity per share is the firm's total common equity—the sum of common shares, contributed surplus, and accumulated retained earnings—divided by the number of shares outstanding. For example, the book value per share of a given firm is $50. The market value, which is what people will actually pay for a share, could be above or below the book value. Maple Leaf Gardens Limited, for example, had a book value per share of $1.83 and a market value of $23.00 as of December 31, 1976; Canron Limited, on the other hand, had a book value of $27.56 and a market value of $23.75 as of the same date. At the end of 1976, the market believed that there was a large growth potential inherent in the assets of Maple Leaf Gardens Limited. For Canron, which manufactures iron, concrete, plastic pipe and fittings along with a number of other steel products, the market did not forsee substantial growth in earnings and dividends. Since market value is dependent upon earnings, while book value reflects historical cost, it is not surprising to find deviations between book and market values in a dynamic and uncertain world.

Market Value versus "Fair" or "Reasonable" Value

The concept of a fair or reasonable value (sometimes called the "intrinsic" value) is widespread in the literature on stock market investments. Although

---

[1] Accountants have termed this difference "goodwill," but "organization value" would be a more appropriate description.

the market value of a security is known at any given time, the security's fair value as viewed by different investors could differ. Graham, Dodd, and Cottle, in a classic investments text, define fair value as "that value which is justified by the facts, e.g., assets, earnings, dividends . . . The computed [fair] value is likely to change at least from year to year, as the factors governing that value are modified."[2]

Although Graham, Dodd, and Cottle develop this concept for security (that is, stock and bond) valuation, the idea is applicable to all business assets. What it involves, basically, is estimating the future net cash flows attributable to an asset; determining an appropriate capitalization, or discount, rate; and then finding the present value of the cash flows. This, of course, is exactly what was done in Chapters 10, 11, and 12, where the concept of reasonable value was developed for application in finding the present value of investment opportunities.

The procedure for determining an asset's value is known as the *capitalization-of-income method of valuation.* This is simply a fancy name for the present value of a stream of earnings, discussed at length in Chapter 10. *In going through the present chapter, keep in mind that value, or the price of securities, is exactly analogous to the present value of assets as determined in Chapters 11 and 12.* From this point on, whenever the word "value" is used, we mean the *present value* found by capitalizing expected future cash flows.

THE REQUIRED RATE OF RETURN, *k*

The first step in using the capitalization of income procedure is to establish the proper capitalization rate, or discount rate, for the security. *This rate is defined as the required rate of return, and it is the minimum rate of return necessary to induce investors to buy or hold the security.* For any given risky security, the required rate of return is equal to the rate of return required in the market place for a riskless asset, R_F , plus a risk premium, ρ, read "rho":

$$k = R_F + \rho . \qquad (18\text{--}1)$$

The current yield on Government of Canada Treasury bills is generally used to measure R_F .

The size of the risk premium will depend on the risk exposure that the equity holder accepts when purchasing the security and on the market determined increment in required yield per unit of risk accepted. This increment in required yield is also referred to as the market's *risk-return tradeoff.* Therefore, Equation 18–1 can be rewritten as follows:

$$k = R_F + \left(\begin{array}{c} \text{increment in required} \\ \text{yield per unit risk} \end{array} \right) \times \left(\begin{array}{c} \text{measure of} \\ \text{risk exposure} \end{array} \right) \qquad (18\text{--}2)$$

[2]B. Graham, D. L. Dodd, and S. Cottle, *Security Analysis* (New York: McGraw-Hill, Inc., 1961), p. 28.

For a given level of risk exposure, the required yield on equity will depend on the increment in required yield per unit risk. The higher this quantity is, the higher will be the required yield. This increment in required yield is set in the marketplace by the investors and reflects the tradeoff of return for risk required by market participants. Since participants in the marketplace are averse to risk, the "return-risk" tradeoff will always be positive—thus, as long as there is some risk, the required rate of return on equity will exceed the riskless rate. For a given level of the "return-risk" tradeoff, the required rate of return on equity will depend on the amount of risk exposure. This risk exposure is related to the business and financial risk of the company. If there is no risk, the required rate of return equals the riskless rate which is generally measured by Government of Canada Treasury Bills. As risk increases, so does the required yield on equity.

Great interest has been shown in the theoretical and empirical literature in the relationship portrayed in Equation 18-2. As a result, there has been considerable analysis of the appropriate measure of risk exposure; given this risk measure, the theoretical literature has derived what the market return-risk tradeoff looks like.

A discussion of these results requires more statistical sophistication than is required for other parts of the book. For expository purposes, we are assuming that risk exposure is measured as the expected standard deviation of the rates of return on the equity of the security in question. In addition, we do not specify the composition of the return-risk tradeoff, but assume that there is a straight-line relationship between the required rate of return on equity and risk exposure.[3] Thus, the required yield on equity for an individual company is written as:

$$k_i = R_F + \alpha \sigma_i \qquad (18\text{-}3)$$

[3]The relationship of required yield to risk is discussed in the literature on the Capital Asset Pricing Model (CAPM). CAPM theory has developed a straight-line relationship between the required yield and a measure of risk. The risk measure used in the CAPM is referred to as a "beta" coefficient. This risk measure for an individual security reflects the movements in the security's rate of return that are related to overall market movements. For example, a portfolio of all stocks in the market would have a risk measure equal to 1. Some companies have rates of return that are not very sensitive to the overall market and have risk measures that are less than 1. Examples of these companies would be some regulated telecommunications companies. All other movements in the firm's rate of return on equity are specific to the company, and hence, can be diversified away by a risk averse investor who holds a portfolio of a large number of securities. The relationship of required rates of return to risk for an individual security is called the *security market line:*

$$k_i = R_F + \lambda \beta_i$$

where λ is the market tradeoff of return for risk, and β is the "beta" coefficient or risk measure.

The standard deviation of the rate of return on equity is composed of both firm-specific events, which can be diversified away, and influences of the general market index. According to CAPM theory, the investor's required yield depends only on the risk that cannot be diversified away.

In our discussion, we attempt to present an intuitive explanation of the relationship of required yield and risk without specifying either the exact risk measure or the tradeoff. The reader can insert whatever measure of risk he or she wants, since the basic conclusions will not be affected. Beta coefficients are discussed in Appendix C to Chapter 19 of Davidson, et. al., *Managerial Finance,* 1975.

where α is the return-risk tradeoff,

σ_i is the expected standard deviation of the rate of return on equity for company i, and

k_i is the required rate of return on equity for company i.

Notice that companies will differ only through the value of σ. In the discussions below, we will drop the subscript i. Finally, the value of the risk premium, ρ, is equal to $\alpha\sigma$ (i.e. it depends on the risk of the equity and α).

Figure 18-1 presents Equation 18-3 in graph form. The required rate of return is shown on the vertical axis and risk (measured here as the expected standard deviation of the rate of return, σ) is shown on the horizontal axis. The slope of the relationship is equal to α.

FIGURE 18–1 The Relationship between Risk and the Required Rate of Return

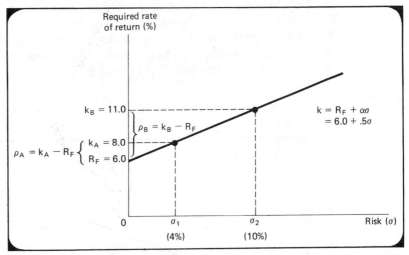

Since a riskless asset, by definition, has no risk, R_F lies on the vertical axis. As risk increases, the required rate of return also increases. A relatively low-risk security, such as that of firm A, might have a risk index of $\sigma_A = 4$ percent and a required rate of return of $k_A = 8$ percent. A more risky security, such as that of firm B, might have a risk index of $\sigma_B = 10$ percent and a required rate of return of $k_B = 11$ percent.

In the illustrative case, the slope of the relationship (α) is 0.5; indicating that the required rate of return rises by 0.5 percent for each 1 percent increase in the standard deviation of expected returns. The standard deviation is 4 percent for firm A, so the risk premium on that security is 2 percent (0.5 × 4 = 2%), while the standard deviation of returns on security B is 10 percent, making its risk premium 5 percent (0.5 × 10 = 5%). When these two risk premiums are added to the riskless rate, R_F, we obtain the required rates of return:

$$k_A = 6\% + 2\% = 8\%.$$

$$k_B = 6\% + 5\% = 11\%.$$

Notice that the graph can also be used to analyze the securities of a single firm. Since a company's bonds have a smaller standard deviation of expected returns than its common shares, k_A might be the required rate of return on the firm's bonds, while k_B might refer to its common shares. The company's preferred shares would lie on the line between k_A and k_B.

Shifts in the Relationship: Changing Interest Rates

We noted in Chapter 7 that interest rates shift markedly over time, and when such shifts occur, the relationship between required rate of return and risk also shifts. Figure 18–2 illustrates the effects of an increase in the riskless rate from 6 to 8 percent, while keeping the slope of the relationship constant. One possible explanation for this type of shift in the relationship is an increase in the rate of inflation expected in the marketplace.[4]

FIGURE 18–2 The Effect of Rising Interest Rates on the Required Rate of Return

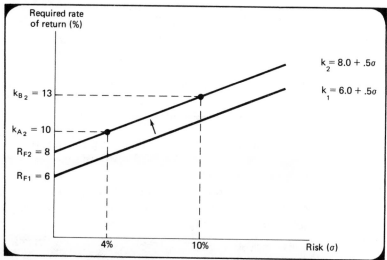

[4]Other types of interest rate changes may not have this impact on the relationship. For example, an increase in interest rates will increase the intercept, but may also reduce the slope of the line. This would result in a rotation of the line, not a parallel shift.

Original relationship: $k = 6.0\% + 0.5$

Revised relationship: $k = 8.0\% + 0.5$

This results in increases in the required rates of return for firms A and B, with k_A rising from 8 to 10 percent and k_B from 11 to 13 percent.

Shifts in the Relationship: Investor Psychology

The slope of the relationship between required return and risk will depend upon the investors' attitudes toward risk. There are times when investors, in aggregate, require a higher expected rate of return per unit of risk; at such times, the slope of the relationship will be relatively steep. Conversely, when investors are optimistic and have a bright outlook, the slope of the line will not be as steep—investors will be willing to bear the same risk for a smaller expected return. Thus, when investors' attitudes change, the relationship will shift. Figure 18–3 illustrates a change in attitudes toward risk which results in an increase in the slope from 0.5 to 0.7.

Original relationship: $k = 6\% + 0.5\,\sigma$

Revised relationship: $k = 6\% + 0.7\,\sigma$

This shift increases the required rates of return for firms A and B, with k_A rising from 8 to 8.8 percent and k_A from 11 to 13 percent.

FIGURE 18–3   The Effect of Changing Investor Attitudes on the Required Rate of Return

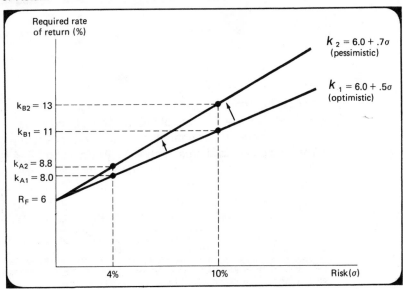

BOND VALUATION

The rate of return concepts developed above may now be used to explain the process of security valuation. In this section we examine bond values; in the two following sections, we go on to study preferred and common shares.

Bond values are relatively easy to determine. As long as the bond is not expected to go into default, the expected cash flows are the annual interest payments plus the principal amount due when the bond matures. Depending upon differences in the risk of default on interest and principal, the appropriate capitalization (or discount) rate applied to different bonds will vary. A Government of Canada bond, for example, would have less risk than a bond with the same term-to-maturity issued by a corporation; and consequently, a lower discount (or capitalization) rate would be applied to the interest payments on the Government bond. The actual calculating procedures employed in bond valuation are illustrated by the following examples.

Perpetual Bond

After the Napoleonic Wars (1814), England sold a huge bond issue which was used to pay off many smaller issues that had been floated in prior years to pay for the war. Since the purpose of the new issue was to consolidate past debts, the individual bonds were called Consols.[5] Suppose the bonds paid $50 interest annually into perpetuity. (Actually, interest was stated in pounds.) What would the bonds be worth under current market conditions?

First, note that the value (V) of any perpetuity is computed as follows:

$$V = \frac{I}{(1 + k_d)^1} + \frac{I}{(1 + k_d)^2} + \cdots + \frac{I}{(1 + k_d)^\infty}$$

$$= \frac{I}{k_d}. \tag{18-4}$$

Here I is the constant annual interest in dollars and k_d is the appropriate interest rate, or required rate of return, for the bond issue. (In this chapter, we use k_d, k_p, and k_s to designate the required rates of return on debt, preferred shares, and common shares, respectively.) Equation 18-4 is an infinite series of $I a year, and the value of the bond is the discounted sum of the infinite series.

---

[5]England was not alone in issuing perpetuities. In 1936, Canada issued a perpetuity with a 3 percent coupon. The issue was not very large ($55 million) and it was callable in 1966. As interest rates increased in the 1970s, the owners of these bonds began to complain about the reduced market values and the low interest payments. In the first quarter of 1975, the government changed some terms of the issue by setting the maturity date equal to the call date, but maintained the $3 coupon per $100 par value. As would be expected, the price of the "perpetual" increased. (See Problem 18-10.) Currently, Canada Pacific Railways (CPR) has a 4 percent perpetual bond outstanding, payable in U.S. dollars. This is the only perpetuity in existence in North America.

We know that the Consol's annual interest payment is $50; therefore, the only other thing we need in order to find its value is the appropriate interest rate. This is commonly taken as the going interest rate, or yield, on bonds of similar risk. Suppose we find such bonds to be paying 4 percent under current market conditions. Then the Consol's value is determined as follows:

$$V = \frac{I}{k_d} = \frac{\$50}{0.04} = \$1,250.$$

If the going rate of interest rises to 5 percent, the value of the bond falls to $1,000 ($50/0.05 = $1,000). If interest rates continue rising, when the rate goes as high as 6 percent the value of the Consol will be only $833.33. Values of this perpetual bond for a range of interest rates are given in the following tabulation:

Current Market Interest Rate	Current Market Value
0.02%	$2,500.00
0.03	1,666.67
0.04	1,250.00
0.05	1,000.00
0.06	833.33
0.07	714.29
0.08	625.00

Short-term Bond

Now suppose the British government issues bonds with the same risk of default as the Consols, but with a three-year maturity. The new bonds also pay $50 interest and have a $1,000 maturity value. What will the value of these new bonds be at the time of issue if the going rate of interest is 4 percent? To find this value, we must solve Equation 18–5 again assuming interest is paid once a year.

$$V = \frac{I_1}{(1 + k_d)^1} + \frac{I_2}{(1 + k_d)^2} + \frac{I_3 + M}{(1 + k_d)^3} \qquad (18\text{–}5)$$

Here M is the maturity value of the bond. The solution is given in the following tabulation:[6]

[6] If the bond has a longer maturity, twenty years for example, we would certainly want to calculate its present value by finding the present value of a twenty-year annuity and then adding to that the present value of the $1,000 principal amount received at maturity. Special bond tables have been devised to simplify the calculation procedure. Note also that k_d will frequently differ for the long- and short-term bonds; as we saw in Chapter 7, unless the yield to maturity curve is flat, long- and short-term rates differ.

Year	Receipt	4 Percent Discount Factors	Present Value
1	$50	.962	$ 48.10
2	$50	.925	46.25
3	$50 + $1,000	.889	933.45
		Bond value =	$1,027.80

At the various rates of interest used in the perpetuity example, this three-year bond would have the following values:

Current Market Interest Rate	Current Market Value
.02%	$1,086.15
.03	1,056.45
.04	1,027.80
.05	1,000.00
.06	973.65
.07	947.20
.08	922.85

FIGURE 18–4 Values of Long-term and Short-term Bonds, 5 Percent Coupon Rate, at Different Market Interest Rates

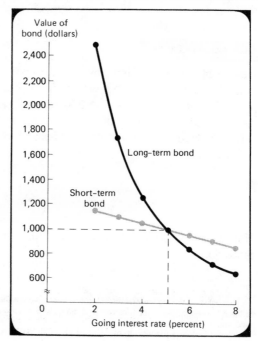

Interest-rate Risk

Figure 18–4 shows how the values of the long-term bond (the Consol) and the short-term bond change in response to changes in the going market rate of interest. Note how much less sensitive the short-term bond is to changes in interest rates. At a 5 percent interest rate, both the perpetuity and the short-term bonds are valued at $1,000. When rates rise to 8 percent, the long-term bond falls to $625, while the short-term security falls only to $923. A similar situation occurs when rates fall below 5 percent. *This differential responsiveness to changes in interest rates always hold true—the longer the maturity of a security, the greater its price change in response to a given change in interest rates.* Thus, even if the risk of default on two bonds is exactly the same, the value of the one with the longer maturity is exposed to more risk from a rise in interest rates. This greater *interest rate risk* is one factor cited to explain why short-term bonds usually have lower yields, or rates of return, than long-term bonds. It also explains why corporate treasurers are reluctant to hold their near-cash reserves in the form of long-term debt instruments—these near-cash reserves are held for precautionary purposes, and a treasurer would be unwilling to sacrifice safety for a little higher yield on a long-term bond.

Yield to Maturity

The rate of return that is expected if a bond is held to its maturity date is defined as the *yield to maturity*. Suppose a perpetuity has a stated par value of $1,000, has a 5 percent coupon rate (that is, pays 5 percent, or $50 annually, on this stated value), and is currently selling for $625. We can solve Equation 18–4 for k_d to find the yield on the bond:

$$k_d = \frac{I}{V} = \frac{\$50}{\$625} = 8\% = \text{yield on a perpetuity.}$$

If the bond sells for $1,250, the formula will show that the yield is 4 percent.

For the three-year bond paying $50 interest a year, if the price of the bond is $922.85, the yield to maturity is found by solving Equation 18–5; the solution *PVIF* is the one for 8 percent:

$$\$922.85 = \$50(PVIF) + \$50(PVIF) + \$1,050(PVIF)$$

$$= \$50(.926) + \$50(.857) + \$1,050(.794)$$

$$= \$46.30 + \$42.85 + \$833.70 = \$922.85 \text{ when } PVIF = 8\%.$$

The interest factors are taken from the 8 percent column of Table A–2. The solution procedure is exactly like that for finding the internal rate of return in capital budgeting, and the trial-and-error method is required unless special tables are available.[7]

TERM STRUCTURE OF INTEREST RATES

An important element in bond valuation is the relationship between yields on long- and short-term bonds. If the financial manager understands the basic theory behind the term structure of interest rates, he or she can avoid making some basic errors. By convention, long-term interest rates are rates on securities with maturities ten years and longer. Short-term rates refer to rates on securities with maturities no longer than 1 year. In Chapter 7, we presented a general discussion of term structure. In this section, we will investigate two explanations of the relationship of long- and short-term bond rates. Although our analysis will be based on Government of Canada bond yields, any conclusions will be applicable to corporate bonds since the yield on a corporate bond of a given maturity will equal the yield on a risk-free bond of the same maturity—a Government of Canada bond—plus a risk premium to reflect the default risk of the corporate bond.

FIGURE 18-5   Interest Rate Differential, Long to Short Term*

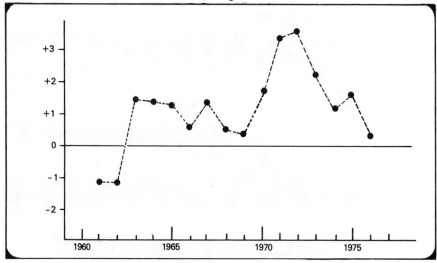

*Source: *Canadian Statistical Review,* February, 1978.
  Long-term: Government of Canada average bond yield, 10 years and over.
  Short-term: three month Treasury Bill yield.

[7]We first tried the *PVIF*'s for 6 percent, found that the equation did not "work," then raised the *PVIF* to 8 percent, where the equation did "work." This indicated that 8 percent was the yield to maturity on the bond. In practice, specialized interest tables called *bond tables,* generated by a computer, are available to facilitate determining the yield to maturity on bonds with different maturities, with different stated interest rates, and selling for various discounts below or premiums above their maturity values.

In Figure 18-5, we present the interest rate differential between long- and short-term rates on Goverment of Canada bonds for the period 1961 to 1976. The interest rate differential is equal to the long-term minus the short-term rate. The interest rates used in this figure are average rates for the year. Throughout this period, the interest rate differential was positive; the average value was 1.54. In addition, there was substantial variability in the differential; the high value was 3.68, in 1972, and the low was 0.29, in 1976. Thus, over this time period, the yearly average long-term rates were in excess of short-term rates.

The first explanation of the structure of bond yields is called the *expectations hypothesis;* under the expectations hypothesis, the long-term interest rate is equal to an average of the expected future short-term interest rates. Thus, the relationship between interest rates on long-term and short-term bonds will depend on what the overall market believes will happen in the future to short-term interest rates.

This is illustrated in Table 18-1. In Panel A of this table, the yield-to-maturity increases as the term-to-maturity on the bond increases (e.g. a one-year bond has a yield-to-maturity of 3 percent per year, whereas a three-year bond has a yield-to-maturity of 5 percent per year). The expected one-year interest rates are presented in Column 3. The interest rate on a two-year bond can be approximated by the average of the one-year rate of 3 percent plus the one-year rate expected to prevail in the following year of 5 percent. That is:

$$4\% = \frac{3\% + 5\%}{2}\text{.}^{8}$$

Similarly, the interest rate on three-year bonds of 5 percent a year is approximately equal to an average of the current interest rate of 3 percent; the one-year rate expected in one year's time (i.e. 5 percent); and the one-year rate expected in two years' time (i.e. 7 percent):

$$5\% = \frac{3\% + 5\% + 7\%}{3}\text{.}$$

From Panel A, we can see that a rising yield curve is related to the market's expectations of increasing short-term interest rates in the future. This type of yield curve, where long-term rates are higher than short-term rates, is observed as the economy comes out of a recession, or when inflation rates are expected to be much higher in the future. In Panel B, we have an example of a falling yield curve; these yield curves have been observed at cyclical peaks. Notice that when there is a falling yield curve, the future interest rates

---

[8]This is only an approximation. The correct technique is to use a geometric average and not a simple average. Let R_t be the annual yield-to-maturity on a bond with t years to maturity. Let r_j be the one-year rate expected to prevail in year j.

Then, $R_t = [(1 + r_1)(1 + r_2)\ldots(1 + r_t)]^{1/t} - 1$. In our example, $t = 2$ and the geometric average is $R_2 = [(1 + .03)(1 + .05)]^{1/2} = 3.995\%$.

are expected to be lower.

If expectations were the only factor operating in the market, then long-term interest rates would be related only to expectations of future interest rates. However, these expected rates do not reflect the risk to the investor of investing in long-term bonds. However, risk may be a factor that is important in determining the relationship of long- and short-term rates. It has been argued that the longer the maturity of the security, the greater the danger that the issuer may not make an effective adaptation to its environment, and therefore, may not be able to meet its obligations in ten or fifteen years. This is an argument that is relevant to corporate, and not government, bonds. The *prices* of long-term bonds are much more volatile than those of short-term bonds when interest rates change. The reason for this is largely arithmetic and was described in this chapter. This will add risk to the investor who has an investment horizon shorter than the maturity of the bond since the investor bears the risk of selling the bond at a low market price.

TABLE 18-1 Relation between Short- and Long-Term Interest Rates: Expectations Hypothesis

	A			B	
(1) *Term to* *maturity* *in years*	*(2)* *Yield to* *maturity:* *percent per year*	*(3)* *Expected* *1 year* *rate*		*(4)* *Yield to* *maturity* *percent per year*	*(5)* *Expected* *1 year* *rate*
1 year	3%			6%	
2 years	4%	5%		5%	4%
3 years	5%	7%		4%	2%

To compensate for this risk of purchasing long-term securities, the investor wants to earn a rate of return in excess of the simple average of the expected future interest rates. Therefore, in Panel A of Table 18-1, when this risk is taken into consideration, the yield to maturity on a three-year bond may be 6 percent, not 5 percent. This difference reflects the risk premium. If this hypothesis is correct, then we would expect to find rising yield curves more often than falling ones, since there is a bias toward higher yields on longer maturity bonds due to the payment for risk. However, regardless of which theory is correct, both have as an important ingredient the market's expectations of the future interest rates.

Notice that, in Figure 18-5, very large interest rate differentials occur in the period 1970 to 1973. This was a period of rapid inflation. The long-term rate is based on a real rate of interest, which depends upon the productivity of the resources in the economy, plus the expected rate of inflation. Since interest rates on bonds are fixed by contract, the investor in bonds will require an interest rate to compensate for the diminished purchasing power of the bond payments. In the 1970 to 1973 period, the market expected high rates of inflation and the long-term yield was very high to reflect this. Currently, the interest rate differential is lower, since the market may expect inflation rates in the future to be lower.

PREFERRED SHARE VALUATION

Most preferred shares promise their owners regular, fixed dividend payments similar to bond interest. Although some preferred issues have a fixed term-to-maturity or are eventually retired, most are perpetuities whose value is found as follows:

$$V = \frac{D}{k_\rho}.$$

(18-6)

In this case, D is the dividend per share on the preferred share, and k_ρ is the appropriate capitalization rate for investment of this degree of risk. For example, Loblaw Companies Limited has a preferred share outstanding that pays a $2.40 annual dividend. The appropriate capitalization rate at the time the preferred was issued (January 1956) was 4.8 percent, so it sold at its par value of $50 at the time of issue. If due to increasing interest rates or increased corporate risk, or both, the appropriate capitalization rate became 10 percent, then the value of the preferred share would fall to $24 per share.

$$V = \frac{2.40}{.10} = \$24.00$$

The yield on a preferred share is similar to that on a perpetual bond and is found by solving Equation 18-6 for k_ρ. For the Loblaw preferred issue, we know that as of the end of January, 1978, the price per share was $26.50 and the annual dividend was $2.40, so the yield is calculated as follows:

$$k_\rho = \frac{D}{V} = \frac{\$ 2.40}{\$26.50} = .0906 \text{ or } 9.06\%.$$

The primary cause of the increase in the yield on the Loblaw preferred was the increase in the general level of interest rates since the date of the issue; in 1956, the yield on long-term government bonds was approximately 4.0 percent, whereas in 1977 the yield was 8.75 percent.

As an example of the impact of risk changes on the yield for preferred shares, consider Electrohome Limited preferred shares issued in 1963 at $100 par with a dividend of $5.75 and a yield of 5.75 percent. As of the beginning of 1978, the price of the preferred share was $33.75 and the resulting yield was 17 percent. This substantial increase in the yield on the

Electrohome preferred cannot be explained solely by the increase in interest rates from 1963 to 1978.

COMMON SHARE VALUATION AND RATES OF RETURN

While the same principles apply to the valuation of common shares as to bonds or preferred shares, two features make their analysis much more difficult. First is the degree of certainty with which receipts can be forecast. For bonds and preferred shares, this forecast presents little difficulty, as the interest payments or preferred dividends are known with relative certainty. However, in the case of common shares, forecasting future earnings, dividends, and common share prices is exceedingly difficult, to say the least. The second complicating feature is that, unlike interest and preferred dividends, common share earnings and dividends are generally expected to grow, not remain constant. Hence, standard annuity formulas cannot be applied, and more difficult conceptual schemes must be used.

Estimating the Value of a Share: The Single Period Case

The price today of a share of common, P_0, depends upon (1) the cash flows investors expect to receive if they buy the share and (2) the riskiness of these expected cash flows. The expected cash flows consist of two elements: (1) the dividend per share expected in each year t, defined as D_t, and (2) the price investors expect to receive when they sell the share at the end of the year n, defined as P_n, which includes the return of the original investment plus a capital gain (or minus a capital loss). If investors expect to hold the share for one year, and if the share price is expected to grow at the rate g, the valuation equation is

$$P_0 = \frac{\text{dividend at end of year 1} + \text{price at end of year 1}}{1.0 + \text{required rate of return}}$$

$$= \frac{D_1 + P_1}{(1 + k_s)} = \frac{D_1 + P_0(1 + g)}{(1 + k_s)},$$

(18–7)

which can be simplied to yield Equation 18–8:[9]

---

[9]
$$P_0 = \frac{D_1 + P_0(1 + g)}{(1 + k_s)}$$

(18–7)

$$P_0(1 + k_s) = D_1 + P_0(1 + g)$$

$$P_0(1 + k_s - 1 - g) = D_1$$

$$P_0(k_s - g) = D_1$$

$$P_0 = \frac{D_1}{k_s - g}.$$

(18–8)

Notice that this equation is developed for a one-year holding period. In a later section, we will show that it is also valid for longer periods, provided the expected growth rate is constant.

$$P_0 = \frac{D_1}{k_s - g}. \qquad (18\text{-}8)$$

Equations 18-7 and 18-8 represent the present value of the expected dividends and the year-end share price, discounted at the required rate of return. Solving Equation 18-8 gives the "fair" or "reasonable" price for the common share. To illustrate, suppose you are contemplating a purchase of the common shares of Consolidated Wrecking Limited. If you buy the stock, you intend to hold it for one year. You note that Consolidated Wrecking earned $3.43 per share last year and paid a dividend of $1.90 per share. Both earnings and dividends have been rising at approximately 5 percent a year, on the average, over the last 10 to 15 years and you expect this growth to continue. In addition, if earnings and dividends grow at this expected rate, you think the stock price will likewise grow at 5 percent.

The next step is to determine the required rate of return on Consolidated's shares. The current rate of interest on one-year Government of Canada bonds, R_F, is 8 percent, but Consolidated is certainly more risky than government bonds—competitors could reduce the company's sales, labor problems could disrupt operations, an economic recession could affect new construction which would have an impact on Consolidated's revenues, and so on. Further, even if sales, earnings, and dividends meet expectations, the overall market may become very pessimistic about the longer term, and this will affect the share prices after you have purchased the shares. Given all these risk factors, you conclude that a 4 percent risk premium is justified, so your required rate of return on Consolidated Wrecking shares, k_s, is calculated as follows:

$$k_s = R_F + \rho_s = 8\% + 4\% = 12\%.$$

Next, you estimate the dividend for the coming year, D_1, as follows:

$$D_1 = D_0 (1 + g) = \$1.90 (1.05) = \$2.$$

Be sure to note that you will not receive the dividend paid last year, $D_0 = \$1.90$; you will receive $D_1 = \$2$.

Now we have the necessary information to estimate the fair value of the share by the use of Equation 18-8:

$$P_0 = \frac{D_1}{k_s - g}$$

$$= \frac{\$2}{.12 - .05} = \$28.57. \qquad (18\text{-}8)$$

To you, $28.57 represents a reasonable price for Consolidated Wrecking's shares. If the actual market price is less, you will buy it; if the actual price is higher, you will not buy it, or you will sell if you own it.[10]

Estimating the Rate of Return on a Share

In the preceding section we calculated the "fair price" of Consolidated's shares to a given investor. Let us now change the procedure somewhat and calculate the rate of return the investor can expect if he or she purchases the common equity at the current market price per share. The expected rate of return, which we define as $\hat{k}_s$, is analogous to the internal rate of return on a capital project. $\hat{k}_s$ is the discount rate that equates the present value of the expected dividends (D_1) and final share price (P_1) to the present share price (P_0):

$$P_0 = \frac{D_1 + P_1}{(1 + \hat{k}_s)} = \frac{D_1 + P_0(1 + g)}{(1 + \hat{k}_s)}.$$

Suppose Consolidated Wrecking is selling for $40 per share. We can calculate $\hat{k}_s$ as follows:

$$\$40 = \frac{\$2 + \$40(1.05)}{(1 + \hat{k}_s)} = \frac{\$2 + \$42}{(1 + \hat{k}_s)}$$

$$\$40(1 + \hat{k}_s) = \$44$$

$$1 + \hat{k}_s = 1.10$$

$$\hat{k}_s = .10 \text{ or } 10\%.$$

Thus, if you expect to receive a $2 dividend and a year-end price of $42, then your expected rate of return on the investment is 10 percent.

Notice that the expected rate of return, $\hat{k}_s$, consists of two components, an expected dividend yield and an expected capital gains yield:

$$\hat{k}_s = \frac{\text{expected dividend}}{\text{present price}} + \frac{\text{expected increase in price}}{\text{present price}}$$

$$= \frac{D_1}{P_0} + g. \tag{18-9}$$

For Consolidated bought at a price of $40,

---

[10]Notice the similarity between this process and the *NPV* method of capital budgeting described in Chapter 11. In the earlier chapter, we (1) estimated a cost of capital for the firm, which compares with estimating k_s, our required rate of return, (2) discounted expected future cash flows, which are analogous to dividends plus the future stock price, (3) found the present value of future cash flows, which corresponds to the "fair value" of the stock, (4) determined the initial outlay for the project, which compares with finding the actual price of the stock, and (5) accepted the project if the *PV* of future cash flows exceeded the initial cost of the project, which is similar to comparing the "fair value" of the stock to its market price.

$$\hat{k}_s = \frac{\$2}{\$40} + \frac{\$2}{\$40} = 5\% + 5\% = 10\%.$$

Given an expected rate of return of 10 percent, should you make the purchase? This depends upon how the expected return compares with the required return. If $\hat{k}_s$ exceeds k_s, buy; if $\hat{k}_s$ is less than k_s, sell; and if $\hat{k}_s$ equals k_s, the share price is in equilibrium and you should be indifferent. In our example, your 12 percent required rate of return for Consolidated Wrecking exceeds the 10 percent expected return, so you should not buy the shares.[11]

Market Equilibrium: Required versus Expected Returns

In the two preceding sections we calculated (1) expected and required rates of return and (2) "fair" or "reasonable" share prices. Further, we saw that buy/no-buy decision can be based upon a comparison of either k_s versus $\hat{k}_s$ or "fair" share value versus actual market price. In this section, we first show that the two decision rules are entirely consistent, then illustrate the process by which stock market equilibrium is maintained.

Consider again the Consolidated Wrecking example, where the following data are applicable:

Expected dividend at year end = D_1 = $2.

Expected growth rate in stock price = g = 5%.

Required rate of return = k_s = 12%.

We calculated a "fair" price of $28.57. We next found that the actual market price, as read from a newspaper or obtained from a stockbroker, is $40, and on the basis of that price we calculated a 10 percent expected rate of return.

By either the rate of return or calculated price criteria, Consolidated's shares are overvalued:

Actual price = $40 > "fair" price = $28.57,

and

required rate of return (k_s) = 12% > expected rate of return $(\hat{k}_s)$ = 10%.

You should not buy Consolidated's common at the $40 price, and if you own it, you should sell.

Now let us assume that you are a "typical" or "representative" investor, so that your expectations and actions actually determine stock market prices. You and others will start selling Consolidated's shares, and this selling pressure will cause the price to decline. The decline will continue until the price

[11]Notice the similarity between this process and the IRR method of capital budgeting. The expected rate of return, $\hat{k}_s$, corresponds to the *IRR* on a project, and the required rate of return, k_s, corresponds to the cost-of-capital cutoff rate used in capital budgeting.

reaches $28.57, which you, the typical investor, feel is reasonable. At this price, the expected rate of return will also equal the required rate of return:

$$\hat{k}_s = \frac{D_1}{P_0} + g = \frac{\$2}{\$28.57} + 5\% = 7\% + 5\% = 12\%,$$

and

$$k_s = R_F + \rho = 8\% + 4\% = 12\%.$$

This situation will always hold—*whenever the actual market price is equal to the "fair" price as calculated by a "typical" investor, required and expected returns will also be equal, and the market will be in equilibrium; that is, there will be no tendency for the stock price to go up or down.*

FACTORS LEADING TO CHANGES IN MARKET PRICES

Let us assume that Consolidated's shares are in equilibrium, selling at a price of $28.57 per share. If all expectations are exactly met, over the next year the price will gradually rise to $30, or by 5 percent.[12] However, many different events could occur to cause a change in the equilibrium price of the shares. To illustrate the forces at work, consider again the share price model, the set of inputs used to develop the price of $28.57, and a new set of assumed input variables:

	Variable Value	
	Original	New
Riskless rate (R_F)	8%	7%
Return-risk tradeoff (α)	.5	.4
Index of common equity risk (σ)	8%	7%
Expected growth rate (g)	5%	6%

The first three variables influence k_s, which declines as a result of the new set of variables from 12 percent to 9.8 percent:

Original: $k_s = 8\% + .5(8\%) = 12\%.$

New: $k_s = 7\% + .4(7\%) = 9.8\%.$

Using these values, together with the new D and g values, we find that P_0 rises from $28.57 to $52.89:

---

[12] $P_0 = \frac{D_1}{k_s - g}$

$P = \frac{D_2}{k_s - g} = \frac{D_1(1+g)}{k_s - g} = P_0(1+g)$

from Equation 18–8

Thus, price per share is expected to grow at a rate of g percent each year.

$$\text{Original: } P_0 = \frac{\$1.90(1.05)}{.12 - .05} = \frac{\$2}{.07} = \$28.57.$$

$$\text{New: } \quad P_0 = \frac{\$1.90(1.06)}{.098 - .06} = \frac{\$2.01}{.038} = \$52.89.$$

At the new price, the expected and required rates of return will be equal:

$$\hat{k}_s = \frac{\$2.01}{\$52.89} + 6\% = 9.8\% = k_s$$

as found above.

Evidence suggests that securities adjust quite rapidly to disequilibrium situations. Consequently, equilibrium ordinarily exists for any given share of equity, and in general, the required and expected returns are equal. Share prices certainly change, sometimes violently and rapidly, but this simply reflects changing conditions and expectations. There are times when it appears that the share price of a particular company continues to react for several months to a favorable or unfavorable development. If upon careful analysis this behavior is confirmed, it need not signify a long adjustment period; rather, it merely shows that as more information about the situation becomes available, the market adjusts to these new bits of information. Throughout the remainder of this book, we will assume that security markets are in equilibrium with $\hat{k}_s = k_s$ [13].

In this section, we have referred to equality of expected and required rates of return on common equity in our discussions of capital market equilibrium. However, the equilibrium concept is, in fact, quite general, and when the capital market is in equilibrium, we will assume that for each type of security in the market, the expected and required yields are equal.

MARKETABILITY AND RATES OF RETURN

Throughout the chapter, when we discussed the required rate of return on securities, we concentrated on two factors, the riskless rate of interest and the risk inherent in the security in question. Before closing, however, we should also note that investors value flexibility, or maneuverability. If one becomes disenchanted with a particular investment, or if one needs funds for consumption or other investments, it is highly desirable to be able to liquidate holdings. Other things being equal, the higher the liquidity, or marketability, the lower an investment's required rate of return. Accordingly, one would expect to find listed stocks selling on a lower yield basis than over-the-counter stocks, and widely traded stocks selling at lower yields than stocks with no established

[13]The market for securities that we are describing is called an *efficient capital market*. In this market, the observed market value of a security at any point in time is the best (i.e. unbiased) estimate of the intrinsic (fair) value of the security. The market is in equilibrium where all information about the company is reflected in the current stock price.

market. Since investments in small firms are generally less liquid than those in large companies, we have another reason for expecting to find higher required returns among smaller companies.

SUMMARY

The basic principles underlying valuation theory were discussed in this chapter, and a number of definitions of value were presented: (1) liquidating value versus going-concern value, (2) book value versus market value, and (3) "fair" value versus current market price. Market value is fundamentally dependent upon discounted cash flow concepts and procedures; it involves estimating future cash flows and discounting them back to the present at an appropriate rate of interest.

Rates of return on bonds and preferred shares are simple to understand and to calculate, but common share returns are more difficult. First, common share returns consist (1) of dividends and (2) of capital gains, not a single type of payment, as in the case of bonds and preferred shares. This fact necessitates the development of a rate of return formula that considers both dividends and capital gains; the rate of return formula for common shares is, therefore, a two-part equation:

$$\text{Rate of return} = \text{dividend yield} + \text{capital gains yield.}$$

The second complicating feature of common shares is the degree of uncertainty involved. Bond and preferred share payments are relatively predictable, but forecasting common share dividends and, even more, capital gains, is a highly uncertain business.

The expected rate of return for common shares can be expressed as $\hat{k}_s = D_1/P_0 + g$ if the growth rate is a constant. P_0 is the price, D_1 is the dividend per share expected this year, and g refers to expected annual, *future growth* per share.

The required rate of return on any security, k, is the minimum rate of return necessary to induce investors to buy or to hold the security. This rate of return is a function of the riskless rate of interest and the investment's risk characteristics. This second equation, when graphed, presents the relationship between the required rate of return and the risk of a security; this relationship shifts over time depending on (1) changes in the riskless rate of interest and (2) investor's psychology, which affects the degree of their risk aversion.

Because investors generally dislike risk, the required rate of return is higher on riskier securities. Bonds, as a class, are less risky than preferred shares, which in turn, are less risky than common shares. As a result, the required rate of return is lowest for bonds, next for preferred shares, and highest for common shares. Within each of these security classes, there are variations among the issuing firms' risks; hence, required rates of return vary among firms.

In equilibrium, the expected rate of return $(\hat{k}_s)$ and the required rate of return (k_s) will be equal. If, however, some disturbance causes them to be different, the market price of the common equity (and thus its dividend yield) will quickly change to establish a new equilibrium where k_s and $\hat{k}_s$ are again equal.

Based on this equality and the existence of efficient capital markets, we are able to use the current market value of the financial asset (bonds, preferreds or common equity) and the expected cash flows from the asset (interest, dividend payments, or capital gains) to calculate the required rate of return.

The required rate of return also depends upon the marketability of a given security issue—the shares and bonds of larger, better known firms are more marketable, hence the required rates of return on such securities are lower than those on smaller, less well known firms. As we shall see in Chapter 20, the required rate of return is, in essence, a firm's cost of capital, so if small firms have relatively high required rates of return, they also have relatively high costs of capital.

QUESTIONS

18-1. Explain what is meant by the term "yield to maturity" (a) for bonds and (b) for preferred shares. (c) Is it appropriate to talk of a yield to maturity on a preferred share that has no specific maturity date?

18-2. Explain why bonds with longer maturities experience wider price movements from a given change in interest rates than do shorter maturity bonds. Preferably give your answer (a) in words (intuitively) and (b) mathematically.

18-3. Explain why a common share of a no-growth company is similar to a preferred share. Use one of the equations developed in the chapter in your explanation.

18-4. Explain the importance in common equity valuation (a) of current dividends, (b) of current market price, (c) of the expected future growth rate, and (d) of the market capitalization rate.

18-5. Suppose a firm's charter explicitly precludes it from ever paying a dividend. Investors *know* that this restriction will never be removed. Earnings last year were $1 a share, and they are expected to grow at a rate of 4 percent forever. If the required rate of return is 10 percent, what is the firm's theoretical P/E ratio?

18-6. Describe the factors that determine the market rate of return on the common equity of a particular company at a given point in time.

18-7. Explain how (a) interest rates and (b) investors' aversion to risk influence common equity and bond prices.

18-8. The Stainless Steel Skate Blade Company Limited is a medium-sized private corporation that is contemplating going public. The company is currently private and the management of Stainless Steel is negotiating with their underwriters as to the price per share of the common equity issue. What advice would you give to the management to assist in establishing the value of the common equity?

18-9. An article in one of the financial reporting services noted that the yield curve, as of September 31, 1978, was falling. The reporter noted that the yield on short-term commercial paper was in excess of the yield on long-term corporate bonds. Is this comparison and the conclusion concerning the shape of the yield curve valid?

PROBLEMS

18-1. Suppose that expected future short-term interest rates have the following alternative patterns.

	Patterns			
Year	A	B	C	D
1	4%	8%	4%	8%
2	5	7	6	7
3	6	6	15	5
4	7	5	6	7
5	8	4	4	8

a. Using a simple arithmetic average, what is the current interest rate on a 5-year bond for each of the 4 patterns?

b. Using a geometric average, answer the same question as in Part a. (Hint: the geometric average is described in Footnote 8.)

c. Is the yield to maturity calculated using the simple average higher or lower than that based on the geometric average? Why?

18-2.a. Criterion Inc. has outstanding a series of *perpetual* bonds that pay $90 interest annually. Bonds of this type currently yield 6 percent. At what price should Criterion's bonds sell?

b. Assume that the required yield for bonds of this type rises to 10 percent. What will be the new price of Criterion's bonds?

c. Assume that the required yield drops to 9 percent. What will be the new price of Criterion's bonds?

d. Now suppose that Criterion has another series of bonds that pay $90 annual interest, mature in ten years, and pay $1,000 on maturity. What will be the value of these bonds when the going rate of interest is (i) 6 percent, (ii) 10 percent, and (iii) 9 percent? (Hint: Use both the *PV* of an annuity and the *PV* of $1 tables.)

e. Why do the longer term bonds (the perpetuities) fluctuate more when interest rates change than do the shorter term bonds (the ten-year bonds)?

18-3. What will be the "yield to maturity" of a perpetual bond with a $1,000 par value, a 5 percent coupon rate, and a current market price of (a) $750, (b) $1,000, and (c) $1,250? Assume interest is paid annually.

18-4. Precision Bearings Ltd. issues a five-year 8 percent note with a maturity value of $1,000. What will be the value of this note at the time of issue if the going rate of interest is 6 percent?

18-5.a. Assuming that a bond has three years remaining to maturity and that interest is paid annually, what will be the yield to maturity on the bond with a $1,000 maturity value, a 7 percent coupon interest rate, and a current market price (1) of $880 or (2) of $1,083? (Hint: Try 12 percent and 4 percent for the two bonds, but *show your work.*)

b. Would you pay $880 for the bond described in part a if your required rate of return for securities in the same risk class is 10 percent; that is, $k_d = 10$ percent? Explain your answer.

18-6. The current market price of a well-established company is $60 per share. It has paid an annual dividend of $3 per share for the last three years and expects to continue the same dividend for the next three years. An investor whose required rate of return is 10 percent is considering buying 100 shares and holding them for two years. What market price per share does the investor expect in two years?

18-7. a. The bonds of the Johnson Corporation Ltd. are perpetuities bearing an 8 percent coupon. Bonds of this type yield 7 percent. What is the price of Johnson bonds? Their par value is $1,000.

b. Interest rate levels rise to the point where such bonds now yield 10 percent. What will be the price of the Johnson bonds now?

c. Interest rate levels drop to 8 percent. At what price will the Johnson bonds sell?

d. How would your answers to parts a, b, and c change if the bonds had a definite maturity date of twenty years?

18-8. a. North-American Aviation is currently earning $6 million a year after taxes. A total of 2,500,000 shares are authorized, and 2,000,000 shares are outstanding. What are the company's earnings per share?

b. Investors require a 15 percent rate of return on equity in the same risk class as North American's ($k_s = 15$%). At what price per share will the common sell if the previous dividend was $1 ($D_0 = $1), and investors expect dividends to grow at a constant compound annual rate of (1) *minus* 5 percent, (2) 0 percent, (3) 5 percent, and (4) 14 percent? (Hint: Use $D_1 = D_0 (1 + g)$, not D_0, in the formula.)

c. In part b, what is the "formula price" if the required rate of return is 15 percent and the expected growth rate is (1) 15 percent or (2) 20 percent? Are these reasonable results? Explain.

d. At what price/earnings (P/E) ratio will the stock sell, assuming each of the growth expectations given in part b?

18-9. Dan Martin plans to invest in common equity for a period of fifteen years, after which he will sell out, buy a lifetime room-and-board membership in a retirement home, and retire. He feels that Computech is currently, but temporarily, undervalued by the market. Martin expects Computech's current earnings and dividend to double in the next fifteen years. Computech's last dividend was $3, and its stock currently sells for $35 a share.

a. If Martin requires a 12 percent return on his investment, will Computech be a good buy for him?

b. What is the maximum that Martin could pay for Computech and still earn his required 12 percent?

c. Given Martin's assumptions, what market capitalization rate for Computech does the current price imply?

18-10. In 1936 the Canadian government raised $55 million by issuing perpetual bonds at a 3 percent annual rate of interest. Unlike most bonds issued today, which have a specific maturity date, these perpetual bonds can remain outstanding forever; they are, in fact, perpetuities.

At the time of issue, the Canadian government stated that cash redemption was *possible* at face value ($100) on or after September 1966; in other words, the bonds were callable at par after September 1966. Believing that the bonds would in fact be called, many investors in the early 1960s purchased these bonds with expectations of receiving $100 in 1966 for each perpetual they held. In 1963 the bonds sold for $55, but a rush of buyers drove the price to just below the $100 par value by 1966. Prices fell dramatically, however, when the Canadian government announced that these perpetual bonds were indeed perpetual and would *not* be paid off. A new thirty-year supply of coupons was sent to each bondholder, and the bond's market price declined to $42 in December 1972.

Because of their severe losses, hundreds of Canadian bondholders have formed the Perpetual Bond Association to lobby for face value redemption of the bonds. Government officials in Ottawa insist that claims for face value payment are nonsense, that the bonds were clearly identified as perpetuals, and that they did not mature in 1966 or at any other time. One Ottawa official states, "Our job is to protect the taxpayer. Why should we pay $55 million for less than $25 million worth of bonds?

a. Would it make sense for a business firm to issue bonds such as the Canadian bonds described above? Would it matter if the firm was a proprietorship or a corporation?

b. If the Canadian government today offered a five-year bond, a fifty-year bond, a "regular perpetuity," and a redeemable perpetuity, what do you think the relative order of interest rates would be; that is, rank the bonds from the one with the lowest to the one with the highest rate of interest. Explain your answer.

c. 1. Suppose that because of pressure by the Perpetual Bond Association, you believe that the Canadian government will redeem this particular perpetual bond issue in five years. Which course of action is more advantageous to you: to sell your bonds today at $42, or to wait five years and have them redeemed? Similar risk bonds earn 8 percent today, and are expected to remain at this level for the next five years.

2. If you have the opportunity to invest your money in bonds of similar risk, at what rate of return are you indifferent between selling your perpetuals today or having them redeemed in five years; that is, what is the expected yield to maturity on the Canadians?

d. Are these more likely to be valued as "regular perpetuities" if the going rate of interest is above or below 3 percent? Why?

e. Do you think the Canadian government would have taken the same action with regard to retiring the bonds if the interest rate had fallen rather than risen between 1936 and 1966?

f. Do you think the Canadian government was "fair" or "unfair" in its actions? Give pros and cons, and justify your reason for thinking that one outweighs the other.

18-11. In a 1972 U.S. study prepared for the Federal Recreation Commission, it was determined that the following equation can be used to estimate the required rates of return on various types of long-term capital market securities (common equity and bonds of various companies): $k_i = R_F + 2\sigma_i$. Here k_i is the required rate of return on the i th security; R_F is the riskless rate of interest as measured by the yield on long-term United States Government bonds; and σ is the standard deviation of the i th security's rate of return during the past five years.

    a. What is the required rate of return, i, if the riskless rate of return is 6 percent and the security in question has a standard deviation of expected return of (1) ½ percent, (2) 1 percent, (3) 2 percent, and (4) 5 percent? Graph your results.

    b. What is the required rate of return, k_i, using the standard deviations given in part a but assuming the riskless rate (1) rises to 8 percent or (2) falls to 4 percent? Graph these results.

    c. Suppose the required rate of return equation changes from $k_i = 6\% + 2\sigma_i$ to $k_i = 6\% + 3\sigma_i$. What does this imply about investors' risk aversion? Illustrate with a graph.

    d. Suppose the equation $k_i = 6\% + 2\sigma_i$ is the appropriate one. Further, suppose a particular stock sells for $20 a share, is expected to pay $1 dividend at the end of the current year, and has a standard deviation of expected return of 3 percent; that is, $\sigma_i = 3$ percent. Information reaches investors that causes them to expect a future growth rate of 3 percent, which is different from the former expected growth rate. σ_i does not change. (1) What was the former growth rate, assuming the security price was in equilibrium before the changed expectations as to growth? (2) What will happen to the price of the stock? that is, calculate the new equilibrium price, and explain the process by which this new equilibrium will be reached. The expected dividend for the current year is still $1.

    e. Suppose the Federal Reserve Board tightens credit in the economy and causes the rate of interest on long-term government bonds to rise from 6 percent to 8 percent. (1) Assuming no other changes, what will happen to the CML; that is, what will be the new CML if the old one was $k_i = 6 + 2\sigma_i$? (2) What will be the new required rate of return for a bond with $\sigma_i = 0$ and a stock with $\sigma_i = 3$ percent? (3) Assume that the average stock had $\sigma = 3$ percent, $D_1 = \$2$, $k_s = 12$ percent, and $g = 6$ percent, thus a price of $33.33, before the change in part 2:

$$P_0 = \frac{D_1}{k_s - g} = \frac{\$2}{0.12 - 0.06} = \$33.33.$$

After the change in part 2 and assuming nothing else changes, what will occur to the market averages, such as the Dow-Jones average?

18-12. Because of ill health and old age, Dale Dinkins contemplates the sale of his shoe store. His corporation has the following balance sheet:

Assets		Liabilities and Net Worth	
Cash	$ 6,000	Notes payable—bank	$ 2,000
Receivables, net	2,000	Accounts payable	4,000
Inventories	13,000	Accruals	1,000
Fixtures and equipment less $10,000 reserve for depreciation	14,000	Common equity plus surplus	28,000
Total assets	$35,000	Total liabilities and net worth	$35,000

Annual before-tax earnings (after rent, interest, and salaries) for the preceding three years have averaged $8,000.

Dinkins has set a price of $40,000, which includes all the assets of the business except cash; the buyer assumes all debts. The assets include a five-year lease on the building in which the store is located and the goodwill associated with the name of Dinkins' Shoes. Assume that both Dinkins and the potential purchaser are in the 50 percent tax bracket.

    a. Is the price of $40,000 a reasonable one? Explain.

    b. What other factors should be taken into account in arriving at a selling price?

    c. What is the significance, if any, of the five-year lease?

18-13. The Callaway Co. Ltd. is a small jewelry manufacturer. The company has been successful and has grown. Now, Callaway is planning to sell an issue of common shares to the public for the first time, and it faces the problem of setting an appropriate price on its common shares. The company feels that the proper procedure is to select firms similar to it with publicly traded common shares and to make relevant comparisons.

The company finds several jewelry manufacturers similar to it with respect to product mix, size, asset composition, and debt/equity proportions. Of these, Sonnet and Mailers are most similar.

Relation	Sonnet	Mailers	Callaway (Totals)
Earnings per share, 1975	$ 4.50	$ 7.50	$1,200,000
Average, 1969–1975	3.00	6.00	900,000
Price per share, 1975	36.00	75.00	—
Dividends per share, 1975	2.25	3.75	600,000
Average, 1969–1975	1.80	3.75	480,000
Book value per share	30.00	75.00	9,000,000
Market-book ratio	120%	100%	—

    a. How would these relations be used in guiding Callaway in arriving at a market value for its stock?

    b. What price would you recommend if Callaway sells 400,000 shares?

18-14. The Data Management Corp. Ltd. is expected to grow at a rate of about 20 percent for the next four years, then at 10 percent for another three years, and finally settle down to a growth rate of 5 percent for the indefinite future. The company's common shares currently pays a $0.50 dividend, but dividends are expected to increase in proportion to the growth of the firm.

    a. What values would you place on the common shares if you require a 10 percent return on your investment?

    b. How would your valuation be affected if you intend to hold the shares for only three years?

    c. What would you expect the trend (1) of market price, (2) of price/earnings ratio, and (3) of dividend yield to be over the next ten years (up, down, or constant)?

Multi-Period Equity Valuation Models

18A Appendix

Our discussion of common equity valuation and rates of return in Chapter 18 focused on a single-period model, where we expect to hold the stock for one year, receive one dividend, and then sell the equity at the end of the year. In this appendix, we expand the analysis to deal with more realistic, but more complicated, multiperiod models.

Expected Dividends as the Basis for Stock Values

According to generally accepted theory, stock prices are determined as the present value of a stream of cash flows. In other words, the capitalization of income procedure applies to common equity as well as to bonds and other assets. What are the cash flows that corporations provide to their shareholders? For an individual investor, cash flows consist of dividends plus capital gains, but, for investors in total, expected cash flows consist only of future dividends—unless a firm is liquidated or is sold to another concern, the cash flows it provides its shareholders as a whole consist of a stream of dividends. Thus, a share of common equity may be regarded as being similar to a perpetual bond or share of perpetual preferreds, and its value may be established as the present value of its stream of dividends:

Per share value of equity $= P_0 = PV$ of expected future dividends

467

$$= \frac{D_1}{(1 + k_s)^1} + \frac{D_2}{(1 + k_s)^2} + \cdots \frac{D_\infty}{(1 + k_s)^\infty} = \sum_{t=1}^{\infty} \frac{D_t}{(1 + k_s)^t}. \quad \text{(A18-1)}$$

Unlike bond interest and preferred dividends, dividends on common equity are not generally expected to remain constant in the future; hence we cannot work with the convenient annuity formulas. This fact, combined with the much greater uncertainty about common equity dividends than about bond interest or preferred dividends, makes common equity valuation a more complex task than bond or preferred share valuation.

Equation A18–1 is a quite general equity valuation model in the sense that the time pattern of D_t can be anything; D_t can be rising, falling, constant, or it can even fluctuate randomly, and Equation A18-1 will still hold. For many purposes, however, it is useful to estimate a particular time pattern for D_t and then develop a simplified (that is, easier to evaluate) version of the equity valuation model expressed in Equation A18-1. In the following sections, we consider the special cases of zero growth, constant growth, and "supernormal" growth.

Share Values with Zero Growth

Suppose the rate of growth is measured by the rate at which dividends are expected to increase. If future growth is expected to be zero, the value of the shares reduces to the same formula as was developed for a perpetual bond:

$$\text{price} = \frac{\text{dividend}}{\text{capitalization rate}} \quad \text{(A18-2)}$$

$$P_0 = \frac{D_1}{k_s}.$$

Solving for k_s, we obtain

$$k_s = \frac{D_1}{P_0}, \quad \text{(A18-3)}$$

which states that the required rate of return on a share of common equity that has no growth prospects is simply the dividend yield.

"Normal," or Constant, Growth

Year after year, the earnings and dividends of most companies have been increasing. The actual growth rate of the dividends per share for a company will depend on (1) the growth rate in GNP, (2) the profitability of investment, and (3) the payout ratio that the company has established. The lower the payout ratio, the more retained earnings re-invested, and hence, the higher the growth rate in dividends per share. The historical relationship of growth in a company's dividends per share relative to growth in GNP can be used to estimate stock values. For example, if GNP has a growth rate of 3 to 5 percent and the company has a growth rate in dividends per share that is 2 percent higher, then the company's growth rate is expected to be 5 to 7 percent. Thus, if such a company's previous dividend per share, which has already been paid, was D_0, its dividend in any future year, t, may be forecast as $D_t = D_0(1 + g)^t$, where g is the expected rate of growth. For example, if Consolidated Wrecking just paid a dividend of $1.90 per share (that is, $D_0 = 1.90), and investors expect a 5 percent growth rate, then the estimated dividend per share one year hence will be $D_1 = ($1.90)(1.05 = $2; D_2$ will be $2.10; and the estimated dividend five years hence will be

$D_1 = ($1.90)(1.05) = $2; D_2$ will be $2.10; and the estimated dividend five years hence will be

$$D_t = D_0(1 + g)^t$$

$$= \$1.90(1.05)^5$$

$$= \$2.42.$$

Using this method of estimating future dividends, the current price, P_0, is determined as follows:

$$P_0 = \frac{D_1}{(1 + k_s)^1} + \frac{D_2}{(1 + k_s)^2} + \frac{D_3}{(1 + k_s)^3} + \cdots$$

$$= \frac{D_0(1 + g)^1}{(1 + k_s)^1} + \frac{D_0(1 + g)^2}{(1 + k_s)^2} + \frac{D_0(1 + g)^3}{(1 + k_s)^3} + \cdots \qquad \text{(A18-4)}$$

$$= \sum_{t=1}^{\infty} \frac{D_0(1 + g)^t}{(1 + k_s)^t}.$$

If g is constant, Equation A18-4 may be simplified as follows:[1]

$$P_0 = \frac{D_1}{k_s - g}. \qquad \text{(A18-5)}$$

Notice that the constant growth model expressed in Equation A18-5 is identical to the single-period model, Equation 18-5, developed in Chapter 18.

---

[1] The proof of Equation A18-5 is as follows. Rewrite Equation A18-4 as:

$$P_0 = D_0\left[\frac{(1 + g)}{(1 + k_s)} + \frac{(1 + g)^2}{(1 + k_s)^2} + \frac{(1 + g)^3}{(1 + k_s)^3} + \cdots + \frac{(1 + g)^N}{(1 + k_s)^N}\right]. \qquad (1)$$

Multiply both sides of Equation (1) by $(1 + k_s)/(1 + g)$:

$$\left[\frac{(1 + k_s)}{(1 + g)}\right] P_0 = D_0\left[1 + \frac{(1 + g)}{(1 + k_s)} + \frac{(1 + g)^2}{(1 + k_s)^2} + \cdots + \frac{(1 + g)^{N-1}}{(1 + k_s)^{N-1}}\right]. \qquad (2)$$

A necessary condition for the constant growth model is that k_s be greater than g; otherwise, Equation A18-5 gives nonsense answers. If k_s equals g, the equation blows up, yielding an infinite price; if k_s is less than g, a *negative* price results. Since neither infinite nor negative prices make sense, it is clear that in equilibrium k_s must be greater than g.

Note that Equation A18-5 is sufficiently general to encompass the no-growth case described above. If growth is zero, this is simply a special case, and Equation A18-5 is identical to Equation A18-2.[2]

"Supernormal" Growth

Firms typically go through "life cycles" during part of which their growth is much faster than that of the economy as a whole. Automobile manufacturers in the 1920s and computer and office equipment manufacturers in the 1960s are examples. Figure A18-1 illustrates such supernormal growth and compares it with normal growth, zero growth, and negative growth.[3]

The illustrative supernormal growth firm is expected to grow at a 20 percent rate for ten years, then to have its growth rate fall to 4 percent, the norm for the economy. The value of a firm with such a growth pattern is determined by the following equation:

Present price = PV of dividends during supernormal growth period + per share value of common equity at end of supernormal growth period discounted back to present

Subtract Equation (1) from Equation (2) to obtain

$$\left[\frac{(1 + k_s)}{(1 + g)} - 1\right] P_0 = D_0 \left[1 - \frac{(1 - g)^N}{(1 - k_s)^N}\right].$$

$$\left[\frac{(1 + k_s) - (1 + g)}{(1 + g)}\right] P_0 = D_0 \left[1 - \frac{(1 + g)^N}{(1 + k_s)^N}\right].$$

Assuming $k_s > g$, as $N \to \infty$ the term in brackets on the right side of the equation $\to 1.0$, leaving

$$\left[\frac{(1 + k_s) - (1 + g)}{(1 + g)}\right] P_0 = D_0 ,$$

which simplifies to

$$(k_s - g) P_0 = D_0 (1 + g) = D_1$$

$$P_0 = \frac{D_1}{k_s - g} \qquad \text{Q.E.D.} \qquad (A18\text{-}5)$$

---

[2] One technical point should at least be mentioned here. The logic underlying the analysis implicitly assumes that investors are indifferent to dividend yield or capital gains. Empirical work has not conclusively established whether this is true or not, but the question is discussed in Chapter 21.

[3] A *negative* growth rate represents a declining company. A mining company whose profits are falling because of a declining ore body is an example.

$$= \sum_{t=1}^{N} \frac{D_0 (1 + g_s)^t}{(1 + k_s)^t} + \left(\frac{D_{N+1}}{k_s - g_n} \right) \left(\frac{1}{(1 + k_s)^N} \right). \tag{A18-6}$$

Here g_s is the supernormal growth rate, g_n is the normal growth rate, and N is the period of supernormal growth.

FIGURE A18–1   Illustrative Dividend Growth Rates

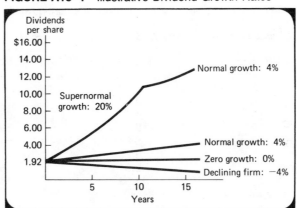

Working through an example will help make this clear. Consider a supernormal growth firm whose previous dividend was $1.92 (that is, D_0 = $1.92), with the dividend expected to increase by 20 percent a year for ten years and thereafter at 4 percent a year indefinitely. If shareholders' required rate of return is 9 percent on an investment with this degree of risk, what is the per share value of the equity? On the basis of the calculations in Table A18-1, the value is found to be $138.19, the present value of the dividends during the first ten years plus the present value of one share at the end of the tenth year.

Comparing Companies with Different Expected Growth Rates

It is useful to summarize this section by comparing the four illustrative firms whose dividend trends were graphed in Figure A18-1. Using the valuation equations developed above, the conditions assumed in the preceding examples, and the additional assumptions that each firm had earnings per share during the preceding reporting period of $3.60 (that is, EPS_0 = $3.60) and paid out 53.3 percent of its reported earnings (therefore dividends per share last year, D_0, were $1.92 for each company), we show prices, dividend yields, and price/earnings ratios (hereafter written P/E) in Table A18-2.

Investors require and expect a return on equity of 9 percent on each of the companies. For the declining firm, this return consists of a relatively high

TABLE A18–1   Method of Calculating the Per Share Value of Common Equity with Supernormal Growth

Assumptions:
a. Shareholders' capitalization rate is 9 percent, i.e., $k_s = 9\%$.
b. Growth rate is 20 percent for ten years, 4 percent thereafter, i.e., $g_s = 20\%$, $g_n = 4\%$, and $N = 10$.
c. Last year's dividend was $1.92, i.e., $D_0 = \$1.92$.

Step 1.   Find present value of dividends during rapid growth period:

End of Year	Dividend $1.92(1.20)^t$	PVIF = $1/(1.09)^t$	Present Value
1	$ 2.30	.917	$ 2.11
2	2.76	.842	2.32
3	3.32	.772	2.56
4	3.98	.708	2.82
5	4.78	.650	3.11
6	5.73	.596	3.42
7	6.88	.547	3.76
8	8.26	.502	4.15
9	9.91	.460	4.56
10	11.89	.442	5.02

$$PV \text{ of first 10 years' dividends} = \sum_{t=1}^{10} \frac{D_0(1+g_s)^t}{(1+k_s)^t} = \$33.83$$

Step 2.   Find present value of year 10 share price:
a. Find value of one share at end of year 10:

$$P_{10} = \frac{D_{11}}{k_s - g_n} = \frac{\$11.89(1.04)}{.05} = \$247.31.$$

b. Discount P_{10} back to present:

$$PV = P_{10}\left(\frac{1}{1+k_s}\right)^{10} = \$247.31(.422) = \$104.36.$$

Step 3.   Sum to find total value of one share today:

$$P_0 = \$33.83 + \$104.36 = \$138.19.$$

current dividend yield combined with a capital *loss* amounting to 4 percent a year. For the no-growth firm, there is neither a capital gain nor a capital loss expectation, so the 9 percent return must be obtained entirely from the dividend yield. The normal growth firm provides a relatively low current dividend yield, but a 4 percent a year capital gain expectation. Finally, the super-normal growth firm has the lowest current dividend yield but the highest capital gain expectation.

What is expected to happen to the prices of the four illustrative firms' shares over time? Three of the four cases are straightforward: The zero growth firm's price is expected to be constant (that is, $P_t = P_{t+1}$); the declining firm is expected to have a falling stock price; and the constant growth firm's stock is expected to grow at a constant rate, 4 percent. The supernormal growth case is more complex, but what is expected can be seen from the data in Table A18–1.

First, note that the present price, P_0, is \$138.19, and the expected price in year ten, P_{10}, is \$247.31. This represents an average growth rate of 6 percent.[4] We do not show, but we could, that the expected growth rate of the share's price is higher than 6 percent in the early part of the ten-year supernormal growth period and less than 6 percent toward the end of the period, as investors perceive the approaching end of the supernormal period. From year eleven on, the company's share price and dividend are expected to grow at the "normal" rate, 4 percent.

TABLE A18–2 Prices, Dividend Yields, and Price/Earnings Ratios for 9 Percent Returns under Different Growth Assumptions

		Price	Current Dividend Yield	P/E Ratio[a]
Declining firm:	$P_0 = \dfrac{D_1}{k_s - g} = \dfrac{\$1.84}{0.09 - (-0.04)}$	\$ 14.15	13%	3.9
No-growth firm:	$P_0 = \dfrac{D_1}{k_s} = \dfrac{\$1.92}{0.09}$	\$ 21.33	9%	5.9
Normal growth firm:	$P_0 = \dfrac{D_1}{k_s - g} = \dfrac{\$2.00}{0.09 - 0.04}$	\$ 40.00	5%	11.1
Supernormal growth firm:	$P_0 =$ (See Table 18–1)	\$138.19	1.7%	38.4

[a] It was assumed at the beginning of this example that each company is earning \$3.60 initially. This \$3.60, divided into the various prices, gives the indicated P/E ratios.

We might also note that as the supernormal growth rate declines toward the normal rate (or as the time when this decline will occur becomes more imminent), the high P/E ratio must approach the normal P/E ratio; that is, the P/E of 38.4 will decline year by year and equal 11.1, that of the normal growth company, in the tenth year. See A. A. Robichek and M. C. Bogue, "A Note on the Behavior of Expected Price/Earnings Ratios over Time," *Journal of Finance* (June 1971).

Note also that D_1 differs for each firm, being calculated as follows:

$$D_1 = EPS_0 (1 + g) (payout) = \$3.60(1 + g) (0.533).$$

The relationships among the P/E ratios, shown in the last column of Table A18-2, are similar to what one would intuitively expect—the higher the expected growth (all other things the same), the higher the P/E ratio.[5]

[4] Found from Table A18-1; \$247.31/\$138.19 = 1.79, and this is approximately the CVIF for a 6 percent growth rate.

[5] Differences in P/E ratios among firms can also arise from differences in the rates of return, k_s, which investors use in capitalizing the future dividend streams. If one company has a higher P/E than another, this could be caused by a higher g, a lower k_s, or a combination of these two factors.

Financial Structure and the Use of Leverage

In the last chapter, we saw that each security has a required rate of return, k, and an expected rate of return, $\hat{k}$. The required rate of return is determined in part by the level of interest rates (the risk-free rate) in the economy, and in part by the riskiness of the individual security. The expected rate of return on a bond or on preferred shares is determined primarily by the interest or preferred dividend, while the expected rate of return on common shares depends upon dividends (which flow from earnings) and the expected growth rates. It was also noted in the previous chapter that, in equilibrium, the expected and required rates of return are equal. In this chapter, we assume that the price of the financial instrument has been adjusted so that equilibrium exists; thus, *expected* and *required* rates of return will be used interchangeably. Both risk and required rates of return are fundamentally affected by financial leverage, as we see in this chapter.

BASIC DEFINITIONS

To avoid ambiguity in the use of key concepts, the meanings of frequently used expressions are given here. *Financial structure* refers to the way the firm's assets are financed: it is the entire right-hand side of the balance sheet. *Capital structure* is the permanent financing of the firm, represented primarily by long-term debt, preferred shares, and common equity, but excluding all short-term credit. Thus, a firm's capital structure is only a part of its financial structure. *Common equity* includes common shares, contributed surplus, and

474

accumulated retained earnings.

Our key concept for this chapter is *financial leverage,* or the *leverage factor;* we define this factor as the ratio of total debt (sum of long and short term) to total assets. For example, a firm with assets of $100 million and a total debt of $50 million would have a leverage factor of 50 percent.[1] Since we are interested in investigating the impact of changes in financial leverage, we make no distinction between long- and short-term debt.

Finally, we return to the distinction presented in Chapter 4 made between business risk and financial risk. By *business risk* we mean the inherent uncertainty or variability of expected pretax returns on the firm's "portfolio" of assets. This kind of risk was examined in Chapter 12, where it was defined in terms of the probability distribution of returns on the firm's assets. By *financial risk* we refer to the additional variability induced to the earnings available to the common equity holders by the use of financial leverage. Throughout the discussions and examples, we assume that financial leverage occurs because of debt financing. However, financial leverage occurs due to the existence of any fixed financial charge; thus preferred shares will result in financial leverage as well. If the company had preferred shares outstanding, the appropriate measure of leverage would be the ratio of debt plus preferred to total assets.

THEORY OF FINANCIAL LEVERAGE

Perhaps the best way to understand the proper use of financial leverage is to analyze its impact on profitability under varying conditions. Suppose there

TABLE 19–1   Alternative Financial Structures

		Firm A	
		Total debt	$ 0
		Net worth	200
Total assets	$200	Total claims	$200
		Firm B	
		Total debt (6%)	$100
		Net worth	100
Total assets	$200	Total claims	$200
		Firm C	
		Total debt (6%)	$150
		Net worth	50
Total assets	$200	Total claims	$200

[1]In our discussions, we measure the leverage ratio by using the book values of debt and assets. Variations

(continued on page 476)

476

are three firms in a particular industry, and these firms are identical except for their financial policies. Firm A has used no debt and consequently has a leverage factor of zero; firm B, financed half by debt and half by equity, has a leverage factor of 50 percent; firm C has a leverage factor of 75 percent. Their balance sheets are shown in Table 19-1.

TABLE 19–2 Shareholder Returns under Various Leverage and Economic Conditions

	Economic Conditions					
	Very Poor	Poor	Indifference Level	Normal	Good	Very Good
Rate of return on assets before interest and taxes	2%	5%	6%	8%	11%	14%
Earnings before interest and taxes (EBIT)	$ 4	$10	$12	$16	$22	$28
Firm A: Leverage factor 0%						
EBIT	$ 4	$10	$12	$16	$22	$28
Less: Interest expense	0	0	0	0	0	0
Taxable income	$ 4	$10	$12	$16	$22	$28
Taxes (50%)[a]	2	5	6	8	11	14
Available to common equity	$ 2	$ 5	$ 6	$ 8	$11	$14
Percent after-tax return on net worth	1%	2.5%	3%	4%	5.5%	7%
Firm B: Leverage factor 50%						
EBIT	$ 4	$10	$12	$16	$22	$28
Less: Interest expense	6	6	6	6	6	6
Taxable income	$ (2)	$ 4	$ 6	$10	$16	$22
Taxes (50%)[a]	(1)	2	3	5	8	11
Available to common equity	$ (1)	$ 2	$ 3	$ 5	$ 8	$11
Percent after-tax return on net worth	−1%	2%	3%	5%	8%	11%
Firm C: Leverage factor 75%						
EBIT	$ 4	$10	$12	$16	$22	$28
Less: Interest expense	9	9	9	9	9	9
Taxable income	$ (5)	$ 1	$ 3	$ 7	$13	$19
Taxes (50%)[a]	(2.5)	.5	1.5	3.5	6.5	9.5
Available to common equity	$ (2.5)	$ .5	$ 1.5	$ 3.5	$ 6.5	$ 9.5
Percent after-tax return on net worth	−5%	1%	3%	7%	13%	19%

[a]The tax calculation assumes that losses are carried back and result in tax credits.

of book value leverage ratios could be used; for example, the ratio of debt to net worth or of debt to the sum of debt plus equity (i.e. total capital).

All of these ratios measure financial leverage. An alternative method would be to use a market value leverage ratio; leverage would be measured as the ratio of the market value of debt to the sum of the market values of debt plus equity. A discussion of the pros and cons of market value weights is presented in Chapter 20 where the cost of capital for a firm is measured.

How do these different financial patterns affect shareholder returns? As can be seen from the top section of Table 19-2, the answer depends partly on the state of the industry's economy. When the economy is depressed, sales and profit margins are low, and the firms earn only 2 percent on assets. When conditions become somewhat better, the return on assets is 5 percent. Under normal conditions, the return goes to 8 percent. In a moderate boom the figure goes to 11 percent, while under extremely favorable circumstances, the companies have a 14 percent return on assets. These percentages, multiplied by the $200 of assets, give the earnings before interest and taxes *(EBIT)* of the three companies under the various states of the economy.

The lower portion of Table 19-2 demonstrates how the use of financial leverage magnifies the impact on the shareholders of changes in the rate of return on assets. When economic conditions go from normal to good, for example, returns on assets go from 8 to 11 percent, an increase of 37.5 percent. Firm A uses no leverage, gets no magnification, and consequently experiences the same 37.5 percent jump in the rate of return to shareholders. However, firm B enjoys a 60 percent increase in shareholder returns as a result of the 37.5 percent rise in returns on assets. Firm C, which uses still more leverage, has an 85.7 percent increase. Just the reverse holds in economic downturns, of course: the 37.5 percent drop in returns on assets when the economy goes from normal to poor results in return-on-net-worth declines of 37.5 percent, 60 percent, and 85.7 percent for firms A, B, and C, respectively.[2]

---

[2] This relationship between the rate of return on net worth and the rate of return on assets can be presented algebraically. Let R_A be the rate of return on assets and R_{NW} be the rate of return on net worth. By definition we have the following relationships:

$$R_A = \frac{EBIT}{Assets} \tag{1}$$

$$R_{NW} = \frac{\text{After-tax net income}}{\text{Net worth}} \tag{2}$$

But Assets = Debt + Net worth (3)

and After-tax net income = *(EBIT* – Interest)$(1-t)$ (4)
where t is the tax rate.

We can expand equation (2) as follows:

$$R_{NW} = \frac{(EBIT - Interest)(1-t)}{\text{Net worth}} = \frac{EBIT(1-t)}{\text{Net worth}} - \frac{Interest(1-t)}{\text{Net worth}} \tag{5}$$

But from (1), $EBIT = R_A \times$ Assets; substituting into (5)

$$R_{NW} = \frac{Interest(1-t)}{\text{Net worth}} + \left(\frac{Assets}{\text{Net worth}}(1-t) \right) R \tag{6}$$

This is a straight-line equation with an intercept equal to $-\frac{Interest(1-t)}{\text{Net worth}}$ and a slope equal to $\frac{Assets}{\text{Net worth}}(1-t)$. As leverage increases, the ratio of assets to net worth becomes larger and the slope of the line is steeper. Thus, a given change in R_A leads to a larger change in R_{NW} as leverage increases. In addition, as leverage increases the interest payments increase and the intercept becomes a larger negative number.

Using the same illustrative numbers, Figure 19-1 gives a graphic presentation of the interaction between the rates of return on assets and net worth, given the three different leverage factors. The interesting point to note here is the intersection of the three lines at the point where assets are returning 6 percent, the interest cost of debt. At this point, the return on net worth is 3 percent. The assumed 50 percent tax rate reduces the 6 percent return on total assets to a return of 3 percent on net worth, regardless of the degree of leverage. When returns on assets are higher than 6 percent, debt-financed assets can pay their interest cost and still leave something over for the shareholders; the greater the leverage factor, the larger the benefit for shareholders. Notice that the absolute amount of earnings available to common shareholders is *not* larger. However, the amount invested by the equity holder —as measured by the net worth—to generate this net income becomes smaller as leverage increases. If the assets earn less than 6 percent, the reverse occurs and rates of return on net worth are small or negative. *In general, whenever the actual or realized rate of return on assets exceeds the interest cost of debt, before taxes, leverage is favorable; and the higher the leverage factor, the higher the rate of return on common equity.*

FIGURE 19–1 Relationship between Rates of Return on Assets and Rates of Return on Net Worth under Different Leverage Conditions

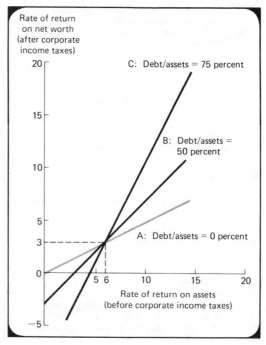

EFFECTS OF FINANCIAL LEVERAGE

The effects of financial leverage can be further clarified by an example. The Universal Machine Co. Ltd., whose latest balance sheet is shown in Table 19-3, manufactures equipment used by steel producers. The major product is a lathe used to trim the rough edges off hot rolls of steel; the lathes sell for $10,000 each. As is typically the case for producers of durable capital assets, the company's sales fluctuate widely, far more than does the overall economy. For example, during nine of the preceding twenty-five years, sales have been below the breakeven point, so losses have been relatively frequent.

TABLE 19-3   Universal Machine Co. Ltd. Balance Sheet[a]
December 31, 19X1

Cash	$ 200,000	Total liabilities having	
Receivables (net)	800,000	an average cost of 5%	$2,000,000
Inventories	1,000,000	Common equity ($10 par;	
Plant (net)	2,200,000	250,000 shares outstanding)	2,500,000
Equipment (net)	2,800,000	Retained earnings	2,500,000
Total assets	$7,000,000	Total claims on assets	$7,000,000

[a] Figures are rounded for convenience.

In addition to the normal fluctuations inherent in the business, Universal faces three additional elements of uncertainty: (1) new methods of processing steel now being discussed in the industry may obsolesce much of Universal's equipment; (2) the long-run demand for steel and steel-processing equipment may decline because of the competitive inroads of plastics, cement, and aluminum; and (3) a tariff conference scheduled for late 19X2 may open the door for increased foreign competition by Japanese machinery manufacturers.

Although future sales are uncertain, current demand is high and appears to be headed higher, and if Universal is to continue sharing in this expansion, it will have to increase capacity. For this increase, $3 million of new capital is required. James Walter, the financial vice-president, learns that he can raise $3 million by selling bonds with a 5 percent coupon. Alternatively, he can raise the money by selling 75,000 shares of common equity at $40 a share.

During the preceding five years, Universal's sales have fluctuated between $500,000 and $4,000,000; at the higher volume, the firm is operating at full capacity and has to turn down orders. With the additional plant expansion, sales capacity will increase to $6 million. Fixed costs, after the planned expansion, will be $400,000 a year, and variable costs (excluding interest on the debt) will be 40 percent of sales.[3] The marketing department has analyzed

[3] The assumption that variable costs will be a constant percentage of sales over the entire range of output is not valid, but variable costs are relatively constant over the output range likely to occur.

TABLE 19-4   Universal Machine Co. Ltd., Profit Calculations at Various Sales Levels

Probability of indicated sales	.025	.10	.20	.35	.20	.10	.025
Sales in units	0	100	200	300	400	500	600
Sales in dollars	$ -0-	$1,000,000	$2,000,000	$3,000,000	$4,000,000	$5,000,000	$6,000,000
Fixed costs	$ 400,000	$ 400,000	$ 400,000	$ 400,000	$ 400,000	$ 400,000	$ 400,000
Variable costs (40% of sales)	-0-	400,000	800,000	1,200,000	1,600,000	2,000,000	2,400,000
Total costs (except interest)	$ 400,000	$ 800,000	$1,200,000	$1,600,000	$2,000,000	$2,400,000	$2,800,000
Earnings before interest and taxes *(EBIT)*	$(400,000)	$ 200,000	$ 800,000	$1,400,000	$2,000,000	$2,600,000	$3,200,000
				Financing with bonds			
Less: Interest on new debt (5% × $3,000,000)	$ 150,000	$ 150,000	$ 150,000	$ 150,000	$ 150,000	$ 150,000	$ 150,000
Interest on old debt (5% × $2,000,000)	$ 100,000	$ 100,000	$ 100,000	$ 100,000	$ 100,000	$ 100,000	$ 100,000
Earnings before taxes	$(650,000)	$ (50,000)	$ 550,000	$1,150,000	$1,750,000	$2,350,000	$2,950,000
Less: Income taxes (50%)[a]	(325,000)	(25,000)	275,000	575,000	875,000	1,175,000	1,475,000
Net profit after taxes	$(325,000)	$ (25,000)	$ 275,000	$ 575,000	$ 875,000	$1,175,000	$1,475,000
Earnings per share on 250,000 shares of common *(EPS)*[d]	$ -1.30	$ -0.10	$1.10	$2.30	$3.50	$4.70	$5.90
Expected *EPS*[b]	$ 2.30						
Coefficient of variation[c]	.67						
				Financing with common equity			
Less: Interest on old debt (5% × $2,000,000)	$ 100,000	$ 100,000	$ 100,000	$ 100,000	$ 100,000	$ 100,000	$ 100,000
Earnings before taxes	$(500,000)	$ 100,000	$ 700,000	$1,300,000	$1,900,000	$2,500,000	$3,100,000
Less: Income taxes (50%)[a]	(250,000)	50,000	350,000	650,000	950,000	1,250,000	1,550,000
Net profit after taxes	$(250,000)	$ 50,000	$ 350,000	$ 650,000	$ 950,000	$1,250,000	$1,550,000
Earnings per share on 325,000 shares of common *(EPS)*[d]	$ -0.77	$ +0.15	$1.08	$2.00	$2.92	$3.85	$4.77
Expected *EPS*[b]	$ 2.00						
Coefficient of variation[c]	.59						

[a] Assumes tax credit on losses.
[b] Calculated by multiplying the *EPS* at each sales level by the probability of that sales level, then summing these products.
[c] Calculated as follows: Coefficient of variation = (standard deviation of *EPS*)/(expected *EPS*).
[d] The *EPS* figures can also be obtained using the following formula:

$$EPS = \frac{(\text{sales} - \text{fixed cost} - \text{variable costs} - \text{interest})(1 - \text{tax rate})}{\text{shares outstanding}}.$$

For example, at $S = \$4$ million,

$$EPS_{equity} = \frac{(4 - .4 - 1.6 - .1)(.5)}{.325} = \$2.92.$$

$$EPS_{bonds} = \frac{(4 - .4 - 1.6 - .25)(.5)}{.250} = \$3.50.$$

Since in this case the equation is linear, the break-even or indifference level of S can be found as follows:

$$EPS_s = \frac{(S - .4 - .4S - .1)(.5)}{.325} = \frac{(S - .4 - .4S - .25)(.5)}{.250} = EPS_b.$$

$$S = \$1.92 \text{ million.}$$

future supply and demand conditions and, on the basis of this analysis, has supplied Walter with a probability distribution for future sales (see Table 19-4).

Although Walter's recommendation will be given much weight, the final decision for the method of financing rests with the company's board of directors. Procedurally, the financial vice-president will analyze the situation, evaluate all reasonable alternatives, come to a conclusion, and then present the alternatives with his recommendations to the board. For his own analysis, as well as for presentation to the board, Walter prepares the materials shown in Table 19-4.

In the top third of the table, earnings before interest and taxes *(EBIT)* are calculated for different levels of sales ranging from $0 to $6 million. The firm suffers an operating loss until sales are almost $1 million, but beyond that point it enjoys a rapid rise in gross profit.

The middle third of the table shows the financial results that will occur at the various sales levels if additional bonds are sold. First, the $250,000 annual interest charges ($100,000 on existing debt plus $150,000 on the new bonds) are deducted from the earnings before interest and taxes. Next, taxes are taken out; notice that if the sales level is so low that losses are incurred, the firm receives a tax credit. Then, net profits after taxes are divided by the 250,000 shares outstanding to obtain earnings per share *(EPS)* for common equity. The various *EPS* figures are multiplied by the corresponding probability estimates to obtain an expected *EPS* of $2.30. Finally, the coefficient of variation is calculated and used as a measure of the riskiness of the financing plan.

The financial results that will occur with common equity financing are calculated in the bottom third of the table. Net profit after interest and taxes is

FIGURE 19–2 Probability Curves for Stock and Bond Financing

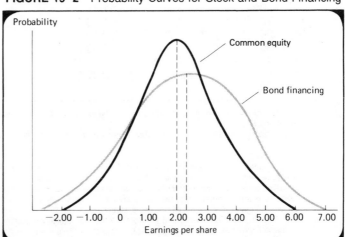

divided by 325,000 shares—the original 250,000 plus the 75,000 new shares—to find earnings per share. Expected *EPS* and the coefficient of variation are computed in the same way as they were for the bond financing.

Figure 19–2 shows the probability distributions of earnings per share. Common equity financing has the tighter, more peaked distribution, and we saw from Table 19–4 that it also has the smaller coefficient of variation; hence, common equity financing is less risky than bond financing. However, the expected *EPS* is lower for common equity than for bonds, so we are again faced with the kind of risk-return tradeoff that characterizes most financial decisions.

The nature of the tradeoff can be made somewhat more specific. First, consider Table 19–5, which shows how both expected earnings per share and the coefficient of variation of these earnings vary with leverage, and Figure 19–3, which graphs the points shown in the table. Two of the items in Table 19–5—the data associated with 20 percent and with 50 percent debt— were obtained directly from Table 19–4, while data on the other leverage ratios were obtained from similar tables.[4] It is clear that in order to obtain the higher expected earnings that go with increased leverage, the firm must accept more risk. What choice should Walter recommend to the board? How much leverage should Universal Machine use? These questions cannot be answered at this point—we must defer answers until we have covered some additional concepts and examined the effects of leverage on the cost of both debt and equity capital.

TABLE 19–5 Risk-return Tradeoff for Various Leverage Ratios, Universal Machine Co. Ltd.

Leverage Ratio	Expected EPS	Coefficient of Variation
0%	$1.87	.552
10	1.93	.570
20	2.00[a]	.591
30	2.08	.615
40	2.18	.651
50	2.30[b]	.669
60	2.44	.700

[a] If stock financing is used, Universal will have 20 percent debt, and we saw in Table 19–4 that the Expected *EPS* is $2.00.
[b] This figure was calculated in Table 19–4; it represents bond financing.

[4] In Table 19–5 we assume that additional debt could be sold at a 5 percent rate of interest. As Chapter 20 shows, interest rates increase with leverage, so the figures shown here overstate the effect of leverage on earnings and understate the effect on risk. In other words, if we consider the fact that increased leverage leads to higher interest rates, the curve shown in Figure 19–3(a) would rise *less* steeply, and the curve shown in Figure 19–3(b) would rise *more* steeply.

Also, in both Table 19–5 and Figure 19–3 we are implicitly assuming that Universal Machine can vary its capital structure while holding its assets constant. This could be done by selling debt and using the proceeds to retire common equity, or vice versa.

FIGURE 19–3 Relationship between Earnings, Risk, and Leverage

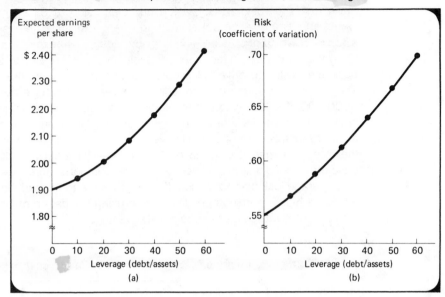

BREAK-EVEN ANALYSIS

Another way of presenting the data on Universal's two financing methods is shown in Figure 19–4, a break-even chart similar to the charts used in Chapter 4. If sales are depressed to zero, the debt financing line would cut the Y axis at – $1.30, well below the – $0.77 intercept of the common equity financing line. The debt line has a steeper slope and rises faster, however, showing that earnings per share will go up faster with increases in sales if debt is used. The two lines cross at sales of $1.92 million. Below that sales volume the firm would be better off issuing common shares; above that level, debt financing would produce higher earnings per share.[5]

[5]Instead of relating earnings per share to sales, we could analyze the relationship of earnings per share to earnings before interest and taxes *(EBIT)* for a particular form of financing.
Algebraically, this latter relationship is written as:

$$EPS = \frac{(EBIT - Interest)(1 - t)}{N}$$

where *N* is number of shares outstanding under the proposed financing scheme. This equation can be rewritten as:

$$EPS = - \frac{Interest(1 - t)}{N} + \frac{1 - t}{N} \; EBIT$$

This is a straight line relationship with a slope of $\frac{1 - t}{N}$ and an intercept of $- \frac{Interest(1 - t)}{N}$.

If the project is to be financed with new equity, *N* increases, the slope falls, and the intercept becomes less negative. If it is to be financed with debt, interest payments are larger and *N* is unchanged, resulting in a shift of the debt line, but not a change in the slope of the line.

If Walter and his board of directors *know with certainty* that sales will never again fall below the break-even sales value of $1.92 million, bonds would appear to be the better method of financing the increase in capacity since *EPS* would always be higher for every sales outcome. But they cannot know this for certain; in fact, they probably have good reason to expect future business cycles to drive sales down to, and even below, this critical level. They know that during the preceding five years sales have been as low as $500,000. If sales fall to this level again, the company would not be earning enough to cover its interest charges. Such a situation, if it continues for several years, could jeopardize the very existence of the firm. Further, if any of the three detrimental long-run events occur—Universal's products become obsolete, steel demand declines, or Japanese imports increase—future sales may average less than $2 million. If sales continue to expand, however, there would be higher earnings per share from using bonds; no officer or director would want to forego these substantial advantages.

FIGURE 19–4   Earnings Per Share for Common Equity and Debt Financing

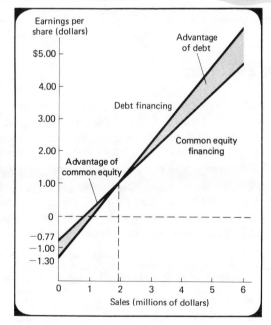

It must be emphasized that we are *not* deciding whether or not to undertake the investment to increase Universal's capacity. This decision has already been made based on the concepts presented for making investment decisions under uncertainty in Chapter 12. The capital budgeting tools were applied to the net cash flows and, employing a risk-adjusted discount rate, it was decided that capacity should be increased. The problem that Walter is considering is a financing decision—the choice of debt or equity or a combination to finance the increased capacity.

Walter's recommendation, and the decision of each director, will depend upon (1) each person's appraisal of the future sales outcomes, and (2) their psychological attitude toward risk.[6] The pessimists, or extreme risk averters, will prefer to employ common equity, while the optimists or the less risk averse directors, will favor bonds.

This example, which is typical of many real-world situations, suggests that the major disagreements over the choice of forms of financing are likely to reflect uncertainty about the future levels of the firm's sales. Such uncertainty, in turn, reflects the characteristics of the firm's environment—general business conditions, industry trends, and quality and aggressiveness of management.

RELATIONSHIP OF FINANCIAL LEVERAGE TO OPERATING LEVERAGE[7]

In Chapter 4 it was shown that a firm has some degree of control over its production processes; it can, within limits, use either a highly automated production process with high fixed costs but low variable costs or a less automated process with lower fixed costs but higher variable costs. If a firm uses a high degree of operating leverage, it was seen that its break-even point is at a relatively high sales level and that changes in the level of sales have a magnified (or "leveraged") impact on profits. Notice that financial leverage has exactly the same kind of effect on profits: the higher the leverage factor, the higher the break-even sales volume and the greater the impact on profits from a given change in sales volume.

The *degree of operating leverage* was defined as the percentage change in operating profits associated with a given percentage change in sales volume, and Equation 4–2 was developed for calculating operating leverage:

$$\text{Degree of operating leverage at point } Q = \frac{Q(P-V)}{Q(P-V)-F} \quad (4\text{--}2)$$

$$= \frac{S-VC}{S-VC-F} \quad (4\text{--}2a)$$

---

[6]In this debt-equity choice, the decision can be based on the subjective judgment of the decision maker. The theory that we have presented permits the decision maker to analyze the implications on earnings per share and risk from the different debt-equity choices. Theory also permits us to structure data collection systems so that they will be of maximum benefit to the decision maker.

[7]This section may be omitted without loss of continuity.

Here Q is units of output, P is the average sales price per unit of output, V is the variable cost per unit, anu F is total fixed costs, while S is sales in dollars and VC is total variable costs. Applying the formula to Universal Machine at an output level of 200 units (see Table 19–4 above), we find its operating leverage to be 1.50, so a 100 percent increase in volume produces a 150 percent increase in profit:

$$\text{Degree of operating leverage} = \frac{200(\$10,000 - \$4,000)}{200(\$10,000 - \$4,000) - \$400,000}$$

$$= \frac{\$2,000,000 - \$800,000}{\$2,000,000 - \$800,000 - \$400,000}$$

$$= \frac{\$1,200,000}{\$800,000} = 1.50 \text{ or } 150\%.$$

Operating leverage affects *earnings before interest and taxes (EBIT),* while financial leverage affects *earnings after interest and taxes,* the earnings available to common shareholders. In terms of Table 19-4, operating leverage affects the top section of the table, financial leverage the lower sections. Thus, if Universal Machine had more operating leverage, its fixed costs would be higher than $400,000, its variable cost ratio would be lower than 40 percent of sales, and earnings before interest and taxes would vary with sales to a greater extent. Financial leverage takes over where operating leverage leaves off, further magnifying the effect on earnings per share of a change in the level of sales. For this reason, operating leverage is sometimes referred to as *first-stage leverage* and financial leverage as *second-stage leverage.*

Degree of Financial Leverage

The *degree of financial leverage* is defined as the percentage change in earnings available to common shareholders that is associated with a given percentage change in earnings before interest and taxes *(EBIT).* An equation has been developed as an aid in calculating the degree of financial leverage for any given level of *EBIT* and interest charges *(I).*[8]

$$\text{Degree of financial leverage} = \frac{EBIT}{EBIT - I}. \qquad (19\text{--}1)$$

[8]The equation is developed as follows for a company with no preferred shares:

1. Notice that $EBIT = Q(P - V) - F.$
2. Earnings per share *(EPS)* $= \frac{(EBIT - I)(1 - t)}{N}$, where *EBIT* is earnings before interest and taxes, *I* is interest paid, *t* is the corporate tax rate, and *N* is the number of shares outstanding.
3. *I* is a constant, so ΔEPS, the change in *EPS,* is

$$\Delta EPS = \frac{\Delta EBIT(1 - t)}{N}.$$

(continued on page 487)

For Universal Machine at 200 units of output and an *EBIT* of $800,000, the degree of financial leverage with bond financing is

$$\text{Financial leverage: bonds} = \frac{\$800,000}{\$800,000 - \$250,000} = 1.45.$$

Therefore, a 100 percent increase in *EBIT* would result in a 145 percent increase in earnings per share. If common equity financing is used, the degree of financial leverage may be calculated and found to be 1.14, so a 100 percent increase in *EBIT* would produce a 114 percent increase in *EPS*.

Combining Operating and Financial Leverage

Operating leverage causes a change in sales volume to have a magnified effect on *EBIT,* and if financial leverage is superimposed on operating leverage, changes in *EBIT* will have a magnified effect on earnings per share. Therefore, if a firm uses a considerable amount of both operating leverage and financial leverage, even small changes in the level of sales will produce wide fluctuations in *EPS*.

Equation 4–2 for the degree of operating leverage can be combined with Equation 19–1 for financial leverage to show the total leveraging effect of a given change in sales on earnings per share.[9]

$$\text{Combined leverage effect} = \frac{Q(P - V)}{Q(P - V) - F - I}. \qquad (19\text{--}2)$$

---

4. The percentage increase in *EPS* is the change in *EPS* over the original *EPS*, or

$$\frac{\dfrac{\Delta EBIT(1 - t)}{N}}{\dfrac{(EBIT - I)(1 - t)}{N}} = \frac{\Delta EBIT}{EBIT - I}.$$

5. The degree of financial leverage is the percentage change in *EPS* over the percentage change in *EBIT,* so

$$\text{Financial leverage} = \frac{\dfrac{\Delta EBIT}{EBIT - I}}{\dfrac{\Delta EBIT}{EBIT}} = \frac{EBIT}{EBIT - I}.$$

[9]Equation 19-2 is developed as follows:

1. Recognize that $EBIT = Q(P - V) - F$, then rewrite Equation 19–1 as

$$\frac{EBIT}{EBIT - I} = \frac{Q(P - V) - F}{Q(P - V) - F - I}. \qquad (19\text{--}1a)$$

2. The total leverage effect is equal to the degree of operating leverage times the degree of financial leverage, or Equation 4–2 times Equation 19–1a:

$$\text{Combined leverage effect} = \text{Equation } 4\text{--}2 \times \text{Equation } 19\text{--}1a$$

$$= \frac{Q(P - V)}{Q(P - V) - F} \cdot \frac{Q(P - V) - F}{Q(P - V) - F - I} \qquad (19\text{--}2)$$

$$= \frac{Q(P - V)}{Q(P - V) - F - I}.$$

For Universal Machine at an output of 200 units (or $2 million of sales), the combined leverage effect, using debt financing, is

$$\frac{\text{Combined}}{\text{leverage effect}} = \frac{200(\$10,000 - \$4,000)}{200(\$10,000 - \$4,000) - \$400,000 - \$250,000}$$

$$= \frac{\$1,200,000}{\$1,200,000 - \$400,000 - \$250,000}$$

$$= 218 \text{ percent.}$$

Therefore, a 100 percent increase in sales from 200 units to 400 units would cause *EPS* to increase by 218 percent, so the new *EPS* figure would be 3.18 times the original *EPS:*

$$EPS_{(400 \text{ units})} = EPS_{(200 \text{ units})} + (EPS_{(200 \text{ units})}) \times 2.18$$

$$= EPS_{(200 \text{ units})} \times (1 + 2.18)$$

$$= \$1.10 \times 3.18 = \$3.50.$$

These figures agree, of course, with those worked out in Table 19–4.

Financial and operating leverage can be employed in various combinations. In the Universal Machine example, the combined leverage factor of 3.18 was obtained by using operating leverage of degree 1.50 and financial leverage of 1.45, but many other combinations of financial and operating leverage would have produced the same combined leverage factor. Within limits, firms can and do make tradeoffs between financial and operating leverage.

The usefulness of the degree of leverage concept lies in the facts (1) that it enables us to specify the precise effect of a change in sales volume on earnings available to common equity and (2) that it permits us to show the interrelationship between operating and financial leverage. The concept can be used to show a businessman, for example, that a decision to automate and to finance new equipment with bonds will result in a situation wherein a 10 percent decline in sales will produce a 50 percent decline in earnings, whereas a different operating and financial leverage package will be such that a 10 percent sales decline will cause earnings to decline by only 20 percent. In our experience, having the alternatives stated in this manner gives the decision-maker a better idea of the ramifications of possible actions.[10]

VARIATIONS IN FINANCIAL STRUCTURE

As might be expected, wide variations in the use of financial leverage may be observed among industries and among the individual firms within a particular

[10]The concept is also useful for investors. If firms in an industry are classified as to their degrees of total leverage, an investor who is optimistic about prospects for the industry might favor those firms with high leverage, and vice versa if he expects industry sales to decline.

industry. Since we are interested in the impact of leverage on the risk of the common equity holder, leverage must reflect the presence of all claims on earnings senior to the common equity holder. Therefore, our examples will include both debt and preferred shares in the leverage ratios. Leverage ratios for various Canadian industry groupings are presented in Table 19-6. Due to data limitations, the leverage ratio is measured as unity minus the ratio of common equity to invested capital, where invested capital is defined as total assets minus current liabilities.

Regulated industries display the highest leverage ratios; this stems from a heavy fixed asset investment coupled with extremely stable sales. The amount of leverage used decreases as the riskiness of the sales and the amount of fixed charges increases. Thus, the oil and gas industry has a low level of leverage. The lowest leverage rates are found in the real estate and construction industry.[11]

TABLE 19-6   Variation in Financial Leverage in Industry Groups, 1976

Industry Group[a]	Ratio of Debt Plus Preferred to Invested Capital[b]
Utilities	.67
Pipelines	.67
Paper and Forest Products	.53
Major Canadian Industries	.50
Merchandising	.47
Metals and Minerals	.46
Industrial Products	.44
Consumer Products	.38
Oil and Gas	.38
Communications and Media	.25
Real Estate and Construction	.17

Source: McLeod, Young, Weir Limited, Performance Summaries, Major Canadian Industries.
a) The industry groups correspond to the TSE 300 groupings.
b) This is calculated as unity minus the ratio of equity to invested capital. This resulting ratio is approximately equal to the ratio of debt plus preferred to total assets.

Even within a given industry grouping, there are wide variations in the use of financial leverage. First, consider the utilities industry. This grouping includes telecommunications companies, electric utilities and gas distributors. In the first part of Table 19-7, we present the leverage ratios for five gas distribution companies. The leverage ratios range from a low of 67 percent for Consumers' Gas to a high of 85 percent for Inter-City Gas. These variations reflect a number of considerations, including the volatility of sales for each company, operating areas, managements' willingness to assume risk, and the influence of the different regulatory boards.

[11] The very low leverage rate in real estate could be increased if short-term liabilities were included in both the numerator and denominator of the leverage ratio.

As a further indication of intra-industry variation, consider the second part of the table where the leverage ratios for gas pipelines are presented. The same influences that were noted for gas distributors are important in this industry as well.

TABLE 19–7   Intra-Industry Variation in Leverage

Industry Group	Firm	Leverage Ratios (1976)[a]
Gas Distributors	Consumers' Gas Company	.67
	Gaz Metropolitain Inc.	.77
	Inland Natural Gas Co. Ltd.	.74
	Inter-City Gas Ltd.	.85
	Union Gas Limited	.73
Gas Pipelines	Alberta Natural Gas Co. Ltd.	.52
	Alberta Gas Trunkline Ltd.	.71
	Trans Canada Pipeline Ltd.	.73
	Westcoast Transmission Co.	.60

Source: The Financial Post Corporation Service
   [a] The leverage ratios are based on the average book value of long-term sources of funds in 1976.

FACTORS INFLUENCING FINANCIAL STRUCTURE

Thus far the discussion has touched on the factors that are generally considered when a firm formulates basic policies relating to its financial structure. The actual capital structure chosen by the firm should reflect the attempt by management to tradeoff a number of factors which influence risk and expected return so that the market value of the firm is maximized. The more important of these financial structure determinants are new listed and briefly discussed.

1. Growth rate of future sales.
2. Stability of future sales.
3. Competitive structure of the industry.
4. Asset structure of the firm.
5. Control position and attitudes toward risk of owners and management.
6. Lenders' attitudes toward the firm and the industry.

Growth Rate of Sales

The future growth rate of sales is a measure of the extent to which the earnings per share of a firm are likely to be magnified by leverage. If sales and earnings grow at a rate of 8 to 10 percent a year, for example, financing by debt with limited fixed charges should magnify the returns to owners of the common equity.[12] This can be seen from Figure 19–4, above.

However, the common equity of a firm whose sales and earnings are growing at a favorable rate commands a high price; thus, it sometimes appears that equity financing is desirable. The firm must weigh the benefits of using leverage against the opportunity of broadening its equity base when it chooses between future financing alternatives. Such firms may be expected to have a moderate-to-high level of debt financing.

Sales Stability

Sales stability and debt ratios are directly related. With greater stability in sales and earnings, a firm can incur the fixed charges of debt with less risk than it can when its sales and earnings are subject to periodic declines; in the latter instance, it will have difficulty in meeting its obligations. In fact, to meet these obligations, the company may be forced to borrow short term with the associated issue costs or forced to hold large safety stocks of marketable securities which do not earn high rates of return.

An additional consideration is the probability of bankruptcy and its associated costs.[13] As leverage ratios increase, the probability of bankruptcy increases. Since bankruptcy is costly, increases in leverage increase the expected value of bankruptcy costs (i.e. the sum of the probability of bankruptcy times the bankruptcy costs), and this will have a depressing impact on the value of the firm. Financial managers, in attempting to maximize the market value of the firm, will choose that leverage rate which includes all factors, including the expected value of bankruptcy costs. Companies with very stable sales may have high bankruptcy costs, but since the probability of bankruptcy is low, the expected costs of bankruptcy are low. Thus, these firms can handle high leverage ratios. For example, the stability of sales for regulated utilities—natural gas pipelines and distributors, and telecommunications companies—has permitted these companies to make use of large amount of debt and preferred shares.

Competitive Structure

Debt-servicing ability is dependent upon the profitability, as well as the volume, of sales. Hence, the stability of profit margins is as important as the stability of sales. The ease with which new firms may enter the industry and the ability of competing firms to expand capacity will influence profit margins. A growth industry promises higher profit margins, but such margins are likely to narrow if the industry is one in which the number of firms can be easily increased through additional entry. For example, the franchised fast-service

[12] Such a growth rate is also often associated with a high profit rate.
[13] The implications of bankruptcy costs on the cost of capital are discussed in Chapter 20. The discussion of bankruptcy and reorganization, and the associated costs are presented in Chapter 24.

food companies were a very profitable industry in the early 1960s, but it was relatively easy for new firms to enter this business and go into competition with the older firms. As the industry matured during the late 1960s and early 1970s, the capacity of the old and the new firms grew at an increased rate. As a consequence, profit margins declined.

Other firms in other industries are better able to resist competitive pressures. For example, there are some firms that have unique technical, service and distribution facilities that are difficult to duplicate. This suggests that profit margins for these firms are less subject to erosion.

Asset Structure

Asset structure influences the sources of financing in several ways. Firms with long-lived fixed assets, especially when demand for their output is relatively assured (for example, utilities), use long-term mortgage debt extensively. Firms whose assets are mostly receivables and inventory whose value is dependent on the continued profitability of the individual firm—for example, those in wholesale and retail trade—rely less on long-term debt financing and more on short term.

Management Attitudes

The management attitudes that most directly influence the choice of financing are those concerning (1) control of the enterprise and (2) risk. Large corporations whose stock is widely owned may choose additional sales of common equity because they will have little influence on the control of the company. Also, because management represents a stewardship for the owners, it is often less willing to take the risk of heavy fixed charges.[14] However, if higher leverage ratios would be of benefit to shareholders and management refuses to increase leverage, the company may be the "victim" of a take-over bid.

In contrast, the owners of small firms may prefer to avoid issuing common equity in order to be assured of continued control. Because they generally have confidence in the prospects of their companies and because they can see the large potential gains to themselves resulting from leverage, managers of such firms are often willing to incur high debt ratios. The converse can, of course, also hold—the owner-manager of a small

---

[14]It would be inappropriate to delve too far into motivational theory in an introductory finance textbook, but it is interesting to note that the managers of many larger, publicly owned corporations have a relatively small ownership position and derive most of their income from salaries. Some writers assert that in such cases managements do not strive for profits, especially if this effort involves using leverage with its inherent risk. Presumably, these managers feel that the risks of leverage for them, the ones who actually decide to use debt or equity, outweigh the potential gains from successful leverage. If sales are low, there is a chance of failure and the loss of their jobs, whereas if sales and profits are high, it is the shareholders, not management, who receive the benefits. Another way of looking at the situation is to say that most shareholders are more diversified than most managers—if the firm fails, a shareholder loses only that percentage of his or her net worth invested in the firm, but the manager loses 100 percent of a job. While there is undoubtedly some merit to this argument, it should be pointed out that companies are increasingly using profit-based compensation schemes—bonus systems and stock-option plans—to motivate management to seek profitability.

firm may be *more* conservative than the manager of a large company. If the net worth of the small firm is, say, $1 million, and if it all belongs to the owner-manager, he may well decide that he is already prosperous enough, and may elect not to risk using leverage, even though the expected returns would be higher.

Lender Attitudes

Regardless of managements' analyses of the proper leverage factors for their firms, there is no question but that lenders' attitudes are frequently important —sometimes the most important—determinants of financial structures. In the majority of cases, the corporation discusses its financial structure with lenders and gives much weight to their advice. But when management is so confident of the future that it seeks to use leverage beyond norms for the industry, lenders may be unwilling to accept such debt increases. They will emphasize that excessive debt reduces the credit standing of the borrower and the credit rating of the securities previously issued.

As we will discuss in Chapter 20, when the leverage ratio increases, the interest rate on debt will increase to compensate the borrowers for the added risk. If bankruptcy is costly, the lenders will also require higher interest rates to cover the expected cost of bankruptcy. The lenders may decide that it is counter-productive to require progressively higher interest rates, since this will almost guarantee that the company becomes bankrupt. Therefore, lenders may impose a credit limit which is equivalent to rationing credit.

SUMMARY

Financial leverage, which means using debt (and preferred shares) to boost rates of return on net worth over the returns available on assets, is the primary topic covered in this chapter. Whenever the return on assets exceeds the cost of debt, leverage is favorable and the return on equity is raised by using it. However, leverage is a two-edged sword, and if the returns on assets are less than the cost of debt, then leverage reduces the returns on equity. This reduction is greater the more leverage a firm employs. As a net result, leverage may be used to boost shareholder returns, but it is used at the risk of increasing losses if the firm's economic fortunes decline.[15]

Probability data, whenever it is available, can be used to make the risk-return tradeoff involved in the use of financial leverage more precise. The expected earnings per share *(EPS)* and coefficient of variation *(v)* of these earnings may be calculated under alternative financial plans, and these *EPS* versus *v* comparisons aid in making choices among plans.

---

[15]The impact of preferred share financing on the breakeven analysis is considered in Problem 19-2.

Financial leverage is similar to operating leverage, a concept discussed in Chapter 4. As is true for operating leverage, financial leverage can be defined rigorously and measured in terms of the *degree of financial leverage*. In addition, the effects of financial and operating leverage may be combined, with the *combined leverage factor* showing the percentage changes in earnings per share that will result from a given percentage change in sales.

In the following chapter the concepts developed to this point in the book will be extended to the formal theory of the cost of capital. The way investors appraise the relative desirability of increased returns versus higher risks is seen to be a most important consideration, one that, in general, invalidates the theory that firms should strive for maximum earnings per share regardless of the risks involved.

QUESTIONS

19-1. How will each of the occurrences listed below affect a firm's financial structure, capital structure, and net worth?

a. The firm retains earnings of $100 during the year.

b. A preferred share issue is refinanced with bonds.

c. Bonds are sold for cash.

d. The firm repurchases 10 percent of its outstanding common shares with excess cash.

e. An issue of convertible bonds is converted.

19–2. From an economic and social standpoint, is the use of financial leverage justifiable? Explain by listing some advantages and disadvantages.

19–3. Financial leverage and operating leverage are similar in one very important respect. What is this similarity and why is it important?

19-4. How does the use of financial leverage affect the break-even point?

19-5. Would you expect risk to increase (a) proportionately, (b) more than proportionately, or (c) less than proportionately, with added financial leverage? Give reasons for your answer.

19-6. What are some reasons for variations of debt ratios among the firms in a given industry?

19-7. Why is the following statement true? "Other things being the same, firms with relatively stable sales are able to incur relatively high debt ratios."

19-8. Why do public utility companies usually pursue a different financial policy from that of trade firms?

19-9. The use of financial ratios and industry averages in the financial planning and analysis of a firm should be approached with caution. Why?

19-10. Some economists believe that swings in business cycles will not be as wide in the future as they have been in the past. Assuming that they are correct in their analysis, what effect might this added stability have on the types of financing used by firms in Canada? Would your answer be true for all firms?

PROBLEMS

19-1. John MacMillan is considering forming a new company, and he is presently investigating the alternative capital structures. Investment dealers tell him that debt capital would cost the following under different debt ratios (Debt/Total Assets):

Debt Ratio	up to 20%	21–40%	41–50%	51–65%
Before-tax cost of debt	8%	9%	11%	14%

Common equity can be issued to net $5 per share. The tax rate is 50 percent. MacMillan plans to raise $5 million. The following alternative capital structures are under consideration:

	(1)	(2)	(3)	(4)	(5)	(6)	(7)	(8)
Debt	0%	20%	21%	40%	41%	50%	51%	65%
Equity	100%	80%	79%	60%	59%	50%	49%	35%

   a. Compute the EPS for each alternative assuming an EBIT of $1 million. Which alternative would maximize EPS?
   b. Discuss the advantages and disadvantages of employing this capital structure.

19-2. Associated Bearings Ltd. is considering an expansion program that would require $10 million in external financing. The alternatives are (1) issue common equity that would net $50 per share (2) issue debt at 8 percent or (3) a combination of 50 percent common equity and 50 percent debt. Assume that the $50 per share and 8 percent rate would exist for the latter alternative.

   The expected earnings before interest and taxes (EBIT) for recessionary, normal, and booming economies are $2 million, $4 million, and $6 million respectively.

   The company has 800,000 shares of common equity outstanding and has a tax rate of 50 percent.

   a. Calculate EPS for each alternative given each economic condition.
   b. If the probabilities of recession, normal and boom economies are 0.2, 0.3 and 0.5 respectively, which financing alternative should be selected? Comment.
   c. Determine the degree of financial leverage for normal economic conditions for each of the three financing alternatives.
   d. Calculate the level of *EBIT* that will make earnings per share equal under the common equity and debt financing alternatives by using a breakeven chart.
   e. Assume that Associated Bearings can also finance the $10 million requirement through an issue of preferred shares at a 6 percent rate. Plot the earnings per share-*EBIT* relationship for preferred share financing on the breakeven chart derived in Part d.

   What is the breakeven level of *EBIT* for common equity and preferred equity financing? Based on this analysis, would the company ever issue preferred shares?

19-3. In early 19X6, the Davis Supply Company Limited planned to raise an additional $100 million for financing plant additions and for working capital. Davis manufactures educational equipment and aids.

   Investment dealers state that the company could sell common equity at a market price of $21 a share to net $20, or it could sell sinking fund debentures to yeild 8 percent. Issue costs would be slightly higher for common equity, but not enough to influence the decision.

Davis Supply Company Limited
Balance sheet, March 31, 19X6
(in millions of dollars)

Current assets	$350	Accounts payable	$ 28
Investments	35	Notes payable to banks	112
Net fixed assets	175	Taxes payable	56
		Other current liabilities	49
		Total current liabilities	$245
		Long-term debt	140
		Common equity, $2 par	40
		Retained earnings	135
Total assets	$560	Total claims	$560

Davis Supply Company Limited
Income statement
For year ended March 31, 19X6
(in millions of dollars)

Sales	$980
Net income before taxes, 10%	98
Interest on debt	8
Net income subject to tax	90
Tax, 50%	45
Net income after tax	$ 45

a. Assuming that net income before interest and taxes remains at 10 percent of sales, calculate earnings per share under both the equity-financing and debt-financing alternatives at sales levels of $600, $900, $1,200, $1,500, and $1,800 million.

b. Assuming that the probability distribution of sales is: (1) 10 percent chance of $600; (2) 25 percent chance of $900; (3) 30 percent chance of $1,200; (4) 25 percent chance of $1,500; and (5) 10 percent chance of $1,800, calculate the expected *EPS* for both debt and common equity financing. (The standard deviations for these *EPS* figures are given to be σ_{debt} = $.86 and σ_{equity}= $.68.)

c. If the market value of the equity has been based on a *P/E* ratio of 11, but it is believed that the use of debt financing will drop the *P/E* ratio to 9, compute expected price per share under each financing alternative. (The standard deviations for these price figures are given to be σ_{debt} = $7.70 and σ_{equity} = $7.53.)

d. Using the data and assumptions given above, which form of financing should Davis adopt? (Answer in terms of both the quantitative factors listed above and the qualitative factors discussed in the chapter.) In your answer, consider the facts that the industry average debt ratio is 30 percent, the current ratio is 2×, and the times interest earned ratio is 7×.

19-4. United Battery Corp. Ltd. produces one product, a long-life rechargeable battery for use in small calculators. Last year 50,000 batteries were sold at $20 each. United Battery's income statement is shown below:

United Battery Corp. Ltd.
Income statement
For year ended December 31, 19X5

Sales		$1,000,000
Less: Variable cost	$400,000	
Fixed cost	200,000	600,000
EBIT		$ 400,000
Less: Interest		125,000
Net income before tax		$ 275,000
Less: Income tax ($t = 0.40$)		110,000
Net income		$ 165,000
EPS (100,000 shares)		$1.65

a. Calculate (1) the degree of operating leverage, (2) the degree of financial leverage, and (3) the combined leverage effect for United Battery for the 19X5 level of sales.

b. United Battery is considering changing to a new production process for manufacturing the batteries. Highly automated and capital intensive, the new process will double fixed costs to $400,000 but will decrease variable costs to $4 a unit. If the new equipment is financed with bonds, interest will increase by $70,000; if the equipment is financed by common equity, total shares outstanding will increase by 20,000 shares. Assuming that sales remain constant, calculate for each financing method (1) earnings per share and (2) the combines leverage if the new process is employed.

c. Under what conditions would you expect United Battery to want to change its operations to the more automated plant?

d. If sales are expected to increase, which alternative will have the greatest impact on EPS? Illustrate with an example.

19-5. The Wilder Corp. Ltd. plans to expand assets by 50 percent; to finance the expansion, it is choosing between a straight 7 percent debt issue and common equity. Its current balance sheet and income statement are shown below.

Wilder Corp. Ltd.
Balance sheet
December 31, 19X5

		Debt, 6%	$140,000
		Common equity, $10 par	350,000
		Retained earnings	210,000
Total assets	$700,000	Total claims	$700,000

Wilder Corp. Ltd.
Income statement
For year ended December 31, 19X5

Sales	$2,100,000	
Total costs (excluding interest)	1,881,600	Earnings per share: $\dfrac{\$105,000}{35,000} = \$3$
Net income before taxes	$ 218,400	Price/earnings ratio = 10 × *
Debt interest	8,400	
Income before taxes	$ 210,000	Market price: 10 × 3 = $30
Taxes at 50%	105,000	
Net income	$ 105,000	

*The price/earnings ratio is the market price per share divided by earnings per share. It represents the amount of money an investor is willing to pay for $1 of current earnings. The higher the riskiness of the equity, the lower its P/E ratio, other things held constant. The concept of price/earnings ratios was discussed at some length in Chapter 18.

If Wilder Corp. Ltd. finances the $350,000 expansion with debt, the rate on the incremental debt will be 7 percent and the price/earnings ratio of the common equity will be 8 times. If the expansion is financed by equity, the new shares can be sold at $25, the rate on debt will be 6 percent, and the price/earnings ratio of all the outstanding common equity will remain at 10 times earnings.

a. Assuming that net income before interest and taxes (*EBIT*) is 10 percent of sales, calculate earnings per share at sales levels of $0, $700,000, $1,400,000, $2,100,000, $2,800,000, $3,500,000, and $4,200,000, when financing is with (1) debt and (2) common equity. Assume no fixed costs of production.

b. Make a break-even chart for *EPS* and indicate the break-even point in sales (that is, where *EPS* using bonds = *EPS* using equity).

c. Using the price/earnings ratio, calculate the market value per share of common equity for each sales level for both the debt and the equity financing.

d. Make a break-even chart of market value per share for the company using data from part c, and indicate the break-even point.

e. If the firm follows the policy of seeking to maximize (1) *EPS* or (2) market price per share, which form of financing should be used?

f. Now assume that the following probability estimates of future sales have been made: 5 percent chance of $0; 7.5 percent chance of $700,000; 20 percent chance of $1,400,000; 35 percent chance of $2,100,000; 20 percent chance of $2,800,000; 7.5 percent chance of $3,500,000; and 5 percent chance of $4,200,000. Calculate expected values for *EPS* and market price per share under each financing alternative.

g. What other factors should be taken into account in choosing between the two forms of financing?

h. Would it matter if the presently outstanding equity was all owned by the final decision-maker, the president, and that this represented her entire net worth? Would it matter if she was compensated entirely by a fixed salary? that she had a substantial number of stock options?

The Cost
of Capital

20 The cost of capital is a critically important topic. First, as we saw in Chapter 11, capital budgeting decisions have a major impact on the firm, and proper capital budgeting requires an estimate of the cost of capital. Second, in Chapter 19 we saw that financial structure can affect both the size and riskiness of the firm's earnings stream, and may even have an impact on the value of the firm. A knowledge of the cost of capital, and how it is influenced by financial leverage, is useful in making capital structure decisions. Finally, a number of other decisions, including those related to leasing, to bond refunding, and to working capital policy, require estimates of the appropriate cost of capital.[1]

In this chapter, we first point out the necessity of using a weighted average cost of capital. Second, the costs of the individual components of the capital structure—debt, preferred shares, and common equity—are considered: because investors perceive different classes of securities to have different degrees of risk, there are variations in the costs of different types of securities. Third, the individual component costs are brought together to form a weighted cost of capital. Fourth, the concepts developed in the earlier sections are illustrated with an example of the cost of capital calculation for an

---

[1]The cost of capital is also of crucial importance in regulated utilities such as gas and oil pipelines, gas distribution companies and telephone companies. The regulatory commission seeks to measure the regulated utility's cost of capital and sets the prices of the utility's products or services such that the utility can earn this rate of return. If the estimate of the cost of capital is below the true cost of capital and the company must raise capital to finance investments, then the investment financed by this capital does not earn the true cost of capital; this will harm the current equity holder. Conversely, if the estimate is above the true cost of capital, customers will pay too much for the service and this gain to current shareholders is reflected in an increase in stock price. Finally, we should note that the cost of capital for regulatory purposes is estimated somewhat differently than the cost of capital for an unregulated company.

actual company. Finally, the interrelationship between the cost of capital and the investment opportunity schedule is developed, and the simultaneous determination of the marginal cost of capital and the marginal return on investment is discussed.

The cost of capital is both a fascinating and controversial topic in the field of finance. Controversy centers around how the overall cost of capital is measured and the influence of leverage and dividend policy on the cost of capital. The latter issue is investigated in Chapter 21, whereas the impact of leverage is discussed at the end of this chapter.

There is still disagreement among financial theorists concerning these issues. In fact it is very likely that the three authors of this book do not agree on every issue. Since this is an introductory textbook, the discussion of the cost of capital will present a point of view with which a majority of financial theorists can agree.

COMPOSITE, OR OVERALL, COST OF CAPITAL

Suppose a particular firm's cost of debt is estimated to be 8 percent, its cost of equity is estimated to be 12 percent, and the decision has been made to finance next year's projects by selling debt. The argument is sometimes advanced that the cost of these projects is 8 percent, because debt will be used to finance them. However, this position contains a basic fallacy. To finance a particular set of projects with debt implies that the firm is also using up some of its potential for obtaining new low-cost debt. As expansion occurs in subsequent years, at some point the firm will find it necessary to use additional equity financing or else the debt ratio will become too large.

To illustrate, suppose the firm has an 8 percent cost of debt and a 12 percent cost of equity. In the first year it borrows heavily, using up its debt capacity in the process, to finance projects yielding 9 percent. In the second year it has projects available that yield 11 percent, well above the return on first-year projects, but it cannot accept them because they would have to be financed with 12 percent equity money. To avoid this problem, the firm should be viewed as an on-going concern, and its cost of capital should be calculated as a weighted average, or composite, of the various types of funds it uses: debt, preferred, and equity.

An additional benefit of using the weighted average approach is that the debt-equity financing decision is totally independent of the investment decision. The firm, having made its decision as to how to finance its operations i.e. the debt-equity choice, then determines the cost of capital for investment decisions. By approaching the cost of capital in this way, the cost of capital to be used for a particular investment project will be independent of how the project is to be financed.

BASIC DEFINITIONS

Both students and practitioners are often confused about how to calculate and use the cost of capital. To a large extent, this confusion results from imprecise, ambiguous definitions, but a careful study of the following definitions will eliminate such unnecessary difficulties.

Capital, or Financial, Components

Capital (or financial) components are the items on the right-hand side of the balance sheet: various types of debt, preferred shares, and common equity. Any net increase in assets must be financed by an increase in one or more capital components.

Component Costs

Capital is a necessary factor of production, and like any other factor, it has a cost. The cost of each component is defined as the *component cost* of that particular component. For example, if the firm can borrow money at 8 percent, the before-tax component cost of debt is defined as 8 percent. Throughout most of this chapter, we concentrate on debt, preferred shares, retained earnings, and new issues of common equity. These are the capital structure components, and their component costs are identified by the following symbols.[2]

k_d = interest rate on firm's new debt = component cost of debt, before-tax.

$k_d(1-t)$ = component cost of debt, after-tax, where t = marginal corporate tax rate; $k_d(1-t)$ is the debt cost used to calculate the marginal cost of capital.

k_p = component cost of preferred shares.

k_r = component cost of retained earnings (or internal equity). k_r is identical to k_s, the required rate of return on common equity as developed in Chapter 18. Here we distinguish between equity obtained from retained earnings versus selling new shares, hence the distinction between k_r and k_s.

k_e = component cost of new issues of common equity (or external equity).

k_a = an average, or "composite," cost of capital. If a firm raises $1 of new capital to finance asset expansion, and if it is to keep its capital structure in balance (that is, if it is to keep the same percentage of debt, preferred, and equity), then it will raise part of the

---

[2] The literature also refers to these component costs as required yields. This terminology is more precise, since the investor in preferred, common equity or debt has an opportunity cost or yield requirement. However, we will continue to refer to the required yields on the sources of capital as the cost of that source of capital.

dollar as debt, part as preferred, and part as common equity (with equity coming either as retained earnings or from the sale of new common shares.[3] It must be emphasized that these are long-run or target proportions. Financing is typically lumpy and any particular project may be financed with one source of funds which moves the capital structure away from the target proportions; this will necessitate that subsequent projects be financed with a different source of funds. The value k_a is also a *marginal cost:* there is a value of k_a for each dollar the firm raises during the year. k_a is, in effect, the marginal cost of capital used in Chapter 11, and the relationship between k_a and the amount of funds raised during the year is expressed as the *MCC* schedule in Figure 11-1.[4]

The fact that the composite cost of capital k_a, is referred to as both a marginal and an average cost is not inconsistent with economic theory. The composite cost of capital will reflect the current opportunity cost or marginal cost of each specific source of funds used by the company. Thus it is a marginal concept. However, since the firm uses these funds in long-run proportions to finance investments, the calculation of the composite cost of capital requires a weighted average of the specific marginal costs be utilized. Since the composite cost is a weighted average of the marginal costs of each source of financing, it is itself a marginal cost.

These definitions and concepts are explained in detail in the remainder of this chapter, where we seek to accomplish two goals: (1) to develop a marginal cost of capital schedule (k_a = *MCC*) which can be used in capital budgeting, and (2) to determine the mix of types of capital that will minimize the *MCC* schedule. If the firm finances so as to minimize its *MCC,* uses this *MCC* to calculate *NPV*'s, and makes capital budgeting decisions on the basis of the *NPV* method, this will lead to a maximization of the common equity share.

In order to emphasize the importance of the marginal cost of capital we present the following simplified example. Assume that a company has two sources of financing – debt with a current interest rate of 8 percent and common equity with a required yield or cost of equity of 15 percent. The total amount of debt plus equity is $100 million of which 70 percent is equity and 30 percent is debt. The firm has invested the full amount of capital to earn a rate of return of 12.9 percent. Finally, all earnings after interest payments are paid out as dividends and there is no corporate income tax.

---

[3] Firms do try to keep their debt, preferred and common equity in balance, but they *do not* try to maintain any propotional relationship between the common equity and retained earnings accounts as shown on the balance sheet.

[4] The value k_a also reflects the average riskiness of the firm's various assets as discussed in Chapter 12, Investment Decisions Under Uncertainty. If a firm uses risk-adjusted discount rates for different projects, k_a should be used only for projects that have a risk level equal to the risk of the overall firm.

The management of the company is contemplating an investment of $10 million which is to be financed in the current proportions of debt and equity; new debt can be issued at 8 percent.

The important point is to determine that minimum rate of return on the investment that will leave the value of the existing equity holders unchanged. This rate of return is the cost of capital.

A summary of the analysis is presented in Table 20-1. In the first column, the capital structure and cash flows before the investment decision are presented. As can be seen the equity holder obtains a rate of return of 15 percent before the investment decision, i.e. dividends divided by the value of equity, or 10,500,000/70,000,000 = .15.

TABLE 20-1

	Column 1 Before Investment Decision	Column 2 Incremental Impact of Invest- ment Decision	Column 3 After the Investment Decision
Capital Structure			
Debt (8%)	$ 30,000,000	$ 3,000,000	$ 33,000,000
Equity	70,000,000	7,000,000	77,000,000
	$100,000,000	$10,000,000	$110,000,000
Earnings before interest	$ 12,900,000	$ 1,290,000	$ 14,190,000
Interest	2,400,000	240,000	2,640,000
Dividends (earnings available to common)	10,500,000	1,050,000	11,550,000

In order to determine the cost of capital, we must determine the incremental impact of the investment decision on the equity holder. Since the firm will issue an additional $3,000,000 in debt at 8 percent, it is obvious that the project must earn at least the incremental interests payments of $240,000. But the project must also earn enough to ensure that existing equity holders are not harmed. In Table 20-1, in the second column, we observe that if the earnings before interest on the project are $1,290,000, there is enough to pay the incremental interest and have $1,050,000 left over to pay the new equity holder. This will give a 15 percent rate of return to the new equity holder and will not impair the dividends to the old shareholders. The overall rate of return on investment that meets these constraints is 12.9 percent, i.e. 1,290,000/10,000,000, and this is the firm's cost of capital. Note also that the rate of return on equity after the investment decision (see Column 3) is 15 percent, as well, i.e. $11,550,000/77,000,000.

Suppose the firm's investment earned 10 percent. This will leave incremental earnings after interest of $760,000 and the total earnings (dividends) after the investment would be $11,260,000. This is a rate of return on equity after the investment of 14.6 percent, a reduction from the pre-investment return on equity of 15 percent. If the project earns in excess of the cost of capital, then the post-investment rate of return on equity will be greater than 15 percent. This is a clear gain to current shareholders.

Suppose the firm decided to finance this project by issuing $5,000,000 of debt instead of $3,000,000. As long as the firm intends to maintain its target capital structure at 30 percent debt and 70 percent equity, this implies that the firm will have to finance subsequent investment opportunities with an equity component in excess of 70 percent. But, as long as the capital structure targets are unchanged, the marginal cost of capital remains at 12.9 percent. If, however, the firm decided to alter its capital structure targets, the marginal cost of capital would be altered as well.

BEFORE-TAX COMPONENT COST OF DEBT (k_d)

If a firm borrows $100,000 for one year at 6 percent interest, the investors who purchase the debt receive, and the firm must pay them, a total of $6,000 interest on their investment:

$$k_d = \text{before-tax cost of debt} = \frac{\text{interest}}{\text{principal}}$$

$$= \frac{\$6,000}{\$100,000} = 6\%. \tag{20-1}$$

For now, assume that there is no corporate income tax on the firm; the effect of income taxes on the analysis of cost of capital is treated in a later section of the chapter. Under this assumption, the firm's dollar interest cost is $6,000, and its percentage cost of debt is 6 percent. As a first approximation, *the component cost of debt is equal to the rate of return required by debt investors or the current interest rate on debt*. If the firm borrows and invests the borrowed funds to earn a return just equal to the interest rate, then the earnings available to common shares remain unchanged.[5] This is demonstrated below.

---

[5] Note that this definition is a *first approximation;* it is modified later to take account of the deductibility of interest payments for income tax purposes. Note also that here the cost of debt is considered in isolation. The impact of debt on the cost of equity, as well as on future increments of debt, is treated when the weighted cost of a combination of debt and equity is derived. Finally, issue costs, or the costs of selling the debt, are ignored. Issue costs for debt issues are generally quite low; in fact, debt placed directly with banks, insurance companies, pension funds, and the like, involves no issue costs. In general the cost of debt is calculated as an internal rate of return as discussed in Chapter 11. The cost of debt is that discount rate that equates the present value of the debt service payments per bond to the net proceeds per bond obtained from the bond issue. The formula for this calculation is presented in the equation on p. 505.

The ABC Company has sales of $1 million, operating costs of $900,000, and no debt. Its income statement is shown in the Before column of Table 20-2. Then it borrows $100,000 at 6 percent and invest the funds in assets whose use causes sales to rise by $7,000 and operating costs to rise by $1,000. Hence, profits before interest rise by $6,000. The new situation is shown in the After column. Earnings are unchanged, as the investment just earns its component cost of capital.

Note that the cost of debt is applicable to *new* debt, not to the interest on any old, previously outstanding debt. In other words, we are interested in the cost of new debt, or the *marginal* cost of debt. Our primary concern with the cost of capital is to use it in a decision-making process—the decision whether to obtain capital to make new investments; whether the firm borrowed at high or low rates in the past is irrelevant.[6]

TABLE 20-2 Income Statement for the ABC Company

	Before	After
Sales	$1,000,000	$1,007,000
Operating costs	900,000	901,000
Earnings before interest	$ 100,000	$ 106,000
Interest (*I*)	—	6,000
Earnings	$ 100,000	$ 100,000

PREFERRED SHARES

Preferred shares described in detail in Chapter 15, are a hybrid between debt and common equity. Like debt, preferreds carry a fixed commitment on the

$$P = \frac{I_1}{1 + k_d} + \frac{I_2}{(1 + k_d)^2} + \dots + \frac{I_t + M}{(1 + k_d)^t}$$

Here, *I* refers to the periodic debt service payment—in this case interest payments—*M* is the par or maturity value of the bond, *P* is the bond's issue price and n is the life of the bond. If there are issue costs, the bond's issue price is less than the par value, *M*. In this case the cost of debt will be higher.

An approximation used to calculate the cost of debt is as follows.

$$k_d = \frac{I_t + \dfrac{M - P}{n}}{\dfrac{M + P}{2}}$$

This equation is an approximation since it does not consider compounding effects. Under most conditions, the approximation is reasonably close; for example, with an 8 percent, 25 year, $1,000 par value bond sold at $980, the formula gives k_d = 8.16 versus 8.19 as found from a bond table.

[6] The fact that the firm borrowed at high or low rates in the past is, of course, important in terms of the effect of the interest charges on current profits and hence on the market value of existing equity, but this past decision is not relevent for *current* decisions. For current financial decision, only current interest rates are relevant.

part of the corporation to make periodic payments, and, in liquidation, the claims of the preferred shareholders take precedence over those of the common shareholders. Failure to make the preferred dividend payments does not result in bankruptcy, as does nonpayment of interest on bonds. Preferred shares are thus somewhat more risky *to the firm* than common equity, but are less risky than bonds. Just the reverse holds for investors. To the investor, preferred is less risky than common but more risky than debt. It would appear logical that if an investor were willing to purchase the firm's bonds to yield a 6 percent return, he or she might, because of risk aversion, ask for a higher yield on the preferred equity, say 8 percent. This would be the case in a taxation system where both interest payments and preferred dividends received equivalent tax treatment in the hands of the investor. However, there are two tax provisions which result in preferred dividends receiving a favorable tax treatment. First, intercompany dividend payments are tax free, and second, investors can take advantage of the dividend tax credit on preferred dividends. Both of these factors are important in determining the yield differentials between the bonds and preferred shares of the same company; it is certainly true that the higher risk of preferreds should result in investors requiring a higher after-personal-tax rate of return on preferreds as compared to bonds. However, with the application of the dividend tax credit it is possible to obtain this required after-personal-tax rate of return on preferreds from a lower before-personal-tax yield on preferreds. In fact, the before-personal-tax yields on preferreds are less than on bonds. For example, as of June 23, 1978, a Bell straight preferred was selling to yield 7.7 percent and, as of the same date, the bond yield on one of its bonds was 9.8 percent. Similarly, as of the same date, Dominion Foundries and Steel, Limited preferreds were yielding 7.2 percent and their debt, 9.85 percent. Assuming the preferred issue is a perpetuity that sells for $100 a share and pays an $8 annual dividend, its before-personal-tax yield is calculated as follows:

$$\text{Preferred yield} = \frac{\text{preferred dividend}}{\text{price of preferred share}} = \frac{D_p}{P_p} = \frac{\$8}{\$100} = 8\%. \qquad (20\text{--}2)$$

Because of issue costs, a firm will receive *less than* the current market price of preferred shares when it sells new preferred. Thus, P_p in the denominator of Equation 20–2 should be the net price received by the firm. Suppose, for example, the firm must incur a selling issue cost of $4 a share. In other words, buyers of the preferred issue pay $100 a share, but investment dealers charge a selling commission of $4 a share, so the firm nets $96 a share. *The cost of new preferred to the firm is calculated as shown in Equation 20–2a:*

$$k_p = \text{cost of preferred} = \frac{D_p}{P_{pn}} = \frac{\$8}{\$96} = 8.33\%. \qquad (20\text{-}2a)$$

where P_{pn} is the net price received by the firm.

TAX ADJUSTMENT

As they stand, the definitions of the component costs of debt and preferred shares are incompatible when we introduce corporate taxes into the analysis, because interest payments are a deductible expense whereas preferred dividends are not. The following example illustrates the point.

The ABC Company can borrow $100,000 at 6 percent, or it can sell 1,000 shares of $6 preferred stock to net $100 a share. Assuming a 48 percent tax rate, its before-investment situation is given in the Before column of Table 20-3. At what rate of return must the company invest the proceeds from the new financing to keep the earnings available to common shareholders from changing?

TABLE 20-3   Tax Adjustment for Cost of Debt

| | | Invest in Assets Yielding | | |
| | | 6% | | 11.538% |
	Before	Debt	Preferred	Preferred
Earnings before interest and taxes (*EBIT*)	$100,000	$106,000	$106,000	$111,538
Interest (*I*)	—	6,000	—	—
Earnings before taxes (*EBT*)	$100,000	$100,000	$106,000	$111,538
Taxes 48% (*T*)	(48,000)	(48,000)	(50,880)	(53,538)
Preferred dividends	—	—	(6,000)	(6,000)
Available for common dividends	$ 52,000	$ 52,000	$ 49,120	$ 52,000

As can be seen from the tabulations in Table 20-3, if the funds are invested to yield 6 percent before taxes, earnings available to common shareholders are constant if debt is used, but they decline if the financing is with preferred shares. To maintain the $52,000 net earnings requires that funds generated from the sale of preferred shares be invested to yield 11.538 percent before taxes or 6 percent after taxes.[7]

---

[7] The 11.538 percent is found as follows: 6%/(1 − tax rate) = 6%/0.52.

Since shareholders are concerned with after-tax rather than before-tax earnings, only the costs of capital *after* corporate taxes should be used. The cost of preferred shares is already on an after-tax basis as defined, but a simple adjustment is needed to arrive at the after-tax cost of debt. It is recognized that interest payments are tax deductible—the higher the firm's interest payments, the lower its tax bill. In effect, the federal government pays part of a firm's interest charges. Therefore, the after-tax cost of debt capital is calculated as follows:

$$k_d(1 - t) = \text{after-tax cost of debt}$$
$$= (\text{before-tax cost}) \times (1.0 - \text{tax rate}). \qquad (20\text{--}3)$$

Whenever the composite, or average cost of capital (k_a) is calculated, $k_d(1 - t)$ and not k_d is used. This after-tax cost of debt capital reflects the true amount of the interest payment that must be paid out of the companies earnings. Equation 20-2 can be written as $k_d - tk_d$. The first term is the actual dollar interest payment and the second term is the tax subsidy given by the federal government. The difference, then, is the actual interest burden of the debt on the company.

Example

Before-tax cost of debt = 6 percent; tax rate = 48 percent.
$$k_d(1 - t) = \text{after-tax cost} = (0.06)(1 - 0.48) = (0.06)(0.52) = 3.12 \text{ percent.}$$

If the tax rate had been 50 percent, the after-tax cost of debt would have been one-half the interest rate. We should also note that the tax rate is zero for a firm with no profits. Therefore, for a corporation without taxable income, the cost of debt is not reduced; that is, in Equation 20–3 the tax rate equals zero, so the after-tax cost of debt is equal to the interest rate.

COST OF RETAINED EARNINGS (k_r)[8]

The cost of preferred shares is based on the return investors require if they are to purchase the preferred shares; the cost of debt is based on the interest rate investors require on debt issues, adjusted for taxes. The cost of equity obtained by retaining earnings can be defined similarly: *it is k_r, the rate of return shareholders require on the firm's common equity.* (k_r is identical to k_s as developed in Chapter 18.)

---

[8] The term "retained earnings" can be interpreted to mean the balance sheet item "retained earnings," consisting of all the earnings retained in the business throughout its history, or it can mean the income statement item "additions to retained earnings." This latter definition is used in the present chapter: *"Retained earnings" for our purpose here refers to that part of current earnings which is not paid out in dividends but, rather, is retained and reinvested in the business.*

"Equity" is defined in this chapter to *exclude* preferred shares. Equity is the sum of capital stock, contributed surplus, and accumulated retained earnings.

As we saw in Chapter 18, the value of a share of common equity with a constant expected growth rate is calculated by use of the following equation:

$$P_0 = \frac{D_1}{k_r - g}. \tag{20-4}$$

Here P_0 is the current price of the share; D is the dividend expected to be paid at the end of the year; k_r is the required rate of return, and g is the expected growth rate. We can solve for k_r to obtain the required rate of return on common equity:

$$k_r = \frac{D_1}{P_0} + \text{expected } g. \tag{20-5}$$

Example

To illustrate this calculation, consider Aubey Rents, a firm expected to earn $2 a share and to pay a $1 dividend during the coming year. The company's earnings, dividends, and share price have all been growing at about 5 percent a year, and this growth rate is expected to continue indefinitely. The equity is in equilibrium and currently sells for $20 a share. Using this information, we compute the required rate of return on the equity in equilibrium, using Equation 20-5, as follows:

$$k_r = \frac{\$1}{\$20} + 5\% = 10\%.$$

The expected growth rate for the price of the shares is 5 percent, which, on the $20 initial price, should lead to a $1 increase in the per share value of the equity, to $21. This price increase will be attained (barring changes in the general level of share prices) if Aubey invests the $1 of retained earnings to yield 10 percent. However, if the $1 is invested to yield only 5 percent, then earnings will grow by only 5 cents during the year, not by the expected 10 cents a share. The new earnings will be $2.05, a growth of only 2½ percent, rather than the expected $2.10, or 5 percent increase. If investors believe that the firm will earn only 5 percent on retained earnings in the future and attain only a 2½ percent growth rate, they will reappraise the per share value of the equity downward according to Equation 20-4 as follows:

$$P_0 = \frac{D_1}{k_r - g} = \frac{\$1}{.10 - .025} = \frac{\$1}{.075} = \$13.33.$$

Note, however, that Aubey Rents will suffer this price decline *only if it invests equity funds—retained earnings—at less than its component cost of capital.*

If Aubey refrains from making new investments and pays all its earnings in dividends, it will cut its growth rate to zero. However, the price of the stock will not fall, because investors will still get the required 10 percent rate of return on their shares:

$$k_r = \frac{D_1}{P_0} + g = \frac{\$2}{\$20} + 0 = 10\%, \text{ or}$$

$$P_0 = \frac{\$2}{.10 - 0} = \$20.$$

All the return would come in the form of dividends, but the actual rate of return would match the required 10 percent.

The preceding example demonstrates a fundamentally important fact: *If investors expect a firm to earn its required rate of return, k_r, on the investment of retained earnings, then when it retains earnings and invests them in its operations, its current share price will not change as a result of this financing and investment. However, if it is expected to earn less than k_r, the share price will fall; if it is expected to earn more, the share price will rise.*

COST OF NEWLY ISSUED COMMON EQUITY, OR EXTERNAL EQUITY (k_e)

The cost of new common equity, or *external* equity capital, k_e is higher than the cost of retained earnings, k_r, because of issue costs involved in selling new common equity. What rate of return must be earned on funds raised by selling equity to make the action worthwhile? To put it another way, what is the cost of new common equity? The answer is found by applying the following formula:[9]

$$k_e = \frac{D_1}{P_0(1-F)} + g = \frac{D_1}{P_n} + g$$

$$= \frac{\text{dividend yield}}{\text{(net price on equity issue)}} + \text{growth},$$

(20–6)

or

$$k_e = \frac{\text{dividend yield}}{(1 - \text{issue percentage})} + \text{growth}$$

$$= \frac{D_1/P_0}{(1-F)} + g.$$

(20–7)

[9] The equation is derived as follows:

Step 1. The old shareholders expect the firm to pay a stream of dividends, D_t; this income stream will be derived from existing assets. New investors will likewise expect to receive the same stream of dividends, D_t. For new investors to obtain this stream *without impairing the D_t stream of the old investors,* the new funds obtained from the sale of equity must be invested at a return high enough to provide a dividend stream whose present value is equal to the price the firm receives:

(continued on page 511)

Here F is the percentage cost of selling the issue, so $P_0(1 - F) = P_n$ is the net price received by the firm. For example, if $P_0 = \$10$ and $F = 10$ percent, then the firm receives \$9 for each new share sold; hence $P_n = \$9$. Notice that Equations 20–6 and 20–7 are strictly applicable only if future growth is expected to be constant.

For Aubey Rents, the cost of new outside equity is computed as follows:

$$k_e = \frac{\$1}{\$20(1 - .10)} + 5\% = 10.55\%,$$

or

$$k_e = \frac{5\%}{.9} + 5\% = 10.55\%.$$

Investors require a return of $k_r = 10$ percent on Aubey's equity. However, because of issue costs, Aubey must earn *more* than 10 percent on common equity financed investments to provide this 10 percent. Specifically, if Aubey Rents earns 10.55 percent on investments financed by new common equity issues, then earnings per share will not fall below previously expected earnings; its expected dividend can be maintained; the growth rate for earnings and dividends will be maintained; and as a result of all this, the price per share will not decline. If Aubey earns less than 10.55 percent, then earnings, dividends, and growth will fall below expectations, causing the price per share to decline. Since the cost of capital is *defined* as the rate of return that must be earned to prevent the price per share of the common equity from falling, we see that the company's cost of external equity, k_e, is 10.55 percent.[10]

$$P_n = \sum_{t=1}^{\infty} \frac{D_t}{(1 + k_e)^t}. \qquad (20\text{--}8)$$

Here P_n is the net price to the firm; D_t is the dividend stream to new shareholders; and k_e is the cost of new outside equity.

Step 2. If issue costs are expressed as a percentage, F, of the gross price of the equity, P_0, we may express P_n as follows:

$$P_n = P_0(1 - F).$$

Step 3. When growth is a constant, Equation 20–8 reduces to

$$P_n = P_0(1 - F) = \frac{D_1}{k_e - g}. \qquad (20\text{--}8a)$$

Step 4. Equation 20–8a may be solved for k_e:

$$k_e = \frac{D_1}{P_0(1 - F)} + g. \qquad (20\text{--}7)$$

[10] The cost of external equity is sometimes defined as follows:

$$k_e = \frac{k_r}{1 - F}.$$

This equation is correct if the firm's expected growth rate is zero; see Equation 20–7. In other cases it tends to overstate k_e.

FINDING THE BASIC REQUIRED RATE OF RETURN ON COMMON EQUITY

It is obvious by now that the basic rate of return investors require on a firm's common equity, k_s as developed in Chapter 18, is a most important quantity. This required rate of return is the cost of retained earnings, and it forms the basis for the cost of capital obtained from new common equity issues. How is this all-important quantity estimated?

Although one *can* use very involved, highly complicated procedures for making this estimation, satisfactory estimates may be obtained through the use of one of two general techniques:

1. Estimate the risk-return tradeoff line as described in Chapter 18; estimate the relative riskiness of the firm in question; and then use these estimates to obtain the required rate of return on the firm's common equity:

$$k_s = k_r = R_F + \rho.$$

Under this procedure, the estimated cost of equity (k_r) will move up or down with changes in interest rates and with changes in "investor psychology."

2. Measure the cost of equity capital for a particular company by using the dividend yield plus growth model as presented in Equation 20-5. In this model, the shareholders' returns are derived from dividends and capital gains. The equity investor's required yield is estimated using the current dividend yield plus an estimate of the expected growth rate. The implementation of this estimation technique depends, crucially, on the estimate of the expected growth rate. While this is a rather involved problem, we will discuss three techniques that have been used to estimate the growth rate. Given the introductory nature of this textbook, we will discus the rationale for these estimates at an intuitive level.

a. Use of Historical Growth Rates.
As noted above, the growth rate used in the calculation of the cost of equity should reflect investors' expectations. In many instances these estimates of growth can be based on historic growth rates.

The theoretical literature on the dividend yield plus growth model notes that, under certain conditions, the expected growth rate refers to growth in per share dividends, earnings and security price; the growth rates should be the same for all three. Therefore, the analyst can use historical growth rates in earnings or dividends per share as a proxy for the expected growth rate.[11] Even though the growth rates should be equal, from a theoretical point of view, the actual growth rates will be different and it remains the responsibility of the analyst to use his or her judgment to choose the appropriate growth rate. In addition, the historical estimates of growth are useful only if there have been no important changes in historical profitability or in either dividend or leverage

[11] Growth rates derived from historical share price performance do not provide good estimates of expected growth, since the share price reflects not only the firm's earnings and dividends but also economy-wide influences.

policies.

b. Estimate the Components of Growth

The expected growth rate can be analyzed into its underlying components. This growth depends on the retention ratio of the company as expected to prevail by investors and the rate of return earned on these retained earnings. These factors reflect the growth rate due to retained earnings.

To see how this works, consider a company that has earned $1 per share. The company has a payout ratio of 40 percent, i.e. the dividend is 40¢, and the retention ratio of 60 percent. Thus, of the $1 earnings per share, the company retains and invests 60¢. Suppose the company earns 20 percent on this investment. Then, the earnings per share in the following year will be higher by the amount invested (60¢) times the return earned on this investment (20 percent). From this information we can measure the growth due to retention financing as the product of the retention ratio and the rate of return on this retention. If we denote b as the retention rate and IRR as the profitability or rate of return on the retention financing, then the expected growth rate, g, is found as follows:

$$g = b \times IRR = (.4)(.20) = .08 \text{ or } 8 \text{ percent}$$

and
$$k_r = \frac{D_1}{P_0} + b \times IRR.$$

There are a number of techniques used to estimate the retention ratio and the rate of return on the retention financing. The former is measured as the most current retention ratio or an average of the past. The rate of return on investment can be measured as the most current rate of return on book equity, or an average of these rates of return over an historical period. Whatever the technique chosen, it should reflect the investors' most current expectations of these variables. This technique is particularly useful if the historical growth experience in earnings or dividends has been unusually unstable, or if there have been important changes in the company's financial policy. In addition, this technique assumes that new outside equity financing is not very important as a long-run source of funds.

c. Outside Estimates of Growth

Security analysts regularly make earnings growth forecasts, looking at such factors as projected sales, profit margins, competitive factors, and the like. Someone making a cost of capital estimate can obtain such analysts' forecasts and use them as a proxy for the growth expectations of investors in general, combine g with the current dividend yield, and estimate k_r as

$$k_r = \frac{D_1}{P_0} + \text{growth rate as projected by security analysts.}$$

Again, note that this estimate of k_r is based upon the assumption that g is expected to remain constant in the future.

Of the two general techniques noted above, the dividend yield plus growth method is used more frequently than the risk-return tradeoff. In estimating the cost of equity for a firm using the first technique, the difficult problem is estimating growth. The use of growth rates estimated from historical data is appropriate only when there are not unusual influences on the company. These "normal" conditions have not generally existed in recent years and the estimated growth rates may be unreliable. The second technique which analyzes growth into its components permits a financial analyst to relate expected growth to the most recent experience of the company. The reliability of the growth rates derived by outside sources, such as security analysts, will depend on the forecasting techniques chosen. In the end, the estimated growth rate may reflect combinations of the results from the three growth measurement techniques presented.

Based on our own experience in estimating equity capital costs, we recognize that both careful analysis and some very fine judgments are required in this process. It would be nice to pretend that these judgments are unnecessary and to specify an easy, precise way of determining the exact cost of equity capital. Unfortunately, this is not possible. Finance is in large part a matter of judgment, and we simply must face this fact.

EFFECT OF LEVERAGE ON THE COST OF EQUITY

We have seen in earlier chapters that investors in general are averse to risk, and that risk aversion leads investors to require higher yields on riskier investments. In Chapter 19, we used the Universal Machine Company case to demonstrate that for any given degree of business risk, the higher the debt ratio, the larger the coefficient of variation (v) in earnings per share.[12] Combining these results leads us to conclude that the more debt a given company employs, other things held constant, the higher its required rate of return on equity capital will be.

To illustrate this relationship, consider Table 20-4, which extends the example of the Universal Machine Company to incorporate the risk-return tradeoff, and Figure 20-1, where the tradeoff function between leverage and rate of return is plotted.[13] The required rate of return on equity is 12 percent if the company uses no debt, but k_r increases with debt and is 19.5 percent if the leverage ratio is as high as 60 percent.[14]

[12] This relationship was worked out for Universal Machine in Table 19–5.

[13] In this example we assume that the risk-return tradeoff function has been estimated, perhaps in a subjective manner, by the financial manager. The precise specification of such risk-return functions is one of the more controversial areas of finance, and having attempted to measure them empirically ourselves, we can attest to the difficulties involved. However, even though the precise shape of the function is open to question, it is generally agreed (1) that the curve is upward sloping and (2) that some estimate, be it better or worse, is necessary if we are to obtain a cost of capital for use in capital budgeting. In this chapter our main concern is that the broad concepts be grasped.

[14] Keep in mind that throughout this analysis we are holding constant the firm's assets and the EBIT on these assets. We wish to consider the effect of leverage on the cost of capital *holding other things constant*.

TABLE 20-4 Universal Machine Company: Leverage, Risk, and Required Rates of Return on Equity

Leverage (Debt/Assets)	Risk (v)	Required Rate of Return (kᵣ)
0%	.552	12.0%
10	.570	12.2
20	.591	12.5
30	.615	13.0
40	.641	14.0
50	.669	16.0
60	.700	19.5

FIGURE 20-1 Relationship between Cost of Equity and Financial Leverage

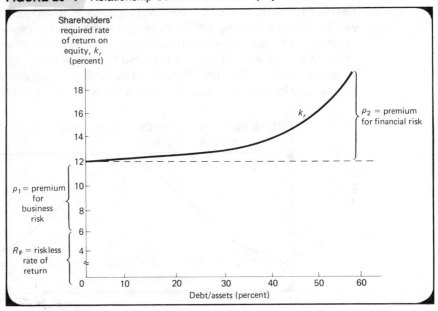

In Chapter 18 we indicated that the required rate of return consisted of the riskless rate plus a risk premium: $k_r = R_F + \rho$. Here we divide ρ into two components, ρ_1 (read "rho one"), a premium for business risk; and ρ_2, a premium required to compensate equity investors for the additional risk brought on by financial leverage. Expressed as an equation,

$$k_r = R_F + \rho_1 + \rho_2. \qquad (20-9)$$

The riskless rate of return, R_F, is a function of general economic conditions, monetary policy, and the like. The premium for business risk, ρ_1, is a function of the nature of the firm's industry, its degree of operating leverage, its diversification, and so on. Financial risk, ρ_2, depends upon the degree of financial leverage employed.[15]

EFFECT OF LEVERAGE ON THE COMPONENT COST OF DEBT

The component cost of debt is also affected by leverage: the higher the leverage ratio, the higher the cost of debt. Further, the cost of debt can be expected to rise at an increasing rate with leverage. To see why this is so, we can again consider the Universal Machine Company example. For simplicity, let us assume the following: (1) the company has $10 million of assets, and this level of assets will be maintained regardless of any financing decisions; (2) the company can adjust its capital structure any way it chooses, selling common equity and using the proceeds to retire bonds if it elects to reduce its leverage, or selling bonds and using the funds to buy and retire its common equity. If it elects to increase leverage; (3) the probability distribution of earnings before interest and taxes (*EBIT*) is represented by Figure 20-2; (4) the company could realize $2 million from the sale of its land, plant, equipment, and inventories if it is forced to liquidate,[16] and (5) risk-free debt yields 6 percent.[17]

FIGURE 20–2 Probability Distribution of *EBIT* for Universal Machine Company

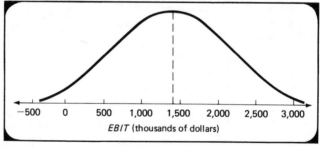

EBIT (thousands of dollars)

---

[15] ρ_2 increases at an increasing rate with leverage because bankruptcy, as opposed to simply lower earnings, becomes an increasing threat as the debt ratio rises, and bankruptcy has some high costs of its own (see Chapter 24). As we saw in Chapter 15, the specific terms of the firm's debt also affect its financial risk. Especially important here is the maturity structure of the debt. In a case where there were no costs of bankruptcy, ρ_2 would still increase at an increasing rate with increases in the ratio of debt to total assets, but the rate of increase would be lower than the case in which bankruptcy costs existed.

[16] The liquidation value should be considered as a probability distribution, but we shall abstract from this and assume that the $2 million is a certain sum.

[17] To simplify the example, we disregard the existing 5 percent debt and assume that all debt bears interest at the new debt cost, k_d.

Suppose Universal raises $1 million of its total funds as debt; how risky would this debt be, and what interest rate would creditors require? First, if the debt is riskless, it should yield the riskless rate, or 6 percent. Since Universal could net $2 million from sale of assets if it is forced into bankruptcy, and since these funds would be available to pay off the bondholders, the first $2 million of debt may be considered riskless.[18]

Next, consider the fact that the more debt the firm has, the higher the interest requirements; and the higher the interest charges, the greater the probability that earnings (*EBIT*) will not be sufficient to meet these charges.[19] Creditors will perceive this increasing risk as the debt ratio rises, and they will begin charging a risk premium above the riskless rate, causing the firm's interest rate to rise. Since creditors are risk averters, they will demand that interest rates be increased to compensate for the increased risk.

One other effect that may operate to raise interest rates at an increasing rate is the fact that a firm may need to use a variety of sources in order to borrow large amounts of funds in relation to its equity base. For example, a firm may be able to borrow from banks only up to some limit set by bank policy. In order to increase its borrowings, the firm would have to seek other institutions, such as insurance companies, finance companies, and so on, that may demand higher interest rates than those charged by banks. Such an effect might tend to cause interest rates to jump whenever the firm was forced to find new lenders.

Table 20–5 shows the estimated relationships between leverage, the interest rate, and the after-tax cost of debt for Universal Machine. Assuming

TABLE 20-5   Universal Machine Company
Effect of Leverage on the Cost of Debt

Leverage (*Debt/Assets*)	Interest Rate (k_d)	After-tax Cost of Debt $k_d(1-t)$
0%	6%	3.0%
10	6	3.0
20	6	3.0
30	7	3.5
40	9	4.5
50	12	6.0
60	17	8.5

[18] Actually, for liquidity (marketability) and for other reasons, corporate debt never sells at yields as low as Treasury securities' rates. So even if Universal Machine's debt is riskless, it would have a marketability premium that would cause its yield to exceed the government bond rate. Also, we abstract here from the many problems that arise in bankruptcy. As we show in Chapter 24, these problems are sufficient to keep corporate debt from ever being truly riskless.

[19] The area under the curve in Figure 20–2 to the left of any level of fixed charges represents the probability of not covering these charges.

a 50 percent tax rate, the after-tax cost of debt is one-half the interest rate; these figures are also shown in Figure 20–3, where they are plotted against the debt ratio. In the example, Universal's cost of debt is constant until the debt ratio passes 20 percent or $2 million; then it begins to climb.

FIGURE 20–3 Universal Machine Company: Leverage and the After-tax Cost of Debt

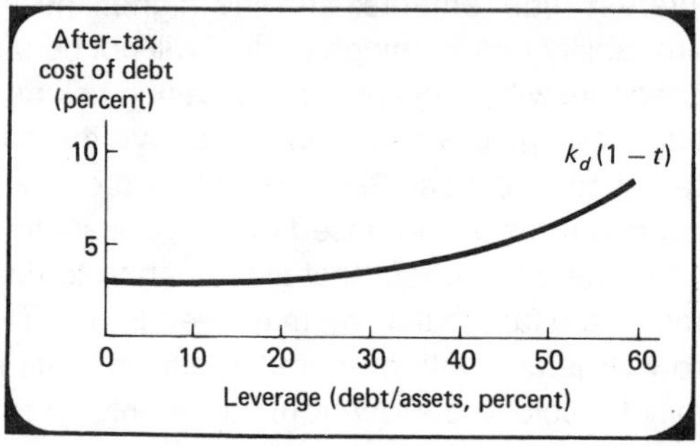

COMBINING DEBT AND EQUITY: WEIGHTED AVERAGE, OR COMPOSITE, COST OF CAPITAL

Debt and equity may now be combined to determine the average, or composite, cost of capital. If we return to Table 20–1, we can see the calculation of the cost of capital in a highly simplified no-corporate tax situation.

Before undertaking the investment decision, the company had interest payments of $2,400,000 and equity requirements of $10,500,000. The cost of capital was the total required earnings divided by the total capital, i.e. 12.9 percent.

By a very simple derivation, the composite cost of capital is measured as a weighted average of the component marginal costs of funds where the weights are the proportion of the total capital structure made up by each type of capital.[20] In the simple example in Table 20–1, debt has a weight of 30

[20]
$$k_a = \frac{\text{cost of}}{\text{capital}} = \frac{\text{interest} + \text{equity requirement}}{\text{total capital}} = \frac{\text{interest} + \text{equity requirement}}{\text{outstanding debt plus equity}}$$

$$= \frac{k_d \left(\begin{array}{c} \text{debt} \\ \text{outstanding} \end{array} \right) + k_e \left(\begin{array}{c} \text{equity} \\ \text{outstanding} \end{array} \right)}{\text{total capital}}$$

$$= k_d \left(\frac{\text{debt}}{\text{total capital}} \right) + k_e \left(\frac{\text{equity}}{\text{total capital}} \right)$$

$$= (k_d \times w_d) + (k_e \times w_e)$$

Where w_d and w_e are the weights assigned to debt and equity respectively in the target capital structure, this equation can be expanded to include other sources of funds with their component costs and associated capital structure weights.

TABLE 20-6 Calculation of Points on Average Cost of Capital Curve (percent), or the Composite Cost of Capital for Different Capital Structures

	Percent of Total (1)	Component Costs (2)	Weighted, or Composite, Cost: $K_a = (1) \times (2) \div 100$ (3)[a]
Debt	0	3.0	0
Equity	100	12.0	12.00
	100		12.00
Debt	10	3.0	.30
Equity	90	12.2	11.00
	100		11.30
Debt	20	3.0	.60
Equity	80	12.5	10.00
	100		10.60
Debt	30	3.5	1.05
Equity	70	13.0	9.10
	100		10.15
Debt	40	4.5	1.80
Equity	60	14.0	8.40
	100		10.20
Debt	50	6.0	3.00
Equity	50	16.0	8.00
	100		11.00
Debt	60	8.5	5.10
Equity	40	19.5	7.80
	100		12.90

[a] We divide by 100 to obtain percentages; figures rounded to nearest hundredth.

percent and a marginal cost of 8 percent. Equity has a weight of 70 percent and a marginal cost of 15 percent. The cost of capital is a weighted average and is equal to 12.9 percent.

$$k_a = (k_d \times w_d) + (k_e \times w_e)$$
$$= k_d(.3) + k_e(.7)$$
$$= (.08)(.3) + (.15)(.7)$$
$$= .129 \text{ or } 12.9 \text{ percent}$$

w_d and w_e are the capital structure weights associated with debt and equity respectively.

When we introduce corporate taxes, the appropriate marginal component costs are measured after corporate tax. Thus, the relevant cost of debt required in an after-tax composite cost of capital calculation is $k_d (1 - t)$ not k_d. However, the capital structure weights are not altered.

Table 20–6 shows the calculations used to determine the after-tax weighted average cost of capital for Universal Machine under a set of assumed capital structures. The resulting average cost, together with the component costs of debt and equity, is plotted against the debt ratio in Figure 20–4. Here we see that the composite cost of capital is minimized when its debt is approximately 35 percent, so Universal's optimal capital structure calls for about 35 percent debt, 65 percent equity.

FIGURE 20–4   Universal Machine Company: Average, or Composite, Cost of Capital

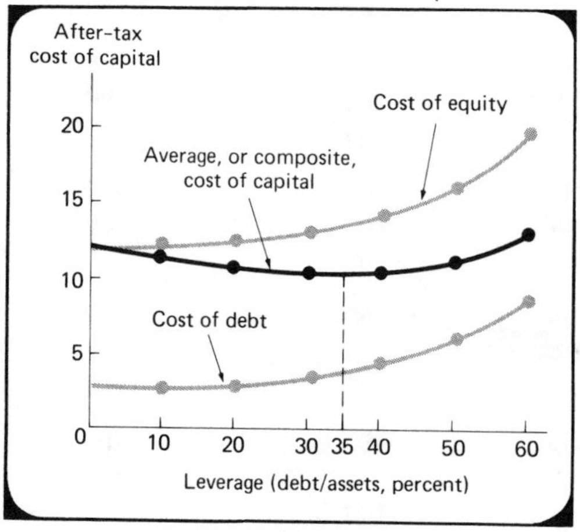

It is important to note that the average cost of capital curve is relatively flat over a fairly broad range: if Universal Machine's debt ratio is in the range of 25 to 45 percent, the average cost of capital cannot be lowered very much by moving to the optimal point. This appears to be a fairly typical situation, as almost any "reasonable" schedule for the component costs of debt and equity will produce a saucer-shaped average cost of capital schedule similar to that shown in Figure 20–4. This gives financial managers quite a degree of flexibility in planning their financing programs, permitting them to sell debt one year, equity the next, in order to take advantage of capital market conditions and to avoid high issue costs associated with small security issues.

The choice of the optimal leverage ratio is consistent with the desire to maximize the market value of the existing equity. As the leverage ratio increases and the weighted average cost of capital falls, the market value of the firm rises. This reflects the fact that the shareholders are obtaining the benefits of the tax subsidy provided by the deductibility of interest payments. This benefit continues to exist at all levels of leverage but is eventually offset by the increasing costs of debt and equity capital due to the existence of bankruptcy costs. Beyond the minimum point on the cost of capital schedule, the market value of the firm begins to fall.

Table 20-6 and Figure 20-4 are based on the assumption that the firm is planning to raise a given amount of new capital during the year. For a larger or smaller amount of new capital, some other cost figures might be applicable; the optimal capital structure might call for a different debt ratio, and the minimum average cost of capital (k_a) might be higher or lower. This point is discussed in detail later in the chapter.

HIGH-RISK AND LOW-RISK FIRMS

Shown in Figure 20-5 are the cost of capital schedules for a firm in a risky industry (R) and for one in a stable industry (S). Firm R, the one on which Figure 20-4 was based, is Universal Machine; firm S is a relatively stable, safe company. We have already examined the interrelationships of the curves of Universal Machine—after declining for a while as additional low-cost debt is averaged in with equity, the average cost of capital for firm R begins to rise after debt has reached 35 percent of total capital. Beyond this point, the fact that both debt and equity are becoming more expensive offsets the fact that the component cost of debt is less than that of common equity.

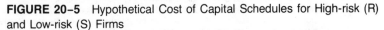

FIGURE 20-5 Hypothetical Cost of Capital Schedules for High-risk (R) and Low-risk (S) Firms

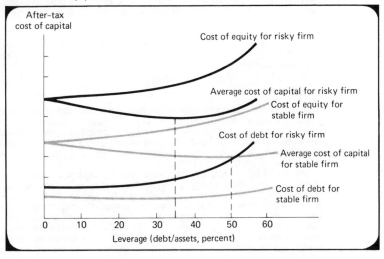

While the same principles apply to the less risky firm, its cost functions are quite different from those of Universal Machine. In the first place, S's overall business risk is lower, giving rise to lower debt and equity costs at all debt levels. Further, its relative stability means that less risk is attached to any given percentage of debt; therefore, its costs of both debt and equity—and, consequently, its average cost of capital—turn up further to the right than do the corresponding curves for Universal Machine. The optimum debt ratio for the firm in the stable industry is 50 percent as compared to only 35 percent for Universal.

Determining the actual optimal capital structure for a specific firm requires both analysis and judgment, and it is up to a firm's financial manager to decide on the best capital structure for his company. Once this decision has been reached, the weighting system for the average cost of capital calculation is also determined. In our calculations of the cost of capital, we will refer to both market and book value capital structure weights. The choice as to which of these weights reflects the optimal capital structure will be discussed later in the chapter.[21]

---

[21]The weights used to calculate the marginal cost of capital, k_a, should be based on the *market value of the capital raised,* not the book value of the existing capital structure. However, if a firm seeks to maintain a constant book value capital structure—as most firms do—*then the market value of the capital raised will be proportional to the book value capital structure.* Consider a firm with assets and capital of $100, whose stock sells at a premium of 40 percent over its book value, and whose debt sells at its book value:

	Book Value Capital Structure		Market Value Capital Structure	
Debt	$ 50	50%	$ 50	42%
Common equity	50	50	70	58
	$100	100%	$120	100%

Suppose this firm plans to raise $50 of new capital. If it raises $25 of debt and $25 of equity, its book value capital structure will remain constant, but its market value percentages will change to 44% debt and 56% equity. Conversely, if it raises new capital as $21 debt and $29 equity, its market value capital structure will remain constant, but its book value structure will change to 47% debt, 53% equity. Thus, we see that a firm whose securities sell at prices different from their book values can maintain a book value capital structure or a market value structure, but not both.

Most firms do, in fact, target on book value capital structures, and there seem to be three reasons for this choice: (1) market values fluctuate widely, and financial planning would be unstable if a market value target was used; (2) it is difficult if not impossible to specify a precise optimal capital structure anyway, whether it is measured in book or market terms; and (3) regardless of which choice is made with regard to the target capital structure, the book and market values of *marginal* capital are approximately equal. Of course, if the *wrong* target capital structure is used as the target, the MCC will be higher than it needs to be, but with the present state of the art, it is almost impossible to *prove* that one capital structure is better than another, at least for capital structures in the broad range of 25–60 percent debt, whether measured at book or market.

CALCULATING THE MARGINAL COST OF CAPITAL FOR AN ACTUAL COMPANY

The procedures discussed above are now applied to an actual company, Dominion Foundries and Steel, Limited (also known as, Dofasco) to illustrate the cost of capital calculation. A number of simplifying assumptions are made in this analysis and the resulting cost of capital number is an approximation to the true value. The company is the second largest producer of steel in Canada and in 1976 it produced over 20 percent of the nation's steel.

Dofasco, a fully integrated steel producer, has subsidiaries and other interests in the manufacture of railway cars, steel tubular products and the production of limestone, coal, and iron ore. It is a large firm with assets, as of 1976, in excess of $1 billion and sales of $900 million. Dividends have been paid continuously since 1937. The indicated annual dividend rate established with the January, 1977, quarterly payment was $1.55 per share; combining this with the end of February, 1977, share price of $25.25 results in a dividend yield of 6.14 percent. From 1971 to 1976, dividends per share grew at a rate of 10.3 percent and earnings per share by 19 percent.[22] The dividends per share displayed a stable growth pattern, whereas earnings per share grew very rapidly in the years 1971 to 1974 and had a negative growth rate during 1975. The alternative method of measuring growth is to combine the expected retention rate with the rate of return on investment. During the period 1971 to 1976 the retention ratio ranged from 48 percent to 72 percent. The 1976 value of 65 percent appeared reasonable as a forecasted retention ratio based on the historical pattern. The historical rates of return on book common equity varied from 9.5 percent in 1970 to 17.5 percent in 1974. The 1976 value was 14 percent. Based on forecasts for the economy and the steel industry, it was unlikely that Dofasco would earn 17 percent. The current value of 14 percent was used.[23] The resulting growth rate was 9.1 percent, i.e. the retention ratio of .65 times the rate of return of 14 percent. Since internally generated funds provide sufficient equity, only the costs of internal equity (found in this case to be the 6.1 percent dividend yield plus the 9.1 percent growth rate, or a total of 15.2 percent) need be considered.

One complication in the Dofasco example is the existence of class A and B common equity introduced in 1975. The difference between these classes was discussed in depth in Chapter 14. For the purposes of this example, it is sufficient to realize that class B shares receive tax deferred dividends and it is likely that the dividend yield on the stock will be different. In our analysis of the Dofasco cost of capital, we will calculate the cost of equity capital for class A

---

[22]Earnings per share for 1971 were $1.74 and for 1976 were $4.17. Dividing $4.17 by $1.74 gives 2.40 which is the *CVIF* for 5 years at approximately 19 percent from Table A-1. Thus, earnings per share grew at approximately 19 percent over the five-year-period.

[23]If the average retention ratio and rate of return on book equity were used, the values would be 62 percent and 13.3 percent respectively. This would result in a growth rate of 8.2 percent, i.e. .62 × .133 × 100.

and assume that this applies to class B shares as well. This assumption avoids the problem of calculating weights for the regular and tax deferred shares.

As of December 31, 1976, the weighted average interest rate on Dofasco's outstanding debt was 9.8 percent. The lowest interest cost debt is 6½ percent and the highest, 10 7/8 percent. Most of the debt has been issued since 1971. To measure the marginal cost of debt capital, we require an estimate of the current yield on Dofasco's debt. Fortunately, Dofasco issued $75 million of sinking fund debentures at 9.375 percent in 1977. Assuming a 40 percent tax rate, the after-tax marginal cost of debt is estimated to be 5.6 percent (i.e. 9.375 (1-.4)). The preferred shares have a stated yield of 4.75 percent, but these shares were issued in 1965 when yields were low. On the basis of the market price of the preferred shares in early 1977, the estimated marginal cost of preferred shares is 8.4 percent.

When considering the sources of funds for any company, a distinction must be made between those funds that are "free" and those that are "non-free". Sources in the first category include accounts payable and accruals and are considered "free" since they provide funding without an explicit interest charge. The long term sources of funds are included in the second category. Some would argue that in the calculation of the overall cost of capital, this "free" capital should be included. Under certain conditions this procedure is valid; usually, however, only "non-free" sources of capital need be considered.[24]

In Table 20–7 the book and market values of non-free sources of funds are presented. The book values are taken from the 1976 annual report.[25] The market values of common (both classes A and B) and preferred equity are based on share prices as of the end of February, 1977. Since the yield on the new debt in 1977 is approximately equal to the average interest cost of the outstanding debt as of year-end 1976, we assume that the book and market values of debt are equal.

---

[24]The primary justification for ignoring "free" capital is that, in the capital budgeting process, these spontaneously generated funds are netted out against the required investment outlay, then ignored in the cost of capital calculation. To illustrate, consider a retail firm thinking of opening a new store. According to customary practices, the firm should (1) estimate the required outlay, (2) estimate the net receipts (additions to profits) from the new store, (3) discount the estimated receipts at the cost of capital, and (4) accept the decision to open the new store only if the net present value of the expected revenue stream exceeds the investment outlay. The estimated accruals, trade payables, and other costless forms of credit are deducted from the investment to determine the "required outlay" before making the calculation. Alternatively, "free" capital could be costed in, and working capital associated with specific projects added in when determining the investment outlay. The two procedures will result in similar decisions.

[25]In estimating the book value of equity, we have taken the sum of retained earnings and common shares and have omitted the reserve for deferred taxes. As of the end of 1976, the reserve for deferred tax was approximately $170 million. The method for handling deferred taxes is an unresolved problem. If we had included the deferred tax reserve as common equity, then the proportion of equity in the capital structure, measured at book value, would be 30 percent. This is a substantial difference from the weight of 36 percent used in the analysis. In using the market value weights, no adjustment for deferred taxes is needed, since the market price will reflect the impact, if any, of this reserve.

TABLE 20-7 Dofasco Capital Structure—Book and Market Values (millions of dollars)

Source of Capital	Book Value Amount	Proportion	Market Value Amount	Proportion
Debentures	$279.6	.36	$279.6	.40
Preferred shares	20.2	.03	11.4	.02
Common equity	470.8	.61	398.0	.58
Total capital	$770.6	1.00	$689.0	1.00

The weighted average cost of capital is calculated in Table 20–8 using both market and book value weights.

TABLE 20-8 Dofasco, Cost of Capital Calculation

Capital	Component Cost (1)	Capital Structure Book Value (2)	Market Value (3)	Weighted Cost Book Value (4) = (1) × (2)	Market Value (5) = (1) × (3)
Debentures	5.6%	.36	.40	2.02	2.24
Preferred shares	8.4	.03	.02	.25	.17
Common equity	15.2	.61	.58	9.27	8.82
				$k_a = 11.54\%$	$k_a = 11.23\%$

As can be observed from this Table, the weighted average costs of capital using market and book weights are approximately equal. However, this will not always be the case. If there is a large discrepancy, which of the two costs of capital should be used? Since the cost of capital is an opportunity cost, we require the inputs used in its calculation to be opportunity costs as well. Book value weights reflect the historical value of the funds invested in the company. The market value of debt reflects the impact of current interest rates and the market value of equity reflects the market's expectations of the profitability of the firm's assets. Clearly, market values of debt and equity reflect opportunity costs. Therefore, market value weights are the correct weights to use from a theoretical point of view and we would favor the measurement of the cost of capital on this basis. If the cost of capital under the book value weights is greater than under market value, using the former as a cut-off rate for investment decisions would result in the rejection of projects that should be accepted.

One problem in using market value weights is that their values fluctuate from year to year and it may be difficult to evaluate the target capital structure. In addition, some companies have debt that is placed privately or not traded on the market. For these companies, the market value of debt must be approximated and the resulting weights are of reduced reliability. Unfortunately, although the theoretical position requires the use of market weights, the measurement problems associated with their use are significant. If possible, the cost of capital under both weighting schemes can be calculated, and a decision made on the basis of the resulting numbers.

The cost of capital estimates we have derived for Dofasco are based on the existing capital structure weights and yields measured as of the beginning of 1977. Note that these costs of capital reflect the tax advantage of debt *and* the overall riskiness of the firm's assets. If Dofasco were contemplating an investment decision which had risk characteristics equivalent to the existing assets, the weighted average cost of capital value could be used.

If management believed that some other capital structure is optimal, then not only would other weights need to be used but also a revised cost of equity, and perhaps even a revised cost of debt would be required since altered leverage targets will have an impact on these yields. For purposes of illustration it is assumed that the existing structure has been determined to be the optimum.

Marginal Cost of Capital When New Common Shares Are Used

In the Dofasco example we have assumed that the company will not issue any new common equity capital and hence that financing would be through debt, preferred shares and *internally generated equity*. On this basis (and assuming the firm financed in its target proportions), we found the weighted average cost of capital to be 11.23 percent using market value weights. What would have happened, however, if the firm's financing requirements were sufficiently large to require an issue of new common equity? The answer is that its marginal cost of new capital would have increased. To show why this is so, we shall extend the Dofasco example.

First, suppose that during 1976 Dofasco had $66 million available for common shareholders, paid $23 million in dividends and retained $43 million. If Dofasco desires to keep its market value capital structure in balance each year, the retained earnings must equal 58 percent of the net additions to capital, the other 42 percent being debt and preferred shares. Therefore, the total amount of new capital that can be obtained on the basis of the retained earnings is

$$\text{Retained earnings} = (\text{percent equity})(\text{new capital})$$

$$\text{New capital} = \frac{\text{retained earnings}}{\text{percent equity}}$$

$$= \frac{\$43 \text{ million}}{0.58} = \$73.5 \text{ million.}$$

Next, we note that 2 percent of the new capital or about $1.5 million, should be preferred shares and that 40 percent, or $29.4 million, should be debt. In other words; Dofasco can raise a total of $73.5 million—$43 million from retained earnings, $29.4 million in the form of debt, and $1.1 million in the form of preferred shares—and still maintain its target capital structure in exact balance.[26]

If all financing up to $73.5 million is in the prescribed proportions, the composite cost of each dollar of new capital *up to $73.5 million* is still 11.23 percent, the previously computed weighted average cost of capital. In Table 20-8, we calculated the weighted average cost of capital of raising funds with the equity component derived from retained earnings. This cost of capital is appropriate for any amount of capital required up to $73.5 million, since this is the maximum that can be raised using the target proportions and only retained earnings for the equity component.

As soon as the total of the required funds exceeds $73.5 million, however, Dofasco must begin relying on more expensive new common shares. Therefore, beyond $73.5 million we must compute a new marginal cost of capital. Assuming Dofasco would incur issue cost on new equity issues equal to 10 percent, we could compute the cost of capital for funds over $73.5 million as shown in Table 20-9.

TABLE 20-9 Calculation of Dofasco's Marginal Cost of Capital Using New Common Shares

1. Find the cost of new equity:

$$\text{Cost of new common shares} = \frac{\text{dividend yield}}{(1 - \text{flotation percentage})} + \text{growth}$$

$$k_e = \frac{6.1\%}{.90} + 5\% = 15.9\%$$

2. Find a new weighted or composite cost of each dollar of new capital in excess of $73.5 million, using only new common shares for the equity component:

Markets proportions × component cost = product

Debentures	.40	5.6	2.24
Preferred shares	.02	8.4	.17
Equity (new)	.58	15.9	9.22
	1.00		$k_a \approx$ 11.63 $\approx$ 11.6%

[26]We have assumed in this discussion that Dofasco wants to maintain its capital structure at the market value target in every period. Of course, the company may prefer to maintain its target capital structure from a long-run point of view. The reliance on debt in one year must be offset in a subsequent year with new share issues and retained earnings. This long-run concept of the target capital structure does not invalidate the discussion in this section, since the investors realize that new outside equity capital must be raised eventually if the firm uses debt in the short run.

According to Table 20-9, for every dollar raised in excess of $73.5 million, the weighted average cost is 11.6 percent so that the marginal cost is 11.6 percent. However, up to a $73.5 million capital requirement, the marginal cost is 11.2 percent.

Other Breaks in the *MCC* Schedule

The *marginal cost of capital schedule* shows the relationship between the average cost of each dollar raised (k_a) and the total amount of capital raised during the year, other things, such as the riskiness of the assets acquired, held constant. In the preceding section, we saw that Dofasco's *MCC* schedule increases at the point where its retained earnings are exhausted and it begins to use more expensive new common shares.

Actually, any time any component cost rises, a similar break will occur. For example, consider the component cost of debt. We noted that the component cost of debt rises as the leverage ratio increases. However, in our analysis we have assumed that the firm has determined its target capital structure weights and will finance its capital requirements with those weights. Thus, if the target weights are maintained, the component cost of debt should not change. How then do we find increases in the component costs that are related to the amount of capital required? It has been argued that, as a company sells more and more shares or other types of securities, it must attract investors who are less and less familiar with the company. In addition, individual investors must be induced to alter their existing portfolios, thereby incurring transaction costs, to hold the new securities issued by the company. The inducement comes about as a higher yield on the new securities. This pressure could affect all securities, new and old. If the sale of new shares permanently lowers the price of existing shares, then this reduction in value must be assessed as a marginal cost of the new shares. Therefore, based on this pressure hypothesis, component costs of capital can increase as the issue size increases.[27]

It is necessary to calculate a different $MCC = k_a$ for the interval between each of the breaks in the *MCC* schedule. The financial manager may obtain information on the relationship of the component costs and the issue size from the underwriter. For example, we have already calculated the *MCC* for a total capital requirement from zero to $73.5 million as 11.2 percent. With the use of new outside equity, the *MCC* curve jumps to 11.6 percent. The values of k_a, assuming component costs increase with the amount of capital required, are plotted as the step-function *MCC* schedule shown in Figure 20-6, Panel a.

This graph is highly idealized; in fact, the actual *MCC* curve looks much more like that shown in Figure 20-6(b). Here we see that the curve is flat until

---

[27]Empirical evidence on the impact of the pressure hypothesis on new security issues has shown that this impact is not very large.

FIGURE 20-6 Relationship between Marginal Cost of Capital and Amount of Funds Raised

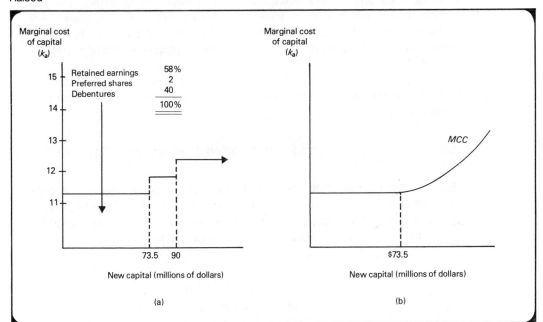

Retained earnings	58%
Preferred shares	2
Debentures	40
	100%

(a)

(b)

it reaches the vicinity of $73.5 million; it then turns up gradually and continues rising. It will go up gradually rather than suddenly because the firm will probably make small adjustments to its target debt ratio, its dividend payout ratio, the actual types of securities it uses, and so on. And the curve will continue to rise, because, as more and more of its securities are put on the market during a fairly short period, it will experience more and more difficulty in getting the market to absorb the new securities.

Ordinarily, a firm will calculate its *MCC* schedule as a step-function similar to the one shown in Figure 20-6(a), then "smooth it out" by connecting the values of k_a shown in the middle of each interval. When one recognizes the types of estimates and approximations that go into the step-function curve, the smoothing process is less arbitrary than it might first appear to be.

COMBINING THE *MCC* AND THE INVESTMENT OPPORTUNITY SCHEDULES

Having developed his firm's *MCC* schedule, and planned its financing mix so as to minimize the schedule, the financial manager's next task is to utilize the *MCC* in the capital budgeting process. How is this done? First, suppose that the k_a value in the flat part of the *MCC* schedule is used as the discount rate for calculating the *NPV* and the total cost of all projects with *NPV* > 0 is less than the dollar amount at which the *MCC* schedule turns up. In this case, the value of k_a that was used is the correct one. For example, if Dofasco used 11.2 percent as its cost of capital and found that the acceptable projects totalled $73.5 million or less, then 11.2 percent is the appropriate cost of capital for capital budgeting.

But suppose the acceptable projects totalled *more than* $73.5 million with a 11.2 percent discount rate. What do we do now? The most efficient procedure is given below:

Step 1   Calculate and plot the *MCC* schedule as shown in Figure 20–6.

Step 2   Ask the operating personnel to estimate the dollar volume of acceptable projects at a range of discount rates, say 14, 13, 12, 11, 10, and 9 percent. There will, thus, be an estimate of the capital budget at a series of k_a values. For Dofasco, some hypothetical values are presented below.

k_a	Capital Budget
16%	$50 million
15	60
14	70
13	80
12	90
11	100

Step 3   Plot the k_a, capital budget points as determined in Step 2 on the same graph as the *MCC*; this plot is labeled *IRR* in Figure 20-7.[28]

Step 4   The correct *MCC* for use in capital budgeting—assuming both the *MCC* and *IRR* curves are developed correctly—is the value at the intersection

---

[28] To see why the k_a, capital budget line is a type of *IRR* curve, consider the following:

1. The *NPV* of a project is zero if the project's *IRR* is equal to k_a. This point was demonstrated in Chapter 11, footnote 11.
2. Now suppose we determine that no projects have *NPV* ≥ 0 at k_a = 17%. This means that no projects have *IRR* ≥ 17%.
3. Next, suppose we determine that $50 million of projects have *NPV* ≥ 0 at k_a = 16%. This means that these projects all have 15% = *IRR* =16%
4. If the projects were completely divisible, and if we examined very small changes in k_a, then we would have a continuous *IRR* curve. As it is, the curve labeled *IRR* in Figure 20–7 is an approximation. In any event, the example does illustrate how an *IRR* curve can be developed even though a company uses the *NPV* capital budgeting method.

FIGURE 20–7 Interfacing the *MCC* and *IRR*
Curves to Determine the Capital Budget

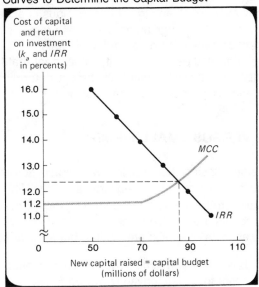

of the two curves, 11.8 percent. If this value of k_a is used to calculate *NPV's*, then projects totalling $92 million will have *NPV's* greater than zero. This is the capital budget that will maximize the value of the firm.

In practice, both the *IRR* and *MCC* schedules are developed on an *ex ante* basis; that is, the schedules are estimated during the planning or budgeting process, when the firm is planning its operations for the coming year. We cannot delve into all the details of this part of the planning process, but the reader is referred to the references at the end of this chapter.

DYNAMIC CONSIDERATIONS

Conditions change over time; when they do, the firm must make adjustments. First, the firm's own individual situation may change. For example, as it grows and matures, its business risk may decline; this may, in turn, lead to an optimal capital structure that includes more debt. Second, capital market conditions could undergo a pronounced, long-run change, making either debt or equity relatively favorable. This too could lead to a new optimal capital structure. Third, even though the long-run optimal structure remains unchanged, temporary shifts in the capital markets could suggest that the firm use either debt or equity, departing somewhat from the optimal capital structure, then adjust back to the long-run optimum in subsequent years. Fourth, the supply and demand for funds varies from time to time, causing shifts in the cost of both debt and equity, and, of course, in the marginal cost of capital. Finally, the firm may experience an almost unconscious change in capital structure because of retained earnings unless its growth rate is sufficient to call for the employment of more debt on a continual basis.

For all these reasons, it is important that the firm reexamine its cost of capital periodically, especially before determining the annual capital budget or engaging in new long-term financing.[29]

LARGE FIRMS VERSUS SMALL FIRMS

Before closing this chapter, we should note that significant differences in capital costs exist between large and small firms; these differences are especially pronounced in the case of small, privately owned firms. The same concepts are involved, and the methods of calculating the average and marginal costs of capital are similar, but several points of difference arise:

1. It is especially difficult to obtain reasonable estimates of equity capital costs for small, privately owned firms.
2. Tax considerations are generally quite important for privately owned companies, as owner-managers may be in the top personal tax brackets. This factor combined with the dividend tax credit and the management's desire to minimize their tax burden may result in the after-tax cost of retained earnings being considerably lower than the after-tax cost of new outside equity.
3. Issue costs for new security issues, especially new stock issues, are much higher for small than for large firms (see Chapter 13).

Points 2 and 3 both cause the marginal cost curves for small firms to rise rapidly once retained earnings are exhausted. These relationships have implications for the growth and development of large versus small firms; recognizing the plight of smaller companies, the federal and provincial governments through crown corporations and agencies provide financial assistance to small business. This assistance, given by means of insurance, subsidies, loans and grants, helps small businesses to obtain capital.

[29]Note that an exact calculation of a firm's need for funds cannot be made until the marginal cost of capital to be used in the capital budgeting process has been calculated. Thus, the marginal cost of capital and the amount of financing required for new projects should be simultaneously determined. This simultaneous determination is considered in Chapter 21, where dividend policy and internal financing decisions are discussed.

SUMMARY

In Chapter 18, the nature of the valuation process and the concept of expected rates of return were considered in some detail. The present chapter used these valuation concepts to develop an average cost of capital for the firm. First, the cost of the individual components of the capital structure—debt, preferred shares, and equity—were analyzed. Next, these individual component costs were brought together to form an average, or composite, cost of capital. Finally, the conceptual ideas developed in the first two sections were illustrated with an example of the cost of capital for an actual company —Dominion Foundries and Steel Limited.

Cost of Individual Capital Components   The *after-tax cost of debt,* $k_d(1-t)$, is defined as the interest rate that must be paid on new increments of debt capital multiplied by (1 – tax rate). The *preferred share cost* to the company is the effective yield and is found as the annual preferred dividend divided by the net price the company receives when it sells new preferred shares. In equation form, the cost of preferred shares is

$$\text{cost of preferred shares} = k_p = \frac{\text{preferred dividend}}{\text{net price of preferred}}.$$

The *cost of common equity* is defined as the minimum rate of return that must be earned on equity-financed investments to keep the value of the existing common equity unchanged. This required rate of return is the rate of return that investors expect to receive on the company's common equity—the dividend yield plus the capital gain yield. The model used to estimate the cost of equity is called the dividend yield plus growth technique. The difficult measurement problem is the estimation of the growth term; the estimated value should reflect the investors' expectations of growth. A number of measurement techniques are presented and their shortcomings are discussed.

Equity capital comes from two sources, retained earnings and sale of new issues of common shares. The basic required rate of return (k_r) is used for the cost of retained earnings. However, new equity has a higher cost because of the presence of issue costs associated with the sale of equity. The cost of new common share issues is computed as follows:

$$\text{Cost of new shares} = k_e = \frac{\text{dividend yield}}{(1 - \text{flotation percentage})} + \text{growth}.$$

New common equity is therefore more expensive than retained earnings.

Weighted Average, or Composite, Cost of Capital   The first step in calculating the weighted average cost of capital, k_a, is to determine the cost of the individual capital components as described above. The next step is to establish the proper set of weights to be used in the averaging process. Unless we have reason to think otherwise, we generally assume that the present capital structure of the firm is at an optimum, where optimum is defined as the capital structure that will produce the minimum average cost of capital for raising a given amount of funds, or a minimum cost of incremental capital. The optimal capital structure varies from industry to industry, with more stable industries having optimal capital structures that call for the use of more debt than in the case of unstable industries.

Marginal cost The marginal cost of capital schedule, defined as the cost of each additional dollar raised during the current year, is of interest for two reasons. First, the firm should finance in a manner that minimizes the *MCC* schedule, and therefore it must measure the *MCC*. Second, the *MCC* is the rate that should be used in the capital budgeting process—the firm should take on new capital projects only if their net present values are positive when evaluated at the marginal cost of capital.

The marginal cost of capital is constant over a range, then begins to rise. The rise is probably gradual, not abrupt, because firms make small adjustments in their target debt ratios, begin to use an assortment of securities, retain more of their earnings, and so on, as they reach the limit of internally generated equity funds.

QUESTIONS

20-1. Suppose that basic business risks to all firms in any given industry are similar.
    a. Would you expect all firms in each industry to have approximately the same cost of capital?
    b. How would the averages differ among industries?

20-2. Why are internally generated retained earnings less expensive than equity raised by selling shares?

20-3. Prior to the 1930s the corporate income tax was not very important, as rates were fairly low. Also prior to the 1930s preferred shares were much more important than they have been since that period. Is there a relation between the rise of corporate income taxes and the decline in importance of preferred shares?

20-4. Describe how each of the following situations would affect the cost of capital to corporations in general.
    a. The federal government solves the problem of business cycles (that is, cyclical stability is increased).
    b. The Bank of Canada takes action to lower interest rates.
    c. The cost of issuing new equity rises.

20-5. The formula $k_r = (D_1/P_0) + g$, where D_1 = expected current dividend, P_0 = the current price of a stock, and g = the past rate of growth in dividends, is sometimes used to estimate k_r, the cost of equity capital. Explain the reasoning behind the formula and this use of it.

20-6. What factors operate to cause the cost of debt to increase with financial leverage?

20-7. Explain the relationship between the required rate of return on common equity (k_r) and the debt ratio.

20-8. How would the various component costs of capital, and the average cost of capital, be likely to change if a firm expands its operations into a new, more risky industry?

20-9. The stock of XYZ Company is currently selling at its low for the year, but management feels that the stock price is only temporarily depressed because of investor pessimism. The firm's capital budget this year is so large that the use of new outside equity is contemplated. However, management does not want to sell new equity at the current low price and is therefore considering a departure from its "optimal" capital structure by borrowing the funds it would otherwise have raised in the equity markets. Does this seem to be a wise move?

20-10. Explain the following statement: "The marginal cost of capital is actually an average cost."

PROBLEMS

20-1. You are planning to form a new company, and several alternative capital structures might be employed. Investment dealers indicate that debt and equity capital would cost the following under different debt ratios (debt/total assets).

Debt Ratio	20% and below	21 to 40%	41 to 50%	51 to 65%
Before-tax cost of debt	8%	9%	11%	14%
Cost of equity capital	12%	13%	18%	25%

a. Assuming a 40% tax rate, what is the after-tax weighted cost of capital for the following capital structures?

	(1)	(2)	(3)	(4)	(5)	(6)	(7)	(8)
Debt	0	20%	21%	40%	41%	50%	51%	65%
Equity	100%	80%	79%	60%	59%	50%	49%	35%

b. Which capital structure minimizes the weighted average cost of capital?

20-2. On January 1, the total assets of the Gould Company Ltd. were $60 million. By the end of the year total assets are expected to be $90 million. The firm's capital structure, shown below, is considered to be optimal. Assume there is no short-term debt.

Debt (6% coupon bonds)	$24,000,000
Preferred shares (7%)	6,000,000
Common equity	30,000,000
	$60,000,000

New bonds will have an 8 percent coupon rate and will be sold at par. Preferred will have a 9 percent rate and will also be sold at par. Common shares, currently selling at $30 a share, can be sold to net the company $27 a share. Shareholders' required rate of return is estimated to be 12 percent, consisting of a dividend yield of 4 percent and an expected growth of 8 percent. Retained earnings are estimated to be $3 million (ignore depreciation). The marginal corporate tax rate is 50 percent.

    a. Assuming all asset expansion (gross expenditures for fixed assets plus related working capital) is included in the capital budget, what is the dollar amount of the capital budget? (Ignore depreciation.)

    b. To maintain the present capital structure, how much of the capital budget must be financed by equity?

    c. How much of the new equity funds needed must be generated internally? externally?

    d. Calculate the cost of each of the equity components.

    e. At what level of capital expenditures will there be a break in the MCC schedule?

    f. Calculate the MCC (1) below and (2) above the break in the schedule.

    g. Plot the MCC schedule. Also, draw in an IRR schedule that is consistent with the MCC schedule and the projected capital budget.

20-3. The Collins Glass Company has the following capital structure as of December 3l, 19X7.

Debt (6½%)		$12,000,000	.375
Preferred (7½%)		4,000,000	1.25
Capital equity	$ 4,000,000		
Retained earnings	12,000,000		
Common equity		16,000,000	.5
Total capitalization		$32,000,000	

Earnings per share have grown steadily from $0.93 in 19X1 to $2 estimated for 19X7. The investment community, expecting this growth to continue, applies a price/earnings ratio of 18 to yield a current market price of $36. Collins' last annual dividend was $1.25, and it expects the dividend to grow at the same rate as earnings. The addition to retained earnings for 19X7 is projected at $4 million; these funds will be available during the next budget year. The corporate tax rate is 50 percent.

    Assuming that the capital structure relations set out above are maintained, new securities can be sold at the following costs:

Bonds: Up to and including $3 million of new bonds, 8 percent yield to investor on all new bonds.

            From $3.01 to $6 million of new bonds, 8½ percent yield to investor on this increment of bonds.

            Over $6 million of new bonds, 10 percent yield to investor on this increment of bonds.

Preferred: Up to and including $1 million of preferred shares, 8½ percent yield to investor on all new preferred shares.

            From $1.01 to $2 million of preferred shares, 9 percent yield to investor on this increment of preferred shares.

            Over $2 million of preferred shares, 10 percent yield to investor on this increment of preferred shares.

Know how to reverse tables.

Common: Up to $4 million of new outside common equity, $36 a share less $2.50 a share issue cost.

Over $4 million of new outside common equity, $36 a share less $5 a share issue cost on this increment of new common.

a. At what dollar amounts of new capital will breaks occur in the *MCC*?

b. Calculate the *MCC* in the interval between each of these breaks, then plot the *MCC* schedule.

c. Discuss the breaking points in the marginal cost curve. What factors in the real world would tend to make the marginal cost curve smooth?

d. Assume now that Collins has the following investment opportunities:

1. It can invest any amount up to $4 million at an 11 percent rate of return.
2. It can invest an additional $8 million at a 10.2 percent rate of return.
3. It can invest still another $12 million at a 9.3 percent rate of return.

Thus, Collins' total potential capital budget is $24 million. Determine the size of the company's optimal capital budget for the year.

20-4. The following tabulation gives earnings-per-share figures for Template Manufacturing during the preceding ten years. The firm's common shares, 140,000 shares outstanding, is now selling for $50 a share, and the expected dividend for the current year is 50 percent of the 1975 *EPS*. Investors expect past trends to continue.

Year	EPS
1966	$2.00
1967	2.16
1968	2.33
1969	2.52
1970	2.72
1971	2.94
1972	3.18
1973	3.43
1974	3.70
1975	4.00

New preferred shares paying a $5 dividend could be sold to the public at a price of $52.50, which includes a $2.50 issue cost (that is, the net price to Template is $50). The current interest rate on new debt is 8 percent. The firm's marginal tax rate is 40 percent. The firm's capital structure, considered to be optimal, is as follows:

Debt (6%)	$ 2,500,000
Preferred shares (7%)	500,000
Common equity	7,000,000
	$10,000,000

a. Calculate the after-tax cost (1) of new debt, (2) of new preferred shares, and (3) of common equity, assuming new equity comes only from retained earnings. Calculate the cost of equity as $k_r = D_1/P_0 + g$.

b. Find the marginal cost of capital, again assuming no new common shares are sold.

c. How much can be spent for capital investments before external equity must be sold? (Assume that retained earnings available for 1976 investment is 50 percent of 1975 earnings.)

d. What is the marginal cost of capital (cost of funds raised in excess of the amount calculated in part c) if the firm can sell new common shares at $50 a share to net $45 a share? The cost of debt and of preferred shares is constant.

e. In the problem, we assume that the capital structure is optimal. What would happen if the firm deviated from this capital structure? Use a graph to illustrate your answer.

Dividend Policy and Internal Financing

21
Dividend policy determines the division of earnings between payments to shareholders and reinvestment in the firm. Retained earnings are one of the most significant sources of funds for financing corporate growth, but dividends constitute the cash flows that accrue to shareholders. Although both growth and dividends are desirable, these two goals could be in conflict. For example, suppose a firm limited its investment budget in a given year to the amount of retained earnings for that year. An increase in the dividend payout ratio would result in less retained earnings and hence a reduced amount of investment. In this instance, dividend policy is equivalent to investment policy and by reducing the amount of retained earnings, the firm may be forced to reject profitable investment opportunities. A more reasonable approach would have the firm determine its investment budget in advance. In this case, the dividend decision has an impact on the amount of new, outside funds that must be raised. A higher dividend rate means less retained earnings and hence a heavier reliance on new, outside equity. This results in a slower rate of growth both in earnings per share and stock price. An important function of the financial manager is to determine the allocation of profits between dividends and retained earnings, as this decision may have a critical influence on the value of the firm. The factors that influence the allocation of earnings to dividends or retained earnings are the subject of this chapter. In addition, we will investigate, briefly, the impact of dividend policy on the market value of shareholder's equity.

FACTORS INFLUENCING DIVIDEND POLICY

What factors determine the extent to which a firm will pay out dividends instead of retain earnings? As a first step toward answering this question, we shall consider some of the factors that influence dividend policy. In this discussion, we will make the realistic assumption that there are issue costs for new outside equity, and thus to minimize costs, the firm would prefer to finance with retained earnings. If there were no issue costs for new, outside equity financing, a number of the factors described below would not have an influence on dividend policy.

Legal Rules

Although the legal restrictions of the relevant corporation's act governing dividend payments can be complicated, their essential nature may be stated briefly. The legal rules provide that dividends must be paid from earnings, either from the current year's earnings or from past years' earnings as reflected in the balance sheet account "retained earnings".

Legislation emphasizes three rules: (1) the net profits rule, (2) the capital impairment rule, and (3) the insolvency rule. The *net profits* rule provides that dividends may be paid from past and present earnings. The *capital impairment* rule protects creditors by forbidding the payment of dividends from capital. Paying dividends from capital would be distributing the investment in a company rather than its earnings.[1] The *insolvency* rule provides that a corporation may not pay dividends while insolvent, or may not pay dividends if the result is to make the company insolvent. Insolvency can be defined either as liabilities exceeding assets or the company not meeting current obligations as they fall due. The payment of dividends in these circumstances would mean giving shareholders funds that rightfully belong to the creditors.

Legal aspects are significant. They provide the framework within which dividend policies can be formulated. Within these boundaries, however, financial and economic factors have a major influence on policy.

Liquidity Position

Profits held as retained earnings (which show up in the right-hand side of the balance sheet in the account labeled "retained earnings") are generally invested in assets required for the conduct of the business. Retained earnings from preceding years are already invested in plant and equipment, inventories, and other assets; they are not held as cash. Thus, although a firm has had a record of earnings, it may not be able to pay cash dividends because

---

[1]It is possible, of course, to return shareholders' capital; when this is done, however, it must be clearly stated as such. A dividend paid out of capital is called a *liquidating* dividend.

of its liquidity position. Indeed, a growing firm, even a very profitable one, typically has a pressing need for funds. In such a situation the firm may elect not to pay cash dividends.

If this point is not clear, refer back to Table 3–1, the Walker-Wilson Company's balance sheet. The retained earnings account shows $400,000, but the cash account shows only $50,000. Since some cash must be retained to pay bills, it is clear that Walker-Wilson's cash position precludes a dividend of even $50,000.

Need to Repay Debt

When a firm has sold debt to finance expansion or to substitute for other forms of financing, it is faced with two alternatives: it can refund the debt at maturity by replacing it with another form of security, or it can make provision for paying off the debt. If the decision is to retire the debt, this will generally require the retention of earnings.

Restrictions in Debt Contracts

Debt contracts, particularly when long-term debt is involved, frequently restrict a firm's ability to pay cash dividends. Such restrictions, which are designed to protect the position of the lender, usually state (1) that future dividends can be paid only out of earnings generated *after* the signing of the loan agreement (that is, future dividends cannot be paid out of past retained earnings), and (2) that dividends cannot be paid when net working capital (current assets minus current liabilities) is below a specified amount. Similarly, preferred share agreements generally state that no cash dividends can be paid on the common shares until all accrued preferred dividends have been paid.

Rate of Asset Expansion

The more rapid the rate at which the firm is growing, the greater will be its needs for financing asset expansion. The greater the future need for funds, the more likely the firm is to retain earnings rather than pay them out.

Profit Rate

The rate of return on investment in new assets determines the relative attractiveness of paying out earnings in the form of dividends to shareholders who will use them elsewhere, compared with the productivity of their use in the present enterprise.

Stability of Earnings

If earnings are relatively stable, a firm is better able to predict what its future earnings will be. A stable firm is therefore more likely to pay out a higher percentage of its earnings than is a firm with fluctuating earnings. The unstable firm is not certain that in subsequent years the hoped-for earnings will be realized, so it is more likely to retain a high proportion of earnings in order to maintain dividends if earnings should fall off in the future.

Access to the Capital Markets

A large, well-established firm with a record of profitability and some stability of earnings will have easy access to capital markets and other forms of external financing. The small, new, or venturesome firm, however, is riskier for potential investors. Its ability to raise equity or debt funds from capital markets is restricted, and it must retain more earnings to finance its operations. A well-established firm is thus likely to have a higher dividend payout rate than is a new or small firm.

Control

Another important variable is the effect of alternative sources of financing on the control situation in the firm. Some corporations, as a matter of policy, will expand only to the extent of their internal earnings. This policy is defended on the grounds that raising funds by selling additional common shares dilutes the control of the dominant group in the company. At the same time, selling debt increases the risks of fluctuating earnings to the present owners of the company. Reliance on internal financing in order to maintain control reduces the dividend payout.

Tax Position of Shareholders

The tax position of the owners of the corporation greatly influences the desire for dividends. The existence of the dividend tax credit makes the effective tax rates applied to dividends and capital gains depend on the marginal tax rate of the individual investor. The effective tax rate on dividends and capital gains for an investor in Ontario is presented in Table 21–1. As can be seen in this table, the effective tax rate on dividends is less than the effective capital gains tax rate for marginal federal tax rates less than the 36 percent category.[2] The

[2]The comparison presented in Table 21–1 assumes that the shares are sold and the capital gains tax is paid after one year. However, an individual can delay the payment of the capital gains tax by holding the shares for a longer period of time before selling them. Thus, the actual capital gains tax may be lower than noted in the table.

TABLE 21-1 Effective Tax Rates on Dividends and Capital Gains[a]

Marginal Federal Tax Rate[c]	Marginal Total Tax Rate, Ontario Investor[c]	Effective Dividend Tax Rate	Effective Capital Gains Tax Rate[b]
16%	23%	- 19.4%	11.5%
23	33	- 4.0	16.5
28	40	6.5	20
32	46	15.0	23
36	52	24.0	26
39	56	30.0	28
43	62	39.0	31

[a] The tax rates are based on an investor who has used up the $1000 deduction on dividends.
[b] The effective capital gains tax rate is one-half the marginal total tax rate.
[c] From Table 2-5 in Chapter 2.

negative effective dividend tax rates for the 16 to 23 percent marginal federal tax rates mean that the dividend tax credit can be used to reduce income taxes on other income. Therefore, a corporation closely held by a few taxpayers with federal marginal tax rates greater than or equal to 36 percent is likely to pay a relatively low dividend. The owners of the corporation are interested in taking their income in the form of capital gains rather than as dividends.

At times there is a conflict of interest in large corporations between shareholders in high income tax brackets and those in low tax brackets. The former may prefer to see a low dividend payout and a high rate of earnings retention in the hope of an appreciation in the stock price of the company. The lower income shareholders may prefer a relatively high dividend payout rate. The dividend policy of such a firm may be a compromise between a low and a high payout—an intermediate payout ratio. If, however, one group dominates and sets, let us say, a low payout policy, those shareholders who seek income are likely to sell their shares over time and shift into higher yielding stocks. *Thus, to at least some extent, a firm's payout policy determines its shareholder types, as well as vice-versa.* This is refered to as the clientele effect—the corporation, by offering a particular dividend policy, attracts a clientele that prefers this dividend policy.

Maintain a Preferred Tax Rate

In Chapter 2 it was noted that for a Canadian controlled private corporation there is a small business deduction which reduces the federal marginal tax rate to 25 percent from 46 percent. This reduced rate is applicable to the first $150,000 of income as long as the cumulative taxable income is below a maximum limit of $750,000. The cumulative taxable income account can be affected by the dividend policy of the firm; for every three dollars of dividends paid, the firm can reduce the cumulative taxable income account by four dollars. Thus, by paying dividends, the firm can extend the period during which the company obtains the small business tax rate.

One purpose of this provision is to prevent the owners of the firm who may be in a high federal marginal tax rate from using the corporation as an incorporated pocketbook. The owners of the firm would attempt to substitute capital gains for dividends even if the retained earnings had to be held in cash or marketable securities.

DIVIDEND POLICY DECISIONS

A fundamental relation observed in dividend policy is the widespread tendency of corporations to pursue a relatively stable dividend policy. Profits of firms fluctuate considerably with changes in the level of business activity, but Figure 21–1 shows that dividends are more stable than earnings.

FIGURE 21-1 Corporate Earnings after Taxes and Dividends

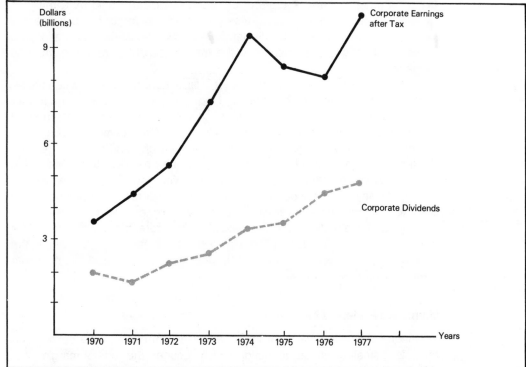

Source: Statistics Canada, Catalogue 61-003. Data excludes non-profit corporations, financial institutions, and firms in construction and forestry.

Most corporations seek to maintain a target dividend per share. However, dividends increase with a lag after earnings rise. Dividends are increased only after an increase in earnings appears clearly sustainable and relatively permanent. When dividends have been increased, strenuous efforts are made to maintain them at the new level. If earnings decline, the existing dividend will generally be maintained until it is clear that an earnings recovery will not take place.

The stability of the earnings of the company will have an impact on the speed with which dividends change after a change in earnings. If the company has relatively stable earnings, for example, a regulated utility, then the permanence of an earnings change can be determined quickly and an appropriate change in dividends is undertaken. However, if the earnings of the company are volatile, then it is difficult for management to determine immediately whether a change in earnings is permanent or transitory. Therefore, management will delay a change in dividends or make a small change until more observations of earnings are available and the permanence of the earnings change can be established.

FIGURE 21–2 Dividends and Earnings Patterns, Walter Watch Co. Ltd.

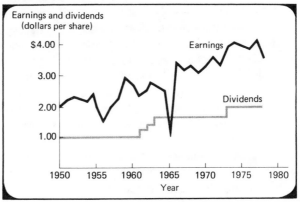

Figure 21-2 illustrates these ideas by showing the earnings and dividends patterns for the Walter Watch Co. Ltd. over a thirty-year period. Initially, earnings are $2 and dividends $1 a share, providing a 50 percent payout ratio. Earnings rise for four years, while dividends remain constant; thus, the payout ratio falls during this period. During 1955 and 1956, earnings fall substantially; however, the dividend is maintained and the payout rises above the 50 percent target. During the period between 1956 and 1960, earnings experience a sustained rise. Dividends are held constant for a time, while management seeks to determine whether the earnings increase is permanent. By 1961, the earnings gain seems permanent, and dividends are raised in three steps to reestablish the 50 percent target payout. During 1965 a strike causes earnings to fall below the regular dividend; expecting the earnings decline to be temporary, management maintains the dividend. Earnings fluctuate on a fairly high plateau from 1966 through 1972, during which time dividends remain constant. A new increase in earnings induces management to raise the dividend in 1973 to reestablish the 50 percent payout ratio.

RATIONALE FOR STABLE DIVIDENDS

Walter Watch, like the great majority of firms, kept its dividend at a relatively steady dollar amount but allowed its payout ratio to fluctuate. Why would it follow such a policy?

Consider the stable dividend policy from the standpoint of the shareholders as owners of a company. Their acquiescence with the general practice must imply that stable dividend policies lead to higher stock prices on the average than do alternative dividend policies. Is this a fact? Does a stable dividend policy maximize equity values for a corporation? There has been no truly conclusive empirical study of dividend policy, so any answer to the question must be regarded as tentative. On logical grounds, however, there is reason to believe that a stable dividend policy will lead to higher stock prices. First, investors might be expected to value more highly dividends they are more sure of receiving, since fluctuating dividends are riskier than stable dividends. Accordingly, the same average amount of dividends received under a fluctuating dividend policy is likely to have a higher discount factor applied to it than is applied to dividends under a stable dividend policy. In the terms used in Chapter 20, this means that a firm with a stable dividend would have a lower required rate of return—or cost of equity capital—than one whose dividends fluctuate.

Second, many shareholders live on income received in the form of dividends, and they would likely pay a premium for a stock with a relatively assured minimum dollar dividend.

A third advantage of a stable dividend from the standpoint of a corporation and its shareholders is the requirement of *legal listing*. Legal lists are lists of securities in which pension funds and insurance companies are permitted to invest. The requirements to be included in the legal list for insurance companies have been amended to include companies that pay dividends or have the ability to pay dividends. In addition, insurance companies can invest limited amounts in stocks of companies that do not pay dividends. Therefore, even though a stable dividend is not essential for a company to be included on a legal list, its existence makes it more likely that the company will be included. Therefore, legal listing may encourage the pursuit of a stable dividend policy.

One explanation of the payment of dividends is that investors use the dividend as a signal of the underlying profitability of the company. Although the reported profit figures can be altered through the creative use of accounting changes, the dividend payment is a cash outflow from the corporation and manipulations of the dividend are less likely to occur. For this signal to be of any use, the dividend must be stable so that any changes in the dividend will be quickly interpreted as a signal of improved future profitability.

On the other hand, if a firm's investment opportunities fluctuate from year to year, should it not retain more earnings during some years in order to take advantage of these opportunities when they appear, then increase dividends when good internal investment opportunities are scarce? This line of reasoning would lead to the recommendation of a fluctuating payout for companies whose investment opportunities are unstable. However, the logic of the argument is diminished by recognizing that it is possible to maintain a reasonably stable dividend by using outside financing, both debt and equity, to smooth out the differences between the funds needed for investment and the amount of money provided by retained earnings.

ALTERNATIVE DIVIDEND POLICIES

Before going on to consider dividend policy at a theoretical level, it is useful to summarize the three major types of dividend policies.

Stable Dollar Amount per Share   The policy of a stable dollar amount per share, followed by most firms, is the policy that is implied when we say "stable dividend policy."

Constant Payout Ratio   A very few firms follow a policy of paying out a constant percentage of earnings. Earnings will surely fluctuate, so following this policy necessarily means that the dollar amount of dividends will fluctuate. If investors prefer stable dividends, this policy is not likely to maximize the value of a firm's shares. Before its bankruptcy, Penn Central Railroad in the U.S. followed the policy of paying out one-half its earnings: "A dollar for the stockholders and a dollar for the company," as one director put it.

This does not imply that the firm does not have a target payout ratio in mind when it pays dividends. Even with the target payout ratio, the firm does not require the target to be met every year; the target ratio is a long-run planning tool of use to both the firm and its shareholders.

Low Regular Dividend plus Extras   The low-regular-dividend-plus-extras policy is a compromise between the first two. It gives the firm flexibility, but it leaves investors somewhat uncertain about what their dividend income will be. The company may set the regular dividend at a level that can be maintained by the company. If earnings are transitorily high, the company can pay out an extra dividend. By labelling the dividend payment as an extra, the company is informing the shareholders that it is transitory. If a firm's earnings are volatile, this policy may well be its best choice.[3]

The relative merits of these three policies can be evaluated better after a discussion of the residual theory of dividends, the topic covered in the next section.

RESIDUAL THEORY OF DIVIDENDS[4]

In the preceding chapters on capital budgeting and the cost of capital, we indicated that, generally, the cost of capital schedule and the investment opportunity schedule must be combined before the cost of capital can be established. In other words, the optimum capital budget, the marginal cost of capital, and the marginal rate of return on investment are determined *simultaneously.* In this section we examine this simultaneous solution in the framework of what is called *the residual theory of dividends.* The theory draws on materials developed earlier in the book—capital budgeting and the cost of capital—and serves to provide a bridge between these key concepts.

The starting point in the theory is that investors prefer to have the firm retain and reinvest earnings rather than pay them out in dividends *if the return on reinvested earnings exceeds the rate of return the investor could, himself, obtain on other investments of comparable risk.* If the corporation can reinvest retained earnings at a 20 percent rate of return, while the best rate the shareholder can obtain if the earnings are passed on in the form of dividends is 10 percent, then the shareholder would prefer to have the firm retain the profits.[5]

We saw in Chapter 20 that the cost of equity capital obtained from retained earnings is an *opportunity cost* that reflects rates of return open to equity investors. If a firm's shareholders could buy the shares of other companies of equal risk and obtain a 10 percent dividends-plus-capital-gains yield, then 10 percent is the firm's cost of retained earnings. The cost of new outside equity raised by selling common shares is higher because of the costs of floating the issue.

Most firms have an optimum debt ratio that calls for at least some debt, so in the long run new financing is done with debt and with equity so as to obtain the target or optimum debt ratio. Debt has a different, and generally lower,

---

[3]If a firm continues to pay an extra dividend, the investor may come to expect the extra dividend and consider it no different than a regular dividend. This would negate the informational and flexibility advantages of the extra dividend.

[4]"Residual" implies *left over.* The residual theory of dividend policy implies that dividends are paid after internal investment opportunities have been exhausted.

[5]If there are no issue costs on a new equity issue, the investor would be indifferent between the policy noted and a policy where a dividend is paid and the funds needed for investment are provided by new equity issues.

component cost than equity so the two forms of capital must be combined to find the *weighted average cost of capital.* As long as the firm finances at the optimum point, using an optimum amount of debt and equity, and provided it intends to use only internally generated equity (retained earnings), its marginal cost of each new dollar of capital will be minimized.

Internally generated equity is available for financing a certain amount of new investment; beyond this amount, the firm must turn to more expensive new common equity. At the point where new stock must be sold, the cost of equity and, consequently, the marginal cost of capital, rises.

These concepts, which were developed in Chapter 20, are illustrated in Figure 21-3. The firm has a marginal cost of capital of 10 percent so long as retained earnings are available; the marginal cost of capital begins to rise when new stock must be sold.

FIGURE 21-3   The Marginal Cost of Capital

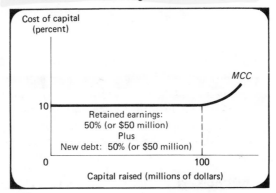

Our hypothetical firm has $50 million of earnings and a 50 percent optimum debt ratio. It can make net investments (investments in addition to asset replacements financed from depreciation) up to $100 million. If the firm intends to finance the investment requirement in the optimum or target proportions, then $50 million will be obtained from retained earnings and $50 million from new debt which is supported by the retained earnings if it does not pay dividends. Therefore, its marginal cost of capital is constant at 10 percent for up to $100 million of capital. Beyond $100 million, the marginal cost of capital begins rising as the firm begins to use more expensive new common equity.

Next, suppose the firm's capital budgeting department draws up a list of investment opportunities, ranked in the order of each project's *IRR*, and plots them on a graph. The investment opportunity curves of three different years—one for a good year (IRR_1), one for a normal year (IRR_2), and one for a bad year (IRR_3)—are shown in Figure 21-4. IRR_1 shows that the firm can invest more money, and at higher rates of return, than it can when the investment opportunities are those given in IRR_2 and IRR_3.

FIGURE 21–4   Investment Opportunities

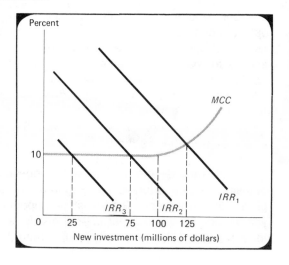

Internal rate of return (percent)

IRR_1

IRR_3 IRR_2

Investment (millions of dollars)

Now we combine the investment opportunity schedule with the cost of capital schedule; this is done in Figure 21–5. The point where the investment opportunity curve cuts the cost of capital curve defines the proper level of new investment. When investment opportunities are relatively poor, the optimum level of investment is $25 million; when opportunities are about normal, $75 million should be invested; and when opportunities are relatively good, the firm should make new investments in the amount of $125 million.

FIGURE 21–5   Interrelation among Cost of Capital, Investment Opportunities, and New Investment

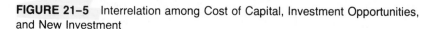

Percent

MCC

10

IRR_3 IRR_2

IRR_1

0   25   75   100   125

New investment (millions of dollars)

Consider the situation where IRR_1 is the appropriate schedule. Suppose the firm has $50 million in earnings and a 50 percent target debt ratio, so it can finance $100 million, $50 million earnings plus $50 million debt, from retained earnings plus new debt *if it retains all its earnings.* If it pays part of the earnings in dividends, then it will have to begin using expensive new common equity sooner, so the cost of capital curve will rise sooner. This suggests that under the conditions of IRR_1, the firm should retain all its earnings and actually sell some new common shares in order to take advantage of its investment opportunities. Its payout ratio would thus be zero percent.

Under the conditions of IRR_2, however, the firm should invest only $75 million. How should this investment be financed? First, notice that if it retains the full amount of its earnings, $50 million, it will need to sell only $25 million of new debt. However, by retaining $50 million and selling only $25 million of new debt, the firm will move away from its target capital structure. If the firm wants to stay on target in this year, it must finance the required $75 million, half by equity (retained earnings) and half by debt, or $37.5 million by retained earnings and $37.5 million by debt. Now if the firm has $50 million in total earnings and decides to retain and reinvest $37.5 million, it must distribute the $12.5 million residual to its shareholders. In this case, the payout ratio is 25 percent ($12.5 million divided by $50 million).

Finally, under the bad conditions of IRR_3, the firm should invest only $25 million. Because it has $50 million in earnings, it could finance the entire $25 million out of retained earnings and still have $25 million available for dividends. Should this be done? Under the assumptions, this would not be a good decision, because it would move the firm away from its target debt ratio. To stay in the 50-50 debt/equity position, the firm must retain $12.5 million and sell $12.5 million of debt. When the $12.5 million of retained earnings is subtracted from the $50 million of earnings, the firm is left with a residual of $37.5, the amount that should be paid out in dividends. In this case the payout ratio is 75 percent.

LONG-RUN VIEWPOINT

There seems to be a conflict between the residual theory and the statement made in an earlier section that firms should and do maintain reasonably stable cash dividends. How can this conflict be reconciled?

Actually, the reconciliation is quite simple if we recognize that the theory is not meant to be applied *exactly.* In other words, we would not recommend that a firm adjust its dividend each and every year—indeed, this is not necessary. Firms do have target debt ratios, but they also have a certain amount of flexibility—they can be moderately above or below the target debt position in any one year with no serious adverse consequences. This means that if an unusually large number of good investments are available in a particular year, the firm does not necessarily have to cut its dividend to take advantage of them—it can borrow somewhat more heavily than usual in that particular year without getting its debt ratio too far out of line. Obviously, however, this excessive reliance on debt could not continue for too many years without seriously affecting the debt ratio, necessitating either a sale of new equity or a cut in dividends and an attendant increase in the level of retained earnings.

HIGH AND LOW DIVIDEND PAYOUT INDUSTRIES

Some industries are experiencing rapid growth in demand for their products affording firms in these industries with many good investment opportunities. In addition, a number of industries have relatively stable earnings. The theory suggests that firms in rapidly growing industries should generally have *IRR* curves that are relatively far out to the right on graphs such as Figure 21-5. These firms would, of course, experience shifts in investment opportunities from year to year, but the curves would *tend* to be in about the same part of the graph. Thus, these firms would *tend* to have more investment opportunities than money, so they would tend to have very low payout ratios.

In Table 21-2 we have presented the payout ratio for 1976 and a five-year average payout ratio ending in 1976 for a number of industrial groups. A good example of a growth industry is the Oil and Gas Industry and the payout ratio for 1976 and the five-year average is well below the corresponding values for all Major Canadian Industries. The industrial classifications are based on the Toronto Stock Exchange Industrial Groups and include 167 Canadian companies.

TABLE 21-2   Payout Ratios on Selected Industrial Categories[a]

	1976	5-Year Average
Major Canadian Industries	41.7	39.8
Consumer Products	45.1	40.0
Industrial Products	34.5	32.8
Merchandising	46.6	38.4
Metals and Minerals	54.6	47.9
Oils and Gas	30.9	33.3
Pipelines	82.2	72.8
Real Estate and Construction	28.3	23.5
Utilities	58.4	58.9

[a]Source: McLeod, Young, Weir Limited, Performance Summaries Major Canadian Industries, 1972-1976.

The theory also suggests that firms with volatile earnings would have lower payout ratios. If we look at Table 21-2, we observe that the Utility and Pipeline groups, both dominated by regulated utilities with relatively stable earnings, have the largest payout ratios.

In evaluating payout ratios it is important to look at the components of the payout ratio in order to prevent incorrect inferences. For example, in the Merchandising group, the 1976 value of the payout ratio is well above the five year average. However, this 1976 payout ratio may not represent the true dividend policy of the company. The Industry group earnings per share went from $0.89 in 1975 to $0.73 in 1976 while the dividends went from $0.35 to $0.34. The dividend stabilization behavior of the industry resulted in a very high—in fact, transitorily high—payout ratio.

CONFLICTING THEORIES ON DIVIDENDS

Two basic schools of thought on dividend policy have been expressed in the theoretical literature of finance. One school, associated with Myron Gordon and John Lintner, among others, holds that the capital gains expected to result from earnings retention are more risky than are dividend expectations. Accordingly, this school suggests that the earnings of a firm with a low-payout ratio, and hence a higher growth rate will typically be capitalized at higher rates than the earnings of a high payout (lower growth) firm, other things held constant.

The other school, associated with Merton Miller and Franco Modigliani, holds that investors are basically indifferent to returns in the form of dividends or of capital gains, assuming no differential taxation. They argue that it is the risk of a company's earnings that is important in determining the capitalization rate. The risk of the earnings does not depend on how the earnings are divided between dividends and capital gains. Empirically, when firms raise or lower their dividends there appears to be a corresponding movement in share prices; does this not prove that investors prefer dividends? Miller and Modigliani argue that it does not. Any effect a change in dividends has on the price of a firm's shares is related primarily to *information about expected future earnings conveyed by a change in dividends*. Recalling that corporate managements dislike cutting dividends, Miller and Modigliani argue that increases in cash dividends raise expectations about the level of future earnings—dividend increases have favorable *information content*. In terms of Figure 21-2, Miller and Modigliani would say that Walter Watch's dividend increases in 1961, 1962, 1963, and 1973 had information content about future earnings—these dividend increases signaled to shareholders that management expected the recent earnings increases to be permanent.

Dividends may be subject to less uncertainty than capital gains, but dividends and capital gains are taxed at different rates. In the pre-1972 time period, capital gains were tax-free and the benefits to retention were obvious. However, with the introduction and subsequent changes in the dividend tax credit provisions, and the taxation of capital gains, the preference for capital gains over dividends is less clear; it will depend on the marginal tax rate of each investor.

If investors value the certainty of dividends, i.e. the Gordon position, the impact on the market value of the stock could be reduced if shareholders, due to their tax position, preferred capital gains to dividends. Unfortunately, it is impossible to generalize the importance of the taxation factor. Depending on the tax status and the current income needs of its set of shareholders (both brokerage costs and capital gains taxes make it difficult for individual shareholders to shift companies), as well as the firm's internal investment opportunities, the opitmum dividend policy will vary from firm to firm.

DIVIDEND PAYMENTS

Dividends are normally paid quarterly. For example, Alberta Gas Trunk Line Co. Ltd. (AGTL) paid dividends of $0.7344 per class A share during 1976, at a rate of $0.1836 per quarter. In common financial language, we say that AGTL's *regular quarterly dividend* is $0.1836, or that its *regular annual dividend* is $0.7344. There is a difference between dividends paid and the *indicated dividend rate*. AGTL announced an increase in its regular quarterly rate to $0.205 as of August 15, 1978. Based on this quarterly rate, the new indicated dividend rate is $0.82 per year. However, during 1978, the actual dividends paid will be $0.7772; composed of two quarterly payments of $0.1836 per share and two of $0.205 per share.

Managements of companies, sometimes by an explicit statement in the annual report and sometimes by implication, convey to shareholders an expectation that the regular dividend will be maintained if at all possible. In fact, Bell Canada goes one step beyond this in its 1976 annual report where it describes its increased dividend as being in line with the company's objective of helping shareholders to maintain the integrity of their investment in the face of inflation.

Under other conditions, a firm's cash flows and investment needs may be too volatile for it to set a very high regular dividend; on the average, however, it needs a high dividend payout to dispose of funds not necessary for reinvestment. In such a case, the directors can set a relatively low regular dividend—low enough that it can be maintained even in low profit years or in years when a considerable amount of reinvestment is needed—and supplement it with an extra dividend in years when excess funds are available. General Motors, whose earnings fluctuate widely from year to year, has long followed the practice of supplementing its regular dividend with an *extra dividend* paid at the end of the year, when its profits and investment requirements are known.

PAYMENT PROCEDURE

The actual payment procedure is of some importance, and the following is an outline of the payment sequence.

1. *Declaration Date.* The directors meet, say on November 15, and declare the regular dividend. On this date, the directors issue a statement similar to the following: "On November 15, 1977, the directors of the XYZ Company met and declared the regular quarterly dividend of 50 cents a share, plus an extra dividend of 75 cents a share, to holders of record on December 15, payment to be made on January 2, 1978."

2. *Dividend-Record Date.* On December 15, the *dividend-record date,* the company closes its share transfer books and makes up a list of the shareholders as of that date. If XYZ Company is notified of the sale and transfer of some shares on or before December 15, the new owner receives the dividend. If notification is received on or after December 16, the old shareholder gets the dividend.

3. *Ex Dividend Date.* Suppose Edward Johns buys 100 shares of stock from Robert Noble on December 13; will the company be notified of the transfer in time to list Johns as the new owner and, thus, pay the dividend to him? To avoid conflict, the stock exchange has set up a convention of declaring that the right to the dividend remains with the shares until two business days prior to the dividend record date; on the second day before the record date, the right to the dividend no longer goes with the shares. The date when the right to the dividend leaves the shares is called the *ex dividend date.*

In this case, the ex dividend date is two business days prior to December 15, or December 13. Therefore, if Johns is to receive the dividend, he must buy the stock by December 12. If he buys it on December 13 or later, Noble will receive the dividend.

The total dividend, regular plus extra, amounts to $1.25, so the ex dividend date is important. Barring fluctuations in the stock market, we would normally expect the price of a share to drop by approximately the amount of the dividend on the ex dividend date.

4. *Payment Date.* The company actually mails the checks to the holders of record on January 2, the payment date.

STOCK DIVIDENDS AND STOCK SPLITS

One of the significant aspects of dividend policy is that of *stock dividends* and *stock splits.* A *stock dividend* is paid in additional shares of stock instead of in cash and simply involves a bookkeeping transfer from retained earnings to the capital stock account.[6] In a *stock split* there is no change in the capital accounts. A larger number of shares of common is issued. In a two-for-one split, each shareholder would receive two shares for each one previously held. Book value per share would be cut in half. The par, or stated, value per share of common shares is similarly changed.[7] Notice that, in both a stock dividend and a stock plit, the proportionate ownership of an investor is not affected. Since no new funds come into the company, the same level of earnings is split among more shares. Hence, the earnings per share will decrease. The dividend per share is still a policy decision of the firm and need not decrease. Therefore, from a practical standpoint, there is little difference between a stock split and a stock dividend. In fact, the major difference is the accounting treatment. Since the two are similar, the issues outlined below are discussed in connection with both stock dividends and stock splits.

Prior to 1972, stock dividends were not taxable. From 1968 to 1971, the average dollar amount of stock dividends declared was $240 million. With the reform of the Income Tax Act, stock dividends were taxable as regular cash dividend distributions and thus were not just changes in the number of pieces of paper issued. It is not surprising to find that the average dollar amount of stock dividends declared for the years 1972 to 1975 fell to $32 million—in 1975 there was $18 million of stock dividends declared. As of March 31, 1977, the tax treatment of stock dividends changed again; they are not treated as a dividend distribution but the shareholder will be subject to a capital gains tax on the shares obtained when they are sold.[8]

Price Effects

The results of a careful empirical study of the effects of stock dividends are available and can be used as a basis for observations on the price effects of stock dividends.[9] The findings of the study are presented in Table 21-3.

---

[6]One point that should be made in connection with stock dividends is that the transfer from retained earnings to the capital stock account must be based on market value. In other words, if a firm's shares are selling for $100 and it has 1,000,000 shares outstanding, a 10 percent stock dividend requires the transfer of $10 million (100,000 × $100) from retained earnings to capital stock. Quite obviously, stock dividends are thus limited by the size of retained earnings. The rule was put into effect to prevent the declaration of stock dividends unless the firm has had earnings. This is another in a long series of rulings designed to prevent investors from being fooled by the practices of unscrupulous firms.

[7]Instead of increasing the number of shares outstanding, the company can reduce them. For example, suppose the company decided to issue one share for each five shares outstanding. This is called a one-to-five *reverse split*. The reverse split maintains the proportional ownership of an investor, and since there are fewer shares, the earnings and price per share increase. However, the total amount invested in the company by the shareholder has not changed.

[8]The shares obtained in a stock dividend receive a zero net cost base in the calculation of capital gains. For private companies, stock dividends will still be considered as a dividend distribution and taxed as regular income.

[9]C.A. Barker, "Evaluation of Stock Dividends", *Harvard Business Review*, 36 (July–August 1958), 99-114. Reprinted by permission. Barker's study has been replicated several times in recent years, but his results are still valid—they have withstood the test of time.

When stock dividends were associated with a cash dividend increase, the value of the company's shares six months after the ex dividend date had risen by 8 percent. On the other hand, where stock dividends were not accompanied by cash dividend increases, share values fell by 12 percent during the subsequent six-month period.

TABLE 21–3   Share Price Effects of Stock Dividends

	Price at Selected Dates (in Percentages)		
	Six Months Prior to ex Dividend Date	At ex Dividend Date	Six Months after ex Dividend Date
Cash dividend increase	100	109	108
No cash dividend increase	100	99	88

Another empirical study,[10] using a more sophisticated analysis, investigated the impact of stock splits and stock dividends (of 25 percent or greater) on rates of return to common equity holders i.e. dividends plus capital gains relative to a stock market index. One finding of this study was that companies which engaged in stock splits had rates or return, before the split date, which were high relative to the market. This reflected dramatic increases in expected earnings and dividends. The authors then investigated the rate of return on the shares after the split date. The overall sample was broken down into two subgroups; those companies with dividend increases after the stock split and those with dividend decreases. The increases and decreases were measured relative to the change in the dividends on the market index. It was found that for the first set of companies, the rates of return after the split were marginally better than the index for approximately one year. However, for the second group, the rates of return were below the index.

The explanation of this differential behavior is straight-forward. It appears that, on average, stock splits are followed by increases in dividends per share—of the 940 splits considered, 672 had dividend increases. It is not the increased dividend per se that affects the rate of return but the information that the increased dividend conveys. As noted before, since managements are adverse to reducing dividends, the increased dividend conveys information about future earnings. Thus, an increased dividend after the split confirms the market's expectations and there is no significant impact on the rate of return after the split. However, a decrease in dividends is completely new and unexpected information and the rate of return falls.

[10]Fama, Fisher, Jensen and Roll, "The Adjustment of Stock Prices to New Information", *International Economic Review*, Vo. 10, No. 1 (February 1969), pp. 1–21.

Both of these studies suggest that stock dividends are seen for what they are—simply additional pieces of paper—and they do not represent true income. When they are accompanied by higher cash dividends, the information in the increased dividend is reflected in the share price. However, when stock dividends are not accompanied by an increase in cash dividends, the share price falls to reflect the new information that earnings are not expected to be higher in the future. Therefore, the fundamental determinant of share price is the underlying expected profitability of the company.

Effects on Extent of Ownership

One alleged benefit of a stock split or stock dividend is the impact on common share ownership. Although there is no information on this phenomenon in the Canadian context, the U.S. experience is instructive.

The results shown in Table 21–4 show that the largest percentage increases in share ownership are associated with large stock dividends. The use of stock dividends increased shareholders by 25 percent on the average. For companies and industries that did not offer stock splits or stock dividends, the increase in ownership was only 5 percent. Furthermore, the degree of increase in ownership increased with the size of the stock dividend.

TABLE 21–4   Effect of Stock Dividends on Share Ownership

	Percentage Increase in Stockholders, 1950–1953
Stock dividend, 25% and over	30
Stock dividend, 5–25%	17
All stock dividends	25
No stock dividends or splits	5

Source: C. Austin Barker, "Evaluation of Stock Dividends," *Harvard Business Review,* 36 (July–August 1958), 99–114. Reprinted by permission.

This evidence suggests that stock dividends increase the number of shareholders. This may be a result in the stock split or stock dividend lowering the price at which shares are traded to a more "popular" range. However, it is unlikely that this increase in a share's popularity has any impact on the total market value of the equity.

In summary, it is difficult to believe that an increase in the number of shares outstanding generated from a stock split or stock dividend can have any impact on the value of the equity unless there is a true economic benefit associated with the stock split or stock dividend. These economic benefits are not present in the lowering the share price to a popular trading range or a substitution of a stock dividend for a cash dividend when a company is in financial difficulty. Since the same pool of earnings are spread among more shares after the split, the total market value of equity will not change; the per share financial variables such as earnings and price may fall. However, financial analysts, when evaluating a company, always adjust the per share quantities so that they will be comparable to previous years. If, however, the stock split or stock dividend is a signal of improved dividends per share, and hence, of improved future earnings, the market value of equity will increase.

SHARE REPURCHASE[11]

Treasury Stock is the term used to refer to common shares that have been repurchased by the issuing firm. Both the Ontario and British Columbia Corporations Act permit the repurchase of shares; the treasury stock has no vote and can be reissued. The Canada Business Corporations Act permits the repurchase of shares by federally incorporated companies, but any repurchased shares must be retired. Hence, no treasury stock is permitted and the repurchased shares can not be reissued.

There are two purposes for share repurchase. First, share repurchase is an alternative to the payment of a cash dividend. Second, share repurchase is being used as a means to remove publicly held shares and permit the company to go private. This latter phenomenon began to occur with surprising frequency in 1970 and has been of concern to the Ontario Securities Commission. We will consider both purposes for share repurchase in the following sections.

As an Alternative to Dividends

If some of the outstanding shares are repurchased, fewer shares will remain outstanding; and assuming the repurchase does not adversely affect the firm's earnings, the earnings per share of the remaining shares will increase. This increase in earnings per share should result in a higher market price per share, so capital gains will have been substituted for dividends. These effects can be seen from the following example.

Example

Canadian Multi Minerals (CMM) earned $4.4 million in 1977; of this amount, 50 percent or $2.2 million has been allocated for distribution to common shareholders. There are currently 1,100,000 shares outstanding, and the market value is $22 a share. This price is measured before the annual dividend is declared. CMM can use the $2.2 million to repurchase 100,000 of its

---

[11] This section is relatively technical and may be omitted without loss of continuity.

shares through a tender offer of $22 a share, or it can pay a cash dividend of $2 per share.[12] If the latter alternative is chosen, the stock price will fall to $20 when the shares go *ex dividend*.

The effect of the repurchase on the *EPS* and market price per share of the remaining shares is determined as follows:

1. Current *EPS* $= \dfrac{\text{total earnings}}{\text{number of shares}} = \dfrac{\$4.4 \text{ million}}{1.1 \text{ million}}$

$$= \$4 \text{ per share.}$$

2. Ex-dividend P/E ratio $= \dfrac{\text{ex-dividend price}}{\text{earnings per share}} = \dfrac{\$20}{\$4} = 5 \times.$

3. *EPS* after repurchase of 100,000 shares $= \dfrac{\$4.4 \text{ million}}{1 \text{ million}} = \$4.40 \text{ per share.}$

4. Expected market price after repurchase $= (P/E)(EPS) = (5)(\$4.40) = \$22 \text{ per share.}$

It should be noted from this example that ignoring tax differences on dividends and capital gains, investors should be indifferent to the method by which the dividend is paid. The wealth of an equity investor is equal under two methods; the per share wealth under the repurchase is $22 whether or not the investor sold his shares and under the cash dividend is $22 i.e. the sum of the dividend per share of $2.00 plus the ex-dividend share price of $20.00. In this example under the share repurchase, the firm pays out the funds but the shareholders whose shares are repurchased receive the dividend as a capital gain.

The equality of shareholder wealth under the share repurchase and cash dividend alternatives occurs because we assumed (1) that the shares could be repurchased at exactly $22 a share, (2) that the P/E ratio would remain constant, and (3) that there is no impact of differential taxes on capital gains and dividends. If shares could be bought for less than $22, the operation would benefit the *remaining* shareholders at the expense of the selling share-holders, but the reverse would hold if CMM paid more than $22 a share. Furthermore, the *P/E* ratio might change as a result of the repurchase operation, rising if investors view it favorably and falling if they view it unfavorably. One important factor that could have an impact on the *P/E* ratio is the differential taxes on capital gains and dividends. If all investors have

---

[12]Share repurchases are commonly made in three ways. First, a publicly owned firm can simply buy its own shares through a broker on the open market. Second, it can issue a *tender* under which it permits share-holders to send in (that is, "tender") their shares to the firm in exchange for a specified price per share. When tender offers are made, the firm generally indicates that it will buy up to a specified number of shares within a specified time period (usually about two weeks); if more shares are tendered than the company wishes to purchase, then purchases are made on a pro rata basis. Finally, the firm can purchase a block of shares from one large holder on a negotiated basis.

marginal federal tax rates in excess of 37.5 percent, then the affective tax rate on dividends exceeds that on capital gains and the share repurchase is preferred. Conversely, at lower federal marginal tax rates the dividend payment is preferred. This would raise the P/E ratio. The problem that the company faces is that its investors will have different marginal tax rates, and thus, unless the company can discern where the majority of tax rates are located, it does not know whether to repurchase or pay cash dividends.

Advantages of Repurchases from the Shareholder's Viewpoint

1. The implied dividend distribution through a common share repurchase is taxed at the capital gains rate and a cash dividend distribution is taxed at an effective tax rate that reflects the dividend tax credit. As noted above, this can be a significant advantage for that group of shareholders with high marginal federal tax rates.[13]
2. The shareholder has a choice; either sell or not sell. On the other hand, with a dividend, he or she has to accept the payment and pay the tax.
3. A qualitative advantage advanced by market practitioners is that repurchase can often remove a large block of shares overhanging the market.

Advantages of Repurchases from Management's Viewpoint

1. Studies have shown that dividends are *sticky* in the short run because managements are reluctant to raise dividends if the new dividend cannot be maintained in the future. Managements dislike cutting cash dividends, so they are reluctant to raise dividends if they are not confident that the dividend can be maintained in the future. Hence, if the excess cash flow is thought to be only *temporary*, management may prefer to "conceal" the distribution in the form of share repurchases rather than to declare a cash dividend they believe cannot be maintained.
2. Repurchased shares can be used for acquisitions or released when share options are exercised. Discussions with financial managers indicate that it is frequently more convenient and less expensive to use repurchased shares than newly issued shares for these purposes, and also when convertibles are converted or warrants exercised.
3. If directors have large holdings themselves, they may have especially strong preferences for repurchases rather than dividend payments because of the tax factor.
4. One interesting use of a share repurchase is to thwart a take-over bid. The management can repurchase shares at a price in excess of the price in the take-over bid. This would permit the management to retain control.

---

[13]However, there are circumstances, as noted in the Income Tax Act, when a repurchase will result in a deemed dividend distribution and shareholders will be taxed accordingly.

5. Repurchases can be used to effect large-scale changes in capital structure. For example, suppose a company had a very low level of long-term debt outstanding. The company decided that its optimal capital structure called for the use of considerably more debt, but even if it financed *only* with debt it would have taken years to get the debt ratio up to the newly defined optimal level. What could the company do? It sold an issue of long-term debt and used the proceeds to repurchase some of its common equity, thus producing an instantaneous change in its capital structure.
6. Treasury shares can be resold in the open market if the firm needs additional funds.

Disadvantages of Repurchases from the Shareholder's Viewpoint

1. Shareholders may not be indifferent between dividends and capital gains, and the price of the shares might benefit more from cash dividends than from repurchase. First, cash dividends may be considered to be relatively dependable, but repurchases are not. Second, the investor's marginal federal tax rate may be at a level for which dividend distributions are preferred. Third, if a firm pursues a regular repurchase program, the likelihood that the repurchase will be interpreted as a dividend distribution increases.
2. The *selling* shareholders may not be fully aware of all the implications of a repurchase or may not have all pertinent information about the corporation's present and future activities. For this reason, firms generally announce a repurchase program before embarking on it.
3. The corporation may pay too high a price for the repurchased shares, to the disadvantage of remaining shareholders. If the shares are inactive and if the firm seeks to acquire a relatively large amount of its shares, the price may be bid above a maintainable price and then fall after the firm ceases its repurchase operations.

Disadvantages of Repurchases from Management's Viewpoint

1. One possible explanation of substantial repurchase activity is that the firm has poorer growth rates and investment opportunities than firms that do not engage in repurchases.[14] Thus, some investors may feel that announcing a repurchase program is like announcing that management cannot locate good investment projects. One could argue that instituting a repurchase program should be regarded in the same manner as announcing a higher dividend payout, but if repurchases are regarded as indicating especially

[14]A recent study of share repurchase activity by S. S. Stewart Jr., "Should a Corporation Repurchase its own Stock?" *Journal of Finance*, June, 1976, pp. 911–21 demonstrates that this conclusion may be invalid. The study found that light repurchasers do not do much better than non-repurchasing firms, whereas very active repurchasers did better. Moderate repurchasers do much poorer than non-repurchasers for approximately two years and from then on, do better than any of the groups considered.

unfavorable growth opportunities, then repurchases can have an adverse impact on the firm's image, and also on the market price of its shares.

Reporting Requirements in Share Repurchase

In the Provincial and Federal Corporations Acts, only the latter has specific reporting provisions for share repurchase. The Canada Business Corporations Act requires that information concerning the repurchase be provided to shareholders of the company as well as to investors in general. The Ontario Securities Commission (OSC) views the lack of required disclosure for share repurchase for non-federally incorporated companies as a serious problem. In 1977, the Province of Ontario introduced a new Securities Act which, when passed, would deal with this problem. Meanwhile, the OSC has investigated the problem and has introduced some regulations under a revised policy toward share repurchase.

There are a number of specific provisions that were introduced; we will consider a few of the more important ones. First, the policy does not apply to federally incorporated companies, private companies or companies which intend to repurchase the shares through the stock exchange.

Share repurchase bids are handled somewhat differently depending on the size of the repurchase bid. If the bid is for less than 5 percent of the outstanding securities in any consecutive 30 day period, an information circular must be presented. Included in this circular must be the reason for the stock repurchase, the income tax consequences on the firm and the investors, and any appraisal or valuation of the assets or securities of the companies made within two years of the date of the repurchase bid and known to the directors or officers of the company.

If the repurchase bid is for an amount greater than 5 percent of the securities in a class, the same basic reporting provisions exist. However, there is one additional requirement. It is noted that where there are reasonable grounds to believe that the repurchase bid price is substantially less than the fair value of the security, a summary of an independent valuation of the fair value, as a going concern, of the company and the class of securities being repurchased must be presented. This valuation cannot be made earlier than three months before the date of the repurchase bid.

It is this past provision which may be somewhat controversial. When the stock market is performing correctly, the fair market value of a security is the current stock price. Thus, a bid which is in excess of the current stock price could be considered fair. The usefulness of an independent valuation may be limited since it does not reflect the expectations of investors.

Conclusion on Share Repurchases as an Alternative to Dividends

When all the pros and the cons on share repurchases are totaled, where do we stand? Our own conclusions may be summarized as follows:

1. Repurchases on a regular, systematic, dependable basis, like quarterly dividends, are not feasible because of uncertainties about such things as the market price of the shares, how many shares would be tendered, and so forth.
2. However, repurchases may offer some significant advantages over dividends, so this procedure should be given careful consideration on the basis of the firm's own unique situation.
3. Repurchases can be especially valuable to effect a significant shift in capital structure within a short period.

Repurchases to Go Private

In the previous section we considered share repurchase where, after the repurchase, the company's stock was still traded on the stock exchange. However, it is possible that a share repurchase can result in a public firm going private. This is not a new development, but it has received prominence beginning in 1976.

This "going private" phenomenon received attention in the United States in 1974. The common scenario is that a junior industrial which went public in a boom stock market at a high market price is faced with relatively low stock price. The management decides that the disadvantages of having the stock listed on an exchange outweigh the advantages and the company becomes private again.

The Ontario Securities Commission is concerned with a problem associated with a company returning to private status. This problem, referred to as a "squeeze-out", occurs when the majority shareholders attempt to eliminate or reduce the importance of minority interest. There are a number of ways to affect a squeeze-out, but the OSC is concerned with the repurchase technique. Their concern reflects a situation where the minority shareholders are bought out at a price per share that is less than the issue price when the firm went public, is less than the appraisal value, but is in excess of the prevailing market price. There are a number of examples where "going private" attempts were undertaken. For example, Sifton Properties Limited made a share repurchase bid at $12 per share, and through other financial arrangements, any remaining public shareholders would have been squeezed out. An independent valuation of the adjusted book value per share was $20.25. The squeeze-out was conditional upon the approval of a majority of the minority shareholders. Sifton Properties Limited ultimately abandoned their plans for a squeeze-out.

There can be a number of benefits for the firm in going private. These include cost savings from reduced reporting requirements, tax advantages, and more flexibility in corporate decision making. The OSC position, however, is that in a squeeze-out situation the majority continues on as an equity participant, whereas the minority does not—therefore, there is a conflict of interest between the majority and the minority.

The temporary rules noted under the reporting requirements for stock repurchase have been applied to the "going private" repurchases. It is not our purpose to comment on these rules or the proposed legislation concerning share-repurchase bids. However, we do have some reservations concerning the usefulness of the independent valuation scheme. It is hard to accept the implication that an independent valuation of the equity is superior to the market's valuation based on expected profitability and risk implicit in the share price. The acceptability of the repurchase bid will depend on the amount by which the bid price exceeds the market price before the announcement of the repurchase bid.

SUMMARY

Dividend policy determines the extent of internal financing by a firm. The financial manager decides whether to release corporate earnings from the control of the enterprise. Because dividend policy affects the financial structure, the flow of funds, corporate liquidity, investor satisfaction, and perhaps even the share price—to list a few ramifications—it is clearly an important aspect of financial management.

In theory, once the firm's debt policy and cost of capital have been determined, dividend policy should automatically follow. Under our theoretical model, dividends are simply a residual after investment needs have been met; if this policy is followed and if investors are indifferent to receiving their investment returns in the form of dividends or of capital gains. Shareholders are better off than they are under any other possible dividend policy. However, the financial manager simply does not have all the information assumed in the theory, and rule-of-thumb guidelines are needed.

As a guide to financial managers responsible for dividend policy, the following check list summarizes the major economic and financial factors influencing dividend policy:

1. Rate of growth and profit level.
2. Stability of earnings.
3. Age and size of firm.
4. Cash position.
5. Need to repay debt.
6. Control.
7. Maintenance of a target dividend.
8. Tax position of shareholders.
9. Maintenance of a preferred tax rate.

Of the factors listed, some lead to higher dividend payouts, some to lower payouts. It is not possible to provide a formula that can be used to establish the proper dividend payout for a given situation; this is a task requiring the exercise of judgment. The considerations summarized above provide a check list for guiding dividend decisions.

Empirical studies indicate a wide diversity of dividend payout ratios not only among industries but also among firms in the same industry. Studies also show that dividends are more stable than earnings. Firms are reluctant to raise dividends in years of good earnings, and they resist dividend cuts as earnings decline. In view of investors' observed preference for stable dividends and of the probability that a cut in dividends is likely to be interpreted as forecasting a decline in earnings, stable dividends make good sense.

Stock Dividends and Splits   Neither stock dividends nor stock splits alone exert a fundamental influence on prices. The fundamental determinant of the price of the company's shares is the company's earning power compared with the earning power of other companies. However, both stock splits and stock dividends can be used as an effective instrument of financial policy. They are useful devices for reducing the price at which shares are traded, and studies in the U.S. indicate that stock dividends and stock splits tend to broaden the ownership of a firm's shares.

Share Repurchases   There are two types of share repurchases undertaken by corporations. First, share repurchases have been used as an alternative to cash dividends. Although repurchases have significant advantages over dividends, they also have disadvantages, in particular the fact that share repurchases necessarily involve greater uncertainty than cash dividends. Second, share repurchases are being used by companies to go private. This results in a control group having all the equity interest after the repurchase. This type of repurchase has been investigated by the Ontario Securities Commission and there are reporting requirements that must be met in any type of repurchase. As with so much in finance, generalizations about share repurchases are difficult—each firm has its own unique problems and conditions, and repurchase policy must be formulated within the context of the firm as a whole.

QUESTIONS

21-1. As an investor, would you rather invest in a firm with a policy of maintaining (a) a constant payout ratio, (b) a constant dollar dividend per share, or (c) a constant regular quarterly dividend plus a year-end extra when earnings are sufficiently high or corporate investment needs are sufficiently low? Explain your answer.

21-2. How would each of the following changes probably affect aggregate payout *ratios*? Explain your answer.

    a. An increase in the personal income tax rate.

    b. An increase in the capital cost allowance rates for all classes.

    c. An increase in the dividend tax credit assuming that the gross-up proportion remains unchanged.

    d. A rise in interest rates.

    e. An increase in corporate profits.

    f. A decline in investment opportunities.

21-3. Discuss the pros and cons of having the directors formally announce what a firm's dividend policy will be in the future.

21-4. Most firms would like to have their shares selling at a high P/E ratio and also have an extensive public ownership (many different shareholders). Explain how stock dividends or stock splits may be compatible with these aims.

21-5. What is the difference between a stock dividend and a stock split? As a shareholder, would you prefer to see your company declare a 100 percent stock dividend or a two-for-one split?

21-6. In theory, if we had perfect capital markets, we would expect investors to be indifferent between cash dividends and an equivalent repurchase of shares outstanding. What factors might in practice cause investors to value one over the other?

21-7. "The cost of retained earnings is less than the cost of new outside equity capital. Consequently, it is totally irrational for a firm to sell a new issue of equity and to pay dividends during the same year." Discuss this statement.

21-8. Would it ever be rational for a firm to borrow money in order to pay dividends? Explain.

21-9. Union spokesmen have presented arguments similar to the following: "Corporations such as General Foods retain about one-half their profits for financing needs. If they financed by selling shares instead of by retained earnings, they could cut prices substantially and still earn enough to pay the same dividend to their shareholders. Therefore, their profits are too high." Evaluate this statement.

21-10. "Executive salaries have been shown to be more closely correlated to size of firm than to profitability. If a firm's board of directors is controlled by management instead of by outside directors, this might result in the firm's retaining more earnings than can be justified from the shareholders' point of view." Discuss the statement, being sure (a) to use Figure 21-5 in your answer and (b) to explain the implied relationship between dividend policy and share prices.

21-11. Assume that capital markets are perfect, and that there are no issue costs when new debt and/or equity is floated; which of the factors noted on page 565 would no longer be relevant?

21-12. Are there any other types of transaction costs, in addition to issue costs, that have an impact on investors and the firm and ultimately are important in determining dividend policy? If so, what are they and what would be their impact on the firm's payout ratio?

21-13. Evaluate the benefits and costs to the shareholders of repurchases to go private. In your analysis, be sure to include the possibility that the majority shareholders have inside information concerning the future profitability of the firm.

PROBLEMS

21-1. Maritime Seafoods Ltd. has a current stock price of $38.50 per share. The firm has consistently earned $3.50 per share and its usual practice is to pay out all the earnings as dividends. There are 1 million shares currently outstanding. This year the firm has decided to use the full earnings available to common to repurchase shares. The ex-dividend P/E multiple is 10 times and the current share price reflects the $3.50 earnings. Suppose the firm repurchases at $38.50 per share. What will be the share price of the remaining shares?

Suppose the firm repurchases at $40.00 per share. What will be the share price of the remaining shares?

21-2. Precision instruments is currently earning $4 per share. The rate of return required by its shareholders, k_s, is 10 percent and the current market price is $40 per share. The company has experienced approximately a 3 percent growth in earnings, dividends, and market value over the past several years, and it is expected that this growth rate will continue. Using the constant growth share valuation model, calculate the dividend anticipated next year. What is the anticipated dividend payout ratio?

21-3. The directors of Lancing Lumber Supply have been comparing the growth of their market price with the growth of one of their competitors, Davidson Panels, Inc. Their findings are summarized below.

Lancing Lumber Supply

Year	Earnings	Dividend	Payout	Price	P/E
1975	$4.30	$2.58	60%	$68	15.8
1974	3.85	2.31	60	60	15.6
1973	3.29	1.97	60	50	15.2
1972	3.09	1.85	60	42	13.6
1971	3.05	1.83	60	38	12.5
1970	2.64	1.58	60	31	11.7
1969	1.98	1.19	60	26	13.1
1968	2.93	1.76	60	31	10.6
1967	3.48	2.09	60	35	10.1
1966	2.95	1.77	60	30	10.2

Davidson Panels, Inc.

Year	Earnings	Dividend	Payout	Price	P/E
1975	$3.24	$1.94	60%	$70	21.6
1974	2.75	1.79	65	56	20.4
1973	2.94	1.79	61	53	18.0
1972	2.93	1.73	59	48	16.4
1971	2.90	1.65	57	44	15.2
1970	2.86	1.57	55	41	14.3
1969	2.61	1.49	57	35	13.4
1968	1.55	1.50	97	20	12.9
1967	2.24	1.50	67	34	15.2
1966	2.19	1.49	68	30	13.7

Both companies are in the same markets, and both are similarly organized (approximately the same degrees of operating and financial leverage). Lancing has been consistently earning more per share yet, for some reason, has not been valued at as high a *P/E* ratio as Davidson. What factors would you point out as possible causes for this lower market valuation of Lancing's shares?

21-4. The Airpac Corporation was organized approximately ten years ago. It has experienced good growth until recently, when a high inflation rate coupled with increased environmental protection concerns caused a serious decline in sales. For the past several years, annual EPS have averaged $6. Throughout that period, the dividend payout was approximately 50 percent or $3 per share, payable 75 cents per quarter.

The fiscal year ending December 31, 19X7 showed an earnings decline to $2.50 per share. Because it was felt that the earnings decline was temporary, the annual dividend of $3 was maintained for that fiscal year, as well as the first six months of the current year. However, recent projections have caused management to revise downward the expected EPS. For this current fiscal year, the forecast of EPS has been reduced to approximately $2 per share, and to approximately $2.20 for next year. The stock is currently selling for $15 per share, and Airpac's latest balance sheet is given below.

Management is considering maintaining the $3 cash dividend for the next two years. (a) Is this feasible? (b) Could the company eliminate the cash dividend and substitute for it a 25 percent stock dividend? (c) What action do you think management should take?

Airpac Corporation
Balance Sheet
December 31, 19X7

Cash	$ 1,000,000		
Inventory	3,500,000		
Accounts receivable	3,000,000	Accts. Payable	$ 2,000,000
Prepaid expenses	500,000	Notes Payable	4,000,000
Total current assets	$8,000,000	Total current liabilities	$ 6,000,000
Net property, plant and		Long term debt	1,800,000
equipment	6,000,000	Common Shares ($10 par)	$ 6,000,000
Other assets	800,000	Retained Earnings	1,000,000
Total assets	$14,800,000	Total liabilities and equity	$14,800,000

21-5. Hazard Tobacco Co. Ltd. has for many years enjoyed a moderate but stable growth in sales and earnings. However, cigarette consumption and, consequently, Hazard's sales have been falling off recently, partly because of a national awareness of the dangers of smoking to health. Anticipating further declines in tobacco sales for the future, Hazard's management hopes eventually to move almost entirely out of the tobacco business and, instead, develop a new diversified product line in growth-oriented industries.

Hazard has been especially interested in the prospects for pollution-control devices—its research department having already done much work on problems of filtering smoke. Right now, the company estimates that an investment of $24 million is necessary to purchase new facilities and begin operations on these products, but the investment could return about 18 percent within a short time. Other investment opportunities total $9.6 million and are expected to return about 12 percent.

The company has been paying a $2.40 dividend on its 6,000,000 shares outstanding. The announced dividend policy has been to maintain a stable dollar dividend, raising it only when it appears that earnings have reached a new, permanently higher level. The directors might, however, change this policy if reasons for doing so are compelling. Total earnings for the year are $22.8 million, common equity is currently selling for $45 per share, and the firm's current leverage ratio (D/A) is 45 percent. Current costs of various forms of financing are:

New bonds	7%
New common shares sold at $45 to yield the firm	$41
Investors required rate of return on equity	9%
Tax rate	50%

a. Calculate the marginal cost of capital above and below the point of exhaustion of retained earnings for Hazard.

b. How large should Hazard's capital budget be for the year?

c. What is an appropriate dividend policy for Hazard? How should the capital budget be financed?

d. How might risk factors influence Hazard's cost of capital, capital structure, and dividend policy?

e. What assumptions, if any, do your answers to the above make about investors' preference for dividends versus capital gains, that is, investors' preference regarding different D/P and g components of k?

21-6. Gemstone, Ltd. has earnings this year of $16.5 million, 50 percent of which is required to take advantage of excellent investment opportunities of the firm. The firm has 206,250 shares outstanding, selling currently at $320 a share. Greg Beaumont, a major shareholder (18,750 shares), has expressed displeasure with a great deal of managerial policy. Management has approached him with the prospect of selling his holdings back to the firm, and he has expressed a willingness to do this at a price of $320 a share. Assuming that the market uses a constant P/E ratio of 4 in valuing the shares, answer the following questions:

a. Should the firm buy Beaumont's shares? Assume that dividends will not be paid on Beaumont's shares if repurchased.

b. How large a cash dividend should be declared?

c. What is the final value of Gemstone's stock after all cash payments to shareholders?

Integrated Topics in Financial Management

Part Six

In the final four chapters we take up important but somewhat specialized topics which draw on the concepts developed in earlier sections.

Chapter 22, "International Financial Management," introduces the problems faced by a Canadian firm that makes investment decisions in other countries. Chapter 23 deals with the growth of firms through mergers and holding companies, and the reasoning behind this development. Throughout the text, we have dealt with growing and successful firms; however, many firms face financial difficulties, and the causes and possible remedies to these difficulties are discussed in Chapter 24. Finally, in Chapter 25, we summarize and integrate the various topics covered in the book.

International Financial Management

22

INTRODUCTION

The financial issues presented in the previous chapters have been analysed from the perspective of financial managers and planners within the Canadian domestic economy. In this chapter, we extend our analysis to consider the role and problems faced by financial managers in the international economic setting.

Any Canadian business that buys or sells goods and services outside of our borders must cope with a more complex financial and economic environment than a firm which carries on business solely within Canada. The Canadian economy cannot be viewed in isolation from the international trade that crosses our borders. A significant proportion of goods and services produced in Canada are sold elsewhere in the world. Similarly, a significant level of the goods and services consumed in Canada originate abroad. This relationship has not only been an important factor in the growth of the Canadian economy but has, over the past seven years become more pervasive.

The cash flows in part (a) of Table 22-1, Current Receipts, represent the cash payments to Canadian individuals and companies for the goods and services provided to foreign buyers plus the receipt of interest and dividends from investments on the financial securities of other countries. It should be noted that these payments are in current or nominal dollars; they have not been adjusted for changes in the purchasing power of the Canadian dollar. Thus, any comparison of flows between years should be made only after an inflation adjustment. All of these cash flows represent a demand for Canadian dollars.

TABLE 22-1 Summary of Canadian Balance of International Payments – Seasonally Adjusted

($ million)

(a) Current Receipts

	Merchandise Exports	Service Receipts	Transfer Receipts	Total
1970	$16,921	$4,246	$ 765	$21,932
1971	17,877	4,304	870	23,051
1972	20,129	4,451	903	25,483
1973	25,461	5,257	1,058	31,776
1974	32,591	6,401	1,360	40,352
1975	33,511	6,941	1,388	41,840
1976	38,132	7,553	1,486	47,171
1977	44,628	8,088	1,465	54,181

(b) Current Payments

	Merchandise Imports	Service Payments	Transfer Payments	Total
1970	$13,869	$ 6,345	$ 612	$20,826
1971	15,314	6,702	604	22,620
1972	18,272	6,978	619	25,869
1973	22,726	8,228	714	31,668
1974	30,902	10,107	803	41,812
1975	33,962	11,627	1,008	46,597
1976	36,793	13,204	975	50,972
1977	41,712	15,520	1,099	58,331

The cash flows in part (b) are what Canadian individuals and firms paid out to import goods and services plus the cost of servicing foreign capital invested in Canada. It can be noted that on current account these cash outflows to foreign sellers and investors which reflect a demand for foreign currencies have outweighed the cash inflows over the past four years. This negative balance is referred to as a deficit on current account. Canada may run a surplus with specific trading partners but, in aggregate, the cash flow with the rest of the world is in a negative position.

This active participation in world trade has resulted in a complex international economic environment. The financial manager must be able to cope with a variety of different monetary units whose values fluctuate over time. As well, each country in the world has its own legal, taxation, political and economic systems of which the financial manager must be aware. Thus a Canadian company that buys and sells in both Canada and some foreign countries must observe the laws of Canada, the laws and political tastes of the other countries and lastly the taxation and trade agreements between Canada and the rest of the world. Since this financial setting is complicated and can add a number of risks, the financial planning for international transactions is an important and difficult task.

In this chapter we will introduce a number of additional factors that must be considered for financial decision making in the international setting. One of the most important factors to be considered is the risk introduced by fluctuating currency exchange rates. We will present a brief discussion of the factors affecting the determination of exchange rates and describe how a financial manager can deal with this risk. In addition, a number of other factors which make international financial transactions more risky than domestic ones will be considered. Finally, an examination of the operations of a multinational firm and its financial planning process will complete the chapter. Through the example of a hypothetical company and its foreign subsidiaries, all of the factors involved will be combined in an illustrative case. This case will highlight the augmented financial planning process that must be performed in an international setting. Multinational corporations are companies with branches or subsidiary companies operating in more than one country.

This chapter is intended to introduce a number of issues or problems. We leave an in-depth analysis of the issues to texts that deal specifically with the whole subject of international financial management and economics. Our purpose is to present some insight into the problems that must be faced in international financial management.

EXCHANGE RATES AND CURRENCY TRANSACTIONS

Let us consider the following highly simplified world. There is only one way to manufacture baubles. They are relatively inexpensive to produce and are in uniform demand by consumers around the world. We will assume that the raw materials for baubles and the labor skills required for their manufacture are available in most countries. Let us further assume that we live in a world where there are no domestic or international tariffs, transportation costs, or other restrictions on trade. We would expect that this product should be priced in each country at roughly the same level. However, not all countries are going to print the price on the baubles in Canadian dollars ($). In France the price will be denominated in French francs (fr.), in the United Kingdom the price will be in pounds sterling (£).

The relationship between any two of these currencies' values is an exchange rate. It is a proportionality factor that should, in the pricing mechanism of relative currency values, maintain the purchasing power of the wealth of the purchasers regardless of which country they acquire the baubles in. If a bauble costs $1.00 in Canada and £0.4 in the United Kingdom, then the exchange rates or proportionality factor which will make the purchasers indifferent as to where they purchase their baubles will be $2.50 Canadian for each pound sterling. For ease of comprehension it is always best to set the foreign country's basic monetary unit as the base and then quote the price or proportion of Canadian dollars required to trade for one unit of the the foreign currency. In this simplified world economy, there should be no difference between paying $1 for a bauble in Canada and trading $1 for $\frac{1}{2.5}$ of a pound sterling and purchasing the exact, same bauble in the United Kingdom.

TABLE 22–2   Foreign Exchange*

MID MARKET RATES IN CANADIAN FUNDS, Dec. 11, 1978.
Prepared by the Bank of Nova Scotia

Country	Currency	Noon	Previous Noon	Country	Currency	Noon	Previous Noon
United States	Dollar	$1.1781	$1.1752	Japan	Yen	.006022	.005938
1 month future		1.1771	1.1745	Jordon	Dinar	4.1116	4.1014
2 months future		1.1767	1.1738	Lebanon	Pound	.4123	.4113
3 months future		1.1760	1.1727	Luxembourg	Franc	.039310	.038864
6 months future		1.1725	1.1694	Malaysia	Dollar	.5384	.5359
12 months future		1.1665	1.1635	Mexico	Peso	.0523	.0522
Britain	Pound	2.3291	2.2946	Netherlands	Guilder	.5731	.5662
1 month future		2.3224	2.2895	New Zealand	Dollar	1.2476	1.2381
2 months future		2.3176	2.2825	Norway	Krone	.2317	.2293
3 months future		2.3127	2.2768	Pakistan	Rupee	.1296	.1293
6 months future		2.2952	2.2586	Poland	Zloty	.0677	.0676
12 months future		2.2607	2.2246	Portugal	Escudo	.0251	.0250
Algeria	Dinar	.3122	.3114	Romania	Leu	.2380	.2374
Argentina	Peso	.0013	.0013	Saudi Arabia	Rival	.3593	.3584
Australia	Dollar	1.3489	1.3404	Singapore	Dollar	.5413	.5380
Austria	Schilling	.0847	.0841	South Africa	Rand	1.3608	1.3574
Bahamas	Dollar	1.1781	1.1752	Spain	Peseta	.0166	.0173
Barbados	Dollar	.5938	.5923	Sudan	Pound	2.4033	2.3974
Belgium	Franc	.039310	.038864	Sweden	Krona	.2673	.2659
Bermuda	Dollar	1.1781	1.1752	Switzerland	Franc	.6974	.6904
Brazil	Cruzeiro	.0575	.0573	Taiwan	Dollar	.0342	.0341
Bulgaria	Lev	1.3548	1.3515	Trinidad, Tobago	Dollar	.5007	.4995
Chile	Peso	.0383	.0382	USSR	Rouble	1.8025	1.7981
China	Renminbi	.7250	.7250	Venezuela	Bolivar	.2751	.2744
Cyprus	Pound	3.2044	3.1965	West Germany	Mark	.6204	.6146
Czechoslovakia	Crown	.2297	.2292	1 month future		.6236	.6181
Denmark	Krone	.2235	.2211	3 months future		.6308	.6248
East Germany	Mark	.5419	.5406	Antigua, Grenada	E.C. Dollar	.4477	.4466
Egypt	Pound	1.7082	1.7040	St. Lucia			
Finland	Markka	.2912	.2903	Yugoslavia	Dinar	.0677	.0676
France	Franc	.2701	.2677	Zambia	Kwacha	1.5197	1.5160
Greece	Drachma	.0324	.0323				
Hong Kong	Dollar	.2456	.2451				
Hungry	Forint	.0648	.0646				
Iceland	Krona	.0047	.0047				
India	Rupee	.1484	.1469				
Israel	Pound	.0677	.0676				
Italy	Lira	.001396	.001387				
Jamaica	Dollar	.7104	.7086				

* Source: Globe and Mail, December 12, 1978

The Financial Post publishes the exchange rates of a wide variety of the more important trading nations' currencies daily. Again the rates are on a Canadian dollar per foreign monetary unit basis. Table 22-2[1] illustrates a snapshot view of the foreign currency market. For example, it requires 1.178 Canadian dollars to purchase 1 U.S. dollar or .2701 Canadian dollars to purchase 1 French franc. Due to transaction costs and other imperfections in the market, the rates quoted will not necessarily be what all participants in the market are going to pay or receive on that day. The larger the trader, the smaller the relative brokerage costs on a dollar basis. This means that the rate published is before the additional holding and trading costs of the intermediary are tacked onto the price of the trade.

So far the reader should understand that the exchange rate between two currencies is a ratio of two countries' monetary units. The ratio should be such that the purchasing power of international consumers is preserved across political boundaries. What sets that ratio is a far more complicated issue and we will now review some of the more important factors that affect the relative prices of world currencies.

THE FUNDAMENTAL FACTORS AFFECTING EXCHANGE RATES

As in all markets there is a buyer and seller or demander and supplier of the commodity traded. This is exactly what is occurring in Foreign Exchange Markets around the world. There exists an orderly market for the more widely traded and stable currencies. All of the Canadian chartered banks buy and sell foreign currencies using a system of bid and ask quotations. There are also other brokers or dealers who perform the same trading functions, sometimes extending the service to other less frequently traded currencies on special orders from clients.

There are a number of reasons why exchange rates shift or change— often many points in one day. To get a better grasp of the factors behind the changes it is necessary to examine who is in the Foreign Exchange Market and why their demands and supplies change over time.

On the demand side for the domestic country's currency are those individuals and companies that need to make payments in that particular currency. These will be participants who need funds to purchase goods from that country and bring them to their own country. Foreign tourists will be consuming goods and services in that country as well as importing goods purchased from there. Foreign investors will either purchase financial assets such as bonds and shares or they will make direct investments in the physical plants and equipment operating and producing in that country.

Finally there are two other demanders of the country's currency. The first, speculators believe, unlike everyone else in the market, that the currency is

---

[1] For this discussion ignore the entries in the table referring to future exchange rates.

going to appreciate in value which means that the exchange ratio of that country's currency with all other world currencies is going to become smaller. The last participant is the government of that country; they may try to establish a stable value for the currency by selling foreign currencies and purchasing the domestic currency as downward pressure on the domestic currency occurs. This last phenomenon has become pervasive for many formerly strong economies in the world.

The suppliers for the domestic country's currency are the reciprocal participants of world trade and travel. Suppliers are the domestic importers who wish to sell their own currency to pay for foreign goods, tourists who plan to travel outside their own country, and speculators and other investors in currencies who do not desire to hold the country's monetary claims. Again the domestic government will be trading in the market, supplying the domestic currency in exchange for foreign currencies. This will occur when there is upward pressure on the relative value of the domestic currency. This last phenomenon has been observed in a limited number of countries in the world that have strong and stable economies. The fingers on one hand will, at the date of writing, be sufficient to count these fortunate few.

What makes these participants change their supply and demand for each country's currency relative to their supply and demand for other currencies? The answer to that question is an explanation of why exchange rates fluctuate over time. If changes in the factors that affect supply and demand can be predicted, then future exchange rates can be predicted. Specifically, there are three main factors; interest rates, changes in internal price levels, and government policy. Again, since all of these factors are interrelated the implications of one cannot be considered in isolation.

Interest Rates

Interest rates will affect exchange rates to the extent that interest rates are not in equilibrium between countries. For example, if the current interest rate in Canada on a one-year Government of Canada bond is 8% and the interest rate on a similar riskless security in the United States is 6%, then if we assume that the inflation rate is the same in both countries and the rate of exchange is $1 Canadian to $1 U.S., there should be a movement by American and foreign investors holding U.S. government securities to sell their securities in the U.S., and purchase Canadian dollars so as to purchase the higher yielding Canadian security. This will increase the supply of U.S. government securities and increase the demand for the Canadian government security. This will reduce the price of the former and increase the price of the latter. The ultimate effect will be to increase U.S. interest rates and reduce Canadian rates. Simultaneously, both the increased supply of U.S. currency and demand for Canadian dollars will force the Canadian dollar above par with the U.S. dollar. In other words, it will take less than one Canadian dollar to purchase one American dollar.

The above forces will continue until an equilibrium of interest rates and exchange rates exists and there is no longer any incentive to move out of the financial assets of one country and into the other's. We must, however, warn that as stated before, the interest rates are also affected by other factors which means that we must in the above example arbitrarily assume that these other factors are, for the moment, fixed.

In Table 22–3 it is clear that exchange rates with respect to the Canadian dollar have not been stable and since 1976 have deteriorated. This is a reflection of Canada's domestic economy relative to the rest of the world and within that the rapid rise in the Canadian consumer price level over this period relative to other countries. This leads us to the second fundamental factor affecting the supply and demand of currencies — inflation.

TABLE 22–3 Exchange Rates; Canadian Dollars per Unit of Foreign Exchange

Year	United States[a] Dollar	Foreign Currency, Closing				
		British[b] Pound	French[b] Franc	German[b] Mark	Swiss[b] Franc	Japanese[b] Yen
1967	1.0787	2.9658	0.2193	0.2706	0.2493	0.002979
1968	1.0775	2.5794	0.2176	0.2699	0.2496	0.002989
1969	1.0768	2.5739	0.2078	0.2746	0.2497	0.003005
1970	1.0440	2.5016	0.1889	0.2863	0.2422	0.002916
1971	1.0098	2.4687	0.1833	0.2900	0.2456	0.002912
1972	0.9905	2.4797	0.1965	0.3108	0.2594	0.003270
1973	1.0001	2.4533	0.2257	0.3782	0.3175	0.003696
1974	0.9780	2.2884	0.2035	0.3785	0.3295	0.003354
1975	1.0173	2.2594	0.2377	0.4144	0.3942	0.003430
1976	0.9861	1.7811	0.2067	0.3920	0.3947	0.003327
1977	1.0635	1.8571	0.2165	0.4586	0.4444	0.003980
1978						
Jan.	1.1011	2.1319	0.2335	0.5203	0.5550	0.004569
Feb.	1.1132	2.1604	0.2301	0.5365	0.5854	0.004637
March	1.1256	2.1467	0.2391	0.5537	0.5937	0.004865
April	1.1416	2.1120	0.2489	0.5594	0.6006	0.005151
May	1.1189	2.0350	0.2409	0.5319	0.5702	0.004952
June	1.1216	2.0610	0.2449	0.5382	0.5952	0.005242
July	1.1245	2.1321	0.2535	0.5476	0.6247	0.005633

Source: Bank of Canada Review, August 1978
[a]Average noon
[b]Average of spot rates

Inflation

This is a more dynamic factor. If the inflation rate in Canada is expected by the participants in the Foreign Exchange Market to be above that in the United States, then investors will prefer to hold securities denominated in United States dollars. As before, investors are concerned about the purchasing power of their wealth. The longer inflation remains a problem, the greater the decline in the value of a country's currency. People prefer to hold a stable currency and the greater the changes in the price level, the greater the uncertainty about future losses in purchasing power. This will be directly reflected in the diminished demand for the currency and the increased demand for the currencies of countries with a relatively more stable price level. Changes in the relative value of two countries' currencies, holding all other factors constant, is a statement by investors and those who must trade in the currencies of these countries about their expectations of the future changes in the price levels of the two countries.

Government Policy

Interest rates and changes in the price level both systematically effect exchange rates. However, governments can influence these factors as well as intervene directly in the trading of the country's currency. Many governments in the world set the price of their currency vis-a-vis all others. This is the practice in the Communist world and some third world countries where rapid changes in the exchange values of their currencies could be disastrous to the internal economic policies of the governments. Further, for a variety of reasons, governments can and do restrict the trading of their currency in and out of the country. They can prohibit their citizens from holding foreign currencies and they can prohibit foreign investors in the country from withdrawing profits and/or capital simply by refusing to sell the investors the foreign currencies.

On a more indirect level the normal process of maintaining an equilibrium of purchasing power among countries will be hampered if countries arbitrarily control the level of trade across their borders. Tariffs and import quotas serve to constrain the supply of domestic currency and the demand for foreign currency in countries that use such practices. These barriers to freer trade may cause similar reactions by other countries and the result is a reduction in the efficient allocation of resources in world markets.

All factors mentioned contribute to the establishment of exchange ratios. The greater stability of the country's economic and political system, the greater the stability in the demand and supply of the country's currency. For the participants in the trading of that country's currency, the less fluctuation in its value and the freer the trade in the currency, the less risk exposure the investors may have to bear. It is ultimately the government of the country and the discretionary powers it holds that will determine the relative rate of exchange of its currency with others. Foreign investors and all those people and corporations who must or are considering dealing in another country's currency should, simultaneously, take a serious look at the government of that country.

INTERNATIONAL MARKETS AND FOREIGN TRADE RISKS

We have up to this point talked about exchange rates in the present tense. That is, we have considered the rate of exchange for currencies that are paid for and delivered all at the same time. This exchange rate is called the *spot rate of exchange.* Another type of trade also occurs in the Foreign Exchange Market. This is the agreement between a demander and supplier to trade currencies at some set date in the future (1 to 12 months) at an exchange rate agreed upon today. These rates are called *forward rates* and will differ from the spot rates depending on the markets' expectations of the future values of the two currencies. The forward exchange markets provide participants in international transactions the opportunity to protect themselves against unexpected future changes in exchange rates.

In what situations would there be an incentive to enter such an agreement? In the international market, sellers of goods to customers in foreign countries face more unknowns than they would operating in their own domestic market. Often credit must be extended to foreign companies for several months while the goods are in transit between countries. The credit worthiness of the purchasers may have to be taken on faith and as well, there is the risk that the purchasing country's government may not allow the company to pay in the selling country's currency because of controls or restrictions. One more risk exists. Suppose the price agreed upon has been set in the purchasing country's monetary unit. If there is a three-month delay on the eventual payment, then there is a chance that the exchange rate may change in the interim. Thus the seller of the goods (the exporter) bears the risk that when the payment is made, the actual amount of the payment received by the seller in his own currency may be different than expected when the transaction was initiated. Conversely, if the price of the products is set in the exporter's currency, the purchaser of the goods bears the risk. At the end of three months when payment is due, the purchaser's currency may be worth less and to complete the transaction will be more costly. Therefore every international transaction exposes one of the parties to exchange rate risk. The party that bears the risk depends on the currency in which the transaction is denominated.

LESSENING FOREIGN TRANSACTIONS RISKS

Forward Markets

The forward exchange market provides foreign trades with the opportunity to remove the risk of fluctuating exchange rates. For example, if a large Canadian company borrows on the U.S. money markets then the interest and principal payments must be made in U.S. dollars. A company such as Ontario Hydro which does raise funds in the U.S. will need to budget its projected cash flow of interest payments to service this debt. To eliminate the risk of exchange rate changes on the day of payment, Ontario Hydro could purchase a forward agreement to buy U.S. dollars at a set rate today for delivery six months from today. Referring to Table 22-2 the six-month forward rate on U.S. dollars is $1.1725 Canadian. This means that Ontario Hydro, by entering the forward market, knows today that it will pay $1.1725 Canadian for each U.S. dollar of interest payments it will make six months from today, regardless of what the actual spot rate happens to be on that date in the future.

This market is useful for both buyers and sellers of currencies as the total cost of the payment is known with certainty sufficient time in advance so that the budgeting of cash flows into the future is evaluated accurately. Table 22-3 indicates the wide swings in value the Canadian dollar has taken relative to other currencies. The forward market provides protection which is necessary, especially when contracts involving millions of dollars must be paid in a foreign currency. Even small fluctuations could be costly to a firm.[2]

Other Techniques   The credit risk of trading with foreign purchases can also, in some cases, be eliminated for Canadian export companies. The Export Development Corporation (E.D.C.), a Crown corporation, sells insurance for foreign receivables. The insurance is available to firms that export consumer goods with credit terms of up to 180 days and for the export of capital goods with credit of up to a maximum of five years. The E.D.C. will not, however, protect exporters against exchange rate fluctuations.

The risk that the foreign purchaser's government will intervene to stop or alter the terms of the agreement can never be avoided. Nevertheless, the risk can be minimized in several ways. The simplest is to demand payment immediately in the selling country's currency. If the foreign government is going to intervene, it will have to do so immediately. This may not be the best answer, however, as this policy may preclude the opportunity of sales to a substantial number of potential customers. The alternative is to research the past actions of the foreign government to determine if it is inclined to restrict trade in such ways as to make the sale unprofitable. This, again, is not an easy

---

[2]If an exporter sells a product priced in the customer's currency, the exchange rate risk can be removed through the forward market. The exporter enters the forward market and promises to provide the foreign currency in (say) three months at the existing forward exchange rate.

task but when the stakes are high, the expenditure of time and funds may be well worthwhile. Large banks and commodity brokers, in many instances, can be of valuable assistance and provide relevant information.

EVALUATION OF FOREIGN INVESTMENT OPPORTUNITIES

More foreign companies have invested in Canada through Canadian subsidiary companies than Canadian companies have established foreign corporate operations. The list of foreign companies (primarily U.S.) that have Canadian subsidiaries is lengthy. Canadian companies that have interests abroad are in most cases in the manufacturing sector. Table 22–4 gives the reader an idea of the diversity of the types of products Canadian companies manufacture and sell abroad.

TABLE 22–4   Example of Canadian Multinational Companies

Company	Products Manufactured
Bata	Footwear products
Inco	Nickel mining and copper mining
Massey Ferguson	Farm machinery
Moore Corporation	Business forms
George Weston	Food products and retail stores

In the following discussion and case example, we will consider the investment analysis required when a firm is considering expansion into a new market and country. This type of evaluation process and its fundamental concepts can be applied to companies found in most Western countries including Canada.

However, many Canadian companies are foreign-controlled subsidiaries. Since the parent company is interested in the maximization of its world-wide profits, it may make financial and investment decisions in its foreign-based subsidiary that are different from the decisions that would be made by the subsidiary if it were domestically owned. In fact, the international organization of a multinational company can be viewed as a totally domestic company with a number of operating divisions.

The potential for different decisions made by a company depending on whether the company is owned by foreigners or nationals has led to extensive debate on the implications for the Canadian economy of foreign-controlled firms. In fact, the purpose for establishing the Foreign Investment Review Agency (FIRA) was to screen take-overs of Canadian companies by foreign companies to ensure that the take-over would be of benefit to Canada.

It is not our intention to evaluate either the arguments for and against foreign ownership of Canadian business or the necessity for a screening agency such as FIRA. However, an understanding of the problems faced by companies setting up foreign subsidiaries and the decision criteria used by the parent companies will provide the reader with an understanding of why foreign-controlled firms and their parents operate as they do.

CASE EXAMPLE

Since 1972, when Mid-West achieved full integration of its domestic and international capital budgeting procedures, all investment proposals, domestic and foreign, have been required to go through an established screening process: each proposal is subjected to a cash flow analysis, which results in a net present value calculation, and all proposals compete for funds on their individual merits.

Although Mid-West uses the *NPV* method to evaluate projects, the firm's management realizes that there are some significant differences between domestic and international investments. These differences relate primarily to two factors: (1) the political and financial environments of the host countries, and (2) the fact that two cash flow analyses must be performed for each of the foreign investment proposals—one for the project itself, and one for cash flows from the foreign project to the parent. The effects of these two factors on the application of capital budgeting theory are discussed in this section.

The Screening Process (Analysis of the Host Country)

In November, 1978, Mr. Bronson was approached by the government of Andovia, a West African republic, with a request that his company establish a cocoa processing plant there. Although this request was received as a direct result of one of Bronson's visits to Africa, it was immediately referred to Mid-West International for screening and analysis, as all foreign proposals are, regardless of their origin.

For administrative purposes, Mid-West International has separated the countries of the world into four areas: Europe, Africa and the Middle East, Latin America, and the Far East. The manager of each area group is responsible for the initial screening of all investment proposals for any country within this area. The primary function of this initial screening is to analyze the political environment of the proposed host country and to determine whether or not the economic environment would be receptive to the proposed project.

The initial screening of the cocoa processing plant proposal showed that Andovia was generally receptive to foreign direct investments. Further, according to the latest industrial policy statement of the Andovian government, food processing plants were to be given highest priority because they would reduce the nation's need for imports and thus save foreign exchange. The country had no plans to nationalize any business, and its constitution states that if nationalization becomes desirable in the public interest, adequate, prompt, and effective compensation is guaranteed. At the time of the analysis, no foreign firm had ever been nationalized, although the electric utilities and railroads were nationalized shortly after the country gained its independence in 1948.

Andovia is one of the world's largest producers of cocoa, but virtually the entire crop of 2.5 million tons a year is exported unprocessed. For such products as chocolate, chocolate milk, Ovaltine, and other beverages made of cocoa, the 62 million Andovians depended almost entirely on imports. Thus, the country found itself in the position of first exporting the raw material and then importing the finished product. The government viewed the correction of this situation as an important economic task, making it likely that Mid-West International would experience very favorable tax treatment.

Analysis of the International Environment

The favorable preliminary report on the project was sent to the office of Robert Harris, the president of Mid-West International, for the second screening stage. Here, the analysis shifts from sole concern with the host country environment to what may be called the "international environment". At this stage, the emphasis centers on such factors as whether the company has the experience to handle the project; whether the project conflicts with other proposals; whether the market could be better served in some other way; and how the project could be integrated into Mid-West's continuing efforts to manage and allocate working capital on a worldwide basis.

Since Mid-West International already had overseas units in the food processing industry, the Andovian proposal would benefit from the company's prior experience. Also, since the host government had indicated that it was willing to place an import tax on cocoa products once production was started, the market would enjoy a protected status. Finally, it was determined that although minor adjustments in some working capital allocations would be required, the anticipated export sales of the project was expected to provide an inflow of hard currency that would reduce the need for some hedging operations and thus reduce costs.

Financial Analysis

The third stage of the screening process involves a standard financial analysis. Although foreign investment proposals are subject to a number of political and international constraints not associated with domestic investments, once these constraints have been considered, Mid-West's policy is that each project should undergo a financial cash flow evaluation to determine whether the project has a positive risk-adjusted *NPV*. There is, however, an important difference in the application of cash flow analysis to a foreign investment: for foreign investments, there must be two sets of cash flow analyses—one for the project itself and one for the parent company.

Factors Affecting the Cash Flows

Demand Forcast   As with any investment proposal, the first step in the analysis of the Andovian project was a forecast of demand. For Andovia, as is often the case for developing countries, there simply were no reliable figures on past cocoa consumption. There were, however, fairly good data on imports of cocoa products, and since almost no cocoa was then processed locally, these figures could be used to estimate past consumption. These past usage estimates were correlated with population, income, and other factors, and, on the basis of population and income projections, were used to develop the estimated demand figures given in Table 22–5.

TABLE 22–5   Estimated Demand for Cocoa Products

Year	Tons
1978	285,000
1979	291,000
1980	297,000
1981	304,000
1982	310,000
1983	316,000
1984	322,000
1985	328,000
1986	335,000
1987	342,000

Duties and Taxes   In arriving at the cash flow figures for a foreign investment, particular attention must be given to the fact that since the transactions to be analyzed flow across national boundaries, a unique set of tax laws and customs duties may be applicable. In the case of Andovia, the government agreed that Mid-West could, under the Andovian Industrial Development Act of 1969, enjoy an income tax holiday for five years, and could also import, duty-free, any new production equipment and materials that could not be obtained from local sources. Used equipment could be imported under a relatively low duty of 10 percent. After five years of production, Mid-West International would be subject to a 40 percent income tax, plus a "super-tax" of 25 percent of all income over 15 percent of equity capital. The super-tax, introduced in 1967 as part of Andovia's Social Reform Act, was originally scheduled to expire in 1980 but it appears that the tax will be extended. If this tax is ever eliminated or reduced, Mid-West's profit potential will, of course, increase.

Applicable Exchange Rates   Another unique feature of foreign investment analysis is that the transactions being examined frequently involve currency transfers, so foreign exchange rates and restrictions must be taken into account. When there is an official rate of exchange and that rate is stable, no problems are presented. However, if the exchange rate is allowed to "float", the evaluation process is more complicated; it becomes necessary to forecast the rate of exchange that may be applicable to future transactions. Although the Andovian government allowed the pound to float for a few months after the U.S. dollar devaluation of February 1973, it soon became apparent that an equilibrium rate of exchange had been reached at about $2.80 Canadian to one Andovian pound. The Andovian government announced in June 1973 that this new rate would be established as the official rate. Mid-West International's screening report indicated that it was safe to assume that the current rate of exchange of $2.80 to one Andovian pound ($2.80:1) would be maintained for the foreseeable future.[3]

Recognizing that many countries closely regulate who may purchase foreign exchange, the screening report also discussed exchange availability. In Andovia, the Central Bank is responsible for the administration of the exchange control regulations. Under those regulations, permission is required to purchase Canadian dollars with Andovian pounds for payment of loan interest, management fees, royalties, home office administration expenses, and most other billings for services rendered by an overseas supplier. Moreover, even if permission to purchase foreign exchange is given, Andovia is frequently so short of foreign exchange that it is simply not available. The screening report indicated that, because of the heavy burden that the armament program had imposed on the country's exchange reserves, applications for permission are subject to considerable delay. Furthermore, the granting of permission does not ensure that the related exchange will be available. In general, the allocation of foreign exchange is administered by the country's commercial banks, and each bank can allocate to its customers only such amounts as are made available to it by the Central Bank.

Reinvestment and Restrictions on Repatriation of Profit   Andovian law restricts repatriation of profits to 70 percent of the net income, as defined by law, during a given accounting period. Thus, regardless of the actual cash flows that might be generated during any period, there is a limit on the amount that can be transferred to the parent company. Since there was nothing to indicate that there would be any change in this law, it would have the effect of forcing Mid-West International to reinvest 30 percent of net income each year in its Andovian operation.

To satisfy this required reinvestment, Mid-West International's analysis

---

[3]The Canadian dollar trades in the world money markets close to the value of the U.S. dollar. After 1973 with the U.S. dollar floating, the Canadian dollar also was permitted to float although its value remained relatively close to that of the U.S. dollar. In more recent times, the Canadian dollar had depreciated to a value considerably below par with the U.S. dollar. See Table 22–3.

suggested that the initial plant should be smaller than actual demand requirements. Then it could use the required retained earnings to expand in later years. Between the expansion required to meet current demand and the normal demand growth, it was anticipated that there would be no difficulty in profitably employing the required investment.

Analysis of Cash Flows

One of the major modifications that must be made when the capital budgeting process is applied to a foreign investment is that two sets of interrelated cash flows must be analyzed. Mid-West invests funds to generate cash flows that can, ultimately, be paid out as dividends to its shareholders. For domestic investments, because no restrictions are placed on the use of funds, simple *NPV* analysis of cash flows is sufficient to evaluate the project. In the case of overseas projects, attention must be given to how and when cash flows can be made available to the parent company. As we have already seen, transfers of funds may be constrained either by direct restrictions or because the host country does not have foreign exchange available.

If the earnings in country A are restricted, while the earnings in country B's currency are freely convertible to dollars and are transferable either to the parent company or to other operating units, a rate of return of 25 percent in country A may be less desirable than a 20 percent return in country B. Although a multinational firm is certainly concerned with the profitability of each investment, it is equally concerned with the amount of earnings that are freely convertible and transferable. Thus, the multinational firm is ultimately concerned with the present value of the *net available inflows to the parent company.*

The general procedures for cash flow analysis are the same for a foreign investment as for a domestic investment. For the foreign investment, however, there are several inflow and outflow items that are not usually associated with the domestic investment. The flow involved in Mid-West's proposed cocoa processing plant investment serves both to illustrate these items and to show the interrelations between cash flows from the project and cash flows to the parent company.

Project Cash Inflows   The major cash inflows shown in the top section of Table 22-6 are from sales in Andovia. These sales show a rapid increase during the first three years as the operation moves toward full production; after that, projected increases in sales are closely related to the growth in population.[4] It is also anticipated that once full production is reached, any surplus over local demand will be exported. Because all foreign exchange earnings must be turned over to the Central Bank, the export sales, like all the amounts in Table 22-6, are in Andovian pounds.

[4]The sales figures given in Table 22-6 are expected values derived from a probability distribution that incorporates the various elements of risk associated with the project.

TABLE 22-6 Andovian Cocoa Processing Plant Proposal, 10-Year Cash Flow (Thousands of Andovian Pounds)*

Year	1	2	3	4	5	6	7	8	9	10
Cash inflows										
Andovian sales		22,500	47,200	72,100	76,400	78,600	81,400	83,600	86,000	88,900
Export sales				500	500	500	500	500	500	500
Terminal value										200
Total Inflows		22,500	47,200	72,600	76,900	79,100	81,900	84,100	86,500	89,600
Cash outflows										
New fixed assets	2,500	178	178	178	178	178	178	178	178	178
Used equipment	1,000									
Plant expansion		200	200							
Out-of-pocket set-up costs	400	200								
Raw material		20,700	41,400	62,000	62,400	62,800	63,000	63,200	63,400	63,600
Labor costs		379	782	1,258	1,332	1,408	1,479	1,553	1,724	1,775
Sales and administrative expense		2,500	5,000	7,500	7,700	7,800	8,200	8,400	8,600	8,800
Supervisory fee		43	57	89	89	89	89	89	89	89
Local taxes							2,890	3,605	4,220	5,075
Total Outflows	3,900	24,200	47,617	71,025	71,699	72,275	75,836	77,025	78,211	79,517
Net Cash Receipts	-3,900	-1,700	-417	1,575	5,201	6,825	6,064	7,075	8,289	10,083

* A token terminal value of 200 Andovian pounds is used for the project.

TABLE 22-7 Cash Flows Associated with Andovian Proposal (Thousands of Canadian Dollars)

	Year	1	2	3	4	5	6	7	8	9	10
Cash inflows											
Yearly inflows from project		-10,924	-4,641	-1,008	4,661	14,817	19,366	17,235	20,067	23,467	28,492
Terminal value											500
Total inflows		-10,924	-4,641	-1,008	4,661	14,817	19,377	17,235	20,067	23,467	28,992
Cash outflows											
Canadian income tax*		-200	-100	-25	2,237	7,112	9,295	117			
Canadian tax on supervisory fee			57	76	119	119	119	119	119	119	119
Div. Withholding tax†			42	132	225	331	438	627	735	832	1,053
Export sales loss (after tax)					800	800	800	800	800	800	800
Total outflows		-200	-1	183	3,381	8,362	10,652	1,723	1,654	1,751	1,972
Net available inflows		-10,724	-4,640	-1,191	1,280	6,455	8,714	15,512	18,413	21,716	27,020
Discount factor (10%)		.91	.83	.75	.68	.62	.56	.51	.47	.42	.39
Present value		-9,759	-3,851	-893	870	4,002	4,880	7,911	8,654	9,121	10,538
Cumulative net present value‡		-9,759	-13,610	-14,503	-13,633	-9,631	-4,751	3,160	11,814	20,935	31,473

* Canadian income taxes decline in the seventh year and disappear thereafter because the firm is given a credit on Canadian taxes for payments of Andovian taxes.
† Tax paid to Andovian government on dividends.
‡ If the project terminates after any given year, its *NPV* will be the figure in this last row under the year in question. For example, if the project operates as projected for ten years, its *NPV* will be $31,473,000.

Project Cash Outflows The lower portion of Table 22-6 shows the expected project outflows. The projected outflows for the first year — the construction period — consist primarily of expenditures for new and used assets and costs of preparing operations. After the first year, the major expenditures are for raw materials, labor, and other normal operating expenses as outlined in the table. Since Mid-West would be expanding the capacity of the processing plant, expenditures for fixed assets would continue, but at a much lower rate.

There are two expenses that are somewhat unusual. The first is a supervisory fee—Mid-West Manufacturing Company would supply the Andovian unit with certain supervisory personnel, for a fee. The second is local taxes—in accordance with Mid-West's agreement with the Andovian government, there would be no tax liability for the first five years of operations. After that, income taxes would be paid at the normal Andovian corporate tax rate.

The final row in Table 22-6 shows the net cash receipts for each year. Cash flows are negative for the first three years, but they rise rapidly thereafter.

Parent Company Cash Flows If this analysis were for a domestic investment, the yearly cash flow figures obtained in Table 22-6 would be discounted at the cost of capital to arrive at a net present value figure. For a foreign proposal, however, this is only the first stage; the multinational firm must be concerned with net inflows that will be available for dividends or employment elsewhere. Since net cash flows calculated in Table 22-6 might be restricted because of various laws and regulations, it is necessary to develop a second cash flow analysis to show the unencumbered net present values that would be available to the parent company.

Inflows to the parent company would come primarily from the project's net cash flows, the figures on the bottom line of Table 22-6. The parent company would also receive supervisory fees, so total potential repatriated cash flows, shown in dollars on the top line of Table 22-7, are the sum of these two items. Note that Table 22-7 is stated in Canadian dollars, whereas Table 22-6 was stated in Andovian pounds.[5] A terminal value for the project is expected in year 10; this figure, added to those in row one, constitutes the tenth year cash inflow.

Offsetting these inflows, however, are the several outflows shown in the lower section of Table 22-7, the first of which is for Canadian income tax. There is a tax liability offset for the first three years, resulting from a Canadian tax regulation that permits Mid-West to offset the losses of the foreign subsidiary against income from its other operations. After the initial loss period, parent company income results in a Canadian tax liability. However, this liability

---

[5]The official rate of exchange established by the Andovian government was $2.8011:1, and this is the rate used to calculate the cash inflow amounts used in Table 22-7.

may be reduced by the amount of taxes paid by the subsidiary in the host country. Since, under Andovian law, Mid-West would not be required to pay any taxes for the first five years of operation, this provision would not be effective until the sixth year of the project. Other Canadian tax liabilities that would be incurred by the parent company are also shown in Table 22–7.

Recall that after the cocoa processing reaches full production, any surplus will be sold in the export market. Since any export sales made by the Andovian operations would be, to some extent, at the expense of Mid-West's other units serving those markets, the after-tax sales losses suffered by those units should be taken into account. This factor is shown as export sales losses (after tax) in Table 22–7.

Assuming that the project works out as planned, the *NPV* for the parent company is obtained by subtracting the present value of the required outflows from the present value of the anticipated inflows. As shown in Table 22–7, cash flows are discounted at the project's estimated cost of capital to arrive at a present value figure for each year,[6] the final amounts given in the table are cumulative net present values. We see that the project, from the parent company's standpoint, is in the black in the fourth year and has broken even on a discounted cash flow basis—that is, the *NPV* is zero—during the seventh year.

Problems Faced by Multinational Firms*

Mid-West's board of directors must give final approval for all capital expenditures in excess of $1 million; since the Andovian project fell into this category, the board had to approve it before the project could be undertaken. Robert Harris, who is president of Mid-West International, and several members of this staff were requested to attend the board's budget meeting in order to answer any questions that might be raised.

During the discussion on the project, Charles Anderson, one of the board members, mentioned that he had just finished reading a survey of 166 international executives who had been asked to list the problems that concerned them most. The consequences of both foreign and domestic government actions, which most of those surveyed saw as beyond their control, were uppermost in their minds. Anderson, to demonstrate that this fear of foreign government action was certainly a legitimate concern, cited the nationalizations that had taken place in Peru and Chile, and the restrictions on foreign businesses being formulated by other South American countries. Specifically, Anderson wondered whether the Andovian government, although it presently had no intention of nationalizing any foreign firms, might not do so

[6] A cost of capital of 10 percent was used on the assumption that 10 percent is the overall company cost of capital and that this project carries about the same risk as the average investment of the company. If the investment were considered to be more risky, then a higher discount rate should be used. Examples that will increase the risk of the project are exchange rate and expropriation risks. To the extent that the firm cannot diversify away these risks, the risk adjusted discount rate must increase.

* This section is based on *Managerial Finance, 6th edition*, by Weston and Brigham.

in the future if this was deemed to be in the Andovian public interest. He went on to say that if nationalization should occur, all of Mid-West's carefully developed cash flow analyses would be useless.

President Harris agreed that since nationalization appeared to be on the rise throughout the world, there was always some risk that a country might decide to nationalize foreign firms. He pointed out, however, that Andovia had recently emphasized its intention of adhering to international law and had promised to pay prompt and adequate compensation if it should ever nationalize a foreign firm. He added that, as long as Mid-West made a net contribution to the Andovian economy, the likelihood of nationalization was relatively small.

Harris explained his position, noting that in some cases host countries do have reasons for being unhappy with foreign businesses: When an industry is controlled from outside, the host country may pay quite a price. For one thing, if exhaustible natural resources such as minerals or oil are involved, the primary wealth of the host nation may be drained off without regard for the local economy. Further, the host country may lose tax revenue because the foreign corporation can report lower profits by manipulating transfer prices between subsidiaries. Also, when the parent company uses its financial network to pull money out of a country with balance of payment problems, or to move money into one struggling to reduce inflation, then the host government rightfully feels that it is losing control over its domestic economy. In addition, if a company uses its international flexibility to reroute a subsidiary's purchases through some other country, then it may cause a sudden drop in the host country's exports. Harris stated that, finally, a country's economy can be upset if a foreign company suddenly decides to pull out, as several had done in Europe because they had overinvested and wanted to consolidate their operations.

Here Bronson, the chairman of the board, entered the discussion to add that it was company policy to maintain good relations with its host governments, and the cocoa processing plant would make several major contributions toward that end. In the first place, according to Bronson, building a large plant and starting a new industry would benefit Andovia's economy in output, employment, and expanded tax revenues. Second, since Mid-West would introduce more advanced equipment than was presently being used, local labor skills would be upgraded. Since Mid-West planned to train local administrators for almost all positions, management talent would be increased. Bronson held that of great importance was the fact that Mid-West would provide Andovian consumers with a better and cheaper product.

To summarize the discussion, Harris pointed out that the presence of foreign businesses could have both advantages and disadvantages for a host country. He felt that the issue was not which side was right or wrong but, rather, whether the two parties could work together to arrive at a mutually beneficial arrangement. He felt that the best way to counter nationalism was to demonstrate that the investment would make a net contribution to the host country's economy. Harris reminded the group that the Andovian government had been first to suggest the project. Since then, there had been several meetings with various Andovian government agencies, and Mid-West had agreed to consult with them on any decision that could adversely affect their country. Harris, concluded that, although there was certainly no way to be sure that the situation would remain stable, at the present time nationalization did not appear to be a problem. Still, he did concede that in the analysis of the Andovian project, Mid-West had not given much weight to the possibility of nationalization when developing the estimated cash flows.[7]

Another board member, John Merriam, vice-president of Mid-West's Toronto bank, spoke up. He pointed out that many countries had recently experienced devaluation. Although the report on the Andovian project mentioned that the official position of the government was to maintain the present exchange, it also stated that foreign exchange had been in short supply recently. He said that it had been Merriam's experience that a short supply of foreign exchange often preceded devaluation, and he wanted to know if a full investigation of the Andovian situation had been made.

In reply, Harris explained that as a result of some unanticipated devaluations in the first year of foreign operations, Mid-West International had developed a devaluation monitoring procedure that, under normal circumstances, is applied on a monthly basis to each country in which the firm has operations. For potentially troublesome areas, the procedure is repeated more frequently either until the trouble has passed or until action has been taken to minimize the loss. The devaluation monitoring procedure consists, basically, of a constant examination of several items that often are indicators of currency weakness: inflation, balance of trade, balance of payments, deficits in the national budget, trends in interest rates, the international reserve position, and foreign exchange quotations.

Harris assured the board members that Andovia had been subjected to the same examination as other countries. It had been determined that, while there was a shortage of foreign exchange and a trade deficit until recently, most of the problems could be attributed to the civil war of three years ago. Improvement had been made in the balance of trade, and for each of the last two years there had been a small net increase in Andovia's international reserve position. In addition, the rate of inflation had been rather low, at about 2 to 3 percent, and the government had been successful in its efforts to hold down budget deficits. With the new petroleum tax decreed in 1970, and with the foreign exchange savings anticipated from import substitutions, it was most probable that the situation would continue to improve. Nevertheless, a close watch over the condition would be maintained.

Harris was also questioned about the steps that were taken when the

[7]The values given in Tables 22–6 and 22–7 are expected values determined from probability distributions of cash flows. The probability of nationalization, and of the losses in this event, was given a low weight in the analysis.

devaluation monitoring procedure indicated that a given currency was vulnerable to devaluation. Before he could answer, Don March, manager of the research division and a new member of the board, asked a more fundamental question: How would an Andovian devaluation hurt Mid-West Manufacturing? Harris replied that there would be an effect since the cash flows (shown in Table 22–6) were stated in Andovian pounds. These pounds were converted to Canadian dollars at the current rate of 2.80 dollars to 1 pound. If the Andovian pound was devalued, fewer dollars could be obtained for each pound, so the dollar value of the Andovian project would be reduced.[8]

Harris stated that if a devaluation appeared imminent the company attempted to accelerate funds flows to the parent, and to take on liabilities payable in local currencies, in order to minimize the danger of losses. In the Andovian case, not very much could be done along those lines, but since Harris felt there was little danger of devaluation, he thought the possibility of devaluation losses should not stand in the way of accepting the project.

John Merriam, the banker on the board who had first brought up the topic of devaluation, reentered the conversation, noting that it was the United States that had twice devalued the dollar with the result that the major trading nations were allowing their currencies to float. Merriam then quizzed Harris as to what action, if any, Mid-West was taking to prevent losses that could arise from changes in the floating rates. Harris readily admitted that the company had little experience in this field but that since March of 1973, when the float was put into effect, the "forward market" had been used several times to hedge certain international transactions. As an example, Harris described a recent contract to purchase machinery made in Germany for delivery six months hence for the equivalent of $200,000 in marks. To lock the dollar price of this machinery, the company had simply purchased a six-month forward contract for marks at a dollar price only slightly higher than the current dollar-to-mark exchange rate. Harris explained that although there was a slight cost involved, the use of the forward market effectively reduced the risk involved with floating exchange rates.

Following this explanation, Merriam and several other directors began to discuss the current international monetary situation and how the trends might affect Mid-West's overseas operations. During this discussion one of the directors pointed out that the International Monetary Fund meeting in September, 1973, had as its main topic international monetary reforms. Merriam noted that as a result of this meeting, it was clear that the direction of future reforms would be toward reestablishment of a modified fixed-rate system, one with a semiautomatic exchange procedure determined by some

[8]A second effect which follows from the first is possible if the Canadian multinational company had listed securities in the United States securities markets. Recognizing that the value to the parent of all projects declines when a devaluation occurs, the U.S. accounting profession requires an immediate write-down to reflect the effects of the devaluation. If the Canadian company has listed securities, the Canadian Annual report will identify the extent of the write-down in a footnote to the annual statements.

A method for determining "exposure" to devaluation is contained in "Hedging Foreign Exchange Risks", Management Monograph No. 49, published by *Business International*.

indicator such as a country's foreign exchange reserves or balance of payments surplus or deficit. Merriam cautioned, however, that it would take some time for the details to be worked out and that implementation of any such reforms would take even longer to analyze.

After these comments, Chairman Bronson moved that the board vote to approve the Andovian project. The motion was seconded, and the project received the board's unanimous approval.

Financing the Project

Once the project was approved, Bronson asked Harris to outline his financing plans. Since the board had to approve any external financing that involved issues in excess of $1 million, Bronson felt that time would be saved by clearing the point up immediately.

Harris outlined the following: Plant construction and equipment costs for the project are estimated at $10 million, with another $7 million required for working capital, or $17 million in total. The Andovian Industrial Development Bank will make a loan of $1.5 million, and two local commercial banks will jointly lend another $1.5 million. Mid-West will supply $5 million of new equipment for which it will accept an 8 percent note; the Andovian government agrees that the interest payment on the note will in no way affect the allowable remittance of earnings.[9] Mid-West will also be permitted to supply, as part of its investment, $3 million worth of used equipment. Since there is no effective capital market in Andovia, the remaining $6 million will have to come from other sources. In accordance with Mid-West's policy of further development of international sources of funds, Harris proposed that the final $6 million be raised in the Euro-bond market.

Although Euro-Canadian dollar[10] loans were currently available at about 9 percent, well below their 1969 – 1970 high of 11 percent, Euro-bond rates were also very advantageous.

Harris noted that one Canadian company had just sold a German mark denominated Euro-bond issue with a yield of 7.26 percent. He felt that the Andovian subsidiary could float an issue at about the same rate if it were denominated in German marks and guaranteed by the parent company. A Mid-West issue in Canada would probably carry an 8½ percent rate. Thus, it was clear that Euro-bonds were less costly at the present time. Following a lengthy discussion of the capital restrictions prevailing in European countries and how they would effect a bond issue, the board approved a $3 million Euro-Canadian dollar loan to finance working capital and a Euro-bond issue of 4.8 million German marks (equivalent to $3 million) to finance the remaining

[9] An intercompany loan has an advantage over an equity investment in that it is unaffected by remittance restrictions and will return the full principal at maturity. Therefore, this aspect of Harris' plan got around the 30 percent freeze on earnings imposed by the Andovian government. Of course, Andovia realized this too, and consequently restricted the extent of intercompany loan financing.

[10] A "Euro-Canadian dollar" is a Canadian dollar deposited in a European bank, frequently a European branch of a Canadian bank.

requirements. Then with the project approved and the financing settled, the board adjourned.

SUMMARY

The level of international trade within the Canadian economy is significant. Goods, services and transfer payments flow continuously across the border to and from many countries of the world. For Canadian businesses, this requires an extra dimension of expertise to manage the planning of international financial decisions.

A number of additional risks must be considered. Fluctuating exchange rates are of a primary concern. The risk involved can be avoided through the use of forward exchange contracts which guarantee a certain rate of exchange of currencies on future deliveries of funds. The fundamental factors which drive exchange rates are reflected in the demand and supply of foreign currencies both on a daily basis and for future trading dates. Current and expected interest rates, inflation rates and government policy all interrelate to affect the exchange rates.

Importers and exporters must also deal with the problems of credit risk and the timing of payments and receipts with foreign companies. All companies must be concerned with the problems of possible exchange controls established by foreign governments to regulate the flow of funds out of their countries. As well, the stability of governments in some countries must be taken into consideration. Firms considering investments in foreign countries must be aware of the risks of nationalization and expropriation of assets as well as the possibility of control of profits and capital leaving foreign economies.

All of these factors were considered in the analysis of Mid-West's plan to establish a cocoa processing plant in Andovia, a country in West Africa. This example provides a synthesis of all issues and concerns and presents the successive stages of the analysis required to determine the economic feasibility of such undertakings. This is the approach that should be used by the holding or parent company. Financial management of a subsidiary or branch company will be quite similar to what is presented in early chapters except for the constraint of a parent which, in most cases, makes the final decisions so as to maximize the global return of the network of companies.

QUESTIONS

22-1. A Canadian commodity merchant has just purchased an order of desiccated coconut from Sri Lanka. The order is for 200,000 100 lb. bags c.i.f. (cost, insurance, freight) Toronto. Payment is to be in U.S. dollars 60 days from ordering. The coconut takes about 1 month to arrive after ordering.

  a. What risks are both the buyer and the seller facing in this transaction?

  b. To what extent can the risks be avoided?

22-2. Explain how each of the following might affect the exchange rates of currencies with the Canadian dollar:

  a. A rise in the Canadian inflation rate.

  b. A drop in the Canadian prime lending rate.

  c. An increase in the level of foreign travel by Canadians.

  d. An increase in the price of oil by OPEC countries.

22-3. Discuss how the imposition of price controls may affect the level of forward exchange rates.

22-4. Discuss what affect exchange controls and import quotas will have on trade and the exchange rate.

22-5. Using the Mid-West company's project as a basis, sketch an outline of the screening process that should be followed to evaluate the problems and worthiness of the foreign project.

22-6. Do you think that a discount rate of 10 percent is appropriate for each year of the Andovian project's life? Why?

22-7. How does Mid-West take account of uncertainty in the Andovian project example? What alternatives might it consider?

22-8. What factors are responsible for the difference between the cash flow of Mid-West's Andovian subsidiary and the cash flow to the parent firm?

22-9. In what ways might it benefit the parent company *not* to own 100 percent of the foreign subsidiary's common stock?

22-10. How useful is the Andovian "tax holiday" to Mid-West?

22-11. If all markets were "free," that is, if there were no trade restrictions such as import and export quotas and tariffs, would this tend to stimulate or retard the development of overseas subsidiaries vis-à-vis branches of a domestic firm?

External Growth: Mergers and Holding Companies

23 Growth is vital to the well-being of a firm; without it, a business cannot attract able management because it cannot give recognition in promotions or offer challenging, creative activity. Without able executives, the firm is likely to decline and die. Much of the material in the previous chapters dealing with analysis, planning, and financing has a direct bearing on the financial manager's potential contribution to the growth of a firm. Because of the central importance of the growth requirement, the present chapter focusses on strategies for promoting growth.

Merger activity is an important ingredient in the growth of firms, and financial managers are required both to appraise the desirability of a prospective purchase and to participate directly in evaluating the respective companies involved in a merger. Consequently, it is essential that the study of financial management provide the background necessary for effective participation in merger negotiations and decisions.

In some instances, business combinations are classified as one of mergers, consolidations or amalgamations. In Canada, the first two types are not defined in law but the third is. However, the U.S. legal definitions of the first two terms are used frequently in Canada. A *merger* is defined as a statutatory procedure whereby one of the constituent companies in a business combination takes title to the assets of the other one which loses its existence. A *consolidation* is a business combination in which none of the constituents remains but a new entity is formed. In Canada, an *amalgamation* has some of the characteristics of the U.S. definition of a merger. In this chapter, we will not distinguish between different types of business combinations and will refer to mergers as any business combination that forms

598

one economic unit from two or more previously independent ones.

ACQUISITION TECHNIQUES

A firm can acquire or merge with another firm by one of the three following techniques:
  i) acquisition of the assets,
  ii) acquisition of the shares, or
  iii) amalgamation.

The choice of the technique used will depend on the impact on the merging firms of a number of legal and tax issues which are the bread and butter of specialists in this area. In this section we will describe briefly each acquisition technique.

Acquisition of the Assets

The acquired company's assets, both fixed and current, are purchased for either cash or shares. The acquired company does not disappear as a result of the acquisition, but it is left with a considerable amount of cash as its only asset. The company then decides whether to pay a liquidating dividend to its shareholders and wind-up; or to use the cash to purchase shares in a number of corporations – i.e. to become a holding company. Under the Federal and most Provincial Corporations Acts, the shareholders of the acquired company must vote on the terms of the purchase. The terms are the result of involved negotiations between the managements of the merging firms. If there are any dissenting shareholders, they have an *appraisal right*; this provides them with the right to have the acquiring company purchase their shares at an appraised price.

Acquisition of the Shares

The most common technique to effect a merger is through the acquisition of shares. The method of payment for these shares can be either cash or shares of the acquiring company. When purchasing the shares, the acquiring company not only obtains the assets but also all the liabilities.

Amalgamation

An amalgamation occurs when two or more companies form one corporate entity based on statutory provisions of the appropriate Corporation Act. The terms of the amalgamation must be voted on by shareholders of all companies in the amalgamation. The terms are determined by negotiations of the managements involved. Finally, an appraisal right for dissenting shareholders exists under this technique.

MERGER CLASSIFICATION AND INCIDENCE

Mergers are generally classified into three categories: conglomerate, vertical and horizontal. Conglomerate mergers occur when the companies involved have unrelated production processes; or a corporation purchases, for control purposes, the shares of a company that is unrelated to it. The acquiring company in the latter type of merger is called a *holding company*. Mergers between companies which are linked in the production process as suppliers or customers are classified as vertical mergers. An example of this type of merger would be the acquisition of a coal company by a steel manufacturer. The final category, horizontal mergers, includes companies producing the same or closely related products.

In Table 23–1, the distribution of types of mergers is presented for both Canada and the United States. In Canada, since 1972, horizontal mergers have declined as a percent of total mergers and conglomerates have increased. Compared to the 1945 to 1961 experience, conglomerate mergers are much more important and vertical mergers have declined in importance. The same general conclusions follow in the U.S. experience.

The total number of major mergers has increased substantially since 1945. A major increase in merger activity began in 1968 and continued until 1973. Since that time period, merger activity has abated somewhat although it is still greater than the pre-1968 period.

In the total merger activity, mergers in which the acquiring company was non-Canadian are classified as foreign mergers. Over the period 1945 to 1976, foreign mergers averaged 33 percent of total merger activity. In 1974, the Canadian Government introduced the *Foreign Investment Review Act* (FIRA). The purpose of this Act was to screen mergers in which the acquiring company was foreign to ensure that the merger would be of ultimate benefit to Canada. If the merger did not meet the criteria set out by FIRA, it was rejected.

MERGERS AS AN INVESTMENT DECISION

As noted in Chapter 11, capital investment decisions involve both the outlay of funds in the present and a series of cash inflows in the future. In that chapter, we were interested in evaluating the profitability of undertaking various investment projects. Our conclusion was that only those projects which increased the stock price of the company should be undertaken. Investment decision criteria were derived which were consistent with the overriding goal of share price maximization. These criteria were to accept all projects which either had a net present value (*NPV*) greater than zero, or equivalently, had an

TABLE 23-1   Canadian Major[a] Merger Activity 1945–1976

| | Number of Mergers | | | Foreign Mergers as Percent of all Mergers | Distribution of Types of Mergers (percents) | | | | | |
| | | | | | Canada | | | United States | | |
Year	Total	Domestic	Foreign		Broad Horizontal	Conglomerate	Vertical	Broad Horizontal	Conglomerate	Vertical
1945	74	51	23	32						
1946	79	64	15	19						
1947	45	32	13	29						
1948	53	39	14	26						
1949	38	27	11	29						
1950	45	36	9	20						
1951	80	61	19	24						
1952	76	59	17	22						
1953	93	68	25	27						
1954	104	61	43	41						
1955	134	78	56	42						
1956	135	81	54	40						
1957	103	68	35	34						
1958	140	80	60	43	68	9	23	67	13	20
1959	186	120	66	36	(1945 through 1961)			(1948 through 1963)		
1960	203	110	93	46						
1961	238	148	90	38						
1962	185	106	79	43						
1963	129	88	41	32						
1964	204	124	80	39						
1965	235	157	78	33						
1966	203	123	80	39						
1967	228	143	85	37				70	21	9
1968	402	239	163	41				(for 1967)		
1969	504	336	168	33						
1970	427	265	162	38						
1971	338	245	143	37						
1972	429	302	127	30	69	19	12			
1973	352	252	100	28	69	19	13	53	35	13
1974	292	220	72	25	68	23	9	63	28	8
1975	299	211	88	29	59	31	10	55	35	10
1976	332	246	86	26	57	31	13	54(b)	35(b)	12(b)

[a] A major merger is defined as a merger that was of sufficient importance to be reported in the financial press.

(b) Estimate.

Source: D. Thompson, "Mergers, Effects, and Competition Policy: Some Empirical Guidance". A discussion paper presented at the National Conference on Competition Policy, University of Toronto, April 6, 1978.

internal rate of return in excess of the cost of capital.

It is our contention that a merger should be undertaken only if it is consistent with the overriding goal of the firm. Hence, the investment decision criteria derived in Chapter 11 are applicable in the merger decision. In the evaluation of a merger, the present value of incremental cash flows generated from the merger must be compared to the initial cost of the merger. The incremental cash flows will equal the cash flows from the acquired company plus any increased earnings (or reduced costs) derived from merging the companies. The estimation of the incremental cash flows is crucial and conditions under which they are expected to exist are considered in a subsequent section.

The cost of the merger is the actual cash paid for the acquired company or the dollar equivalent of the shares exchanged, based on the price per share of the acquiring company's shares, and the share exchange terms. For example, suppose the acquiring Company B, has a price per share of $50 as of the merger date, and the share exchange terms are one share of B in exchange for two shares of A, the acquired company. This means that B has paid $25 per share to obtain the shares of Company A. The total cost of the merger will equal the price paid by B times the number of shares of A outstanding.

To demonstrate the interrelationship between the net present value of a merger and the value of the acquiring firm, assume that a company with a stock price of $50 per share decides to take over a company in a totally unrelated field. The market price of the acquired company is $100 per share and this price reflects the value of the company as an independent, going concern. Suppose that the acquiring company anticipates that the incremental cash flows due to the merger will just equal the cash flows of the acquired firm, i.e. the total cash flow to the new merged firm is the sum of the cash flows of the constituent companies. If the acquiror pays the current market price per share to the acquired company's shareholders, i.e. the terms of the share exchange are two shares of the acquiror for every share of the acquired, then the *NPV* of the merger is zero and there will be no impact on the stock price of the acquiror. If the acquiror gives more favorable terms, i.e. pays a higher price, the net present value of the merger is negative. The acquired company's shareholders gain and the price per share of the acquiring company's shares falls. Therefore, if the post-merger earnings are expected to equal the sum of the pre-merger earnings of the merging companies, any share exchange that differs from the pre-merger stock price values will result in benefits to one set of shareholders and equivalent losses to the other set.

If the acquiror believes that the post-merger earnings will be in excess of the sum of the pre-merger earnings of the companies, then there are gains to the merger which can be divided between the companies. If the acquiror exchanges shares at the pre-merger stock prices, then the *NPV* of the merger is positive and the stock price of the acquiror will increase. This occurs because the stock price of the acquired firm does not reflect the benefits of the merger to the acquiring firm. With the increased benefits from the merger, the acquiring company can afford to give the acquired company a more generous price and still find the *NPV* of the merger profitable. In this case, the shareholders of both firms will gain.

The concept of a merger as an investment decision has been embraced by Molson Companies Ltd. of Montreal. Molson's president, as reported in the *Globe and Mail,* stated that in planning an acquisition "You'll only be ahead if you see a value in a company which the market cannot perceive". As a specific example, he referred to the acquisition of Diversey Corp. of Chicago where Diversey's compatability with Molson's marketing and distribution orientation is something the market would not have seen. Molson, then, appeared to undertake a merger only if it was expected to result in incremental earnings to Molson's in excess of the earnings of the acquired firm.

Finally, the decision whether to merge or to grow internally (given that the growth will be profitable) is also a form of investment decision. If the internal growth route is used, it will take longer for earnings to be realized, and there will be start-up problems such as finding managerial talent. If the merger route is taken, the problems noted above are reduced, but there may be problems integrating the new company's operations into the existing coimpany. In addition, the cost of merger may be higher than the cost of internal growth. All of these factors must be considered and evaluated within the investment decision framework.

MOTIVATIONS FOR MERGER

Since mergers can be considered as a form of an investment decision for the acquiring company, the acquiror must identify those potential merger partners which will result in an increase in earnings (or cash flows) over and above those that derive from the acquired company as an independent entity. In this section, we will describe the conditions under which these incremental earnings are most likely to occur. In the next section, we will investigate the second factor in the investment decision – the price that will be paid for the acquired firm.

Economic Motivations

Synergy   It is possible that a well-conceived merger will produce what is called a *synergistic* or a "two plus two equals five" effect. Through the merger, more profits are generated than could be achieved by the individual firms operating separately. Synergistic influences arise in two general ways. First, there is the classical argument from economics that as the firm grows in size, its costs grow less than proportionally. This is referred to as "economies of scale" and would result in increased profits. An example of this benefit would be the increased efficiency derived from integrating small plants. This type of synergistic effect occurs predominantly in horizontal mergers.[1] Second, there may be imperfect markets in the purchase and sale of certain assets such as management expertise, personnel, production facilities, and marketing. A merger may permit a more economical use of the asset and hence result in higher profits. For example, suppose Company A hires an efficient management team but they are so efficient that there is excess capacity. Company A would have preferred to pay only for the services needed in running its company, but the market is imperfect – Company A had to buy all of the management services or none. In this case, a merger will permit fuller use of the services of the management team without any increase in cost. This will result in an increase in profits to the acquiror in excess of the profits of the acquired firm. Of course, the excess capacity in the specialized assets may be found in the acquiring company. For example, a merger may result in the acquisition of a technically competent scientific or engineering staff which is required by the acquiring company. Or the acquiror may need to develop an effective sales organization to make up for a lack of an industrial sales organization, and merger is a solution to this problem.

This concept of using specialized assets more intensively appears to be an important ingredient in Molson's plans. Molson views itself as a multi-unit conglomerate, comprising several larger groups that have marketing and distribution expertise in common.

Financial Motivations

Risk Reduction   As noted in Chapter 12, combining products with different risk characteristics into a portfolio may reduce the variability of the earnings of the resulting company. Since it is questionable that this pure risk-reduced merger will increase the stock price of the firm, this motive for mergers may not be very crucial. In fact, if the company pays a premium to acquired companies, there could be a negative impact on the stock price of the acquiror. However, the risk reduction will reduce the default risk on the company's debt and this will be of benefit to the existing bondholders. With the lower default risk, interest rates will be lower and the maximum amount of debt that the firm can issue (the firm's debt capacity) will increase. Since interest payments on debt are a tax deductible expense, there is a benefit from higher leverage which accrues to current shareholders.[2]

---

[1]Another possible benefit from horizontal mergers is the acquisition of monopoly power. If this type of merger is not stopped by Anti-Combines legislation, then post-merger profits will be higher than the sum of pre-merger profits. This is not a benefit from synergy.
[2]In a pure conglomerate merger, the reduction of default risk will reduce the interest rate on new debt and thus increase the market value of debt. Since the merger has no synergistic effects, the increased market value of debt is matched by a reduction in the market value of equity. Thus, this pure financial effect will hurt existing

(Continued on page 605)

Changing Financial Variables   Suppose an existing independent company has a very low leverage rate or is paying out very little in dividends and investing the retained earnings in cash or marketable securities. If the acquiring company intends to change the leverage rate and thus obtain the benefits of the tax subsidy on debt, then the market value of the equity of the acquiring company will increase. If the acquiring company believes that a sub-optimal dividend policy of the acquired firm has depressed its stock price, then an acquisition will be of benefit. If, however, investors realize that the leverage or dividend policies of a company are inapproprioate, they also recognize that the company is a merger candidate. Thus, the current stock prices of these firms will reflect some part of the potential merger gains that will be obtained when these policies are changed and the potential benefits to the acquiring companies are reduced.

Increased Growth   It has been argued in the literature on mergers that growth, either in earnings per share or in sales, is an important motivation for mergers. This argument is based on the desire of the acquiring company's management to maintain an historic, or target, level of growth. To the extent that investors value growth *per se,* or if growth and profitability are correlated, then growth can be a legitimate motivation for mergers. If, however, growth is desired only by the management of the acquiring company, its impact on the market value of the acquiring firm will not be positive.

TERMS OF MERGERS

For every merger actually consummated, a number of other potentially attractive combinations fail during the negotiating stage. In some of these cases, negotiations are broken off when it is revealed that the companies' operations are not compatible. In others, tangible benefits would result, but the parties are unable to agree on the merger terms. Of these terms, the most important is the price to be paid by the acquiring firm for the firm acquired. Factors that influence this important aspect of a merger are now considered.

Effects on Price and Earnings

A merger carries potentialities for either favorable or adverse effects on earnings, on market prices of shares, or on both. Previous chapters have shown that investment decisions should be guided by the effects on market values,

---

shareholders. This effect is known as the *co-insurance effect.* Co-insurance occurs as follows: as a separate entity, the bondholders face a certain risk of default. When the company is merged, it is possible that poor earnings in one company, which would have resulted in default had the company been independent, will be offset by good earnings in the other companies in the merged entity. Hence, the risk of default has been reduced.

and these effects should in turn be determined by the impact on future earnings and dividends. These future events are difficult to forecast, however, so shareholders, as well as managers may attrribute great importance to the immediate effects of a contemplated merger on earnings per share. Directors of companies are interested in the market price of the shares of the company, and if the merger meets the investment decision criteria, i.e. net present value greater than zero, then the stock price should increase. However, management may use the impact on earnings per share due to the merger as a proxy for the impact on market price, since the effect on earnings per share can be seen directly.

An example will illustrate the effects of a proposed merger on earnings per share and thus suggest the kinds of problems that are likely to arise. Assume the following facts for two companies:

	Company A	Company B
Total earnings	$20,000	$50,000
Number of shares of common equity	5,000	10,000
Earnings per share of common	$ 4.00	$ 5.00
Price/earnings ratio	15×	12×
Market price per share	$ 60.00	$ 60.00

Suppose the firms agree to merge, with B, the surviving firm, acquiring the shares of A by a one-for-one exchange of common equity. The exchange ratio is determined by the respective market prices of the two companies. Assuming no increase in earnings, the effects on earnings per share are shown in the following tabulation:

	Shares of Company B Owned after Merger	Earnings per Share	
		Before merger	After merger
A's shareholders	5,000	$4	$4.67
B's shareholders	10,000	5	4.67
Total	15,000		

Since total earnings are $70,000 and a total of 15,000 shares will be outstanding after the merger has been completed, the new earnings per share will be $4.67. Earnings will increase by 67 cents for A's shareholders, but they will decline by 33 cents for B's.

The effects on market values are less certain. If the combined company sells at company A's price/earnings ratio of 15, the new market value per share of the new company will be $70. In this case, shareholders of both companies will have benefited. This result comes about because the combined earnings are now valued at a multiplier of 15, whereas prior to the merger one portion of the earnings was valued at a multiplier of 15 and another portion was valued at a multiplier of 12.

If, on the other hand, the earnings of the new company are valued at B's multiplier of 12, the indicated market value of the shares will be $56. The shareholders of each company will have suffered a $4 dilution in market value. Obviously, the ultimate impact on the market price of B will depend on the price/earnings ratio applied to the earnings of the merged entity. In order to determine this, management could investigate why the P/E ratios for the two companies are different.

The higher ratio for A may reflect the lower risk of that company relative to B. Thus, the merged entity will have risk, and thus a P/E multiple, that is somewhere between the values for the companies operating as independent entities. In the example we are analyzing, there is no increase in earnings due to the merger and the net present value of the acquisition is zero. Therefore, the price per share of B's equity should remain at $60. With earnings per share of $4.67, this implies a P/E ratio for the post-merger company of 12.8 times. This is approximately equal to a weighted average of the pre-merger P/E ratios of the individual companies; the weight applied to company B's P/E ratio is the ratio of the market value of B's equity to the market value of the equity of the post-merger firm.

A general principle concerning the impact on earnings per share is that when the terms of the merger are based on the market price per share and the price/earnings ratios of the two companies are different, then the resulting earnings per share will be somewhere between the earnings per share of the merging companies. The company with a higher price/earnings ratio will have an increase in *EPS,* while the company with the lower P/E ratio will have a reduction in *EPS*. If the sizes of the companies are very different, the effect on the larger company will be relatively smaller and the effect on the smaller company will be large.

Of the numerous factors affecting the valuation of the constituent companies in a merger, all must ultimately be reflected in the earnings per share, or market price, of the companies. Hence, all the effects on the earnings position or wealth position of shareholders are encompassed by the foregoing example. We will now consider both quantitative and qualitative factors that will influence the terms on which a merger is likely to take place.

Factors Affecting Merger Terms

The terms of the merger refer to the actual cost of consummating the merger. The cost equals either the actual cash per share paid to the acquired company's shareholders, or the implicit dollar cost of the exchange of the acquiror company's shares per share of the acquired company. This rate of exchange is called the *exchange ratio*. If we were to look at the companies involved in a merger, either before the merger is announced or before information of the merger is leaked to the market[3], then the stock prices of the companies will reflect their going concern values as independent entities. Any influence of the potential benefits from the merger will not be reflected in these stock prices.

These prices are the base from which to determine the terms of the merger, regardless of whether the merger is to be paid for with cash or shares. In fact, studies have demonstrated that these prices are the best explanation of the ultimate exchange ratios. However, the final terms for the merger are unlikely to be exactly equal to these stock prices for a number of reasons. First, the prospective purchaser may be interested in acquiring the company for the synergistic or financial contribution it may make to the acquiring company. Thus, there is scope to pay a higher price, since the acquired company is worth more to an informed purchaser than to the general market. Second, some inducement to current shareholders may be necessary to give them the incentive to sell (or exchange) their shares. This compensation, over and above the market price of the acquired company, is called the *merger premium*. Due to tax reasons, the premiums paid in mergers for cash are higher than in mergers in which shares are exchanged. In addition, the premium will depend upon a number of additional factors including the amount of shares the acquiring company already owns of the acquired company and the uniqueness of fit between the acquiring and acquired company; i.e. the premium is likely to be smaller if the benefits of the merger are available only to one acquiring company, since there would not be a large number of potential acquiring companies to bid up the merger terms.

In this section, we will investigate some factors which can result in the terms of the merger being in excess of the pre-merger stock prices. In order to be legitimate factors, they must not be reflected in the pre-merger stock prices of the merging companies.[4]

Earnings and Growth Rates

Both expected earnings and capitalization rates as reflected in P/E ratios may be important in determining the values that

---

[3]One study has found that information of the impending merger is reflected in the stock price of the merging firms, on average, seven months before the announcement of the merger and its terms.

[4]A factor such as differential dividend policies of the merging firms is unlikely to be important, since it is already reflected in the pre-merger stock prices. Other factors, such as the book values per share of the merging companies, are likely to be unimportant, since they represent the historical investments that have been made in the company and will have no relation to current market values of either the assets or the equity.

will be established in a merger. The analysis necessarily begins with historical data on the firms' earnings, whose past growth rates, future trends, and variability are important determinants of the earnings multiplier, or *P/E* ratio, that will prevail after the merger.

How future earnings growth rates affect the multiplier can be illustrated by extending the preceding example. First, we know that high *P/E* ratios are commonly associated with rapidly growing companies. Since company A has the higher *P/E* ratio, it is reasonable to assume that its earnings are expected to grow more rapidly than those of company B. Suppose A's expected growth rate is 10 percent and B's 5 percent. Looking at the proposed merger from the point of view of company B and its shareholders, and assuming that the exchange ratio is based on present market prices, it can be seen that B will suffer a dilution in earnings when the merger occurs. However, B will be acquiring a firm with more favorable growth prospects; hence, its earnings after the merger should increase more rapidly than before. In this case, the new growth rate is assumed to be a weighted average of the growth rates of the individual firms, weighted by their respective total earnings before the merger. In the example, the new expected growth rate is $(20/70)(10\%) + (50/70)(5\%) = 6.43$ percent.

With the new growth rate it is possible to determine just how long it will take company B's shareholders to regain the earnings dilution, that is, how long it will take earnings per share to revert back to their previous position be-

FIGURE 23–1 Effect of Merger on Future Earnings

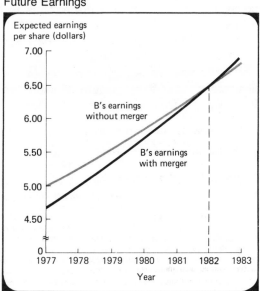

fore the merger. This can be determined graphically from Figure 23–1[5]. Without the merger, B would have initial earnings of $5 a share, and these earnings would have grown at a rate of 5 percent a year. With the merger, earnings drop to $4.67 a share, but the rate of growth increases to 6.43 percent. Under these conditions, the earnings dilution is overcome after five years; from the fifth year on, B's earnings will be higher, assuming the merger is consummated.

This same relationship could be developed from the point of view of the faster growing firm. Here there would be an immediate earnings increase but a reduced rate of growth. Working through the analysis would show the number of years before the earnings accretion would be eroded.

It is apparent that the critical variables are (1) the respective rates of growth of the two firms; (2) their relative sizes, which determine the actual amount of the initial earnings per share dilution or accretion, as well as the new weighted average growth rate; (3) the firms' P/E ratios; and (4) the exchange ratio. These factors interact to produce the resulting pattern of earnings per share for the surviving company. It is possible to generalize the relationships somewhat; for our purposes, it is necessary simply to note that in the bargaining process the exchange ratio is the variable that must be manipulated in an effort to reach a mutually satisfactory earnings pattern.[6]

Net Current Assets per Share   Net current assets (current assets minus current liabilities) per share are likely to have an influence on merger terms because they represent the amount of liquidity that may be obtained from a company in a merger. In the U.S. postwar textile mergers, net current assets were very high, and this was one of the characteristics making textile companies attractive to the acquiring firms. By buying a textile company, often with securities, an acquiring company was in a position to look for still other merger candidates, paying for the new acquisition with the just-acquired liquidity. Similarly, if an acquiring company is debt-free, the acquiring firm may be able to borrow funds required for the purchase, using the acquired firm's assets and earning power as security for the loan.[7] To the extent that these liquidity factors are reflected already in the acquired company's stock

---

[5]The calculation could also be made algebraically by solving for N in the following equation: $E_1(1 + g_1)^N = E_2(1 + g_2)^N$, where E_1 = earnings before the merger, E_2 = earnings after the merger, g_1 and g_2 are the growth rates before and after the merger, and N is the break-even number of years.

[6]We should also mention at this point that certain companies, especially the "conglomerates," are reported to have used mergers to produce a "growth illusion" designed to increase the prices of their stocks. When a high P/E ratio company buys a low P/E ratio company, the earnings per share of the acquiring firm rise *because* of the merger. Thus, mergers can produce growth in reported earnings for the acquiring firm. This growth by merger, in turn, can cause the acquiring firm to keep its high P/E ratio. With this ratio, the conglomerates can seek new low P/E merger candidates and thus continue to obtain growth through mergers. The chain is broken (1) if the rate of merger activity slows, or (2) if the P/E ratio of the acquiring firm falls. Note, however, that there is no evidence that this "contrived" growth had a major, positive influence on stock prices. Even though some of the more famous conglomerates had drastic reductions in stock prices, these may have been caused by changes in tax laws, anti-trust actions, a down-turn in the economy, or a reduction in the expected profitability of the company.

[7]By the same token, a firm seeking to *avoid* being acquired will reduce its liquid position and use up its borrowing potential.

price, the impact of this factor on merger terms is reduced.

Contingent Payments

Suppose the acquired firm in a merger was a closely-held company whose profitability is based on the effectiveness of the current management-owners. The acquiring company recognizes the importance of the current management and agrees that, after the merger, the acquired firm will operate as an independent entity. The acquiring firm will want to structure incentives to ensure that the managers either stay with the company for a certain number of years during which time new management can be trained, or manage the company so as to maximize the profit contribution from the acquired firm to the total entity.

One way to accomplish these results is to make the payment for the merger to the owner-managers contingent on the occurrence or non-occurrence of specified events at specified periods in the future. For example, the total consideration paid for the merger can be composed of a down payment and the remainder placed in escrow. This remaining payment will be released from escrow if the managers meet certain requirements, e.g. remain with the company for, say, five years. Alternatively, there may be a down payment and a future payment contingent on the firm maintaining or achieving specified earnings levels in periods subsequent to the merger.

These forms of contingent payments will provide an incentive for the manager to perform in the desired manner. However, in setting these contingent payments, the acquiring company must specify the terms very carefully. For example, if the payment is contingent on achieving a certain level of earnings per share, the management may not undertake investment decisions which have a long-run earnings potential but may result in reduced earnings per share in the short-run. Also, the acquiring company must be aware of accounting changes which result in increased reported earnings per share.

Another form of contingent payment which has no incentive impact on management behavior relates to the market price of the acquiring company's shares at some specified date in the future. If this market price does not reach a specified level by a specified date, the acquiring company will be required to issue additional shares or cash so as to make the total amount paid for the acquisition equal to the amount that would have been paid if the share price reached the specified level.

TAKE-OVER BIDS

If one firm wishes to gain control over another, it typically approaches the other firm's management and seeks its approval of the merger. The shareholders of the acquired firm are then asked to vote in favor of the merger.

In a take-over bid, the process is different. The acquiring company, called the bidder, offers to purchase the shares of the target company at a stated price which is in excess of the prevailing market price.[8] The offer is sent to shareholders and they in turn send their agreement to sell their shares to the agent for the bidder; this agent is typically a trust company. The consideration involved can be cash, shares or other securities. The offer may be conditional on obtaining a certain percentage of the outstanding shares.

What we have described above is called a *tender offer*, since the bidder has asked the shareholders of the target firm to submit or tender their shares. A take-over bid is a tender offer that meets the following legal requirements: if the tender offer results in the acquiring company owning in excess of 20 percent of the outstanding listed shares of the acquired company (including the shares already owned by the acquiring company), then the tender offer is called a take-over bid.

In most of the Provincial Securities Acts, there are regulations concerning the form of the offer and the notification requirements. In Ontario, for example, the bidder must file with the Ontario Securities Commission (OSC) a take-over bid circular which is equivalent in form to a prospectus. All shares must be treated equally. Therefore, if a take-over bid is for 40 percent of the shares and 50 percent are tendered, then the acquiring company must pro-rate the offer, i.e. each shareholder who tendered shares will have 80 percent of their offer accepted. In the new Ontario Securities Act, the concept of treating all shareholders equally has been applied such that the bidder must pay the same amount per share to each shareholder. Thus, any premiums that would be paid for a control block are no longer possible.

Since the take-over bid is a direct appeal to the shareholders, it need not be approved by the management of the target firm. However, OSC regulations require the management of the target company to send to its shareholders a circular which recommends either acceptance or rejection of the bid.

There are four exemptions to the take-over bid requirements of the Ontario Securities Act. The most important of these is an exemption to take-over bids effected through the facilities of a stock exchange or the over-the-counter market. However, as of December 1976, the Toronto Stock Exchange introduced a new by-law which stipulated certain reporting requirements for take-over bids. The net effect of this by-law was to remove the exemption, since, on a take-over bid through the exchange, notice must be given to the Exchange, the OSC and the target company, and prescribed information concerning the bid must be published in a daily newspaper. Not all purchases through the exchange must meet these reporting requirements. The TSE by-law exempts "normal-course" purchases which are defined as purchases for an amount of no more than 5 percent of the outstanding shares within the preceding 30 days.

[8]The premium as a percent of the prevailing market price is approximately 10 to 20 percent.

The take-over bid route can be used either when the management of the target company is hostile to a merger or when there is a large block of shares of the target company that has agreed to a sale and a bid to the minority shareholders is needed. In the former case, there is no reason to believe that existing management and current shareholders have identical interests when a take-over bid is in the works. If the take-over bid is successful and the management of the target firm is hostile to the bid, then they are certain to be removed from their positions. In addition, they may believe that it is not in the long-run economic interests of the shareholders for the firm to be taken over. There are a number of tactics available to the management of a target firm to defend against a take-over bid. For example, if a take-over bid is in the formative stages, the potential target company will undertake certain actions to discourage the making of the bid. These would include an increase in the dividend per share or a stock split. Once the bid is made, the target company can attempt to show that the bid is too low - for example, by increasing the value of the assets and advising shareholders of the new values. Alternatively, as a last resort, the target company may decide to find another company to make a counter bid; management of the target firm, having decided that shareholders may accept the first bid, prefer to be taken over by a firm with which they have common interests. Finally, the management of the target company may merge with a company in the same industry as the bidder; this may prevent the take-over since the resulting merger would be between companies in the same industry and thus be subject to anti-combines regulations. Note that these last two strategies are undertaken as a last resort and may not be justifiable on economic grounds.

To illustrate the discussions on take-over bids, we will consider some recent examples. The first example concerns a bid by Kaiser Resources Limited for the shares of Ashland Oil Canada Limited, whose parent, Ashland Oil Inc. of Kentucky, owns 83 percent of the equity. The offer made by Kaiser and agreed to by Ashland Oil Inc. management was that Kaiser would pay $32.50 per share for Ashland Canada Ltd. shares. Since the parent's shares have been committed to Kaiser, a similar offer would be made to the remaining shareholders once approval by FIRA had been obtained. However, all bids do not run smoothly and a last minute counterbid was made by a U.S. owned conglomerate. As a result of this bid, the price per share offered to Ashland was raised by $1 to $33.50. Ashland management accepted this offer. As of July 20, 1978, Ashland stock closed at $31.375 which is 6 percent below the offer price. This difference in price reflects the risk that the deal will not go through because FIRA may not give approval to the take-over.

This risk of regulation can be compared to the Air Canada-Nordair take-over. Air Canada offered $11.50 per share to Nordair shareholders - both for the controlling block of 60 percent of the shares and the minority interest. Approval for this take-over had to be obtained from the Canadian Transport Commission (CTC). On July 28, 1978, approval was given. However, before that date, Nordair was trading at $10 to $10.50 per share. This was equal to a discount of 9 to 13 percent from the offer price. It appears that the risk of not obtaining regulatory approval was greater for the CTC than for FIRA.

The second example will probably go down in financial history as one of the most exciting and puzzling take-over bids in Canada. The sequence of events that we will describe concerns the take-over of Husky-Oil, an American owned company which has stock listed on both the Toronto and American Stock Exchanges. The reasons for the take-over, be they political or economic, are not crucial to the present discussion and will be omitted. On June 10, 1978, Petro Can, the Federal Government's presence in the energy industry, offerred $45 cash per share of Husky stock in a take-over bid. Husky Oil, as a defence to the Petro Can offer, worked out an agreement with Occidental Petroleum Limited of California. The offer made by Occidental and accepted by Husky's board was a securities exchange equivalent to $49 Canadian. The Occidental offer was conditional on obtaining at least 80 percent of the shares and of course, approval by FIRA was necessary.

On June 15, 1978, Petro Can raised its offer to $52 per share and Occidental retaliated by increasing its offer to $54 Canadian. While this battle of bid and counterbid was raging. Alberta Gas Truck Line (AGTL) quietly acquired 35 percent of the equity of Husky Oil by purchasing the shares on the American Stock Exchange. When AGTL's holdings were announced, Occidental's offer was stopped, since they could only obtain the required 80 percent by purchasing shares from an unwilling seller, AGTL. Petro Can then withdrew its offer and control was in AGTL's hands, although the President of Husky still owns 20 percent of the shares.

The AGTL purchase was very expensive. On June 28, 1978, when trading in Husky shares was stopped on the TSE, the stock price was $48½ Canadian; this was about $1 per share higher than the price in the previous week. On June 30, 1978, after the dust had cleared and trading was re-opened, Husky stock fell to $38.625, a loss of approximately $10 per share. Thus, the value of Husky shares purchased by AGTL fell substantially.

This AGTL involvement was of some concern both to the TSE and the Ontario Securities Commission. As we noted under the discussion of take-over bids, market purchases in excess of five percent must be reported and AGTL's activity would have become public. However, there is an exemption in the regulations for purchases on other exchanges where the acquiror need abide only by the rules of that exchange; based on AGTL's activity, no reporting was required on the American Stock Exchange.

At the beginning of this discussion we described this sequence of events as both exciting and puzzling. The excitement is obvious. The puzzle arises from the AGTL involvement – why did AGTL intervene, given that Occidental's offer was subject to approval from FIRA? Second, although control has changed, there has been no take-over! – will the AGTL presence solve any of the problems that motivated Petro Can's original offer?

SUMMARY

Growth is vital to the well-being of a firm, for without it a business cannot attract able management because it cannot give employees recognition in promotions and challenging, creative activity. Mergers have played an important part in the growth of firms, and since financial managers are required both to appraise the desirability of a prospective merger and to participate in evaluating the respective companies involved in the merger, the present chapter has been devoted to background materials on merger decisions.

Throughout the discussion on mergers we have stressed the similarity of the merger decision to the capital budgeting decision. The incremental cash inflows from the merger represent not only the flows from the acquired company but any financial or economic gains from combining the companies. The cost of the merger is the price paid for either the assets or shares of the acquired company. The acquisition can be paid for by cash, shares, or other securities.

Merger Terms The most important term that must be negotiated in a merger arrangement is the price the acquiring firm will pay for the acquired business. The most important factor in determining the terms of the merger is the relationship of the pre-merger stock prices of the firms in the merger. A number of other factors that are not fully reflected in these stock prices are important in setting the merger terms. These include the resulting earning growth rates and net working capital. Finally, the price paid for the merger may be contingent on specific performance of the management-owners of the merged firm. The contingency may be a certain level or growth of earnings per share.

QUESTIONS

23-1. The number of mergers tends to fluctuate with business activity, rising when GNP rises and falling when GNP falls. Why does this relationship exist?

23-2. A large firm has certain advantages over a smaller one. What are some of the *financial* advantages of large size?

23-3. What are some of the potential financial and economic benefits that can be expected by a firm that merges with a company in a different industry?

23-4. Distinguish between a holding company and an operating company. Give an example of each.

23-5. Discuss the reasons why a firm might decide to expand and grow by the acquisition of other companies' shares instead of direct capital investment in plant and equipment within its own corporate structure.

23-6. Is the public interest served by an increase in merger activity? Give arguments both pro and con.

23-7. Would the book value of a company's assets be considered the absolute minimum price to be paid for a firm? Why? Is there any value that would qualify as an absolute minimum?

23-8. Discuss the situation where one firm calls off merger negotiations with another because the management of the former firm believes that the latter's stock price is overvalued. What assumption concerning dilution is implicit in the above situation?

23-9. There are many methods by which a company can raise additional capital. Can a merger be considered a means of raising additional equity capital? Explain.

23-10. Are the negotiations for merger agreements more difficult if the firms are in different industries or in the same industry? If they are about the same size or quite different in size? If the ages of the firms are about the same or if they are very different? Why?

23-11. How would the existence of long-term debt in a company's financial structure affect its valuation for merger purposes? Could the same be said for any debt account regardless of its maturity?

23-12. During 1964–1965, the Heavy Oil Company Limited was involved in merger negotiations with at least three other firms. The terms of these arrangements varied from a transfer of stock to a direct cash purchase of Heavy Oil. Discuss the relative advantages to a corporation of paying for an acquisition in cash or in stock.

23-13. a. Discuss the requirements in Canada with respect to both the acquiring and target companies during a take-over bid.

b. Are the interests of all relevant parties protected?

c. When might the management of a target company be averse to a take-over bid and how could the management ward off the take-over while still protecting the rights of its shareholders?

23-14. Why is the target company in a take-over usually considered the underdog? What attributes does a target company *usually* display?

23-15. In late 1968 the SEC and the New York Stock Exchange each issued sets of rulings on disclosure of information which, in effect, required that firms disclose that they have entered into merger discussions as soon as they start such discussions. Since the previous procedure had been to delay disclosure until it was evident that there was a reasonably good expectation the merger under discussion would actually go through (and not to bring the matter up at all if the merger died in the early stages), it can safely be predicted that, in a statistical sense, a larger percentage of prospective mergers will be "abandoned" in the future than in the past.

a. Why do you suppose the new rulings were put into effect?

b. Will the new rulings have any adverse effects? Why?

PROBLEMS

23-1. The following companies are of a similar asset size and have equal earnings per share, but their market values per share are quite different.

	Heath Co. Ltd.	Kwan Co. Ltd.
Total earnings	$100,000	$120,000
Number of common shares	20,000	24,000
Earnings per common share	$ 5.00	$ 5.00
Price/earnings ratio	8X	6X
Market price per share	$40.00	$30.00

If the firms agree to merge and the Health Co. survives by acquiring the shares of Kwan Co. on a 3 for 4 basis:

    a. What will be the EPS of the new Heath Co. given that there are no economies of scale?

    b. If the price/earnings ratio of the new Heath Co. stays somewhere between the price/earning ratios of the original two firms, what is the possible range of market prices for the new Heath Co.?

    c. Why might the market value of the original Heath Co.'s equity in total be greater than that of Kwan Co. despite the fact they have assets of a similar size?

23-2. Texas Mining Company is a holding company owning the entire common shares of Metco Company Ltd. and Jenkins Company Ltd. The balance sheet as of December 31, 19X5, for each subsidiary is identical with the following one.

Balance sheet, December 31, 19X5

Current assets	$ 7,500,000	Current liabilities	$ 1,250,000
Fixed assets, net	5,000,000	First mortgage bonds (9%)	2,500,000
		Preferred shares (7%)	2,500,000
		Common shares	5,000,000
		Retained earnings	1,250,000
Total assets	$12,500,000	Total claims on assets	$12,500,000

Each operating company earns $1,375,000 annually before taxes and before interest and preferred dividends. A 50 percent tax rate is assumed.

    a. What is the annual rate of return on each company's net worth (common shares plus retained earnings)?

    b. Construct a balance sheet for Texas Mining Company based on the following assumptions: (1) The only assets of the holding company are the common shares of the two subsidiaries; these shares are carried at par (not book) value. (2) The holding company has $1.2 million of 8 percent coupon debt and $2.8 million of 6 percent preferred shares.

    c. What is the rate of return on the book value of the holding company's common shares if (1) Texas Mining files a consolidated income tax return, and (2) subsidiary earnings available to common are taken as dividends by the holding company?

    d. With regard to part c, which method of income taxation should Texas Mining employ?

    e. How can the rate of return in part c be increased?

    f. What investment is necessary to control the three companies under the assumptions specified in part b?

    g. If ownership of 25 percent of the holding company's common shares ($6 million of common) could control all three firms, what percentage would this be of the total operating assets?

23-3. Every merger agreement is subject to negotiation between the companies involved. One significant indicator of the compensation received by the acquired company is the respective market prices of the companies' stocks in relation to the merger terms. Some actual merger data are given below.

Calculate the percent premium, or discount, received by the acquired company, using market prices as the criteria. Compare the results of your calculations on the basis of the stock prices of the two previous quarters with that of your results on the basis of the prices immediately preceding the merger. Which is the proper measure of the actual discount or premium received: the one indicated by the earlier stock prices or the one indicated by the stock prices immediately preceding the merger? Explain.

Company	Terms	Market Price Two Quarters before Merger		Market Price Immediately Preceding Merger	
		A	B	A	B
1 { A Celanese Corporation B Champlain Oil	2 shares of Celanese for every 3 shares of Champlain	62	34	67	42
2 { A Cities Service Company B Tennessee Corporation	0.9 shares (2.25 pref.) for each Tenn. Corp. share (common)	65	48	61	55
3 { A Ford Motor Company B Philco Corporation	1 share of Ford for every 4½ shares of Philco	81	22	113	25
4 { A General Telephone B Sylvania Electric	Share-for-share basis	52	46	69	69

23-4. To meet its growth objectives, Waters Manufacturing Ltd. is planning to expand via acquisition. It has two potential acquisition candidates. Apex Corporation and Allied Engineering. The latest balance sheet for Waters is given below, along with certain statistical data for all three companies. Assume that the pre-tax cost of new debt to Waters is 9 percent, that its cost of equity is 10 percent, and that Waters has an effective tax rate of 50 percent.

Waters Manufacturing
Balance sheet
December 31, 19X6

Current Assets	$120,000	Current liabilities	$ 50,000
Net fixed assets	150,000	Long-term debt (9%)	70,000
		Common equity	150,000
Total	$270,000	Total	$270,000

Statistical Data

	EPS	DPS	Growth Rate	Market Price	Shares Outstanding
Waters	$3.00	$1.80	6%	$45.00	5,000,000
Apex	$2.00	$0.50	7.5%	$50.00	2,000,000
Allied	$4.00	$3.00	2%	$42.00	3,000,000

a. Based on the above information, determine an appropriate price for Waters to pay for each acquisition candidate. Waters computes the value of an acquisition candidate's stock using the constant growth model, based on the target company's growth rate and projected dividends. Waters uses its own marginal cost of capital as the minimum required rate of return.

b. If Waters is forced to make a tender offer for each of the two candidates at 20 percent above their current market value, compute the following items.

    1. The exchange ratio based on a stock offering.

    2. Waters' new earnings growth rate for next year after the acquisition of each company—Apex and Allied.

    3. Calculate Waters' new EPS following each acquisition.

c. Chart Waters' growth in EPS for the next ten years with and without each acquisition to illustrate the dilutive effect of the purchase price computed in part 2-b above.

23-5. The Prideaux Percolator Company Ltd. is considering the acquisition of the Parker Perambulator Co. Ltd. Each firm has 100 shares of common equity outstanding. Prideaux's market share price is $70 and it has an earnings per share of $10. Parker's share price is $35 with an earnings per share of $9.

Pre-Merger Balance Sheets

	Prideaux Co. Ltd.				Parker Co. Ltd.		
Assets	$10,000	Liabilities	$ 5,000	Assets	$7,000	Liabilities	$4,000
		Owners Equity	$ 5,000			Owners Equity	$3,000
Total Assets	$10,000	Total Liabilities and Owners Equity	$10,000	Total Assets	$7,000	Total Liabilities and Owners Equity	$7,000

Prideaux Percolator proposes to give 50 shares for the 100 shares of Parker Perambulator that are outstanding. Prideaux has 100 shares outstanding.

a. What would the post-merger balance sheet for Prideaux look like under each of the purchase and pooling-of-interest approaches?

b. If there are no economies of scale, what would be the new EPS under each method? What would be the rate of return on book assets and book equity before and after the merger for all three firms?

Accounting Policies in Mergers

23A Appendix

After merger terms have been agreed upon, the financial manager must be familiar with the accounting principles for recording the financial results of the merger and for reflecting the initial effect on the earnings of the surviving firm. This appendix deals with these matters briefly.

There has been considerable discussion in both the United States and Canada on the accounting treatment for mergers. In 1970, the Accounting Principles Board of the American Institute of Certified Public Accountants issued policy papers dealing with guidelines for corporate mergers and with goodwill arising from mergers. In 1974, the Canadian Institute of Chartered Accountants presented their recommendations on these issues. These recommendations set out the circumstances for the use of the "pooling of interest" and "purchase" methods of accounting for business combinations. For reasons that will become clear later in this Appendix, corporate managements generally prefer pooling. Although the pooling technique was used frequently in the United States, its use in Canada was very infrequent.

The CICA recommendations concerning the appropriate accounting treatment revolve around one key factor—is it possible to identify one of the combining companies as the acquiror? The CICA recommendations include a set of guidelines to assist in finding the acquiror. The easiest case occurs when one company distributes cash or other assets, or incurs liabilities, to obtain the assets or shares of another company. Clearly, the former company is the acquiror. Another test would designate the acquiror as that company whose shareholders hold more than 50 percent of the voting shares of the combined company.

In the case where the acquiror can be identified, the purchase method of accounting is to be used. The "pooling of interest" method is to be used on those rare occasions where it is not possible to identify one of the parties to the business combination as the acquiror. In these cases, the shareholders of the previously independent companies have combined their resources to carry on their previous businesses in combination.

In a purchase, the excess of the purchase price paid over the book value (restated to reflect the appraised value of physical assets) is set up as goodwill, and the shareholders' equity section reflects the actual purchase price. The goodwill created should be amortized to income on a straight line basis over the estimated life of the goodwill; the maximum period for this amortization is forty years. In addition, in a purchase the reported income in the acquired firm should be included in the new company's statements only from the date of acquisition.

In a pooling of interest, the total assets and liabilities after the merger represent a simple sum of the assets and liabilities at the values recorded by the constituent companies. Thus, the shareholders' equity section of the combined company is the sum of the share capital of the constituents. Notice that under a pooling of interest, no goodwill is set up, since the market value of the consideration paid is not included. Finally, under the pooling alternative, reported income of the combined firm includes the full reported income of the constituent companies for the entire year in which the acquisition occurred.

As we will demonstrate, the earnings per share and the rate of return on book equity will be higher if the accounting treatment is a pooling rather than a purchase. Thus, from a strict accounting point of view, it appears that managements should prefer to have their post-merger statements prepared under the pooling technique. However, the crucial question is the impact of the accounting technique chosen on the market price of the merged company. Since the amortization of goodwill is not a tax deductible expense, the true after-tax earnings of the new company will not depend on the accounting treatment chosen. Unless the stock market can be fooled very easily, it is hard to believe that the choice of accounting techniques for reporting purposes will have an impact on the market price of the new company.

To demonstrate the impact of the pooling of interest versus purchase methods of accounting for business combinations, we will utilize a very simple example[1]. We will start with the balance sheet and earnings of the acquiror and acquired companies. Then, the impact on earnings per share and on the balance sheets will be calculated using first the purchase method, and then the pooling of interest technique. To simplify matters further, we will assume that the combination occurs at the beginning of the fiscal year.

[1]This example is taken from the Department of Financial and Commercial Affairs, Report of the Committee of the Ontario Securities Commission on the Problems of Disclosure Raised for Investors by Business Combinations and Private Placements, February 1970, Appendix VIII.

Acquiror Company—Balance Sheet

Assets	12000	Liabilities		$1000
		Shareholders' equity		
		50 no par value	$500	
		Retained earnings	500	1000
		Total liabilities and		
Total assets	$2000	shareholders' equity		$2000

The market value of the acquiror shares is assumed to be $50 per share and earnings per share are $3 and expected to continue at this level in the future. This results in a 15 percent rate of return on book equity. The book value per share is $20 and the price/earnings ratio is 16.67 i.e. $50/$3.

Acquired Company—Balance Sheet

Assets	$1000	Liabilities		$500
		Shareholders' equity		
		50 no par value shares	$250	
		Retained earnings	250	500
Total assets	$1000	Total		$1000

The earnings per share of this company are $2 and expected to continue at this level. The market value is assumed to equal the book value of $10 per share. This firm has a price/earnings ratio of 5 (i.e. $10/$2) and it is earning a 20 percent rate of return on book equity.

Under the acquisition terms, all the shares of the acquired company will be obtained through an exchange of 20 shares of the acquiring company. At the market price of $50 per share, the fair value of the compensation is $1000 which is a premium of $500 above the book value of the shareholders' equity in the acquired company.

Purchase Method

If the balance sheet of the new company is prepared using the purchase method, then we know that an element of goodwill is included to reflect the compensation which was in excess of the book value. The resulting balance sheet is presented as follows:

Combined Company—Balance Sheet

Assets	$3000	Liabilities		$1500
Goodwill	500	Shareholders equity		
		50 NPV shares	$500	
		20 NPV shares	1000	
		Retained earnings	500	2000
Total	$3500	Total		$3500

The new balance sheet is obtained by adding the assets of the constituent companies and by adding the liabilities. The shareholders' equity section is equal to the pre-merger acquiror shareholder equity plus the fair value of the compensation. Any premium paid for the shares of the acquired company is included in the assets section.

What will be the new earnings per share of the combined entity? If no economies of scale occur, then the earnings per share are calculated as follows:

Earnings—acquired company	$100
Earnings—acquiring company	150
Total	250
Goodwill amortized over 20 years	25
	$225
Number of shares outstanding	70
Earnings per share:	$3.21

Notice in this case the earnings per share is higher than the earnings per share for either of the companies before the combination. The rate of return on book equity has become 11.3 percent, which is below the rates of return earned on either of the constituent companies.

Pooling of Interest

Using the pooling of interest technique, no goodwill is set up. The balance sheet of the combined company is obtained by increasing the accounts of the acquiror company by the book value of the corresponding accounts in the acquired company. The resulting combined balance sheet is presented as follows:

Combined Company—Balance Sheet

Assets	$3000	Liabilities		$1500
		Shareholders equity		
		50 *NPV* shares	$500	
		20 *NPV* shares	250	
		Retained earnings	750	1500
Total	$3000	Total		$3000

Notice in the shareholders' equity account that the increase is equal to book value of equity of the acquired company; the retained earnings increased by $250; the book value of the shares increased by the par value of the old shares, i.e. $250.

The earnings per share under a pooling will not include the amortization of goodwill. Thus, earnings per share will be equal to the total earnings of $250 divided by 70 shares or $3.57. The rate of return on book equity is 17 percent, i.e. $250 divided by $1500. Notice that under pooling both the earnings per share and the rate of return on book equity are higher than under the purchase method.

Failure, Reorganization, and Liquidation

24 Thus far the text has dealt with issues associated mainly with the growing, successful enterprise. Not all businesses are so fortunate, however, so we must examine financial difficulties, their causes, and their possible remedies. This material is significant for the financial managers of successful, as well as of potentially unsuccessful, firms. The successful firm's financial manager must know the firm's rights and remedies as a creditor and must participate effectively in efforts to collect from financially distressed debtors. Conversely, the financial manager of a less successful firm must know how to handle his or her own firm's affairs if financial difficulties arise. Such understanding may often mean the difference between loss of ownership of the firm and rehabilitation of the operation as a going enterprise.

THE FIRM'S LIFE CYCLE

The life cycle of an industry or firm is often depicted as an S-shaped curve, as shown in Figure 24–1. The figure represents a hypothetical life cycle of a firm, and although it is an oversimplification, it does provide a useful framework for analysis. The hypothesis represented by the four-stage life-cycle concept is based on a key assumption—competent management in the growth periods and insufficient management foresight prior to the decline phase. Obviously, one of management's primary goals is to prolong phase B and to forestall completely phase D; many firms are apparently successful in these endeavors.

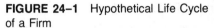

FIGURE 24–1 Hypothetical Life Cycle
of a Firm

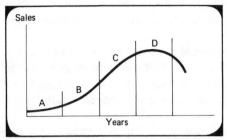

If an industry experiences the period of decline, financial readjustment problems will arise, affecting most firms in the industry. Furthermore, specific events may result in business failure—for example, a prolonged strike, a fire not adequately covered by insurance, or a bad decision on a new product.

There appears to be a significant risk of bankruptcy in the first few years after a firm has started. This reflects the start-up problems associated with management ability and competitive pressures. For example, of the failures in 1976, Dun & Bradstreet has noted the years in which these failed businesses started operation. For these concerns, 70.5 percent started in business in the years 1971 to 1976; 16.2 percent in the period 1966 to 1970, 5.6 percent in 1961 to 1965, and 3.0 percent in 1956 to 1960.

FAILURE

Although failure can be defined in several ways according to various applications of the term, it does not necessarily result in the collapse and dissolution of a firm.

Economic Failure

Failure in an economic sense usually signifies that a firm's revenues do not cover costs. Another definition of economic failure states that a firm has failed if the rate of earnings on the historical cost of investment is less than the firm's cost of capital. According to still another definition, a firm can be considered a failure if its actual returns have fallen below expected returns. There is no consensus on the definition of failure in an economic sense.[1]

---

[1]In still another economic sense, a firm that goes bankrupt may not be a failure at all. To illustrate, suppose someone starts a business to *attempt* to develop a product that, if successful, will produce very large returns and, if unsuccessful, will result in a total loss of invested funds. The entrepreneur *knows* that he is taking a risk but thinks the potential gains are worth the chance of loss. If a loss in fact results, then the outcome simply occurred in the left tail of the distribution of returns.

Financial Failure

Although financial failure is a less ambiguous term than the concept of economic failure, even here, two aspects are generally recognized:

Technical Insolvency   A firm can be considered a failure if it is insolvent in the sense that it cannot meet its current obligations as they fall due, even though its total assets may exceed its total liabilities. This is defined as *technical insolvency* and reflects the financial condition of the company.

Bankruptcy   A firm is a failure, in a legal sense, or is *bankrupt,* if its total liabilities exceed a fair valuation of its total assets. The "real" net worth of the firm is negative.

When we use the word "failure" hereafter, we include both technical insolvency and bankruptcy.

CAUSES OF FAILURES

Dun and Bradstreet have compiled a list of the underlying causes of failure in Canada.[2]

Underlying Cause of Failure, 1976	Percentage of Total Failures
Neglect	1.7%
Fraud	0.3
Lack of experience in the line	11.7
Lack of managerial experience	14.3
Unbalanced experience	7.4
Incompetence	63.0
Disaster	0.8
Reasons unknown	0.8

The most important cause of failure is management incompetence. We can group the third, fourth and fifth causes noted in the table under the general title of insufficient experience in the management function. This would include those cases in a partnership where two or more of the partners are specialized in one facet of management, for example, in sales. This grouping accounts for 33.4 percent of the total failures. Both of these management inadequacies were evidenced by the inability to avoid conditions which resulted in inadequate sales, heavy operating expenses, excessive fixed assets, or

[2]Dun & Bradstreet Canada Limited. Research Division Report, 1.

difficulties in receivables and inventories. The failures induced by the impact of recession are included in the two managerial categories. The classification is logical because managements should be prepared to operate in environments in which recessions occur and should frame their policies to cope with downturns as well as to benefit from business upswings. Also, managements must anticipate unfavorable industry trends.

A number of financial remedies are available to management when it becomes aware of the imminence or occurrence of insolvency. These remedies are described in the remainder of this chapter.

THE FAILURE RECORD

How widespread is business failure? Is it a rare phenomenon, or do failures occur fairly often? In Table 24–1, we see that a fairly large number of businesses do fail, although the failures in any one year are not a large percentage of the total number of businesses. In 1976, for example, there were 2,976 failures, but these represented only .82 percent of all business firms. The average firm owed $394,300 when it failed. It is interesting to observe that the average liabilities per failure have increased substantially from 1973 to 1976. In the last column of Table 24–1, the annual percentage growth in constant dollar Gross National Product (GNP) is presented. In 1970, a significant increase in the failure rate is associated with a low rate of growth in GNP. The same relationship is found in 1975.

TABLE 24-1 Historical Failure Rate Experience of Canadian Business

Year	Number of Failures	Average Failure Rate[a]	Average Liability per Failure	Annual Percent: Growth in constant dollar GNP[b]
1966	2418	93	$ 72,300	6.9%
1967	1967	75	109,600	3.3
1968	1697	67	76,700	5.8
1969	1861	69	78,300	5.3
1970	2287	82	115,800	2.5
1971	2627	90	124,600	6.9
1972	2848	98	87,700	6.1
1973	2718	91	117,800	7.5
1974	2512	78	150,300	3.7
1975	2863	84	164,800	1.1
1976	2976	82	394,300	4.9

[a] Per 10,000 concerns.
[b] Bank of Canada Review.

The failure statistics are further subdivided into a number of categories such as manufacturing and trade. The liabilities per failure will be very different for each category. For example, in 1976, there were 457 manufacturing failures (approximately 15 percent of the total failures), and the average liabilities per failure were $1,703,527. For the wholesale trade sector, there were 245 failures in 1976 and the average liabilities per failure were $181,327. The size of the liabilities per failure for each industry reflects the average size of the business establishment within the industry. The largest number of failures, by far, occurred in the retail trade area—in 1976 there were 1242 failures which was 42 percent of the total failures.

While it appears that most failures occur to smaller establishments, large firms are not immune to failure. However, there are a number of offsetting factors which keep the failure rate of large companies lower. These factors include governmental intervention to assist the firm, or mergers of a failing firm with a solvent one. In fact, merger has been called a civilized alternative to bankruptcy.

Why do government and industry seek to avoid bankruptcy among larger firms? There are many reasons—to prevent an erosion of confidence in the case of financial institutions, and to avoid disrupting a local community. Also, bankruptcy is a very expensive process, so even when "the public interest" is not at stake, private industry has strong incentives to avoid out-and-out bankruptcy. The costs of bankruptcy, as well as some further alternatives to it, are discussed in subsequent sections.

EXTENSION AND COMPOSITION

Extension and *composition* are discussed together because they both represent voluntary concessions by creditors. Extension postpones the date of required payment of past-due obligations. Composition voluntarily *reduces* the creditors' claims on the debtor. Both have the purpose of keeping the debtor in business and avoiding court costs. Although creditors absorb a temporary loss, the recovery is often greater than if one of the formal procedures has been followed, and the hope is that a stable customer will emerge. Both extension and composition are used more frequently by smaller concerns.

Procedure

The debtor files a proposal for an extension or a composition. Subsequently, a meeting of the debtor and the creditors is held. The creditors appoint a committee consisting of some of the largest creditors and perhaps one or two of the smaller ones. The purpose of the meeting, and any subsequent meetings, is to work out a proposal that is acceptable to all parties. Usually a vote with a two-thirds majority of each creditor class is required to have the proposal accepted and binding on all creditors.

Necessary Conditions

At least three conditions are usually necessary to make an extension or a composition feasible:

1. The debtor is a good moral risk.
2. The debtor shows ability to make a recovery.
3. General business conditions are favorable to recovery.

Extension

An extension is preferred by creditors because it provides for payment in full. The debtor buys current purchases on a cash basis and pays off his past balance over an extended time. In some cases, creditors may agree not only to extend time of payment but also to subordinate existing claims to new debts incurred in favor of vendors extending credit during the period of the extension. The creditors must have faith that the debtor will solve his problems. Because of the uncertainties involved, however, creditors will want to exercise controls over the debtor while waiting for their claims to be paid.

As examples of controls, the committee may insist that an assignment (turnover of assets to the creditors' committee) be executed, to be held in escrow in case of default. The committee may obtain security in the form of notes, mortgages, or assignment of accounts receivable.

Composition

In a composition, a pro rata cash settlement is made. Creditors receive in cash from the debtor a uniform percentage of the obligations. The cash received is taken as full settlement of the debt. The ratio may be as low as 10 percent. Bargaining will take place between the debtor and the creditors over the savings that result from avoiding certain costs associated with the bankruptcy: costs of administration, legal fees, expenses of outside experts, and so on. In addition to avoiding such costs, the debtor gains in that the stigma of bankruptcy is avoided, and thus the debtor may be induced to part with most of the savings that result from avoiding bankruptcy.

Combination Settlement

Often the bargaining process will result in a compromise involving both an extension and a composition. For example, the settlement may provide for a cash payment of 25 percent of the debt and six future installments of 10 per-cent each. Total payment would thereby aggregate 85 percent. Installment payments are usually evidenced by notes. Creditors will also seek protective controls.

Appraisal of Voluntary Settlements

The advantages of voluntary settlements are informality and simplicity. Inves-tigating, legal, and administrative expenses are held to a minimum. The proce-dure is the most economical and results in the largest return to creditors.

One possible disadvantage is that the debtor is left in control of the busi-ness. This situation may involve legal complications or erosion of assets still operated by the debtor. However, numerous controls are available to give the creditors protection. In fact, one of the requirements for a voluntary settlement may be that the creditors' committee take an active interest in operating the firm.

REORGANIZATION OR COMMERCIAL ARRANGEMENTS

Bankruptcy legislation should have as one of its aims the efficient allocation of resources. If a firm has no long-run promise of profitability and is bankrupt, the company should be liquidated as quickly and as costlessly as possible so that the resources tied up in the bankrupt firm can be put to a more profitable use. However, a firm can be viable in the long-run but have short-run financial problems. To force this firm into costly bankruptcy procedures would not be an efficient use of resources. To assist in the rehabilitation of a firm in this position, the Bankruptcy Act provides for proposals for *reorganization* or *commercial arrangements.*

Commercial arrangements are a form of extension or composition of the firm's obligations and have the following features:

1. The firm is insolvent either because it is unable to meet cash obligations as they come due or because claims on the firm exceed its assets. Hence, some modifications in the nature or amount of the firm's obligations must be made. A scaling down of terms or amounts must be formulated. This procedure may represent scaling down fixed charges or converting short-term debt into long-term debt.
2. New funds may have to be raised for working capital and for property rehabilitation.
3. The operating and managerial causes of difficulty must be discovered and eliminated.

A proposal for a commercial arrangement can be filed by a debtor either before or after bankruptcy. The proposal stops all legal actions against the debtor by all creditors except the secured creditors. In order to be acceptable, the proposal must provide for payment of the trustee's expenses, and the creditors with a priority under the Bankruptcy Act must be paid in full. If the proposal is accepted by a majority of the creditors representing three-quarters of the value of the claims, all unsecured creditors are bound. Unless stated otherwise, the debtor continues to operate the business. The proposal must also be accepted by the court. This acceptance is usually forthcoming if the proposal is considered to be fair to all unsecured creditors. If the proposal is rejected by the creditors or by the court, the debtor is declared bankrupt, or if bankruptcy proceedings were already underway, they are continued.

In a commercial arrangement, the creditors must assess the likelihood of successful rehabilitation and profitable future operations against the sacrifices that they must make in terms of a restructuring of their claims. The elements in this financial decision for creditors are assessed in the following section.

FINANCIAL DECISIONS IN REORGANIZATION

When a business becomes insolvent, a decision must be made whether to dissolve the firm through liquidation or to keep it alive through reorganization. Fundamentally, this decision depends upon a determination of the value of the firm if it is rehabilitated versus the value of the sum of the parts if it is dismembered.

Liquidation values depend upon the degree of specialization of the capital assets used in the firm and hence their resale value. In addition, liquidation itself involves costs of dismantling, including legal costs. Successful reorganization also involves costs. Typically, better equipment must be installed, obsolete inventories must be disposed of, and improvements in management must be made.

Net liquidation values are compared with the value of the firm after reorganization, net of the costs of rehabilitation. The procedure that promises the higher returns to the creditors and owners will be the course of action favored. Often the greater indicated value of the firm in reorganization, compared with its value in liquidation, is used to force a compromise agreement among the claimants in a reorganization, even when they feel that their relative position has not been treated fairly in the reorganization proposal.

Example of Commercial Arrangement

In evaluating the important concerns in a commercial arrangement, we will utilize a simple hypothetical example. Then we will use, as an illustration of the types of arrangements actually made, a simplified version of a successful commercial arrangement. Even though the Bankruptcy Act permits proposals for arrangements, the number of successful arrangements is very small.

In Table 24–2 the balance sheet as of December 31, 19X6, for New-Life Furniture Company, Limited is presented. The company is a medium-size manufactuer of furniture and has been suffering substantial losses for the past two years. During March, 19X7, the company filed a proposal for a commercial arrangement.

TABLE 24–2 New-Life Furniture Company, Limited
Balance Sheet
December 31, 19X7
(thousand of dollars)

Assets:	
Current assets	200
Net property	800
Total assets	$1,000
Liabilities and capital:	
Accounts payable	80
Notes payable	100
8% First-mortgage bonds	500
Common shares	120
Retained earnings	(100)
8½% Sinking fund debentures	300
	$1,000

In preparing the proposal, the company provided an evaluation of its prospective value as a going concern. After a survey and discussion with various experts, an estimate of future earnings was derived. Based on a reasonable price-earnings multiple for furniture manufacturers, a valuation of New-Life as a going concern was $750,000.

The proposal was to restructure the company and have the company issue debt and new common equity for the outstanding claims of New-Life. The new company would issue $500,000 of 20-year, 12 percent debentures in exchange for the first mortgage bonds. This provided for the first priority claim in full and resulted in a net value available to ordinary unsecured creditors of $250,000. Their claims, however, totalled $480,000. With only $250,000 available, each claimant was entitled to 52 percent of its claim. The proposal provided for the ordinary unsecured creditors receiving, in aggregate, 100,000 shares of the new company to settle their claims in full. The claims and settlement are shown in Table 24–3.

TABLE 24–3 Proposal for Commercial Arrangement

Prior Claims	Amount	Receives
First mortgage bonds	$500,000	$500,000 in debentures of new company

Ordinary Unsecured Creditors	Amount	52 Percent of Claim	Number of Common Shares
Notes payable	$100,000	$ 52,000	20,800
Sinking funds debentures	300,000	156,000	62,400
Accounts payable	80,000	42,000	16,800
	$480,000	$250,000	100,000

Of course, the proposal must include payment for the trustee's costs and payment of any outstanding taxes. In this proposal, the common shareholders of the firm did not receive anything. Also, the highest priority claim must be settled in full before the claim of any lower priority class can be considered. This is known as the *absolute priority* rule. This rule does not imply that the first mortgage bondholders must receive securities of the same class in the reorganized company. In fact, if the valuation of the company were much lower, the first mortgage bondholders may receive common shares. The absolute priority rule specifies the order in which claims must be settled in full.

Clearly, the larger the valuation of the company, the more likely it is that the original common shareholders will receive something in the arrangement. If the valuation of the common were in excess of $980,000, the claims of the ordinary, unsecured creditors could be settled in full and the shareholders would receive some new shares.

In addition to satisfying the priority claims of the creditors, the proposal must present a new financial structure that is feasible, given the forecasted earnings for the company. It is essential that the new capital structure be determined so that the firm is not forced into bankruptcy again because of earnings that are not adequate to service a very large debt component.

Up to this point, we have considered the concept of commercial arrangements in general terms with reference to an artificial example. We will now consider an actual commercial arrangement to demonstrate the absolute priority rule and the types of securities that are given to creditors in an arrangement. The arrangement concerns Rideau Carleton Raceway Investments Limited, (hereafter called Investments) and a wholly owned subsidiary, Rideau Carleton Raceway Holdings Limited (hereafter called Holdings). Both companies had their head offices in Ottawa. The first company was incorporated under federal jurisdiction and the second in the Province of Ontario.

On April 2, 1962, Investments issued $1,000,000 of 6¾ percent first mortgage bonds secured by the outstanding shares of Holdings. In addition, $1,000,000 of 6½ percent sinking fund debentures were also issued and secured by a floating charge on the assets of Investments. Interest had not been paid on these bonds since November 15, 1962. In addition, there was a mechanic's lien of $897,621 on the real property of Holdings. This lien was outstanding since March 5, 1966. On May 19, 1962, Investments issued 100,000 preferred shares with a par value of $5 per share. The preferred shares were entitled to a dividend only if the consolidated net income of Investments was in excess of $30,000. Since net earnings never exceeded this value, no dividends were paid, and upon liquidation, the preferred holders were entitled to the paid up value of the shares. Finally, Investments issued 250,000 common shares of no par value in 1962. The aggregate consideration for the shares was $112,500. In the first column of Table 24–4, the creditors claims are presented.

TABLE 24–4 Proposed Compensation in Reorganization of "Investments" and "Holdings"

Creditors	Claims	Proposed Compensation
1st Mortgage bonds	$1,000,000	$900,000 + 200,000 common shares
Sinking fund debentures	1,000,000	500,000 common shares
Mechanic's lien	897,621	$500,000 + 750,000 common shares (income bonds)
Preferred shares; 100,000 shares	500,000	100,000 common shares
Common shares; 250,000 shares	112,500	25,000 common shares
	$3,510,121	

The actual form of the arrangement is somewhat complicated, since Holdings was to take over all obligations of Investments, and any shares issued by Investments were convertible into shares of Holdings on a one-for-one basis. In this example, we will consider that all shares issued by Investments are converted into Holdings so that only the shares of Holdings are outstanding. The proposal was dated August 9, 1971, and had the following provisions.

The first mortgage bondholders received $900,000 in 12 percent, first mortgage bonds of Holdings plus 200,000 common shares. In addition, for each $1,000 of principal amount of existing bonds, a cash payment of $100 was made in respect of the accrued interest. The holders of the sinking fund debentures received 500,000 common shares in settlement of their claim. The holders of the mechanic's lien received $500,000 worth of 8 percent secured income bonds. These bonds were subordinated to the 12 percent first mortgage bonds. In addition, they received 750,000 common shares of

Holdings. The preferred shares received one new share of Holdings for each preferred share. Finally, the common shareholders received one new share for each ten shares of Investments held. This resulted in the issuance of 25,000 common shares.

One way of evaluating this plan is to assume that the payment given to the old first mortgage bonds is equal to $1,000,000. Thus, the implicit price per share on the common is $0.50. Thus, the preferred share claim of $500,000 was settled for $50,000 and the old common received $12,500 in common shares of Holding.

Included in the proposal was the payment in cash for the fees, costs and expenses of the receiver and the trustee. The acceptance of the proposal by the creditors is equivalent to the granting of a complete and full discharge of all claims of the creditors against Holdings and Investments.

In the United States, federal bankruptcy laws specify that reorganization plans must be worked out by court-appointed officials and must be reviewed by the Securities and Exchange Commissions (SEC). Both the SEC and the courts are called upon to determine the "fairness" and the feasibility of the proposed reorganization plan, based on precedents set in court decisions. In Canada, the courts must ultimately accept or reject the proposal based on the concept of fairness. However, the Canadian system implicitly assumes that a proposal agreed to by all parties must, by definition, be fair.

LIQUIDATION PROCEDURES

Liquidation of a business occurs when the estimated value of the firm is greater "dead than alive."

Assignment is a liquidation procedure that does not go through the courts, although it can be used to achieve full settlement of claims on the debtor. *Bankruptcy* is a legal procedure carried out under the jurisdiction of courts in which a business firm is formally liquidated and claims of creditors are completely discharged.

Assignment

Assignment (as well as bankruptcy) takes place when the debtor is insolvent and the possibilities of restoring profitability are so remote that the enterprise should be dissolved—that is, when the firm is "worth more dead than alive." Assignment is a technique for liquidating a debt and yielding a larger amount to the creditors than is likely to be achieved in formal bankruptcy.

Technically, there are three classes of assignments: (1) common law assignment, (2) statutory assignment, and (3) assignment plus settlement.

Common Law Assignment   The common law provides for an assignment whereby a debtor transfers his title to assets to a third person, known as an assignee or a trustee. The trustee is instructed to liquidate the assets and to distribute the proceeds among the creditors on a pro rata basis.

The assignee may liquidate the assets through what is known as a bulk sale, which is a public sale through an auctioneer. The auction is preceded by sufficient advertising so that there will be a number of bids. Liquidation may also be by a piecemeal auction sale conducted on the premises of the assignor by a competent licensed auctioneer, rather than by a bulk sale. On-premises sales are particularly advantageous in the liquidation of large machine shops of manufacturing plants.

The common law assignment, as such, does not discharge the debtor from his obligations. If a corporation goes out of business and does not satisfy all its claims, there will still be claims against it, but in effect the corporation has ceased to exist. The people who have been associated with the company can then proceed to organize another corporation free of the debts and obligations of the previous corporation. There is always the danger, however, that the court may hold the individuals responsible: therefore, it is usually important to obtain a statement from creditors that claims have been completely settled. Such a statement is, of course, even more important for an unincorporated business.

Statutory Assignment   Statutory assignment is similar in concept to common law assignment. Legally, it is carried out under statutes regulating assignment; technically, it requires more formality. The debtor executes an instrument of assignment, which is recorded. This recordation provides notice to all third parties. The proceedings are handled under court order: the court appoints an assignee and supervises the proceedings, including the sale of the assets and distribution of the proceeds. As in the common law assignment, the debtor is not automatically discharged from the balance of his obligations.

Assignment Plus Settlement   Both the common law assignment and the statutory assignment may take place with recognition and agreement beforehand by the creditors that the assignment will represent a complete discharge of obligation. Normally, the debtor communicates with the creditors at a meeting of the creditors, and a trust instrument of assignment is drawn. The assets are disposed of through regular trade channels, by bulk sales, by auction, or by private sale. The creditors, typically, leave all responsibility for the liquidation procedure with the assignee or the trustee.

Having disposed of the assets and obtained funds, the trustee will then distribute the proceeds pro rata among the creditors in full settlement of the claims on the debtor. Ordinarily, a release is not agreed upon before the execution of the assignment. After full examination of the facts, the creditors' committee will usually make a recommendation for the granting of a release following the execution of the assignment.

Assignment has substantial advantages over bankruptcy. Bankruptcy through the courts involves much time, legal formalities, and accounting and legal expenses. An assignment saves the costs of bankruptcy proceedings, and it may save time as well. Furthermore, an assignee usually has much more flexibility in disposing of property than does a bankruptcy trustee. He or she may be more familiar with the normal channels of trade. Since action is taken much sooner, before the inventories become more obsolete, better results may be achieved.

BANKRUPTCY

The Federal Acts under which bankruptcy proceedings currently can be instituted represent two main achievements: (1) They provide safeguards against fraud by the debtor during liquidation, and, simultaneously, they provide for an equitable distribution of the debtor's assets among the creditors. (2) Insolvent debtors may discharge all their obligations and start new businesses unhampered by a burden of prior debt.

Prerequisites for Bankruptcy

A voluntary petition of bankruptcy (or assignment) may be filed by the debtor, but the creditors may petition for an involuntary bankruptcy if the following two conditions are met.

1. Creditor(s) must have $1,000 or more owing.

2. Within the six months preceding the filing of a creditor's petition, the debtor must have committed one or more acts of bankruptcy. These acts of bankruptcy raise the presupposition that the debtor is either unable to pay the debts, or is attempting to avoid payment.

Acts of Bankruptcy

The ten acts of bankruptcy can be summarized briefly.

1. Fraudulent Conveyance   Fraudulent conveyance is a transfer of property to a third party without adequate consideration and with intent to defraud creditors.

2. Preferential Transfer   A preferential transfer is the transfer of money or assets by an insolvent debtor to a creditor, giving the creditor a greater portion of his or her claim than other creditors would receive on liquidation. This is also referred to as a fraudulent preference.

3. Concealment or Removal Concealment constitutes hiding of property with the intent to defraud creditors. Removal refers to the removal of property with the same intent.

4. Assignment If a debtor makes a general assignment for the benefit of creditors, an act of bankruptcy exists. This enables creditors who have become distrustful of the debtor in the process of assignment to transfer the proceedings to an involuntary bankruptcy.

5. Sudden Departure If the debtor absconds in order to defeat or delay the creditors, then a petition for bankruptcy can be filed.

6. Admission at Creditor's Meeting The debtor commits an act of bankruptcy if, at a meeting of the creditors, he or she presents either a statement of assets and liabilities showing that he or she is insolvent or admits, in writing, that he or she is unable to pay debts.

7. Default on a Proposal In order to prevent bankruptcy, the debtor may have presented a proposal for a commercial arrangement under the Bankruptcy Act. Any default under this proposal is an act of bankruptcy.

8. Notice to Creditors If the debtor presents notice to any creditor that he or she has or will suspend payments on the debt, then an act of bankruptcy has occurred.

9. Execution Order An act of bankruptcy occurs if the debtor fails to redeem goods that were seized under an execution issued against the debtor.

10. Technical Insolvency The most common act of bankruptcy occurs when the debtor is unable to meet liabilities generally as they become due.

Interim Receiver

After a petition for involuntary bankruptcy has been filed, the court may appoint a trustee to be an *interim receiver*. The purpose of the interim receiver is to protect the estate for the creditors. If the receiving order is issued by the court and bankruptcy procedures continue, the interim receiver is usually appointed as the trustee of the estate.

In a voluntary bankruptcy, there is no petition or receiving order and the trustee is appointed directly. However, after appointment of the trustee, the procedures for an involuntary and voluntary bankruptcy are identical.

First Creditors' Meeting

The first meeting of the creditors is called by the trustee within five days after his or her appointment. The purpose of this meeting is to inform the creditors of the financial state of the company, to appoint a board of inspectors, to confirm the appointment of the trustee (or elect a replacement if necessary), and to permit the creditors to give directions to the trustee with regard to the administration of the bankrupt estate. The board of inspectors represents the creditors in the administration of the estate and subsequent meetings of the creditors are not necessary.

Typically, there is little left over for the ordinary, unsecured creditors after those creditors with claims of higher priority receive their payments. Thus, unless the estate is large, unsecured creditors feel that attending the first meeting is a waste of time. This leads to delays in the process, since it becomes difficult to obtain a quorum for the meeting.

Subsequent Procedure

The trustee obtains control of the assets and converts them into cash. The trustee has the power to sell property, carry on business, bring or defend legal actions, and make compromises with creditors. Upon the bankruptcy of the debtor, any legal proceedings against the bankrupt are postponed except for secured creditors. In fact, secured creditors may, by prompt repossession and disposal of assets in which they have a security interest, leave few assets for the trustee to liquidate and distribute to the remaining creditors.

Discharge

After the proceeds from the liquidation of the bankrupt estate have been distributed, the bankrupt applies to the court for a discharge. The court has wide discretion to grant a discharge. If the bankrupt is a corporation, a discharge may be granted if the claims of all the creditors have been satisfied in full; this is an unlikely event.

Even though the bankrupt corporation is not discharged, the directors and officers of the corporation are free to pursue new ventures. There is a problem for these directors and officers only if it has been demonstrated that they are to blame for the corporate bankruptcy.

Priority of Claims on Distribution of Proceeds of a Bankruptcy

Four classes of creditors can be identified in the bankruptcy process and each class has a different priority. These classes are:
1. Secured creditors
2. Preferred creditors

3. Ordinary unsecured creditors

4. Deferred creditors

In the first pass, the secured creditors are not included in the priority ranking for the distribution of the liquidation proceeds. Typically, the secured creditors will take possession of their security and apply the proceeds of sale of this security against their claims. To the extent that their claims exceed the proceeds from the liquidation of the security, the secured creditors join the ordinary, unsecured creditors to obtain the balance owing. Notice that the secured creditors have an absolute priority to the extent of their security interest.

Preferred creditors have the highest priority in the distribution of the proceeds. The highest priority claim is the costs of administration of the estate. After these costs are paid, the remaining proceeds are divided among the other preferred creditors on a pro rata basis. The other preferred creditors include arrears in rent, unpaid wages and salaries, municipal taxes and claims of the Crown or province.

The claim of the ordinary unsecured creditors consists of the remaining balances after payment in full to preferred creditors. These unsecured creditors include trade creditors, holders of debentures, and unsatisfied claims of secured creditors. Holders of subordinated debt fall into the unsecured creditor class, but they must turn over required amounts to the holders of senior debt.

The final class of creditor is the deferred creditor. An example of a deferred creditor is the spouse of the bankrupt who has a claim in respect of wages or compensation. These creditors are paid with any remaining funds. It is unlikely that these creditors will receive any payment. If, by some surprising combination of events, the deferred creditors are paid in full, then the preferred shareholders have a claim to the remaining funds.

All creditors in a specific class, except for the secured creditors, are paid on a pro rata basis. The order of priority is strict—no payment is made to a class of a lower priority until all claims of a higher priority are paid in full.

To illustrate how this priority of claims works out, let us take a specific example. The balance sheet of a bankrupt firm is shown in Table 24–5. Assets total $90 million. The claims are those indicated on the right-hand side of the balance sheet. It will be noted that the subordinated debentures are subordinated to the notes payable to commercial banks.

Now assume that the assets of the firm are sold. These assets as shown in the balance sheet in Table 24–5 are greatly overstated—they are, in fact, worth much less than the $90 million at which they are carried. The following amounts are realized on liquidation:

Current assets	$28,000,000
Net property	5,000,000
Total assets	$33,000,000

TABLE 24-5   Bankrupt Firm
                 Balance sheet

Current assets	$80,000,000	Accounts payable	$20,000,000
Net property	$10,000,000	Notes payable (due bank)	10,000,000
		Accrued wages,	
		1,400 @ $500	700,000
		Federal and	1,000,000
		provincial taxes	1,300,000
		Current debt	$32,000,000
		First mortgage	$ 6,000,000
		Second mortgage	1,000,000
		Subordinated debentures[a]	8,000,000
		Long-term debt	$15,000,000
		Preferred shares	2,000,000
		Common equity	26,000,000
		Contributed surplus	4,000,000
		Retained earnings	11,000,000
		Net worth	$43,000,000
Total assets	$90,000,000	Total claims	$90,000,000

[a] Subordinated to $10 million notes payable to the First Provincial Bank.

The order of priority of payment of claims is shown by Table 24-6. Fees and expenses of administration are assumed to be $6 million. Next in priority are wages due workers, which total $700,000. The total amount of taxes to be paid is $1.3 million. Thus far, the total of claims paid for the $33 million is $8 million. The first mortgage is then paid from the net proceeds of $5 million from the sale of fixed property, leaving $20 million available to the ordinary unsecured creditors.

The claims of the general creditors total $40 million. Since $20 million is available, each claimant would receive 50 percent of his claim before the subordination adjustment. This adjustment requires that the subordinated debentures turn over to the notes to which they are subordinated all amounts received until the notes are satisfied. In this situation, the claim of the notes payable is $10 million, but only $5 million is available; the deficiency is therefore $5 million. After transfer by the subordinated debentures of $4 million, there remains a deficiency of $1 million, which will be unsatisfied. It will be noted that 90 percent of the bank claim is satisfied, whereas only 50 percent of other unsecured claims will be satisfied. These figures illustrate the usefulness of the subordination provision to the security to which the subordination is made. Since no other funds remain, the claims of the holders of preferred and common shares are completely wiped out.

In the U.S., studies of the proceeds in bankruptcy liquidations reveal that unsecured creditors receive, on the average, about 15 cents per dollar of

TABLE 24-6 Bankrupt Firm
Order of priority of claims

Distribution of Proceeds on Liquidation	
1. Proceeds of sale of assets	$33,000,000
2. Fees and expenses of administration of bankruptcy	$ 6,000,000
3. Wages due workers earned three months prior to filing of bankruptcy petition	700,000
4. Taxes	1,300,000
	$25,000,000
5. First mortgage, paid from sale of net property	5,000,000
6. Available to ordinary unsecured creditors	$20,000,000

Claims of General Creditors	Claim (1)	Application of 50 Percent (2)	After Subordination Adjustment (3)	Percentage of Original Claims Received (4)
Unsatisfied portion of first mortgage	$ 1,000,000	$ 500,000	$ 500,000	92
Unsatisfied portion of second mortgage	1,000,000	500,000	500,000	50
Notes payable	10,000,000	5,000,000	9,000,000	90
Accounts payable	20,000,000	10,000,000	10,000,000	50
Subordinated debentures	8,000,000	4,000,000	0	0
	$40,000,000	$20,000,000	$20,000,000	56

Notes: 1. Column 1 is the claim of each type of creditor. Total claims equal $40 million.
2. From line 6 in the upper section of the table we see that $20 million is available. This sum, divided by the $40 million of claims, indicates that general creditors will receive 50 percent of their claims. This is shown in column 2.
3. The debentures are subordinated to the notes payable. Four million dollars is transferred from debentures to notes payable in column 3.
4. Column 4 shows the results of dividing the column 3 figure by the original amount given in Table 24-7, except for first mortgage, where $5 million paid on sale of property is included. The 56 percent total figure includes the first mortgage transactions, that is, ($20,000,000 + $5,000,000) ÷ ($40,000,000 + $5,000,000) = 56%.

credit extended. Consequently, where assignment to creditors is likely to yield more, assignment is to be preferred to bankruptcy.

Role of the Trustee

The trustee plays an important role in both voluntary and involuntary bankruptcy proceedings. A trustee must be licensed by the Superintendent of

Bankruptcy and is an officer of the court. The main function of the trustee is to obtain control of the assets, liquidate them, and distribute the proceeds according to the legislated priority rules. If any persons have claims against the bankrupt estate, they must prove their claims. The trustee has the power to disallow a claim, or approve it, in part or in total. Upon completion of the administration of the estate, the trustee applies for a discharge. This discharge releases the trustee from any liabilities incurred during the administration of the estate, and it is granted if the inspectors and court are satisfied with the results.

In taking possession of the property for liquidation, the trustee goes beyond the outward appearance of ownership. There are a number of transfers of property which, having taken place within a prescribed period before the date of becoming bankrupt, may be examined and reversed. These transfers of property include the following: (a) transfers of property intended to defraud the creditors, (b) certain types of gifts made by the debtor within one year before becoming bankrupt, (c) transfers which give certain creditors a preference, if these transfers occurred three months before the bankruptcy. An example of the latter type of preference would be the taking of additional security, such as a floating charge on the assets of a company's subsidiary, to improve the security of an existing claim.

PROPOSED NEW BANKRUPTCY ACT (BILL S-11)

Currently, there are a number of federal laws concerning bankruptcy. These include the Bankruptcy Act, the Winding-Up-Act, the Companies' Creditors Arrangement Act, and the Farmers' Creditors Arrangement Act. The purpose of the proposed, new Bankruptcy Act is to draw together into one act a number of rules contained in these statutes. In addition, the new Act is intended to clarify a number of provisions and to streamline procedures. There are in excess of 100 amendments to the existing Bankruptcy Act. These include increasing the priority of the claims of wage earners to the level of an absolute priority and reducing the priority of claims of the Crown. In addition, the new Act imposes personal liability where an officer acted in his or her own interests which was contrary to that of the company, or did business with the purpose of defrauding creditors. Directors of a bankrupt company will become liable for unpaid wages owed to employees up to $2500 per employee.

There is an important change in philosophy in this proposed Act as compared to the existing one. In the existing Act, there appear to be significant obstacles to a company that wishes to introduce a proposal for an arrangement, and thus avoid the costs of bankruptcy. Even though the filing of a proposal is sufficient to stop a creditor from filing an action to enforce a claim, secured creditors are not affected by the proposal and they are interested in recovering as much of their loan as possible from existing assets. However, the new Act is intended to promote proposals for commercial arrangements which will not be thwarted by the secured creditors' enthusiasm to recover their funds. To this end, not only can the debtor make a proposal as under the existing legislation, but the trustee, liquidator, or creditor may make a proposal. The new Act introduces the Notice of Intention; once filed, the notice of intention stops all creditors from any further action for ten days. This provides the debtor with time to prepare a proposal. After ten days, or longer if provided by the court, the proposal for a commercial arrangement must be filed or bankruptcy proceedings will continue, or are automatically instituted.

Some rough estimates suggest that, under the existing legislation, one in five companies entering a commercial arrangement is saved from liquidation. It is hoped that, with the new Act, there will be an improvement in the success ratio.

SUMMARY

Problems associated with the decline and failure of a firm, and methods of rehabilitating or liquidating one that has failed, were the subjects treated in this chapter. The major cause of failure is incompetent management. Bad managers should, of course, be removed as promptly as possible; if failure has occurred, a number of remedies are open to the interested parties.

The first question to be answered is whether the firm is better off "dead or alive"—whether it should be liquidated and sold off piecemeal or be rehabilitated. Assuming the decision is made that the firm should survive, it must be put through what is called a *commercial arrangement* or *reorganization.* Legal procedures are always costly, especially in the case of a business failure. Therefore, if it is at all possible, both the debtor and the creditors are better off if matters can be handled on an informal basis rather than through the courts. The informal procedures used in reorganization are (1) *extension,* which postpones the date of settlement, and (2) *composition,* which reduces the amount owed.

If voluntary settlement through extension or composition is not possible, the matter is thrown into the courts. If the court decides on reorganization rather than liquidation, it will appoint a trustee (1) to control the firm going through reorganization, and (2) to prepare a proposal for a commercial arrangement. The plan must be approved by both creditors and the courts, and it should be both fair and feasible.

Finally, where liquidation is treated as the only solution to the debtor's insolvency, the creditors should attempt procedures that will net them the largest recovery. *Assignment* of the debtor's property is the cheaper and the faster procedure. Furthermore, there is more flexibility in disposing of the debtor's property and thus providing larger returns. *Bankruptcy* provides formal procedures in liquidation to safeguard the debtor's property from fraud and provides equitable distribution to the creditors. The procedure is long and cumbersome. Moreover, the debtor's property is generally poorly managed during bankruptcy proceedings unless the trustee is closely supervised by the creditors.

A new bankruptcy law has recently been proposed which will introduce a number of innovations and consolidate into one act the provisions that currently exist under four separate acts. A major policy in the new act is an attempt to facilitate the use of proposals for commercial arrangements.

QUESTIONS

24-1. "A certain number of business failures is a healthy sign. If there are no failures, this is an indication (a) that entrepreneurs are overly cautious, hence not as inventive and as willing to take risks as a healthy, growing economy requires, (b) that competition is not functioning to weed out inefficient producers, or (c) that both situations exist." Discuss, giving pros and cons.

24-2. How can financial analysis be used to forecast the probability of a given firm's failure? Assuming that such analysis is properly applied, can it always predict failure?

24-3. Why do creditors usually accept a plan for financial rehabilitation rather than demand liquidation of the business?

24-4. Would it be possible to form a profitable company by merging two companies, both of which are business failures? Explain.

24-5. Distinguish between a reorganization and a bankruptcy.

24-6. Would it be a sound rule to liquidate whenever the liquidation value is above the value of the corporation as a going concern? Discuss.

24-7. Why do all liquidations usually result in losses for the creditors or the owners, or both? Would partial liquidation or liquidation over a period limit their losses? Explain.

24-8. Are liquidations likely to be more common for public utility or industrial corporations? Why?

PROBLEMS

24-1. The financial statements of the Johnston Publishing Co. Ltd. for 19X5 are shown below.

A recapitalization plan is proposed in which each share of the $6 preferred will be exchanged for one share of $2.40 preferred (stated value, $37.50) plus one 8 percent subordinated income debenture (stated principal, $75). The $10.50 preferred would be retired from cash.

    a. Show the *pro forma* balance sheet (in millions of dollars) giving effect to the recapitalization and showing the new preferred at its stated value and the common stock at its par value.

    b. Present the *pro forma* income statement (in millions of dollars carried to two decimal places).

    c. How much does the firm increase income available to common shares by the recapitalization?

    d. How much less is the required pretax earnings after the recapitalization compared to those before the change? Required earnings is the amount that is just

enough to meet fixed charges, debenture interest, and/or preferred dividends.
e. How is the debt-to-net-worth position of the company affected by the recapitalization?
f. Would you vote for the recapitalization if you were a holder of the $6 prior preferred shares?

Johnston Publishing Co. Ltd.
Balance sheet
December 31, 19X5
(in millions of dollars)

Current assets	$120	Current liabilities	$ 42
Investments	48	Advance payments for subscriptions	78
Net fixed assets	153	Reserves	6
Goodwill	15	$6 preferred shares, $112.50 par	
		($1,200,000 shares)	135
		$10.50 preferred shares, no par	
		(60,000 shares, callable at $150)	9
		Common equity, par value	
		of $1.50 (6,000,000 shares outstanding)	9
		Retained earnings	57
Total assets	$336	Total claims	$336

Johnston Publishing Co. Ltd.
Consolidated statement of income and expense for year ended
December 31, 19X5
(in millions of dollars)

Operating income		$540.0
Operating expense		516.0
Net operating income		$ 24.0
Other income		3.0
Other expense		0.0
Earnings before income tax		$ 27.0
Income tax at 50 percent		13.5
Income after taxes		$ 13.5
Dividends on $6 prior preferred shares	$7.2	
Dividends on $10.50 preferred shares	0.6	7.8
Income available for common equity		$ 5.7

24-2. The Sun Instrument Co. Ltd. produces precision instruments. The company's products are designed and manufactured according to specifications set out by its customers and are highly specialized.

Declines in sales and increases in development expenses in recent years resulted in a large deficit at the end of 19X8.

Sun Instrument Co. Ltd.
Balance sheet
December 31, 19X8
(in thousands of dollars)

Current assets	$375	Current liabilities	$450
Fixed assets	375	Long-term debt (unsecured)	225
		Capital stock	150
		Retained earnings (deficit)	(75)
Total assets	$750	Total claims	$750

Sun Instrument Co. Ltd.
Sales and profits, 19X5 – 19X8
(in thousands of dollars)

Year	Sales	Net Profit after Tax before Fixed Charges
19X5	$2,625	$ 262.5
19X6	$2,400	$ 225.0
19X7	$1,425	$(75.0)
19X8	$1,350	$(112.5)

Independent assessment led to the conclusion that the company would have a liquidation value of about $600,000. As an alternative to liquidation, the management concluded that a reorganization was possible with additional investment of $300,000. The management was confident of eventual success of the company and stated that the additional investment would restore earnings to $125,000 a year after taxes and before fixed charges. The appropriate multiplier to apply is 8 times. The management is negotiating with a local investment group to obtain the additional investment of $300,000. If the funds are obtained, the holders of the long-term debt would be given one-half the common equity in the reorganized firm in place of their present claims.

Should the creditors agree to the reorganization or should they force liquidation of the firm?

24-3. During the past several months, the Canadian Industrial Corporation has had difficulty meeting its current obligations. Attempts to raise additional working capital have failed. To add to CIC's problems, its principal lenders, The National Bank and the General Insurance Company, have been placing increased pressure on CIC because of its continued delinquent loan payments and apparent lack of fiscal responsibility.

The National Bank is first mortgage holder on CIC's production facility and, in addition, the bank has a $1 million, unsecured, revolving loan with CIC that is past due and on which certain restrictive clauses have been violated. The General Insurance Company is holding $5 million of CIC's subordinated debentures. These debentures are subordinate to the notes payable.

Because of the bank's increasing concern for the long-term future of CIC, it exercised its right of offset and attached $750,000 of CIC's deposits. Because of this action, the bank has forced the company into reorganization or bankruptcy.

General Insurance has located a large manufacturing company that is interested in taking over CIC's operations. This company has offered to assume the $8 million mortgage, pay all back taxes, and in addition pay $4.3 million in cash for the company.

a. Given the data in Exhibit 1 and the fact that CIC cannot be reorganized internally, show the effect of the above reorganization plan on claims of CIC's creditors.

b. Comment on the actions of the bank in offsetting CIC's deposits.

c. Do you feel the bank and the insurance company were right in not advancing CIC additional money?

EXHIBIT I
($000's)

Current assets	$ 3,000
Net property, plant, and equipment	12,000
Other assets	2,800
Total assets	$17,800
Accounts payable	2,000
Taxes	200
Notes payable to bank	250
Other current liabilities	1,350
Total current liabilities	3,800
Mortgage	8,000
Subordinated debentures	5,000
Common shares	1,000
Paid-in capital	2,000
Retained earnings	(2,000)
Total liabilities and shareholders' equity	$17,800

EXHIBIT II
(000's)

Estimated Sales	$20,000
Estimated Earnings	1,294
Capitalization factor	10×

Managerial Finance: A Summary

25
Perhaps the biggest single failing of both finance texts and finance courses is that they often leave the student with the impression that managerial finance consists of a series of discrete, unconnected parts. *This is decidedly not true.* Because the nature of each element must be understood before the inter-relationships among elements can be made meaningful, we have considered the various topics in semi-isolation. But to truly understand finance, one simply must recognize the interdependencies and see how the pieces fit together. Our purpose in this chapter is to draw together the various components in order to present a unified, integrated view of managerial finance.

ROLE OF MANAGERIAL FINANCE WITHIN THE ECONOMY

Because business firms produce the vast majority of the economy's goods and services, if the economy is to function efficiently so must the firms within it. By efficient operations we mean that firms must accurately determine what goods and services consumers desire, then produce and distribute these products at the lowest possible cost.[1]

---

[1] In order to have an efficient allocation of resources from the social point of view, cost must include all social costs, such as air and water pollution. One possible procedure for forcing the inclusion of such costs in operating decisions of firms is for a governmental agency to assess charges to polluters, with the charges being an increasing function of the level of pollution and the estimated social cost of the particular pollution. This is a thorny problem, but it is perfectly obvious that business firms can and will reduce pollution, just as they reduce labor usage or raw materials wastage, if their pollution costs are assessed against them. Charges based on the extent to which a firm creates pollution would provide this incentive. We might also note that it is unrealistic to expect voluntary controls to work in a competitive industry, as even one non cooperative firm can gain an advantage over other firms and literally force them to abandon voluntary controls. Thus, mandatory industry-wide controls are necessary. Alternatively, it has been suggested that individuals be given property rights to a pollution free environment. Thus, any firm causing pollution will be held liable for damages. This will force firms to negotiate with individuals who would be directly affected by pollution in order to determine an appropriate payment to the individuals, if any, that will compensate for the loss of the property right.

The financial manager plays a key role in the operations of a firm. Through the exercise of internal controls he or she helps insure that the resources available to the firm are used as efficiently as possible. Included here are both cost control and cost analysis designed to achieve the most efficient use of assets. The financial manager also plays a key role with regard to the use of external resources or to the decision to acquire resources not presently under the control of the firm. In the first place, the capital budgeting decision is designed to insure that the firm makes desirable investments but forgoes undesirable ones. If all costs, social as well as private, are taken into account, and if the cost of capital is estimated appropriately, then the capital budgeting process will ensure that the firm's capital expenditures are optimal from the points of view of both shareholders and society as a whole. The cost of capital, when determined in the correct manner, will reflect the opportunity cost of employing resources in the particular firm versus using them elsewhere in the economy. Further, if the firm is to produce funds in the least-cost manner, it must provide the package of investment securities that investors (that is, savers) consider to be the most desirable.

Finance, then, plays an important role both in increasing operating efficiency within individual business units and in allocating productive resources among firms.

FINANCIAL ANALYSIS, PLANNING, AND CONTROL

Managerial finance consists, in essence, of a set of decision rules designed to help management maximize the market value of existing shareholders' equity. *Market value* is defined as the present value of the firm's expected future cash flows, discounted at a rate that reflects the uncertainty inherent in the projected cash flows. In theory, we can set up a simultaneous equation model, then solve the model for the set of controllable variables that maximizes the firm's value. In practice, such a mathematical approach is out of the question. We recognize that everything is related to everything else, but we cannot specify the full set of relationships well enough to optimize in the mathematical sense.

We wish to optimize, but we cannot. What can we do? The best alternative, and the one followed by both academicians and financial managers, is to suboptimize, or examine one aspect of a given decision and explicitly assume that the decision at hand has only a minimal effect on other dimensions of the firm's operations. The EOQ inventory model is an example of a suboptimizing model.

Suboptimization is dangerous, however—there is always the possibility that a series of suboptimal decisions will work at cross-purposes and produce very bad overall results. Because of this, we must constantly keep "the big picture" in mind, altering individual decisions if it becomes clear that they are inconsistent. In Part II of this book, An Overview of Finance: Analysis, Planning, and Control, we examined certain tools and techniques that are useful in developing an overall framework into which suboptimizing models can be fitted.

Ratio Analysis

First, we examined a number of financial ratios and saw how ratio analysis could be used to appraise key aspects of a firm's operating position. *Liquidity ratios*—especially the current and the quick ratios—were seen to provide information on the firm's ability to meet its short-run obligations. *Leverage ratios*—particularly the debt ratio, the times interest earned, and the fixed charge coverage—were used to make judgments about the firm's risk of financial leverage. *Activity ratios*—relating to the turnover of such asset categories as inventories, accounts receivable, and fixed assets, as well as total assets—were studied to see how intensively the firm is employing its assets. Finally, *profitability ratios*—the profit margin on sales, and the rate of return on net worth and total assets—were examined. The firm's primary operating objective is to earn a good return on its invested capital, and the rate-of-return ratios show how successfully the firm is meeting this objective.

The ratios are interrelated, and the set of relationships can be studied through the so-called du Pont system. Basically the du Pont system makes use of the fact that the profit margin on sales times the turnover of total assets equals the rate of return on investment.

$$\text{Return on assets} = \frac{\text{profit}}{\text{sales}} \times \frac{\text{sales}}{\text{assets}} = \frac{\text{profit}}{\text{assets}}.$$

This equation can be expanded to include financial leverage, in which case the final product is the rate of return on net worth.

$$\text{Return on net worth} = \frac{\text{percentage return on assets}}{1.0 - \text{debt ratio}}.$$

The significant advantage of the du Pont approach is that it helps the financial manager focus on problem areas. If his rate of return on net worth is lower than that of other firms in the same industry, he can trace back through the du Pont system to see where the trouble lies—for example, is some category of assets (such as inventories) too high, or are labor costs excessive? Note that in addition to comparing a firm with others in its industry, the financial manager can use the du Pont system of ratio analysis to study the trend in his firm's performance over time, thus helping to forestall developing problems.

By categorizing the ratios into four groups, we stressed the uses of the ratios rather than their definitions. Our emphasis was on the generality of ratio analysis, and we sought to show that the purpose of a ratio determines how it is defined. The financial manager faces a myriad of situations calling for analysis—for example, appraising the credit-worthiness of his firm's customers and analyzing the performance of his own firm's various operating divisions. Ratios facilitate this analysis, and because of their simplicity and flexibility they are one of the most widely used tools in the financial manager's kit.

Profit Planning

Ratio analysis is used to examine the firm's current operating posture. Such constant surveillance is a critical part of the control process, but even if no current weaknesses are detected, the firm must still plan for future growth. One important element of such planning relates to decisions about expansion of existing operations, as well as movements into new product lines. Also, whatever type of expansion occurs, the firm must choose between using more or less highly automated productive processes. If a greater degree of auto-mation is to be employed, then relatively heavy investments in fixed assets must be made, and this will increase fixed costs. Variable costs will, however, be relatively low in such cases. The extent to which fixed costs are incurred in the production process is defined as *operating leverage,* while the relation-ship between changing levels of sales and profits is known as *break-even analysis.*

Financial Forecasting

Although each specific asset expansion decision must be evaluated in detail in reaching the capital budgeting decision, the financial manager should also make broad-brush, aggregate forecasts of future asset requirements to as-sure that funds will be available to finance new investment programs. These forecasts are, in effect, made because of the explicit recognition that the capi-tal budgeting procedures used in practice are suboptimizing models.

The first step in the aggregate forecast is to obtain an estimate of sales during each year of the planning period. This estimate is worked out jointly by the marketing, production, and finance departments—the marketing manager estimates demand, the production manager estimates capacity, and the financial manager estimates the availability of funds to finance new accounts receivable, inventories, and fixed assets.

Given the approximate level of sales, the financial manager must deter-mine, as accurately as possible, the amount and timing of financial require-ments over the planning horizon. On the basis of past relationships between sales and individual balance sheet items, the funds requirements can be forecast by using either (1) the *percent-of-sales method,* or (2) *regression analysis* (simple or multivariate, linear or curvilinear). Asset requirements by balance sheet category are forecast, spontaneously generated funds (increases in accounts payable plus retained earnings) are estimated, and the difference is determined. If the growth rate is quite rapid, asset require-ments will exceed internal sources of funds, so plans must be made to obtain new debt or external equity money. If growth is slow, then more funds will be generated than are required to support the estimated growth in sales. In this case the financial manager will consider a number of alternatives, including increasing the dividend payout ratio, retiring debt, repurchasing shares, using excess funds to acquire other firms, or, perhaps, going back to the operating departments to encourage more R&D expenditures and a further search for profitable investment opportunities.

Control through Budgeting

Once the firm's broad goals for the planning period have been established, the next step is to set up a detailed plan of operation—the *budget*. A complete budget system encompasses all aspects of the firm's operations over the planning horizon; modifications in plans as required by variations in factors outside the firm's control, especially the level of economic activity, are accounted for by use of *flexible budgets.*

A good budgeting system is a most important management tool. It starts with a sales forecast, then works through various intermediate schedules to the *cash budget, budgeted income statement,* and *budgeted,* or *projected* (pro forma), *balance sheet.* The cash budget provides a relatively precise estimate of when funds will be needed and the extent of the firm's short-run financing requirements. The budgeted income statement gives an indication of projected profits, and the budgeted balance sheet indicates the firm's financial picture at the end of the period. If projected profits are too low, or if the *pro forma* balance sheet suggests that the financial ratios are getting out of line, actions can be taken to correct these imbalances.

Interrelationships among Ratio Analysis, Profit Planning, Forecasting, and Budgeting

Ratio analysis is used to highlight certain key features of a firm's operations. Such an analysis can be conducted relatively quickly, and it can be updated frequently to permit early detection of developing problems. Further, ratio analysis is useful in that it facilitates a comparison between the firm in question and other firms in the industry. Once ratio analysis has been used to take stock of the firm's present condition, actions must be taken to exploit its strong points and to strengthen its weak ones. Here, the planning techniques come into play. Break-even analysis can be used both to appraise the prospects of new product decisions and to analyze the effects of expansion or plant modernization decisions on earnings variability.

Sales forecasts are made and used to determine asset requirements and the funds needed to finance these assets. Specific, detailed plans for the current year are drawn up to implement the firm's long-run goals and objectives—this is the annual budget. A key part of the total budget—the cash budget—pinpoints when and how much money will be required during the budget period.

Finally, the financial manager continually compares actual operating results with budgeted figures: Are sales running at the forecast level? Are costs being kept within the estimated limits? Are cash flows running on schedule? Are all divisions meeting their own individual budgeting objectives? This process, called *budgetary control,* is an important key to successful operations.

WORKING CAPITAL MANAGEMENT

In theory, investments in current assets should be analyzed in the same way as investments in capital assets. In practice, however, important differences in the two classes of assets lead to variations in the way the financial manager controls current and fixed asset investments. The most important difference is the fact that investments in capital assets commit the firm to a certain course of action over an extended period, while current asset investments can be modified relatively quickly. This means that capital budgeting must emphasize long-run projections, discounting procedures, and the like. Current asset management, in contrast, is more short-run oriented; the primary objective is to use current assets efficiently. There is an opportunity cost of tying funds up in inventories, cash, and accounts receivable. If the investment in these assets can be reduced without increasing costs or reducing sales, then such a reduction increases the firm's profitability. However, operating with low levels of current assets involves risks, so in working capital policy we encounter the familiar risk-return tradeoff.

LONG-TERM INVESTMENT DECISIONS

In addition to the role in the analysis-planning-control process described above, the financial manager must make decisions on specific individual investments. These capital budgeting decisions involve the whole process of evaluating projects whose returns are expected to extend beyond one year.

Compound Interest

Since long-term returns are involved, the effects of compound interest must be considered. Chapter 10 was devoted to a discussion of compound interest and the ways of taking it into account in financial analysis. Perhaps the most fundamental idea developed in Chapter 10 was that of *present value:* The present value of any asset is equal to the sum of future cash flows from the asset, discounted at an "appropriate" interest rate, later defined as the firm's cost of capital.

Capital Budgeting

Capital budgeting, as it is practiced by sophisticated firms, involves (1) estimating the cost of each prospective project, (2) estimating annual net cash flows from each project, (3) determining the appropriate risk-adjusted discount rate (cost of capital) for the project, and (4) using the present value equation to see if the project's net present value (NPV) is positive. If the NPV is positive or, alternatively, if the internal rate of return (the IRR) exceeds the cost of capital, the project should be accepted.

This sketch of capital budgeting is, of course, highly simplified. At times it is difficult to estimate either the cost of a project or the cash flows that will come from it. Ordinarily, the NPV and the IRR give identical answers to these questions: Which of two mutually exclusive projects should be selected? How large should the total capital budget be? However, under certain circumstances conflicts may arise. In general, the NPV is preferred.

Uncertainty, or Risk Analysis

Both logic and empirical evidence suggest that investors prefer investments with relatively certain returns, other things the same. This being the case, investment decisions should encompass more than just the *expected return* from a project—the decision maker should also take into account any *risk differentials* that may exist among projects.

The first task in risk analysis is to measure the riskiness of various projects. The measure of risk that we employ, and the one used most frequently in practice, is the *coefficient of variation* of the probability distribution of expected returns from a project. The larger the coefficient of variation, the greater the probability that the actual return will deviate significantly from the expected return, and the greater the riskiness of the project.

The risk to the firm embodied in a single project is dependent upon the correlation between returns on the project at hand and the remainder of the firm's assets. If these returns are perfectly, positively correlated, returns on the project are high when other assets are providing high returns, and vice versa. As the correlation becomes less than perfect, but is still positive, the association of returns is not as direct and there is a diversification effect. However, if the correlation is negative, returns on the project will be high when those on other assets are low, so taking on the project in question will reduce earnings fluctuations for the firm as a whole. In this case, favorable *portfolio effects* are said to be present, because the overall risk to the firm is less than the apparent risk of the project considered alone.

The typical method for dealing with risk in capital budgeting is to employ a lower cost of capital for less risky projects and a higher cost for more risky ones—this is called the *risk-adjusted discount rate method*. For example, a firm may determine that its average cost of capital is 10 percent and may use this discount rate to find the NPV of "average risk" projects. It will use rates less than 10 percent for low-risk projects and more than 10 percent for high-risk investments.

LONG-TERM FINANCING

In our discussion of capital structure and the cost of capital, we emphasized the risk differences between debt and equity. We did not consider other differences, nor did we attempt to show the alternative ways "debt" and "equity" securities can be packaged. These points, which are essential to a thorough understanding of managerial finance, were covered in Chapters 13, 14, 15, 16, and 17.

One critical distinction between debt and equity is the fact that equity—common shares—have control of a firm's operations. In theory, management should operate in strict accordance with "what is best for shareholders"—subject to external constraints imposed by labor, government, and so on. In practice, however, if a firm's managers are not also its major shareholders, management will also be concerned about maintaining its control position. This factor can influence the stock-versus-bonds decision and thus perhaps affect the firm's capital structure.

Long-term debt can be issued with a number of alternative features. Depending on the firm's own position and investor's preferences, it will be advantageous for the financial manager to use different ones of these features at different times. For example, if the financial manager feels that interest rates are presently high and are likely to decline in the near future, he will probably insist on making new long-term debt callable. Similarly, if investors think that a sinking fund will reduce the riskiness of the firm's bonds, they will accept a lower interest rate if the bonds have a sinking fund. However, a sinking fund will increase the cash flow requirements for servicing the debt, and this may be unattractive from the firm's standpoint. The financial manager must balance all these alternatives and decide upon the specific set of features that will be in the best interests of his firm.

Two particularly important financial instruments are *term loans* and *leases.* A term loan is generally of intermediate maturity—over one year but less than five, although some term loans run for fifteen years. Leases have maturities similar to those for term loans, and these two forms of financing are frequently alternatives to each other. The recommended procedure for comparing the cost of a loan versus a lease calls for determining the present value cost differential between the two instruments and choosing the one with the lower present value cost.

Convertible debt and preferred shares, or bonds with warrants, can be issued to raise new money. When either convertibles or bonds with warrants are used, the purchaser receives a package consisting of both a fixed income component and the possibility of a capital gain. Thus, the investor is able to hedge his position somewhat—he is more protected against losses than if he owned only common shares, yet he can still share the benefits if the firm is highly successful or if inflation dilutes the value of fixed return securities. Because of this protection, investors may be willing to accept lower overall expected rates of return on convertibles or bonds with warrants than on straight debt plus common shares. The usefulness of convertibles and warrants varies over time. They are most attractive in times of uncertainty such as the early 1970s, and at such times the financial manager can use them to lower his firm's cost of capital.

Why do firms issue so many different types and forms of securities? The primary reason has to do with the risk-return tradeoff function. Different classes of investors, as well as different individual investors within a given class, exhibit differing degrees of willingness to assume risks. Recognizing these investor preferences, an astute financial manager can create a whole array of different securities with differential risk characteristics, thereby appealing to many kinds of investors and broadening the market for his or her firm's issues. Also, having an array of instruments permits the financial manager to issue the types of securities that are most popular at any given point in time.

FINANCIAL STRUCTURE AND THE COST OF CAPITAL

In Chapter 12 we saw that risk aversion leads investors to seek higher returns on more risky investments—the riskier the investment, the greater the *risk premium* (the amount by which the expected return on a risky investment exceeds the riskless rate of return). These concepts were extended in Chapters 18, 19, and 20, where we showed the effect of capital structure on risk and thus on the firm's cost of capital.

Financial Leverage

Whenever a firm uses debt capital, it is employing *financial leverage.* Since debt typically involves a fixed interest charge, any fluctuation in operating income will produce a magnified fluctuation in earnings available to common equity. The greater the extent of financial leverage, the greater the earnings variability of the common equity.

The impact of financial leverage can be examined graphically, but it can also be studied more rigorously and can be measured in terms of its effect on the coefficient of variation. Typically, the higher the leverage factor, the larger the variability in earnings per share. Finally, the effects of leverage can be examined in terms of the *degree of financial leverage.* In addition, the effects of financial and operating leverage may be combined, with the *combined leverage factor* showing the percentage change in earnings per share that results from a given percentage change in sales.

Valuation and Rates of Return

When the present value concepts developed in Chapter 10 were used in Chapter 11 to determine the desirability of investing in specific assets, we determined the value of the asset *to the firm* by discounting the expected cash flows by the appropriate cost of capital. This same valuation technique may be applied to the firm as a whole by investors—common and preferred shareholders, and bondholders. In this latter case, the cash flows are the expected returns on the firm's securities—interest plus maturity value on bonds, dividends depends on preferred shares, and dividends plus the market value of the shares on the date of sale on common shares. The appropriate discount rate is dependent primarily on the riskiness of the particular security and supply and demand conditions in the capital market—the riskier the security, the higher the appropriate discount rate, and the greater the demand for funds vis-à-vis the supply of funds, the higher the rate.

Notice particularly that the firm can influencē its cost of capital. If it uses a high degree of operating leverage and invests in assets which produce highly uncertain returns, then it will be subject to a high degree of *basic business risk,* which will cause its cost of capital to be relatively high. If it superimposes financial leverage on top of its basic business risk, it further increases the risk borne by investors.

Cost of Capital

Each component of the capital structure has what is called a *required yield* or *component cost,* and each individual component cost is a function of the capital market's evaluation of the riskiness of the income stream generated by the particular component security (e.g., debt and common equity). The component cost is also related to the opportunity cost which reflects the rate of return an investor in a particular security expects to earn if the funds were invested in another security of equivalent risk. The firm can influence the opportunity cost, and hence the component cost of any particular security, only if the risks of the income stream accruing to the holders of the security are altered, either through asset purchases or changes in financial leverage.

Both theory and empirical evidence suggest that for each firm there is an *optimum capital structure,* that is, a mix of debt and equity securities that minimizes the cost of raising any given amount of capital.[2] Shifts in this optimum structure as capital market conditions vary is the issue discussed in Chapter 20. However, at any point in time there is an optimum structure.[3]

[2]Theories have been advanced by Modigliani and Miller, among others, that no optimum capital structure would exist if there were no corporate taxes and if capital markets were perfect. The existence of a corporate tax, where interest payments are a tax-deductible expense would lead to a preference for very high leverage. The perfection of capital markets requires, for example, that bankruptcy is costless and that individuals and corporations can borrow on identical terms. To the extent that imperfections in the capital market are sufficiently large in the real world, an optimal capital structure will exist.

[3]Empirical evidence suggests that the average cost of capital curve is U-shaped, not V-shaped, so

Recall that we have two primary reasons for wishing to know the cost of capital: (1) we need it for capital budgeting purposes, and (2) we want to minimize it. The cost of capital we need is the *marginal cost,* which is determined as follows:

1. Decide on a tentative optimum capital structure.
2. Determine the cost of the various capital components under this capital structure:
   a. Debt cost = (current interest rate) (1 – tax rate)
   b. Preferred cost = (preferred dividend)/(price of preferred net of issue costs).
   c. Retained earnings cost = $k = (D_1/P_0) + g$. Alternatively, k may be thought of as consisting of a riskless return plus a premium for business and financial risk: $k = R_F + \rho$.
   d. Newly issued common equity = $k_e = [D_1/P_0(1 - F)] + g$, where F is the issue cost as a proportion of the total proceeds of the issue and g is the expected (and constant) growth rate.
3. Use the capital structure percentages and the estimated component costs to calculate a weighted average cost.
4. The marginal cost is constant until retained earnings have been used up. At this point, newly issued common stock must be sold, raising the component cost of equity. Here, the marginal cost begins to rise.

Dividend Policy

Our study of the cost of capital makes it clear that because of issue costs, if for no other reason, retained earnings have a lower cost than new outside equity. However, dividends, which constitute an important part of the return to common shareholders, must be lowered if a firm increases its retained earnings. Thus, dividend policy—or the determination of how net income will be split between dividends and reinvestment—is an important component of overall financial policy.

We found in Chapter 21 that because of capital budgeting and cost of capital considerations, a firm with many good investment opportunities will tend to have a low dividend payout ratio, while a firm with few good investments will have a high payout. We also found that the firm's own individual situation—its cash or liquidity position, its access to capital markets, the tax position of its shareholders, and so on—has an important bearing on its dividend policy.

there is generally a *range* of capital structures within which the average cost of capital is *approximately* minimized. This greatly facilitates the financial manager's task, as it is much easier to locate a range than a unique point.

REVIEW OF FINANCIAL THEORY

It is useful to review developments to this point. First, the operating goal of the firm is to maximize the market value of the equity of existing (not new) shareholders, or equivalently, to maximize the current share price. To achieve this maximization, the firm must satisfy a number of conditions.

Operating Efficiency

The firm must operate efficiently in the sense of recognizing customer demands, both actual and potential, and of producing to meet this demand at a minimum cost. The planning and control techniques introduced earlier are designed to enhance operating efficiency.

Rate of Expansion

Expansion decisions (capital budgeting) should be made if, and only if, the expected present value of a specific project exceeds the cost of undertaking the project. In this connection, note that since more efficient firms have higher expected cash flows than inefficient ones, resources shift over time to efficient businesses.

Risk Characteristics

The degree of business risk inherent in a firm's assets combines with any additional risk resulting from financial leverage to determine its overall risk characteristics. These, in turn, affect the firm's cost of capital.

Average Cost of Capital

To maximize its value the firm must minimize the cost of capital for financing its chosen set of assets. This means selecting the set of securities—long-term and short-term debt, preferred and common shares, retained earnings and new outside equity, convertibles or bonds with warrants, and the specific provisions attached to each of these instruments—that minimizes capital costs.

Marginal Cost of Capital

The marginal cost of capital is dependent upon basic business risk and financial leverage. It is also a function of the amount of capital the firm raises during a given period. If the rate of expansion is quite rapid, the firm must bring in new outside equity capital, which causes the marginal cost of capital to rise.

Simultaneous Determination

The cost of capital is a necessary ingredient in asset expansion decisions, because we must know the marginal cost of capital to determine if each particular project should be accepted or rejected. We must also know the size of the capital budget before we can determine the marginal cost of capital. Therefore, the cost of capital and the capital budget must be determined simultaneously. If we knew the cost of capital schedule and the investment opportunity schedule *precisely,* then we could use mathematical techniques to obtain the simultaneous solution to a system of equations and thus determine a precise value-maximizing set of investments. As a practical matter, we do not have sufficient information to warrant using this approach.

Although we cannot obtain the simultaneous solution, the pragmatic usefulness of the theoretical concepts that have been developed should not be ruled out. The financial manager can obtain an estimate of his cost of capital which, if not exact, is sufficiently accurate to use in the capital budgeting process. Further, under normal conditions the rate of expansion, or even changes in the firm's mix of assets that would cause significant changes in its basic business risk, is not large enough to alter its cost of capital seriously. If the cost of capital is relatively constant, the simultaneity conditions are not important, and straightforward capital budgeting techniques, such as the risk-adjusted NPV method, are appropriate. Further, even if the firm is contemplating a significant change in operations—such as a shift in product lines, entry into a new industry, or an important change in dividend or capital structure policy—the wisdom of such a move can certainly be better ascertained if it is considered within the framework of our theory of financial policy.

INTERNATIONAL FINANCE

The evaluation of financial and investment decisions by a Canadian firm which engages in international business requires more complex and sophisticated analysis to identify and cope with the relevant cash flows that pass across political boundaries.

Exchange rate risk, credit risk, stability of governments and their economic policies are factors which can affect both the profitability of a project abroad and the ability of the parent company to repatriate profits for reinvestment in profitable projects.

MERGER POLICY

Because of his or her strategic position, the financial manager has a key role in corporate mergers and acquisitions. In a sense, a merger is like any other long-term investment decision—one firm acquires another in much the same way that it would acquire a new plant or office building. From this point of view, the merger decision should be analyzed in the capital budgeting framework, and the acquisition should be made if it increases the acquiring firm's net present value as reflected in the price of its stock. However, mergers are frequently quite significant in terms of their impact both on the acquiring firm and on the economy. Not only can a bad merger decision literally wreck a firm, but mergers among competing firms can turn a competitive market into an oligopolistic one. Accordingly, both managements and the federal government are generally more concerned over merger decisions than over most other decisions made by corporations.

CONCLUSION

Finance is a complex subject, blending abstract theory, practical decision models, and a description of the institutional setting in which financial decisions are made. Further, it is a dynamic area, ever changing in response to new technology and developments within the economy. These characteristics make finance a difficult subject, but one which is exciting and challenging. Finance is also important to the economy, for we must have efficient firms if the economy is to cope with the problems it faces. We can only hope that this book has, by helping the reader to understand the theory and methodology of finance, assisted in preparing the student to meet the challenges of the future.

QUESTIONS

25-1. Assume that an operating company is analyzing a potential acquisition candidate. The target firm, if acquired, will operate completely independently of the parent company, and the only cash flows from the subsidiary to the parent will be dividends. There will be no synergistic effects.

a. How would you determine a "fair" price to pay for the target firm? Be explicit, giving (1) a valuation model, (2) an idea of the cash flows that should be used, and (3) the appropriate discount rate. Justify your answers.

b. Now assume that the parent would truly merge the target company into its operations and that synergistic effects would occur. How would this affect your answers to part a?

25-2. In what sense is an inventory model an example of suboptimization? Could the same thing be said about the NPV capital budgeting model? Explain.

25-3. Why do firms use different types of securities? In your discussion of this question, use a graph and be sure to include considerations that would apply over time as well as those that would apply at any one instant of time.

25-4. Assume that a firm uses, in addition to long-term debt and equity, the following types of financing:

1. convertible bonds
2. bonds with warrants
3. accounts payable
4. long-term financial leases

a. Explain how to calculate the component cost of each type of capital.

b. How would you calculate the average cost of capital for a firm with a large amount of long-term leases outstanding?

25-5. An important ingredient in any financial decision is the impact of the decision on the after-tax income of the investors. We have demonstrated that a share repurchase is an alternative to the payment of dividends in which the dividend is paid as a capital gain. If a company has a long history of a high payout ratio and has attracted a particular clientele, will a share repurchase be in the best interest of the shareholders?

PROBLEMS

25-1[4] To obtain a position in the underwriting department of a major investment banking house is difficult, but it is especially hard to land a job that calls for contact with the top partners so that one may really learn the inside of the business. Through family connections, however, Gordon Hammrick was fortunate enough to get the job of assistant to William Murray, senior partner and managing officer of Murray, Finch, Price, Farmer & Smith. Hammrick received his bachelor's degree in history only two weeks before getting his job, and this was his first day on the job. After a rather pleasant morning spent meeting various people around the office, including some attractive secretaries, Hammrick was given his first task.

Murray had not only been forced to miss his regular Thursday afternoon golf match, but he also had to stay up long after midnight finishing some recommendations on the types of financing that a group of clients should use. The next morning, having completed the analyses and made his recommendations, Murray turned over to Hammrick the folder on each client and, attached to each of the folders, his recommendation on the type of financing that each should use. He then told Hammrick, first, to have the analyses and financing recommendations typed and sent immediately to each of the client companies and, second, that he was taking his secretary away for a weekend of uninterrupted dictation. Murray particularly stressed that he should be consulted during the weekend only in the event of an emergency.

The first thing Hammrick did was to detach the analyses and recommendations from the folders and give them to a secretary to type. When the secretary returned the typed reports, Hammrick discovered that he did not know which recommendation belonged to which company! He had folders on nine different companies and financing recommendations for nine companies, but he could not match them up. Hammrick's major was history, so he could not be expected to be able to match the financing recommendations with the appropriate companies. You, as a finance student, should be able to help Hammrick by telling him which companies (listed on the following pages) should use which financing methods.

[4]This case study is taken from E.F. Brigham, Timothy J. Nantell, Robert T. Aubey, and Richard H. Pettway, *Cases in Managerial Finance, Third Edition* (New York: Holt, Rinehart and Winston, Inc., 1977).

Financing Methods

1. Common stock: nonrights
2. Debt with warrants
3. Factoring
4. Friends or relatives
5. Preferred stock (nonconvertible)
6. Common stock: rights offering
7. Long-term bonds
8. Leasing arrangement
9. Convertible debentures

Companies

a. **Arizona Mining Company**   Arizona Mining needs $10 million to finance the acquisition of mineral rights to some land in south-central Arizona, as well as to pay for some extensive surveys, core borings, magnetic aerial surveys, and other types of analyses designed to determine whether the mineral deposits on this land warrant development. If the tests are favorable, the company will need an additional $10 million. Arizona Mining's common stock is currently selling at $12, while the company is earning approximately $1 a share. Other firms in the industry sell at from 10 to 15 times earnings. Arizona Mining's debt ratio is 25 percent, which compares with an industry average of 30 percent. Total assets at the last balance sheet date were $105 million.

b. **New York Power Company**   Since New York Power, a major electric utility, is organized as a holding company, the Securities and Exchange Commission must approve all security issues; such approval is automatic if the company stays within conventional norms for the electric utility industry. Reasonable norms call for long-term debt in the range of 55 to 65 percent, preferred stock in the range of 0 to 15 percent, and common equity in the range of 25 to 35 percent. New York Power Company currently has total assets of $1 billion, financed as follows: $600 million debt, $50 million preferred stock, and $350 million common equity. The company plans to raise an additional $25 million at this time.

c. **Wilson Brothers, Inc.**   Wilson Brothers, Inc., a wholesale grocery business in Cincinnati, Ohio, is owned by the three Wilson brothers; each owns one-third of the outstanding stock. The company is profitable, but rapid growth has put it under a severe financial strain. The real estate is all under mortgage to an insurance company, the inventory is being used under a blanket chattel mortgage to secure a bank line of credit, and the accounts receivable are being factored. With total assets of $5 million, the company now needs an additional $100,000 to purchase twenty forklift trucks and related equipment to facilitate handling in the shipping and receiving department.

d. **Alabama Milling Company**   Alabama Milling manufactures unbleached cotton cloth, then bleaches the cloth and dyes it in various colors and patterns. The finished cloth is packaged in bulk and is sold on sixty-day credit terms, largely to relatively small clothing companies operating in the New York City area. The company's plant and equipment have been financed in part by a mortgage loan, and this is the only long-term debt. Raw materials—cotton and dyes—are purchased on terms calling for payment within thirty days of receipt of goods, but no discounts are offered. Because the national economy is currently so prosperous, apparel sales have experienced a sharp increase, which, in turn, has produced a marked increase in the demand for Alabama Milling's products. To finance a higher level of output, Alabama Milling needs approximately $500,000.

e. **Florida-Pacific Corporation**   Florida-Pacific is a major producer of plywood, paper, and other forest products. The company's stock is widely held, actively traded, and listed on the New York Stock Exchange; recently it has been trading in the range of $30 to $35 a share. The latest twelve-months earnings were $2.12; the current dividend rate is 80 cents a year, and earnings, dividends, and the price of the company's stock have been growing at a rate of about 7 percent over the preceding few years. Florida-Pacific's debt ratio is currently 42 percent versus 25 percent for other large forest product firms. Other firms in the industry, on the average, have been growing at a rate of about 5 percent a year, and their stocks have been selling at a price/earnings ratio of about 13. Florida-Pacific has an opportunity to acquire a substantial stand of forest in Northern California. The current owners of the property are asking $20 million in cash for the land and timber.

f. **Toy World**   Joseph Marino, an employee of the state of Pennsylvania and an avid model airplane and model automobile builder, has just learned that some of the stores in a new neighborhood shopping center are still available for lease. Marino knows that no good toy and hobby store exists in the southwest section of the city of Harrisburg, and he believes that if he can obtain approximately $20,000 for fixtures and stock, he can open a successful store in the new shopping center. His liquid savings total $5,000, so Marino needs an additional $15,000 to open the proposed store.

g. **Knight Electronics Corporation**   Knight Electronics is a medium-size electronics company whose sales distribution is approximately 30 percent for defense contracts and 70 percent for nonmilitary uses. The company has been growing rapidly in recent years, and projections based on current research and development prospects call for continued growth at a rate of 10 to 12 percent a year. Although recent reports of several brokerage firms suggest that the firm's rate of growth might be slowing down, Knight's management believes, on the basis of internal information, that no decline is in sight. The company's stock, which is traded on the Pacific Stock Exchange, is selling at 20 times earnings; this is slightly below the 23 times ratio of Standard & Poor's electronics industry average. The firm's debt ratio is 40 percent, just above the 38 percent average for the industry. The company has assets of $28 million and needs an additional $4 million, over and above retained earnings, to support the projected level of growth during the next twelve months.

h. **Utah Chemical Company**   Utah Chemical is a closely held company that was founded in 1952 to extract from the Great Salt Lake minerals used in agricultural fertilizers. The company's debt ratio is 48 percent versus an average ratio of 36 percent for agricultural fertilizer producers in general. The stock is owned in equal parts by ten individuals, none of whom is in a position to put additional funds into the business. Sales for the most recent year totaled $10 million, and earnings after taxes amounted to $600,000. Total assets, as of the latest balance sheet, amounted to $8 million. Utah Chemical needs an additional $3 million to finance expansion during the current fiscal year; given the worldwide growth in demand for agricultural chemicals, the firm can anticipate additional outside capital needs in the years ahead.

i. **Universal Container Corporation**   Universal Container is engaged in the manufacture of cans, glass bottles, paper boxes of various sorts, a variety of plastic tubes, and other packaging materials. Since the firm sells to a great many producers of nondurable consumer goods, sales are relatively stable. The current price of the company's stock, which is listed on the New York Stock Exchange, is $42, and the most recent earnings and dividends per share are $4 and $2, respectively. The rate of growth in sales, earnings, and dividends in the last few years has averaged 5 percent. Universal Container has total assets of $360 million. Current liabilities, which consist primarily of accounts payable and accruals, are $25 million; long-term debt is $75 million; and common equity totals $260 million. An additional $30 million of external funds is required to build and equip a new can manufacturing complex in central California and to supply the new facility with working capital.

25-2. a. A firm with $60 million of assets judges that it is at the beginning of a three-year growth cycle. It is a manufacturing firm with a total-debt-to-assets ratio of 16 percent. It expects sales and net earnings to grow at a rate of 10 percent a year.

   Share prices are expected to rise 30 percent a year over the three-year period. The firm will need $6 million at the beginning of the three-year period and another $3 million by the middle of the third year. It is at the beginning of a general business upswing and money and capital costs are relatively low. By the middle of the third year, it is expected that money and capital costs will have risen substantially.

How should the firm raise the $6 million and the $3 million?

b. An aerospace company with sales of $25 million a year needs $5 million to finance expansion. It has a debt-to-total-assets ratio of 65 percent. Its common equity, which is widely held, is selling at a price/earnings ratio of 25 times. It is comparing the sale of common shares and convertible debentures.

Which do you recommend? Why?

c. A chemical company has been growing steadily. To finance a growth of sales from $40 million a year to $50 million over a two-year period, it needs $2 million in additional equipment. When additional working capital needs are taken into account, the total additional financing required during the first year is $5 million. Profits will rise by 50 percent after the first ten months. The shares are currently selling at 20 times earnings. It can borrow on straight debt at 7 ½ percent or with a convertibility or warrant "sweetener" for ¾ percent less. The present debt-to-total-assets ratio is 25 percent.

Which form of financing should it employ?

25-3. Allied Chemists, Inc., has experienced the following sales, profit, and balance sheet patterns. Identify the financial problem that has developed and recommend a solution for it.

Allied Chemists, Inc.
Financial data, 19X1 –1X10
(in millions of dollars)

Income Statements	19X1	19X2	19X3	19X4	19X5	19X6	19X7	19X8	19X9	1X10
Sales	$100	$140	$180	$200	$240	$400	$360	$440	$480	$680
Profits after tax	10	14	18	20	24	40	36	44	48	68
Dividends	8	10	12	12	14	20	20	28	36	48
Retained earnings	$ 2	$ 4	$ 6	$ 8	$ 10	$ 20	$ 16	$ 16	$ 12	$ 20
Cumulative retained earnings	$ 2	$ 6	$ 12	$ 20	$ 30	$ 50	$ 66	$ 82	$ 94	$114

Balance Sheets	19X1	19X2	19X3	19X4	19X5	19X6	19X7	19X8	19X9	1X10
Current assets	$ 20	$ 30	$ 40	$ 50	$ 60	$100	$ 80	$110	$120	$160
Net fixed assets	30	40	50	50	60	100	100	110	120	180
Total assets	$ 50	$ 70	$ 90	$100	$120	$200	$180	$220	$240	$340
Trade credit	$ 8	$ 12	$ 16	$ 18	$ 20	$ 36	$ 30	$ 40	$ 40	$120
Bank credit	8	12	20	20	26	58	28	40	40	40
Other	2	10	12	12	14	16	16	18	16	16
Total current liabilities	$ 18	$ 34	$ 48	$ 50	$ 60	$110	$ 74	$ 98	$ 96	$176
Long-term debt	0	0	0	0	0	10	10	10	20	20
Total debt	$ 18	$ 34	$ 48	$ 50	$ 60	$120	$ 84	$108	$116	$196
Common equity	$ 30	$ 30	$ 30	$ 30	$ 30	$ 30	$ 30	$ 30	$ 30	$ 30
Retained earnings	2	6	12	20	30	50	66	82	94	114
Net worth	$ 32	$ 36	$ 42	$ 50	$ 60	$ 80	$ 96	$112	$124	$144
Total claims on assets	$ 50	$ 70	$ 90	$100	$120	$200	$180	$220	$240	$340

Appendix A
Mathematical
Tables

TABLE A–1 Compound Sum of $1: $CVIF = (1 + k)^t$

Period	1%	2%	3%	4%	5%	6%	7%
1	1.010	1.020	1.030	1.040	1.050	1.060	1.070
2	1.020	1.040	1.061	1.082	1.102	1.124	1.145
3	1.030	1.061	1.093	1.125	1.158	1.191	1.225
4	1.041	1.082	1.126	1.170	1.216	1.262	1.311
5	1.051	1.104	1.159	1.217	1.276	1.338	1.403
6	1.062	1.126	1.194	1.265	1.340	1.419	1.501
7	1.072	1.149	1.230	1.316	1.407	1.504	1.606
8	1.083	1.172	1.267	1.369	1.477	1.594	1.718
9	1.094	1.195	1.305	1.423	1.551	1.689	1.838
10	1.105	1.219	1.344	1.480	1.629	1.791	1.967
11	1.116	1.243	1.384	1.539	1.710	1.898	2.105
12	1.127	1.268	1.426	1.601	1.796	2.012	2.252
13	1.138	1.294	1.469	1.665	1.886	2.133	2.410
14	1.149	1.319	1.513	1.732	1.980	2.261	2.579
15	1.161	1.346	1.558	1.801	2.079	2.397	2.759
16	1.173	1.373	1.605	1.873	2.183	2.540	2.952
17	1.184	1.400	1.653	1.948	2.292	2.693	3.159
18	1.196	1.428	1.702	2.026	2.407	2.854	3.380
19	1.208	1.457	1.754	2.107	2.527	3.026	3.617
20	1.220	1.486	1.806	2.191	2.653	3.207	3.870
25	1.282	1.641	2.094	2.666	3.386	4.292	5.427
30	1.348	1.811	2.427	3.243	4.322	5.743	7.612

Period	8%	9%	10%	12%	14%	15%	16%
1	1.080	1.090	1.100	1.120	1.140	1.150	1.160
2	1.166	1.186	1.210	1.254	1.300	1.322	1.346
3	1.260	1.295	1.331	1.405	1.482	1.521	1.561
4	1.360	1.412	1.464	1.574	1.689	1.749	1.811
5	1.469	1.539	1.611	1.762	1.925	2.011	2.100
6	1.587	1.677	1.772	1.974	2.195	2.313	2.436
7	1.714	1.828	1.949	2.211	2.502	2.660	2.826
8	1.851	1.993	2.144	2.476	2.853	3.059	3.278
9	1.999	2.172	2.358	2.773	3.252	3.518	3.803
10	2.159	2.367	2.594	3.106	3.707	4.046	4.411
11	2.332	2.580	2.853	3.479	4.226	4.652	5.117
12	2.518	2.813	3.138	3.896	4.818	5.350	5.926
13	2.720	3.066	3.452	4.363	5.492	6.153	6.886
14	2.937	3.342	3.797	4.887	6.261	7.076	7.988
15	3.172	3.642	4.177	5.474	7.138	8.137	9.266
16	3.426	3.970	4.595	6.130	8.137	9.358	10.748
17	3.700	4.328	5.054	6.866	9.276	10.761	12.468
18	3.996	4.717	5.560	7.690	10.575	12.375	14.463
19	4.316	5.142	6.116	8.613	12.056	14.232	16.777
20	4.661	5.604	6.728	9.646	13.743	16.367	19.461
25	6.848	8.623	10.835	17.000	26.462	32.919	40.874
30	10.063	13.268	17.449	29.960	50.950	66.212	85.850

TABLE A–1   *(continued)*

Period	18%	20%	24%	28%	32%	36%
1	1.180	1.200	1.240	1.280	1.320	1.360
2	1.392	1.440	1.538	1.638	1.742	1.850
3	1.643	1.728	1.907	2.067	2.300	2.515
4	1.939	2.074	2.364	2.684	3.036	3.421
5	2.288	2.488	2.932	3.436	4.007	4.653
6	2.700	2.986	3.635	4.398	5.290	6.328
7	3.185	3.583	4.508	5.629	6.983	8.605
8	3.759	4.300	5.590	7.206	9.217	11.703
9	4.435	5.160	6.931	9.223	12.166	15.917
10	5.234	6.192	8.594	11.806	16.060	21.647
11	6.176	7.430	10.657	15.112	21.199	29.439
12	7.288	8.916	13.215	19.343	27.983	40.037
13	8.599	10.699	16.386	24.759	36.937	54.451
14	10.147	12.839	20.319	31.961	48.757	74.053
15	11.974	15.407	25.196	40.565	64.359	100.712
16	14.129	18.488	31.243	51.923	84.954	136.97
17	16.672	22.186	38.741	66.461	112.14	186.28
18	19.673	26.623	48.039	85.071	148.02	253.34
19	23.214	31.948	59.568	108.89	195.39	344.54
20	27.393	38.338	73.864	139.38	257.92	468.57
25	62.669	95.396	216.542	478.90	1033.6	2180.1
30	143.371	237.376	634.820	1645.5	4142.1	10143.

Period	40%	50%	60%	70%	80%	90%
1	1.400	1.500	1.600	1.700	1.800	1.900
2	1.960	2.250	2.560	2.890	3.240	3.610
3	2.744	3.375	4.096	4.913	5.832	6.859
4	3.842	5.062	6.544	8.352	10.498	13.032
5	5.378	7.594	10.486	14.199	18.896	24.761
6	7.530	11.391	16.777	24.138	34.012	47.046
7	10.541	17.086	26.844	41.034	61.222	89.387
8	14.758	25.629	42.950	69.758	110.200	169.836
9	20.661	38.443	68.720	118.588	198.359	322.688
10	28.925	57.665	109.951	201.599	357.047	613.107
11	40.496	86.498	175.922	342.719	642.684	1164.902
12	56.694	129.746	281.475	582.622	1156.831	2213.314
13	79.372	194.619	450.360	990.457	2082.295	4205.297
14	111.120	291.929	720.576	1683.777	3748.131	7990.065
15	155.568	437.894	1152.921	2862.421	6746.636	15181.122
16	217.795	656.84	1844.7	4866.1	12144.	28844.0
17	304.914	985.26	2951.5	8272.4	21859.	54804.0
18	426.879	1477.9	4722.4	14063.0	39346.	104130.0
19	597.630	2216.8	7555.8	23907.0	70824.	197840.0
20	836.683	3325.3	12089.0	40642.0	127480.	375900.0
25	4499.880	25251.	126760.0	577060.0	2408900.	9307600.0
30	24201.432	191750.	1329200.	8193500.0	45517000.	230470000.0

TABLE A–2 Present Value of $1: $PVIF = \dfrac{1}{(1+k)^t} = \dfrac{1}{CVIF}$

Period	1%	2%	3%	4%	5%	6%	7%	8%	9%	10%	12%	14%	15%
1	.990	.980	.971	.962	.952	.943	.935	.926	.917	.909	.893	.877	.870
2	.980	.961	.943	.925	.907	.890	.873	.857	.842	.826	.797	.769	.756
3	.971	.942	.915	.889	.864	.840	.816	.794	.772	.751	.712	.675	.658
4	.961	.924	.889	.855	.823	.792	.763	.735	.708	.683	.636	.592	.572
5	.951	.906	.863	.822	.784	.747	.713	.681	.650	.621	.567	.519	.497
6	.942	.888	.838	.790	.746	.705	.666	.630	.596	.564	.507	.456	.432
7	.933	.871	.813	.760	.711	.665	.623	.583	.547	.513	.452	.400	.376
8	.923	.853	.789	.731	.677	.627	.582	.540	.502	.467	.404	.351	.327
9	.914	.837	.766	.703	.645	.592	.544	.500	.460	.424	.361	.308	.284
10	.905	.820	.744	.676	.614	.558	.508	.463	.422	.386	.322	.270	.247
11	.896	.804	.722	.650	.585	.527	.475	.429	.388	.350	.287	.237	.215
12	.887	.788	.701	.625	.557	.497	.444	.397	.356	.319	.257	.208	.187
13	.879	.773	.681	.601	.530	.469	.445	.368	.326	.290	.229	.182	.163
14	.870	.758	.661	.577	.505	.442	.388	.340	.299	.263	.205	.160	.141
15	.861	.743	.642	.555	.481	.417	.362	.315	.275	.239	.183	.140	.123
16	.853	.728	.623	.534	.458	.394	.339	.292	.252	.218	.163	.123	.107
17	.844	.714	.605	.513	.436	.371	.317	.270	.231	.198	.146	.108	.093
18	.836	.700	.587	.494	.416	.350	.296	.250	.212	.180	.130	.095	.081
19	.828	.686	.570	.475	.396	.331	.276	.232	.194	.164	.116	.083	.070
20	.820	.673	.554	.456	.377	.312	.258	.215	.178	.149	.104	.073	.061
25	.780	.610	.478	.375	.295	.233	.184	.146	.116	.092	.059	.038	.030
30	.742	.552	.412	.308	.231	.174	.131	.099	.075	.057	.033	.020	.015

Period	16%	18%	20%	24%	28%	32%	36%	40%	50%	60%	70%	80%	90%
1	.862	.847	.833	.806	.781	.758	.735	.714	.667	.625	.588	.556	.526
2	.743	.718	.694	.650	.610	.574	.541	.510	.444	.391	.346	.309	.277
3	.641	.609	.579	.524	.477	.435	.398	.364	.296	.244	.204	.171	.146
4	.552	.516	.482	.423	.373	.329	.292	.260	.198	.153	.120	.095	.077
5	.476	.437	.402	.341	.291	.250	.215	.186	.132	.095	.070	.053	.040
6	.410	.370	.335	.275	.227	.189	.158	.133	.088	.060	.041	.029	.021
7	.354	.314	.279	.222	.178	.143	.116	.095	.059	.037	.024	.016	.011
8	.305	.266	.233	.179	.139	.108	.085	.068	.039	.023	.014	.009	.006
9	.263	.226	.194	.144	.108	.082	.063	.048	.026	.015	.008	.005	.003
10	.227	.191	.162	.116	.085	.062	.046	.035	.017	.009	.005	.003	.002
11	.195	.162	.135	.094	.066	.047	.034	.025	.012	.006	.003	.002	.001
12	.168	.137	.112	.076	.052	.036	.025	.018	.008	.004	.002	.001	.001
13	.145	.116	.093	.061	.040	.027	.018	.013	.005	.002	.001	.001	.000
14	.125	.099	.078	.049	.032	.021	.014	.009	.003	.001	.001	.000	.000
15	.108	.084	.065	.040	.025	.016	.010	.006	.002	.001	.000	.000	.000
16	.093	.071	.054	.032	.019	.012	.007	.005	.002	.001	.000	.000	
17	.080	.060	.045	.026	.015	.009	.005	.003	.001	.000	.000		
18	.069	.051	.038	.021	.012	.007	.004	.002	.001	.000	.000		
19	.060	.043	.031	.017	.009	.005	.003	.002	.000	.000			
20	.051	.037	.026	.014	.007	.004	.002	.001	.000	.000			
25	.024	.016	.010	.005	.002	.001	.000	.000					
30	.012	.007	.004	.002	.001	.000	.000						

TABLE A–3 Sum of an Annuity of \$1 for N Periods: $CVIF_a = \sum_{t=0}^{n-1} (1+k)^t = \dfrac{(1+k)^n = 1}{k}$

Period	1%	2%	3%	4%	5%	6%
1	1.000	1.000	1.000	1.000	1.000	1.000
2	2.010	2.020	2.030	2.040	2.050	2.060
3	3.030	3.060	3.091	3.122	3.152	3.184
4	4.060	4.122	4.184	4.246	4.310	4.375
5	5.101	5.204	5.309	5.416	5.526	5.637
6	6.152	6.308	6.468	6.633	6.802	6.975
7	7.214	7.434	7.662	7.898	8.142	8.394
8	8.286	8.583	8.892	9.214	9.549	9.897
9	9.369	9.755	10.159	10.583	11.027	11.491
10	10.462	10.950	11.464	12.006	12.578	13.181
11	11.567	12.169	12.808	13.486	14.207	14.972
12	12.683	13.412	14.192	15.026	15.917	16.870
13	13.809	14.680	15.618	16.627	17.713	18.882
14	14.947	15.974	17.086	18.292	19.599	21.051
15	16.097	17.293	18.599	20.024	21.579	23.276
16	17.258	18.639	20.157	21.825	23.657	25.673
17	18.430	20.012	21.762	23.698	25.840	28.213
18	19.615	21.412	23.414	25.645	28.132	30.906
19	20.811	22.841	25.117	27.671	30.539	33.760
20	22.019	24.297	26.870	29.778	33.066	36.786
25	28.243	32.030	36.459	41.646	47.727	54.865
30	34.785	40.568	47.575	56.805	66.439	79.058

Period	7%	8%	9%	10%	12%	14%
1	1.000	1.000	1.000	1.000	1.000	1.000
2	2.070	2.080	2.090	2.100	2.120	2.140
3	3.215	3.246	3.278	3.310	3.374	3.440
4	4.440	4.506	4.573	4.641	4.770	4.921
5	5.751	5.867	5.985	6.105	6.353	6.610
6	7.153	7.336	7.523	7.716	8.115	8.536
7	8.654	8.923	9.200	9.487	10.089	10.730
8	10.260	10.637	11.028	11.436	12.300	13.233
9	11.978	12.488	13.021	13.579	14.776	16.085
10	13.816	14.487	15.193	15.937	17.549	19.337
11	15.784	16.645	17.560	18.531	20.655	23.044
12	17.888	18.977	20.141	21.384	24.133	27.271
13	20.141	21.495	22.953	24.523	28.029	32.089
14	22.550	24.215	26.019	27.975	32.393	37.581
15	25.129	27.152	29.361	31.772	37.280	43.842
16	27.888	30.324	33.003	35.950	42.753	50.980
17	30.840	33.750	36.974	40.545	48.884	59.118
18	33.999	37.450	41.301	45.599	55.750	68.394
19	37.379	41.446	46.018	51.159	63.440	78.969
20	40.995	45.762	51.160	57.275	72.052	91.025
25	63.249	73.106	84.701	98.347	133.334	181.871
30	94.461	113.283	136.308	164.494	241.333	356.787

TABLE A-3 *(continued)*

Period	16%	18%	20%	24%	28%	32%
1	1.000	1.000	1.000	1.000	1.000	1.000
2	2.160	2.180	2.200	2.240	2.280	2.320
3	3.506	3.572	3.640	3.778	3.918	4.062
4	5.066	5.215	5.368	5.684	6.016	6.362
5	6.877	7.154	7.442	8.048	8.700	9.398
6	8.977	9.442	9.930	10.980	12.136	13.406
7	11.414	12.142	12.916	14.615	16.534	18.696
8	14.240	15.327	16.499	19.123	22.163	25.678
9	17.518	19.086	20.799	24.712	29.369	34.895
10	21.321	23.521	25.959	31.643	38.592	47.062
11	25.733	28.755	32.150	40.238	50.399	63.122
12	30.850	34.931	39.580	50.985	65.510	84.320
13	36.786	42.219	48.497	64.110	84.853	112.303
14	43.672	50.818	59.196	80.496	109.612	149.240
15	51.660	60.965	72.035	100.815	141.303	197.997
16	60.925	72.939	87.442	126.011	181.87	262.36
17	71.673	87.068	105.931	157.253	233.79	347.31
18	84.141	103.740	128.117	195.994	300.25	459.45
19	98.603	123.414	154.740	244.033	385.32	607.47
20	115.380	146.628	186.688	303.601	494.21	802.86
25	249.214	342.603	471.981	898.092	1706.8	3226.8
30	530.312	790.948	1181.882	2640.916	5873.2	12941.0

Period	36%	40%	50%	60%	70%	80%
1	1.000	1.000	1.000	1.000	1.000	1.000
2	2.360	2.400	2.500	2.600	2.700	2.800
3	4.210	4.360	4.750	5.160	5.590	6.040
4	6.725	7.104	8.125	9.256	10.503	11.872
5	10.146	10.846	13.188	15.810	18.855	22.370
6	14.799	16.324	20.781	26.295	33.054	41.265
7	21.126	23.853	32.172	43.073	57.191	75.278
8	29.732	34.395	49.258	69.916	98.225	136.500
9	41.435	49.153	74.887	112.866	167.983	246.699
10	57.352	69.814	113.330	181.585	286.570	445.058
11	78.998	98.739	170.995	291.536	488.170	802.105
12	108.437	139.235	257.493	467.458	830.888	1444.788
13	148.475	195.929	387.239	748.933	1413.510	2601.619
14	202.926	275.300	581.859	1199.293	2403.968	4683.914
15	276.979	386.420	873.788	1919.869	4087.745	8432.045
16	377.69	541.99	1311.7	3072.8	6950.2	15179.0
17	514.66	759.78	1968.5	4917.5	11816.0	27323.0
18	700.94	1064.7	2953.8	7868.9	20089.0	49182.0
19	954.28	1491.6	4431.7	12591.0	34152.0	88528.0
20	1298.8	2089.2	6648.5	20147.0	58059.0	159350.0
25	6053.0	11247.0	50500.0	211270.0	824370.0	3011100.0
30	28172.0	60501.0	383500.0	2215400.0	11705000.0	56896000.0

TABLE A–4 Present Value of an Annuity of $1: $PVIF_a = \sum_{t=1}^{n} \frac{1}{(1+k)^t} = \frac{1 - \frac{1}{(1+k)^n}}{k}$

Period	1%	2%	3%	4%	5%	6%	7%	8%	9%	10%
1	0.990	0.980	0.971	0.962	0.952	0.943	0.935	0.926	0.917	0.909
2	1.970	1.942	1.913	1.886	1.859	1.833	1.808	1.783	1.759	1.736
3	2.941	2.884	2.829	2.775	2.723	2.673	2.624	2.577	2.531	2.487
4	3.902	3.808	3.717	3.630	3.546	3.465	3.387	3.312	3.240	3.170
5	4.853	4.713	4.580	4.452	4.329	4.212	4.100	3.993	3.890	3.791
6	5.795	5.601	5.417	5.242	5.076	4.917	4.766	4.623	4.486	4.355
7	6.728	6.472	6.230	6.002	5.786	5.582	5.389	5.206	5.033	4.868
8	7.652	7.325	7.020	6.733	6.463	6.210	5.971	5.747	5.535	5.335
9	8.566	8.162	7.786	7.435	7.108	6.802	6.515	6.247	5.995	5.759
10	9.471	8.983	8.530	8.111	7.722	7.360	7.024	6.710	6.418	6.145
11	10.368	9.787	9.253	8.760	8.306	7.887	7.499	7.139	6.805	6.495
12	11.255	10.575	9.954	9.385	8.863	8.384	7.943	7.536	7.161	6.814
13	12.134	11.348	10.635	9.986	9.394	8.853	8.358	7.904	7.487	7.103
14	13.004	12.106	11.296	10.563	9.899	9.295	8.745	8.244	7.786	7.367
15	13.865	12.849	11.938	11.118	10.380	9.712	9.108	8.559	8.060	7.606
16	14.718	13.578	12.561	11.652	10.838	10.106	9.447	8.851	8.312	7.824
17	15.562	14.292	13.166	12.166	11.274	10.477	9.763	9.122	8.544	8.022
18	16.398	14.992	13.754	12.659	11.690	10.828	10.059	9.372	8.756	8.201
19	17.226	15.678	14.324	13.134	12.085	11.158	10.336	9.604	8.950	8.365
20	18.046	16.351	14.877	13.590	12.462	11.470	10.594	9.818	9.128	8.514
25	22.023	19.523	17.413	15.622	14.094	12.783	11.654	10.675	9.823	9.077
30	25.808	22.397	19.600	17.292	15.373	13.765	12.409	11.258	10.274	9.427

Period	12%	14%	16%	18%	20%	24%	28%	32%	36%
1	0.893	0.877	0.862	0.847	0.833	0.806	0.781	0.758	0.735
2	1.690	1.647	1.605	1.566	1.528	1.457	1.392	1.332	1.276
3	2.402	2.322	2.246	2.174	2.106	1.981	1.868	1.766	1.674
4	3.037	2.914	2.798	2.690	2.589	2.404	2.241	2.096	1.966
5	3.605	3.433	3.274	3.127	2.991	2.745	2.532	2.345	2.181
6	4.111	3.889	3.685	3.498	3.326	3.020	2.759	2.534	2.339
7	4.564	4.288	4.039	3.812	3.605	3.242	2.937	2.678	2.455
8	4.968	4.639	4.344	4.078	3.837	3.421	3.076	2.786	2.540
9	5.328	4.946	4.607	4.303	4.031	3.566	3.184	2.868	2.603
10	5.650	5.216	4.833	4.494	4.193	3.682	3.269	2.930	2.650
11	5.938	5.453	5.029	4.656	4.327	3.776	3.335	2.978	2.683
12	6.194	5.660	5.197	4.793	4.439	3.851	3.387	3.013	2.708
13	6.424	5.842	5.342	4.910	4.533	3.912	3.427	3.040	2.727
14	6.628	6.002	5.468	5.008	4.611	3.962	3.459	3.061	2.740
15	6.811	6.142	5.575	5.092	4.675	4.001	3.483	3.076	2.750
16	6.974	6.265	5.669	5.162	4.730	4.033	3.503	3.088	2.758
17	7.120	5.373	5.749	4.222	4.775	4.059	3.518	3.097	2.763
18	7.250	6.467	5.818	5.273	4.812	4.080	3.529	3.104	2.767
19	7.366	6.550	5.877	5.316	4.844	4.097	3.539	3.109	2.770
20	7.469	6.623	5.929	5.353	4.870	4.110	3.546	3.113	2.772
25	7.843	6.873	6.097	5.467	4.948	4.147	3.564	3.122	2.776
30	8.055	7.003	6.177	5.517	4.979	4.160	3.569	3.124	2.778

Appendix B
Answers to Selected
End-of-Chapter
Problems

We present here some partial answers to selected end-of-chapter problems. For the most part, the answers given are only the final answers (or answers at intermediate steps) to the more complex problems. Within limits, these answers will be useful to see if the student is "on the right track" toward solving the problem. The primary limitation, which must be kept in mind, is that some questions may have more than one solution, depending upon which of several equally plausible assumptions are made in working the problem. Also, many of the problems involve some verbal discussion as well as numerical calculations. We have not presented any of this verbal material here.

2-1. Dividends after tax: $20,371.20.
2-2. 0.48 [$0.6M + ½ ($2.5M)] = $888,000.
2-3. Earnings after tax: $212,680 and $241,000.
2-4. $32,569.10.
2-5. $144.

3-1. (a) TIE = 5.8, ACP = 37, ROE = 4.8%.
3-4. $100,000.

4-1. (a) ($40,000); (b) 6,000 units; (c) 8,000 units: 4.0; (d) 4,800 units.
4-2. (a) FC = $50,000, VC = $600,000; (c) 1.5.
4-4. BEP = 500 and 1,000 units.
4-5. (a) (ii) BEP = 64,286 units; (b) (iii) OL = 9.71; (c) (i) $382,500; (f) $631.3, $620.6, $570.4.

5-2. (a) Total assets, $2,800,000, 5-year addition to R/E, $360,000.
5-3. (a) Total assets, $1,440,000.

5-4. (a) Total assets, $8,760,000; (b) $229,200; (c) Total assets, $9,198,000; (d) (2) (i) $304,800.

6-1. (a) $85,250, $233,000, ($151,750), ($26,500), $91,250, $160,250.

7-2. Aggressive, 11.31%; Average, 10.36%; Conservative, 8.75%.

7-5. (a) $65,600, $66,800, $66,200; (b) Worst: ($28,000), ($6,400), ($17,200), Best: $142,800, $136,800, $139,800.

8-1. 20.99%

8-2. (b) $196,000.

8-3. $8,125, ($18,750).

8-4. (c) $750,000, ($3,250,000)

8-5. (a) $9,000; (b) $4,163; (c) $458; (d) $4,379.

8-6. (a) 4,000 units; (b) 75; (c) 22,000 units.

9-1. (b) 14.69%; (e) 12.12%.

9-2. (c) 11.8%.

9-4. $59,728, $49,375.

9-5. (a) $125,000, $112,360.

9-6. $2,583.34, $4,000, $2,000.

10-2. Nine years.

10-3. (c) $1,086.14.

10-5. $5,990.13

10-7. $29,464.

10-8. (c) $1,044.58.

10-9. (b) $24,927.25.

10-12. 6%.

10-14. $1,150,000, $1,322,000, $1,521,000, $1,749,000, $2,011,000.

10-16. (a) $1.15, $1.32, $1.52, $1.75, $2.01; (b) $5.00; (c) $10.00, (d) $15.00.

10-17. (a) $140,350.

11-2. (a) NPV = ($3,226.45); (b) NPV = ($1,588.65); (c) NPV = $411.35; (d) NPV = $3,519.60.

11-7. Project S
(a) (i) $8,000, (ii) $7,332, (iii) $6,944, (iv) $6,112; (b) 21.5%.

12-1. (a) E(CF) = $19,500, E(NPV) = $10,175, E(IRR) = 14%.

12-3. 5 years: NPV = ($207.60), 8 years: NPV = $8,546, 10 years: NPV = $13,406.

12-4. (b) E(CF) = $16,200, E(NPV) = ($8,470); (e) 41%.

13-1. 11.5%.

13-2. 13.6%.

13-3. (1) 5.02%; (2) 12.0%, 10.7%.

14-1. 224,517 shares.

14-2. $5.00.

14-4. (a) $3.00.

14-5. (a)

	$25	$50	$80
(iii)	$3.10	$4.65	$5.72
(v)	$1.74	$2.60	$3.20

15-1. NPV = $11,782.

15-3. (c) $23,648, $23,662.

16-1. The present value of leasing is $4,831.38.
The present value of the purchase/borrow is $2,425.22.

17-1. (a) $1,150.60; (b) $53.52.

17-2. (b) $2.00, (d) $10.00.

17-3. (b) subscription price = $51.00.

17-5. (a) $.90; (b) $14.40; (d) Total assets = $500,000; (f) Total assets = $687,500.

17-6. (b) 45%, 47%, 47%; (c) $.45, $.47, $.61; (d) 22%, 22%, 50%.

18-2. (a) $1,500; (d) (ii) $939.

18-4. $1,084.

18-5. (a) (i) 12%, (ii) 4%.

18-6. $66.30.

18-7. (b) $800.

18-8. (a) $3.00; (b) (ii) $6.67; (d) (ii) 2.22.

18-9. (c) (i) (a) $42.00, (b) $80.08; (d) $41.96, $150.

18-11. (a) (i) 7%, (iii) 10%; (b) (i) (1) 9%, (ii) (1) 5%; (d) (i) 7%; (e) (ii) 14%.

18-12. (a) Net assets = $22,000.

18-14. (a) PV of price at end of year 7 = $14.88.

19-1. (a) EPS = $.50, $.58, $.57, $.68, $.66, $.73, $.66, $.78.

19-2. (a)

	Stock	Debt	Both
EPS	$1.00, $2.00, $3.00	$.75, $2.00, $3.25	$.89, $2.00, $3.11
(b)	$2.30	$2.38	$2.33
(c)	1.0	1.25	1.11

19-3. (a) Debt EPS: $1.10, $1.85, $2.60, $3.35, $4.10; Stock: $1.04, $1.64, $2.24, $2.84, $3.44; (b) debt: E(EPS) = $2.60, σ = $.86; (c) debt: E(Price) = $23.40, σ = $7.70.

19-4. (a) (i) 1.5, (ii) 1.45, (iii) 2.18.

19-5. (a) Bond: EPS = ($.47), $.53, $1.53, $2.53, $3.53, $4.53, $5.53; (f) Bond: E(EPS) = $2.53, E(Price) = $20.24.

20-1. (b) 40%.

20-2. (b) $15,000,000; (c) $12,000,000; (e) $6,000,000; (f) MCC below = 8.5%, MCC above = 8.7%.

20-3. (a) $8,000,000 $16,000,000; (b) MCC_1 = 9.47%, MCC_2 = 9.76%, MCC_3 = 10.33%.

20-4. (a) (i) 4.8%, (ii) 10%, (iii) 12%; (b) 10.10%; (d) (i) 12.44%, (ii) 10.41%.

21-2. $2.80.

21-5. (a) with dividend: total financing = $15,270,000, MCC_1 = 6.53%, MCC_2 = 6.82%.

21-6. (b) $12; (c) $352.

21-2. (a) 6.4%; (c) (i) 9.73%, (ii) 8.73%.

21-5. (1) 20%; (2) 22%; (4) 13%.

21-6. (a) Apex: $45,000, Allied: $45.67; (b) (2) growth with Apex = 6.3%, growth with Allied = 4.2%.

24-1. (a) Total assets = $327,000,000; (c) $1,320,000.

24-3. (b) Percent of claims = 57.4%.

25-1. (1) h; (2) a; (3) d; (4) f; (5) b; (5) b; (6) e; (7) i; (8) c; (9) g.

Glossary

Accruals   Continually recurring short-term liabilities. Examples are accrued wages, accrued taxes, and accrued interest.

Aging Schedule   A report showing how long accounts receivable have been outstanding. It gives the percent of receivables not past due and the percent past due by, for example, one month, two months, or other periods.

Amortize   To liquidate on an installment basis; an amortized loan is one in which the principal amount of the loan is repaid in installments during the life of the loan.

Annuity   A series of payments of a fixed amount for a specified number of years.

Arbitrage   The process of selling overvalued and buying undervalued assets so as to bring about an equilibrium where all assets are properly valued.

Arrearage   Overdue payment; frequently, omitted dividends on preferred shares.

Asset Pool   Each depreciable asset fits into one of many asset classes. When there are a number of assets in a particular class, these assets are grouped into one unit called a pool for capital cost allowance calculations.

Assignment   A relatively inexpensive way of liquidating a failing firm that does not involve going through the courts.

Baloon Payment   When a debt is not fully amortized, the final payment is larger than the preceding payments and is called a "balloon" payment.

Banker's Acceptance   A bill of exchange drawn by a borrowing firm on its bank and sold by the borrowing firm to an investment dealer.

Banking Group   A group of investment dealers which accepts the risk of a new security issue.

Bankruptcy   A legal procedure for formally liquidating a business, carried out under the jurisdiction of courts of law.

Beta Coefficient   Measures the extent to which the returns on a given stock move with a market index. The Beta coefficient is a measure of relative risk.

Bond   A long-term debt instrument.

Book Value   The accounting value of an asset. The book value of a share of common equity is equal to to the net worth (common equity plus retained earnings) of the corporation divided by the number of shares of common outstanding.

682

Break-even Analysis An analytical technique for studying the relation between fixed cost, va̶r̶.̶.̶ cost, and profits. A break-even *chart* graphically depicts the nature of break-even analysis. The break-even *point* represents the volume of sales at which total costs equal total revenues (that is, profits equal zero).

Business Risk The basic risk inherent in a firm's operations. Business risk plus financial risk resulting from the use of debt equals total corporate risk.

Call (1) An option to buy (or "call") a share of common equity at a specified price within a specified period. (2) The process of redeeming a bond or preferred share issue before its normal maturity.

Call Premium The amount in excess of par value that a company must pay when it calls a security.

Call Price The price that must be paid when a security is called. The call price is equal to the par value plus the call premium.

Call Privilege A provision incorporated into a bond or a preferred share that gives the issuer the right to redeem (call) the security at a specified price.

Capital Asset An asset with a life of more than one year that is not bought and sold in the ordinary course of business.

Capital Budgeting The process of planning expenditures on assets whose returns are expected to extend beyond one year.

Capital Cost Allowance The amount of depreciation expense allowed in the computation of taxable income. The CCA is calculated by applying a fixed capital cost rate to a declining capital cost balance.

Capital Cost Rate The rate of depreciation that may be used for a particular asset pool in calculating taxable income. The capital cost rate multiplied by the capital cost balance yields the capital cost allowance for an asset class. The maximum capital cost rate applicable to a particular class is specified in the Income Tax Regulations.

Capital Gains Profits on the sale of capital assets held for six months or more.

Capital Losses Losses on the sale of capital assets.

Capital Rationing A situation where a constraint is placed on the total size of the capital investment during a particular period.

Capital Structure The permanent long-term financing of the firm represented by long-term debt, preferred shares, and net worth (net worth consists of capital, contributed surplus, and retained earnings). Capital structure is distinguished from *financial structure,* which includes short-term debt plus all reserve accounts.

Capitalization Rate A discount rate used to find the present value of a series of future cash receipts; sometimes called *discount rate.*

Carry-back; Carry-forward For income tax purposes, losses that can be carried backward or forward to reduce federal income taxes.

Cash Budget A schedule showing cash flows (receipts, disbursements, and net cash) for a firm over a specified period.

Cash Cycle The length of time between the purchase of raw materials and the collection of accounts receivable generated in the sale of the final product.

Certainty Equivalents The amount of cash (or rate of return) that someone would require *with certainty* to make him or her indifferent between this certain sum (or *rate of return*) and a particular uncertain, risky sum (or rate of return).

Chattel Mortgage A mortgage on personal property (not real estate). A mortgage on equipment would be a chattel mortgage.

Coefficient of Variation Standard deviation divided by the mean.

Collateral Assets that are used to secure a loan.

Commercial Paper Unsecured short-term promissory notes of large firms, usually issued in denominations of $50,000 or more. The rate of interest on commercial paper is typically somewhat below the prime rate of interest.

Commitment Fee   The fee paid to a lender for a formal line of credit.

Compensating Balance   A required minimum chequing account balance that a firm must maintain with a chartered bank. The required balance is generally equal to 15 or 20 percent of the amount of loans outstanding. Compensating balances can raise the effective rate of interest on bank loans.

Composite Cost of Capital   A weighted average of the component cost of debt, preferred shares, and common equity. Also called the "weighted average cost of capital", but it reflects the cost of each additional dollar raised, not the average cost of all capital the firm has raised throughout its history.

Composition   An informal method of reorganization that voluntarily reduces creditors' claims on the debtor firm.

Compound Interest   An interest rate that is applicable when interest in succeeding periods is earned not only on the initial principal but also on the accumulated interest of prior periods. Compound interest is contrasted to *simple interest,* in which returns are not earned on interest received.

Compounding   The arithmetic process of determining the final value of a payment or series of payments when compound interest is applied.

Conditional Sales Contract   A method of financing new equipment by paying it off in installments over a one-to-five-year period. The seller retains title to the equipment until payment has been completed.

Consolidated Tax Return   An income tax return that combines the income statement of several affiliated firms.

Continuous Compounding (Discounting)   As opposed to discrete compounding, interest is added continuously rather than at discrete points in time.

Conversion Price   The effective price paid for common shares when the shares are obtained by converting either convertible preferred shares or convertible bonds. For example, if a $1,000 bond is convertible into twenty shares, the conversion price is $50 (= $1,000/20).

Conversion Ratio or Conversion Rate   The number of shares of common that may be obtained by converting a convertible bond or share of convertible preferred.

Convertibles   Securities (generally bonds or preferred shares) that are exchangeable at the option of the holder for common shares of the issuing firm.

Correlation Coefficient   Measures the degree of relationship between two variables.

Cost of Capital   The discount rate that should be used in the capital budgeting process.

Coupon Rate   The stated rate of interest on a bond.

Covenant   Detailed clauses contained in loan agreements. Covenants are designed to protect the lender and include such items as limits on total indebtedness, restrictions on dividends, minimum current ratio, and similar provisions.

Cumulative Dividends   A protective feature on preferred shares that requires all past preferred dividends to be paid before any common dividends are paid.

Cut-off Point   In the capital budgeting process, the minimum rate of return on acceptable investment opportunities.

Debenture   A long-term debt instrument that is not secured by a mortgage on specific property.

Debt Ratio   Total debt divided by total assets.

Decision Tree   A device for setting forth graphically the pattern of relationship between decisions and chance events.

Default   The failure to fulfil a contract. Generally, default refers to the failure to pay interest or principal on debt obligations.

Degree of Leverage   The percentage increase in profits resulting from a given percentage increase in sales. The degree of leverage may be calculated for financial leverage, operating leverage, or both combined.

Devaluation The process of reducing the value of a country's currency stated in terms of other currencies; e.g., the British pound might be devalued from $2.30 for one pound to $2.00 for one pound.

Discount Rate The interest rate used in the discounting process; sometimes called *capitalization rate.*

Discounted Cash Flow Techniques Methods of ranking investment proposals. Included are (1) internal rate of return method, (2) net present value method, and (3) profitability index or benefit/cost ratio.

Discounting The process of finding the present value of a series of future cash flows. Discounting is the reverse of compounding.

Discounting of Accounts Receivable Short-term financing where accounts receivable are used to secure the loan. The lender does not *buy* the accounts receivable but simply uses them as collateral for the loan. Also called *pledging of accounts receivable.*

Dividend Gross-up For tax calculation, the marginal federal tax rate is applied to the adjusted dividends received. The adjusted dividend is the actual dividend received, grossed-up by 50 percent of the dividends received.

Dividend Tax Credit A tax credit equal to 75 percent of the dividend gross-up is allowed against the federal tax payable an individual received.

Dividend Yield The ratio of the current dividend to the current price of a share of stock.

Du Pont System A system of analysis designed to show the relationship between return on investment, asset turnover, and the profit margin.

EBIT Acronym for "earnings before interest and taxes".

Economical Ordering Quantity (EOQ) The optimum (least cost) quantity of merchandise which should be ordered.

EPS Acronym for "earnings per share".

Equity The net worth of a business, consisting of capital stock, capital (or paid-in) surplus, earned surplus (or retained earnings), and, occasionally, certain net worth reserves. *Common equity* is that part of the total net worth belonging to the common shareholders. *Total equity* would include preferred shareholders. The terms "common shares", "net worth", and "common equity" are frequently used interchangeably.

Eurobonds Bonds sold to investors in a foreign country denominated in a currency other than the domestic currency of the investor.

Excise Tax A tax on the manufacture, sale, or consumption of specified commodities.

Ex Dividend Date The date on which the right to the current dividend no longer accompanies a stock.

Exercise Price The price that must be paid for a share of common equity when it is bought by exercising a warrant.

Expected Return The rate of return a firm expects to realize from an investment. The expected return is the mean value of the probability distribution of possible returns.

Ex Rights The date on which share purchase rights are no longer transferred to the purchaser of the shares.

Extension An informal method of reorganization in which the creditors voluntarily postpone the date of required payment on past-due obligations.

External Funds Funds acquired through borrowing or by selling new common or preferred shares.

Factoring A method of financing accounts receivable under which a firm sells its accounts receivable (generally without recourse) to a financial institution (the "factor").

Field Warehousing A method of financing inventories in which a "warehouse" is established at the place of business of the borrowing firm.

Financial Lease A lease that does not provide for maintenance services, is not cancellable, and is fully amortized over the life of the lease.

Financial Leverage The ratio of total debt to total assets. There are other measures of financial leverage, especially ones that relate cash inflows to required cash outflows. In this book, the debt/total asset ratio is generally used to measure leverage.

Financial Risk That portion of total corporate risk, over and above basic business risk, that results from using debt.

Financial Structure The entire right-hand side of the balance sheet—the way in which a firm is financed.

Fixed Charges Costs that do not vary with the level of output, especially fixed financial costs such interest, lease payments, and sinking fund payments.

Float The amount of funds tied up in cheques that have been written but are still in process and have not yet been collected.

Floating Exchange Rates Exchange rates may be fixed by government policy ("pegged") or allowed to "float" up or down in accordance with supply and demand. When market forces are allowed to function, exchange rates are said to be floating.

Forward Exchange Markets The market for trading of foreign currencies in which the exchange rate is set for currency to be delivered at a future date.

Funded Debt Long-term debt.

Funding The process of replacing short-term debt with long-term securities.

Goodwill Intangible assets of a firm established by the excess of the price paid for the going concern over its book value.

Hedging The creation of cash flows in a currency in the forward exchange market at rates set in advance so that cash flows from operations in that currency are matched. The hedging process permits business to cover cash inflows or outflows for a currency for a specific maturity.

Holding Company A corporation operated for the purpose of owning the common shares of other corporations.

Hurdle Rate In capital budgeting, the minimum acceptable rate of return on a project; if the expected rate of return is below the hurdle rate, the project is not accepted. The hurdle rate should be the marginal cost of capital.

Income Bond A bond that pays interest only if the current interest is earned.

Incremental Cash Flow Net cash flow attributable to an investment project.

Incremental Cost of Capital The average cost of the increment of capital raised during a given year.

Indenture A formal agreement between the issuer of a bond and the bondholders.

Insolvency The inability to meet maturing debt obligations.

Interest Factor (IF) Numbers found in compound interest and annuity tables.

Internal Financing Funds made available for capital budgeting and working capital expansion through the normal operations of the firm; internal financing is approximately equal to retained earnings plus depreciation.

Internal Rate of Return (IRR) The rate of return on an asset investment. The internal rate of return is calculated by finding the discount rate that equates the present value of cash flows to the cost of the investment.

Investment Dealer One who underwrites and distributes new investment securities; more broadly, one who helps business firms to obtain financing.

Investment Tax Credit Investment in prescribed buildings, machinery and equipment permits a company to claim an investment tax credit of between 5 and 10 percent of the capital cost of the asset. The tax credit is applied to federal taxes in the year of acquisition; however, there are some limitations. The tax credit causes the undepreciated capital cost of the asset to be reduced by the value of the credit.

Issue Costs The costs of issuing new securities.

Legal List A list of securities in which pension funds, insurance companies, and other fiduciary institutions are permitted to invest.

Leverage Factor The ratio of debt to total assets.

Lien A lender's claim on assets that are pledged for a loan.

Line of Credit An arrangement whereby a financial institution (bank or insurance company) commits itself to lend up to a specified maximum amount of funds during a specified period. Sometimes the interest rate on the loan is specified; at other times, it is not. Sometimes a commitment fee is imposed for obtaining the line of credit.

Liquidity Refers to a firm's cash position and its ability to meet maturing obligations.

Listed Securities Securities traded on an organized security exchange.

Lock-box Plan A procedure used to speed up collections and to reduce float.

Margin—Profit on Sales The *profit margin* is the percentage of profit after tax to sales.

Margin—Securities Business The buying of stocks or bonds on credit, known as *buying on margin*.

Marginal Cost The cost of an additional unit. The marginal cost of capital is the cost of an additional dollar of new funds.

Marginal Efficiency of Capital A schedule showing the internal rate of return on investment opportunities.

Marginal Revenue The additional gross revenue produced by selling one additional unit of output.

Merger Any combination that forms one company from two or more previously existing companies.

Money Market Financial markets in which funds are borrowed or lent for short periods. (The money market is distinguished from the capital market, which is the market for long-term funds.)

Mortgage A pledge of designated property as security for a loan.

Net Present Value (NPV) Method A method of ranking investment proposals. The NPV is equal to the present value of future returns, discounted at the marginal cost of capital, minus the present value of the cost of the investment.

Net Worth The capital and surplus of a firm—capital stock, capital surplus (paid-in capital), earned surplus (retained earnings), and, occasionally, certain reserves. For some purposes, preferred shares are included; generally, net worth refers only to the common shareholders' position.

Nominal Interest Rate The contracted or stated interest rate, undeflated for price level changes.

Normal Probability Distribution A symmetrical, bell-shaped probability function.

Objective Probability Distributions Probability distributions determined by statistical procedures.

Operating Income Income from the normal operations of a firm. Operating income specifically excludes income from the sale of capital assets.

Operating Leverage The extent to which fixed costs are used in a firm's operation. Break-even analysis is used to measure the extent to which operating leverage is employed.

Opportunity Cost The rate of return on the best *alternative* investment of the same risk that is available. It is the highest return that will *not* be earned if the funds are invested in a particular project. For example, the opportunity cost of *not* investing in bond A yielding 8 percent might be 7.99 percent, which could be earned on bond B.

Organized Security Exchanges   Formal organizations having tangible, physical locations. Organized exchanges conduct an auction market in designated ("listed") investment securities. For example, the Toronto Stock Exchange is an organized exchange.

Overdraft System   A system where a depositor may write cheques in excess of his or her balance, with the bank automatically extending a loan to cover the shortage.

Over-the-counter Market   All facilities that provide for trading in unlisted securities, that is, those not listed on organized exchanges. For example, corporate bonds are traded in this market.

Par Value   The nominal or face value of a share or bond.

Payback Period   The length of time required for the net revenues of an investment to return the cost of the investment.

Payout Ratio   The percentage of earnings paid out in the form of dividends.

Pegging   A market stabilization action taken by the manager of an underwriting group during the offering of new securities. The manager does this by continually placing orders to buy at a specified price in the market.

Perpetuity   A stream of equal future payments expected to continue forever.

Pledging of Accounts Receivable   Short-term borrowing from financial institutions where the loan is secured by accounts receivable. The lender may physically take the accounts receivable but typically has recourse to the borrower; also called *discounting of accounts receivable.*

Pooling of Interest   An accounting method for combining the financial statements of two firms that merge. Under the pooling-of-interest procedure, the assets of the merged firms are simply added to form the balance sheet of the surviving corporation. This method is different from the "purchase" method, where goodwill is put on the balance sheet to reflect a premium (or discount) paid in excess of book value.

Portfolio Effect   The extent to which the variation in returns on a combination of assets (a "portfolio") is less than the sum of the variations of the individual assets.

Portfolio Theory   Deals with the selection of optimal portfolios, i.e., portfolios that provide the highest possible return for any specified degree of risk.

Preemptive Right   A provision contained in the corporate charter and bylaws that gives holders of common shares the right to purchase on a pro rata basis new issues of common shares (or securities convertible into common shares).

Present Value (PV)   The value today of a future payment, or stream of payments, discounted at the appropriate discount rate.

Price/Earnings Ratio (P/E)   The ratio of price earnings. Faster growing or less risky firms typically have higher *P/E* ratios than either slower growing or riskier firms.

Prime Rate   The lowest rate of interest chartered banks charge very large, strong corporations. Typically, interest rates charged to less secure borrowers are set a number of percentage points above the prime rate.

Pro Forma   A projection. A *pro forma* financial statement is one that shows how the actual statement will look if certain specified assumptions are realized. *Pro forma* statements may be either future or past projections. An example of a backward *pro forma* statement occurs when two firms are planning to merge and show what their consolidated financial statements would have looked like if they had been merged in preceding years.

Profit Center   A unit of a large, decentralized firm that has its own investments and for which a rate of return on investment can be calculated.

Profit Margin   The ratio of profits after taxes to sales.

Profitability Index (PI)   There are a number of definitions of the profitability index currently in use. One widely used definition is the present value of future returns divided by the present value of the investment outlay.

Progressive Tax   A tax that requires a higher percentage payment on higher incomes. The personal income tax in Canada, which is at a rate of 6 percent on the lowest increments of income to 61.9 percent on the highest increments, is progressive.

Prospectus   A document issued for the purpose of describing a new security issue. The Securities Commissions of the provinces in which the issue is to be sold examine the prospectus to insure that statements contained therein are not "false and misleading".

Proxy   A document giving one person the authority or power to act for another. Typically, the authority in question is the power to vote shares of common equity.

Put   An option to sell a specific security at a specified price within a designated period.

Rate of Return   The internal rate of return on an investment.

Recourse Arrangement   A term used in connection with accounts receivable financing. If a firm sells its accounts receivable to a financial institution under a recourse agreement, then, if the account receivable cannot be collected, the selling firm must repurchase the account from the financial institution.

Rediscount Rate   The rate of interest at which a bank may borrow from the Bank of Canada.

Refunding   Sale of new debt securities to replace an old debt issue.

Regression Analysis   A statistical procedure which is based on historical data and is used to determine a relationship between one variable (dependent variable) and one or more other variables (independent variables).

Reinvestment Rate   The rate of return at which cash flows from an investment are reinvested. The reinvestment rate may or may not be constant from year to year.

Reorganization   When a financially troubled firm goes through reorganization, its assets are restated to reflect their current market value, and its financial structure is restated to reflect any changes on the asset side of the statement. Under a reorganization the firm continues in existence; this is contrasted to bankruptcy, where the firm is liquidated and ceases to exist.

Required Rate of Return on Equity   The rate of return that shareholders expect to receive on common equity investments.

Residual Value   The value of leased property at the end of the lease term.

Retained Earnings   That portion of earnings not paid out in dividends. The figure that appears on the balance sheet is the sum of the retained earnings for each year throughout the company's history.

Right   A short-term option to buy a specified number of shares of a new issue of securities at a designated "subscription" price.

Rights Offering   A securities issue offered to existing shareholders.

Risk   The probability that actual future returns will be below expected returns. Measured by standard deviation or coefficient of variation of expected returns.

Risk-adjusted Discount Rates   The discount rate applicable for a particular risky (uncertain) stream of income; the riskless rate of interest plus a risk premium appropriate to the level of risk attached to the particular income stream.

Risk Premium   The difference between the required rate of return on a particular risky asset and the rate of return on a riskless asset with the same expected life.

Risk-Return Tradeoff Function   (see *Security Market Line.*)

Sales and Leaseback   An operation whereby a firm sells land, buildings, or equipment to a financial institution and simultaneously executes an agreement to lease the property back for a specified period under specific terms.

Salvage Value   The value of a capital asset at the end of a specified period. It is the current market price of an asset being considered for replacement in a capital budgeting problem.

Securities, Junior   Securities that have lower priority in claims on assets and income than other securities *(senior securities)*. For example, preferred shares are junior to debentures, but debentures are junior to mortgage bonds. Common equity is the most junior of all corporate securities.

Securities, Senior   Securities having claims on income and assets that rank higher than certain other securities *(junior securities)*. For example, mortgage bonds are senior to debentures, but debentures are senior to common shares.

Security Market Line   A relationship between the required rate of return on a security and its measure of risk.

Selling Group   A group of brokerage firms formed for the purpose of distributing a new issue of securities; part of the investment banking process.

Sensitivity Analysis   Simulation analysis in which key variables are changed and the resulting change in the rate of return is observed. Typically, the rate of return will be more sensitive to changes in some variables than it will in others.

Service Lease   A lease under which the lessor maintains and services the asset.

Short Selling   Selling a security that is not owned by the seller at the time of the sale. The seller borrows the security from a brokerage firm and must at some point repay the brokerage firm by buying the security on the open market.

Simulation   A technique whereby probable future events are simulated on a computer. Estimated rates of return and risk indexes can be generated.

Sinking Fund   A required annual payment designed to amortize a bond or preferred share issue. The sinking fund may be held in the form of cash or marketable securities, but more generally the money put into the sinking fund is used to retire each year some of the securities in question.

Small Business Deduction   The basic federal tax rate of 46 percent is reduced by the small business deductions of 21 percent to a rate of 25 percent on the first $150,000 of active business income for Canadian controlled private companies. A provincial small business deduction applicable to income eligible for the federal deduction is allowed in five provinces.

Squeeze-Out   An attempt by majority shareholders to eliminate or reduce the importance of the minority shareholders.

Standard Deviation   A statistical term that measures the variability of a set of observations from the mean of the distribution.

Stock Dividend   A dividend paid in additional shares of common equity rather than in cash. It involves a transfer from retained earnings to the capital stock account; therefore, these dividends are limited by the amount of retained earnings.

Stock Split   An accounting action to increase the number of shares outstanding; for example, in a 3-for-1 split, shares outstanding would be tripled and each shareholder would receive three new shares for each one formerly held. Stock splits involve no transfer from surplus to the capital account.

Subjective Probability Distributions   Probability distributions determined through subjective procedures without the use of statistics.

Subordinated Debenture   A bond having a claim on assets only after the senior debt has been paid off in the event of liquidation.

Subscription Price   The price at which a security may be purchased in a rights offering.

Synergy   A situation where "the whole is greater than the sum of its parts"; in a synergistic merger, the postmerger earnings exceed the sum of the separate companies' premerger earnings.

Systematic Risk   That part of a security's risk which cannot be eliminated by diversification.

Tangible Assets   Physical assets as opposed to intangible assets such as goodwill and the stated value of patents.

Tender Offers   A situation wherein one firm offers to buy the shares of another, going directly to the shareholders, frequently over the opposition of the management of the firm whose shares are being sought.

Term Loan   A loan generally obtained from a bank or an insurance company with a maturity greater than one year. Term loans are generally amortized.

Trade Credit   Interfirm debt arising through credit sales and recorded as an account receivable by the seller and as an account payable by the buyer.

Treasury Shares   Common shares that have been repurchased by the issuing firm.

Trust Receipt   An instrument acknowledging that the borrower holds certain goods in trust for the lender. Trust receipt financing is used in connection with the financing of inventories for automobile dealers, construction equipment dealers, appliance dealers, and other dealers in expensive durable goods.

Trustee   The representative of bondholders who acts in their interest and facilitates communication between them and the issuer. Typically these duties are handled by a department of a trust company.

Underwriting   (1) The entire process of issuing new corporate securities. (2) The insurance function of bearing the risk of adverse price fluctuations during the period in which a new issue of shares or bonds is being distributed.

Underwriting Syndicate   A syndicate of investment firms formed to spread the risk associated with the purchase and distribution of a new issue of securities. The larger the issue, the more firms typically are involved in the syndicate.

Unlisted Securities   Securities that are traded in the over-the-counter market.

Unsystematic Risk   That part of a security's risk associated with random events; unsystematic risk can be eliminated by proper diversification (also called "diversifiable risk").

Utility Theory   A body of theory dealing with the relationships among money income, utility, and the willingness to accept risks.

Warrant   A long-term option to buy a stated number of shares of common equity at a specified price. The specified price is generally called the "exercise price".

Weighted Cost of Capital   A weighted average of the component costs of debt, preferred shares, and common equity. Also called the "composite cost of capital".

Working Capital   Refers to a firm's investment in short-term assets—cash, short-term securities, accounts receivable, and inventories. *Gross working capital* is defined as a firm's total current assets. *Net working capital* is defined as current assets minus current liabilities. If the term "working capital is used without further qualification, it generally refers to gross working capital.

Yield   The rate of return on an investment; the internal rate of return.

Index